COMPETITIVE AGRICULTURE

Multi-subject Competition Explorer

K. Vanangamudi

N. Chezhiyan

M. Kokila

P. Shyni

S. Kamalesh

nipa® books for everyone

PAPERBACKS

New Delhi – 110 034

nipa® books for everyone
PAPERBACKS

A Paperback Division of

NEW INDIA PUBLISHING AGENCY

101, Vikas Surya Plaza, CU Block, LSC Market
Pitam Pura, New Delhi – 110 034, India
Email: info@nipabooks.com
Web: www.nipabooks.com

For customer assistance, please contact
Phone: +91-11-27 34 17 17 Fax: +91-11- 27 34 16 16
E-Mail: feedbacks@nipabooks.com

ISBN: 978-93-89907-00-1

Composed and Designed by NIPA.

Preface

"Agriculture was the first occupation of man, and as it embraces the whole earth, it is the foundation of all other industries". -Edward W. Stewart

Agriculture is essentially a way of lifestyle and not a mere economic engine. Generations together, Indian agriculture which is primarily monsoon dependent, has faced tumultuous ups and downs leaving the farmers in lambasting hypocrises. Indian agriculture is ought to undergo a critical surgery to provide panglossian disposition to the plowman.

According to NITI Aayog, since 1970-71, trend growth in Indian agriculture has been approximately 3%, above that in population but, well below that in the entire economy consisting of agriculture, industry and services. By implication, while per-capita agricultural output has seen a steady rise, the share of agriculture in the Gross Domestic Product (GDP) has fallen. The rise in per-capita agricultural production has gone a long way towards easing pressure on meeting food and nutritional security of the country.

Agricultural research and development (R&D) in India has made impressive contribution in the past. Today, the agricultural sector has witnessed the infusion of digital intervention. In India, an encouraging sign for the exchanges is the growing popularity among farmers of the e-National Agriculture Market (e-NAM). During this era of Industrial revolution 4.0, Agriculture should tap the verdure of avant-garde technologies such as Artificial intelligence, Internet of Things (IoT) etc., and use such other spin of technologies thereby, Climate resilient smart agriculture is not a nightmare anymore.

To instill fortitude and double the farmer's income, corralling of agriculture knowledge is need of the hour. To get into service of the billions through competitive examinations, outrageous support by this book "**Competitive Agriculture**" is guaranteed.

January, 2020 **Authors**

Contents

UNIT III: PLANT BREEDING AND GENETICS

UNIT IV: SOIL SCIENCE AND AGRICULTURAL CHEMISTRY

UNIT XII: AGRICULTURAL ECONOMICS, FINANCE AND AGRI BUSINESS

UNIT XIII: AGRICULTURAL MARKETING AND INTELLIGENCE

UNIT XIV: AGRICULTURAL EXTENSION AND RURAL SOCIOLOGY

UNIT XV: HORTICULTURE

UNIT XVI: FORESTRY

UNIT XVII: FARM MACHINERY AND RENEWABLE ENERGY

UNIT XVIII: LIVESTOCK AND POULTRY REARING

UNIT I: IMPORTANCE OF AGRICULTURE

1

General Agriculture

I. Choose the correct answer

1. Agricultural sector contribution to GDP in the year 2018-19 is

   A. 16% B. 17-18%

   C. 19% D. 20 %

2. Through yellow revolution, oil seed production increased in compare to independence

   A. 5 to 25 million tons B. 17 to 108.5 million tons

   C. 0.75 to7.6 million tons D. 2 to 28 billion tons

3. Aadhar card was introduced in the year

   A. 2008 B. 2009

   C. 2010 D. 2011

4. Pink revolution is related with

   A. Onion and prawn B. Prawn and grapes

   C. Onion and pulses D. Prawn and Pulses

5. Father of green revolution in the world is

   A. M.S. Swaminathan B. Norman Borlaug

   C. Ramaiah D. Robertson

6. Expand HACCP?

   A. Hazard Analysis and Critical Control Point

   B. Hazard Analysis and Common Control Point

   C. Hazard Accounting and Critical Control Point

   D. Hazard Accounting and Common Control Point

7. The present union Minister for Agriculture in India

   A. Rajnath Singh B. Duraikannu

   C. Radha Mohan Singh D. Narendra Singh Tomar

8. The word 'agriculture' is derived from ____ word.

A. Greek B. Dutch
C. Latin D. English

9. Who is known as father of white revolution in India?

A. M.S.Swaminathan B. V. Kurien
D. B.P.Pal D. K.N.Bahal

10. Which was the principle crop used in green revolution?

A. Japonica rice B. Indica rice
C. Emmer wheat D. Mexican wheat

11. The Tamil Nadu farmer who received progressive farmer award in all India level is

A. PRM Ravichandran B. R. Rasathi
C. S. Samynathan D. S. Jayaraman

12. First cultivated crops in the world are

A. Rice and wheat B. Wheat and barley
C. Oats and barley D. Wheat and millets

13. The term green revolution is coined by

A. William Gaud B. Robert Ransome
C. Muller D. J. B. Bossinggault

14. The importance of agriculture in Indian economy is indicated by its contribution to which of the following ?

A. National income and employment
B. Industrial development and international trade
C. Supply of food grains
D. All of the above

15. The impact of the green revolution was felt most in the production of

A. Rice B. Pulses
C. Oilseeds D. Wheat

16. The blue revolution is related with

A. Fish production B. Food grain production
C. Oilseed production D. Milk production

17. The main components of evergreen revolution are
    (i) Upgradation of soil health
    (ii) Promote lab to land demonstrations
    (iii) Promoting rain water harvesting
    (iv) Increasing cash crop production
    Which statements are correct?
    A. (i), (ii) and (iii) are correct
    B. (ii), (iii) and (iv) are correct
    C. (i), (iii) and (iv) are correct
    D. All of these
18. Which of the following statement is correct about sustainable agriculture?
    A. It focuses on producing long-term crops and livestock without harming the environment.
    B. It is a technique and method that protect the environment, public health, human communities and animal welfare while producing food, fibre, or plant or animal products.
    C. Both A and B
    D. Only A
19. Green revolution refers to
    A. Use of green manure
    B. Grow more crops
    C. High yield variety programme
    D. Green vegetation
20. Which of the following state was chosen as the initiation site in India for green revolution?
    A. Punjab
    B. Tamil Nadu
    C. Andhra Pradesh
    D. Bihar
21. When did the department of agriculture in Tamil Nadu was established?
    A. 1870
    B. 1880
    C. 1890
    D. 1895
22. Which of the following crop production is maximized after the independence?
    A. Rice
    B. Jute
    C. Wheat
    D. Pulses
23. Consider the following
    (i) Continued expansion of farming areas
    (ii) Double-cropping in existing farmland
    (iii) Using seeds with improved genetics

Which of the above statement (s) is/are not the one of the three basic elements in the method of the Green Revolution?

A. (i) alone is correct B. (ii) alone is correct

C. (i) and (iii) are correct D. None of the above

24. Green revolution in India was introduced in 19th century during decade's of________for adopting new agricultural strategy.

A. 1960s B. 1970s

C. 1950s D. 1990s

25. Who among the following used the term evergreen revolution for increasing agricultural production in India?

A. Norman Borlaug B. M.S Swaminathan

C. Raj Krishna D. R.K.V Rao

26. Norman Borlaug was from which country?

A. United States of America B. Mexico

C. Australia D. New Zealand

27. The green revolution in India was an introduction of high-yielding varieties (HYV) of seeds for

A. Millet B. Pulse

C. Wheat D. Oilseed

28. Which one of the following is the correct sequence in the decreasing order of production (in million tonnes) of the given food grains in India?

A. Wheat - Rice - Pulses - Coarse cereals

B. Rice - Wheat - Pulses - Coarse cereals

C. Wheat - Rice - Coarse cereals – Pulses

D. Rice - Wheat - Coarse cereals - Pulses

29. What is slash and burn agriculture?

A. Method of sugarcane cultivation B. Process of deforestation

C. Agriculture without irrigation D. Jhum cultivation

30. Which is the largest cotton growing state in India?

A. Maharashtra B. Madhya Pradesh

C. Andhra Pradesh D. Gujarat

31. The United Nations General Assembly has declared 2013 as the International year of

A. Quinoa B. Buckwheat

C. Rice D. Jatropha

32. The term agronomy is derived from
    A. German word
    B. Latin word
    C. Spanish word
    D. Greek word
33. Primary resources for agriculture are
    A. Land, air and water
    B. Seed, fertilizer and pesticide
    C. Seed, air and water
    D. Land, fertilizer and water
34. Cultivation of rice begins in
    A. 2200 BC
    B. 5700 BC
    C. 7700 BC
    D. 8700 BC
35. The book Horse hoeing husbandry was published by
    A. Van Helmont
    B. Gregor Johann Mendel
    C. Jethro Tull
    D. None
36. The Annals of Agriculture was published by
    A. Jethro Tull
    B. Arthur Young
    C. Van Helmont
    D. None
37. The book Element of Agricultural Chemistry was published by
    A. Justus Von Liebig
    B. Sir Humphry Davy
    C. Van Helmont
    D. J.B. Lawes
38. Experiments on effect of manures on crop were initiated by
    A. Sir John Bannet Lawes
    B. G. J. Mendel
    C. Van Helmont
    D. Justus Von Liebig
39. Kharif, rabi and zaid words belong to
    A. Urdu
    B. French
    C. Persian
    D. Arabic
40. First state in India to launch a policy to establish Special Agriculture Zones (SAZs)
    A. Uttar Pradesh
    B. Haryana
    C. Gujarat
    D. Uttarkhand
41. Which industry employs the largest number of women in India?
    A. Tea
    B. Textile
    C. Jute
    D. Coal
42. The Barak valley of Assam is famous for cultivation of which crop?
    A. Oil palm
    B. Tea
    C. Sugarcane
    D. Coffee

43. The green gold revolution is related to the

A. Coffee B. Gold

C. Bamboo D. Tea

44. The first Director General of ICAR

A. Dr. B.P. Paul B. Dr. R.S. Paroda

C. Dr. M.S. Swaminathan D. Dr. B. Vishwanath

45. Indian agriculture is typically characterized as

A. Land surplus, labour scare economy

B. Land surplus, lablour surplus economy

C. Land scare, labour surplus economy

D. Land scare, labour scare economy

46. Dr. M.S. Swaminathan has distinguished himself in which of the following fields?

A. Nuclear Physics B. Agriculture

C. Astrophysics D. Medicine

47. The *green revolution* in India was the outcome of the efforts of whom amongst the following?

A. M.S. Swaminathan B. C. Rangarajan

C. K.V. Kamath D. Rakesh Mohan

48. Nearly ______ per cent of population is dependent on agriculture presently in India.

A. 72% B. 54%

C. 22% D. None

49. The main source of India's national income is?

A. Industry B. Agriculture

C. Forestry D. None of these

Answer keys

1.	B	11.	A	21.	B	31.	A	41.	A
2.	A	12.	B	22.	C	32.	D	42.	C
3.	B	13.	A	23.	D	33.	A	43.	C
4.	A	14.	D	24.	A	34.	A	44.	A
5.	B	15.	D	25.	B	35.	C	45.	C
6.	A	16.	A	26.	A	36.	B	46.	B
7.	D	17.	A	27.	C	37.	B	47.	A
8.	C	18.	C	28.	D	38.	A	48.	B
9.	B	19.	C	29.	D	39.	D	49.	B
10.	D	20.	A	30.	D	40.	D		

2

Agricultural Development through Five Years Plans

I. Choose the correct answer

1. In first five year plan, how much per cent of total plan outplay devoted to agriculture

   A. 21% B. 16%

   C. 31% D. 45%

2. Minor irrigation and HYV of seed are the important programs allocated during

   A. Sixth plan B. Third plan

   C. Fifth plan D. Seventh plan

3. Second green revolution occurs during the year

   A. 2002-2007 B. 2007-2012

   C. 1997-2002 D. 1992-1997

4. MMA stands for

   A. Micro Management of Agriculture

   B. Macro Management of Agriculture

   C. Micro Mission on Agriculture

   D. Macro Mission on Agriculture

5. Growth rate of agriculture and allied sectors increased during

   A. 8th five year plan B. 9th five year plan

   C. 10th five year plan D. 11th five year plan

6. NABARD was established in the

   A. Fourth five year plan B. Fifth five year plan

   C. Sixth five year plan D. Eighth five year plan

7. Under which five year plan, agriculture registered negative growth?

   A. Third B. Fifth

   C. Seventh D. Ninth

8. Who gives the final approval to the five year plans of India?
   A. National Development Council (NDC)
   B. Ministry of Finance
   C. Planning Commission (now NITI Aayog)
   D. President of India
9. What was the prime target of the first five year plan of India?
   A. Development of the industries B. Development of Agriculture
   C. Development of infrastructure D. Development of ports
10. What is the planned rate of agriculture growth in the 12th five year plan?
    A. 3.5% B. 4%
    C. 5.5% D. 6%
11. FCI was set up during the
    A. 3rd five year plan B. 4th five year plan
    C. 5th five year plan D. 7th five year plan
12. Five year plan in India is borrowed from
    A. Soviet union B. USA
    C. Russia D. None of these
13. The government forced to declare plan holiday during
    A. 1963-1966 B.1966-1969
    C. 1959-1962 D.1969-1972
14. NITI Aayog is planning a new framework for
    A. Five-year plans B. Finance commission
    C. Budget D. All of the above
15. Under which plan did the Government introduce an agricultural strategy which gave rise to green revolution?
    A. Third five-year plan (FYP) B. Fourth FYP
    C. Fifth FYP D. Second FYP
16. Consider the following statements and identify the correct ones.
    (i) The 11th five year plan was based on the planning commission model
    (ii) The plan main objective was to faster and inclusive growth.
    A. (i) only B. (ii) only
    C. Both (i) and (ii) D. None

17. Consider the following statements and identify the correct ones.
    (i) The 12th five year plan targeted the real GDP growth rate of 8%
    (ii) The plan aimed at generating 50 million new work opportunities in agricultural sector during the 8th plan period.

    A. (i) only B. (ii) only
    C. Both (i) and (ii) D. None

18. What is the main objective of the 12th five year plan?
    A. Faster and inclusive growth
    B. Faster and sustainable growth
    C. Inclusive and sustainable growth
    D. Faster, sustainable and more inclusive growth

19. Which of the following five year plans laid the foundation for industrialization?
    A. 1st FYP B. 2nd FYP
    C. 3rd FYP D. 7th FYP

20. Which of the following five year plans was officially announced as a failed plan?
    A. 1st FYP B. 2nd FYP
    C. 3rd FYP D. 7th FYP

21. Who is known as father of green revolution in India?
    A. MS Swaminathan B. Vikram Sarabhai
    C. Somnath Desai D. S. Radhakrishnan

22. In which year, Indian Council of Agricultural Research was established in India?
    A. 1919 B. 1929
    C. 1939 D. 1949

23. The Minimum Support Price (MSP) for food grains was introduced in the year?
    A. 1954 B. 1964
    C. 1974 D. 1984

24. Under which plan, did the Government introduced an agricultural strategy which gave rise to green revolution?
    A. First five year plan B. Second five year plan
    C. Third five year plan D. Fourth five year plan

25. National Horticulture Mission (NHM) promoted by Government of India was launched under which five year plan?

A. 9th five-year plan
B. 10th five-year plan
C. 5th five-year plan
D. 6th five-year plan

26. When was the first five year plan of India started?

A. 1949
B. 1950
C. 1952
D. 1951

Answer keys

1.	C	11.	A	21.	A
2.	C	12.	A	22.	B
3.	B	13.	B	23.	B
4.	B	14.	A	24.	C
5.	D	15.	B	25.	B
6.	C	16.	C	26.	D
7.	A	17.	A		
8.	A	18.	D		
9.	B	19.	B		
10.	B	20.	C		

3

Area, Production and Productivity of Crops in India

I. Choose the correct answer

1. India ranks first in the world in terms of production of

   A. Fruits B. Spices and condiments

   C. Vegetables D. Pulses

2. India stands which position in terms of production of vegetables

   A. First B. Second

   C. Third D. Fourth

3. Third advance estimates of production of food grains during 2018-2019 is

   A. 283.37 MT B. 115.63 MT

   C. 400.37 MT D. 101.20 MT

4. Position of Tamil Nadu at National level in productivity of rice

   A. First B. Second

   C. Third D. Fourth

5. Which Indian state produces the highest quantity of pulses?

   A. Maharashtra B. Uttar Pradesh

   C. Madhya Pradesh D. Rajasthan

6. Which of the following state of India is the largest producer of coconut?

   A. Kerala B. Karnataka

   C. Tamil Nadu D. Andhra Pradesh

7. In the year 2016-17, leading states in the order of 1st, 2nd and 3rd in terms of total food grain production is

   A. UP>MP>Rajasthan B. MP>UP>Tamil Nadu

   C. TN>UP>MP D. UP>MP>Punjab

8. Which of the following statement is not correct?

   A. India is the second largest producer of fruits in the world.

   B. India is the biggest producer of vegetables in the world.

   C. Production of fruits, vegetables and spices is called as horticulture.

   D. Uttar Pradesh is the largest producer of the wheat in India.

9. The correct arrangement of Indian states according to their capacity of sugar production in decreasing order is

   A. Uttar Pradesh > Maharashtra> Karnataka > Tamil Nadu

   B. Maharashtra > Uttar Pradesh > Karnataka > Tamil Nadu

   C. Maharashtra > Uttar Pradesh > Tamil Nadu > Karnataka

   D. Uttar Pradesh > Karnataka > Maharashtra > Tamil Nadu

10. State growing mostly tea is

   A. Maharashtra B. Uttar Pradesh

   C. Gujarat D. Assam

11. Productivity of paddy in Tamil Nadu is

   A. 5494 kg/ha B. 3494 kg/ha

   C. 4494 kg/ha D. 2494 kg/ha

12. Per capita availability of food grains in 2016 is

   A. 450.25 g B. 486.8 g

   C. 495.75 g D. 475. 25 g

13. WHO recommendation of vegetable consumption per day is about

   A. 200-250 g/day B. 150g/day

   C. 300 g/day D. 450 g/day

14. Which among the following is the largest food grain producing state of India?

   A. Uttar Pradesh B. Punjab

   C. Madhya Pradesh D. Rajasthan

15. In which state / Union Territory is located Kuttanad a place which is with the lowest altitude in India and is one of the places in the world, where agriculture is carried out below sea level?

   A. Tamil Nadu B. Kerala

   C. Andaman and Nicobar islands D. Lakshadweep

16. Which is the highest oilseeds producing Indian state, as per 2013-14?
    A. Gujarat B. Madhya Pradesh
    C. Rajasthan D. Andhra Pradesh
17. What is the correct descending order of rice producing states in India?
    A. Uttar Pradesh, Punjab, West Bengal and Andhra Pradesh
    B. Punjab, West Bengal, Uttar Pradesh and Andhra Pradesh
    C. West Bengal, Punjab, Uttar Pradesh and Andhra Pradesh
    D. West Bengal, Uttar Pradesh, Punjab and Andhra Pradesh
18. What is the correct descending order of food grain producing states?
    A. Uttar Pradesh, Punjab, Madhya Pradesh and West Bengal
    B. Punjab, Uttar Pradesh, Madhya Pradesh and West Bengal
    C. Uttar Pradesh, Punjab, West Bengal and Madhya Pradesh
    D. Uttar Pradesh, Madhya Pradesh, Punjab and West Bengal
19. Which of the following is not matched correctly?
    A. Rabi crop.........Mustard, cucumber
    B. Rabi crop.........Mustard, barley
    C. Zaid crop.........Moong, vegetables
    D. Kharif crop.....Cotton
20. Which of the following state is the largest producer of cotton in India?
    A. Karnataka B. Gujarat
    C. West Bengal D. Tamil Nadu
21. Which of the following plantation crop produces in India more than its need?
    A. Tea B. Food grains
    C. Petroleum D. Rubber
22. Which of the following Indian State is the largest producer of rubber?
    A. Tamil Nadu B. Andhra Pradesh
    C. Karnataka D. Kerala
23. Which of the following state is not known for the production of cardamom?
    A. Kerala B. Karnataka
    C. Odisha D. Tamil Nadu
24. Which of the following Indian state is popularly known as garden of spices?
    A. Karnataka B. Kerala
    C. Andhra Pradesh D. Tamil Nadu

25. Which one of the following sequence is correct in the context of three largest wheat producing states in India?

A. Punjab, Uttar Pradesh and Haryana

B. Uttar Pradesh, Haryana and Punjab

C. Uttar Pradesh, Punjab and Haryana

D. Punjab, Haryana and Uttar Pradesh

26. Match the following

Set I	Set II
a. Largest litchi producing state in India	1. Rajasthan
b. Cocoa producing state in India	2. Uttar Pradesh
c. Largest wheat producing state in India	3. Kerala
d. Largest rice producing state in India	4. Bihar

	a	b	c	d
A.	1	2	3	4
B.	4	3	2	1
C.	3	1	4	2
D.	1	4	3	2

27. Which of the following state is a not top soyabean growing state in India?

A. Madhya Pradesh B. Maharashtra

C. Rajasthan D. Chattisgarh

28. What is the rank of India in the production of linseed in the world?

A. First B. Second

C. Third D. Fourth

29. Which state is the leading producer of redgram?

A. UP B. AP

C. MP D. HP

30. Which state is the leading producer o rapeseed and mustard?

A. Gujarat B. Rajasthan

C. Punjab D. Haryana

31. ________m ha is the irrigated area in India during 2018.

A. 66.0 B. 67.0

C. 64.7 D. 65.0

Answer keys

1.	A	11.	B	21.	A	31.	C
2.	B	12.	B	22.	D		
3.	A	13.	A	23.	C		
4.	B	14.	A	24.	B		
5.	C	15.	B	25.	C		
6.	A	16.	B	26.	B		
7.	D	17.	D	27.	D		
8.	B	18.	A	28.	D		
9.	B	19.	A	29.	A		
10.	D	20.	B	30.	B		

4

Government Agricultural Policies

I. Choose the correct answer

1. The procurement policy announced by the Government of India in September 2018 is
   A. Pradhan Mantri Annadata Aay Sanraks Han Abhiyan
   B. Pradhan Mantri Accounts Aay Sanraks Han Abhiyan
   C. Pradhan Mantri Amounts Aay Sanraks Han Abhiyan
   D. Pradhan Mantri Analysis Aay Sanraks Han Abhiyan
2. e NAM (Electronic National Agriculture Market) was launched in the year
   A. 2018 B. 2017
   C. 2016 D. 2015
3. SAMPADA stands for
   A. Scheme for Agricultural Management and Development of Agriculture
   B. Scheme for Agro Mantri Processing and Development of Agriculture
   C. Scheme for Agro Market Products and Development of Agriculture
   D. Scheme for Agro Marine Processing and Development of Agro Processing
4. National Agricultural Policy was announced in the year
   A. 2000 B. 2007
   C. 2012 D. 1997
5. Electricity subsidy was provided by
   A. State Government
   B. Central Government
   C. Both State and Central Government
   D. Electricity Control board
6. Rastriya Krishi Vikas Yojna also known as
   A. National Agricultural Development Programme
   B. Integrated scheme on Agricultural Cooperation
   C. National Mission for Sustainable Agriculture
   D. National Agricultural Insurance Scheme

7. The aim of PM – Krishi Sinchayee Yojana is
   A. To provide financial assistance to the farmers
   B. To enhance reach and impact of extension services
   C. To promote sustainable agricultural practices
   D. To ensure access to protective irrigation to all agricultural farms in the country
8. SAMPADA is renamed as
   A. PM-Kisan Sampada Yojana B. PM-Krishi Sinchayee Yojana
   C. Rashtriya Krishi Vikas Yojana D. NADP
9. MGNREGA was implemented in the year
   A. 2008 B. 2005
   C. 2009 D. 2006
10. Which of the following Yojana of Government of India entered the Guinness World Record in 2014?
   A. PMKSY B. PMJDY
   C. RKVY D. SAGY
11. SFC stands for
   A. State Finance Corporation B. Small Farmers Corporation
   C. State Fisheries Corporation D. Small Farmers Centre
12. From the year 2009-10, the pricing policy followed for sugarcane is
   A. Minimum Support Price (MSP)
   B. Statutory Minimum Price (SMP)
   C. Issue Price (IP)
   D. Fair and Remunerative Price (FRP)
13. The soil health card was first introduced in which state of India by PM Narendra Modi?
   A. Rajasthan B. Haryana
   C. Maharashtra D. Jharkhand
14. When the government did introduce kisan credit card scheme?
   A. 1853 B. 1998
   C. 1991 D. 1995
15. When was the National Policy for Farmers established?
   A. 2000 B. 2002
   C. 2007 D. 2004

16. Which among the following is the largest food grain producing state of India?

    A. Uttar Pradesh B. Punjab

    C. Madhya Pradesh D. Rajasthan

17. Consider the following statements

    (i) Minimum support price is used to procure the food grains from the farmers at the remunerative prices.

    (ii) Central issue price is used to issue the food grains to the sections of society particularly poor and vulnerable section.

    Which among the following statement is /are correct?

    A. Only (i) B. Only (ii)

    C. Both (i) and (ii) D. Neither (i) or (ii)

18. Which among the following welfare scheme doesn't belong to farmers

    A. Kisan card scheme

    B. SHG linkage programme

    C. National Agricultural Insurance scheme

    D. Employee Referral scheme

19. For how many crops, MSP is announced in India?

    A. 20 B. 24

    C. 25 D. 23

20. Who regulates the market in agricultural products in India?

    A. Essential commodities Act 1955

    B. Agricultural produce market committee act enacted by states

    C. Agricultural produce (grading and marketing) act 1937

    D. Food products order 1956

21. The amount allocated to the Rashtriya Gokul Mission under dairy development during union budget 2019 is

    A. Rs. 750 crores B. Rs. 500 crores

    C. Rs. 450 crores D. Rs. 350 crores

22. NAFED stands for

    A. National Association Cooperative Marketing and Formation of India Ltd.

    B. National Agricultural Cooperative Marketing and Federation of India Ltd.

C. Norms on Agricultural Cooperative Marketing and Federation of India Ltd.

D. Norms on Agricultural Cooperative Mission and Federation of India Ltd.

23. Soil health card covers about

A. 10 parameters B. 13 parameters

C. 12 parameters D. 11 parameters

24. The MSP for paddy (fair average quality) in 2019-2020 is

A. Rs. 1550 B. Rs. 1500

C. Rs. 1600 D. Rs. 1815

25. Uzhavan App was launched in the year

A. 2016 B. 2017

C. 2018 D. 2019

26. PSF stands for

A. Project on stabilization of fund

B. Programme on stabilization of fund

C. Price stabilization fund

D. Price stabilization for farmers

27. TRYSEM, a programme made for the

A. Employment to rural youths

B. Employment to urban youths

C. Development of nutrition intake in the food of poor of the country

D. Providing road connectivity to the villages

28. The price at which the government purchases food grains for maintaining the public distribution system and for building up buffer stocks are known as

A. Minimum Support Prices B. Procurement prices

C. Issue prices D. Ceiling prices

29. Who announced the launch of Rashtriya Krishi Vikas Yojana?

A. Narendra Modi B. Dr. Manmohan Singh

C. Atal Bihari Vajpayee D. I.K.Gujral

30. Soil health card was launched in the year

A. 2018 B. 2017

C. 2015 D. 2016

31. National urban mission was launched by PM Modi in which state?
    A. New Delhi B. Chattisgarh
    C. Haryana D. Gujarat
32. Which year is the deadline for completion of PMGSY (Pradhan Mantri Gram Sadak Yojana)?
    A. 2018 B. 2020
    C. 2021 D. 2019
33. Rural Infrastructure Development Fund (RIDF) was instituted by which of the following?
    A. NABARD B. RBI
    C. Government of India D. Finance Ministry
34. The Integrated Child Development Services (ICDS) Scheme was launched in which year to provide food, preschool education, and primary healthcare to children less than 6 years of age and their mothers?
    A. 1980 B.1975
    C. 1982 D.1993
35. The magazine Panchayat Darpan launched to monitor the progress of which Yojana?
    A. Bhamashah Yojana B. Saansad Adarsh Gram Yojana
    C. Pradhan Mantri Awas Yojana D. Pradhan Mantri Jan-Dhan Yojana
36. Which of the following estimates the national income in India?
    A. Central Statistical Organization B. National Income Committee
    C. Planning Commission D. Reserve Bank of India
37. Which of the following is a new sub-scheme under the Rashtriya Krishi Vikas Yojana?
    A. Bringing green revolution to eastern region
    B. Special programme on oil palm area expansion
    C. Accelerated fodder development programme
    D. All the above
38. The Rashtriya Krishi Vikas Yojana of 2011-12 has 9 new sub-schemes under it. Which of the following is a new sub-scheme under the Rashtriya Krishi Vikas Yojana?
    A. Integrated development of pulses in rainfed areas
    B. Vegetable initiative for urban clusters
    C. National mission for protein supplements
    D. All the above

39. Which of the following is an area of focus under RKVY?
    A. Agriculture mechanization
    B. Support to state seed farms
    C. Encouraging non-farm activities
    D. All the above
40. Which of the following is not an area of focus under RKVY?
    A. Animal husbandry and fisheries development activities
    B. Special schemes for beneficiaries of land reforms
    C. Study tours of farmers
    D. None of the above
41. Who announced the introduction of National Food Security Act?
    A. Pranab Mukherjee
    B. Manmohan Singh
    C. P.Chidambaram
    D. Arun Jaitley
42. When was NFSM launched?
    A. Mid of 9th five-year plan
    B. End of 10th five-year plan
    C. Mid of 11th five-year plan
    D. End of 11th five-year plan
43. Which among the following does not belong to welfare schemes for the farmers?
    A. Kisan Credit Card Scheme
    B. SHG Bank Linkage Programme
    C. National Agricultural Insurance Scheme
    D. Employee Referral Scheme
44. When was On Farm Water Management Scheme launched?
    A. July 2000
    B. March 2002
    C. March 2004
    D. January 2004
45. When were kisan call centres established?
    A. July 2000
    B. March 2002
    C. March 2004
    D. January 2004
46. When was micro irrigation launched?
    A. March 2000
    B. March 2004
    C. January 2004
    D. January 2006
47. When was the new agricultural policy established?
    A. July 2000
    B. March 2002
    C. March 2004
    D. January 2004

48. The minimum guaranteed price at which the government offers to purchase any quantity is known as

A. Procurement price B. Minimum Support Price

C. Issue price D. Market price

49. In which state of India the famous cooperative AMUL is situated?

A. Gujarat B. Maharashtra

C. Delhi D. M P

50. When was the Antyodaya Anna Yojana (AAY) scheme launched?

A. In January 1999 B. In May, 2000

C. In December 2000 D. In October, 2005

51. Buffer stock is the stock of food grains procured by the government through

A. IFCI B. FCI

C. IDBI D. FICCI

52. What does food security mean?

A. Availability of food

B. Accessibility of food

C. Availability and accessibility of food to all at all times.

D. Availability, accessibility and affordability of food to all at all the times

53. Annapurna scheme provide food requirements of

A. Children B. Women

C. Senior citizens D. Students

54. The official document entitling the holder to a ration of food issued by the government of India is cknown as

A. Ration card B. Food card

C. Health card D. Insurance card

55. The color of Antyodaya Anna Yojana scheme card is

A. Pink B. Black

C. Blue D. Yellow

56. PMJDY stands for

A. Pradhan Mantri Jan Dhan Yojana

B. Prime Minister Jan Dhan Yojana

C. Pradhan Mantri Jeevan Dhan Yojana

D. None of these

57. The primary role of MANAGE

    A. Develop management skills   B. Generate employment

    C. Promote entrepreneurship   D. Promote spiritual talent

58. The toll free telephone number of the Kisan call centre is

    A. 1515   B. 1551

    C. 5115   D. 5151

59. The minimum support price for food grains was introduced in the year

    A. 1954   B. 1944

    C. 1964   D. 1974

60. In which year National Seed Policy was announced?

    A. 2000   B. 2002

    C. 2004   D. 2006

Answer keys

1.	A	11.	A	21.	A	31.	B	41.	A	51.	B
2.	C	12.	D	22.	B	32.	D	42.	D	52.	D
3.	D	13.	A	23.	C	33.	A	43.	D	53.	C
4.	A	14.	B	24.	D	34.	B	44.	B	54.	A
5.	A	15.	C	25.	C	35.	B	45.	D	55.	D
6.	A	16.	A	26.	C	36.	A	46.	D	56.	A
7.	D	17.	C	27.	A	37.	D	47.	A	57.	A
8.	A	18.	D	28.	B	38.	D	48.	B	58.	B
9.	B	19.	D	29.	B	39.	D	49.	A	59.	C
10.	B	20.	B	30.	C	40.	D	50.	C	60.	B

5

Import and Export

I. Choose the correct answer

1. Export earnings from agricultural sector is about

   A. 18% B. 15%

   C. 17% D. 20%

2. Indian food processing industry accounts for about what per cent of the total food market

   A. 52% B. 42%

   C. 32% D. 22%

3. Export potential of coffee in 2017-18 is about

   A. 300000 tons B. 395000 tons

   C. 350000 tons D. 385000 tons

4. Agricultural product is the ———largest exported principle commodity of the total export of the country

   A. Fourth B. Third

   C. Fifth D. Sixth

5. India is the largest exporter of

   A. Basmati rice B. Pulses

   C. Spices D. Fruits

6. India is the largest importer of

   A. Vegetables and fruits B. Vegetable oils

   C. Spices and condiments D. Pulses

7. Which of the following agricultural commodity of India gives the largest in terms of export value?

   A. Cotton B. Tea

   C. Rice D. Spice

8. Important export rice variety of India is

A. CO 51 B. Triveni

C. Basmati D. Jaya

9. Variety suitable for exporting to South Asian countries

A. GEB 24 B. ADT 27

C. TPS 4 D. BPT 5204

10. EIC stands for

A. Export information council B. Export inspection council

C. Export information committee D. Export inspection committee

11. Which organization is the nodal agency for export and import of agricultural commodities?

A. APEDA B. ICAR

C. MANAGE D. MPEDA

12. When agricultural export policy for farmers was launched?

A. 2016 B. 2017

C. 2018 D. 2019

13. Highest export produce is

A. Cereals B. Pulses

C. Oil seeds D. Cotton

14. India's total agricultural export in 2018-2019 accounts for

A. 2.00 lakh crores B. 1.58 lakh crores

C. 1.38 lakh crores D. 1.18 lakh crores

15. India's total agricultural import in 2018-19 accounts for

A. 1.51 lakh crores B. 1.41 lakh crores

C. 1.31 lakh crores D. 1.21 lakh crores

16. In which year, National food security mission was launched?

A. 2006 B. 2007

C. 2008 D. 2009

17. Which among the following is having the largest export value in India?

A. Groundnut B. Sunflower

C. Sesame D. Safflower

18. Which country is the largest supplier of almond?

    A. UK   B. USA

    C. Russia   d. Australia

19. Which crop is produced, consumed and imported in larger quantities in India?

    A. Cereals   B. Pulses

    C. Oil seeds   D. Millets

20. Which among the following crop is imported nearly 40%?

    A. Redgram   B. Blackgram

    C. Chickpea   D. Peas

Answer keys

1.	B	11.	A
2.	C	12.	C
3.	B	13.	A
4.	D	14.	D
5.	A	15.	A
6.	B	16.	B
7.	D	17.	A
8.	C	18.	B
9.	A	19.	B
10.	B	20.	D

6

Role of National Organisations in Agriculture

I. Choose the correct answer

1. NITI Aayog – NITI stands for

   A. National Institution for Transforming India

   B. National Innovation for Transforming India

   C. National Institute for Transferring India's Product

   D. National Integration of Transforming India

2. Apex body in development of agriculture and empowerment of rural people as a refinancing institution is

   A. RRB　　B. NBFC

   C. NABARD　　D. RBI

3. Minimum support price was announced by

   A. Central Government

   B. Directorate of Marketing and Inspection

   C. Planning Commission

   D. Commission on Agricultural Costs and Prices

4. Doubling farmers income in five years is the aim of

   A. NITI Aayog

   B. Ministry of Agriculture and Farmers welfare

   C. Directorate of economics and statistics

   D. Agricultural price commission

5. NITI-Aayog has formulated a model agricultural land leasing act in the year

   A. 2015　　B. 2016

   C. 2017　　D. 2018

6. Which state stands the highest in implementation of agricultural reforms as per NITI Aayog's index?

   A. Karnataka B. Tamil Nadu

   C. Maharashtra D. Gujarat

7. Public distribution system was established by GOI under

   A. Ministry of Agriculture and Farmers welfare

   B. Ministry of Rural Development

   C. Ministry of Health and Family welfare

   D. Ministry of Consumer Affairs, Food and Public distribution

8. National Seed Corporation was established in the year

   A. 1962 B. 1963

   C. 1964 D. 1965

9. Procurement of the marketable surplus food grains at incentive prices from the farmers on behalf of the central and state government is a function of

   A. AGMARK NET B. Food Corporation of India

   C. National Seed Corporation D. Public Distribution System

10. Who is the current CEO of the NITI Aayog?

    A. Rajeev Kumar B. Arvind Subramaniam

    C. Amitabh Kant D. Narendra Modi

11. When was the planning commission established?

    A. 10th March 1950 B. 15th March 1950

    C. 20th March 1950 D. 16th March 1951

12. Which agency is responsible for procurement, distribution and storage of food grain production in India?

    A. Ministry of Agriculture B. Food Corporation of India

    C. NAFED D. TRIFED

13. Who approves the Fair and Remunerative Price (FRP) of sugarcane?

    A. Cabinet Committee on Economic Affairs

    B. Commission for Agricultural Costs and Prices

    C. Directorate of Marketing and Inspection, Ministry of Agriculture

    D. Agricultural Produce Market Committee

14. National Development Council consists of

A. Members of planning commission

B. Governors of the states

C. Chief Ministers of the states

D. Both A and C

15. Consider the following statements regard to food stocks

(i) Food stock maintenance comes to the responsibility of state government

(ii) It ensures food security

(iii) It stabilizes open market prices.

(iv) Monthly supply through public distribution system.

Select a correct answer from the codes given below

A. (i) and (ii) are correct B. (ii) and (iii) are correct

C. (ii), (iii) and (iv) are correct D. All are correct

16. Food corporation of India was started in the year

A. 1975 B. 1985

C. 1965 D. 1995

17. The organization which advices the Government of India regarding agricultural price policy is

A. RBI B. NABARD

C. CACP D. FCI

18. The Targeted Public Distribution System (TPDS) is operated under the joint responsibility of Central Government and State/Union Territory Governments. The Central Government will be responsible for which of the following jobs/ duties under TPDS?

(i) Identifying the eligible Below Poverty Line (BPL) families

(ii) Lifting and distributing the allocated food grains within the States/UTs

(iii) Procurement, allocation and transportation of food grains upto the designated depots of FCI

(iv) Supervising the distribution of allocated food grains to eligible card holders through Fair Price Shops.

A. Only (i) B. (iii) and (iv) only

C. (i) and (iii) only D. (ii) and (iii) only

19. Public Distribution System (PDS) is aimed at
    A. Providing food security to the poor
    B. To prevent hoarding and black-marketing
    C. To prevent overcharging by traders
    D. All of these
20. CGIAR means
    A. Consultative Group on International Agricultural Research
    B. Consultative Group on Indian Agricultural Research
    C. Consultative Group on Innovative Agricultural Research
    D. Consultative Group on Indian Agricultural Review
21. Expansion of IFOAM is
    A. International Foreign Agriculture Meeting
    B. International Federation of Organic Agriculture Movement
    C. International Forum of Agricultural Movement
    D. International Federation of Agricultural Countries Meeting

Answer keys

1.	A	11.	B	21.	B
2.	C	12.	B		
3.	D	13.	A		
4.	A	14.	D		
5.	B	15.	C		
6.	C	16.	C		
7.	D	17.	C		
8.	B	18.	A		
9.	B	19.	D		
10.	C	20.	A		

UNIT II: AGRONOMY AND AGROMETEOROLOGY

1

Fundamentals of Crop Production

I. Choose the correct answer

1. Climatic factors influences ______ % of yield in crop production.
   A. 50% B. 60%
   C. 70% D. 40%

2. The range of temperature for most agricultural crops is
   A. 10-15°C B. 15-40°C
   C. 20-25°C D. >40°C

3. RH suitable for most of the agricultural crops is
   A. 50-90% B. 80%
   C. 70-90% D. 40-60%

4. Photosynthetic active radiation essential for carbohydrate production is
   A. 0.4-0.7μ B. 0.2-0.3μ
   C. 0.3-0.5μ D. 0.7-0.9μ

5. Wind velocity suitable for most of the crops is
   A. 2-3 km/hr B. 7-8 km/hr
   C. 4-6 km/hr D. 3-5 km/hr

6. Oxygen content in atmosphere is about
   A. 20% B. 20.95%
   C. 21% D. 20.87%

7. Which gas is toxic to plants
   A. CO B. CO_2
   C. H_2 D. Both A and B

8. Crops requiring low oxygen content is
   A. Pulses B. Groundnut
   C. Rice D. Maize

9. Crops requiring higher oxygen content is

A. Sugarcane B. Cotton

C. Legumes D. Both B and C

10. Synergistic effect is observed in

A. Cereals and legumes B. Cereals and weeds

C. Sugarcane and Striga D. Both B and C

11. Watermelon is a

A. Kharif crop B. Rabi crop

C. Zaid season crop D. Both B and C

12. Kar season in rice is

A. December – January B. February – March

C. May – June D. July - August

13. Suitable cropping pattern in Tamil Nadu

A. Rice - wheat B. Rice – rice - pulse

C. Rice - sugarcane - wheat D. Wheat - maize

14. Tamil Nadu comes under

A. Central tropical zone B. Southern tropical zone

C. Coastal humid zone D. Subtropical zone

15. Agroclimatic zones of Tamil Nadu is

A. 7 zones B. 15 zones

C. 20 zones D. 12 zones

16. Shifting cultivation is practiced in the zone of

A. Western Himalayan region B. Eastern Himalayan region

C. Middle gangetic plains D. Central plateau and hills region

17. Example of salt tolerant crop is

A. Groundnut B. Maize

C. Cotton D. Grams

18. The substance used to inhibit the growth of parasite which are secreted by plant tissues is called

A. Phytohormone B. Phytoalexin

C. Phytoauxin D. Phytogen

19. Match the following

List I	List II
A. Millets	1. 50-10 cm (Rainfall)
B. Sugarcane	2. High sandy loam
C. Cotton	3. 75-150 cm (Rainfall)
D. Oilseeds	4. Loamy soil

	A	B	C	D
A.	4	1	2	3
B.	2	1	4	3
C.	4	3	1	2
D.	3	4	2	1

20. Statement
   (i) Western Himalayan region consists of Jammu and Kashmir
   (ii) Kerala consists of eight Agro climatic zones
   A. (i) alone is correct B. (ii) alone is correct
   C. Both are correct D. Both are wrong

21. The district having lesser area of growing cotton and sugarcane in Tamil Nadu
   A. Salem and Thiruvannamalai B. Cuddalore and Thiruvarur
   C. Kancheepuram and Thiruvallur D. Thiruvannamalai and Cuddalore

22. The name of the rice growing season between the months of May to September in Tamil Nadu is known as
   A. Kuruvai B. Kar
   C. Swarnavari D. Samba

23. The length of crop growing season (days) in Cauvery delta zone of Tamil Nadu is
   A. 100-120 days B. 250-270 days
   C. 165-180 days D. 100-140 days

24. Water core in tomato is due to
   A. Low temperature B. High temperature
   C. High light intensity D. Low light intensity

25. Multitier cropping in cereals is
   A. Pearl millet – Greengram – Sorghum – Cowpea
   B. Pearl millet – Blackgram – Groundnut – Barnyard millet
   C. Sorghum – Dewgram – Roselle – Finger millet
   D. Sorghum – Cumbu – Cowpea /greengram – Moth bean

26. IFS system followed in wetlands commonly is

A. Rice + Fish + Poultry + Dairy
B. Paddy + Dairy + Maize
C. Groundnut + Dairy+Mushroom
D. Maize + Mushroom + Fish

27. Minimal tillage causes

A. Low infiltration
B. High resistance to root growth
C. Less soil compaction
D. Higher soil erosion

28. Minimal tillage can be practiced by

A. Complete disc ploughing
B. Complete disc harrowing
C. Plough plant tillage
D. Complete cultivator ploughing

29. Vertical mulching is

A. To improve infiltration and storage of rainwater
B. To protect soil from erosion
C. To reduce transpiration loss
D. To reduce evaporation loss

30. Alley cropping refers to

A. Growing trees and agricultural crops
B. Planting trees with companion crops in between rows
C. Growing mixed cropping
D. Growing intercropping in alleyways

31. (i) Subsistence farming is defined as crop grown just for the farmer and his family

(ii) The ownership of collective farming is constituted by state government

(iii) Extensive farming is done with low inputs of labour

A. (i) and (ii) are correct
B. (iii) alone is correct
C. (i) and (iii) are correct
D. All the statements are correct

32. Maximum number of operational land holdings in India is

A. Small holdings
B. Marginal land holdings
C. Medium holdings
D. Large land holdings

33. Match the following

A. Marginal holdings	1. > 25 acres
B. Small holdings	2. 2.5 – 5 acres
C. Medium holdings	3. < 2.5 acres
D. Large holdings	4. 10-25 acres

	A	B	C	D
A.	3	4	2	1
B.	3	2	1	4
C.	3	2	4	1
D.	4	3	1	2

34. Which of the following soil test parameters would give the best indication of general fertility?
A. Phosphorus
B. Potassium
C. Organic matter
D. Sulphur

35. Summer ploughing is essential to
A. Increase the water holding capacity
B. Kill weeds
C. Destroy insect pupae
D. All the above

36. Any direct or indirect harmful effect of one plant on another through chemical substances is called
A. Allelopathy
B. Inhibition
C. Annidation
D. Annihilation

37. What do you mean by conservational tillage?
A. Zero and minimum tillage
B. Primary tillage
C. Secondary tillage
D. Disc ploughing and harrowing

38. Which farming system is highly useful to achieve more sustainable biological and economic profitability on long run?
A. Conventional farming
B. State farming
C. Alternate land use farming
D. Commercial farming

39. Growing two or more crops in the same field simultaneous in definite proportion
A. Companion cropping
B. Sequential cropping
C. Inter cropping
D. Mixed cropping

40. Cropping intensity is higher in
A. Monocropping
B. Intercropping
C. Monoculture
D. Both B and C

41. Example of strip cropping is
A. Groundnut + Redgram
B. Maize + Greengram
C. Turmeric + Onion
D. Rice + Rice fallow pulse

42. Crop suitable for ratooning is

A. Sugarcane
B. Sorghum and brinjal
C. Both A and B
D. Pulses

43. Growing two or more crops simultaneously with no distinct row arrangement is called as

A. Relay intercropping
B. Mixed cropping
C. Ratoon cropping
D. Double cropping

44. A farmer owns 5 ha of land and cultivate crop in 5 ha during kharif season and again he raises 3 ha of crop during rabi season. Work out the cropping intensity?

A. 100%
B. 160 %
C. 62.5%
D. 125%

45. Example of primary tillage implement

A. Harrows
B. Rotavators
C. Cultivator
D. Bed furrow former

46. Most commonly followed IFS component for wetlands are

A. Rice culture + Fish culture
B. Rice culture + Apiculture
C. Rice culture + Sericulture
D. Rice culture + Dairy culture

47. Tillage under saturated condition is termed as

A. Contour tillage
B. Strip tillage
C. Wet tillage
D. Deep tillage

48. Land Equivalent Ratio (LER) is related to

A. Inter cropping
B. Sequential cropping
C. Ratooning
D. None of the above

49. The practice of allowing the regrowth of the planted crops is known as

A. Mixed cropping
B. Ratooning
C. Sequential cropping
D. Intercropping

50. Alley cropping is known as

A. Ley system
B. Silvi-pastural system
C. Food-cum-fruit system
D. Hedgerow inter cropping

51. Growing two or more crops in the same field simultaneous in definite proportion

A. Companion cropping
B. Sequential cropping
C. Inter cropping
D. Mixed cropping

52. Relative Yield Total (RYT) in cropping system is

A. $\frac{Y\ ba + Y\ bb}{Y\ aa + Y\ ab}$ B. $\frac{Y\ bb + Y\ ba}{Y\ aa + Y\ bb}$

C. $\frac{Y\ aa + Y\ bb}{Y\ ba + Y\ ba}$ D. $\frac{Y\ ab + Y\ ba}{Y\ aa + Y\ bb}$

53. The crops recommended for the tannery waste affected soils are

A. Tomato (PKM1) and brinjal

B. Rice (ASD 16) and finger millet (CO 12)

C. Sunflower (CO 4) and mustard

D. All the above

54. The country plough produced in one of the following places is very famous in Tamil Nadu

A. Thiruppachethi B. Melur

C. Kangeyam D. Cholavandhan

55. Which one of the following implements is not used for wet land operations?

A. Helical blade puddler B. Green manure trampler

C. Cage wheel D. Junior hoe

56. Planting of succeeding crop before harvesting the proceeding crop is known as

A. Ratoon cropping B. Mono cropping

C. Sequence cropping D. Relay cropping

57. Growing of coconut, black pepper and ginger simultaneously in the same field is called

A. Relay cropping B. Inter cropping

C. Mixed cropping D. Multistoreyed cropping

58. Lac dye contains _______ and used as manure

A. Phosphorus B. Potash

C. Ammonium sulphide D. Nitrogen

59. When was the Agriculture act enacted?

A. 1967 B. 1929

C. 1947 D. 1935

60. Who is the father of Agronomy?

A. Jethro tull
B. Pietro de' Crescenzi
C. Robinson
D. Munsell

61. Match list I with list II and choose the correct options given below

List I	List II
a. Blue revolution	1. Fertilizer
b. Green revolution	2. Cotton
c. Grey revolution	3. Fish
d. Silver revolution	4. High yielding varieties

	a	b	c	d
A.	2	3	4	1
B.	3	4	1	2
C.	3	1	4	2
D.	2	4	3	1

62. The term Agronomy is derived from which language

A. Greek
B. Latin
C. German
D. French

63. Consider the statement and choose the correct answer - Agronomy

(i) To identify proper season for cultivation of wide range of crops

(ii) Package of practices to explore full potential of new varieties

(iii) It does not maintain ecological balance

A. (i) alone is correct
B. (ii) alone is correct
C. (i) and (ii) are correct
D. All the statements are correct

64. What is the optimum range of temperature for agricultural crops?

A. 15-30°C
B. 30-35°C
C. 15-20°C
D. 20-30°C

65. For fixing atmospheric nitrogen what is the symbiotic microorganism involved in soil

A. *Trichoderma*
B. Azotobacter
C. *Rhizobium*
D. *Azospirillum*

66. What are the minerals derived from weathering of rocks and minerals?

A. N, Cu, Zn
B. Ca, Mg, S
C. P, Cu, B
D. Zn, Cl, Ni

67. What is the carbon content range in soil organic matter?

A. 0.5 – 3.0% B. 5 -6 %

C. 0.05 – 0.03% D. 4 – 5%

68. What is the ideal range of pH for most of the field crops?

A. < 7 B. > 7

C. 7 D. 10

69. Consider the statement and choose the correct answer regarding multiple cropping

(i) Mixed intercropping – Growing two (or) more crops simultaneously

(ii) Row intercropping – Growing two (or) more crops simultaneously but planted in rows

(iii) Strip intercropping – Growing two (or) more crops in ridges

(iv) Relay intercropping – Raising second crop at the maturity stage of first crop but before harvesting

A. (i) (ii) and (iii) are correct B. (ii) and (iv) are correct

C. All the statements are correct D. (i), (ii) and (iv) are correct

70. The term tillage is derived from which word

A. Anglo – saxon B. Greek

C. Latin D. Swedish

71. Consider the statement and choose the correct answer regarding tillage

(i) Primary tillage is done after harvest of the crop

(ii) Secondary tillage operation is performed on the soil after summer tillage

(iii) Inter tillage is done in the standing crop

(iv) Zero tillage – residues of previous crop is left in the soil and no tillage will be done

A. (i), (ii) and (iii) are correct B. (i), (iii) and (iv) are correct

C. (i), (ii) and (iv) are correct D. All the statements are correct

72. Match list I with list II and choose the correct options given below

List I	**List II**
a. Sub – soil tillage	1. Increases water holding capacity
b. Bind tillage	2. Puddling
c. Dry tillage	3. Break the hard pan beneath plough layer
d. Wet tillage	4. Pre-emergence stage

	a	b	c	d
A.	2	3	1	4
B.	3	4	2	1
C.	3	4	1	2
D.	2	1	3	4

73. What is the depth of stubble mulch tillage

A. 10 – 11 cm
B. 8 – 10 cm
C. 18 – 20 cm
D. 12 – 15 cm

74. Match List I with List II and choose the correct options given below

List I	**List II**
a. Tractor operated pit digger	1. Sowing equipment
b. Rice transplanter	2. Harvesting and threshing implement
c. Banana clump removal	3. Tillage implement
d. Impact type groundnut stripper	4. Miscellaneous farm equipments

	a	b	c	d
A.	3	1	4	2
B.	2	3	4	1
C.	2	4	3	1
D.	3	2	4	1

75. Which among the following is a shallow rooted crop?

A. Onion
B. Coconut
C. Pulses
D. Maize

76. What is the ideal depth of deep rooted crops?

A. 30-60 cm
B. 90-150 cm
C. 50-100 cm
D. 20-30 cm

77. Indian Institute of Pulses Research is suited at

A. Lucknow
B. Kanpur
C. Almora
D. Cuttack

78. When was Madras Agricultural college was established?

A. 1976
B. 1906
C. 1876
D. 1971

79. Central Institute of Cotton Research is situated at

A. Coimbatore
B. Varanasi
C. Trivandrum
D. Nagpur

80. Agriculture sector contribution to GDP is during 2017

A. 16% B. 17.9%

C. 18% D. 15%

81. Name a mixed cropping sequence suitable for drought prone and irrigated areas

A. Sesamum, maize, oats B. Sorghum, wheat

C. Maize, upland rice, berseem D. Sesamum, pearl millet, niger

82. Which one of the following crop rotation is the best for maintaining soil fertility?

A. Maize-toria-wheat B. Paddy-wheat-cowpea

C. Paddy-potato-greengram D. Soybean-wheat-greengram

83. The main objectives of growing a catch crop is to

A. Add more residues to the soil

B. Prevent cracking of soil

C. Suppress weeds

D. Get an additional income without further investment

84. The ratio between total crop area and actual net cultivated area is

A. Cropping ratio B. Cropping intensity

C. Cropping pattern D. Cropping multiple

85. The process of loosening and turning the soil is called

A. Broadcasting B. Irrigation

C. Ploughing D. Levelling

86. The organic substance obtained from dead plants and animal wastes is

A. Manure B. Fertilizer

C. Irrigation D. Agriculture

87. Rotation of crops means

A. Growing of different crops in the same area in sequential seasons.

B. Shifting of area of same crops.

C. Growing two or more crops simultaneously to increase productivity.

D. Alternating crops with fruits over a period of years.

88. Which of the following is a cash crop in India?

A. Rice B. Wheat

C. Sugarcane D. Sorghum

89. Which of the following crops would be preferred for sowing in order to enrich the soil with nitrogen?
    A. Wheat B. Mustard
    C. Sunflower D. Gram
90. Which one of the following is known as a pseudocereal?
    A. Wheat B. Quinoa
    C. Horse gram D. Barley
91. Besides rabi and kharif, which is the third crop season in India?
    A. Zaid B. Barsati
    C. Sharad D. Jhum
92. Kharif crops are harvested in
    A. June – July B. October - November
    C. May – June C. March - April
93. Which one among the following agricultural crops/groups of crops may be grown in abundant in lowlands and river deltas of fertile alluvial soil where there is high summer temperature and rainfall varies from 180 cm to 250 cm?
    A. Wheat and sugarcane B. Cotton
    C. Maize and coarse crops D. Rice, jute and tea
94. Golden rice variety has been developed to combat the deficiency of
    A. Iron B. Vitamin C
    C. Calcium D. Vitamin A

Answer keys

1. A	16. B	31. C	46. A	61. B	76. B	91. A
2. B	17. C	32. B	47. C	62. A	77. B	92. B
3. D	18. B	33. C	48. A	63. C	78. C	93. D
4. A	19. C	34. C	49. B	64. D	79. D	94. D
5. C	20. C	35. D	50. D	65. C	80. B	
6. B	21. C	36. A	51. C	66. B	81. D	
7. A	22. C	37. A	52. D	67. A	82. D	
8. C	23. A	38. C	53. D	68. C	83. D	
9. D	24. B	39. C	54. B	69. D	84. B	
10. A	25. D	40. B	55. D	70. A	85. C	
11. C	26. A	41. A	56. D	71. B	86. A	
12. C	27. C	42. C	57. D	72. C	87. A	
13. B	28. C	43. B	58. D	73. D	88. C	
14. B	29. A	44. B	59. C	74. A	89. D	
15. A	30. B	45. C	60. B	75. A	90. B	

2

Production Technology of Field Crops

2.1 CEREALS

2.1.1 Rice

1. Choose the correct answer

1. In rice, the panicle initiation takes place in about

   A. 10 days after transplanting B. 15 days after transplanting

   C. 20 days after transplanting D. 40 days after transplanting

2. Seed hardening of rice seeds is usually done with

   A. Potassium chloride B. Sodium sulphate

   C. Super phosphate D. Urea

3. The upgrading of paddy seeds by a density grading is done by using

   A. Potassium chloride B. Ammonium chloride

   C. Zinc chloride D. Sodium chloride

4. *Azospirillum* application to paddy crop supplements

   A. Nitrogen requirement B. Phosphorous requirement

   C. Potassium requirement D. Sulphur requirement

5. The nutrient that is usually applied to paddy crop in split doses is

   A. Gypsum B. Super phosphate

   C. Muriate of potash D. Urea

6. The optimum temperature for rice growth is

   A. 10 – 20°C B. 20 – 30°C

   C. 30 – 40°C D. 40 – 50°C

7. The original seed produced for the first time by the plant breeder is called

   A. Certified seed B. Foundation seed

   C. Breeder seed D. Nucleus seed

8. The term employed for exploitation for hybrid vigour is called

A. Apomixis B. Heterosis

C. Polygamous D. Hermaphrodite

9. Name the growth regulator extensively used in hybrid seed production of rice.

A. IAA B. GA_3

C. Cytocyme D. Ethrel

10. Rice nursery area required for planting 1 ha of main field is

A. 1500 m^2 B. 2000 m^2

C. 500 m^2 D. 800 m^2

11. The cohesiveness and tenderness of cooked rice depends largely on

A. The percentage of amylase

B. The percentage of amylopectin

C. The proportion of amylase and protein

D. The proportion of amylase and amylopectin

12. Propanil (Stamp F-34) herbicide should be applied in rice after transplanting

A. 2 – 4 DAT (Days after transplanting)

B. 6 – 8 DAT (Days after transplanting)

C. 14 – 15 DAT(Days after transplanting)

D. 2 weeks after transplanting

13. Tungro virus of rice is transmitted by

A. Stem borer B. Leaf roller

C. Green leaf hopper D. Gundhi bug

14. Idea of super rice was given by

A. GH Shull B. GS Khush

C. VL Chopra D. Yoshida

15. The N fertilizer use efficiency in rice can be increased by using

A. S-coated urea B. Ammonium chloride

C. BGA D. Azophos

16. Which gas is released from paddy fields?

A. CH_4 B. H_2S

C. CO_2 D. NH_3

17. The duration of paddy varieties as short medium and long is based on
    A. Reproductive phase B. Vegetative phase
    C. Germination to flowering D. Ripening phase
18. Rice is usually cultivated as
    A. Low land rice B. Upland rice
    C. Semi dry rice D. Dry land rice
19. An example for warm season crop is
    A. Rice B. Wheat
    C. Barley D. Oats
20. In rice, dapog nursery would be ready for transplanting in
    A. 11 – 14 days B. 14 – 17 days
    C. 17 – 20 days D. 20 – 23 days
21. In wet bed method of nursery of rice, seedling would be ready for transplanting at an age of
    A. 14 days B. 15 – 20 days
    C. 20 - 25 days D. 25 –30 days
22. The optimum seed rate for broadcasted rice crop is
    A. 10 – 15 kg/ha B. 15 – 20 kg/ha
    C. 30 – 40 kg/ha D. 80-120 kg/ha
23. The highest productivity of rice is recorded in
    A. Assam B. Andhra Pradesh
    C. West Bengal D. Punjab
24. The country that ranks second after China in commercial production of hybrid is
    A. Japan B. India
    C. Thailand D. Russia
25. The ideal pH for rice cultivation is
    A. 5.5 - 6.5 B. 4.5 - 5.5
    C. 6.5 - 7.5 D. 7.5- 8.0
26. Ideal soil type for paddy cultivation is
    A. Sandy loam B. Silty and clay loam
    C. Clay or clay loamy D. Sandy soil

27. Paddy prefers

A. Alkaline soil B. Saline soil

C. Saline-sodic D. Acidic soil

28. Paddy grows under

A. Dry condition B. Submerged condition

C. Marshy D. Deep water condition

29. Paddy crop needs

A. Hot and humid climate B. Temperate climate

C. Sub-humid climate D. Sub-tropical climate

30. Average temperature required for crop growth of paddy is

A. 15-20°C B. 21-37°C

C. 40-45°C D. 35-40°C

31. Sornavari season in rice is

A. April - May B. December – January

C. June - July D. September - October

32. Pishanam season in rice is

A. April - May B. December – January

C. June - July D. September - October

33. Seed rate for hybrid rice is

A. 30 kg/ha B. 40 kg/ha

C. 60 kg/ha D. 20 kg/ha

34. Fungicide used for seed treatment in paddy is

A. Ridomil B. Carbendazim

C. Hinoson D. Vitavax

35. Pre-emergence herbicide used for paddy is

A. 2, 4 -D B. Glyphosate

C. Pretilachlor/butachlor D. Atrazine

36. To avoid root snapping problem in paddy cultivation, quantity of gypsum applied to nursery is

A. 2.5 kg/cent B. 1 kg/cent

C. 5 kg/cent D. 10 kg/cent

37. Depth of water to be maintained in paddy field is

A. 5 cm B. 2.5 cm

C. 1 cm D. 10 cm

38. Optimum age for transplanting in rice (dry nursery field)

A. 3rd leaf stage B. 4th leaf stage

C. 5th leaf stage D. 2nd leaf stage

39. Amount of zinc sulphate to be applied for sodic soils in paddy cultivation is

A. 37.5 kg/ha B. 25 kg/ha

C. 12.5 kg/ha D. 10 kg/ha

40. Spacing for paddy under high fertility soils of long duration varieties is

A. 15 x 10 cm B. 20 x 10 cm

C. 20 x 20 cm D. 20 x 15 cm

41. Fertilizer recommendation for hybrid rice is

A. 120:40:40 kg NPK/ha B. 150:50:50 kg NPK/ha

C. 175:50:50 kg NPK/ha D. 175:60:60 kg NPK/ha

42. Moisture content suitable for storage of rice is

A. 8% B. 12%

C. 15% D. 13%

43. Maturity can be hastened by 3-4 days by spraying of

A. 20% KCl B. 20% NaCl

C. 25% NaCl D. 25% KCl

44. Rice bowl of India is

A. Andhra Pradesh C. Karnataka

C. Maharashtra D. Gujarat

45. Rice hulling percentage is

A. 68-72% B. 82-92%

C. 60-65% D. 50-65%

46. The suitable temperature for good tillering habit is

A. below 15°C B. 25-37°C

C. 20-25°C D. 16-20°C

47. Match list I with list II and choose the correct options given below

List I	**List II**
a. Rice	1. Abyssinia
b. Wheat	2. Asia minor
c. Barley	3. South East Asia
d. Oats	4. Pakistan and Afghanistan

	a	b	c	d
A.	4	3	2	1
B.	3	4	2	1
C.	3	2	4	1
D.	4	2	3	1

48. What is the recommended fertilizer schedule for medium and long duration variety of paddy?
   A. 120:40:40 kg NPK/ha
   B. 175:60:60 kg NPK/ha
   C. 150:50:50 kg NPK/ha
   D. 175:50:50 kg NPK/ha

49. Consider the statement and choose the correct answer
   (i) Short duration (latest) variety of rice: RMD (R) 1, TPS (R) 4, PMK (R) 4
   (ii) Medium duration (latest) variety: CO(R) 48, CO(R) 50, TRY (R) 3
   (iii) Long duration variety of rice: BPT 5123, IR 64
   A. (i) and (ii) are is correct
   B. (i) and (iii) are correct
   C. (ii) and (iii) are is correct
   D. All the statements are correct

50. Match list I with list II and choose the correct options given below

List I	List II
a. Navarai	1. >150 days
b. Samba	2. 115-120 days
c. Late thaladi	3. <120 days
d. Late pishanam	4. 130-135 days

	a	b	c	d
A.	4	1	2	3
B.	4	3	2	1
C.	3	2	1	4
D.	3	1	2	4

Answer keys

1	B	11	D	21	C	31	A	41	C
2	A	12	B	22	D	32	D	42	B
3	D	13	C	23	D	33	D	43	B
4	A	14	B	24	B	34	A	44	A
5	D	15	D	25	A	35	B	45	A
6	B	16	A	26	C	36	B	46	D
7	C	17	B	27	D	37	A	47	B
8	B	18	A	28	B	38	B	48	C
9	B	19	A	29	A	39	A	49	A
10	D	20	A	30	B	40	C	50	D

2. One word question and answer

1. Which country has got marketing patent of basmati rice?

Ans. USA

2. Which is the most outstanding green manure crop?

Ans. Sunhemp

3. Mention the soil suitable for rice growing

Ans. Alluvial

4. In which crop, the use of BGA as a biofertilizer will be most useful?

Ans. Rice

5. What is the characteristic root system in rice?

Ans. Fibrous

6. In which state the floating rice is popular?

Ans. West Bengal

7. What causes dead heart and white head damage to rice?

Ans. Stem borer

8. Name the insect that causes the silvery shoot or onion leaf symptom of rice tillers

Ans. Gall midge

9. What is the test weight of basmati rice?

Ans. 20-21g

10. Which metal toxicity is named as Akiochi disease in rice?

Ans. Hydrogen sulphide

11. What is the name of the disease due to zinc deficiency in rice?

Ans. Khaira

12. What is the form of nitrogen absorbed by all crops except rice?

Ans. Nitrate

13. Rice can survive and grow under water logged conditions since

Ans.
- It uptakes oxygen from water
- Supplies oxygen from leaves to roots
- Anaerobic respiration in roots
- Roots grow above ground level

14. The seed dormany in paddy can be eliminated by

Ans. Treating the seeds with HNO_3 for 12 – 16 h

15. Mention few benefits of SRI system of rice cultivation

Ans.
- Saving seeds
- Saving water
- Better root growth
- Improve tillering
- Low cost

16. Mention few rice growing seasons

Ans.
- Navari
- Sornavari
- Early kar
- Kuruvai
- Early samba
- Samba
- Late samba
- Late thaladi

17. For mitigating water stream situation in paddy cultivation foliar application is done

Ans.
- CCC(Cycocel)
- Application of kaolin clay as antitranspirant
- Foliar spray with potassium chloride.

18. Mention few reasons favoring blast disease in rice

Ans.
- Heavy dose of nitrogen
- High atmospheric humidity
- Night temperature around 20°C

19. Name the superfine, aromatic, basmati hybrid

Ans. Pusa RH 10

20. Name the deep water rice

Ans. Jai suriya

21. Name the saline tolerant rice variety

Ans. SR26B

22. The first dwarf variety introduced in India

Ans. IR 8

23. What is the acceptable moisture content for safe storage of rice?

Ans. 12%

24. What is the optimum seed rate for transplanted rice?

Ans. 50 kg/ha.

25. The best nitrogenous fertilizer suited for rice crop

Ans. Ammonium sulphate

26. What is the type of fruit in cereals?

Ans. Caryopsis

27. What is the seed rate of paddy required for adopting SRI technique?

Ans. 5 kg/ha

2.1.2 Wheat

1. Choose the correct answer

1. *Phlaris minor* is a major weed in

   A. Rice B. Wheat

   C. Sorghum D. Tobacco

2. Dr. Norman Borlaug of Mexico introduced the following crop in India

   A. Mexican dwarf wheat B. Hybrid rice

   C. Maize D. Pearl millet

3. King of cereals is

   A. Rice B. Maize

   C. Wheat D. Pearl millet

4. The maximum area in wheat crop is in the state of

   A. Tamil Nadu B. Bihar

   C. Uttar Pradesh D. Punjab

5. The acceptable moisture content for safe storage of wheat is

   A. 6% B. 10%

   C. 12% D. 14%

6. The optimum seed rate for wheat crop is

   A. 60 kg/ha B. 60 – 75 kg/ha

   C. 80 – 90 kg/ha D. 100-125 kg/ha

7. The major diseases of wheat are caused by

   A. Bacteria B. Nutrient deficiency

   C. Virus D. Fungi

8. Sowing time of wheat in peninsular zones in India

   A. Middle of November B. Middle of December

   C. First week of December D. First week of November

9. Zinc deficiency in wheat can be corrected by foliar spray of
   A. 0.25% $ZnSO_4$ B. 0.5% $ZnSO_4$
   C. 0.75% $ZnSO_4$ D. 1% $ZnSO_4$
10. Water requirement for wheat is
   A. 500-800 mm B. 450-650 mm
   C. 1200-1500 mm D. 800-900 mm
11. Commercially used herbicide for wheat is
   A. Pendimethalin B. Isoproturon
   C. Butachlor D. 2,4-D
12. Under which condition wheat is harvested earlier?
   A. Irrigated B. Rainfed
   C. Both irrigated and rainfed D. None of these
13. Tetraploid wheat is
   A. Einkorn wheat B. Bread wheat
   C. Durum wheat D. Summer wheat
14. Durum wheat is also known as
   A. Winter wheat B. Emmer wheat
   C. Common wheat D. Macroni wheat
15. Which is the commonly used wheat species for preparation of noodles, vermicelli?
   A. Common wheat B. Duram wheat
   C. Emmer wheat D. Short wheat
16. What is triticale?
   A. Wheat x Rye B. Wheat x Oats
   C. Wheat x Barely D. Wheat x Wheat
17. Which is the commonly used wheat (Allohexaploid species) for diet
   A. *Triticum durum* B. *Triticum dicoccum*
   C. *Triticum monococcum* D. *Triticum aestivum*
18. The inflorescence of wheat is known as
   A. Ear B. Raceme
   C. Panicle D. Umbel
19. The rainfed wheat is usually grown during the month of
   A. October - November B. March – April
   C. August – September D. June – July

20. Loose smut of wheat can be controlled by
    A. Crop rotation
    B. Soil treatment with non systemic fungicides
    C. Seed treatment with systemic fungicides
    D. Spraying the crop with fungicides
21. The most critical stage for water requirement in wheat is
    A. Booting B. Tillering
    C. Crown root initiation D. Heading
22. Shelling percentage of wheat is
    A. 30% B. 40%
    C. 50% D. 60%
23. Temperature for germination of wheat seed is
    A. 10-15°C B. 20-25°C
    C. 30-35°C D. 40-45°C

Answer keys

1	B	11	B	21	C
2	A	12	B	22	D
3	C	13	C	23	B
4	C	14	D	24	
5	C	15	B		
6	D	16	A		
7	D	17	D		
8	C	18	A		
9	B	19	A		
10	B	20	C		

2. One word question and answer

1. Which crop is used for intercropping in wheat?

Ans. Mustard

2. At what temperature proper grain filling takes place in wheat?

Ans. 23 - 25 °C

3. What is the substance responsible for bread making quality of wheat?

Ans. Gluten

4. What crop is having maximum area under irrigation?

Ans. Wheat

5. Mention few dwarf varieties of wheat under cultivation

Ans. • Kalyan sona
• Lerma Rojo 64-A
• Sonara 64

6. Mention photo nonsensitive varieties of wheat suitable for rainfed cultivation

Ans. • Sonalika
• Sharbati sonara

7. Mention few varieties of wheat useful in bread making.

Ans. • Deccan queen
• Sharbati sonara

8. For improving yield of wheat during green revolution the dwarfing gene introduced is

Ans. Norin-10

9. What is the temperature required for wheat seed germination?

Ans. 20°C

10. Mention a few selections in wheat

Ans. • Kalyan sona
• Sonalika

2.1.3 Barley

1. Choose the correct answer

1. Crop which is tolerant to salinity is

A. Rice B. Barely

C. Wheat D. Oats

2. Origin of barely is

A. Ethiopia B. South East Asia

C. Kenya D. Egypt

3. Spacing recommended for barley is

A. 22.5 cm row spacing B. 20 cm row spacing

C. 27.5 cm row spacing D. 25 cm row spacing

4. Depth of sowing under rainfed condition in barley is

A. 1 - 2 cm B. 4 - 6 cm

C. 6 - 8 cm D. 2 - 3 cm

5. Barley is raised as mixed crop with

   A. Chickpea B. Greengram

   C. Niger D. Blackgram

Answer keys

1 B
2 A
3 A
4 C
5 A

2.1.4 Oats

1. Choose the correct answer

1. Crop which is best adapted to cotton belt is

   A. Banana B. Sugarcane

   C. Oats D. Jute

2. Best time of sowing for oats is

   A. Mid November – mid December

   B. Mid August - mid September

   C. Mid June - July

   D. Mid October to mid November

3. Critical stage for irrigation of oats is

   A. Flowering stage B. Tillering stage

   C. Panicle stage D. Maturation stage

4. The crop which is used as fodder cum grain is

   A. Wheat B. Sorghum

   C. Oats D. Barley

5. ____ also cultivated as green manure crop and cover crop

   A. Rye B. Oats

   C. Triticale D. Barley

Answer keys

1 C
2 D
3 B
4 C
5 A

2.2 MILLETS

2.2.1 Maize

1. Choose the correct answer

1. The charcoal rot in maize crop is due to infection by

   A. Bacteria B. Fungi

   C. Mycoplasma D. Virus

2. Maize was introduced in India in 17th century by

   A. Japanese B. Portuguese

   C. Chinese D. Americans

3. First hybrid maize, Ganga – 1 was developed in India in

   A. 1957 B. 1961

   C. 1964 D. 1965

4. Bund former is used for making

   A. Furrows B. Ridges/bunds

   C. Soil smooth D. Levelling

5. In maize plants

   A. Silk appears first B. Tassel appears first

   C. Flowers appears first D. Cob appears first

6. Which one of the following crops is most sensitive to both excess moisture and drought?

   A. Direct seeded rice B. Maize

   C. Sunflower D. Sorghum

7. The water requirement for maize crop is

   A. 200 – 300 mm B. 300 – 450 mm

   C. 500-800 mm D. 800 – 1000 mm

8. The fertilizer recommendation for maize crop is

   A. 100:50:50 kg/NPK/ha B. 80:60:40 kg/NPK/ha

   C. 135:62:50 kg/NPK/ha D. 120:150:80 kg/NPK/ha

9. Origin of maize is

   A. Mexico B. Abyssinia

   C. South East Asia D. India

10. Sugar content in sweet corn (white) is
    A. 8.2 g per 100g B. 5.2 g per 100g
    C. 1.2 g per 100g D. 3.2 g per 100g
11. Type of corn which contains soft starch with little or the hard starch is
    A. Waxy corn B. Pop corn
    C. Flour corn D. Flint corn
12. Type of corn which contains amylopectin only is
    A. Waxy corn B. Pop corn
    C. Flour corn D. Flint corn
13. Maximum rate of temperature for maize growth is
    A. 20°C B. 30°C
    C. 40°C D. 10°C
14. Maize grown in thaipattam season occurs during
    A. January - February B. July – August
    C. September - October D. November - December
15. The herbicide which is not used when sorghum intercrop with pulses is
    A. Pendimethalin B. Atrazine
    C. Butachlor D. 2, 4 -D
16. Depth of sowing in maize is
    A. 2.5 inches/4-5 cm B. 4 inches/3-4 cm
    C. 1.5 inches/4-5 cm D. 1.0 inches /1-2 cm
17. The recommended rate of water requirement for maize is
    A. 700 - 800 mm B. 600 - 700 mm
    C. 500 - 600 mm D. Above 800 mm
18. Fertilizer recommendation for rainfed maize is ____ NPK kg/ha.
    A. 60:30:30 B. 40:20:20
    C. 70:35:35 D. 100:50:50
19. Shelling percentage of normal ears in maize is
    A. 50% B. 60%
    C. 80% D. 70%

20. Match list I with list II and choose the correct options given below

List I	List II
a. Maize	1. Africa
b. Sorghum	2. Ethiopa
c. Pearl millet	3. Mexico and Central America
d. Finger millet	4. Africa and India

	a	b	c	d
A.	4	2	3	1
B.	3	2	1	4
C.	3	4	1	2
D.	4	3	2	1

21. Consider the statement and choose the correct one

(i) Flint corn: hard starch in outer portion

(ii) Dent corn: hard starch confined to kernel only

(iii) Sweet corn: 20% dry matter is sugar

(iv) Pop corn: kernel is big and extreme form of dent corn

A. (i), (ii) and (iii) are correct B. All the statement are correct

C. (i) and (ii) are correct D. (i), (iii) and (iv) are correct

22. What is the fertilizer recommendation for maize under irrigated condition?

A. 125:65:75 kg/NPK/ha B. 130:65:70 kg/NPK/ha

C. 135:62.5:50 kg/NPK/ha D. 135:70:50 kg/NPK/ha

23. Match list I with list II and choose the correct options given below

List I	List II
a. Maize	1. Rainfed crop (June – July)
b. Sorghum	2. Adipattam (July – August)
c. Pearl millet	3. Chithiraipattam (March – April)
d. Finger millet	4. Thaipattam (January – February)

	a	b	c	d
A.	2	3	1	4
B.	2	4	3	1
C.	3	4	2	1
D.	2	1	3	4

24. What is the cob called after extraction of grains in maize?

A. Sheath B. Tassel

C. Arrow D. Shank

25. Consider the statement and choose the correct one in respect of spacing

(i) Maize	60 x 25 cm
(ii) Sorghum	45 x 25 cm
(iii) Minor millets	22.5 x 10 cm

A. (i) and (ii) are correct B. (ii) and (iii) are correct

C. All the statements are correct D. (i) and (iii) are correct

26. Match list I with list II and choose the correct options given below

List I	**List II**
a. Maize	1. CO 3
b. Sorghum	2. APK 1
c. Pearl millet	3. Paiyur 1
d. Little millet	4. COH (M) 5

	a	b	c	d
A.	4	3	2	1
B.	4	2	3	1
C.	3	1	2	4
D.	4	1	2	3

Answer keys

1	B	11	C	21	A
2	B	12	A	22	C
3	B	13	B	23	B
4	B	14	A	24	D
5	B	15	B	25	C
6	B	16	A	26	A
7	C	17	B		
8	C	18	A		
9	A	19	D		
10	B	20	C		

2. One word question and answer

1. What is the most critical stage of maize from irrigation point of view?

Ans. Tasseling stage

2. How much water required for growth of maize per day per plant?

Ans. 2 – 3 litres

3. Mention any one common herbicide used in maize cultivation

Ans. Atrazine

4. What is the nutrient that is causing deficient disorder known as white bud of maize.

Ans. Zinc

5. Name the state in India where the maize productivity is maximum

Ans. Andhra Pradesh

6. What is the soil best suited for maize growing?

Ans. Clay loam

7. Mention few hybrids of maize.

Ans. Ganga – 5, COH – 1,COH – 2

2.2.2 Sorghum

1. Choose the correct answer

1. Camel food crop is

   A. Maize B. Sorghum

   C. Millets D. Pearl millet

2. The optimum plant population per hectare of sorghum is

   A. 50,000 plants B. 1,00,000 plants

   C. 1,50,000 plants D. 2,00,000 plants

3. The fertilizer schedule for rainfed sorghum

   A. 20:20:10 kg NPK/ha B. 30:10:10 kg NPK/ha

   C. 40:20:10 kg NPK/ha D. 50:30:10 kg NPK/ha

4. CSH – 1 was first sorghum hybrid released in

   A. 1961 B. 1962

   C. 1963 D. 1964

5. The vegetative phase in cereals is characterized as

   A. Seed germination to panicle initiation

   B. Germination to tillering

   C. Germination to flowering

   D. Germination to maturity

6. Most of the stored form of food in cereal grain is

   A. Protein B. Fat

   C. Carbohydrate D. Glycoprotein

7. Cereal crops are highly valued food because they provide
   A. Large amount of minerals B. Large amount of energy
   C. Large amount of proteins D. Large amount of fat
8. The water requirement for sorghum crop
   A. 250 – 300 mm B. 300 – 450 mm
   C. 450-650 mm D. 650 – 800 mm
9. Test weight of sorghum is
   A. 20 – 25 gram B. 25 – 30 gram
   C. 30 – 35 gram D. 70 – 75 gram
10. Seed rate of transplanted sorghum is
   A. 7.5 kg/ha B. 10 kg/ha
   C. 15 kg/ha D. 25 kg/ha
11. Parasitic weed in sorghum is
   A. Dodder B. Striga
   C. Cuscutta D. Orabanche
12. Fertilizer recommendation for irrigated sorghum is ____ NPK kg/ha.
   A. 50:25:25 B. 100:50:50
   C. 90:45:45 D. 70:35:35
13. Mixed crop in sorghum is
   A. Blackgram B. Redgram
   C. Horsegram D. Bengalgram
14. Iron deficiency in sorghum (direct sown) can be overcome by
   A. $FeSO_4$ @ 75 kg/ha B. $FeSO_4$ @ 50 kg/ha
   C. $FeSO_4$ @ 60 kg/ha D. $FeSO_4$ @ 80 kg/ha

Answer keys

1	B	6	C	11	B
2	C	7	B	12	C
3	C	8	C	13	A
4	D	9	B	14	D
5	A	10	A	15	

2. One word question and answer

1. Name the chemical commonly used for inducing drought tolerance in cereal crops like sorghum is

Ans. Potassium dihydrogen phosphate.

2. Mention few drought tolerant sorghum varieties.

Ans. K9, K10

3. Mention few varieties suited for ratoon sorghum.

Ans. CSH5,K Tall

4. What is the oldest of the cultivated grain crop?

Ans. Sorghum

2.2.3 Pearl millet

1. Choose the correct answer

1. Poor man's food is called

   A. Maize B. Pearl millet

   C. Sorghum D. Millets

2. General sowing season for rainfed pearl millet is

   A. January – February B. March – April

   C. June – July D. September – October

3. The fat content in pearl millet is around

   A. 2% B. 3%

   C. 4% D. 5%

4. The depth of sowing of pearl millet is

   A. 1-2 cm B. 3-4 cm

   C. 4-5 cm D. 5-6 cm

5. Where is Indian Institute of Millet Research located at?

   A. Sholapur B. Hyderabad

   C. Cuttack D. Jhansi

6. Which among the following is not a variety of pearl millet?

   A. BN 1 B. NB21

   C. FD275 D. CO2

Answer keys

1	B
2	C
3	B
4	A
5	B
6	C

2. One word question and answer

1. Mention few varieties of pearl millet.

Ans. CO7, K3, X7

2. Mention few herbicides used in millet crop cultivation.

Ans. Butachlor, Pendimethalin, Fluchloralin

3. The important nutrient favoring quality improvement in cereals is

Ans. Potassium

2.2.4 Finger millet

1. Choose the correct answer

1. Soil sickness is caused by

   A. Maize B. Pearl millet

   C. Linseed D. Finger millet

2. Nursery area required for raising finger millet seedlings to plant 1 ha main field is

   A. 25 cents B. 10 cents

   C. 12.5 cents D. 50 cents

3. Crop can tolerate salinity of pH upto > 11.0 is

   A. Finger millet B. Kodo millet

   C. Proso millet D. Foxtail millet

Answer keys

1 D
2 C
3 A

2. One word question and answer

1. Mention few cultivated varieties of finger millet

Ans. TRY 1, INDAF 5, K7

2.2.5 Minor millets

1. Choose the correct answer

1. Scientific name of foxtail millet is

   A. *Setaria italica* B. *Paspalum scrobiculatum*

   C. *Panicum miliaceum* D. *Echinochloa frumentacea*

2. Minor millet suitable for continuous drought
   A. Barnyard millet B. Kodo millet
   C. Proso millet D. Little millet

Answer keys

1 A
2 B

2. One word question and answer

1. Mention few varieties of foxtail millet

Ans. K2, K3, CO5

2.3 PULSES

2.3.1 Pigeon pea (Redgram)

1. Choose the correct answer

1. The sucking insects infesting redgram can be controlled by spraying
   A. Systemic insecticides B. Contact pesticides
   C. Non systemic insecticides D. Systemic fungicides
2. The root rot disease of redgram can be controlled by carbendazim by
   A. Mixing with irrigation water B. Foliar spray
   C. Spot drenching D. Seedling dip
3. The storage pest, bruchids, can be easily controlled in storage
   A. By increasing the seed moisture level by 15%
   B. By reducing seed moisture level to 10%
   C. By reducing the seed moisture level to 5%
   D. By increasing the seed moisture level to 18%
4. The seed rate for mixed cropping of redgram
   A. 5 – 10 kg/ha B. 2 -3 kg/ha
   C. 20 - 25 kg/ha D. 25 – 30 kg/ha
5. The common seed rate followed for long duration redgram is
   A. 5 kg/ha B. 10 kg/ha
   C. 15 kg/ha D. 20 kg/ha

6. The fertilizer dose for rainfed pigeon pea
   A. 12.5 kg N + 25 kg P_2O_5 + 12.5 kg K_2O + 10 kg sulphur /ha
   B. 15 kg N + 15 kg P_2O_5 + 12.5 kg K_2O
   C. 20 kg N + 15 kg P_2O_5 + 25 kg K_2O
   D. 15 kg N + 10 kg P_2O_5 + 10 kg K_2O
7. The redgram is raised as rainfed crop with the intercrop of groundnut in the ratio of
   A. 1:6 B. 4:2
   C. 4:5 D. 1:10
8. Spacing for long duration redgram is
   A. 60 x 30 cm B. 45 x 30 cm
   C. 90 x 30 cm D. 100 x 30 cm
9. Zinc deficiency in redgram can be rectified by spraying with
   A. 5 kg $ZnSO_4$ + 2.5 kg lime /ha B. 5 kg $ZnSO_4$ + 5 kg lime /ha
   C. 10 kg $ZnSO_4$ + 5 kg lime /ha D. 20 kg $ZnSO_4$ + 2.5 kg lime /ha
10. Which one of the following varieties of pigeon pea is an extra early maturing
    A. Pusa Ageti B. Prabhat
    C. UPAS – 120 D. Mukta
11. The technique of growing legumes and ploughing back into the soil is known as
    A. Symbiotic fixation B. Nitrification
    C. Green manuring D. Fertilization
12. Pulses are well suited in any cropping system as they are
    A. Short duration B. Long duration
    C. Disease resistant crop D. Moisture stress resistant crop
13. The second most important Indian pulse crop is
    A. Chickpea B. Pigeon pea
    C. Cowpea D. Field pea
14. Variety of redgram suited for intercropping
    A. VAM 1 B. CO 6
    C. CO 5 D. SA1
15. Origin of redgram is
    A. India B. Nigeria
    C. Africa D. Burma

16. First hybrid in redgram is

    A. VBN 3 B. COH 2

    C. UPAS 120 D. ICPH 8

17. Perennial redgram variety is

    A. BSR 1 B. APK 1

    C. CO 7 D. VBN 3

Answer keys

1	A	11	C
2	C	12	A
3	B	13	B
4	A	14	C
5	B	15	A
6	A	16	D
7	A	17	A
8	C		
9	A		
10	B		

2. One word question and answer

1. Mention the common redgram growing seasons

Ans.
- June-August
- September-October
- February-March

2. Name the important pests occurring in pulses cultivation

Ans.
- Pod borer
- Plume moth
- Pod bug

3. Mention few important pests of redgram

Ans.
- Aphids
- Pod borer
- Pod bug

4. Mention some important diseases of redgram

Ans.
- Wilt
- Root rot
- Sterility mosaic

5. What is multi bloom technology of pulses?

Ans. Inducing second new flushes of flowers by applying extra dose of nitrogen.

6. Mention the fertilizer schedule for rainfed redgram

Ans. 12.5:25 kg NP/ha

7. Mention a perennial red gram variety

Ans. BSR 1

8. What fertilizer is used to correct Zn deficiency in redgram?

Ans. Zinc sulphate

9. Name the seed treatment chemicals used in redgram

Ans.
- *Trichoderma viride*
- *Rhizobium*

10. Name the biocontrol agents used for seed treatment of redgram.

Ans.
- *Trichoderma viride*
- *Pseudomonas fluorescens*

11. Name the suitable multistoreyed cropping system of rainfed soils receiving more than 300 mm rainfall.

Ans. Agathi + redgram + cotton + blackgram

12. What is the seed treatment method for controlling bruchid infestation in redgram?

Ans. Treating with turmeric powder or neem leaf powder.

13. Name the growth regulator used for controlling flower drop in redgram?

Ans. NAA

14. Which climate is suitable for redgram cultivation?

Ans. Tropical and sub tropical

15. Which disease of pigeon pea is transmitted by mite?

Ans. Sterility mosaic

16. Name the fertilizer used for foliar spray after flowering of redgram.

Ans. DAP 2%

17. What is the symptom of interveinal chlorosis?

Ans. Veins remain green and tissues become yellow

18. Which storage container is best for storing redgram seeds?

Ans. Polylined gunny bag

2.3.2 Blackgram

1. Choose the correct answer

1. Duration of short duration variety of blackgram is

   A. 60 – 65 days B. 70 – 75 days

   C. 80 – 90 days D. 90 – 100 days

2. The place of origin of blackgram is

   A. India B. Burma

   C. Bangladesh D. Ceylon

3. Recently released variety in blackgram in the year 2017 is

   A. VBN 8 B. ADT 6

   C. CO 6 D. MDU 1

4. Match list I with list II and choose the correct options given below

List I	List II
a. Redgram	1. 30 x 10 cm
b. Bengalgram	2. 90 x 30 cm
c. Soyabean	3. 45-90 x 20-30 cm
d. Field lablab	4. 30 x 50 cm

	a	b	c	d
A.	3	4	2	1
B.	3	1	4	2
C.	4	3	2	1
D.	4	1	2	3

5. Which among the following is incorrect regarding blackgram varieties?

   A. CO 5 B. VBN 7

   C. ADT 3 D. BSR 1

6. Recommended row spacing for summer season, blackgram is

   A. 10-15 cm B. 15-20 cm

   C. 20-25 cm D. 30-35 cm

7. For *kharif* season blackgram, the recommended optimum seed rate is

   A. 8-10kg ha B. 12-15 kg ha

   C. 15 -20 kg ha D. 22-25 kg ha

8. Time of sowing for rice fallow pulses

   A. January – February B. April – May

   C. August – September D. November – December

9. Blackgram originated in

   A. India B. Tropical America

   C. China D. Indonesia

Answer keys

1	A	6	A
2	A	7	B
3	B	8	A
4	B	9	A
5	D	10	

2. One word question and answer

1. Which fungicide is used to control powdery mildew in blackgram?

Ans. Wettable sulphur

2. Blackgram, grown well in which climate

Ans. Hot and humid

3. If blackgram is being grown for the first time in a field, the seed should be inoculated with

Ans. *Rhizobium*

2.3.3 Greengram

1. Choose the correct answer

1. King of pulses is

   A. Pea B. Gram

   C. Horsegram D. Lab-lab

2. Variety suitable for rice fallow pulse is

   A. ADT 6 B. ADT 5

   C. ADT 4 D. All the above

3. Flowering in pulse can be induced by foliar spray of

   A. 1% KCl B. 2% DAP

   C. 1% Urea D. 2% KCl

4. Seed rate of greengram is

   A. 15-20 kg/ha B. 10 kg/ha

   C. 20-30 kg/ha D. 10-15 kg/ha

5. Pulse which uses residual soil moisture effectively is

   A. Blackgram B. Horsegram

   C. Greengram D. Cowpea

6. Legumes are planted in pasture to

A. Build up soil nitrate B. Remove soil minerals

C. Being moisture to the surface D. Provide drymatter

7. The type of germination in blackgram is known as

A. Epigeal B. Hypogeal

C. Hypoepigeal D. Epihypogeal

8. The 100 grain weight of greengram is

A. 3 – 4 g B. 6 – 7 g

C. 8 – 10 g D. 10 – 15 g

9. The leaf curl virus in pulses is generally transmitted by

A. Aphids B. Jassids

C. Mites D. Thrips

10. When greengram are allowed to sprout, which vitamin is synthesized

A. Vitamin A B. Vitamin B

C. Vitamin C D. Vitamin D

11. The recommended optimum seed rate of kharif season greengram is

A. 8-10 kg/ha B. 12-15 kg/ha

C. 18-20 kg/ha D. 22-25 kg/ha

12. Greengram cultured with package of improved technological practices may yield

A. 8-10 q/ha B. 12-15q/ha

C. 18-20q/ha D. 22-25 q/ha

13. The herbicide recommended for control of weeds in greengram is

A. Basalin @ 1 kg B. 2,4-D @ 1 litre

C. Simazine @ 1 kg D. Atrazine @ 1 kg

Answer keys

1	B	6	A	11	D
2	D	7	A	12	B
3	B	8	A	13	A
4	A	9	D	14	
5	B	10	C	15	

2. One word question and answer

1. What is the seed rate for rice fallow greengram?

Ans. 25 kg/ha

2. What is the most important critical stage for irrigation in pulse?

Ans. Flowering

3. Name the commercial product of NAA which is applied to pulse crop for flowering and pod set.

Ans. Planofix

2.3.4 Cowpea

1. Choose the correct answer

1. For the successful cultivation of pulses

    A. Water stagnation should be avoided

    B. Water must be allowed to stand for 1 cm depth

    C. Water must be given as and when required

    D. Flood irrigation

2. Where is National Pulses Research Centre located?

    A. Kanpur B. Anand

    C. Kovilpatti D. Vamban

3. The fertilizer used for mitigating water stress in pulses at vegetative stage is

    A. Calcium chloride B. Manganese sulphate

    C. Sodium phosphate D. Potassium chloride

4. Foliar spray recommended for rice fallow pulse in Tamil Nadu is

    A. DAP 5% B. DAP 2%

    C. DAP 10% D. Urea 5%

5. In pulses, the need for nitrogen is specific at

    A. Germination stage B. Vegetative stage

    C. Post flowering stage D. Pre flowering stage

6. Cowpea grown for grain purpose should be seeded at

    A. 10-15 kg/ha B. 15 – 20 kg/ha

    C. 20 - 25 kg/ha D. 25-30 kg/ha

7. The recommended row and plant spacing for *kharif* cowpea is
   A. 30-45 x 8-10 cm B. 30-45 x 4-6 cm
   C. 25-30 x 8-10 cm D. 25-30 x 4-6 cm
8. Which one of the following pulse crops is used as a pulse, a fodder and a green manure crop?
   A. Mung bean B. Urd
   C. Cowpea D. Pea
9. Which one of the following operations is associated with the process of nipping?
   A. Plucking the apical buds to promote branches
   B. Treating the seed with *Rhizobium* culture
   C. Tying the branches to avoid lodging
   D. Picking green leaves for vegetable purposes
10. The origin of cowpea
   A. USA B. China
   C. Russia D. India
11. Mention a vegetable type of cowpea grown in Tamil Nadu
   A. CO5 B. Paiyur
   C. VBN1 D. VBN2

Answer keys

1	A	6	C	11	D
2	D	7	A		
3	D	8	C		
4	B	9	A		
5	C	10	D		

2. One word question and answer

1. What is the average productivity of pulses in India?

Ans. 623 kg/ha

2. Name the state in which the productivity of pulses is maximum

Ans. Uttar Pradesh

3. Application of nitrogen in cowpea at the time of planting is known as what

Ans. Starter dose

4. Mention a drought resistant legume

Ans. *Stylosanthus*

2.3.5 Bengalgram (Chickpea)

1. Choose the correct answer

1. The moisture content for storage of bengalgram is about

   A. 8 – 9 % B. 9 – 10%

   C. 10 – 12% D. 12 – 15%

2. The bengalgram usually raised under rainfed condition during the months of

   A. March – April B. May – June

   C. July – August D. September – October

3. Seed rate for bengalgram is

   A. 20 – 40 kg/ha B. 30 – 40 kg/ha

   C. 50 – 75 kg/ha D. 75 – 100 kg/ha

Answer keys

1 A
2 D
3 C
4 9
5 10

2. One word question and answer

1. Which herbicide is recommended for weed control in chick pea?

Ans. Basalin

2. Name the pathogen causing chick pea wilt.

Ans. *Fusarium orthocerus*

3. Name the most serious pest of bengalgram

Ans. Pod borer

2.3.6 Soybean

1. Choose the correct answer

1. The optimum seed rate for soybean for normal planting is

   A. 50-60 kg/ha B. 60-70 kg/ha

   C. 70-80 kg/ha D. 80-90 kg/ha

2. Yellow mosaic viral disease of soybean is transmitted by

   A. Thrips B. White fly

   C. Mite D. Aphid

3. The ideal moisture content in soybean seed at the time of threshing has been estimated as

A. 10-11 per cent B. 11-12 per cent
C. 13-14 per cent D. 14-15 per cent

4. Fluchloralin can be used in soybean as

A. Pre – emergence B. Post – emergence
C. Pre – plant incorporation D. None of these

5. The protein content of soybean is about

A. 10 per cent B. 20 per cent
C. 30 per cent D. 40 per cent

6. The pH range suitable for soybean cultivation is

A. 5.0-6.0 B. 6.0-7.5
C. 7.5-8.0 D. 8.0-8.5

7. The origin of soybean

A. China B. USA
C. India D. Germany

8. The state having largest production of soybean in India.

A. Madhya Pradesh B. Uttar Pradesh
C. Rajasthan D. Maharashtra

9. The optimum moisture content of the soybean grain

A. 6 – 8% B. 8 – 10%
C. 10 – 12% D. 12 – 14%

10. The oil content of the soybean is

A. 43% B. 20%
C. 25% D. 60%

11. Poor man's meat is

A. Soybean B. Cowpea
C. Dolichus lab D. Gram

Answer keys

1	C	6	B	11	A
2	B	7	A		
3	C	8	A		
4	C	9	D		
5	D	10	B		

2. One word question and answer

1. What is the optimum time for kharif soybean sowing?

Ans. First fortnight of July

2. What is the recommended plant to plant distance for soybean?

Ans. 4-5 cm

3. What is the optimum seed rate of soybean?

Ans. 70 – 80 kg/ha

4. Which bacteria is responsible for nitrogen fixation in nodules of legumes?

Ans. *Rhizobium*

5. What is the oil content of soybean, besides good quality protein?

Ans. 20%

6. In which country, soybean in largely cultivated?

Ans. China

7. Mention a grain legume which is also grown as an oilseed

Ans. Soybean

8. What is the common cereal intercrop with soybean?

Ans. Maize

9. Which amino acid is rich in soybean?

Ans. Methionine

2.3.7 Lentil

1. Choose the correct answer

1. The average protein content of the lentil grain is

   A. 10% B. 15%

   C. 20% D. 25%

2. Name the important lentil growing country in the world

   A. India B. Nepal

   C. Canada D. Bangladesh

3. RMO – 40 is a variety of

   A. Mung bean B. Urd bean

   C. Horse bean D. Moth bean

4. The protein percentage in lentil has been estimated as

   A. 20 B. 25

   C. 30 D. 35

Answer keys

1	D	2	A	3	D	4	B

2.4 OILSEEDS

2.4.1 Groundnut

1. Choose the correct answer

1. The maximum productivity of oil seeds is in the state
   A. Tamil Nadu B. Andhra Pradesh
   C. Karnataka D. Punjab
2. Water uptake by groundnut seed is enhanced by
   A. Increasing temperature B. Decreasing temperature
   C. Increasing humidity D. Freezing.
3. Flowering in most of the groundnut varieties starts at
   A. 15 - 20 DAS B. 25 - 30 DAS
   C. 45 - 60 DAS D. 60 - 70 DAS
4. Physical and mechanical damages caused during groundnut harvest affect
   A. Seed colour B. Seed growth
   C. Seed strength D. Seed quality
5. Immature groundnut seed contains
   A. Higher free fatty acids B. Lower free fatty acids
   C. Higher carbohydrates D. Higher oil
6. In groundnut, seed protein and oil content have
   A. Direct relationship B. Indirect relationship
   C. Inverse relationship D. No relation
7. The predominant sugar in groundnut seed is
   A. Glucose B. Fructose
   C. Sucrose D. Lactose
8. The number of irrigations required for groundnut crop in Tamil Nadu for rabi summer
   A. 3 – 4 B. 4 – 8
   C. 8 – 13 D. 15 – 18
9. In acid soils, which of the following micronutrients becomes deficient
   A. Molybdenum and boron B. Calcium and magnesium
   C. Potassium and phosphorus D. Iron and zinc

10. Seed priming technique in groundnut is meant for improving

A. Pest resistance
B. Disease resistance
C. Heat resistance
D. Drought resistance

11. Iron chlorosis in groundnut can be controlled by foliar application of

A. Ferrous sulphate
B. Zinc sulphate
C. Copper sulphate
D. Urea

12. Fertilizer dose recommended for groundnut crop is

A. 20-40 + 50-60 + 30-40 kg NPK/ha
B. 20-40 + 60-80 + 30-50 kg NPK/ha
C. 40-50 + 50-60 + 30-40 kg NPK/ha
D. 40-50 + 60-80 + 30-50 kg NPK/ha

13. Water requirement for groundnut crop

A. 240 – 300 mm
B. 400 – 550 mm
C. 750 – 850 mm
D. 850 – 1000 mm

14. The groundnut cake contains NPK in the proportions of

A. 3.8:1.1:0.9
B. 4.9:1.2:1.0
C. 6.2:0.8:0.8
D. 7.3:1.5:1.3

15. The herbicide formulation for effective control of weeds in groundnut is

A. 2, 4 – D
B. Simazine
C. Isoproturon
D. TOKE – 25

16. Ammonium sulphate is preferred for nitrogen application in groundnut because it also provides

A. Calcium
B. Magnesium
C. Sulphur
D. Boron

17. Application of gypsum is required more for

A. Paddy
B. Berseem
C. Lucerne
D. Groundnut

18. Name the state where the National Centre for Groundnut Research is located.

A. Tamil Nadu
B. Gujarat
C. Karnataka
D. Orissa

19. The developing groundnut pegs are known to produce
    A. Ethylene B. Oxygen
    C. Carbon dioxide D. Nitrogen
20. The hollow heart disorder in groundnut is due to
    A. Zinc B. Boron
    C. Magnesium D. Calcium
21. The keeping quality of groundnut oil is determined by
    A. Free fatty acids B. Saturated fatty acids
    C. Unsaturated fatty acids D. Glycerol content
22. Earthing up in groundnut crop as an inter culture is given to
    A. Improve aeration B. To reduce pest infestation
    C. To check pest incidence D. Check the root growth
23. Percentage of seed protein in groundnut is
    A. 20% B. 25%
    C. 30% D. 35%
24. The recommended row to row spacing for bunchy type of groundnut is
    A. 20-30 cm B. 30-40 cm
    C. 40-50 cm D. 45-60 cm
25. The recommended row spacing for spreading type of groundnut is
    A. 25-30 cm B. 35-50 cm
    C. 45-60 cm D. 55-70 cm
26. Directorate of Groundnut Research is located at
    A. Junagadh B. Jabalpur
    C. Jaipur D. Tindivanam
27. The seed rate for bunch type of groundnut is
    A. 60-80 kg/ha B. 70-90 kg/ha
    C. 80-100 kg/ha D. 100-120 kg/ha
28. Name the state where the groundnut area and production are maximum
    A. Karnataka B. Assam
    C. Bihar D. Gujarat
29. The oil content of groundnut
    A. 20– 30% B. 30– 40%
    C. 44 – 50% D. 50– 60%

30. The origin of groundnut

A. India B. Brazil

C. Africa D. USA

31. The maximum productivity of oilseeds is in the state

A. Tamil Nadu B. Andhra Pradesh

C. Karnataka D. Punjab

32. The dormancy of groundnut seeds can be reduced by the treatment with

A. Abscisic acid B. Indole acetic acid

C. Ethylene D. Gibberellic acid

33. The changes in groundnut seed quality is indicated by

A. Oxygen production B. Ethylene production

C. Carbon dioxide production D. SO_2 production

34. The cotyledon of groundnut mainly contains

A. Starch B. Fat

C. Protein D. Oil

35. Root nodules in groundnut appear due to infection by *Rhizobium* which is

A. Bacteria B. Fungi

C. Algae D. Virus

36. Stalk like elongating pegs in groundnut generally grows

A. Above the ground B. Below the ground

C. Horizontally D. Vertically

37. A fertilized flower in groundnut first produces

A. Peg B. Seed

C. Fruit D. Root

38. The biofertilizer Arbuscular Mycorrhizae belongs to the group

A. Bacteria B. Fungi

C. Virus D. Nematodes

39. A non dormant variety of groundnut can be made dormant by foliar application of

A. MH B. GA

C. NAA D. IAA

40. Rotting of groundnut seeds during storage is due to
    A. Fungus B. Bacteria
    C. Virus D. Nematode
41. The fungus responsible for toxin production in groundnut seed storage is
    A. *Penicillium* B. *Phytophthora*
    C. *Pythium* D. *Aspergillus flavus*
42. The typical colour of the roasted groundnut is due to the production of
    A. Melanin B. Phytochromes
    C. Carotenoids D. Xanthophylls
43. High yield of groundnut is obtained in soils with
    A. High alkalinity B. Moderate acidity
    C. High salinity D. High nitrogen
44. Soil application of gypsum is recommended for groundnut to
    A. Improve vegetative growth
    B. Improve flower production
    C. Improve pegging and pod development
    D. Improve maturity
45. Which type of groundnut is drought tolerant?
    A. Spreading B. Bunch
    C. Semi spreading D. Both A and B
46. Shelling percentage in groundnut is
    A. 50% B. 60%
    C. 70% D. 80%
47. Gypsum rate in groundnut is
    A. 250 kg/ha B. 500 kg/ha
    C. 400 kg/ha D. 100 kg/ha
48. Highest peg formation is observed in which type of groundnut?
    A. Spreading and semi spreading B. Semi spreading
    C. Spreading D. Bunching
49. Intercrop in groundnut is
    A. Bengalgram B. Redgram
    C. Maize D. Pearl millet

50. Which crop is called King of oilseeds?

A. Sunflower B. Coconut

C. Sesame D. Groundnut

Answer keys

1	A	11	A	21	A	31	A	41	D	51	
2	A	12	A	22	A	32	C	42	A	52	
3	B	13	C	23	B	33	B	43	B	53	
4	D	14	D	24	B	34	C	44	C	54	
5	A	15	D	25	C	35	A	45	A		
6	C	16	C	26	A	36	B	46	C		
7	C	17	D	27	B	37	A	47	C		
8	C	18	B	28	D	38	B	48	D		
9	A	19	A	29	C	39	A	49	B		
10	D	20	B	30	B	40	A	50	D		

2. One word question and answer

1. Name the oil cake containing highest nitrogen

Ans. Groundnut cake

2. When the interculture operation is to be avoided?

Ans. Pegging stage

3. What is the moisture content of groundnut seed suitable for storage?

Ans. 6%

4. At which stage, the gypsum application is recommended in groundnut cultivation.

Ans. At the time of earthing up operation.

5. Name the farm implement used for stripping the pods from groundnut plant.

Ans. Groundnut stripper

6. Name the best intercrop for groundnut which serves as trap crop for cut worm or *Spodoptera* menace.

Ans. Castor

7. What is the bait used to control the *Spodoptera* cutworms in groundnut?

Ans. Rice bran + brown sugar + carbaryl

8. Name the farm equipment used for separating kernel from harvested pods.

Ans. Decorticator

9. When does groundnut podding starts?

Ans. 60 – 70 DAS

10. Which fertilizer is applied to correct the calcium deficiency in groundnut.

Ans. Gypsum

11. How many days does groundnut crop require for root nodule formation?

Ans. 15 DAS

12. Which compound is responsible for dormancy in groundnut

Ans. Abscisic acid

13. What is the toxic compound present in deteriorated groundnut under storage.

Ans. Aflatoxins

14. Name the fertilizers which increases groundnut oil content.

Ans. Sulphur containing

15. What is the energy supplied by 1g of raw groundnut kernel

Ans. 5 – 64 k calories

16. Lack of which nutrient causes black heart disorder in groundnut kernel

Ans. Boron

17. What is the plant protection measure for controlling leaf spot diseases of groundnut?

Ans. Foliar spray using carbendazim and mancozeb.

18. What is the optimum seed rate for groundnut?

Ans. 120 – 140 kg/ha

19. Mention the name of the leaf spot disease caused by fungus

Ans. Tikka leaf spot

20. Name the group of microorganism to which the *Rhizobium* belongs to

Ans. Bacteria

21. Name the growth regulator applied to a non-dormant variety which is made dormant

Ans. Maleic hydrazide

22. Which irrigation system is the best for higher water use efficiency?

Ans. Sprinkler and drip irrigation

23. Name a herbicide formulation which provides effective control of weeds in groundnut

Ans. Toke-25

24. During which stage of crop growth, the intercultural operations in groundnut should be avoided?

Ans. Pegging stage

25. What is the plant growth regulator commonly used for fruit set in groundnut?

Ans. NAA

26. What imparts the colour of the roasted groundnut?

Ans. Melanin

27. What group of microorganisms causes rotting of groundnut seeds in storage?

Ans. Fungus

28. Name the fungal biofertilizer recommended for groundnut cultivation

Ans. AM

29. Name the part that is first produced from a fertilized groundnut flower

Ans. Peg

30. The elongating pegs generally grow and where it enters to produce the pod

Ans. Below the soil

31. In which part of the seed, the protein and fats are stored

Ans. Cotyledons

32. Ethylene production from the stored groundnut seed result in

Ans. Determination of seed quality

33. Name the anti oxidant commercially used in preparation of edible groundnut products

Ans. BHA (Butylated Hydroxyl Anisole)

34. What is the basis of grading in groundnut seeds?

Ans. Percentage sound mature kernals, per cent splits

35. What is the average shelling percentage of groundnut?

Ans. 70 – 80 %

36. Name a semi spreading variety of groundnut cultivated in Tamil Nadu.

Ans. TMV10, COGN5

37. What is the approximate 100 seed weight of groundnut (VRI 2)?

Ans. 50 g

38. How to prevent soil crusting in groundnut cultivation?

Ans. Lime application along with FYM or composted coirpith.

39. What is the biofertilizer applied along with coir pith for composting in groundnut cultivation?

Ans. *Pleurotus*

40. Name the products from groundnut kernels

Ans. Groundnut oil, groundnut cake

41. What for groundnut shells are used?

Ans. Composting, source of fire for cooking, poultry rearing

42. The seed yield in groundnut is determined by

Ans.
- Pod number
- Seed number
- Seed size
- Seed weight

43. The mature groundnut seed contains

Ans.
- Embryo
- Two cotyledom
- Hypocotyl and plumule
- Twin testa

44. Ground seed germination is dependent on

Ans.
- Parents
- Soil fertility
- Climatic factors (Temperature, relative humidity)
- Crop nutrition

45. Mention few measures to prevent aflatoxin production in groundnut.

Ans.
- Avoid mechanical damage while harvesting
- Harvesting at proper maturity
- Drying as rapid and possible
- Preventing rewetting
- Removing at safe moisture level

46. Which International organization is involved in groundnut research in India?

Ans. ICRISAT

47. Name few detoxification methods to remove toxins in groundnut seed.

Ans.
- Autoclaving
- Cooking
- Roasting
- Irradiation

48. Application of lime to groundnut is better than gypsum because

Ans. Gypsum is subjected for leaching by water

49. Mention few common methods of irrigation used for groundnut.

Ans.
- Border strip
- Check basin
- Sprinkler
- Broad bed and furrow

50. Mention the reasons for high cost of groundnut production.

Ans.
- High cost of seed
- Cost of labour
- Cost on weed control
- Cost of harvesting
- Stripping and preparation of the produce.

51. Name the few equipments/instruments used in groundnut production.

Ans.
- Seed drill
- Bund former
- Weeders
- Diggers
- Mould board ploughs for inter cultivation and earthing up
- Strippers
- Decorticator

52. Mention few foliar diseases of groundnut

Ans.
- Tikka leaf spot
- Cercospora leaf spot
- Leaf rust

53. Mention few management practices to control insects damaging foliage.

Ans.
- Use of natural enemies.
- Use of insecticides
- Use of resistant cultivars
- Use of cultural practices

54. Mention few byproducts obtained from groundnut.

Ans.
- Groundnut oil
- Groundnut butter
- Salted groundnut
- Roasted groundnut
- Groundnut flakes
- Groundnut grits
- Candies
- Concentrates

55. Mention other industrial products obtained from groundnut.

Ans. • Groundnut shells used for litter
- Mushroom growing medium
- Carrier for pesticide and fertilizer
- Mulch, flour sweetening compounds
- Metal polisher
- Activated charcoal
- Raisin making
- Hardboard

56. Proper drying of harvested groundnut pod is ensured by the following tests

Ans. • Pods when shaken given rattling sound.
- Splitting of kernel when pressed between thumb and index finger.
- Pebing of testa when kernal is rubbed.

57. The ancient method of storing groundnut pods for seed purpose.

Ans. • Earthern pots
- Mud bin
- Bamboo baskets

58. The peg growth and development are influenced by

Ans. • Light intensity
- Soil moisture content
- Daily mean temperature
- Species differences

59. For getting good groundnut crop and pod yield in groundnut

Ans. • Seeds must be pure, viable and free from diseases.
- Minimum germination percent of 70%
- Damaged seeds should be rejected.

60. Mention the varieties cultivated in both rainfed and irrigated conditions.

Ans. VRI 2, VRI 3

61. The marketing functions performed by groundnut seed trader

Ans. • Assembly
- Transportation
- Broking
- Storage and movement of produce to the mill

62. Mention few drying systems for groundnut after harvest.

Ans.
- Solar drying
- Heat pump systems
- Infra red drying
- Vaccum drying
- Sac drying

63. Mention the types of warehouses used as storage structures for groundnut

Ans.
- Concrete silo
- Flat type storage
- Warehouses

64. How to reduce the post harvest losses in groundnut?

Ans.
- Appropriate harvest maturity
- Proper handling
- Effective drying
- Proper storage

65. Name few improved storage methods of groundnut.

Ans.
- Low temperature storage
- Controlled atmosphere storage

66. What is the pre treatment given for ambient open storage of groundnut?

Ans. Treatment of groundnut pods with hot water at 80° for 90 seconds.

67. Name the chemical method of controlling post harvest losses.

Ans. Use of pyrethrins/ fumigants

68. Name few groundnut processing operations.

Ans.
- Pre cleaning
- Pre sizing
- Shelling (Decortication)
- Separating
- Sorting
- Milling
- Oil extraction

69. Shelling property of groundnut is dependent on

Ans.
- Variety
- Growing condition
- Harvesting
- Curing treatment
- Method of storage

70. In groundnut, shelling efficiency and seed thickners are dependent on

Ans. Pod shape, seed thicknes

71. Milling quality of groundnut is influenced by

Ans. Temperature at the time of shelling

72. The methods of oil extraction from groundnut seeds

Ans.
- Hydraulic pressing
- Expeller pressing
- Solvent extraction

73. What is the traditional method of oil extraction?

Ans.
- Grinding
- Boiling the paste with water

74. What is the quantity of groundnut shelled when manually by a hand operated device?

Ans. 10 kg/ha

75. Deoiling of groundnut is done to obtain

Ans.
- Crisp texture
- Sweet taste
- White colour

76. Name the reliable seed quality testing method.

Ans. Germination

77. What is the chemical used for testing the seed viability of groundnut?

Ans. Tetrazoluim salt (2, 3, 5 - Triphenyl tetrazolium chloride)

78. In groundnut cost of cultivation, which component contributed more?

Ans. Cost of seed

79. Which factor contributes for the poor productivity of groundnut crop?

Ans.
- Poor seed multiplication ratio
- Poor quality seed

80. What is the farm equipment used for forming beds for groundnut cultivation?

Ans. Bed former

81. What is the dose of micronutrient mixture recommended for soil application immediately after sowing?

Ans. 12.5 kg/ha

82. When the groundnut seeds are to be treated with *Trichoderma*?

Ans. Just before sowing

83. Name the equipment commonly used for groundnut sowing in lines.

Ans. Kovai seed drill / gorru

84. When the gypsum application is recommended in groundnut cultivation?

Ans. At the time of earthing up operation.

85. How to identify visually the maturity of groundnut crop ready for harvest?

Ans. Drying of leaves and yellowing of leaves

86. What is the problem associated with harvested bunch varieties of groundnut when they are wet?

Ans. Sprouting of pods.

87. Name the farm implement used for stripping the pods from groundnut plant.

Ans. Groundnut stripper

88. What is the mulching material recommended in groundnut for conserving soil moisture?

Ans. Polythene film mulching

89. Name the pesticide used to control the earwig or pod borer in groundnut.

Ans. Malathoin

90. What is the seed hardening chemical used for presowing treatment?

Ans. $CaCl_2$ 0.5%

91. Which environment factor causes high percentage of shrivelled seed in groundnut?

Ans. Higher temperature

92. Deficiency of which nutrient causes watery hypocotyl of groundnut seedling.

Ans. Nitrogen

93. What is the type of pollination in groundnut?

Ans. Self pollination

94. What is the favourable soil temperature for getting more number of pods in groundnut?

Ans. 23°C

95. Which chemical increases the rate of germination in groundnut seeds?

Ans. Ethephon

96. Which pigment is responsible for green colouration of leaf?

Ans. Chlorophyll

2.4.2 Sunflower

1. Choose the correct answer

1. The anti cholesterol property in sunflower is due to the presence of

   A. Linolenic acid B. Linoleic acid
   C. Nicotinic acid D. Capric acid

2. In sunflower, the days taken to mature during kharif

   A. 80-90 days B. 100-110 days
   C. 105-130 days D. 120-130 days

3. The fertilizer dose recommended for sunflower is

   A. 30 + 60 + 40 NPK kg/ha B. 30 + 30 + 20 NPK kg/ha
   C. 70 + 40 + 30 NPK kg/ha D. 70 + 60 + 40 NPK kg/ha

4. For better quality of sunflower oil, the extraction should be done within

   A. 80 days after harvesting B. 85 days after harvesting
   C. 90 days after harvesting D. 95 days after harvesting

5. Sunflower acts as an indicator plant to diagnose the deficiency of

   A. P_2O_5 B. Fe
   C. N_2 D. Mg

6. Mention the chemical used to improve the germination of sunflower seeds

   A. Urea B. Ethrel
   C. Zinc sulphate D. Potassium sulphate

7. The high oxidative stability of sunflower oil is due to

   A. High oleic acid B. Low oleic acid
   C. High linoleic acid D. High palmitic acid

8. The phenolic compound identified in sunflower seed is

   A. Catechin B. Chlorogenic acid
   C. Benzoic acid D. Coumarin

9. What is the best intercropping sequence in sunflower?
   A. Soybean - maize – sunflower
   B. Finger millet – blackgram – sunflower
   C. Maize – sesamum – sunflower
   D. Sorghum -blackgram – sunflower
10. The storage container suitable for storing sunflower seeds in large quantities
   A. Cloth bag B. Polythene bag
   C. Gunny bag D. Polythene lined gunny bag
11. Name the insect which is highly beneficial in pollination of sunflower
   A. Wasp B. Honeybees
   C. Mite D. Aphids
12. Sunflower is a
   A. Self pollinated crop B. Cross pollinated crop
   C. Often cross pollinated crop D. Self sterility crop
13. The optimum time for sowing of sunflower during kharif in India is
   A. First fortnight of June B. Second fortnight of June
   C. First fortnight of July D. Second fortnight of July
14. What is the plant population in sunflower/acre?
   A. 14,000 – 17,000 plants B. 18,000 – 20,000 plants
   C. 20,000 – 25,000 plants D. 26,000 – 28,000 plants
15. What is the 100 seed weight of sunflower?
   A. 3.6 - 4.2 g B. 5.8 – 7.1 g
   C. 8.0 – 9.5 g D. 10 – 12.5 g
16. Sunflower oil cake contains higher amount of protein
   A. 40 – 44% B. 30 – 38%
   C. 38 – 40% D. 45 – 50%
17. The sunflower was introduced to India during
   A. 1965 B. 1966
   C. 1968 D. 1969
18. The flowering of sunflower occurs during
   A. Short day B. Short- Long day
   C. Long day D. Day neutral

19. The economic part of sunflower is

A. Capitulum B. Square

C. Hypanthodium D. Panicle

20. Season for irrigated sunflower is

A. June-July B. October-November

C. December-January D. February-March

21. Intercropping system followed in sunflower is

A. Groundnut and sunflower B. Pigeon pea and sunflower

C. Castor and sunflower D. All the above

22. Match list I with list II and choose the correct options given below

List I	**List II**
a. Ground nut	1. North America
b. Sesamum	2. Ethiopia and Eastern Africa
c. Sunflower	3. Brazil and South America
d. Castor	4. Africa and India

	a	b	c	d
A.	4	3	2	1
B.	3	4	1	2
C.	3	4	2	1
D.	4	3	1	2

23. Match list I with list II and choose the correct options given below

List I	**List II**
a. Groundnut	1. 5 kg/ha
b. Sesamum	2. 7-20 kg/ha
c. Safflower	3. 5-30 kg/ha
d. Sunflower	4. 120 kg/ha

	a	b	c	d
A.	3	4	1	2
B.	3	4	2	1
C.	4	3	1	2
D.	4	1	2	3

Answer keys

1	B	11	B	21	D
2	A	12	B	22	B
3	D	13	C	23	C
4	C	14	A	24	
5	D	15	B	25	
6	B	16	A		
7	A	17	D		
8	B	18	C		
9	A	19	A		
10	D	20	C		

2. One word question and answer

24. Mention the growth regulator applied as foliar spray for increasing seed set in sunflower.

Ans. TIBA

25. Mention few pesticides used in sunflower cultivation.

Ans. Phosalone

26. What is the most sensitive stage of sunflower to water stress?

Ans. Flowering and grain filling

27. Mention the biocontrol agent used for controlling charcoal rot in sunflower

Ans. *Pseudomonas fluorescens, Trichoderma viride*

28. Mention sunflower varieties used for cultivation on a large scale

Ans. Morden, CO4, TCSH1

29. Name the major sunflower growing states in India

Ans. Karnataka, Maharashtra and Andhra Pradesh

30. What is the maturity index for harvesting sunflower?

Ans. The bracts of sunflower should turn lemon yellow colour, back of head turns brown to black colour

31. What is the micronutrient used for seed treatment of sunflower.

Ans. 2% $ZnSO_4$ for 12 h soaking

32. What are the different types of sunflower?

Ans.
- Giant types: 180 – 420 cm tall
- Semi dwarf types: 130 – 180 cm tall
- Dwarf types: 60 – 130 cm tall

33. What are the bad effects, when the sunflower oil extraction is delayed?

Ans. Becomes bitter in taste, rancidity

34. Name a pre-emergence herbicide used for increasing the seed yield in sunflower

Ans. Pendimethalin

35. Which climate is required for germination to seedling stage of sunflower?

Ans. Cool climate

36. Mention the best season suitable for cultivation of irrigated sunflower

Ans. December – January, April – May

37. Mention the season suited for rainfed cultivation of sunflower

Ans. June – July, October – November

38. What is the optimum pH range for sunflower crop growth?

Ans. 5.5-7.5

39. What is the spacing for sunflower crop?

Ans. 60 x 20 cm

40. Name the nutrient that helps in translocation of food materials from leaf to developing grain in sunflower

Ans. Boron

41. What is the average yield of sunflower obtained from a hectare?

Ans. 1000 – 1500 kg/ha

42. Which factor decides the quality of sunflower oil?

Ans. High quantities of unsaturated fatty acids.

43. Mention the optimum season for the cultivation of sunflower

Ans. February – March

44. Mention the hybrids of sunflower

Ans. KBSH 1, KBSH 44, DRSH 1, TNAU Sunflower Hybrid CO 2, AP SH-11, BSH-1, and PSFH-67

45. Name the term which is used to call seed of sunflower

Ans. Achene

46. How will you separate seeds from the head of sunflower?

Ans. By beating with sticks

47. What is the safe moisture content for storing the sunflower seeds?

Ans. 7 – 8%

48. What is the important factor which decreases sunflower productivity in saline soils?

Ans. Decreased water availability

49. Mention few mechanical methods for improving seed set in sunflower.

Ans.
- Rubbing the capitulum with hand covered with soft muslin cloth
- Rubbing the two flower heads face to face gently

50. Mention few serious pests that affect the productivity of sunflower

Ans. Weevil, cutworm, pod borer

51. Mention the management strategies for controlling pest incidence in sunflower

Ans.
- Collect and destroy the *Helicoverpa* larvae
- Spray malathion or phosalone @ 100 ml/ha
- Spray fenthion or phenthoate @ 500 ml/ha
- Dust malathion or phosalone @ 25 kg/ha

52. Which fungicide is used for treating the sunflower seeds?

Ans. Carbendazim @ 2 - 4g/kg

53. High temperature stress during grain filling period of sunflower affects what?

Ans.
- Grains yield
- Grain quality
- Alters the unsaturation ratio of oleic to linoleic acid

54. The yield of sunflower is determined by

Ans.
- Achene number
- Achene weight
- Oil content

55. Mention the reasons for wide spread cultivation of sunflower in India

Ans.
- Wider adaptability
- Photoperiod insensitiveness
- Shorter duration (60 – 100 days)
- High quality edible oil
- Remunerative

56. Mention a few phenophases of the life cycle of sunflower

Ans.
- Sowing to emergence
- Emergence to floral initiation
- Floral initiation to first anthesis
- First anthesis to last anthesis
- Last anthesis to physiological maturity

57. Mention the factors that affect the growth and yield of sunflower

Ans. • Drought

• High temperature leads to early bud formation, anthesis and physiological maturity

• Water stress

• Depth of sowing

58. Mention the important diseases which affects the productivity of sunflower

Ans. • Alternaria blight

• Head rot

• Charcoal rot

• Rust

• Bacterial leaf blight

59. Which biofertilizer is used for seed treatment in sunflower?

Ans. • *Azospirillum* @ 600g/ha

• Azophos @ 1200g/ha

60. Which biocontrol agent is recommended for sunflower seed treatment?

Ans. *Trichoderma viride* @ 4g/kg of seed

61. Which state leads in productivity of oil seeds?

Ans. Tamil Nadu

62. What is the bioinoculant recommended for seed treatment of sunflower?

Ans. *Trichoderma*

63. What is the pre sowing weedicide used in sunflower?

Ans. Fluchloralin

64. What is the optimum time for irrigation for getting higher yield in sunflower?

Ans. Flowering

2.4.3 Sesamum

1. Choose the correct answer

1. Poor man's substitute for ghee is

A. Groundnut B. Sunflower

C. Sesame D. Safflower

2. Economic part of sesame is

A. Head B. Panicle

C. Capsule D. Capitulum

3. Origin of sesame is

A. India B. South Africa

C. Mexico D. South East Asia

4. White seeded sesame variety is

A. TMV1 B. Paiyur 1

C. SVPR 1 D. TMV 6

5. Name the quantity of N + $P_2 O_5$ + K_2O in sesamum cake

A. 6.0-6.2 + 2.0-2.2 + 1.0-1.2 B. 2.0-2.2 + 6.0-6.2 + 1.0-1.2

C. 6.0-6.2 +1.0-1.2 + 2.0-2.2 D. 2.0-2.2 + 1.0-1.2 + 6.0-6.2

6. The recommended spacing for planting sesame is

A. 4 x 15 cm B. 25 x 15 cm

C. 30 x 10 cm D. 30 x 15 cm

7. Sesamum yields well in the pH range of

A. 3 - 4.5 B. 5.0 – 6.0

C. 5.5 – 8.0 D. 7.0 – 8.0

8. Powdery mildew disease in sesamum can be controlled by the application of

A. Metasystox B. Malathion

C. Wettable sulphur D. Dithane

9. In South India, sesamum is grown in

A. Rabi season only B. Kharif season only

C. Rabi and kharif seasons D. Summer season only

10. The seed normally required for planting of sesamum is

A. 2-3 kg/ha B. 3-4 kg/ha

C. 4-5 kg/ha D. 5-6 kg/ha

11. Oil percentage in sesamum is

A. 20 – 25% B. 25 – 30%

C. 35 – 40% D. 46 – 52%

12. Consider the statement and choose the correct one

(i) Groundnut - TMV 10, JL 24

(ii) Sesamum - Paiyur 1, VRI 1

(iii) Castor - SA 1, TMVCH 1

A. (i) alone is correct B. (ii) alone is correct

C. All the statements are correct D. (i) and (ii) are correct

Answer keys

1	C	6	D	11	D
2	C	7	C	12	D
3	A	8	C		
4	C	9	C		
5	A	10	B		

2. One word question and answer

13. Mention the best season for sowing sesamum.

Ans. April – May

14. Name the micronutrient essential for sesamum.

Ans. Manganese sulphate

15. What is the seed rate for sesamum?

Ans. 3 – 4 kg

16. Mention the optimum temperature for sesamum cultivation.

Ans. 25 – 27°C

17. What is the optimum rainfall required for sesamum cultivation?

Ans. 500 – 600 mm

18. What is the type of soil required for sesamum cultivation?

Ans. Well drained sandy loam

19. What is the pesticide used for controlling pod borer of sesamum?

Ans. Malathion

20. Mention the rice fallow sesamum.

Ans. VRI – 1

21. Mention few tips for harvesting sesamum.

Ans.
- Harvest at appearance of yellow colour pods.
- Harvested plants to be stacked perpendicular for aeration.
- Sun dry the pods until the seed moisture is 7- 8%

22. Mention few rainfed varieties of sesamum.

Ans. VR1, TMV5, TMV 6

23. Mention few varieties of irrigated sesamum.

Ans.
- SVPR1
- Paiyur 1
- CO6

2.4.4 Mustard

1. Choose the correct answer

1. Maximum yield of mustard is obtained at a plant spacing of

   A. 45 x 20 cm B. 60 x 30 cm

   C. 90 x 30 cm D. 90 x 60 cm

2. Which one of the following causes pungency of mustard oil?

   A. Phenols B. Amino acids

   C. Glucosinolates D. Erucic acid

3. Canola is a group of plants belongs to

   A. Mustard B. Safflower

   C. Oilseeds D. Vegetables

4. The oil content of mustard is

   A. 30% B. 40%

   C. 60% D. 70%

5. The origin of mustard is

   A. USA B. India

   C. China D. Pakistan

6. The largest producer of rapeseed and mustard in the world is

   A. China B. Japan

   C. India D. Canada

7. The mustard crop is regarded ready for harvest when its pods turn to

   A. Greenish-yellow B. Greenish-black

   C. Yellowish green D. Yellowish-brown

8. The fruit of rapeseed and mustard is known as

   A. Pod B. Grain

   C. Siliqua D. Caryopsis

9. Rape seed and mustard oil contains

   A. Oleic acid B. Erucic acid

   C. Lauric acid D. Stearic acid

10. Scientific name of Indian mustard

   A. *Brassica juncea* B. *Brassica napus*

   C. *Brassica campestris* D. *Brassica oleratea*

11. King of oil seed is

    A. Sesame B. Sunflower

    C. Groundnut D. Mustard

Answer keys

1	A	6	D	11	D
2	C	7	D	12	
3	A	8	C		
4	C	9	B		
5	C	10	A		

2. One word question and answer

12. Name the mustard selection used in cultivation

Ans. Kalyani, Pusa bold, Varuna

13. What is the colour of pod which indicates that the mustard crop is ready for harvest?

Ans. Yellowish – brown

14. Mention few varieties of mustard

Ans. Pusa bold, Karanthi, Jawahar, Sita

15. Name the state where the mustard is produced in large quantities.

Ans. Rajasthan

2.4.5 Safflower

1. Choose the correct answer

1. The seed of safflower should be treated with agrosan G.N. @

   A. 30 g/kg of seed B. 30mg/kg of seed

   C. 30 decigram/kg of seed D. 100 decigram/kg of seed

2. The fertilizer recommendation for irrigated safflower is

   A. 80 + 60 + 20 NPK kg/ha B. 80 + 40 + 20 NPK kg/ha

   C. 40 + 20 + 20 NPK kg/ha D. 40 + 40 + 20 NPK kg/ha

3. The recommended row spacing for safflower planting is

   A. 25 cm B. 35 cm

   C. 45 cm D. 55 cm

4. Nitrogen application of safflower influences

   A. Seed yield B. Seed composition

   C. Seed yield and composition D. Seed quality

5. Safflower is a _____ plant

   A. Long day B. Short day

   C. Day neutral D. Both B and C

6. The maximum duration for the safflower is

   A. 110 days B. 120 days

   C. 125 days D. 140 days

7. The recommended seed rate for the cultivation of safflower is

   A. 10 kg/ha B.15 kg/ha

   C. 17 kg/ha D. 20 kg/ha

8. The optimum spacing adopted for safflower cultivation is

   A. 30 x 45 cm B. 45 x 15 cm

   C. 60 x 45 cm D. 45 x 60 cm

9. Safflower is a

   A. Dry season crop B. Summer crop

   C. Arid season crop D. Cool crop

10. Safflower can be grown as an intercrop with

    A. Wheat B. Greengram

    C. Maize D. Sorghum

11. Safflower as an oilseed crop was introduced into India in

    A. 1965 B. 1969

    C. 1972 D. 1985

Answer keys

1	C	6	C	11	B
2	D	7	A		
3	B	8	B		
4	C	9	C		
5	C	10	A		

2. One word question and answer

12. Mention the nitrogen dosage recommended as basal application for the safflower cultivation is

Ans. 20 kg of N/ha

13. Mention the maturity index for safflower harvesting

Ans. The leaves turn to brown.

14. Which season is optimum for safflower sowing?

Ans. Cool season crop

15. Topping of safflower plants is beneficial

Ans.
- To reduce the lodging
- To reduce the water losses
- To promote branching and flowering
- To reduce losses of seed and fruit

16. Safflower rust can be controlled by

Ans.
- Spray of zineb
- Treatment of seed with carbendazim
- Destroying the infected material

2.4.6 Castor

1. Choose the correct answer

1. High temperature above 41°C at flowering of castor results in
   A. Rotting of pollens and poor fertilization
   B. Blasting of flowers and poor seed set
   C. Delayed pollination and poor fertilization
   D. Reduced pollination and rotting of seed
2. The optimum time for planting of castor varies between
   A. 20th May and 5th June B. 5th June and 20th June
   C. 20th June and 5th July D. 5th July and 20th July
3. The recommended seed rate of castor varies from
   A. 10 to 12 kg/ha B. 14 to 16 kg/ha
   C. 16 to 18 kg/ha D. 18 to 70 kg/ha
4. Irrigated crop of castor should normally be planted at a row and plant distance of
   A. 45 x 45 cm B. 60 x 45 cm
   C. 60 x 60 cm D. 90 x 45 cm
5. Fertilizer requirement of castor is (N + P_2O_5+K_2O kg/ha)
   A. 60+40+40 B. 120+60+60
   C. 120+40+40 D. 60+60+30
6. Castor (*Ricinus communis*) is originated from
   A. India B. Tropical Africa
   C. Tropical America D. Tropical Asia

7. The oil content of castor is

   A. 10 – 15% B. 18 – 25%

   C. 20 – 25% D. 35 – 58%

8. Linseed can be used as a crop for

   A. Oilseed B. Fibre

   C. Oilseed and fibre D. Oil and protein

9. Castor is a _____ plant

   A. Long day B. Short day

   C. Day neutral D. Both B and C

Answer keys

1	B	6	A
2	C	7	B
3	D	8	A
4	C	9	A
5	A		

2. One word question and answer

10. Mention few varieties of rainfed castor.

Ans. TMV CH1
TMV 6
TMV 5
SA 2

11. Mention few varieties of irrigated castor.

Ans. Kranthi
RC 8
Aruna

12. What is the optimum time for planting of castor?

Ans. 20th June and 5th July

13. What is the depth of sowing in castor?

Ans. 8 cm

14. What is the optimum temperature required for castor cultivation?

Ans. 20 – 26°C with low relative humidity.

15. Which is the best suited crop for cultivating castor as an inter crop?

Ans. Groundnut

16. Mention few pesticides and fungicides recommended for castor cultivation

Ans. Malathion, Neem Seed Kernal Extract, Mancozeb

17. What is the oil content of castor?

Ans. 18 – 25%

2.4.7 Linseed

1. Choose the correct answer

1. Retting is practiced in which oilseed crop
   A. Niger B. Linseed
   C. Groundnut D. Safflower
2. The recommended row to row spacing for linseed planting is
   A. 20 cm B. 30 cm
   C. 40 cm D. 50 cm
3. The weeds can be controlled in linseed by the application of MCPB @
   A. 0.5 kg a.i./ha B. 1.5 kg a.i./ha
   C. 1.0 kg a.i./ha D. 2.0 kg a.i./ha
4. The protein content in linseed cake has been estimated at
   A. 12 per cent B. 24 per cent
   C. 36 per cent D. 48 per cent
5. Linseed is regarded as
   A. Warm season B. Cool season crop
   C. Hot season crop D. Dry season crop

Answer keys

1	B	5	B
2	B		
3	A		
4	C		

2. One word question and answer

6. Which season is best for linseed cultivation?

Ans. Cool season crop

2.4.8 Niger

1. Choose the correct answer

1. The recommended seed rate for the cultivation of niger is

   A. 5 – 8 kg/ha B. 8 – 10 kg/ha

   C. 10 – 12 kg/ha D. 12 – 15 kg/ha

2. Example of xerophytic plant is

   A. Sunflower B. Groundnut

   C. Safflower D. Niger

3. What is the botanical name for niger?

   A. *Linum usitatissimum* B. *Brassica napus*

   C. *Guizotia abyssinica* D. *Carthamus tinctorius*

4. Where is Indian Institute of Oil Seed Research located at

   A. Jungadh B. Bhopal

   C. Rajendra Nagar D. Tindivanam

5. In nuts and oilseeds, the limiting amino acid is

   A. Threonine B. Tryptophan

   C. Cystine D. Methionine

Answer keys

1	C	5	C
2	D	6	
3	C		
4	C		

2. One word question and answer

6. Mention the uses of niger

Ans. Oil extraction
Cosmetics
Feed for cattle
Oil cakes for feeding cattle
Green fodder

7. Mention the optimum temperature for the cultivation of niger

Ans. 18 – 23°C

2.4.9 Oil palm

1. Choose the correct answer

1. Orange frond of oil palm is due to the deficiency of

   A. Manganese B. Magnesium

   C. Calcium D. Boron

2. The oil palm will give yield after

   A. 2 – 3 years after planting B. 3 - 4 years after planting

   C. 4 – 5 years after planting D. 5 – 6 years after planting

3. The seeds of oil palm require temperature to break the dormancy

   A. 30 – 40 °C B. 40 – 50 °C

   C. 50 – 60 °C D. 60 – 70 °C

Answer keys

1 B

2 C

3 C

2. One word question and answer

4. Mention the planting system followed in oil palm cultivation.

Ans. Triangular system

5. Mention the effect when the excess application of nitrogen is given to oil palm.

Ans.
- Increases in the production of male inflorescence
- Decreases the female inflorescence thereby reducing the sex ratio

6. What do you mean by ablation in oil palm?

Ans. The process of removal of small and low oil content branched inflorescence.

7. Ripeness of the fruit of oil palm can be determined by

Ans.
- The degree of detachment of the fruit from bunches.
- Change in fruit colour
- Change in texture of the fruit.

8. Mention the cost of one tonne of fresh fruit bunches of oil palm.

Ans. Rs.2, 500/-

2.4.10 Coconut

1. Choose the correct answer

1. Pencil point disease in coconut is
   A. Micronutrient disorder B. Fungal disease
   C. Viral disease D. Bacterial disease
2. Crown choke deficiency in coconut is caused due to the deficiency of
   A. Calcium B. Magnesium
   C. Iron D. Boron
3. How many coconut seedlings are required for planting 1 ha?
   A. 100 B. 150
   C. 175 D. 200

Answer keys

1	A	3	C
2	D		

2. One word question and answer

4. Mention the intercropping sequence for coconut cultivation

Ans. Groundnut, sesame, sunflower, tapioca, turmeric and banana

5. What is the best legume fodder suited for growing below the coconut for *in-situ* incorporation?

Ans. Sunhemp

6. Mention the control measure for red palm weevil in coconut

Ans. Root feeding of monocrotophos @ 5ml/lit

7. What is the common method for the control of rhinocerous beetle?

Ans. Application of 3-4 camper balls

8. How to manage the drought and conserve the soil moisture in coconut garden?

Ans.
- Mulching with coconut husk / leaves / coir pith
- Burial of coconut husk or coir pith
- Manuring with 50 kg of FYM or green manure

9. Mention the biofertilizers recommended for coconut cultivation

Ans.
- 50 g of *Azospirillum*/tree
- 50 g of phosphobacteria (or) 100 g of Azophos / tree
- 50 g of AM/ tree

10. How will you manage the rhinoceros beetle menace in coconut?

Ans.
- Collect and destroy all the bio-stages of beetles
- Incorporate the fungus to check the perpetuation of the pest
- Set up the pheromone traps
- Root feeding

11. What are all the causes for button shedding in coconut?

Ans.
- Excess acidity or alkalinity
- Severe drought
- Hormone deficiency
- Pests and diseases
- Lack of pollination

12. Mention few products obtained from coconut

Ans.
- Coconut milk
- Coconut paste
- Coconut cake
- Tender coconut
- Copras
- Coconut oil

13. Mention few varieties of coconut

Ans.
- East coast tall
- West coast tall
- Tall x Tall

14. Mention the fertilizer dosage recommended for the cultivation of 5 years old coconut tree

Ans.
- 50 kg of compost / tree
- Urea 1.3 kg / tree
- Super phosphate 2 kg / tree
- Murate of potash 2 kg / tree

2.5 CASH CROPS

2.5.1 Cotton

1. Choose the correct answer

1. The country which ranks third in the production of cotton next to USA and China is

A. India B. Germany

C. Russia D. Thailand

2. Which of the following herbicides that cannot be used for cotton crop?
   A. Diuron B. Basalin
   C. 2,4-D D. Trifluorolin
3. The trap crop in cotton cultivation is
   A. Cowpea B. Bajra
   C. Paddy D. Bhendi
4. Heavy rainfall during fruiting period of cotton cause
   A. Lodging B. Shedding of flowers
   C. Yellowing D. Resurgence of pests
5. The seed rate for hybrid cotton is
   A. 2.5 kg/ha B. 8 kg/ha
   C. 12 kg/ha D. 15 kg/ha
6. Cotton variety suitable for dryland is
   A. Varalaxmi B. LRA 5166
   C. G4 D. Jayalaxmi
7. The optimum temperature for cotton is
   A. 20 – 30° C B. 32° C
   C. 35° C D. 40° C
8. The optimum water requirement for cotton is
   A. 300 – 350 mm B. 350 – 400 mm
   C. 400 – 550 mm D. 500 – 700 mm
9. The origin of cotton is
   A. China B. Russia
   C. India D. USA
10. Delinting of cotton seed is done using
   A. Sulphuric acid B. Citric acid
   C. Sodium hydroxide D. Ammonium chloride
11. The optimum sowing period of cotton in Northern regions of India is
   A. First fortnight of May B. Second fortnight of May
   C. First fortnight of June D. Second fortnight of June
12. Cotton is classified under
   A. Shallow rooted crop B. Medium rooted crop
   C. Deep rooted crop D. Very deep rooted crop

13. Optimum soil moisture range for cotton crop is from field capacity to
    A. 20 per cent B. 30 per cent
    C. 45 per cent D. 50 per cent
14. The seed rate for suvin variety of cotton is
    A. 4 kg/ha B. 5 kg/ha
    C. 6 kg/ha D. 7 kg/ha
15. The inter crop suitable for obtaining higher returns with cotton is
    A. Greengram/ soybean B. Black gram / cowpea
    C. Soybean / cowpea D. Cowpea / green gram
16. The state which ranks first in cotton production is
    A. Punjab B. Tamil Nadu
    C. Gujarat D. Madhya Pradesh
17. Best climate suited for higher yield in cotton.
    A. Rainy B. Arid
    C. Semi Arid D. Humid climate
18. In cotton, cool night temperature is required for
    A. Vegetative growth B. Flowering
    B. Fruiting D. Maturity
19. In cotton, the bud and boll shedding usually occur to the tune of
    A. 5 – 10% B. 20 – 30%
    C. 30 – 40% D. 60 - 70%
20. Bacterial blight is caused by
    A. Bacteria B. Fungi
    C. Virus D. Mycoplasma
21. The root rot caused by *Rhizoctonia* is
    A. Soil borne B. Air borne
    C. Water borne D. Seed borne
22. Which among the following is incorrect regarding cotton varieties?
    A. MCU 5 B. K 11
    C. SVPR 2 D. TCHB 213
23. Black arm of cotton occurs severely in
    A. Summer Cambodia tract B. Winter Cambodia tract
    C. Rainfed cotton D. Garden land cotton

24. Average water requirement of cotton is
    A. 250 mm B. 300 mm
    C. 600 mm D. 150 mm
25. Leaf reddening in cotton is commonly noticed during
    A. November – December B. January – February
    C. June – July D. August – September
26. NAA is recommended in cotton to
    A. Avoid boll and flower shedding B. Increase boll size
    C. Increase crop biomass D. Increase the ginning percentage
27. The number of known species in genus *Gossypium* have been estimated as
    A. 10 B. 15
    C. 20 D. 25
28. American cotton should normally be planted with the spacing of
    A. 45 x 30 cm B. 60 x 30 cm
    C. 60 x 45 cm D. 90 x 45 cm
29. The optimum plant population for cotton has been estimated as
    A. 25000 – 50000 plants/ha B. 30000 – 60000 plants/ha
    C. 50000 – 80000 plants/ha D. 80000 – 100000 plants/ha
30. Boll shedding in cotton is due to
    A. Overloading of plant with reproductive structures
    B. Inhibitory effect of ABA (Abscisic acid)
    C. Heavy dressing of urea
    D. Frequent irrigation
31. Where is Central Institute of Cotton Research located?
    A. Nagpur B. Coimbatore
    C. Ludhiana D. Hisar
32. Name the crop which records the highest pesticide consumption
    A. Rice B. Wheat
    C. Cotton D. Maize
33. What is the recommended NPK fertilizer dosages for MCU7 and SVPR3 varieties of cotton?
    A. 50:20:20 kg/ha B. 60:30:30 kg/ha
    C. 70:40:40 kg/ha D. 50:60:70 kg/ha

34. At what concentration, the cotton kapas yield will be higher when DAP and KCl are given as foliar application?

A. 2% DAP + 1% KCl B. 3% DAP + 2% KCl

C. 3% DAP + 1% KCl D. 1% DAP + 2% KCl

35. How will you correct the nutrition disorder of zinc deficiency?

A. $ZnSO_4$ application B. $MgSO_4$ application

C. $CuSO_4$ application D. $FeSO_4$ application

36. Luxuriant growth of cotton is favourable for

A. High cotton lint yield

B. Severe incidence of pests and diseases

C. For development of reproductive growth

D. Stress tolerance

37. The soil reaction which favours cotton growth is

A. Acid pH B. Alkaline pH

C. Neutral pH D. Saline alkali

38. Intercrop sowing in cotton is taken up

A. 20 days prior to sowing of cotton

B. 10 days after sowing of cotton

C. Sown along with cotton

D. Sown at flowering stage

39. Red leaf disease in cotton is due to infection by

A. Virus B. Fungus

C. Insects D. Mineral deficiency

40. The potassium deficiency in cotton is easily visible as

A. Apical bud necrosis

B. Inverted 'V' shaped chlorosis in leaves

C. Interveinal chlorosis

D. General chlorosis

41. Name the foliar spray recommended for controlling boll shedding in cotton

A. NAA B. IBA

C. Cytokinin D. Ethrel

42. The moisture content recommended for storage for better germination of seeds is

A. 5% B. 8%

C. 11% D. 15%

43. The best time suited for hand pollination of cotton crops with pollen dusting is

A. 5 – 6 am B. 9 – 12 noon

C. 2 – 5 pm D. 6 – 8 pm

44. Nipping or topping is practiced in cultivation of

A. Maize B. Tobacco

C. Sugarcane D. Cotton

45. The ginning percentage of cotton is calculated using the formula

A. $\frac{\text{Seed cotton weight (g)}}{\text{Lint weightt (g)}} \times 100$ B. $\frac{\text{Kapas weight (g)}}{\text{Lint weightt (g)}}$

C. $\frac{\text{Lint weight (g)}}{\text{Seed cotton weight (g)}} \times 100$ D. $\frac{\text{Lint weight (g)}}{\text{Kapas weight (g)}}$

46. The king of fibres is

A. Cotton B. Jute

C. Sunnhemp D. Agave

47. Delinting in cotton is done using

A. Con. H_2SO_4 @ 100 ml/kg B. Con. HCl @ 100 ml/kg

C. Con. HNO_3@ 100 ml/kg D. Con. H_3PO_4 100 ml/kg

48. Reddening in cotton can be corrected by foliar spray of

A. 5% $MgSO_4$ B. 2% $MnSO_4$

C. 5% $MnSO_4$ D. 2% $MgSO_4$

49. Variety suitable for rainfed cotton is

A. K11 B. SVPR 1

C. Suvin D. MCU 12

50. The suitable soil type for the cultivation of cotton is

A. Black soil B. Sandy soil

C. Silty soil D. Red soil

51. Better season for the growth of cotton in Tamil Nadu is

A. January B. August

C. May D. March

52. Cotton seed oil contains
    A. Saturated fatty acid
    B. Polyunsaturated fatty acid
    C. Polyunsaturated fatty acid + cholesterol
    D. Saturated fatty acid + cholesterol

53. How many kg is equivalent to a bale of cotton?
    A. 217 kg B. 177 kg
    C. 330 kg D. 225 kg

Answer keys

1. A	11. D	21. A	31. A	41. A	51. B
2. C	12. C	22. D	32. C	42. C	52. B
3. D	13. A	23. B	33. B	43. B	53. B
4. B	14. C	24. C	34. A	44. D	
5. A	15. A	25. B	35. A	45. C	
6. B	16. C	26. A	36. B	46. A	
7. A	17. C	27. C	37. C	47. A	
8. D	18. B	28. C	38. A	48. A	
9. C	19. D	29. A	39. D	49. A	
10. A	20. A	30. B	40. B	50. A	

2. One word question and answer

54. What is the major constraint in cotton production?

Ans. Vagaries of monsoon, insect pest problems

55. Mention the criteria for harvesting cotton.

Ans. Fully opened bolls.

56. Where the Central Institute for Cotton Research is located?

Ans. Nagpur

57. Who is called as the father of hybrid cotton?

Ans. C.T.Patel

58. Mention few varieties of cotton that are suitable for Tamil Nadu.

Ans.
- MCU 5
- MCU
- Suvin
- Sumangala

59. Mention the rainfed varieties of cotton.

Ans.
- LRA 5166
- K 11
- KC 2
- SVPR 2

60. Mention the varieties suitable for rice fallow cultivation of cotton.

Ans.
- MCU 7
- SVPR 3
- Anjali

61. Mention the bioinocluant used for cotton production.

Ans. *Azospirillum*

62. Name the presowing seed treatments followed in cotton cultivation.

Ans.
- Carbendazim
- *Trichoderma*
- *Azospirillum*

63. Mention the seed hardening chemicals used for improving drought tolerance.

Ans.
- Potassium chloride
- Pungam leaf extract.

64. Name the pests that attack the bolls of cotton.

Ans. Pink boll worm

65. Name the serious pest causing damage upto 90 – 100% to the cotton crop.

Ans. Stem weevil, boll worms (American, pink and spotted boll worms)

66. Name the botanical insecticide largely used for controlling pests in cotton.

Ans. Neem Seed Kernel Extract (NSKE) – 3 to 5 per cent

67. What is the optimum seed moisture content favourable for ginning in seed cotton?

Ans. 15 - 17%

68. Name the transgenic genotype of cotton

Ans. Bt Cotton

69. When the transgenic cotton crop was developed?

Ans. 1987 in USA by Monsanto

70. From which part of the seed, cotton fibre develops?

Ans. Epidermal growth.

71. Which operation contributes more cost for total cost of production of cotton?

Ans. Plant protection cost.

72. What are the products obtained from cotton for export?

Ans.
- Raw cotton
- Cotton yarn
- Textile finished products – garments
- Cotton oil
- Animal feed

73. What are all the adverse factors that affect cotton productivity in Northern zone?

Ans.
- Rising water table
- Salinity
- High temperature in early phases
- Pest and disease problems

74. Mention the varieties of cotton which are resistant to pest and diseases.

Ans.
- Verticillium wilt : MCU 5 VT, Savitha
- White fly : Kanchana
- Boll worm : Abhadita

75. Mention the importance of cotton.

Ans.
- Primarily for lint
- Medical and surgical purpose – Raw cotton
- Linters – Cushions, pillows
- Stalk – Fuel
- Cakes and meals – cattle feed.

76. What are all the practices that are carried out after sowing in cotton?

Ans. Thinning, Gap filling on 10th day, Earthing up, Nipping

77. Mention the methods of irrigation followed in cotton.

Ans. Flooding through furrows, Surge may be followed, Drip fertigation

78. Mention the methods of harvesting for cotton.

Ans. Hand picking, Strippers, Using machineries

79. What are all the quality parameters adapted in cotton cultivation?

Ans.
- Ginning percentage
- Colour
- Trash
- Fibre quality

- Fibre fineness
- Fibre strength
- Spinning performance
- Oil content of the seed

80. Mention the cropping sequence in irrigated cotton areas.

Ans.
- Cotton – wheat
- Cotton – pulse – millets
- Rice – cotton

81. Mention the advantages of delinting in cotton

Ans.
- Grading the seed (Removal of damaged and ill filled seeds)
- Killing of hibernating boll worm larvae and disease pathogens
- Quick germination

82. Mention the machines that are used for ginning of kapas.

Ans.
- Hand gins
- Power gins
- Single roller gin
- Double roller gin
- Saw gin

83. What do you mean by ginning?

Ans. The act of separating fibres (lint) from seed cotton is known as ginning.

84. Mention the growth phases of cotton.

Ans.
- Germination phase (1 – 15 days)
- Vegetative phase (16 – 44 days)
- Flowering phase (45 – 100 days for hybrids and 45 – 87 days for varieties)

85. Mention the cotton growing seasons in Tamil Nadu.

Ans.
- Winter irrigated
- Summer irrigated
- Short duration
- Medium duration
- Rainfed
- Rice fallow

86. Severe drought during maturity phase influences.

Ans.
- Seed quality
- Lint quality
- Lint yield
- Fibre length
- Fibre quality

87. Mention few steps in cotton field preparation

Ans.
- Deep ploughing
- Harrowing 2 – 3 times
- Chiselling
- Levelling
- Uniform irrigation

88. Name the farm equipments used in cotton cultivation.

Ans.
- Dibbler
- Mould board plough
- Chisel plough
- Harrows
- Bund former/Ridger
- Cotton harvester

89. Briefly mention the delinting methods followed in cotton.

Ans.
- Mechanical delinting
- Acid delinting
- Gas delinting
- Foam delinting

90. Seed pelleting for cotton is practiced for sowing in soil to over come

Ans.
- Moisture stress
- Nutritional disorder
- Drainage problems
- Against toxic elements

91. Mention the seed coating sequence followed in cotton.

Ans. Delinted seed + Polykote + Carbendazim + Imidachloprid + *Pseudomonas* + *Azophos.*

92. Mention the cultural practices for cotton crop.

Ans.
- Application of organic and inorganic fertilizers
- Formation of ridges
- Rectification of ridges and furrows
- Sowing treated seeds
- Gap filling
- Thinning seedlings

93. Name the important insects affecting cotton crop cultivation.

Ans.
- White flies
- Aphids
- Boll worms
- Leaf eating insects / sucking pests

94. What are all the IPM technologies for cotton cultivation?

Ans. • Crop rotation
- Avoiding monocropping
- Use of resistant cultivars
- Correct time of sowing and fertilization
- Use of trap crops

95. Mention the control measure for *Fusarium* wilt in cotton.

Ans. Growing tolerant (resistant) varieties, Crop rotation

96. What are the facilities offered by regulated markets for cotton marketing?

Ans. • Correct weighing
- Commercial grading
- Godown facilities
- Sale through licensed traders
- Banking facilities
- Price intelligence information

97. What is the packaging material commonly used for the storage of cotton?

Ans. Gunny bag

98. Mention the common method of picking in cotton

Ans. Hand picking

99. In India, the cotton kapas is harvested by hand picking, why?

Ans. Cheap availability of labour

100. Before sowing, cotton kapas has to be dried for safer storage. Which method you can recommend?

Ans. Sun drying

101. Mention the method of separation of seed from kapas?

Ans. Ginning

102. Mention the method of marketing of cotton kapas in regulated market

Ans. Auctioning

103. Mention few important fibre crops grown in India.

Ans. Cotton, Jute, Mesta

104. Which factors are responsible for lesser production of cotton in Southern Zone?

Ans. Vagaries of monsoon and extensive damage due to pests.

105. Mention the important hybrids of cotton.

Ans. Super long staple : Hybrid – 4, Varalaxmi, Suvin, DCH 32.

Medium staple : Dhanalaxmi, TSH 289, CDHB 1, DHB – 105.

106. Mention the pre – emergence herbicides used for better crop cultivation in cotton.

Ans. Fluchloralin, pendimethalin

107. Mention the cropping systems followed for cotton in rainfed areas.

Ans. Mono cropping, mono with mixed crops. – pulses, millets, groundnut

108. Mention the critical stages for irrigation requirement in cotton.

Ans. Flowering stage, boll formation

109. Mention the soil types where the cotton is grown predominately.

Ans. Alluvial soil, black cotton soil, red sandy loam to loam soil, lateritic soil

110. The optimum seed rate for fuzzy and delinted seeds to obtain maximum yield of cotton.

Ans. Fuzzy seed – 15 kg/ha, delinted seed– 7.5 kg/ha

111. Mention irrigation methods followed for cotton.

Ans. Skip furrow method, alternate furrow irrigation

112. Mention the causes for heavy shedding of buds and young bolls in cotton.

Ans. Drought, rain, high humidity, Wind, lack of nutrition, attack of pests

113. Rain received during maturity period of cotton results in

Ans.
- Spoilage of link
- Lowers spinning per cent
- Increases pests and diseases

114. What is the purpose of nipping of terminal portions of cotton plant?

Ans. Nipping of main stem in cotton is done to arrest the growth of main stem.

115. What is the environmental factor that influences the flower bud formation in cotton?

Ans. Day length temperature

116. Name the biological insecticide used for controlling *Spodoptera* pest

Ans. NPV virus

117. Mention the trap crop ideal for cotton to control boll worm

Ans. Castor

118. Mention the predators for controlling sucking pests in cotton.

Ans. Chrysoperla

119. Name the premier cotton association in India

Ans. East India Cotton Association

120. What is the government agency involved in cotton marketing?

Ans. Cotton Corporation of India

2.5.2 Jute

1. Choose the correct answer

1. Species of jute which has higher quality is

   A. *C.olitorius* B. *C.cordifolius*

   C. *C.capsularis* D. *C.marua*

2. National Institute of Research on Jute and allied Fibre is situated at

   A. Lucknow B. Barrackpore

   C. Kolkata D. Jhansi

3. During retting practice, jute bundles are kept in submerged condition for about

   A. 7 - 10 days B. 10 - 12 days

   C. 14 - 16 days D. 16 - 20 days

4. Harvesting stage of jute is

   A. Flowering stage B. Pod initiation stage

   C. Small pod stage D. Mature pod stage

Answer keys

1. C 2. C 3. A 4. C

2.5.3 Sugarcane

1. Choose the correct answer

1. Which is a special season for sugarcane during the month of

   A. September - October B. February – March

   C. December - January D. June - July

2. Scientific name of noble cane is

   A. *Saccharum barberi* B. *Saccharum sinense*

   C. *Saccharum spontaneum* D. *Saccharum officinarun*

3. SSI in sugarcane stands for

   A. Sustainable Sugarcane Invention

   B. Sustainable Sugarcane Implementation

   C. Sustainable Sugarcane Innovative

   D. Sustainable Sugarcane Initiative

4. _____ prevents lodging in sugarcane.
   A. Earthing up B. Propping
   C. Detrashing D. Removal of H_2O shoots
5. Sugar content in sugarcane is about
   A. 10-15% B. 13-18%
   C. 20% D. 20-25%
6. Variety which has multi ratooning capacity is
   A. TNAU SCSi 8 B. CO 86032
   C. COC 23 D. COC 671
7. Highest ratoon practicing country in sugarcane in the world is
   A. Cuba B. South Africa
   C. Brazil D. India
8. Example of riperers in sugarcane is
   A. Sodium sulphate B. Sodium metasilicate
   C. Sodium thiosulphate D. Sodium metabisulphate
9. Parasitic weed in sugarcane is
   A. Striga B. Orabanche
   C. Cusutta D. Dodder
10. For effective photosynthesis, how many leaves are sufficient in sugarcane?
   A. 8 - 10 leaves B. 30 - 35 leaves
   C. 15 - 20 leaves D. 20 - 30 leaves
11. Water requirement in sugarcane is about
   A. 100 - 550 mm B. 400 - 450 mm
   C. 1300 - 1350 mm D. 2000 - 2500mm
12. What is the recommended sett rate for sugarcane (3 bud setts)?
   A. 75000 B. 187500
   C. 50000 D. 60000
13. Which of the following is correct regarding commercial crops?
   A. *Morus alba* B. *Medicago sativa*
   C. *Saccharum officinarum* D. *Arachis hypogea*
14. Where is Indian Institute of Sugarcane Research located?
   A. Coimbatore B. Lucknow
   C. Cuddalore D. Sirugamani

15. Where is Sugarcane Breeding Institute located?
    A. Sirugamani B. Cuddalore
    C. Pantnagar D. Coimbatore
16. Which city is called as sugar bowl of India?
    A. Akola B. Lucknow
    C. Guntur D. Trichy
17. When should detrashing be done in sugarcane?
    A. 2nd and 4th month after planting
    B. 3rd and 5th month after planting
    C. 5th and 7th month after planting
    D. 6th and 8th month after planting

Answer keys

1.	D	6.	B	11.	D	16.	B
2.	D	7.	A	12.	C	17.	C
3.	D	8.	B	13.	C		
4.	B	9.	A	14.	B		
5.	A	10.	A	15.	B		

2.5.4 Tobacco

1. Choose the correct answer

1. Critical stage of tobacco is
   A. Flowering B. Tapping stage
   C. Booting stage D. Primodia development
2. Predominant parasitic weed in tobacco is
   A. Orobanche B. Cuscutta
   C. Striga D. Loranthus
3. Desuckering is commonly practiced in
   A. Sugarcane B. Tobacco
   C. Cotton D. Linseed
4. To suppress the growth of suckers in tobacco, the chemical used is
   A. Pungam oil + sandivit B. Neem oil + sandivit
   C. Iluppai oil + sandivit D. Mahua oil + sandivit

5. Curing is a post harvest operation carried out in
   A. Rice B. Blackgram
   C. Groundnut D. Tobacco
6. Which among the following is incorrect regarding varieties of *Nicotiana tabacum*
   A. Cauvery B. OK 1
   C. VV 2 D. VKT 1

Answer keys

1. B 2. A 3. B 4. B 5. D 6. A

2.5.5 Mulberry

1. Choose the correct answer

1. Which among the following is incorrect regarding mulberry?
   A. MR 2 B. S36
   C. S1635 D. DD (Viswa)
2. What type of pruning is done in mulberry at ground level?
   A. Bottom pruning B. Kolar pruning
   C. Middle pruning D. Rajuvenation pruning
3. What is the transplanting age of mulberry saplings?
   A. 90-120 days B. 70-80 days
   C. 130-135 days D. 60-70 days
4. In mulberry cultivation, first leaf harvesting can be made at
   A. Three months after planting
   B. Six months after planting
   C. Nine months after planting
   D. Twelve months after planting
5. Water requirement for mulberry is
   A. 500-750 mm B. 800-900 mm
   C. 100-1500 mm D. 1600-7500 mm
6. Among the following, which mulberry variety is unsuitable for rainfed condition?
   A. S 13 B. S 34
   C. V 1 D. RFS 135

7. Which is the yield potential of V 1 mulberry variety (express in tons/ha/ year)?

   A. 20 B. 40

   C. 30 D. 80

8. What is the quantity of farm yard manure (FYM) recommended for one hectare of rainfed crop per year?

   A. 10 tons B. 20 tons

   C. 30 tons D. 40 tons

9. What is the fertilizer schedule (kg NPK/ha) for V 1 mulberry variety?

   A. 200:100:100 B. 300:120:120

   C. 375:140:140 D. 500:160:160

10. What is the recommended dose of *Azospirillum* for mulberry crop?

    A. 5 kg/ha B. 10 kg/ha

    C. 20 kg/ha D. 30 kg/ha

11. Which mulberry variety is resistant to powdery mildew?

    A. Kanna 2 B. S 36

    C. S 13 D. MR 2

Answer keys

1.	C	6.	C	11.	D
2.	B	7.	C		
3.	A	8.	A		
4.	B	9.	C		
5.	D	10.	C		

3

Irrigation Management

I. Choose the correct answer

1. In which moisture point resistant to wind erosion in soil

   A. Permanent wilting point B. Hygroscopic point
   C. Field capacity D. None of the above

2. When a plant is under soil moisture stress, the roots

   A. Shrink in size B. Expand in size
   C. Remain unaffected D. Both A and B

3. The water held with a water potential lessar than1/3 bar is known as

   A. Field capacity B. Gravitational water
   C. Available water D. Unavailable water

4. Water not available to the plants is

   A. Field capacity B. Permanent wilting point
   C. Available water capacity D. Gravitational water

5. Water available to the plants is called

   A. Gravitational water B. Hygroscopic water
   C. Capillary water D. Both B and C

6. Which of the following is incorrectly matched?

Soil water	Soil moisture tension
A. Gravitational water	- 0 or less than 1/3 atmospheric pressure
B. Capillary water	- 1/3 and 31 atmospheric pressure
C. Hygroscopic water	- Less than 30 atmospheric pressure
D. Available water	- Between wilting coefficient and field capacity

7. Water saving percentage in drip irrigation is

   A. 50% B. 70%
   C. 45% D. 60%

8. In Tamil Nadu, how much area is being cultivated under irrigation?

A. 2 million hectares B. 3 million hectares

C. 4 million hectares D. 5 million hectares

9. Workout the water use efficiency for the rice, if yield is 6200 kg/ha and evopotranspiration is 500 mm

A. 12.4 kg/ha/mm B. 0.8 kg/ha/mm

C. 1 kg/ha/mm D. 13.4 kg/ha/mm

10. Ratio of irrigation water consumed by crop to the water delivered from the source is called as

A. Water application efficiency B. Water use efficiency

C. Irrigation efficiency D. Consumptive use efficiency

11. Tamil Nadu receives more water through river called

A. Vaigai B. Cauvery

C. Thamirabarani D. Thenpennai

12. Which of the following water sources is utilized to the maximum for crop production in India?

A. Godaveri B. Chambal

C. Chinav D. Ganga

13. The soil water potential is

A. Of gravitational, osmotic, capillary and pressure potential

B. Of gravitational, osmotic and capillary potential

C. Of gravitational and osmotic potential

D. Equal to gravitational potential

14. The best agronomic practices to improve the water use efficiency is

A. Minimum tillage B. Mulching

C. Planting geometry D. All of these

15. WUE is the highest in

A. Flood irrigation B. Border irrigation

C. Sprinkler irrigation D. Drip irrigation

16. Darey's law in water management explains

A. Flow of water in dam B. Flow of water in soil

C. Flow of water in forest trees D. Flow of soil in hills

17. Average water requirement of cotton is
    A. 250 mm B. 300 mm
    C. 600 mm D. 150 mm
18. Critical stage of irrigation in groundnut is
    A. Seed set/formation B. Throughout the growth period
    C. Flowering D. Peg formation
19. Crop water requirement is represented as
    A. WR = T + E + WP + WL + WSP
    B. WR = Irrigation requirement + Effective rainfall + Contribution from groundwater table
    C. WR = Consumptive use + Water loss + Water for special needs
    D. All the above
20. Critical stage of irrigation for wheat is
    A. Primodial initiation B. Blooming
    C. Crown root initiation D. Grain formation
21. A day is said to be a rainy day, if rainfall is
    A. More than 2.5 mm B. More than 5 mm
    C. More than 7.5 mm D. More than 1 mm
22. Irrigation requirement is expressed in terms of
    A. Hectare centimetre B. Centimetre
    C. Millimetre D. All the above
23. Water requirement of mango per day is
    A. 80-100 lit/plant (tree) B. 30-40 lit/plant (tree)
    C. 20-30 lit/plant (tree) D. 8-12 lit/plant (tree)
24. The field water efficiency of trickle irrigation is
    A. 50-55% B.55-85%
    C. 80-90% D. 60-70%
25. Fertigation is a process in ___________ irrigation
    A. Sprinkler B. Surface
    C. Drip D. Centre pivot
26. Which of the following instrument is used for measuring evaporation?
    A. Pan evaporometer B. Penetrometer
    C. Tentiometer D. All of the above

27. Chemical precipitation in irrigation water occurs due to increase in

A. Fe and HCO_3 B. HCO_3

C. Ca D. CO_3

28. Basic irrigation is commonly adopted for

A. Cardamom B. Cabbage

C. Coconut D. Coffee

29. Available water is between

A. FC and PWP B. FC and saturation

C. PWP and hygroscopic coefficient D. None of the above

30. Higher water use efficiency can be achieved with the help of

A. Furrow irrigation B. Drip irrigation

C. Corrugation D. Basin irrigation

31. Ground water contamination is mainly due to

A. Nitrate leaching B. Erosion

C. Nitrous oxide emission D. None of the above

32. Water requirement for sugarcane is

A. 1100 mm B. 900 mm

C. 2500 mm D. 1600 mm

33. Channel flowing irrigation water is measured by

(i) Submerged orifice (ii) Pipe orifice

(iii) Parshall flume (iv) V – Notches

Of the above

A. (i) and (ii) B. (iii) and (iv)

C. (iii) alone D. (iv) alone

34. What is the upper limit of soil moisture range?

A. -0.01 to -0.02 Mpa B. -0.01 to -0.03 Mpa

C. 0.01 to 0.02 Mpa D. 0.01 to 0.03 Mpa

35. Match list I with list II and choose the correct options given below

List I	**List II**
a. Border irrigation	1. Finger millet
b. Check basin irrigation	2. Greengram
c. Furrow irrigation	3. Sunflower
d. Surge irrigation	4. Cotton

	a	b	c	d
A.	3	1	2	4
B.	2	3	1	4
C.	2	1	4	3
D.	3	2	1	4

36. Consider the statement and choose the correct answer

    (i) The diameter of emitter in trickle irrigation is 0.2 – 2 mm

    (ii) The emitter average discharge rate is 2 – 10 l/hr

    (iii) The emitter's discharge rate at pressure 2.5 kg/cm^2 is 1-4 l/hr

    A. (i) and (iii) are correct B. (ii) alone is correct

    C. (i) and (ii) are correct D. All the statements are correct

37. Which one of the following arrangements is correct regarding drip irrigation system?

    A. Ventury, filter, pressure regulators, mains, laterals, emitters

    B. Filter, ventury, mains, pressure regulators, laterals, emitters

    C. Pressure regulators, ventury, filter, laterals, emitters

    D. Ventury, pressure regulators, filter, mains, laterals, emitters

38. What is the average percentage of water saving in sprinkler irrigation system?

    A. 70 – 80 % B. 60 -70 %

    C. 25 – 50 % D. 10 -20 %

39. Consider the statement and choose the correct answer

    (i) The average annual rainfall of Tamil Nadu is 945 mm

    (ii) The average annual rainfall of India is 1190 mm

    (iii) The average annual rainfall of Tamil Nadu is 998 mm

    A. (ii) and (iii) are correct B. (i) and (ii) are correct

    C. (i) alone is correct D. (i) and (iii) are correct

40. Match list I with list II and choose the correct options given below

List I	List II
a. Groundnut	1. 550-600 mm
b. Sugarcane	2. 200-450 mm
c. Pulses	3. 500-550 mm
d. Cotton	4. 1800-2200 mm

	a	b	c	d
A.	4	1	2	3
B.	4	2	3	1
C.	4	3	2	1
D.	3	4	2	1

41. Match list I with list II and choose the correct options given below

List I	List II
a. Maize	1. Two weeks before and after flowering
b. Finger millet	2. Full growing period
c. Sunflower	3. Just prior to tasseling and grain filling
d. Cotton	4. Primordial initiation and flowering

	a	b	c	d
A.	4	3	2	1
B.	3	4	1	2
C.	4	3	1	2
D.	3	1	4	2

42. What is the range of soil moisture tension at permanent wilting point?

A. 5 to 15 atm B. 3 to 18 atm

C. 7 to 32 atm D. 8 to 40 atm

43. Soil moisture between field capacity and permanent wilting point is referred as

A. Saturation capacity B. Moisture equivalent

C. Wilting co-efficient D. Available water

44. Consider the statement and choose the correct answer

(i) Mild stress – 8-10%

(ii) Moderate moisture stress – 10-20%

(iii) Severe stress - >20%

A. (i) and (ii) are correct B. (ii) alone is correct

C. All the statements are correct D. (iii) alone is correct

45. How much tension is present in available water

A. 0.33 and 15 atm B. 0 and 1/3 atm

C. 0 and 0.03 atm D. 0 and 2/3 atm

46. Which among the following is incorrect regarding poor quality water?

A. Salinity B. Toxicity

C. Sodicity D. Presence of high chloride ions

47. Application gypsum to the irrigation water is to increase the proportion of

A. Magnesium B. Sulphate

C. Calcium D. Phosphorus

48. ________ is the anerobically decomposed organic matter present in sewage water

A. Microbes B. Sludge

C. *Rhizobium* D. Algae

49. Consider the statement and choose the correct answer regarding excess irrigation

(i) It causes poor aeration

(ii) Stagnation and salinity

(iii) Results in gain of fertilizer

A. (i) alone is correct B. (ii) alone is correct

C. All the statements are correct D. (i) and (ii) are correct

50. Which one of the following plant is used as an indicator of stress?

A. Sunflower B. Groundnut

C. Sorghum D. Cowpea

51. Consider the statement and choose the correct answer regarding irrigation scheduling

(i) Micro plot technique - field soil with sand (1:2 ratio)

(ii) Phonological stage approach – Growing of indicator plant

(iii) Meteorological approach – Evapotranspiration rates

A. (i) alone is correct B. (ii) alone is correct

C. (i) and (iii) are correct D. (i) and (ii) are correct

52. What is the formula for irrigation efficiency?

A. $E_i = \frac{W_t}{W_f} \times 100$ B. $E_i = \frac{W_s}{W_f} \times 100$

C. $E_i = \frac{W_c}{W_r} \times 100$ D. $E_i = \frac{W_{cu}}{W_d} \times 100$

53. What is the formula for water use efficiency?

A. $E_u = \frac{W_s}{W_w} \times 100$ B. $E_u = \frac{W_{cu}}{W_d} \times 100$

C. $E_u = \frac{W_s}{W_f} \times 100$ D. $E_u = \frac{W_{cu}}{W_d} \times 100$

54. What is the formula for crop water use efficiency?

A. $\frac{Y}{ET}$ B. $\frac{Y}{WR}$

C. $\frac{Y}{ER}$ D. $\frac{Y}{WE}$

55. Which of the following is the largest irrigation canal in India?

A. Buckingham canal B. Sirhind canal

C. Indira Gandhi canal D. Sutlej Yamuna Link canal

56. In which of the following methods of irrigation, rotating nozzles are used?

A. Moat B. Drip system

C. Chain pump D. Sprinkler system

57. The term PET was coined by

A. Sarkar and Biswas B. Haigreaves

C. Thornthwaite D. Mendel

58. High Water Use Efficiency (WUE)

A. Flood irrigation B. Sprinkler

C. Drip D. All of the above

59. The pump is mostly made up of

A. Iron B. Zinc

C. Brass D. Plastic

60. Crop water need (mm/total growing period) for maize crop is

A. 350-500 B. 900-1200

C. 500-800 D. 400-600

61. What is the right combination for irrigated upland farming system?

A. Crop + Dairy + Mushroom

B. Crop + Dairy + Piggery

C. Crop + Goat + Fish

D. Crop + Dairy + Biogas + Mushroom

62. An example of integrated farming system in Tamil Nadu

A. Duck and fish rearing B. Goat and buffalo rearing

C. Sheep and buffalo rearing D. Sheep and rabbit rearing

Answer keys

1	A	11	B	21	A	31	A	41	B	51	C	61	D
2	A	12	D	22	D	32	C	42	C	52	C	62	A
3	B	13	A	23	B	33	B	43	D	53	D		
4	D	14	D	24	C	34	B	44	C	54	A		
5	C	15	D	25	C	35	C	45	A	55	C		
6	C	16	B	26	A	36	D	46	D	56	C		
7	B	17	C	27	A	37	A	47	C	57	C		
8	B	18	D	28	C	38	C	48	B	58	C		
9	A	19	D	29	A	39	A	49	D	59	C		
10	C	20	C	30	B	40	D	50	A	60	C		

4

Dry Farming

I. Choose the correct answer

1. __________ refers to cultivation of crops in regions with annual rainfall more than 750 mm.

   A. Rainfed farming B. Semi arid farming

   C. Dryland farming D. Irrigated farming

2. What is the total geographical area under rainfed cultivation?

   A. 141 Mha B. 80 Mha

   C. 70 Mha D. 120 Mha

3. Where is Central Research Institute for Dryland Agriculture (CRIDA) located?

   A. Hyderabad B. Bikaner

   C. Jaipur D. Kovilpatti

4. Consider the statement and choose the correct one regarding management practices in dryland agriculture

   (i) Growing early maturing crop with deep root

   (ii) Maintaining optimum plant population

   (iii) Avoid mixed or intercropping

   A. (i) and (ii) are correct B. (ii) and (iii) are correct

   C. (i) and (iii) are correct D. All the statements are correct

5. Among the following which is not a dry farming crop?

   A. Sorghum B. Bajra (Pearl millet)

   C. Rice D. Maize

6. __________ is a ideal land use option for degraded lands

   A. Horti – pastoral system B. Silvi – pastoral system

   C. Agri-silvi pastoral system D. Pastoral system

7. SALT refers to

A. Straight Agricultural Land Technology

B. Slope Agricultural Land Technology

C. Saline Alkali Land Technology

D. Sodic Acidic Land Technology

8. Which among the following species is used as live fence in dry areas

A. *Zizyphus nummularia* B. *Sesbania grandiflora*

C. *Leucaena leucocephala* D. *Sesbania rostrata*

9. Which one of the following crops is not cultivated under dryland farming

A. Ragi B. Groundnut

C. Jowar (Sorghum) D. Sugarcane

10. Consider the following statements. Identify the correct ones.

(i) On the basis of main source of moisture for crops, the farming can be classified as irrigated and rainfed.

(ii) While irrigated farming is dependent on irrigation facilities, but rainfed farming is done with the help of rainfall received during Southwest monsoon.

A. (i) only B. (ii) only

C. Both (i) and (ii) D. None

11. Consider the following statements about dryland farming. Identify the correct ones.

(i) The dryland farming is largely confined to the regions having annual rainfall less than 75cm.

(ii) These regions grow hardy and drought resistant crops.

A. (i) only B. (ii) only

C. Both (i) and (ii) D. None

12. Dry farming in India is extensively practised in

A. Punjab plains B. Deccan region

C. Kanara plains D. Coromendal plains

13. Which of the following is/are correct about dry farming in India?

(i) Dry farming is mainly practised is western India

(ii) Generally only one crop in grown in a year

(iii) Repeated ploughing of field is avoided

Select the correct option from codes given below

A. (i) and (ii) only
B. (iii) only
C. (ii) and (iii) only
D. (i), (ii) and (iii)

14. Dryland farming mean

A. Multiple cropping
B. Forming of high yielding varieties of maize, jowar and bajra
C. Cultivation of soil degradation and reclaiming problematic lands
D. Cultivation of drought resistant, short duration and high yielding varieties of crops, with package of soil and water management including water harvesting

15. How soil resistance can increase against erosion?

A. By maintaining the water inflow
B. By maintaining the physical structure of soil
C. By maintaining the environmental conditions
D. By increasing the manure given to the plants

16. __________ is a soil binder crop which controls wind and water erosion

A. *Kigelia pinnata*
B. *Parkinsonia aculeata*
C. *Spathodea companulata*
D. *Pandanus odoratissimus*

17. (i)The area of macro watershed ranges from 400 to 2000 ha

(ii) Mini watershed area ranges from 1 to 100 ha

(iii) Strip cropping refers to growing two or more crops in strip across the slope

A. (i) and (iii) are correct
B. (i) and (ii) are correct
C. (iii) alone is correct
D. (i), (ii) and (iii) are correct

18. (i) Contour bunding is followed in areas having less than 600 mm

(ii) Graded bunding is not suitable for soils having low permeability and low infiltration

A. (i) alone is correct
B. (ii) alone is correct
C. Both are correct
D. Both are wrong

19. Command Area Development Authority was setup in

A. Tamil Nadu
B. Haryana
C. New Delhi
D. Jodhpur

20. (i) Wind breaks which obstruct the wind flow and reduce wind speed
(ii) Shelter belts are row of trees planted for protection of crop against wind
(iii) The direction from which wind is blowing is called windward side
A. (i) and (iii) are correct B. (ii) and (iii) are correct
C. (i) and (ii) are correct D. All the statements are correct

21. Most efficient land management practice evolved by ICRISAT for moisture conservation in deep black soil is known as
A. Narrow bed conservation system
B. Broad bed furrow system
C. Furrow improvement system
D. Moisture conservation system

22. Mechanical measures of soil conservation include
(i) Contour bunding (ii) Bench terracing
(iii) Check dams (iv) Percolation ponds
A. (i), (ii) and (iv) B. (i), (iii) and (iv)
C. (i), (ii) and (iii) D. All the four

23. Which of the following is a multi purpose tree species?
A. *Albizia amara* B. *Azadirachta indica*
C. *Albizia lebeck* D. All the above

24. It is a well accepted conservation measure in controlling run-off and soil erosion and thereby maintaining fertility of soil
A. Strip cropping B. Inter cropping
C. Contour farming D. Mixed cropping

25. A watershed is a
A. Physical land B. Geohydrological unit of land
C. Vegetative unit of land D. Water holding topography

26. Match the following
a. Contour cultivation 1. Groundnut and cowpea
b. Efficient in checking soil erosion 2. 1 ½ % slope
c. Graded bunding 3. Grasses
d. Interception of rainfall 4. Less than 600 mm rainfall

	a	b	c	d
A.	2	1	4	3
B.	4	3	2	1
C.	1	4	2	3
D.	3	4	2	1

27. Match the following

a. Dryland farming	1. > 750 mm rainfall
b. Rainfed farming	2. Hosiarpur
c. Submontane soil	3. Hisar
d. Sierozemic soils	4. > 115 mm rainfall

	a	b	c	d
A.	4	3	2	1
B.	1	4	3	2
C.	1	4	2	3
D.	1	4	4	2

28. Find out the correct answer

(i) Growing late maturing varieties with deep root system

(ii) Premonsoon sowing is recommended

(iii) Adoption is inter cropping – cereals and cotton

A. (i) alone is correct B. (i) and (ii) are correct

C. (ii) and (iii) are correct D. (ii) alone is correct

29. Find out the live fence tree

A. *Leucaena leucocephala* B. *Tectona grandis*

C. *Albizia lebeck* D. *Hardwickia binata*

30. Which one of the following area (million hectare) is classified as waste lands in India?

A. 175 B. 250

C. 75 D. 300

31. Which among the following is the correct arrangement of gully development stages

A. Initiation, development, healing and stabilization stage

B. Development, healing, initiation and stabilization stage

C. Healing, initiation, development and stabilization stage

D. Stabilization, healing, development and initiation stage

32. Consider the statement and choose the correct answer in gully control measure

(i) Treatment of catchment area – bench terrace and contour bunds

(ii) Diversion of gully – Stabilization by masonry construction or sodding of grasses

(iii) Stabilization of gully (biological measure) – vegetation decreases and velocity of gully is increased

A. (i) alone is correct B. (ii) alone is correct

C. (i) and (ii) are correct D. (iii) alone is correct

33. Match list I with list II and choose the correct options given below

List I	List II
a. Graded bunds	1. Slope between 10 and 16%
b. Broad base terrace	2. Slope between 16 and 33%
c. Contour stone wall	3. Slope between 6 and 10%
d. Bench terracing	4. Slope between 2 and 6%

	a	b	c	d
A.	4	2	1	3
B.	4	3	1	2
C.	4	1	2	3
D.	3	4	1	2

34. Consider the statement and choose the correct answer regarding bench terracing

(i) Level bench terrace – table top terrace

(ii) Inward sloping bench terrace – to drain off excess water

(iii) Outward sloping bench terrace – increases the excess slope to mild slopes

(iv) Californian type of terrace – digging soil little by little

A. (i) and (ii) are correct B. (i), (ii) and (iii) are correct

C. (i), (ii), (iii) and (iv) are correct D. (i), (ii) and (iv) are correct

35. When adjacent ridges are joined at regular intervals by barriers are called as

A. Contour bunding B. Graded bunding

C. Tie ridging D. Bench terracing

36. Tiny finger like channels are formed in what type of erosion?

A. Rill erosion | B. Sheet erosion
C. Gully erosion | D. Stream erosion

37. What is the permissible value of soil erosion?

A. 16.35 t/ha | B. 15 t/ha
C. 13.3 t/ha | D. 11 t/ha

38. Central Soil and Water Conservation Research and Training Institute is located?

A. Ooty | B. Bhopal
C. Dehradun | D. Karnal

39. Who proposed "Soil without water is desert and water without soil is useless"?

A. Hennings | B. H.H.Bennett
C. Bernald | D. Robinson

40. ___________ association is ideal for soil conservation

A. Grass + legume | B. Tree + legume
C. Creeper + legume | D. Hedge + legume

41. Consider the statement and choose the correct one

(i) Mulching is essential because 60 to 75% rain water is lost through evaporation
(ii) Mulch is material that is applied to soil surface
(iii) Application of mulch increases soil salinity

A. (i) and (ii) are correct | B. (ii) and (iii) are correct
C. (i) and (iii) are correct | D. All the statements are correct

42. Match list I with list II and choose the correct options given below

List I	**List II**
a. Kaolin	1. Film forming type
b. Phenyl mercuric acetate	2. Growth retardant
c. Hexadeconol	3. Stomatal closing type
d. Cycocel	4. Reflectant type

	a	b	c	d
A.	3	2	4	1
B.	4	2	1	3
C.	4	3	1	2
D.	3	4	2	1

43. Spraying of which nutrient will be useful in regeneration of legumes and castor after rain

A. MOP
B. SSP
C. SOP
D. DAP

44. Match list I with list II and choose the correct options given below

List I	**List II**
a. Sub watershed	1. 1000 to 10000 ha
b. Multi watershed	2. 1 to 100 ha
c. Micro watershed	3. 10000 to 50000 ha
d. Mini watershed	4. 100 to 1000 ha

	a	b	c	d
A.	3	4	1	2
B.	3	1	4	2
C.	4	1	3	2
D.	4	2	3	1

45. Initial stage of soil erosion is

A. Rill erosion
B. Gully erosion
C. Sheet erosion
D. Wave erosion

46. Average annual rate of erosion of Indian soil is

A. 12 tons/ha
B. 16.35 tons/ha
C. 17.8 tons/ha
D. 20.5 tons/ha

47. According to National Commission on Agriculture, area of eroded soil in India is

A. 167 million ha
B. 119 million ha
C. 162 million ha
D. 150 million ha

48. Example of erosion permitting crop is

A. Pulses
B. Maize
C. Cowpea
D. All the above

49. Erosion losses of nitrogen is _____ kg N/ha/ year

A. 10-40
B. 20-60
C. 40-80
D. 60-90

50. Dryland based cropping system followed in India is

A. Sorghum + Sheep + Fish
B. Maize + Dairy + Biogas + Sericulture
C. Sorghum + Goat + Agroforestry
D. Rice + Dairy + Biogas + Mushroom

51. Low and uneven rainfall is a common in

    A. Semi arid B. Dryland farming

    C. Wetland farming D. Garden land

52. Rainfed farming receives rainfall of about

    A. More than 750 mm B. Less than 750 mm

    C. More than 1150 mm D. Less than 1150 mm

53. Bench terracing is also called as

    A. Hill farming B. Staircase farming

    C. Erosion control farming D. None of these

54. Broad base terrace is also known as

    A. Bench terrace B. Channel terrace

    C. Drainage type terrace D. None of these

Answer keys

1	C	11	C	21	B	31	A	41	A	51	B
2	B	12	D	22	C	32	C	42	C	52	C
3	A	13	D	23	D	33	B	43	D	53	B
4	A	14	D	24	A	34	D	44	B	54	C
5	C	15	B	25	B	35	C	45	C		
6	A	16	D	26	A	36	A	46	B		
7	B	17	D	27	C	37	D	47	D		
8	A	18	A	28	D	38	C	48	B		
9	D	19	B	29	A	39	B	49	B		
10	C	20	D	30	A	40	A	50	A		

5

Weeds and Their Management

I. Choose the correct answer

1. Which statement is the wrong statement?

   (i) *Convolvulus arvensis* seeds viable for 50 years

   (ii) Yield loss due to weeds in rice is 11%

   (iii) Yield loss due to weeds in cotton is >70%

   A. (i) alone is correct B. (ii) alone is wrong

   C. (iii) alone is correct D. (i) and (ii) are wrong

2. Match the following

Crop pest	Alternate host
a. Redgram gram caterpillar	1. *Echinochloa*
b. Rice stem borer	2. *Saccharum spontaneum*
c. Castor hairy caterpillar	3. Amaranthus
d. Maize downy mildew	4. *Crotalaria*

	a	b	c	d
A.	3	1	4	2
B.	2	1	4	3
C.	3	4	2	1
D.	4	2	1	3

3. Statement (i): *Pistia lanceolata* causes malaria and encephalitis

   Statement (ii): Dermatitis is caused by *Parthenium hysterophorus*

   A. (i) alone is correct B. (ii) alone is correct

   C. Both are correct D. Both are wrong

4. Which can be conserved by ground cover of weeds?

   A. K B. P

   C. N D. Ca

5. Match the following

a. Perennial weed	1. *Cynodon dactylon*
b. Wetland weed	2. *Parthenium hysterophorus*
c. Exotic weed	3. *Datura stramonium*
d. Poisonous weed	4. *Echinochloa colona*

	a	b	c	d
A.	1	4	2	3
B.	4	3	2	1
C.	3	2	4	1
D.	2	4	1	3

6. Example of total stem parasite is
   A. *Orabanche cernua* B. *Loranthus longiflorus*
   C. *Striga lutea* D. *Cuscuta chinensis*

7. Match the following

a. Rodenticide	1. Metaldehyde
b. Molluscicides	2. 2, 4 – D
c. Fungicide	3. Zinc phosphide
d. Herbicide	4. Copper oxychloride

	a	b	c	d
A.	2	3	4	1
B.	3	1	4	2
C.	2	1	4	3
D.	3	4	2	1

8. Which herbicide is having higher persistence in soil?
   A. Atrazine B. Pendimethalin
   C. Paraquat D. 2, 4-D

9. Key elements in weed management are
   A. Prevention B. Control
   C. Eradication D. All the above

10. Solarisation is a weed control method which comes under
    A. Chemical control B. Biological control
    C. Physical control D. Cultural control

11. Match the weed and its type and select the correct code

Weed	**Type**
a. Nut grass	1. Grassy
b. Carpet weed	2. Aquatic

c. Bermuda grass — 3. Broad leaved

d. Water hyacinth — 4. Sedges

	a	b	c	d
A.	1	3	4	2
B.	4	3	1	2
C.	1	4	3	2
D.	4	1	3	2

12. The herbicides which move from place of application to place which show ultimate effect is known as

A. Contact herbicide B. Translocated herbicide

C. Selective herbicide D. Non selective herbicide

13. Butachlor application in rice is effective against

A. Sedges B. Grasses

C. Broad leaved weeds D. None of the above

14. What is the per cent of total loss caused by weeds in agricultural production?

A. 125% B. 35%

C. 45% D. 55%

15. Who was the first to define the word weed?

A. Jethro Tull B. Robinson

C. Whitaker D. Ramaiah

16. Which weed ranks first in obnoxious weed in world level?

A. *Cyanadon dactylon* B. *Cyperus rotundus*

C. *Chenopodium* D. *Amaranthus viridis*

17. Which among the following is a annual weed?

A. *Alteranthera echinata* B. *Acalypha benghalensis*

C. *Trianthema protulacastrum* D. *Commelina benghalensis*

18. Which among the following is a biennial weed?

A. *Cyanadon dactylon* B. *Cyperus rotundus*

C. *Alteranthera echinata* D. *Amaranthus viridis*

19. Which among the following is a perennial weed?

A. *Boerhavia erecta* B. *Convolvulus arvensis*

C. *Phyllanthus maderaspatensis* D. *Croton sparsiflorus*

20. Which among the following is correct regarding ephemerales?

A. Annual B. Biennial

C. Perennial D. Short lived annual

21. Consider the statement and choose the correct one

(i) Wetland weed - *Eclipta alba*

(ii) Gardenland weed - *Argemone mexicana*

(iii) Dryland weed - *Achyranthes aspera*

A. (i) alone is correct B. (i) and (ii) are correct

C. (ii) and (iii) are correct D. (i) and (iii) are correct

22. Consider the statement and choose the correct one

(i) Black soil - *Solanum elaeagnifolium*

(ii) Red soil - *Corchorus trilocularis*

(iii) Laterite soil - *Spergula arvensis*

A. (i) alone is correct B. (ii) alone is correct

C. (iii) alone is correct D. All the statement are correct

23. Match list I with list II and choose the correct options given below

List I	List II
a. Indigenous weeds	1. *Indigofera tinctoria*
b. Exotic weeds	2. *Parthenium hysterophorus*
c. Monocot weeds	3. *Abutilon indicum*
d. Dicot weeds	4. *Panicum flavidum*

	a	b	c	d
A.	3	2	4	1
B.	3	1	2	4
C.	4	2	1	3
D.	4	1	2	3

24. Match list I with list II and choose the correct options given below

List I	**List II**
a. Basophile	1. *Sporobolus trimulus*
b. Grasses	2. *Taraxacum platycarpum*
c. Sedges	3. *Digera arvensis*
d. Broad leaved weeds	4. *Fimbrystylis miliceae*

	a	b	c	d
A.	4	1	2	3
B.	2	1	4	3
C.	3	1	4	2
D.	3	2	1	4

25. Consider the statement and choose the correct one
    (i) Woody stem weeds: *Lantana camara*
    (ii) Semi-woody stem : *Prosopis juliflora*
    (iii) Herbaceous weeds: *Amaranthus tricolor*
    A. (i) alone is correct
    B. (ii) alone is correct
    C. (iii) All the statements are correct
    D. (i) and (iii) are correct

26. Which among the following is a poisonous weed?
    A. *Nymphaea pubescens* B. *Eichhornia crassipes*
    C. *Datura stramonium* D. *Utricularia stellaris*

27. Match List I with List II and choose the correct options given below

List I	List II
a. Total stem parasite	1. *Striga lutea*
b. Total root parasite	2. *Cuscuta chinensis*
c. Partial root parasite	3. *Loranthus longiflorus*
d. Partial stem parasite	4. *Orabanche cernua*

	a	b	c	d
A.	4	3	1	2
B.	2	3	1	4
C.	2	4	1	3
D.	4	2	1	3

28. Which among the following is a floating weed?
    A. *Ceratophyllum demersum* B. *Nelumbium speciosum*
    C. *Cephalanthus occidentalis* D. *Pistia stratiotes*

29. Which among the following is incorrect regarding herbicide classification in soil (selective)
    A. Nitrofen B. Simazine
    C. Butachlor D. Propanil

30. Match list I with list II and choose the correct options given below

List I	List II
a. Contact non selective herbicide	1. Atrazine
b. Translocated non selective herbicide	2. Paraquat
c. Soil fumigants	3. Glyphosate
d. Soil sterilant	4. Trifluralin

	a	b	c	d
A.	2	4	3	1
B.	2	3	4	1
C.	4	3	1	2
D.	4	2	1	3

31. Match list I with list II and choose the correct options given below

List I	List II
a. 2, 4, D	1. Basalin
b. Fluchloralin	2. Gesprim
c. Pendimethalin	3. Fernoxone
d. Atrazine	4. Stomp

	a	b	c	d
A.	4	3	2	1
B.	3	2	4	1
C.	3	1	4	2
D.	4	2	3	1

32. __________ is the application of herbicides with irrigation water?
    A. Fumigation B. Herbigation
    C. Fertigation D. Band application
33. Among the following which is the commonly used herbicide for rice crop
    A. Butachlor B. Atrazine
    C. Thiobencarb D. Alachlor
34. Which among the following crop should not be sprayed with atrazine?
    A. Sorghum B. pearl millet
    C. Finger millet D. Sugarcane
35. Which is the biological control method for aquatic weeds?
    A. Netting B. Water weed cutters
    C. Tilapia D. Submergence

36. Which is commonly used herbicide for the control of phanerogamic parasite?

A. Glyphosate
B. Butachlor
C. Alachlor
D. Paraquat

37. Where is the Directorate of Weed Research situated

A. Bhopal
B. Raichur
C. Cuttack
D. Jabalpur

38. Which one of the following is correct regarding stale seed bed weed control?

A. Weeds are destroyed before planting of a crop
B. Weeds are destroyed after planting of crop
C. Weeds are destroyed in standing crop
D. Weeds are destroyed before flowering

39. Match list I with list II and choose the correct options given below

List I	**List II**
a. Devine	1. *Aeschyomene virginica*
b. Collego	2. *Sorghum halepense*
c. Bipolaris	3. General vegetation
d. Biolophos	4. *Morrenia odorata*

	a	b	c	d
A.	4	1	2	3
B.	3	1	2	4
C.	4	3	1	2
D.	3	4	1	2

40. Match the common weeds with their crops

Crops	**Weeds**
a. Wheat	1. *Marsilea quadrifolia*
b. Rice	2. *Chenopodium album*
c. Sugarcane	3. *Achyranthes aspera*
d. Cotton	4. *Parthenium hysterophorus*

	a	b	c	d
A.	2	1	4	3
B.	4	3	2	1
C.	1	4	3	2
D.	4	3	1	2

41. Match the following

a. Maize	1. *Amaranthus viridis*
b. Redgram	2. *Chloris barbata*
c. Groundnut	3. *Cyperus rotundus*
d. Sunflower	4. *Pennisetum cenchroides*

	a	b	c	d
A.	2	1	4	3
B.	4	3	2	1
C.	1	4	3	2
D.	4	3	1	2

42. Which one of the following weed is very common in rice?
A. *Dactyloctenium aegyptium*
B. *Convolvulus arvensis*
C. *Echinochloa colona*
D. *Argemone mexicana*

43. *Convolvulus arvensis* is a common weed in
A. Rice
B. Groundnut
C. Bhendi
D. Wheat

44. Which one of the following statement is correct?
(i) Mango - Orabanche
(ii) Tobacco - Cuscuta
(iii) Sugarcane- Striga
A. (i) and (ii) are correct
B. (ii) and (iii) are correct
C. (ii) alone is correct
D. (iii) alone is correct

45. In upland rice, most of the weeds are controlled by
A. *Trichoderma viride*
B. *Heterorhabditis bacteriophora nematode*
C. *Hirschmanniella spinicaudata nematode*
D. *Aphelenchoides bessey*i

46. In which system of rice cultivation, cono weeder is very effectively used to control weeds?
A. Transplanted puddled lowland rice
B. System of rice intensification
C. Wet seeded puddled lowland rice
D. Wet seeded puddled upland rice

47. In sunflower, _____ is used as pre-emergence weedicide.

A. Fluchloralin @ 2.0 l/ha
B. 2, 4-D @ 1.25 kg/ha
C. Trifluralin @ 0.75 l/ha
D. Atrazine @ l/ha

48. Find out the correct herbicide and its dosage used to control weeds in sugarcane.

A. Atrazine @ 1 kg/ha
B. Atrazine @ 1.5 kg/ha
C. Atrazine @ 2 kg/ha
D. Atrazine @ 2.5 kg/ha

49. _____ is a post-emergence herbicide used to control weeds in banana.

A. Fluchloralin @ 2.0 lit/ha
B. Paraquat @ 1.8 kg a.i./ha
C. Atrazine @ 1.5 kg a.i./ha
D. 2, 4-D @ 1.25 kg a.i./ha

50. Which is the incorrect statement?

Weeds	**Biological control**
A. Water hyacinth	- Rhizoctonia blight
B. Weed control in sorghum	- Cowpea intercrop
C. Alligator weed	- Flea beetle
D. Prickly pear weed	- Snails

51. _____ seed bed is used to control weeds in horticultural crops.

A. Sunken
B. Raised
C. Stale
D. *In situ*

52. What is the temperature followed in solarization method of controlling weeds?

A. 40°C
B. 45°C
C. 50°C
D. 35°C

53. Match the following

a. Bhendi	1. *Datura* spp
b. Potato	2. *Nothoscordum gracile*
c. Cabbage	3. *Malva parviflora*
d. Onion	4. *Lepidium* spp

	a	b	c	d
A.	4	3	2	1
B.	3	1	4	2
C.	3	4	2	1
D.	2	1	4	3

54. _____ is the pre-emergence herbicide to control weeds in tomato

A. Pendimethalin @ 1.0 kg/ha B. Pendimethalin @ 2.0 kg/ha

C. Pendimethalin @ 0.5 kg/ha D. Pendimethalin @ 2.5 kg/ha

55. Which one of the following herbicide is non-selective in action?

A. Atrazine B. Butachlor

C. Alachlor D. Paraquat

Answer keys

1	B	11	B	21	D	31	C	41	B	51	C
2	A	12	B	22	D	32	B	42	C	52	A
3	C	13	B	23	A	33	A	43	D	53	B
4	C	14	C	24	B	34	C	44	D	54	A
5	A	15	A	25	D	35	C	45	C	55	D
6	D	16	B	26	C	36	D	46	B		
7	B	17	D	27	C	37	D	47	A		
8	A	18	C	28	D	38	A	48	C		
9	D	19	B	29	D	39	A	49	B		
10	C	20	D	30	B	40	A	50	D		

6

Agrometeorology

1. Choose the correct answer

1. Increase in altitude doesn't cause

   A. Decrease in temperature B. Increase in precipitation

   C. Increase in wind velocity D. Increase in RH

2. Average rainfall of Tamil Nadu is about

   A. 750 mm B. 800 mm

   C. 950 mm D. 1500 mm

3. High rainfall zone covers

   A. Erode B. Coimbatore

   C. Kanyakumari D. Ramnad

4. For artificial rainfall, the chemical used is

   A. KI B. KCl

   C. HCl D. $AgCl_2$

5. Total solar radiation is measured by

   A. Sunshine recorder B. Anemometer

   C. Pyranometer D. Pyrheliometer

6. At lower latitude, temperature is low because it is

   A. Near to equator B. Near to sun

   C. Near to meridian D. Near to poles

7. In altitude, for every vertical rise of 165 metres the temperature decreases at the rate of

   A. 1°C B. 2°C

   C. 3°C D. 4°C

8. Cloudless sky is observed under

   A. Tropical region B. Subtropical region

   C. Temperate region D. Desert region

9. Cardinal temperature points includes
   A. Minimum temperature
   B. Optimum temperature
   C. Maximum temperature
   D. All the above
10. Low temperature causes
   A. Heating injury
   B. Scorching
   C. Suffocation
   D. Drying
11. Hoar frost is due to
   A. Sublimation of ice crystals
   B. Reduction of air temperature
   C. Incursion of large masses of cold air
   D. Radiation from all exposed objects
12. IITM stands for
   A. International Institute of Tropical Monsoon
   B. International Institute of Tropical Meteorology
   C. Indian Institute of Tropical Meteorology
   D. Indian Institute of Tropical Monsoon
13. Validity period of forecasting about 10 days upto a month is termed as
   A. Short range forecast
   B. Long range
   C. Very short range
   D. Medium range forecasting
14. Pan evapotranspiration is measured by
   A. Lysimeter
   B. Pyrheliometer
   C. Photometer
   D. Hygrometer
15. A day is said to be a rainy day, if the rainfall is
   A. 5 mm and above
   B. 1 mm and above
   C. 2.5 mm and above
   D. 7.5 mm and above
16. Conversion factor of centigrade to Fahrenheit is
   A. F = (C-32) x 5/9
   B. F = (C+32) x 5/9
   C. F = C x 9/5 + 32
   D. F = C x 9/5 - 32
17. IMD was established during the year
   A. 1885
   B. 1905
   C. 1975
   D. 1875
18. Which layer of atmosphere is known as "seat of weather phenomenon"?
   A. Stratosphere
   B. Troposphere
   C. Mesosphere
   D. Thermosphere

19. Predominant gases found in the exosphere is

    A. H and He B. H and Ne

    C. H and Ar D. H and CO

20. The layer of atmosphere which extends upto 400km is

    A. Troposphere B. Exosphere

    C. Thermosphere D. Ionosphere

21. The average lapse rate of air temperature is

    A. 1°C/km B. 6.5°C/km

    C. 2.5°C/km D. 5°C/km

22. The percentage of rainfall received through southwest monsoon in the country is

    A. 48-50% B. 20-25%

    C. 80-95% D. 70-75%

23. Winter rainfall is major source in the states of

    A. Punjab, Rajasthan, Central India

    B. Uttar Pradesh, Bihar, West Bengal

    C. Uttaranchal, Uttarkand, Kashmir

    D. Madhya Pradesh, Chandigarh, Tripura

24. Layer which separates the troposphere from the stratosphere known as

    A. Stratosphere B. Tropopause

    C. Mesopause D. Stratopause

25. Ozonosphere is also known as

    A. Seat of photochemical reactions B. Seat of weather phenomenon

    C. Ionosphere D. Chemosphere

26. Contribution of rainfall through northwest monsoon in TN is

    A. 25% B. 48%

    C. 72% D. 80%

27. Clouds exist in the atmosphere in the layer of

    A. Stratosphere B. Mesosphere

    C. Troposphere D. Exosphere

28. Clouds which doesn't produce precipitation is

    A. Nimbostratus B. Cumulonimbus

    C. Stratus D. Cirrus

29. Type of cloud seen in winter season is

A. Cumulus B. Stratus

C. Nimbus D. Cirrus

30. Match the following

List I	**List II**
A. Troposphere	1. 50-55 km
B. Stratosphere	2. Ion enriched zone
C. Mesosphere	3. 75% of total gases
D. Thermosphere	4. Coldest region

	a	b	c	d
A.	4	2	1	3
B.	1	3	2	4
C.	3	1	4	2
D.	2	4	1	3

31. Identify the statements

(i) Relative humidity is low, there is a chance for outbreak of pests and diseases.

(ii) Wind dispersal of pollen and seeds are necessary for certain crops.

(iii) Soil temperature controls the microbial activity.

(iv) Soil air is not essential for nutrient availability.

A. (ii) and (iii) are correct B. All the statements are correct

C. (ii), (iii) and (iv) are correct D. (i) and (ii) are correct

32. Expand WMO?

A. World Management Organization

B. World Meteorological Organogram

C. World Meat Organization

D. World Meteorological Organization

33. CIAT stands for

A. Centro International de Aquaculture Tropical

B. Centro International de Agricultural Tropical

C. Centro International de Agricultural Temperate

D. Centro International de Aquaculture Temperate

34. IMD stands for
    A. Indian Mining Department
    B. International Meteorological Department
    C. Indian Meteorological Department
    D. Institute of Meteorological Department
35. Consider the statements
    Statement (i): Water takes long time to heat and long time to cool.
    Statement (ii): Temperature decreases with increase in altitude
    A. (i) and (ii) are wrong
    B. (i) and (ii) are correct
    C. (i) is correct and (ii) is wrong
    D. (i) is wrong and (ii) is correct
36. Identify the incorrectly matched pair
    (i) Family C - Stratus
    (ii) Family B - Cumulonimbus
    (iii) Family A - Cirrus
    (iv) Family D - Cumulus
    A. (iii) alone is incorrect
    B. (ii) and (iv) are incorrect
    C. (i) alone is incorrect
    D. (ii) alone is incorrect
37. Stem gridle is an important symptom due to high temperature in
    A. Sugarcane
    B. Cotton
    C. Tea
    D. Coffee
38. Statement (i): IMD comes under Ministry of Environment, Forests and Climate Change
    (ii): The present Director General of Meteorology is K.J.Ramesh
    A. (i) alone is correct
    B. (ii) alone is correct
    C. Both are correct
    D. Both are wrong
39. Where is the Indian Meteorological Department (IMD) located?
    A. New Delhi
    B. Kolkata
    C. Pune
    D. Chennai
40. Where is the headquarters for World Meteorological Organization located?
    A. Mumbai
    B. London
    C. Geneva
    D. Tokyo
41. Consider the statement and choose the correct one
    (i) Weather: Physical state of atmosphere at a given place and time.
    (ii) Climate: Long term regime of atmospheric variables
    (iii) Meteorology means chemistry of atmosphere
    A. (i) and (ii) alone is correct
    B. (i) alone is correct
    C. (iii) alone is correct
    D. All the statements are correct

42. Coordinates of India lies between .... and ....

A. 25°N 90°E
B. 28°N 95°E
C. 27°N 85°E
D. 21°N 78°E

43. What is the percentage of ozone gas present in the atmosphere?

A. 0.0004%
B. 0.004%
C. 0. 04%
D. 0.00004%

44. Match list I with list II and choose the correct options given below

List I	**List II**
A. Troposphere	1. Above 80 km
B. Stratosphere	2. 16 km from earth
C. Thermosphere	3. 50-80 km
D. Mesosphere	4. 50-55 km

	a	b	c	d
A.	2	3	1	4
B.	2	4	1	3
C.	4	2	3	1
D.	3	2	4	1

45. The ozone layer absorbs ___________ rays.

A. UV rays
B. Violet rays
C. UR rays
D. X- rays

46. What is the predominant gases present in exosphere?

A. Neon and Argon
B. Nitrogen and oxygen
C. Methane and ethane
D. Hydrogen and Helium

47. Match List I with List II and choose the correct options given below

List I	**List II**
A. North Eastern zone	1. Nilgris and Dindigul
B. Western zone	2. Trivallur and Vellore
C. Southern zone	3. Coimbatore and Theni
D. Hilly zone	4. Ramanathapuram and Tirunelveli

	a	b	c	d
A.	3	2	4	1
B.	2	4	3	1
C.	2	3	4	1
D.	3	4	3	1

48. What is the major type of soil present in Coimbatore?

A. Clay soil
B. Laterite soil
C. Red loamy
D. Sandy soil

49. What is the optimum temperature for rice crop?

A. 10-12°C
B. 30-32°C
C. 20-25°C
D. 12-20°C

50. In which crop, freezing injury occurs?

A. Tea
B. Broccoli
C. Turnip
D. Brussels sprout

51. Lifting of plants along with soil from its actual position by ice crystals is called

A. Suffocation
B. Frost damage
C. Chilling injury
D. Heaving

52. High temperature causes ________ in stem

A. Gridling
B. Scald
C. Ringing
D. Burning

53. What is the validity period for now casting short range?

A. 72 hours
B. 12 hours
C. 2 hours
D. > 3 days

54. Match list I with list II and choose the correct options given below

List I	**List II**
A. Cup Anemometer	1. Direct solar radiation
B. Hygrometer	2. Direction and speed of wind
C. Sunshine recorder	3. Tempeture and humidity
D. Pyrheliometer	4. Sunshine

	a	b	c	d
A.	4	3	2	1
B.	2	3	4	1
C.	4	2	3	1
D.	2	4	3	1

55. The ratio between incoming and outgoing radiation is called

A. Heating efficiency
B. Specific heat
C. Heat capacity
D. Albedo

56. The rate of solar radiation reaching the earth's atmosphere is

A. 2.9 cal /cm^2/min
B. 2.5 cal/cm^2/min
C. 2 cal/cm^2/min
D. 1.5 cal/cm^2/min

57. For effective on farm management practices, a reliable system of

A. Short range weather forecast is needed
B. Medium range weather forecast is needed
C. Short and medium range weather forecast is needed
D. Long range weather forecast is needed

58. ET (Evapo transpiration) can be measured using

A. Lactometer
B. Lysimeter
C. Heliometer
D. Hydrometer

59. The nitrogen present in the atmosphere is

A. Of no use to plants
B. Injurious to plants
C. Directly utilized by plants
D. Utilized through microorganisms

60. Climate pertains to a

A. Long period of time
B. Short duration
C. Medium duration
D. None

61. Principles of mercury barometers was discovered by

A. Torricelli
B. Aristotle
C. Pliny
D. Galileo

62. Instrument used for measuring wind velocity is known as

A. Hydrometer
B. Pyranometer
C. Altimeter
D. Anemometer

63. A rainy day called when rainfall received in 24 h

A. >2.5 mm
B. >3.0 mm
C. >5.0 mm
D. >1.0 mm

64. Increasing atmospheric pressure is an indicator of

A. Rainfall
B. Thunderstorm
C. Storm
D. None of the above

65. Ringle man chart is used to determine

A. Smoke concentration
B. Relative humidity
C. Transpiration
D. None of the above

66. High intensity rain bearing cloud is

A. Cumulonimbus B. Cirrus

C. Stratus D. Altocumulus

Answer keys

1	D	11	A	21	B	31	A	41	A	51	D	61	A
2	C	12	C	22	C	32	D	42	D	52	A	62	D
3	C	13	B	23	A	33	B	43	D	53	C	63	A
4	A	14	A	24	B	34	C	44	B	54	B	64	A
5	C	15	C	25	D	35	B	45	A	55	D	65	A
6	D	16	C	26	B	36	D	46	D	56	C	66	A
7	A	17	D	27	C	37	B	47	C	57	C		
8	D	18	B	28	D	38	B	48	C	58	B		
9	D	19	A	29	B	39	C	49	B	59	D		
10	C	20	C	30	C	40	C	50	A	60	A		

UNIT III: PLANT BREEDING AND GENETICS

1

Principles of Genetics and Cytogenetics

I. Choose the correct answer

1. Indian Institute of Millets Research is located at

   A. Karnal B. Coimbatore

   C. Hyderabad D. Mirzapur

2. Central Institute of Cotton Research is situated at

   A. Hyderabad B. Nagpur

   C. Mumbai D. Coimbatore

3. Headquarters of Cotton Corporation of India is

   A. Mumbai B. Hyderabad

   C. Bhopal D. Cuttack

4. Nuclear Magnetic Resonance Analyzer is used to determine oil content in

   A. Groundnut B. Castor

   C. Linseed D. Sunflower

5. CIMMYT was established at

   A. Mexico B. India

   C. Australia D. Argentina

6. Scientific name of kodo millet is

   A. *Paspalum scrobiculatum* B. *Setaria italica*

   C. *Panicum miliare* D. *Eleusine coracana*

7. Who coined the term linkage?

   A. Correns B. Mendal

   C. Morgan D. Hugo de Vries

8. Mendal did not observe linkage due to

   A. Crossing over B. Mutation

   C. Synapsis D. Independent Assortment

9. The phenomenon of linkage was first observed in
   A. *Lathyrus odoratus* B. *Pisum sativum*
   C. *Datura* sp. D. *Mirabilis jalapa*
10. Crossing over occurs during
   A. Pachytene B. Diplotene
   C. Diakinesis D. Zygotene
11. Crossing over is more frequent in
   A. Males B. Females
   C. Both D. None
12. Crossing over in diploid organisms is responsible for
   A. Dominance of gene B. Segregation of alleles
   C. Recombination of linked genes D. Linkage between genes
13. Complete linkage is observed in
   A. Maize B. Human female
   C. Male drosophila D. Female drosophila
14. Coupling and repulsion is concerned with
   A. Linkage B. Crossing over
   C. Mutation D. All of these
15. Linkage prevents
   A. Homogeneous condition B. Segregation of alleles
   C. Hybrid formation D. Heterozygous condition
16. When two dominant alleles of gene present, this condition is called?
   A. Incomplete dominance B. Codominance
   C. Epistasis D. None of these
17. Independent assortment is absent in the case of
   A. Genes located on the same chromosome
   B. Genes located on the homologous chromosome
   C. Genes located on the non homologous chromosome
   D. All the above
18. When alleles of two contrasting characters are present together, one of the characters remain hidden and the other character express. This is called
   A. Law of dominance B. Law of segregation
   C. Law of independent assortment D. Law of purity of gametes

19. The character that express in the F_1 generation is called as
    A. Dominant character B. Codominant character
    C. Recessive character D. None of these
20. Mendalian hybridization was use of two plants of
    A. Differencing in a pair of contrasting character
    B. Differencing in a two pairs of contrasting character
    C. Differencing in a many pairs of contrasting character
    D. None of these
21. F_3 generation is obtained by
    A. Selfing of F_1 B. Selfing of F_2
    C. Crossing of F_1 and F_2 D. None of these
22. The term ideotype was proposed by
    A. Rimpau B. Watson
    C. Jennings D. Donald
23. Insect resistance is governed by
    A. Polygenes B. Plasmagenes
    C. Oligogenes D. All the above
24. Vertical resistance is otherwise called as
    A. Major gene resistance B. Oligogenic resistance
    C. Qualitative resistance D. All the above
25. The nonsense codon ______ is called opal codon.
    A. UAG B. UGA
    C. AUG D. All the above
26. ____ DNA has no function and contributes nothing to the cell where it is found.
    A. Selfish DNA B. Ignorant
    C. Junk D. All the above
27. Sensor genes were proposed by
    A. Garrod B. Britten and Davidson
    C. Crick D. Watson
28. The process of quarantine at NBPGR takes atleast
    A. Four weeks B. Three weeks
    C. Five weeks D. Two weeks

29. National Research Centre for Mustard is located at

A. Bharatpur B. Rajmundry

C. Nagpur D. Hisar

30. The method used for fixation of heterosis are

A. Apomixis B. Sexual reproduction

C. Monoploid D. Vegetative propagation

31. The dominance hypothesis of heterosis was first proposed by

A. Davenport (1908) B. East (1908)

C. Hull (1945) D. Shull (1914)

32. The genotypic ratio of monohybrid cross is

A. 3:1 B.1:2:1

C. 2:1:1 D. 9:3:3:1

33. Muller in 1911 discovered

A. Linkage B. Mutation

C. Interference D. Repulsion

34. C. B. Bridges in 1930 discovered

A. Non disjunction B. Crossing over

C. Linkage D. Mutation

35. ______ introduced the term polygenes

A. K.Mather B. Muller

C. Batizar D. Painter

36. The concept that new cells arise from preexisting cells was proposed by

A. Strasberger B. Rudolf Virchow

C. Watson and Crick D. Hugo de Vries

37. Who proposed theory of pangenesis in 1838?

A. Mendal B. Charles Darwin

C. Waldeyer D. T.H. Morgan

38. Golgi bodies was discovered by

A. Camillo golgi B. Benda

C. Lamark D. Bonnet

39. The RNA rich region in the nucleus is

A. Chromosome B. Nuclear membrane

C. Nucleolus D. Ribosomes

40. The organelle present in animal cell, but absent in plant cell
A. Nucleolus B. Centriole
C. Mitochondria D. Chloroplast

41. ______ is the site of transcription
A. Chromosome B. Ribosome
C. Nucleolus D. Mitochondria

42. Who discovered mRNA?
A. Jacob and Monod B. Benzer and Jacob
C. Baltimore D. Nathan and Smith

43. Which is called dictyosome in plants?
A. Vacuole B. Golgi bodies
C. Plastid D. Centriole

44. The chromosome with diffused centromere
A. Acentric chromosome B. Monocentric
C. Holokinetic D. Dicentric

45. The fluid portion of cytoplasm excluding the formed elements is called as
A. Cytosol B. Plastids
C. Centrioles D. Endoplasmic reticulum

46. The ________ components of the nucleus contain materials for building DNA and messenger RNA.
A. Non chromatin B. Chromatin
C. Plastids D. Vacuole

47. ______ stores the excess water
A. Golgi complex B. Vacuole
C. Mitochondria D. Hyaloplasm

48. The arrangement of chromosome on the equatorial plate occurs during
A. Early prophase B. Late prophase
C. Early metaphase D. Late metaphase

49. Nucleus reappears at
A. Metaphase I B. Telophase
C. Metaphase II D. Prophase

50. During interphase, which of the following takes place
A. DNA synthesis B. RNA synthesis
C. Protein synthesis D. All the above

51. _____ phase is the post replication phase

A. S phase B. G1 phase

C. G2 phase D. Prophase

52. The characteristic feature, general morphology of the chromosome of a species is called

A. Idiogram B. Karyotype

C. Chromosome model D. None

53. The germplasm theory was proposed by

A. Weisman B. Mendel

C. Darwin D. Hugo de vries

54. The alternative forms of a gene are known as

A. Transgene B. Pseudogene

C. Mixed gene D. Alleles

55. Which of the following is the controlling centre of a cell

A. Chloroplast B. Nucleus

C. Nucleolus D. Mitochondria

56. Which of the following produces pseudo-dominance

A. Inversion B. Deletion

C. Duplication D. Translocation

57. Which of the following bases is not present in DNA

A. Adenine B. Thymine

C. Uracil D. Cytosine

58. Balbiani rings are found in which of the following

A. Lampbrush chromosomes B. Sex chromosomes

C. Polytene chromosomes D. B chromosomes

59. In which of the following sub stages of meiosis-I, chromatin exchange between non- sister chromatids is completed

A. Pachytene B. Diplotene

C. Zygotene D. Diakinesis

60. The theory of origin of species through natural selection was proposed by

A. Darwin B. Lamarck

C. Mendel D. Vilmorin

61. In 1909, multiple factor hypothesis was given by

A. Levene
B. Brown
C. Nilsson Ehle
D. Waldeyer

62. Mendel's laws were rediscovered in which of the following years

A.1890
B. 1905
C. 1900
D. 1898

63. The term 'genotype' and 'phenotype' were introduced by

A. W.L. Johannsen
B. W.Bateson
C. G.J. Mendel
D. R. C. Punnet

64. Gene which affects the expression of more than one character is known as

A. Multiple gene
B. Pleiotropic gene
C. Epistatic gene
D. Hypostatic gene

65. Effect of one gene on the phenotypic expression of other non-allelic gene is termed as

A. Dominance
B. Pleiotropy
C. Epistatic
D. Over-dominance

66. Supplementary gene action in F_2 generation shows phenotypic ratio of

A. 9:3:4
B. 9:7
C. 12:3:1
D. 9:6:1

67. Deletion causes

A. Codominance
B. Incomplete dominance
C. Pseudo dominance
D. All the above

68. Translocation leads to changes in

A. Gene number
B. Gene structure
C. Sequence of genes
D. Linkage map

69. Balanced lethal system in *Oenothera* was reported by

A. T H Morgan
B. C B Bridges
C. Renner
D. Sturtevant

70. Chromosomal aberration in aged seed is due to

A. Physical mutagens
B. Chemical mutagens
C. Both
D. None of these

71. Johannsen has coined the term

A. Phenotype B. Genotype

C. Phenotype and genotype D. Genetics

72. The publication of Mendel's work was found in

A. Journal of genetics

B. Journal of heredity

C. Proceeding of natural history society of Brunn

D. All the above

73. —— gene action is otherwise called as duplicate recessive epistasis.

A. Inhibitory gene action B. Complementary gene action

C. Supplementary gene action D. Polymeric gene action

74. Two gene pair that produce the same effect is called as

A. Unstable genes B. Complementary genes

C. Duplicate genes D. Recessive genes

75. The number of genotypic class is ________ phenotypic class.

A. Higher than B. Lower than

C. Equal to D. None

76. The nitrogenous base found in DNA, but not in RNA is

A. Cytocine B. Guanine

C. Adenine D. Thymine

77. Which gene is transcribed during repression?

A. Structural B. Regulator

C. Promoter D. Operator

78. What is the minimum effective size of an operator for lac repressor binding?

A. 30 base pairs B. 15 base pairs

C. 25 base pairs D.17 base pairs

79. The chemical basis of heredity is

A. RNA B. DNA

C. Gene D. Chromosome

80. The purine base of DNA is

A. Guanine B. Thymine

C. Adenine D. Cytosine

81. The percentage of recombination varies between

A. 0-25% B. 0-50%

C. 0-75% D. 0-100%

82. In a completely linked gene, the crossing over frequency will be

A. 100 B. <100

C. <50 D. Nil

83. Which RNA transports amino acid to the site of protein synthesis?

A. mRNA B. tRNA

C. rRNA D. cRNA

84. RNA is the genetic material in

A. TMV B. Retrovirus

C. Paramyxo virus D. All the above

85. Dehydrated DNA occurs in

A. A form B. B form

C. C form D. Z form

86. The B form of DNA is found in the fibres with ____ percent relative humidity

A. 62 B. 72

C. 82 D. 92

87. Selection coefficient is also known as

A. Selective advantage B. Selective disadvantage

C. Adaptive value D. All the above

88. Selection coefficient is 1, there will ______ survival

A. 100% survival B. 0% survival

C. 50% survival D. 0-50% survival

89. Artificial selection favours the characters of organism which are

A. Advantageous for survival B. Useful for mankind

C. Decided by environment D. All the above

90. The rate of elimination of different genotypes of a population in the sane environment under natural selection is

A. Fitness B. Genetic drift

C. Genetic load D. Genetic homeostasis

91. Meiotic drive is

A. Selection coefficient B. Segregation distortion
C. Selection D. All the above

92. D^2 statistics was first used for the assessment of variability in plant breeding by

A. C.R. Rao B. Smith
C. Wright D. Anderson

93. Polygenic traits are

A. Additive B. Cumulative
C. Environmental sensitive D. All the above

94. The concept of biparental mating was developed by

A. Comstock and Robinson B. Smith
C. Jinks and Jones D. Rawlings and Cockerham

95. Green revolution in India occurred during

A. 1960 B. 1970
C. 1980 D. 1950

96. 2n denotes

A. Number of homozygote produced by selfing a F_1
B. Number of types of gametes produced by F_1
C. Number of types of heterozygote produced
D. Number of types of male gametes produced by F_1

97. A cybrid is

A. A sex hybrid B. A hybrid formed by cell fusion
C. A plant produced by cell culture D. Symptom to hybrid

98. In 1866, Mendel postulated laws of inheritance based on his work with

A. Garden pea B. Field beans
C. Drosophila D. Pigeon pea

99. Which one of the following crop is a biennial

A. Maize B. Sugar beet
C. Sugarcane D. Tapioca

100. Who coined the term genetics?

A. Hugo de vries B. W.L. Johannsen
C. T.H. Morgan D. W. Bateson

101. Match list I with list II and choose the correct options given below

List I	**List II**
A. ex situ conservation	1. Hyderabad
B. in situ conservation	2. New Delhi
C. NPBGR	3. Conservation in laboratory
D. ICRISAT	4. Conservation in the field

	a	b	c	d
A.	4	3	2	1
B.	3	4	1	2
C.	4	3	1	2
D.	2	4	3	1

Answer keys

1	C	26	D	51	C	76	D	101	A
2	B	27	B	52	B	77	B		
3	A	28	B	53	A	78	D		
4	D	29	A	54	D	79	B		
5	A	30	A	55	B	80	C		
6	A	31	A	56	B	81	B		
7	C	32	B	57	C	82	D		
8	D	33	B	58	C	83	B		
9	A	34	A	59	A	84	D		
10	A	35	A	60	A	85	A		
11	B	36	B	61	C	86	D		
12	C	37	B	62	C	87	B		
13	C	38	A	63	A	88	A		
14	A	39	C	64	B	89	B		
15	B	40	B	65	C	90	A		
16	B	41	C	66	A	91	B		
17	B	42	B	67	C	92	A		
18	A	43	B	68	D	93	D		
19	A	44	C	69	C	94	A		
20	A	45	A	70	B	95	A		
21	A	46	A	71	C	96	B		
22	D	47	B	72	C	97	B		
23	D	48	C	73	B	98	A		
24	D	49	B	74	C	99	B		
25	B	50	D	75	A	100	D		

2

Plant Domestication and Plant Introduction

I. Choose the correct answer

1. Plant introduction from one state to another state is named as

   A. Indigenous introduction B. Foreign introduction

   C. Foreign collection D. State to district introduction

2. Which of the following wheat variety is introduced to India?

   A. IR 8 B. IR 20

   C. Sonara 64 D. TN 1

3. What is domestication?

   A. Bringing wild species under animal management

   B. Bringing wild species under wildlife management

   C. Bringing wild species under human management

   D. Bringing wild species under stress management

4. Acclimatisation is

   A. A process of adjustment by crop plants to environment

   B. Removal of female parts of a flower

   C. Related with the clay

   D. Changing of climatical condition

5. Introduction of plant from western countries is called as

   A. Indigenous introduction B. Foreign introduction

   C. Indigenous collection D. Country to country collection

6. Shifting of plants from native environment to new environment is called as

   A. Plant domestication B. Plant collection

   C. Plant introduction D. Germplasm collection

7. Which one of the following variety of rice was introduced to India?

   A. IR8 B. IR 20

   C. Basmati rice D. Jawahar

8. Which organization is involved in the introduction of a variety from exotic source?

   A. IARI B. ICRISAT

   C. NBPGR D. ICAR

Answer keys

1	A	6	C
2	C	7	A
3	C	8	C
4	A		
5	B		

3

Breeding Methods for Self Pollinated Crops

I. Choose the correct answer

1. Consider the statements and choose the correct answer
   (i) Pureline variety is highly uniform
   (ii) Mass selection produces moderately uniform variety
   (iii) Bulk method of breeding takes 14 years duration
   A. (i) and (iii) are correct B. (ii) and (iii) are correct
   C. (i) and (ii) are correct D. (iii) alone correct
2. The new varieties of plants are produced by
   A. Introduction and mutation B. Selection and hybridization
   C. Mutation and selection D. Selection and introduction
3. Pureline refers to
   A. Homozygosity only B. Heterozygosity only
   C. Homozygosity and self assortment D. Heterozygosity and linkage
4. In which breeding method, ancestor of an individual is determined
   A. Pureline selection B. Pedigree method
   C. Mass selection D. Bulk method
5. In which crop, lantern method is used for hybridization?
   A. Tapioca B. Potato
   C. Sugar beet D. Sugarcane
6. How many parents are involved in double cross hybrid?
   A. 4 parents B. 3 parents
   C. 2 parents D. 1 parent
7. Parentage of triticale is
   A. Wheat x rice B. Wheat x rye
   C. Wheat x oats D. Wheat x barely

8. Pollen stored for periods ranging from
   A. 1 day to 1 year B. 1 day to 2 years
   C. 1 day to 3 years D. 1 day to 4 years
9. Highest uniformity is present in
   A. Single cross hybrid B. Double cross hybrid
   C. Three way cross hybrid D. Double top cross hybrid
10. The name triticale was first appeared in
   A. Scotland B. Ireland
   C. Germany D. England
11. In which crop, CMS method of hybridization is used?
   A. Maize B. Rice
   C. Cotton D. Redgram
12. In which crop, PGMS method of hybridization is followed?
   A. Rice B. Maize
   C. Sorghum D. Cumbu
13. What is the optimum temperature for induction of male sterility in rice?
   A. 24°C/18°C B. 20°C/16°C
   C. 30°C/22°C D. 32°C/24°C
14. Which of the following is a maintainer line?
   A. A line B. B line
   C. R line D. M line
15. If a character is cytoplasmically controlled then
   A. The progeny resembles female parent
   B. The progeny resembles male parent
   C. It is segregated to 3:1 in F_1
   D. In F_1, 15:1 segregation is observed.
16. If a dihybrid without genic interaction is selfed, the following ratio is obtained in F_2
   A. 1:1:1:1 B. 9:3:3:1
   C. 9:7 D. 9:6:1
17. The first generation progenies of a hybrid are called
   A. Purelines B. Segregates
   C. Inbreds D. F_1 plants

18. Who has listed out the factors of apparent and real deterioration of varieties
    A. Kadam (1942) B. Bateman (1947)
    C. Dettann (1953) D. Martin (1942)
19. Where MLT is conducted?
    A. KVK's of SAU's
    B. Research stations of SAU's
    C. Central Agricultural Universities
    D. CSIR Institutes
20. A maintainer line is
    A. Male fertile and can restore fertility
    B. Male sterile but can restore fertility
    C. Male sterile but cannot restore fertility
    D. Male fertile but maintain the sterile line
21. A restorer gene is present in
    A. Nucleus B. Cytoplasm
    C. Protoplsm D. Golgi apparatus
22. Cross between cytoplasmic male sterile x cytoplasmic male fertile is to
    A. Produce sterile F_1 B. Produce fertile F_1
    C. Produce fertile, sterile in 1:1 ratio D. Produce restorer F_1
23. Hybrid seeds can be produced through open pollination with the use of
    A. Inbreds B. Clones
    C. Purelines D. Male sterile lines
24. Which sterility is exploited in hybrid seed production of redgram?
    A. Male genetic sterility B. Cytoplasmic male sterility
    C. Cytoplasmic genic male sterility D. Genetic male sterility
25. Specific combining ability of the parents should be high in order to develop
    A. Hybrids B. Composites
    C. Varieties D. Synthetics
26. To produce hybrid seed, we need
    A. A male sterile line, restorer, maintainer
    B. A male fertile line and maintainer
    C. A maintainer and restorer
    D. Only male sterile line

27. Which one of the following is a top cross hybrid?
    A. $(A \times R) = F_1$ B. $(A \times B) \times (C \times D) = F_1$
    C. $(A \times B) \times C = F_1$ D. $(A \times B) \times OPV = F_1$
28. Semi dwarf rice variety IR 8 was developed in
    A. India B. Taiwan
    C. China D. Philippines
29. Sonalika and kalyan sona are the hybrid varieties of
    A. Rice B. Wheat
    C. Maize D. Sugarcane
30. First inter specific hybrid in dianthus was developed by
    A. Mendal B. Hugo de Vries
    C. Thomas Fairchild D. Andrew Knight
31. Hinderence of self pollination due to some physical barriers in the flower is known as
    A. Heterostyly B. Dichogamy
    C. Herkogamy D. Dicliny
32. The source of male sterile cytoplasm for rice is
    A. Wild abortive type B. Chinsurah boro II
    C. Gambiaca D. All the above
33. In gametophytic system, self incompatility is eliminated by
    A. Bud pollination B. Double pollination
    C. Removal of stigmatic surface D. Chromosome doubling
34. At what temperature level, TGSM line becomes fertile
    A. > 34°C / 26°C (day / night) B. > 32°C / 24°C (day / night)
    C. < 24°C / 18°C (day / night) D. < 22°C / 16°C (day / night)
35. What is the incorrect answer with respect to effects of inbreeding?
    A. Appearance of lethal and sublethal alleles
    B. Reduction in vigour
    C. Time consuming
    D. Increase in homozygosity
36. Which one of the following is a correct answer with respect to inbreeding?
    A. Time consuming B. Inbreeding depression
    C. Poor performance D. Identical to recurrent parent

37. In pedigree breeding, single plants are selected in which one of the following generation

A. F_2 B. F_3

C. F_4 D. F_5

38. Bulk method is otherwise called as

A. Pedigree method B. Selection method

C. Mass method D. Single seed descent method

39. What is the most effective method for transfer of on oligogenic character in an otherwise agronomically superior genotype?

A. Backcross B. Bulk population

C. Pedigree D. Recurrent selection

40. After emasculation, the spike of the male parent in wheat is

A. Covered with a butter paper bag

B. Not be covered

C. Crossed with selected male parent pollen

D. Crossed and covered

41. CO 43 paddy variety was evolved by crossing

A. ADT 5 x IR 50 B. ASD 5 x IR 20

C. Dasal x IR 20 D. Dasal x IR 8

42. How the genes for drought resistance are transferred to high yielding variety?

A. Hybridization B. Mass selection

C. Pureline selection C. Pure line selection

43. Which one of the following is correct with respect to mass selection?

A. Narrow adaptation B. Difficult to identity

C. Easily identified D. Highly uniform

44. Bulk population breeding is suitable for

A. Fruit crops B. Vegetables

C. Small grains D. Flower crops

45. In which type of crop, the progeny test method is used for breeding purpose

A. Cross pollinated crop B. Often cross pollinated crop

C. Self incompatible crop D. Self pollinated crop

46. First cotton hybrid variety in the world developed in India, the variety is

A. Varalaxmi
B. H4
C. Suguna
D. None of these

47. A and B lines behave differently because

A. Genetically dissimilar
B. Genetically similar for all traits
C. They are isogenic for sterility
D. Derived from different genetic sources

48. In India male sterility is used in

A. Wheat
B. Maize
C. Pearl millet
D. Chickpea

49. In ———— pollen dispersal is poor and seed set is likely to be low on male sterile plants

A. Tomato
B. Carrot
C. Broccoli
D. Cauliflower

50. Selfing of a plant increases

A. Homozygosity
B. Heterozygosity
C. Homogeneity
D. Heterogeneity

51. Bagging is done to avoid

A. Avoid self pollination
B. Avoid cross pollination
C. Achieve desired pollination
D. Prevent contamination from foreign pollen

52. A hybrid is always

A. Heterozygous
B. Homozygous
C. Often heterozygous
D. Often homozygous

53. Which one of the following rice variety was developed by inter specific hybridization?

A. CO 30
B. ADT 30
C. CO 31
D. ADT 31

54. Match list I with list II and choose the correct options given below

List I	List II
A. Maize	1. Female parent
B. Cotton	2. Male parent
C. A line	3. Detasseling
D. R line	4. Emasculation & dusting

	a	b	c	d
A.	4	3	2	1
B.	3	4	2	1
C.	3	4	1	2
D.	2	1	3	4

55. Which method is followed in rice hybrid seed production?

A. Detasseling B. Self incompatability

C. GMS D. TGMS

Answer keys

1	C	16	B	31	C	46	B
2	B	17	B	32	D	47	C
3	A	18	A	33	D	48	C
4	B	19	B	34	C	49	A
5	D	20	D	35	C	50	A
6	A	21	A	36	B	51	D
7	B	22	A	37	A	52	A
8	C	23	A	38	C	53	C
9	A	24	D	39	A	54	C
10	C	25	A	40	B	55	D
11	B	26	A	41	C	56	
12	A	27	D	42	A	57	
13	D	28	D	43	B	58	
14	B	29	B	44	C	59	
15	A	30	C	45	D	60	

4

Breeding Methods for Cross Pollinated Crops

I. Choose the correct answer

1. In which type of crops, synthetic varieties are bred?

   A. Cross pollinated crop
   B. Self pollinated crop
   C. Often cross pollinated crop
   D. Asexually propagated crop

2. African tall variety belongs to

   A. Single cross hybrid
   B. Double cross hybrid
   C. Three way cross hybrid
   D. Composites

3. Find out the correct answer for working out average or relative heterosis.

   A. $[(F_1\text{-BP})/\text{MP}]\text{x}100$
   B. $[(F_1\text{-MP})/\text{BP}]\text{x}100$
   C. $[(F_1\text{-SH})/\text{SH}]\text{x}100$
   D. $[(F_1\text{-MP})/\text{MP}]\text{x}100$

4. In which type of crops, hybrids perform well and released in more numbers?

   A. Self pollinated crops
   B. Cross pollinated crops
   C. Often cross pollinated crops
   D. Asexually propagated crops

5. Match list I with list II and choose the correct options given below

List I	List II
A. Double cross hybrid	1. ICMS - 7703
b. Synthetic variety	2. Hugo de Vries
c. Mutation breeding	3. Carl Linnaeus
d. Botanical classification	4. Deccan

	a	b	c	d
A.	3	4	1	2
B.	2	1	3	4
C.	4	2	1	3
D.	4	1	2	3

6. How to estimate the heterobeltiosis?

A. $[(F_1 - AP) / AP] \times 100$ B. $[(F_1 - BP) / BP] \times 100$

C. $[(F_1 - MP) / MP] \times 100$ D. $[(F_1 - SH) / SH] \times 100$

7. Heterosis over the better parent is called as

A. Relative heterosis B. Standard heterosis

C. Pseudoheterosis D. Heterbeltiosis

8. Heterosis lost due to continuous inbreeding is

A. Inbreeding depression B. Out breeding depression

C. Hybrid vigour D. None of these

9. Which one of the manifestations is incorrect with regard to heterosis?

A. Increased opportunity for recombination

B. Increased yield

C. Increased reproductive ability

D. Increased resistance to pests and diseases

10. What is the effect of dominance hypothesis?

A. Unfavourable effect B. Harmful effect

C. Deleterious effect D. Favourable effect

11. The increased performance of F_1 hybrid over its parents is called

A. Dominance B. Crossing over

C. Heterosis D. Over dominance

12. Heterosis is

A. Appearance of spontaneous mutation

B. Induction of mutation

C. Mixture of two or more traits

D. Superiority of hybrids over parents

13. Specific combining ability of the parents should be high in order to develop

A. Synthetics B. Varieties

C. Composites D. Hybrids

14. High performance is noted in hybrid coconuts of

A. Tall x Dwarf B. Dwarf x Tall

C. Tall x Tall D. Dwarf x Dwarf

15. Heterosis is commercially exploited in

A. Self pollinated species B. Cross pollinated species

C. Often cross pollinated species D. Vegetatively propagated species

16. Which one of the following is a correct answer with respect to inbreeding?

A. Time consuming

B. Inbreeding depression

C. Poor performance

D. Identical to recurrent parent

17. The number of three way crosses are

A. $n(n + 1)(n + 2)/2$ B. $n(n - 1)(n - 2)/2$

C. $n(n - 1)(n - 2)(n - 3)/8$ D. None of these

18. Which one of the following is the simplest method for testing the general combining ability of an inbred line?

A. Top cross B. Test cross

C. Single cross D. Multiple cross

19. Which system is used for hybrid seed production in onion?

A. Self incompatibility B. Dioecious

C. Genetic male sterility D. Cytoplasmic male sterility

20. The first inbreeding experiments with maize were those reported by

A. Sprengel in 1866 B. Darwin in 1876

C. Sprague in 1886 D. Baird in 1896

21. A homozygous line developed by self fertilization in a cross pollinated crop is termed as

A. Mutant B. Clone

C. Inbred D. Pureline

22. In cross pollinated species, a true breeding line obtained by continuous inbreeding is called

A. Synthetic variety B. Composite variety

C. Clone D. Inbred

23. The production of double cross hybrid in maize was first suggested by

A. Shull B. E.M. East

C. Jones D. Hull

24. In cross pollinated species, a true breeding line obtained by continuous inbreeding is

    A. Inbred
    B. Hybrid
    C. Cybrid
    D. All of these

25. Find out the incorrect answer

    A. Hybrids are high yielders
    B. Ganga is a double cross hybrid
    C. Deccan is double cross hybrid
    D. A line is sterile line

26. Which one of the following is the example for maize composite?

    A. Ganga
    B. Deccan
    C. Vikram
    D. Ganga 5

27. An example for synthetics is

    A. Ganga
    B. CSH 5
    C. Vikram
    D. ICMS 7703

28. Which of the following is not true in inbreeding?

    A. It causes inbreeding depression after few generation
    B. It leads to homozygosity
    C. It is used to produce pureline
    D. It increases the productivity

Answer keys

1	A	6	B	11	C	16	B	21	C	26	C
2	D	7	D	12	D	17	B	22	D	27	D
3	D	8	A	13	D	18	B	23	C	28	D
4	B	9	A	14	A	19	D	24	A		
5	D	10	D	15	B	20	B	25	B		

5

Breeding Methods for Asexually Propagated Crops

I. Choose the correct answer

1. Breeding crops for improved nutritional quality is

   A. Biomagnification B. Biomining

   C. Biofortification D. Bioremediation

2. Which one of the following answer is a incorrect answer with regard to asexually reproduced crop?

   A. Mostly monoploids B. Mostly perennials

   C. Mostly cross pollinated D. Show reduced flowering and seed set

3. Which one of the following statement is correct pertaining to clones?

   A. Identical individuals B. No phenotype x environment interactions

   C. No phenotypic variations D. Intra specific hybrids

4. Which one of the following answer is not correct with regard to the effect of clonal selection?

   A. Genotype effect B. Environment effect

   C. G x E interaction effect D. P x E interaction effect

5. Which one of the following potato variety was developed from a complex cross (*Solanum curtilobum* × *S.tuberosum*) × *S.andigena*?

   A. Kufri muthu B. Kufri kuber

   C. Kufri red D. Darjeeling red

6. Which one of the following varieties is a selection from Darjeeling red round and pusa savani bhendi for YMV resistance?

   A. Kufri red B. Kalyan sona

   C. Sonalika D. Kufri muthu

7. In which crop, leaf gall resistant type is introduced from USA.

   A. Potato B. Grapes

   C. Mango D. Tapioca

8. …… is a rice variety which is resistant for flood.

   A. Kufri red B. ADT 43

   C. MTU 1001 D. CR 1009

9. Which rice variety is salt resistant?

   A. CSR 36 B. ASD 30

   C. IR 50 D. Pusa red

Answer keys

1	C	6	A
2	A	7	B
3	A	8	C
4	D	9	A
5	B		

6

Mutation Breeding

I. Choose the correct answer

1. Which one the following is a chemical mutagen?
   A. EMS B. GMS
   C. CMS D. None of these
2. Mendok is a gametocide used for inducing male sterility in
   A. Onion B. Sunflower
   C. Maize D. Cotton
3. The chemical mutagens usually induce
   A. Chromosomal breakages B. Gene mutation
   C. Chromosomal translocation D. None of these
4. Mutation due to change in gene because of
   A. Addition B. Loss
   C. Degeneration D. All of these
5. Recommended concentration of EMS for induced mutagenesis is
   A. 1.00 to 3.5% B. 0.03 to 1.5%
   C. 0.30 to 3.0% D. Above 4%
6. Quickest method of plant breeding is
   A. Introduction B. Selection
   C. Hybridization D. Mutation breeding
7. Mutation is an altered phenotype and results in a change which is
   A. Temporarily inherited B. Inherited
   C. Partly inherited D. Unstable
8. The word mutation was first used by
   A. Muller B. S.Wright
   C. Morgan D. Hugo de Vries

9. What is the effect of mutation at chromosome level?
   A. Transcription B. Transversion
   C. Translation D. Replication
10. Which one of the following plant part is used for mutagen treatment?
   A. Ovule B. Ovary
   C. Zygote D. Seed
11. Ethyl methane sulphonate is
   A. Base analogue B. Acridine dye
   C. Alkylating agent D. Hormone
12. ______is the classical chemical mutagen that is used in mutation breeding
   A. Sodium chloride B. Calcium chloride
   C. Ethyl methyl sulphonate D. Ethyl methyl carbonate
13. ______is the dosage of mutagen that produces maximum frequency of mutation and causes minimum killing
   A. LD 30 B. LD 40
   C. LD 60 D. LD 50
14. Most of the mutation have _______ effect
   A. Deleterious B. Good
   C. Bad D. Both B and C
15. Which one of the following mutagens is non-ionizing types?
   A. Gamma rays B. Beta rays
   C. X – rays D. Ultra - violet rays
16. Sudden and sharp change in individual directly inherited by the offspring is called
   A. Adaptation B. Heredity
   C. Mutation D. Continuous variation

Answer keys

1	A	6	D	11	C	16	C
2	A	7	B	12	C		
3	B	8	D	13	D		
4	D	9	B	14	A		
5	B	10	D	15	D		

7

Polyploid and Resistance Breeding

I. Choose the correct answer

1. In polyploidy breeding, the dosage of colchicines for seed treatment is

   A. 0.1 to 1% | B. 0.5 to 1%

   C. 0.001 to 1% | D. 0.01 to 1%

2. In which polyploidy, chromosome doubling within species takes place?

   A. Autopolyploidy | B. Heteropolyploidy

   C. Both A and B | D. None of these

3. Under drought conditions , there is an increase in

   A. Abscisic acid content | B. Ethylene level

   C. Proline level | D. NAA level

4. Polyploidy is induced through

   A. Irradiation | B. Colchichine

   C. Mutagenic chemicals | D. Ethylene

5. Which of the following chemical is used for polyploidy breeding?

   A. MH | B. CCC

   C. NAA | D. Colchicine

6. Which one of the following is a polyploidy?

   A. Haploid | B. Diploid

   C. Monoploid | D. Triploid

7. Breeding method for transferring monogenic disease resistance from wild species to improved variety of wheat is

   A. Bulk method | B. Backcross method

   C. Pedigree method | D. Pureline selection

8. The concept of vertical and horizontal resistance was introduced by

   A. Robinson (1971) | B. Nelson (1973)

   C. Van der Plank (1963) | D. Russell (1978)

9. Which one of the following variety of bhendi is resistant to YVMV?

   A. Parbhani kranti B. Varsha uphar

   C. CO 1 D. Arka anamika

10. How the genes for drought resistance are transferred to high yielding variety?

   A. Hybridization B. Mass selection

   C. Pureline selection D. Pedigree method

Answer keys

1	B	7	B
2	A	8	C
3	C	9	A
4	B	10	A
5	D		
6	D		

UNIT IV: SOIL SCIENCE AND AGRICULTURAL CHEMISTRY

1

Soil and its Formation

I. Choose the correct answer

1. Which of the following is an igneous rock?

   A. Quartz B. Marble

   C. Mica schist D. Slate

2. Who initially started the soil testing programme

   A. Liebig B. Munsell

   C. Fitt's D. Whitaker

3. How soil develops

   A. Decomposed crust B. Decomposed plant residues

   C. Decomposed rock D. Decomposed animal residues

4. Soil colour inherited from its parent material is referred to as

   A. Lithochromic B. Monochromic

   C. Polychromic D. Dichromic

5. International year of soil is

   A. 2013 B. 2015

   C. 2016 D. 2017

6. Indian Institute of Soil Science is located at

   A. Ludhiana B. Pantnagar

   C. New Delhi D. Bhopal

7. AI refers to

   A. Arid Inlands B. Aridity Index

   B. Actual Index D. Actual Initial Moisture

8. Intermediate textured rock is

   A. Granite B. Diorite

   B. Ryolite D. Felsite

9. 'A' horizon of the soils also designated as

A. Eluviated horizon
B. Illuviated horizon
C. Both A and B
D. None of these

10. A combination of many taxonomic units like soil series, phase or types is called

A. Soil variant
B. Soil series
C. Soil complex
D. Soil association

11. A man made epipedon in many characters except P_2O_5 content (more than 250 ppm) is

A. Hisitic epipedon
B. Ochric epipedon
C. Anthropic epipedon
D. Umbric epipedon

12. The soil solum includes

A. A horizon
B. B horizon
C. A and B horizon
D. None of the above

13. Tarai soils are generally deficient in

A. Potassium
B. Graphite
C. Quartz
D. Basalt

14. The mass of organisms in the soil are termed as

A. Soil biota
B. Soil biomass
C. Soil microorganism
D. None of these

15. Soil is biochemically weathered part of

A. Regolith
B. Bedrock
C. Clay minerals
D. Organic matter

16. Petrology is the science of

A. Petrol
B. Mineral oils
C. Earth
D. Rocks

17. What is called for the matured soils which are arranged in a series of zones?

A. Soil zones
B. Soil layers
C. Soil horizons
D. Soil benches

18. Mica is

A. Primary mineral
B. Secondary mineral
C. Accessory mineral
D. None of the above

19. In soil profile, the horizon which is called parent material
    A. A horizon B. B horizon
    C. C horizon D. E horizon
20. If the sand material transported by wind is called
    A. Aeolian B. Alluvium
    C. Colluvium D. Loess
21. End product of weathering is
    A. Bed rock B. Parent material
    C. B horizon D. None
22. In which stage of weathering, decomposition of easily weathered minerals occur
    A. Initial B. Juvenile
    C. Virile D. Senile
23. Soils formed under the predominat influence of parent material, where the climatic effects are obliterated, are known as
    A. Ectodynamomoprphic soils B. Endodynamomorphic soils
    C. Hydromorphic soils D. None
24. The following nutrient deficient in Tarai region occurs
    A. Cu B. Zn
    C. Fe D. Mn
25. Increase in clay content occur, at which stage of weathering
    A. Initial B. Juvenile
    C. Virile D. Senile
26. O horizon is absent in
    A. Grassland B. Forest land
    C. Arable land D. Both A and B
27. Dark coloured horizon in soil profile is
    A. A horizon B. B horizon
    C. C horizon D. Bedrock
28. In soil profile, solum means
    A. A+ B horizons B. A+ B + C horizons
    C. Chorizon D. Bedrock (R)

29. Emigration also called
    A. Illuviation B. Elluviation
    C. Haplodization D. Neosynthesis
30. Alkalization also called
    A. Solonization B. Solodization
    C. Gleization D. Pedoturbation
31. Mechanical movement of clay and iron oxides from A horizon without undergoing chemical alteration is called
    A. Lessivage B. Soil fluxion
    C. Eluviation D. Illuviation
32. The terms pedocal and pedalfer are given by
    A. Dokuchaev B. Marbut
    C. Jenny D. Joffe
33. Hardness in minerals is measured by
    A. Moh's scale B. Talc scale
    C. Clastic scale D. Beaufort's scale
34. Centre for Environment management of degraded ecosystem (CEMDE) is located at
    A. Jodhpur B. Ranchi
    C. Delhi D. Hyderabad
35. Which of the following mineral does not belong to primary mineral?
    A. Quartz B. Orthoclase
    C. Biotite D. Hematite
36. In India, which soil order has the highest area
    A. Entisols B. Alfisols
    C. Inceptisols D. Ultisols
37. The word soil has been derived from
    A. Latin B. Greek
    C. Arabic D. French
38. The study of soil in relation to the higher plants is known as
    A. Edaphology B. Pedology
    C. Climatology D. Petrology

39. Which element is used in maximum amount in earth's crust?
    A. Silicon B. Sodium
    C. Aluminium D. Iron
40. Father of soil pedology is
    A. Dokuchaev B. Marbut
    C. Liebig D. Jenny
41. The process which operates in hydromorphic soils is known as
    A. Gleying B. Drying
    C. Wetting D. Waterlogging
42. Which is not a isomorph of SiO_2?
    A. Quartz B. Cristobalite
    C. Opal D. Siderite
43. Age of soil can be known from
    A. Development of genetic horizon B. Development of soil colour
    C. Development of vegetation D. None of these
44. Total number of agro-ecological sub- regions in India delineated by NBSS-LUP is
    A. 21 B. 42
    C. 60 D. 76
45. Sediments deposited in fresh water lakes are called
    A. Delta B. Aeolian
    C. Lacustrine D. Outwash
46. Which one of the following mineral will weather most rapidly?
    A. Muscovite B. Albite
    C. Quartz D. Microcline
47. In subordinate horizons "t" stands for
    A. Accumulation of clay B. Accumulation of OM
    C. Accumulation of Fe D. All of the above
48. Onion type of weathering is
    A. Exfoliation B. Diagenesis
    C. Graded bedding D. Lessivage
49. Halite or rock salt is
    A. HCl B. NaCl
    C. KCl D. All of the above

50. Example for non foliated rock is

A. Schist
B. Marble
C. Slate
D. All of the above

51. If the fragments of conglomerate rock are angular rather than rounded, then the rock is called as

A. Breccias
B. Arkose
C. Mull
D. Coal

52. The capacity of the soil to recover its functional capacity after disturbance is called as

A. Soil capacity
B. Soil resilience
C. Soil productivity
D. Soil reaction

53. The region of soil above the water table is called

A. Vadose zone
B. Oxic zone
C. Mollic zone
D. Cambic zone

54. Molybdenum present in the following mineral is

A. Wulfenite
B. Kaolinite
C. Pyrite
D. Pyrolusite

55. Fool's gold is

A. Pyrite
B. Pyrolusite
C. Manganite
D. Quartz

56. Alluvial deposits of soft $CaCO_3$ is called as

A. Catena
B. Calena
C. Caliche
D. None

57. Plant capable of growing in rock crevices called

A. Lithophytes
B. Xerophytes
C. Sciophytes
D. Halophytes

58. Very much effective process in chemical weathering is

A. Hydration
B. Carbonation
C. Oxidation
D. Reduction

59. The moisture regime having enough water throughout year

A. Aquic
B. Ustic
C. Udic
D. Xeric

60. The appearance of mineral in reflected light is known as

A. Lustre B. Cleavage

C. Tenacity D. Lattice

61. The elements which remain in atmosphere

A. Lithophile B. Chalcophile

C. Biophiles D. Atmosphiles

62. If the temperature always less than 0°C, which is called as

A. Plinthite B. Permafrost

C. Fragipan D. None

63. When the albic horizon material penetrate into argillic or natric horizon called

A. Plinthite B. Permafrost

C. Fragipan D. Tonguing

64. The epipedon having sandy horizon 100cm or more thick over an argillic horizon is

A. Grossarenic B. Umbric

C. Folistic D. Plaggen

65. Well developed profile occurs in

A. Azonal soils B. Zonal soils

C. Intra zonal soils D. All

66. World soil day

A. Dec 5th B. Dec 14th

C. May 10th D. April 6th

67. National Wasteland Development Board was established in

A. 1975 B. 1995

C. 1985 D. 1965

68. A unit of CSWCR & TI (Central Soil and Water Conservation Research and Training Institute) in Tamil Nadu is located at

A. Ooty B. Kodaikanal

C. Palani D. Yercaud

69. CAZRI (Central Arid Zone Research Institute) is located at

A. Raipur B. Jaipur

C. Hyderabad D. Jodhpur

70. The headquarters of CSWCRI (Central Soil and Water Conservation Research Institute) is located at

A. Jodhpur B. Dehradhun

C. Jaipur D. New Delhi

71. Fine-grained rocks formed on earth crust are called

A. Intensive igneous rock B. Extrusive rock

C. Sedimentary rock D. Plutonic

72. Weathering of gabbros gives

A. Sand and clay B. Clay and iron oxide

C. Clay and Mg oxide D. Sand and iron oxide

73. Soil formation is a

A. Slow process B. Fast process

C. Rapid process D. None of these

74. The increasingly dominant active factor in soil formation is

A. Climate B. Nature of parent rock

C. Man and animal D. Microorganisms

75. Feldspars is primary mineral that occurs predominantly in

A. Igneous rock B. Sedimentary rock

C. Metamorphic rocks D. All of the above

76. In 5 master horizon, which horizon is called elluvial/washout horizon

A. A B. B

C. E D. All of the above

77. The active soil forming factor

A. Climate B. Relief

C. Organism D. Both A and C

78. The parent material transported by gravity is called as

A. Lacustrine B. Colluvium

C. Alluvium D. None of the above

79. Removal of silica from soil and accumulation of sesquioxide is known as

A. Podzolization B. Laterization

C. Gleization D. Both A and B

80. Mixing process of soil is called

A. Pedoturbation B. Podzolization

C. Laterization D. None of the above

81. Which element is found the highest in earth crust?

A. Oxygen
B. Silicon
C. Aluminium
D. Iron

82. _____ of igneous rock is found in earth crust

A. 45%
B. 65%
C. 75%
D. 95%

83. The rocks formed by alteration by heat and pressure is called as

A. Sedimentary rock
B. Metamorphic rock
C. Igneous rock
D. None of the above

84. Slate metamorphs from which rock

A. Shale
B. Sandstone
C. Granite
D. Dolomite

85. Elements which are absorbed from the soil are known as

A. Plants nutrients
B. Plant components
C. Pant feeders
D. Plant supplements

86. Elluviation refers to

A. Removal of clay from above horizons to lower horizons
B. Removal of clay and sequioxide from above horizons to lower horizons
C. Removal of sesquioxide from above horizons to lower horizons
D. None of the above

87. 'The law of limiting factors' was proposed by

A. Liebig
B. Hatch and Slack
C. Blackman
D. Arnon

88. ______ play a key role in the transformation of rock to soil

A. Cyanobacteia
B. Pectin decomposing bacteria
C. Nitrifying bacteria
D. De-nitrifying bacteria

89. Chemical formula of muscovite is

A. $KAl_2Si_3O_{10}(OH)_2$
B. $KAl_3Si_4O_{10}(OH)_2$
C. $KAl_2(AlSi_3O_{10})(F\ OH)_2$
D. $KAl_3Si_2O_{10}(OH)_2$

90. Jarosote is a

A. Mineral of Fe and K
B. Mineral of Fe and Al
C. Mineral of boron
D. Mineral of Mo

91. Which of the following is the source of sulphur

A. Epsomite
B. Hematite
C. Geothite
D. Chalcocite

Answer keys

1	A	21	B	41	A	61	D	81	A
2	C	22	D	42	D	62	B	82	D
3	C	23	B	43	A	63	D	83	B
4	A	24	B	44	C	64	A	84	A
5	B	25	C	45	C	65	B	85	A
6	D	26	C	46	A	66	A	86	B
7	B	27	A	47	B	67	C	87	C
8	B	28	A	48	A	68	A	88	A
9	A	29	B	49	B	69	D	89	C
10	D	30	A	50	B	70	B	90	A
11	C	31	A	51	A	71	A	91	A
12	C	32	B	52	B	72	B	92	
13	C	33	A	53	A	73	A		
14	B	34	C	54	A	74	A		
15	A	35	D	55	A	75	A		
16	D	36	C	56	C	76	C		
17	C	37	A	57	A	77	D		
18	A	38	A	58	B	78	B		
19	C	39	A	59	C	79	B		
20	A	40	A	60	A	80	A		

2

Soil Types

I. Choose the correct answer

1. Most of the copper deficiencies appear in

   A. Sandy soil B. Clay soil

   C. Mineral soil D. Organic soil

2. Which mineral imparts black colour to the soil?

   A. Glauconite B. Manganese oxide

   C. Lepidocrosite D. Hematite

3. Buffering capacity is high for

   A. Sand B. Silt

   C. Clay D. Humus

4. At the pH range of 2-5, phosphorous is mainly fixed by

   A. Fe and Al B. Clay

   C. Ca and Mg D. Organic matter

5. Peat soils are generally having the nature of

   A. Acidic B. Basic

   C. Neutral D. Senile

6. New alluvial soils are called

   A. Bhangar B. Khadar

   C. Usar D. Kallar

7. Red soils are developed at

   A. Higher topographic regions B. Lower topographic regions

   C. Medium topography D. None

8. The black cotton soils of India are derived from

   A. Limestone B. Graphite

   C. Quartz D. Basalt

9. Which soil is very sticky when wet and very hard when dry?

A. Entisols | B. Oxisols
C. Vertisols | D. Andisols

10. Name of the twelfth order of taxonomy

A. Vertisols | B. Oxisols
C. Andisols | D. Gelisols

11. Black colour of vertisol is due to the presence of

A. Oragnic matter | B. Titanium
C. Selenium | D. Montmorillonite clay

12. The order developed without horizons or little development of horizons are called

A. Inceptisol | B. Entisol
C. Alfisol | D. Aridisol

13. Major area of arable soils in India falls under the climatic region of

A. Semi arid | B. Arid
C. Humid | D. Sub humid

14. Presence of mottles in some part of soil profile indicates

A. Continuous oxidizing | B. Fluctuating water table
C. Continuous reducing condition | D. Static water table

15. A bleached E (A2) horizon and dark coloured B2 horizon characterize the soil order

A. Oxisol | B. Utlisol
C. Spodosol | D. Aridisol

16. Match list I with list II and choose the correct options given below

List I	**List II**
a. Alluvial soil	1. Dark-grey
b. Black soil	2. Coastal belt
c. Red soil	3. Hilly regions
d. Laterite soil	4. Ferric oxide

	a	b	c	d
A.	4	3	2	1
B.	3	4	2	1
C.	1	2	3	4
D.	2	1	4	3

17. Consider the statements and choose the correct answer
    (i) Parental material of soil is metamorphic rock
    (ii) Granite is a parental material of black soil
    (iii) Parental material of soil is sedimentary rock
    A. (i) and (iii) are correct B. (i) and (ii) are correct
    C. (i) alone is correct D. (ii) alone is correct
18. Find out the wrong answer
    A. Alluvial soil is found in Godavari
    B. Black soil is found in Kovilpatti of Tamil Nadu
    C. Laterite soil is found in Yercaud of Tamil Nadu
    D. Desert soils is found in New Delhi
19. Match list I with list II and choose the correct options given below

List I	**List II**
a. Alluvial soil	1. Groundnut
b. Black soil	2. Sugarcane
c. Red soil	3. Coffee
d. Laterite soil	4. Rice

	a	b	c	d
A.	4	2	1	3
B.	2	1	3	4
C.	4	2	1	3
D.	3	1	2	4

20. Find out the correct answer.
    (i) Desert soil contains more sodium
    (ii) Peaty and marshy soil is suitable for all crops
    (iii) Problem soil ESP : >15, pH: > 8.5
    (iv) Black soil is not suitable for growing cotton
    A. (i) and (ii) are correct B. (iii) and (iv) are correct
    C. (i) alone is correct D. (iii) alone is correct
21. Match list I with list II and choose the correct options given below

List I	**List II**
a. Red soil	1. 3%
b. Black soil	2. 7%
c. Laterite soil	3. 62%
d. Coastal soils	4. 12%

	a	b	c	d
A.	4	3	1	2
B.	4	2	1	3
C.	3	2	1	4
D.	3	4	1	2

22. What is the diameter of soil particles that is excluded for soil textural determinations?

A. >0.002 mm
B. <0.002 mm
C. >0.2 mm
D. <0.2 mm

23. Match list I with list II and choose the correct options given below

List I	**List II**
a. Clay	1. 1.00 – 2.00 mm
b. Silt	2. <0.002 mm
c. Fine sand	3. 0.002 – 0.05 mm
d. Very coarse sand	4. 0.10-0.25 mm

	a	b	c	d
A.	4	3	2	1
B.	2	4	3	1
C.	2	3	4	1
D.	4	3	1	2

24. Soil moisture availability is more in

A. Red soil
B. Laterite soil
C. Sandy soil
D. Clay soil

25. Soil which is a good conductor of heat is

A. Stony soil
B. Sandy soil
C. Clay soil
D. Both A and B

26. Upward swelling of soil due to frost is called as

A. Freezing injury
B. Heaving
C. Suffocation
D. Buffering of soil

27. Major soil found in hilly areas

A. Red loamy soil
B. Black soil
C. Coastal alluvium
D. Lateritic soil

28. Major soil type found in Tamil Nadu is

A. Black soils
B. Laterite soil
C. Red soil
D. Coastal soil

29. Statement 1: Newer alluvium is called as Khadar which is sandy, light colour and less kankar nodules

Statement 2: Black soil contain higher proportion of calcium and magnesium carbonates

Choose the correct statements.

A. Statement 2 alone is correct B. Statement 1 alone is correct

C. Both are correct D. Both are wrong

30. Match the following

a. Entisol	1. Alluvial soil
b. Alfisol	2. Sandy soil
c. Vertisol	3. Part of red soil and part of black soil
d. Inceptisol	4. Red soil

	a	b	c	d
A.	2	4	1	3
B.	2	1	3	4
C.	4	3	2	1
D.	3	4	1	2

31. (i) Red soil is always acidic in nature

(ii) Alluvial soils are medium in phosphorus content and high in potassium content

(iii) Clay content in desert soil is <8%

A. (ii) and (iii) are correct B. (i) and (ii) are correct

C. (i) and (iii) are correct D. All the statements are correct

32. Proportion of clay in black soil is about

A. 5-10% B. 30-40%

C. 70-80% D. 80-90%

33. Which of the following is incorrectly matched?

A. Red soil - 62% B. Black soil - 25%

C. Laterite soil - 3% D. Coastal soil - 7%

34. Swelling and shrinkage is a specific characteristics of

A. Alfisol B. Entisol

C. Vertisol D. Mollisol

35. Crop grown in desert soil is

A. Mango
B. Litchi
C. Datepalm
D. Apple

36. Red colur of red soil is due to

A. Haematite
B. Quartz
C. Calcite
D. Geothite

37. Match the following

a. Black soil — 1. Ferric oxides
b. Red soil — 2. Organic matter
c. Peat soil — 3. Ca and Mg carbonates
d. Laterite soil — 4. Fe and Al oxides

	a	b	c	d
A.	2	1	3	4
B.	3	4	1	2
C.	4	3	2	1
D.	3	1	2	4

38. Which of these will add calcium to the soil without changing the soil pH?

A. Lime
B. Gypsum
C. Superphosphate
D. Dolomite

39. The soil type of dry lands in India is dominated by

A. Sandy soil
B. Clayey soil
C. Alluvial soils
D. Black soils

40. Which type of soil is commonly known as hungry and thirsty soil?

A. Black soil
B. Alluvial soil
C. Laterite soil
D. Red soil

41. Organic matter is abundantly available in

A. Sandy loam
B. Clay loam
C. Silt
D. None of the above

42. Which of the following pairs is correctly matched?

A. Red soil — Calcareous
B. Alkali soil — pH 9
C. Black soil — Rich in kaolinite
D. Laterite soil — pH 8

43. Pore space is higher in
    A. Sandy soil B. Clayey soil
    C. Loamy soil D. Silty soil
44. The soil order which has high content of clays that swell when wetted
    A. Alfisols B. Ultisols
    C. Vertisols D. Mollisols
45. Oilseed suitable for growing in red soil is
    A. Groundnut B. Sunflower
    C. Safflower D. Soybean
46. Bedrock is absent in which soil?
    A. Black soil B. Red soil
    C. Alluvial soil D. Forest soil
47. The honey comb structure is found in
    A. Alluvial soil B. Black soil
    C. Saline soil D. Laterite soil
48. Black colour of soil is due to
    A. Titaniferous magnetite B. Geothite
    C. Glauconite D. Organic matter
49. Total soil order found in world?
    A. 9 B. 10
    C. 11 D. 12
50. Number of soil orders according USDA classification is
    A. 8 orders B. 12 orders
    C. 16 orders D. 18 orders
51. The phenomenon slickenside found in which soil
    A. Inceptisol B. Vertisol
    C. Gelisol D. Spodosol
52. Laterite soil develops as a result of
    A. Deposits of alluvial B. Deposition of loss
    C. Leaching of sedimentary rocks D. Windblown dust
53. What kind of soil is treated with gypsum to make it suitable for cropping?
    A. Alluvial B. Acidic
    C. Water-logged D. Soil with excessive clay content

54. For which of the following is black soil not very suitable?

A. Cotton B. Wheat

C. Ground nut D. Potato

55. To which group does the black cotton soil of India belong?

A. Laterite B. Podzol

C. Chernozem D. Sierozem

56. Which of the following is grown mainly on mountain slopes?

A. Paddy B. Tea

C. Groundnut D. Potato

57. Irreversible shrinkage of organic soils upon excessive drainage occurs due to

A. Mineralization of organic matter

B. Internal pairing of proton donor and acceptor groups

C. Production of clays for swelling-shrinking type

D. None of these

Answer keys

1	D	11	B	21	D	31	D	41	B	51	B
2	B	12	B	22	B	32	A	42	B	52	C
3	D	13	A	23	C	33	B	43	B	53	D
4	A	14	B	24	D	34	C	44	C	54	C
5	A	15	C	25	D	35	C	45	A	55	C
6	B	16	D	26	B	36	A	46	C	56	B
7	A	17	A	27	D	37	D	47	D	57	B
8	D	18	D	28	C	38	C	48	A		
9	C	19	A	29	A	39	C	49	D		
10	D	20	C	30	A	40	D	50	B		

3

Soil Physical Properties

I. Choose the correct answer

1. V = 2rg (PP-Pm)/gm is

   A. Darcy's law B. Stoke's law

   C. Beer's law D. None of these

2. Upper plastic limit is also known as

   A. Liquid limit B. Lower limit

   C. Index of plasticity D. None of these

3. Which is the most common colour in the soil?

   A. Red B. Yellow

   C. Blue D. Brown

4. In munsell colour chart, value of '0' indicate

   A. White B. Black

   C. Red D. Yellow

5. What is the bulk density of sandy soil?

   A. 1.4 g/cm^3 B. 1.3 g/cm^3

   C. 1.1 g/cm^3 D. 1.36 g/cm^3

6. Consider the statement and choose the correct one

   (i) In sandy soil, pore space is low

   (ii) In clay soil, pore space is high

   (iii) Presence of organic matter decrease pore space

   A. (i) and (ii) are correct B. (ii) alone is correct

   C. (iii) alone is correct D. All the statements are correct

7. The composition of soil consists of

   A. 50% mineral matter + 45% soil air and water + 5% organic matter

   B. 25% soil air + 25% soil water + 45% mineral matter + 5% organic mater

C. 30% soil air + 30% soil water + 35% mineral matter + 5% organic matter

D. 5% soil air + 5% soil water + 85% mineral matter + 5% organic matter

8. The relative proportion of particles of sand, silt and clay refers to

A. Soil structure
B. Soil texture
C. Soil density
D. Soil consistency

9. Match the following

a. Silt	1. < 0.002mm
b. Clay	2. 0.02-0.2 mm
c. Coarse sand	3. 0.002-0.02 mm
d. Fine sand	4. 0.2-2.0 mm

	a	b	c	d
A.	4	2	1	3
B.	2	3	4	1
C.	3	1	4	2
D.	3	2	1	4

10. Soil physical property which cannot be changed or altered is

A. Soil structure
B. Soil texture
C. Soil colour
D. Soil particles

11. Soil structure suitable for crop cultivation is

A. Platy structure
B. Prism type
C. Crumby structure
D. Blocky type

12. The percentage of CO_2 content in soil air is about

A. 0.03%
B. 0.003%
C. 0.30%
D. 3.0%

13. Which of the following is incorrect statement?

A. Particle density of normal soil is 2.65 gms/cubic cm
B. Bulk density is always higher than particle density
C. Average bulk density of soil is 1.33 g/cc
D. Particle density also known as true density

14. Bulk density is low for

A. Sandy soil
B. Loamy soil
C. Silty loam
D. Clayey soil

15. The mass (weight) per unit volume of a dry soil including pore space is called

A. Particle density B. Soil density
C. Soil porosity D. Bulk density

16. The arrangement of primary soil particles and their aggregates into a certain definite pattern is called as

A. Soil structure B. Soil monolith
C. Soil texture D. Soil reaction

17. The total porosity of the soil is higher in

A. Sandy soils B. Silty soils
C. Clayey soils D. Loamy soils

18. Bulk density of organic matter is

A. 1.6 g/cm^2 B. 0.5 g/cm^2
C. 1.0 g/cm^2 D. 0.7 g/cm^2

19. Hue denotes

A. Dominant spectrum B. Lightness or brightness
C. Purity D. Intensity

20. In munsell colour chart, hue 10 represents as

A. Red B. Black
C. Grey D. Yellow

21. Available water is the water held between

A. Saturation to wilting point B. Field capacity to hygroscopic coefficient
C. Only field capacity D. Field capacity to wilting point

22. Which plant is used for indication of permanent wilting point?

A. Safflower B. Sunflower
C. Marigold D. Both A and C

23. Quantity of soil to be taken for texture analysis is

A. 10g B. 20g
C. 30g D. 40g

24. When organic matter is added into the soil, effect on bulk density is

A. Increased B. No effect
C. Decreased D. Both A and C

25. Loose soil has a relative density within a range of

A. 60-85 B. 85-100
C. 10-35 D. 35-60

26. _________ apparatus is used to test liquid limit of a soil.

A. Mohr B. Casagrande
C. Otto D. Terzaghi

27. How many types of pores are present in a soil mass?

A. 6 B. 3
C. 5 D. 4

28. Father of agricultural chemistry is

A. Justus Von Liebig B. Neil Brady
C. Neuron D. J. Jones

29. Process of mixing soil by fauna and flora is called

A. Lessivage B. Pedoturbation
C. Leaching D. Enrichment

30. Diameter of most erodible soil particles is

A. 0.2mm B. 0.4mm
C. 0.3mm D. 0.1mm

31. A soil absorbs about ______ of incoming solar radiation

A. 5% B. 10%
C. 15% D. 20%

32. Stokes' law is used for determination of

A. Soil texture B. Soil structure
C. Soil air D. Soil water movement

33. Ratio between the weight of a mineral to the weight of an equal volume of water is called

A. Specific gravity B. Bulk density
C. Particle density D. None of these

34. At 20% soil moisture content by volume, the sequence of soil moisture tension (negative potential) in the soils of three different textures will be

A. Sand>silt loam>silty clay B. Silty clay>silt loam>sand
C. Silt loam>silty clay>sand D. Silty clay>sand>silt loam

35. The infiltration rate of ponded water is measured with the help of
    A. Hydrometer B. Conductivity meter
    C. Tensiometer D. Ring-infiltrometer
36. A device for measuring percolation, leaching and evaporation losses from a column of soil under controlled conditions is known as
    A. Hydrometer B. Lysimeter
    C. Infiltrometer D. Thermometer
37. Water infiltration rate will be higher in a soil having a bulk density of
    A. 0.8 g/cc B. 1.3 g/cc
    C. 1.7 g/cc D. 7.0 g/cc
38. In no tillage system, the surface soil layers have
    A. Higher bulk density B. Lower bulk density
    C. Higher total pore space D. Low water infiltration
39. If the voids of a soil mass are full of air only, the soil is termed as
    A. Air entrained soil B. Partially saturated soil
    C. Dry soil D. Dehydrated soil
40. A fully saturated soil is said to be
    A. One phase system
    B. Two phase system with soil and air
    C. Two phase system with soil and water
    D. Three phase system
41. Percolation rate of water is least in
    A. Sandy soil B. Clayey soil
    C. Loamy soil D. None of these
42. The size of macro pores
    A. >0.05mm B. >0.09mm
    C. >0.04mm D. >0.06mm
43. Which of the following structure is heavier than the other?
    A. Loamy sand B. Silty clay loam
    C. Sandy loam D. Silty loam
44. Unit of surface tension is
    A. Dynes/cm (or) Newton/metre B. Dynes/g
    C. Cm D. Cal

45. Henry's law describes

A. Solubility of gases B. Sedimentation

C. Heat conduction D. Diffusion of gases

46. The mean albedo of the earth is

A. 0.36 B. 0.46

C. 0.25 D. 0.12

47. In addition to the rock particles, the soil contains

A. Air and water

B. Water and plants

C. Minerals, organic matter, air and water

D. Water, air and plants

48. pF scale for field capacity is

A. 2 B. 2.5

C. 3.5 D. 4.5

49. Which chemical compound is used to improve soil aeration, infiltration and water holding capacity of soil

A. Jalshakti B. Fentachlore

C. Hydrotech D. None of the above

50. Bhata soil is also known as

A. Clayey B. Clay loam

C. Gravely D. Sandy loam

51. A property of fluids by virtue of which it reduces the relative motion among different layers of fluid, is termed as

A. Soil consistency B. Soil specificity

C. Soil viscosity D. None of these

52. Amount of heat required to raise temperature of 1 gm soil from 14 to 15 °C is known as

A. Heat capacity B. Specific heat

C. Thermal conductivity D. None of these

53. Bulk density is denoted by

A. Weight of the given soil sample volume of the same soil sample (g/c.c.)

B. Volume of the soil sample/weight of the soil sample (g/c.c.)

C. Weight of the soil sample x 100/volume of the soil sample (g/c.c.)

D. None of these

54. Capillary movement of water is complemented by

A. Stem elongation
B. Root extension
C. Leaf orientation
D. None of these

55. Diameter of clay particle is

A. Less than 0.002 mm
B. 0.05 - 0.5 mm
C. 0.5 - 1.0 mm
D. 0.7 - 0.9 mm

56. If a soil has a bulk density of 1.50 mg/m^3 and a particle density of 2.65 mg/m^3, then the percentage pore space of the soil will be

A. 35
B. 38.5
C. 43.4
D. 48.5

57. If the particle size is 2mm to 7.5 cm, then it is known as

A. Gravels
B. Stones
C. Sand
D. Silt

58. In no-tillage systems, the surface soil layers have

A. Higher bulk density
B. Lower bulk density
C. Higher total pore space
D. Lower water infiltration

59. In the diffusion, the movement of ions takes place

A. From the region of higher concentration to the lower concentration
B. From the region of lower concentration to the higher concentration
C. Both are correct
D. None of the above

60. Which one of the following sets of soil condition is more suitable for plant growth?

A. Sandy soils with high aeration and low water holding capacity
B. Clay soils with higher water holding capacity and low aeration
C. Organic soils with high water holding capacity and low aeration
D. Loamy soils with medium aeration and medium water holding capacity

61. Flux of the gas across the plane directly proportional to concentration gradient indicates

A. Stoke's law
B. Fick's law
C. Darcy's law
D. Henry's law

62. Mass flow of gases into the soil occurs due to the difference of

A. Surface tension B. Pressure gradient

C. Both of the above D. None of the above

63. The mean annual temperature of soil is 22°C or more present in which of the following temeperature regimes

A. Pargelic B. Cryic

C. Frigid D. Hyper thermic

64. Ratio between thermal conductivity to volumetric heat capacity is called as

A. Thermal diffusivity B. Specific heat

C. Heat capacity D. None

65. The following constituent is having lowest specific heat of

A. Quartz B. Humus

C. Water D. Organic matter

66. In which type of atterberg limit, there is no further decrease in volume occurs

A. Lower plastic limit B. Upper plastic limit

C. Both A and B D. Shrinkage limit

67. The main source of recharge of ground water is

A. Percolation B. Seepage

C. Infiltration D. All the above

68. Hysteresis occur due to the

A. Alternate wetting and drying B. Temperature

C. High rainfall D. None

69. Physical classification of water is given by

A. Briggs B. Richards

C. Gardner D. Marshall

70. Skeleton of the soil is

A. Sand + silt B. Sand + clay

C. Clay D. Only sand

71. Boundary layer between water and air is called

A. Catena B. Calena

C. Meniscus D. Cutan

72. When ions are hydrated large amount of energy released which is called
    A. Heat of wetting B. Heat of solution
    C. Heat of drying D. None
73. The notation number of value range from 0-10 and in this 0 indicates
    A. Absolute black B. Absolute white
    C. Absolute red D. Absolute yellow
74. Weakly joining of soil particle is referred to as
    A. Granular structure B. Crumb structure
    C. Platy structure D. None of the above
75. The mean particle diameter of sand particles is
    A. 2.0 – 0.05 mm B. < 0.02 mm
    B. < 0.002 mm D. 0.05 – 0.002 mm
76. The total pore space of the soil occupied by air and water is on
    A. 50:50 basis B. 25:75 basis
    B. 5:95 basis D. 45:55 basis
77. Arrangement of soil particles is known as
    A. Soil texture B. Soil structure
    B. Soil contour D. Soil order
78. Value of soil colour denotes the
    A. The dominant spectral colour B. Intensity of a colour
    C. Purity of the colour D. Soil density
79. CO_2 concentration in soil air
    A. 0.25% B. 0.025%
    C. 0.0025% D. 2.5%
80. Soil shows plasticity
    A. > 15% clay B. < 15% clay
    C. 10% silt D. 5 -10% clay
81. Diffusion in soil is
    A. The movement of ions down a concentration gradient
    B. PO_4 moving with water via gravity flow
    C. Movement of ions by electrostatic attraction
    D. Evapotranspiration in plants
82. Heat transmission in soil through the process of
    A. Conduction B. Convection
    C. Diffusion D. Both a and b

83. Who found out the soil colour chart?

A. Liebeg
B. Jenny
C. Joffy
D. Munsell

84. Hydraulic conductivity of soils varies directly with

A. Capillary porosity
B. Non-capillary porosity
C. Total porosity
D. Water holding capacity

85. Hygroscopic moisture is held at

A. 31 atm
B. 1000 atm
C. 99 atm
D. 200 atm

86. Thermal conductivity of different textural classes of the soils follows the following order

A. Sand < Loam < Clay < Peat
B. Sand > Loam > Clay > Peat
C. Sand = Clay = Loam = Sand
D. None of the above

87. pF scale for field capacity is

A. 2
B. 2.5
C. 3.5
D. 4.5

88. Match the following:

a. Coarse sand — 1. 2.798
b. Fine sand — 2. 2.659
c. Silt — 3. 2.837
d. Clay — 4. 2.655

	a	b	c	d
A.	4	2	1	3
B.	2	3	4	1
C.	3	1	4	2
D.	3	2	4	1

89. Match the following:

a. Gravitational water — 1. Held in macropores
b. Capillary water — 2. Held tightly on the surface of soil colloidal particles
c. Hygroscopic water — 3. Held between wilting coefficient and field capacity
d. Available water — 4. Held in micropores

	a	b	c	d
A.	2	4	1	3
B.	2	4	3	1
C.	1	4	2	3
D.	3	2	1	4

90. Match the following

a. Gravimetric method	1. Suction method
b. Electrical conductivity method	2. Drying the sample in oven at 105°C
c. Tensiometer	3. Moisture content at different tension during wetting and drying
d. Hysteresis	4. Gypsum block present

	a	b	c	d
A.	3	4	2	1
B.	4	2	1	3
C.	1	2	3	4
D.	2	4	1	3

Answer keys

1	B	21	D	41	B	61	B	81	A
2	A	22	B	42	D	62	B	82	A
3	D	23	B	43	B	63	D	83	D
4	B	24	C	44	A	64	A	84	C
5	D	25	C	45	A	65	A	85	A
6	A	26	A	46	A	66	D	86	B
7	B	27	C	47	C	67	A	87	B
8	B	28	B	48	B	68	A	88	D
9	C	29	B	49	A	69	A	89	C
10	B	30	D	50	C	70	A	90	D
11	C	31	B	51	C	71	C		
12	C	32	A	52	A	72	B		
13	B	33	A	53	A	73	A		
14	D	34	C	54	B	74	B		
15	D	35	D	55	A	75	A		
16	A	36	B	56	C	76	A		
17	C	37	A	57	A	77	B		
18	B	38	A	58	A	78	B		
19	A	39	C	59	A	79	A		
20	D	40	C	60	D	80	A		

4

Soil Chemical Properties

I. Choose the correct answer

1. The positive and high value of redox potential indicates

   A. Reducing conditions

   B. Strong oxidizing conditions

   C. Equally reducing and oxidizing conditions

   D. None of these

2. The concept of soil as a natural body was first developed by

   A. C.F.Marbut B. K.D.Glinka

   C. V.V.Dokuchaev D. E.W.Hillgard

3. In water logged soil, the concentration of ______ is high.

   A. Ethane B. Methane

   C. Carbondioxide D. Carbonmonoxide

4. Particles less than 0.001 mm size possess colloidal properties called as

   A. Soil organic matter B. Soil colloids

   C. Soil texture proportions D. Clay soil

5. (i) Adhesion, a property of soil colloids means the attractive force between different molecules or materials.

   (ii) Sesquioxides are mixture of Cl $(OH)_3$ and Fe_2O_3.

   A. (ii) alone is correct B. (i) alone is correct

   C. Both are correct D. Both are wrong

6. Power to resist a change in pH is called as

   A. Reserve acidity B. Reserve alkalinity

   C. Buffering action D. CEC

7. (i) TDS = EC x 640

   (ii) SAR = Na^+/" (Ca + Mg)/2

   (iii) RSC = $(CO_3^{2-} + HCO_3^{3-}) - (Ca^{2+} + Mg^{2+})$

A. (ii) and (iii) are correct
B. (i) and (iii) are correct
C. (i) and (ii) are correct
D. All the statements are correct

8. The RSC content which is unsafe (water suitability) is
A. > 7.50 me/L
B. > 10 me/L
C. > 2.50 me/L
D. > 5 me/L

9. Choose the correct formula for calculating TDS.
A. TDS (ppm) = EC (dSm^{-1}) x 640
B. TDS (ppm) = EC (dSm^{-1}) x 600
C. TDS (ppm) = EC (dSm^{-1}) x 620
D. TDS (ppm) = EC (dSm^{-1}) x 660

10. Soils containing heavy amount of _____ show white colour
A. Organic matter
B. Iron compounds
C. Silica and lime
D. OM + iron oxides

11. _____ is the second most important reaction in nature.
A. Photosynthesis
B. Cation exchange
C. Respiration
D. Humification

12. Which is the formula for SAR (Sodium absorption ratio)
A. $SAR = \frac{Na^{++}}{\sqrt{Ca^{++} + Mg^{++} / 2}}$
B. $SAR = \frac{Na^{++}}{Ca^{++} + Mg^{++}}$
C. $SAR = \frac{Na^{++}}{Ca^{++} + Mg^{++} / 2}$
D. $SAR = \frac{Na^{++}}{\sqrt{Ca^{++} + Mg^{++}}}$

13. Which is the formula for RSC (Residual sodium carbonate)
A. $(CO_3^{2-} + HCO_3^-) - (Ca^{2+} + Mg^{2+})$
B. $(CO_3^{2-} - HCO_3^-) + (Ca^{2+} + Mg^{2+})$
C. $(CO_3^{2-} + HCO_3^-) \times (Ca^{2+} + Mg^{2+})$
D. $(CO_3^{2-} - HCO\text{–}) - (Ca^{2+} + Mg^{2+})$

14. What is the formula for permeability index?
A. Na (HCO_3) / (Ca + Mg + NA)
B. Na (HCO_3) / (Ca + Mg + NA) x 100
C. Na (HCO_3) x (Ca + Mg + NA)
D. Na (HCO_3) x (Ca + Mg + NA) x 100

15. A good quality irrigation water should have an EC of
A. < 4.5 dSm^{-1}
B. < 1.5 dSm^{-1}
C. < 0.5 dSm^{-1}
D. 3 to 5 dSm^{-1}

16. Base saturation in lateritic soil is

    A. < 40 %   B. > 40%

    C. < 20%   D. > 20%

17. Which chemical compound is used for improving soil aeration, infiltration and water holding capacity of soil

    A. Jalshakti   B. Fentachlore

    C. Hydrotech   D. None of the above

18. What is the ESP of saline-alkaline soils?

    A. >15   B. <15

    C. =15   D. None

19. Which of the following is harmful to the higher plants?

    A. Phenol carboxylic acid   B. Vanillic acid

    C. Dihydroxystearic acid   D. All of these

20. The correct unit of cation exchange capacity of soil is

    A. C mol (p^+)/L   B. M mol (p+)/m^3

    C. C mol (p^+)/kg   D. me/l

21. Long term effect of urea application in soil is

    A. Alkaline   B. Acidic

    C. Neutral   D. Increase in organic matter

22. Compounds behaving as weak acid as well as weak base are known as

    A. Isoelectric compounds   B. Amphoteric compounds

    C. Amorphous compounds   D. None of these

23. Excess of which of the following element in soil may encourage a deficiency of zinc, but may enhance the absorption of molybdenum by growing plants

    A. Nitrogen   B. Phosphorus

    C. Potassium   D. Iron

24. The concept of equilibrium phosphate potential (EPP) was introduced by

    A. Schofield   B. Mitscherlich

    C. Ramamoorthy and Subramanian D. Bajaj and Ramamoorthy

25. Which of these conditions do not favour dispersion of colloids?

    A. High hydration

    B. Absence of oppositely charged colloids in the system

    C. pH near isoelectric point

    D. Low electrolyte

26. At isoelectric point on zero point of charge, zeta potential is

A. Positive B. Negative

C. Zero D. Variable

27. Among the following ions, maximum hydration is shown by

A. Ca^{++} B. Na^{+}

C. Al^{++} D. K^{+}

28. Exchangeability of a cation also depends on the degree of saturation and exchangeability of accompanying cations. This is known as

A. Raman effect B. Cationic effect

C. Jarusov effect D. Chatterjee effect

29. Replacement of other cations from exchange complex across a semi permeable membrane by the H^{+} ions from water is termed as

A. Donnan equilibrium B. Donnan hydrolysis

C. Mineral decomposition D. None of these

30. Due to increase in temperature, cation adsorption is generally

A. Increased B. Decreased

C. Not changed D. Variable

31. Higher concentration of anions in the bulk of solution of soil than in the diffuse double layer is termed as

A. Anion effect B. Cation effect

C. Cataphoresis D. Negative adsorption

32. When a medium moves under the influence of applied potential as a direct consequence of the existence of a zeta potential between the colloidal particles and the medium, this phenomenon is referred as

A. Cataphoresis B. Electrophoresis

C. Electroosmosis D. Electrodialysis

33. The amount of P that is associated with the solid phase which would readily equilibrate with its isotope in the same ionic form is known as

A. Intensity factor B. Quantity factor

C. Rate factor D. Potential buffering capacity

34. Quickest method of saturating the clay with H^{+} is

A. Electrolysis B. Dialysis

C. Dilute acid washing D. Cation exchange resin

35. The kind of equilibria existing in the soil systems are referred as

A. Static equilibria
B. True equilibria
C. Dynamic equilibria
D. None of these

36. The colloidal system with the liquid as disperse phase and solid as dispersion medium in termed as

A. Suspension
B. Aerosol
C. Gel
D. Emulsion

37. Aggregation or clumping together of individual, tiny soil particles called

A. Flocculation
B. Deflocculation
C. Tyndall effect
D. Adsorption

38. The term colloid was coined by

A. Thomas Graham
B. Sorenson
C. Schofield
D. Marshall

39. In which type of colloid, surface tension is lower and viscosity is higher than the dispersion medium

A. Lyophilic
B. Lyophobic
C. Both A and B
D. None

40. The substitution of one ion with another ion of similar size and with lower positive charge called

A. Adsorption
B. Isomorphous substitution
C. CEC
D. None

41. Amphoteric nature means

A. They hold only anions
B. They hold only cations
C. They hold both anions and cations
D. None of these

42. The dominant exchangeable cation is

A. Ca^{+2}
B. Mg^{+2}
C. Na^{+}
D. Al^{+3}

43. The weight of one hectare furrow slice layer (0-15cm) is

A. 2.24×10^{4} kg
B. 2.24×10^{6} kg
C. 2.24×10^{5} kg
D. 2.24×10^{3} kg

44. Ligand adsorption of P by soil results in

A. Increase of CEC
B. Increase of AEC
C. Decrease of pH
D. Increase specific surface area

45. P fixation is more in

A. Montmorillonite
B. Vermiculite
C. Kaolinite
D. Illite

46. Solid to solid (Roots and clay surface) exchange phenomena is called

A. CEC
B. AEC
C. Contact exchange
D. All

47. The potential difference between fixed part and freely mobile portions of diffuse double layer is called as

A. Zeta potential
B. Osmotic potential
C. Matric potential
D. Pressure potential

48. Zero point charge is also called as

A. Iso electric point
B. Zeta potential
C. Matric potential
D. None

49. If the concentration of the adsorbate is less on the surface of the adsorbant than in the bulk, it is known as

A. Negative adsorption
B. Positive adsorption
C. Adsorption
D. Absorption

50. Redistribution of ions either side of semi permeable membrane for both ions of same salt related to

A. Stoke's law
B. Fick's law
C. Donnan membrane equilibrium
D. Darcy's law

51. 2:1 minerals are also called as

A. Dimorphic minerals
B. Trimorphic minerals
C. Tetramorphic minerals
D. Absorption

52. Bruchite layer ($Mg_3(OH)_6$) present in which of this following minerals

A. Montmorillonite
B. Kaolinite
C. Halloysite
D. Chlorite

53. High specific surface area present in which of this minerals

A. Montmorillonite
B. Kaolinite
C. Vermiculite
D. None

54. One milli equivalent of Ca is equal to

A. 0.04mg B. 0.01mg

C. 0.02mg D. 0.42mg

55. Dielectric constant of water is

A. 75 B. 81

C. 63 D. 85

56. Enthalpy is

A. Total heat content of a system B. Liberation of heat

C. Change of heat D. All

57. The substance having different chemical composition and crystallizing in same form is called as

A. Potash alum B. Ammonium alum

C. Carbon D. Both A and B

58. Most predominant anion present in silicate clay mineral is

A. Chlorine B. Molybdenum

C. Oxygen D. Vanadium

59. Base saturation is more in

A. 1:1 minerals B. 2:1 minerals

C. 2:2 minerals D. None

60. Lignin is polymer of

A. Carbohydrates B. Alcohol

C. Polyphenol D. Glucose

61. Biochar related to

A. Carbon sequestration B. Nitrification inhibitor

C. Slow release nitrogen fertilizer D. None of the above

62. Influence of one adsorbed ion on the release of another from the surface of colloid is

A. Specific ion effect B. Complementary ion effect

C. Zeta potential D. Iso electric point

63. CEC/AEC ratio for mineral vermiculite is

A. 6.7 B. 2.3

C. 0.5 D. 9.5

64. Root CEC is given by
    A. Devaux B. Marshall
    C. Puri D. Jenny and overstreet
65. Chlorites belongs to
    A. Ino silicates B. Phyllosilicates
    C. Ortho silicates D. Tekto silicates
66. Heat insulating mineral is
    A. Kaolinite B. Montmorillonite
    C. Vermiculite D. Illite
67. Ionic strength introduced by
    A. Lewis B. Rendol
    C. Schofield D. Both A and B
68. The chemical bond which is developed due to opposite charged ions is called
    A. Ionic bond B. Hydrogen bond
    C. Covalent bonding D. Vander wall bonding
69. Colloidal solutions is also called as
    A. Sols B. Zols
    C. Jells D. None
70. pE concept was given by
    A. Silen B. Sorenson
    C. Beckett D. Puri
71. Total porosity of puddle soil is
    A. High B. Medium
    C. Low D. None
72. The colour of permanently reduced zone is
    A. Black B. Bluish green
    C. Brown D. Red
73. The following mineral belongs to trioctahedral
    A. Serpentine B. Kaolinite
    C. Montmorillonite D. Nantronite
74. Bemmelon factor is
    A. 1.754 B. 1.724
    C. 1.342 D. 1.524

75. Surface area of clay particles can be measured by using

A. Alcohol B. HCl

C. Cetylpyridinum bromide D. All

76. Electric conductivity method is also called as

A. Gypsum block method B. Neutron probe method

C. Gravimetric method D. All

77. (i) Stokes law related with particle size analysis

(ii) Liebig (1851) was the first to suggest the relationship between the radius of the particle and its rate of fall in liquid

(iii) EC of alkali soil is $< 4\ dSm^{-1}$.

A. (ii) and (iii) are correct B. (i) and (ii) are correct

C. (i) and (ii) are correct D. All the statements are correct

78. Soil colloidal particle shows the phenomena of

A. Plasticity B. Adhesion and cohesion

C. Flocculation D. All of the above

79. The central cation on silica tetrahedran is

A. Al^{3+} B. Si^{4+}

C. Fe^{2+} D. None of the above

80. A non expanding type of clay mineral is

A. Chlorite B. Illite

B. Kaolinite D. Montmorillonite

81. Small particles of organic matter and clay particles are known as

A. Micelle B. Illite

C. Chlorite D. Kaolinite

82. Which of the following is 1:1 type clay mineral

A. Vermiculite B. Nacrite

C. Illite D. Saponite

83. The specific surface area of colloidal particle among the following clay particles is the highest for

A. Mica B. Vermiculite

C. Chlorite D. Kaolinite

84. Silaxane bond is

A. 0-Si-0 B. Si-0-Si

C. HO-Si-OH D. Al-0-Al

85. Dickite belongs to which group of minerals?

A. Kaolinite B. Mica

C. Smectite D. Amorphous

86. Mica is a _____ type of clay mineral

A. 1:1 B. 2:1

C. 2:1:1 D. None of the above

87. Hydrogen bond found in which clay minerals

A. Kaolinite B. Montmorillonite

C. Vermiculite D. Beidelite

88. Identify the incorrect statement

A. The specific heat of water is 1.00 cal/g

B. Dry soil heats up quickly than a moist soil

C. Specific heat of dry soil is higher than wet soil

D. Dry soil conduct heat slower than wet soil

89. The basic building blocks of layer silicate clays are

A. Silica tetrahedral and Aluminium pentahedral

B. Silica pentahedral and Alluminium tetrahedral

C. Silica octahedral and Aluminium tetrahedral

D. Silica tetrahedral and Alluminium octahedral

90. Match the following

a. 1:1 type clay mineral — 1. Montmorillonite and vermiculite

b. 2:1 type clay mineral (expanding) — 2. Chlorite

c. 2:1 type (non expanding) — 3. Kaolinite group

d. 2:2 type clay mineral — 4. Muscovite and biolite

	a	b	c	d
A.	3	4	2	1
B.	2	3	4	1
C.	3	1	4	2
D.	4	3	2	1

91. Saturated hydraulic conductivity is measured by

A. Pycnometer B. Tensiometer

C. Amoozemeter D. Hydrometer

92. Flocculation order is appropriate

A. Al > Ca and H > Mg > K > Na

B. Al > Na and H > Mg > K > Ca

C. Al > Ca and K > Mg > H > Na

D. Na > Ca and H > Mg > K > Al

93. Maximum CEC found in

A. Vermiculite B. Humus

C. Montmorillonite D. Kaolinite

94. Beidellite mineral has isomorphous substitution in tetrahedral sheet is an example of ____type clay mineral.

A. 1:1 B. 2:1

C. 2:1:1 D. None of these

95. A soil is considered to be fertile when the base saturation percentage is

A. More than 50 B. More than 60

C. More than 75 D. More than 80

96. Attraction between similar particles is called as

A. Adhesion B. Cohesion

C. Vander wall D. All the above

97. Vermiculite is similar to illite except vermiculite has

A. A higher CEC

B. A lower CEC

C. Not an expansive layer

D. K-bridge between the layers

Answer keys

1	B	21	B	41	C	61	A	81	A
2	C	22	B	42	C	62	B	82	B
3	B	23	B	43	B	63	D	83	B
4	B	24	C	44	A	64	A	84	B
5	C	25	C	45	A	65	B	85	A
6	C	26	C	46	C	66	C	86	B
7	D	27	B	47	A	67	D	87	A
8	C	28	C	48	A	68	A	88	C
9	A	29	B	49	A	69	A	89	D
10	C	30	B	50	C	70	A	90	C
11	B	31	D	51	B	71	A	91	C
12	A	32	C	52	D	72	B	92	A
13	A	33	B	53	C	73	C	93	B
14	B	34	C	54	C	74	B	94	B
15	B	35	C	55	B	75	C	95	D
16	B	36	C	56	A	76	A	96	B
17	A	37	A	57	D	77	C	97	A
18	A	38	A	58	C	78	D		
19	C	39	A	59	B	79	B		
20	C	40	B	60	C	80	D		

5

Problem Soils and their Corrective Measures

I. Choose the correct answer

1. Highly salt tolerant crop

   A. Datepalm B. Mango

   C. Potato D. Bael

2. Recommended rate of lime in fluffy paddy soil is

   A. 1 ton/ha B. 2 ton/ha

   C. 5 ton/ha D. 7.5 ton/ha

3. Which of the following is a correct statement?

   (i) Hard pan soil occurs due to movement of clay and iron hydroxide and settling at shallow depth

   (ii) Surface crusted soil can be prevented by application of lime or gypsum

   (iii) River sand is added to reclaim sandy soil

   A. (i) and (iii) are correct B. (ii) and (iii) are correct

   C. (i) and (ii) are correct D. All the statements are correct

4. (i) Tie ridging refers to adjacent ridges are joined at regular interval by barriers or ties of the same height

   (ii) Saline soil can be reclaimed by adding sulphur

   (iii) Dry farming refers to crop cultivation in regions with annual rainfall less than 750 mm

   A. (i) and (ii) are correct B. (i) and (iii) are correct

   C. (ii) and (iii) are correct D. All the statements are correct

5. Tolerant crops for sodium is

   A. Soybean B. Beans

   C. Rice D. Maize

6. Permissible limit of fluorine in irrigation water is

A. 5.0 ppm B. 1.00 ppm

C. 0.20 ppm D. 0.75 ppm

7. Central Soil Salinity Research Institute was located at

A. Karnal B. Nagpur

C. Ranchi D. Dehradun

8. Sand dunes are commonly seen in

A. Dry areas B. Hilly areas

C. Desert and coastal areas D. Coastal areas only

9. An electrical conductivity of less than one milli mhos per cm indicates that the soil condition for plant growth is

A. Above normal B. Critical

C. Injurious D. Normal

10. Causes of soil salinity

(i) The soluble salts are leached from high lying to low lying areas due to high rainfall.

(ii) Irrigation of soils with saline water.

A. (i) alone is correct B. (ii) alone is correct

C. Both are correct D. Both are not correct

11. Acid soils are characterized by a pH of

A. > 8 B. < 6

C. 8 to 10 D. 7 to 8

12. A common phenomenon in areas with good canal irrigation but poor drainage is

A. Salinisation / alkalisation B. Calcification

C. Laterisation D. Cheluviation

13. Alkali soils are characterized by a pH of

A. > 6 B. 6 to 7

C. > 8 D. 4 to 6

14. Absorption of water by roots in saline soils is affected by

A. Transpiration B. Transportation

C. Osmotic effect D. Shallow depth

15. The crops recommended for the tannery waste affected soils are
    A. Tomato (PKM 1) and brinjal B. Rice (ASD 16) and ragi (CO 12)
    C. Sunflower (CO 4) and mustard D. All the above
16. What should be done to reclaim saline soils?
    A. Lime B. Gypsum
    C. Sulphur D. Potassium
17. Which among the following is a soil stabilizing chemical?
    A. CO_3 B. Na_2
    C. HCO_3 D. $MgCO_3$
18. The ideal green manure crop suitable for reclamation of salt affected soils is
    A. Sunhemp B. Daincha
    C. Pillipesara D. All
19. If the parent material is granite, then soils become
    A. Acidic B. Basic
    C. Neutral D. None
20. If an acid soil is limed to the pH level ________, it enhances nitrification
    A. 3.5-4.5 B. 4.5-5.5
    C. 5.5-6.5 D. 6.5-7.5
21. Which is generally used for correcting soil acidity?
    A. Gypsum B. Lime
    C. Iron pyrites D. Urea
22. Acid sulphate is also known as
    A. Reh B. Thur
    C. Usar D. Cat clays
23. Acid soil is injurious to plants because of presence of
    A. Ca and Mg B. K and boron
    C. Fe and Al D. Mn and sulphur
24. Alkaline soils contain more of
    A. Fe and Al ions B. Cl and SO_4 ions
    C. CO_3 and HCO_3 ions D. H^+ ions

25. (i) Saline soil contains more of chlorides and sulphates of Na, Ca, Mg
(ii) Saline soil is also known as white alkali
(iii) Sodic soil is also known as alkali soil
(iv) Acid soils are rich in H^+ and Al^{3+}
A. (i), (iii) and (iv) are correct B. (ii) and (iv) are correct
C. (ii) and (iii) are correct D. (i), (ii), (iii) and (iv) are correct

26. Gypsum recommendation for alkali soil is
A. 250 kg/ha B. 400 kg/ha
C. 750 kg/ha D. 500 kg/ha

27. Which among the following is not a chemical constraint?
A. Salinity B. Sodicity
C. Acidity D. Permeability

28. Consider the statement and choose the correct one
(i) Saline soil: Application of FYM @ 5 t/ha in paddy field.
(ii) Sodic soil : Gypsum application based on requirement
(iii) Iron and Aluminium toxicity: Application of organic manure
A. (i) and (ii) are correct B. All the statements are correct
C. (ii) and (iii) are correct D. (i) and (ii) are correct

29. Electrical conductivity of saline water should be less than
A. 4.0 dSm^{-1} B. 5.0 dSm^{-1}
C. 6.0 dSm^{-1} D. 7.0 dSm^{-1}

30. Reclamation of sodic soils can be achieved by
(i) Applying gypsum (ii) Green manuring
(iii) Leaching (iv) Ponding
A. (i) (ii) and (iii) are correct B. (ii), (iii) and (iv) are correct
C. (i), (iii) and (iv) are correct D. (i), (ii), (ii) and (iv) are correct

31. Gypsum, an amendment applied to alkali soils belongs to ________type
A. Acid former B. Low solubility
C. Soluble calcium salt D. None of these

32. Match list I with list II and choose the correct options given below

List I	**List II**
a. High salt tolerant	1. Sugarbeet
b. Medium salt tolerant	2. Sesame
c. Low salt tolerant	3. Pearl millet
d. Tolerant crops	4. Barley

	a	b	c	d
A.	2	3	1	4
B.	4	3	2	1
C.	4	3	1	2
D.	1	2	3	4

33. Gypsum can be applied for saline and alkali soil having pH up to
    A. 9
    B. 5
    C. 8
    D. 7
34. Farm yard manure
    A. Balanced food for plants
    B. Recommended for salinity reclamation
    C. Tends to make soil acidic
    D. Tends to make soil alkaline
35. In saline soils, plant growth is adversely affected
    A. Through toxicity of specific ions, e.g. Na, Cl, B, etc.
    B. Through the effect of excess salts on the osmotic pressure of soil solution resulting in reduced availability of water
    C. Through the dispersive effect of excess exchangeable sodium resulting in poor physical properties
    D. Both A and B
36. Excess soil salinity causes
    A. Poor and spotty stands of crops
    B. Uneven and stunted growth
    C. Poor yields
    D. All the above are correct
37. Amelioration of soil acidity can be done by
    A. Amount of lime added to increase the pH
    B. Amount of sodium added to increase the pH
    C. Amount of carbonate added to increase the pH
    D. Amount of sulphate added to increase the pH
38. Which of the following are acid soils?
    A. Laterite
    B. Laterite red
    C. Podosolic brown
    D. All of the above
39. Which of the following is a salt tolerant rice variety grown in water logged coastal regions of Kerala?
    A. Navara
    B. Pokkali
    C. Ponni
    D. Samba

Answer keys

1	A	11	B	21	B	31	C
2	B	12	A	22	D	32	B
3	C	13	C	23	C	33	A
4	D	14	C	24	C	34	B
5	C	15	D	25	D	35	D
6	B	16	C	26	B	36	D
7	A	17	B	27	D	37	A
8	C	18	B	28	B	38	D
9	D	19	A	29	A	39	B
10	C	20	C	30	A		

6

Fertilizers

I. Choose the correct answer

1. Which of the following are the slow release fertilizers?

   A. Surface coated urea B. Neem cake and super grain urea

   C. N-serve D. All of the above

2. Which of the following element is mobile in soil?

   A. Ca B. Mg

   C. K D. N

3. Where is Indian Institute of Soil Science located?

   A. Bhopal B. Dehradun

   C. Karnal D. Hisar

4. What is the average population of mold in 1 sq.m?

   A. 1-10 billion/m^2 B. 10-200 billion/m^2

   C. 8-9 billion/m^2 D. 5-6 billion/m^2

5. Which is the major nitrogen fertilizer used in our country?

   A. DAP B. CAN

   C. Urea D. Anhydrous ammonia

6. What is the percentage of nitrogen present in DAP?

   A. 20% B. 16%

   C. 18% D. 15%

7. What is the percentage of phosphorus present in triple super phosphate?

   A. 26% B. 46%

   C. 36% D. 16%

8. What is the chemical formula for MOP?

   A. K_2SO_4 B. $KMnO_4$

   C. K_2PO_4 D. KCl

9. What is the percentage of potash in sulphate of potash?

A. 18% B. 48%

C. 32% D. 46%

10. What is the chemical formula for urea?

A. $CaCN_2$ B. $[Ca\ (H_2PO_4)_2]$

C. $[CO\ (NH_2)_2]$ D. $CaCO_4$

11. What is the right ratio for the given fertilizer schedule 14-28-14?

A. 1:2:1 B. 2:1:1

C. 2:2:1 D. 1:1:2

12. What is the average sulphate content of magnesium sulphate?

A. 15% B. 17%

C. 13% D. 19%

13. What is the average concentration of molybdenum in plant tissue?

A. 6 ppm B. 1 ppm

C. 0.01 ppm D. 0.1 ppm

14. Match list I with list II and choose the correct options given below

List I	**List II**
a. Magnesium	1. Mirabilite
b. Calcium	2. Magrulite
c. Iron	3. Anorthite
d. Sulphur	4. Hornblende

	a	b	c	d
A.	4	2	3	1
B.	4	3	1	2
C.	3	2	4	1
D.	2	4	3	1

15. Who developed phosphorus extraction method?

A. Waugh and Fitts B. Olsen and Bray

C. Munsell and Fisher D. Buckman and Brandy

16. Ammonical form of N is taken up by

A. Cotton B. Sugarcane

C. Maize D. Rice

17. (i) The nutrient content of CAN is about 26% N
    (ii) The only neutral fertilizer applied to the crops is calcium ammonium nitrate
    (iii) The chemical formula of urea is $CO(NH_2)_2$
    (iv) 80% of fertilizers used in the country are made up of nitrogenous fertilizer particularly urea
    A. (i) (iii) and (iv) are correct B. (ii) and (iv) are correct
    C. (i) (ii) (iii) and (iv) are correct D. (iii) alone is correct
18. Ca and sulphur content in gypsum is about
    A. 20% Ca and 20% S B. 27% Ca and 25% S
    C. 15% Ca and 21% S D. 23% Ca and 18.5% S
19. Urea is a/an ——— of N fertilizers
    A. Ammoniacal form B. Nitrate form
    C. Both A and B D. Amide form
20. (i) VFI is worked out for every revenue village
    (ii) VFI above 5 is considered as high
    (iii) VFI stands for village fertility index
    A. (i) and (ii) are correct B. (i) and (iii) are correct
    C. (ii) and (iii) are correct D. All the statements are correct
21. The N fertilizer use efficiency in rice can be increased by using
    A. S-coated urea B. Urea super granules
    C. BGA D. Both A and B
22. Which of the following elements are considered as energy storers?
    A. Hydrogen, oxygen, sodium and boron
    B. Carbon, nitrogen, phosphorus and sulphur
    C. Potassium, calcium and magnesium
    D. Iron, manganese, molybdenum, copper and zinc
23. Ammonia is transformed in to nitrate by
    A. Algae B. Bacteria
    C. Fungi D. Actinomycetes
24. Agricultural grade gypsum contains
    A. 70% purity B. 90% purity
    C. 30% purity D. 35% purity

25. Biuret content in urea should be less than

A. 2 B. 1.5

C. 10 D. 3

26. In India, potassic fertilizers are manufactured at

A. Tamil Nadu B. Karnataka

C. Andhra Pradesh D. None of the above

27. Fertilizer control order of 1985 implemented by Government of Tamil Nadu ensures

A. Application B. Distribution

C. Quality D. Transport

28. Water soluble phosphatic fertilizer is

A. Rock phosphate B. DAP

C. SSP D. Orthophosphoric acid

29. Match list I correctly with list II

List I	**List II**
a. Calcium	1. Major nutrient
b. Molybdenum	2. Micro element
c. Phosphorus	3. Micronutrient
d. Silicon	4. Secondary nutrient

	a	b	c	d
A.	2	4	1	3
B.	3	4	1	2
C.	4	3	1	2
D.	2	3	1	4

30. Paddy takes nitrogen in the form of

A. NO_2^- B. N_2

C. NH4 D. NO_3^-

31. Integrated nutrient management involves

(i) Biofertilizers (ii) Chemical fertilizers

(iii) Crop residues (iv) Organic manures

A. (i) (ii) and (iv) of the above B. (i) (iii) and (iv) of the above

C. (i) (ii) and (iii) of the above D. (i) (ii) (iii) and (iv) of the above

32. N use efficiency of fertilizers can be enhanced by

A. Coating B. Split application

C. Placement D. All the above

33. Potassium chloride is not suitable for

A. Tomato B. Cassava

C. Sweet potato D. Potato

34. Choose the wrong answers

(i) K_2SO_4 contains 60% K_2O

(ii) Zinc sulphate contains 23% Zn

(iii) Sodium molybdate contains 50% Mo

(iv) Urea ammonium nitrate is a liquid fertilizer

A. (i) and (ii) are correct B. (ii) and (iii) are correct

C. (i) and (iv) are wrong D. (i) and (iii) are wrong

35. Phosphorus uptake in alkali soil is in the form of

A. $H_2PO_4^-$ B. HPO_4^{2-}

C. PO_4^{3-} D. H_3PO_4

36. Which fertilizer produces acidity in soil?

A. Ammonium sulfate B. Sodium nitrate

C. Calcium ammonium nitrate D. Calcium nitrate

37. Maximum N content found in which of the following fertilizers.

A. Urea B. Anhydrous ammonia

C. Sodium nitrate D. Ammonium sulphate

38. Rock phosphate has P_2O_5

A. 10-20% B. 20-40%

C. 30-50 % D. 20-30%

39. The conversion factor for calculating P from P_2O_5

A. P_2O_5 x 2.29 B. P x 0.44

C. P x 2.29 D. P_2O_5 x 0.44

40. Thiourea is type of fertilizer

A. Slow release B. Nitrification inhibitor

C. Natural nitrification inhibitor D. Artificial nitrification inhibitor

41. Chemical formula of thiourea is

A. $CO\ (NH_2)_2$ B. $SC\ (NH_2)_2$

C. HCN D. None of the above

42. N content in thiourea is

A. 46% B. 36.8%

C. 22.5% D. 33%

43. The K_2O content in illite varied between

A. 6 to 10% B. 2 to 4%

C. 10 to 15% D. 33%

44. Reddish colour in muriate of potash is due to

A. KCl B. Colour reagent

C. Impurities D. All of the above

45. Which instrument is used for the estimation of potash?

A. Spectrophotometer B. Flamephotometer

C. Colorimeter D. Atomic absorption

46. Highest P_2O_5 consumption in which crop

A. Wheat B. Groundnut

C. Maize D. Legume

47. The Neubauer seedling method is used to evaluate the soil fertility. The test plant used in this method is

A. Barely seedling B. Wheat seedling

C. Rye or oat seedling D. All of the above

48. The soil layer of maximum leaching is indicated by the symbol

A. A1 B. A2

C. B1 D. B2

49. Which of the following is not a method of placement of fertilizers?

A. Plough sole B. Deep

C. Side D. None of these

50. Which one of the following fertilizers has zero equivalent acidity?

A. Ammonium sulphate B. Ammonium nitrate

C. Anhydrous ammonia D. Calcium ammonium nitrate

51. In Jenny pot culture technique, test crop is

A. Oat B. Lettuce

C. Wheat D. None

52. CAN is also called

A. Nitro chalk B. Nitro lime

C. Lime ammonium nitrate D. All of these

53. KCl manufacturing process is done by

A. Floatation process B. Crystallization

C. Both A and B D. Trona process

54. Phosphogypsum contains impurity like

A. Chlorine B. Fluorine

C. Cadmium D. Calcium

55. Examples for water soluble P fertilizers are

A. SSP B. DSP

C. TSP D. All of these

56. Physiologically acid fertilizers are

A. Urea B. Ammonical fertilizers

C. $CaCN_2$ D. None

57. Aluminum ions contribute to soil acidity through their tendency to

A. Oxidize B. Reduce

C. Hydrolyze D. Solubulize

58. Surface application of urea in alkaline soil is not advisable as

A. NH_4^+ is formed and fixed

B. $(NH_4)_2CO_3$ is formed and volatilized

C. NH_3 is formed and volatilized

D. Ammonia is formed and become toxic to plants

59. Predominance of P mineralization over immobilization is regulated by

A. Organic P in soil

B. Inorganic P in soil

C. C/P ratio of decomposing residue

D. N/P ratio of decomposing residue

60. The value of 'nutrient index' for medium category soil under Indian condition range from

A. 1.25-2.25 B. 1.67-2.33

C. 2.25-3.25 D. None of these

61. Which of the following methods is most useful to increase the availability of soil applied phosphorus?

A. Broadcast
B. Placement
C. Broadcast and soil incorporation
D. None of these

62. Which of the following nutrient elements are regarded as energy exchangers?

A. Hydrogen and oxygen
B. Carbon and nitrogen
C. Potassium and magnesium
D. Iron, manganese and molybdenum

63. Phosphate solubilization from inorganic sources by soil microorganisms is mainly through production of

A. Carbonic acid
B. Volatile fatty acids
C. Organic acids
D. Microbial enzymes

64. _______in 1909 developed an equation that related growth to the supply of plant nutrients

A. V. J. Kilmer
B. R. B.Mckercher
C. J.W. Friedrich
D. E. A.Mitscherlich

65. The sufficiency range of iron is normally between _____ppm

A. 10-40
B. 50-250
C. 300-400
D. None of these

66. Permissible biuret level in most of urea fertilizers is_____%

A. 5
B. 4
C. 2
D. 3

67. The essentiality of copper for higher plants was first recognized in

A. 1911
B. 1921
C. 1931
D. 1941

68. First manufactured fertilizer in India is

A. DAP
B. Urea
C. SSP
D. $CaCN_2$

69. The following fertilizer which is physiologically neutral

A. CAN
B. Ammonium nitrate
C. Ammonium sulphate
D. Urea

70. For conversion of P to P_2O_5 it should be multiplied % P with

A. 2.29
B. 3.29
C. 1.29
D. 0.09

71. Formula for salt peter

A. $NaNO_3$
B. KNO_3
C. $CaCO_3$
D. None

72. If the deficiency symptoms occur on younger leaves, then the elements is called as

A. Mobile elements
B. Immobile element
C. Partly mobile elements
D. None

73. Nitrapyrin is also called as

A. N-Serve
B. AM
C. ST
D. KN_3

74. Nitrogen percentage in sulphur coated urea is

A. 36-38
B. 30-35
C. 55-60
D. 20-30

75. The anaerobic breakdown of protein rich material is known as

A. Putrefaction
B. Aminization
C. Denitrification
D. Ammonification

76. Lime potential is given by

A. Aslynge and Schofield
B. Milne
C. Stevenson
D. Larsen

77. Bone meal is well suitable for

A. Acid soils
B. Neutral soils
C. Alkaline soils
D. All soils

78. High specificity of potassium occurs at

A. Planar position
B. Interlayer position
C. Edges position
D. All the above

79. Calcicoles are

A. Ca loving plants
B. Ca hating plants
C. Ca transfer plants
D. All the above

80. Luxury consumption is more in

A. Forage crops
B. Forest trees
C. Coniferous trees
D. None

81. Critical nutrient concept is given by

A. Chapman and Gay B. Cate and Nelson

C. Ramamoorthy D. Troug

82. The value which is used for calculating phosphorus supply of soil is

A. A-value B. E-value

C. L-value or Y-value D. None of these

83. Major raw material for ammonia in India

A. Natural gas B. Naphtha

C. Both A and B D. None of these

84. Law of maximum was proposed by

A. Wallace and Wallace B. Kohnke

C. Philip D. Baul

85. The size of prilled urea is

A. 2-4mm B. 5-10mm

C. 15-20mm D.25-30mm

86. Most sulphur loving crop is

A. Mustard B. Rice

C. Wheat D. None of the above

87. Which of the following is the best nitrogenous fertilizer as far as physical condition is concerned?

A. Ammonium chloride B. Ammonium sulphate

C. Ammonium nitrate D. Anhydrous ammonia

88. Basic slag enriched with rock phosphate is marketed as

A. Pelophos B. TSP

C. Both A and B D. None of these

89. Nutrient that is mobile in plant and immobile in soil is

A. N B. P

C. K D. S

90. Diffusion is measured by following technique

A. Half-cell technique B. Neutron scattering

C. TDR method D. None of these

91. Nutrient mobility concept was given by

A. Mitscherlich B. Bray

C. Whitney D. Marshall

92. Burnt lime (or) quick lime formula is

A. CaO B. Ca $(OH)_2$

C. $CaCO_3$ D. None of these

93. What is the optimum pH for availability of most of the nutrients?

A. 5.0-6.0 B. 6.0-7.0

C. 6.5-7.5 D. >8.0

94. The movement of nutrients, ions by mass flow is reduced at low temperatures because of

A. Low respiration B. Low photosynthesis

C. Low transpiration D. None of these

95. The concentrations of ____ SO_4^{2-} ion in the soil or solution cultures have proved adequate for the growth of many plant species

A. 1-2 ppm B. 3-5 ppm

C. 6-8 ppm D. 9-11 ppm

96. The maximum phosphorus availability in most of the soils is in the pH range of

A. 4.0-4.5 B. 5.0-5.5

C. 6.0-6.5 D. 7.0-7.5

97. The highest percentage content of nitrogen among the commonly used nitrogenous fertilizers is embodied by

A. Urea B. Urea sulphate

C. Ammonium nitrate D. Anhydrous ammonia

98. The losses of ammonia usually become greater with

A. Increase in soil pH B. Decrease in soil pH

C. Decrease in calcium D. Decrease in temperature

99. What is the salt index of ammonium sulphate?

A. 1.61 B. 2.99

C. 6.83 D. 3.25

100. Fertilizer quality control organization is located in

A. Faridabad B. Delhi

C. Mumbai D. Chennai

101. Triacid method of plant sample is not used for the estimation of

A. N, P and K B. P and K

C. S only D. N and S

102. Single super phosphate is best suitable for
    A. Neutral and alkaline soils   B. Neutral and acid soils
    C. Acid and alkaline soils   D. Neutral soils only
103. The method used to measure a nutrient concentration in soil at equilibrium with the same in soil solution is
    A. E - value   B. A- value
    C. L - value   D. All
104. First permanent manurial experiment in India was started at
    A. Coimbatore   B. Kanpur
    C. Pusa (Bihar)   D. None of these
105. Which nutrient is called traffic police man ?
    A. B   B. K
    C. P   D. Ca
106. Readily available form of K in soil ranges from?
    A. 0.1-0.2%   B. 1-10%
    C. 30-40%   D. 90-98%
107. Water is the sole nutrient of plants and is given by?
    A. Glauber   B. Liebig
    C. Lawes and gilbert   D. Van Helmont
108. The critical nutrient concentration for N is?
    A. 3 %   B. 0.3%
    C. 2 %   D. 0.2 %
109. The P content in poultry manure
    A. 3 %   B. 2.5%
    C. 2 %   D. 1.5 %
110. Urea was first isolated by?
    A. Wohler   B. Rouelle
    C. Haber   D. Bosch
111. Which fertilizer is called kisan khad ?
    A. MAP   B. DAP
    C. CAN   D. MOP
112. Which among the following has high amount of P?
    A. Meat meal   B. Guano
    C. Raw bone meal   D. Streamed bone meal

113. The mineral element that is immobile in soil and mobile in plants is
   A. Potassium B. Phosphorus
   C. Calcium D. Boron
114. Molybdenum is adsorbed strongly by
   A. Calcium and magnesium oxides B. Iron and aluminium oxides
   C. Carbon compounds D. Calcium carbonate
115. Contaminant in phosphatic fertilizers is
   A. Fluoride B. Chloride
   C. Bromide D. Iodide
116. Which fertilizer is not manufactured in India?
   A. DAP B. Nitro phosphate
   C. Murate of potash D. CAN
117. Sugarbeet is an indicator of
   A. Mo B. Na
   C. Bo D. P
118. Fortified fertilizer is
   A. Zincated urea B. DAP
   C. MOP D. None of these
119. What is the P_2O_5 content of various rock phosphates?
   A. 20 - 35% B. 35%
   C. 11 - 20% D. 18 - 20%
120. Availability of phosphorus at the pH is
   A. 6-7 B. 5-6
   C. 8-9 D. 3-4
121. Which acid is used in the production of fertilizers?
   A. Nitric acid B. Hydrochloric acid
   C. Sulphuric acid D. Carbonic acid
122. Coating urea with which of the following has been found to increase the yield of crops?
   A. Lime B. Ash
   C. Neem oil D. Eucalyptus oil
123. Which one of the following is not a nitrogenous fertilizer?
   A. KCl B. $CaCN_2$
   C. NH_4NO_3 D. Urea

124. Efficiency of applied fertilizers in rice crop is

A. 5-50% B. 10-75%

C. 50-75% D. 60-90%

125. Efficiency of applied fertilizers in wheat crop is

A. 20-50% B. 35-50%

C. 60-80% D. 44-64%

126. Single super phosphate (SSP) was first manufactured by

A. Lawes J.B. B. Stuart John

C. Frank A.B. D. All of the above

127. Value of nutrient index (NI) less than 1.5 is called

A. Low B. Medium

C. High D. None of these

128. Solubility of $CaCO_3$ is

A. 4.0% B. 0.04%

C. 0.4% D. 40%

129. Which of the following essential elements is chiefly taken up by plant roots through diffusion in soil

A. Nitrogen B. Phosphorus

C. Sulphur D. Copper

130. Interaction of phosphorus and nitrogen is generally

A. Positive B. Negative

C. Additive D. None of these

131. The mineral which resembles some properties to one mineral and some to other mineral is termed as

A. Interstratified B. Intergrade

C. Intermicellar D. None of these

132. Which of the following methods is most useful to increase the availability of soil applied phosphorus?

A. Broadcast B. Placement

C. Broadcast and soil incorporation D. None of these

133. Nitrogen fertilizer which supplies approximately 46% nitrogen is

A. Aqueous ammonia B. Ammonium phosphate

C. Ammonium sulphate D. Urea

Answer keys

1	D	21	D	41	B	61	B	81	B	101	D	121	A
2	D	22	B	42	B	62	A	82	C	102	A	122	C
3	A	23	B	43	A	63	C	83	B	103	A	123	A
4	B	24	A	44	C	64	D	84	A	104	B	124	B
5	C	25	B	45	B	65	B	85	A	105	B	125	D
6	C	26	D	46	B	66	C	86	A	106	A	126	A
7	B	27	C	47	C	67	C	87	B	107	D	127	A
8	D	28	D	48	B	68	C	88	A	108	A	128	C
9	B	29	C	49	D	69	A	89	B	109	B	129	B
10	C	30	C	50	D	70	A	90	A	110	B	130	A
11	A	31	D	51	B	71	B	91	A	111	C	131	B
12	B	32	D	52	D	72	B	92	A	112	D	132	B
13	D	33	D	53	C	73	A	93	C	113	B	133	D
14	B	34		54	B	74	A	94	C	114	B		
15	A	35	C	55	D	75	A	95	B	115	A		
16	D	36	A	56	B	76	A	96	C	116	C		
17	C	37	B	57	C	77	A	97	D	117	B		
18	D	38	B	58	C	78	B	98	A	118	A		
19	D	39	D	59	C	79	A	99	D	119	A		
20	B	40	D	60	B	80	A	100	A	120	A		

7

Nutrient Deficiencies and their Corrective Measures

I. Choose the correct answer

1. When emerging leaves of maize show yellow to white bleached bands in lower parts, it shows the deficiency of

   A. Zinc   B. Iron

   C. Copper   D. Boron

2. The essential element which is an essential component of the enzyme nitrogenase, involved in N-fixation and present in very low concentration in plant is

   A. Boron   B. Molybdenum

   C. Zinc   D. Copper

3. In normal Indian soils, available boron content ranges from

   A. 0.1 to 6.0 ppm   B. 10 to 60 ppm

   C. 0.01 to 0.06 ppm   D. None of these

4. Weeping disease in cotton is caused by

   A. Mo deficiency   B. B deficiency

   C. Cl deficiency   D. Co deficiency

5. Low concentration of ______ is beneficial for the growth of microorganisms

   A. Sodium   B. Nickel

   C. Copper   D. Vanadium

6. Marsh spot in peas is caused by deficiency of

   A. Zn   B. Mn

   C. S   D. N

7. In which form, the inorganic nutrients are present in the soil

   A. Macronutrients   B. Parasites

   C. Atom   D. Electrically charged ion

8. The value above ______ ppm is associated with boron toxicity

A. 150 B. 200

C. 250 D. 300

9. When a nutrient takes active part in growth and development of plant, it is called as

A. Beneficial B. Essential

C. Required D. None of above

10. Critical limit approach is generally more suited for

A. Secondary nutrients B. Primary nutrients

C. Micronutrients D. Labile nutrients

11. Hidden hunger means

A. Deficiency symptoms are seen when the nutrient is deficient

B. Severe yield reduction may occur without appearance of deficiency symptoms

C. The nutrient is not deficient, but apparently seems to be deficient

D. Visual deficiency symptoms are suppressed by other elements

12. Which of the following nutrient effects in plant being colourless length of unfolded leaves at the top leaving gelatinous material

A. Mg B. Zn

C. Ca D. Mn

13. The availability of this micronutrient is more in alkaline condition

A. Iron B. Zinc

C. Molybdenum D. Copper

14. Impeded drainage increases the toxicity of Mo because of

A. Increased Mo in plant B. Increased solubility

C. No change D. None of these

15. Match the following

a. Marsh spot in peas 1. B

b. White bud in cotton 2. Cu

c. Fruit cracking in guava 3. Zn

d. Blackened plumule in groundnut 4. Mn

	a	b	c	d
A.	3	2	4	1
B.	1	2	3	4
C.	4	3	1	2
D.	4	3	2	1

16. In which crop, 25 kg of $ZnSO_4$ is applied through soil to correct zinc deficiency?

A. Rice B. Sorghum

C. Maize D. Pearl millet

17. To correct boron deficiency in groundnut, what is your recommendation?

A. Soil application of 5 kg borax + 200 kg gypsum/ha

B. Soil application of 10 kg borax + 200 kg gypsum/ha

C. Soil application of 5 kg borax + 250 kg gypsum/ha

D. Soil application of 10 kg borax + 250 kg gypsum/ha

18. Integrated nutrient management includes

(i) Cultural practices of soil (ii) Use of microbial inoculants

(iii) Use of organic sources (iv) Use of mineral fertilizers

A. (ii), (iii) and (iv) are correct B. (ii) and (iii) are correct

C. (i), (ii) and (iii) are correct D. All are correct

19. What is the deficiency symptom for calcium?

A. Crinkling B. Mottling

C. Dieback D. Stunted growth

20. What is the deficiency symptom for magnesium?

A. Puckering B. Yellowing

C. Browning D. Greening

21. Among the following, which is not a micronutrient

A. Copper B. Zinc

C. Magnesium D. Boron

22. What is the deficiency symptom of zinc?

A. Reddening B. Chlorosis

C. Brown heart D. Rosette and little leaf

23. Micronutrient involved in pollen production, fertility and fruit formation is

A. Chlorine B. Boron

C. Magnesium D. Potassium

24. Puckering in brassica is due to deficiency of

A. Manganese B. Magnesium

C. Calcium D. Sulphur

25. Match the following

a. Cotton reddening	1. Zinc
b. Pahala blight of sugarcane	2. Copper
c. White bud in maize	3. Magnesium
d. Cracking of guava	4. Molybdenum
e. Black heart of apple	5. Manganese
f. Whiptail of cauliflower	6. Boron

	a	b	c	d	e	f
A.	6	5	4	3	2	1
B.	2	1	4	3	6	5
C.	3	5	1	2	6	4
D.	4	3	5	1	2	6

26. Khaira disease in rice is corrected by foliar spray of

A. 2% $MnSO_4$ B. 0.2% $CuSO_4$

C. 0.5% $ZnSO_4$ D. 0.2% Borax

27. (i) The term functional nutrients is coined by D.J.Nicholas

(ii) Example of regulator and carriers are K, Ca, and Mg

(iii) Number of essential elements is 16

(iv) Number of essential elements is 17

A. (ii) and (iv) are correct B. (i) (ii) and (iii) are correct

C. All the statements are correct D. (i) and (ii) are correct

28. Match the following

a. Phosphorus	1. Brown *et. al*
b. Molybdenum	2. Arnor and Stout
c. Nickel	3. Priestly
d. Carbon	4. Von Liebig

	a	b	c	d
A.	3	2	4	1
B.	4	2	1	3
C.	3	4	2	1
D.	2	1	4	3

29. Whiptail is a malady associated with the nutrient

A. Molybdenum B. Manganese

C. Zinc D. Copper

30. Shortening in bhendi is due to the deficiency of

A. Fe B. B
C. N D. P

31. Who proposed the term functional or metabolic nutrient in plant nutrition?

A. D.J. Nicholas B. Arnon
C. Stout D. Arnon and Stout

32. Lattice hole theory of potassium fixation was proposed by

A. F.E. Bear B. M.L. Jackson
C. Page and Baver D. McLean

33. Two elements which are associated with biological nitrogen fixation are

A. Fe and Mo B. Mo and Co
C. Mo and B D. Co and Zn

34. White tip is related to deficiency of following element

A. B B. Cu
C. Mo D. Fe

35. Sickle leaf development is due to the deficiency of

A. Ca B. Mg
C. K D. P

36. The rice variety which serves as an indicator for manganese deficiency

A. IR 8 B. IR 7
C. IR 6 D. IR 4

37. The family which needs less boron is

A. Cruciferae B. Fabaceae
C. Malvaceae D. Graminae

38. 1.6 to 2.3 value of nutrient index indicates

A. Average fertility of soil B. Adequate fertility of soil
C. Both of the above D. None of the above

39. Element essential for the deflocculation of soil particles is

A. Potassium B. Calcium
C. Magnesium D. Sodium

40. Little leaf symptom in citrus is called as

A. Frenching B. Drenching
C. Hen and chicken D. All the above

41. Fe deficiency mostly occurs in
    A. Calcareous soils B. Alluvial soils
    C. Red soils D. Black soils
42. Example (s) for chloride sensitive crops is/are
    A. Citrus B. Peaches
    C. Grapes D. All
43. Effective method of iron application is/are
    A. Spraying B. Soil application
    C. Dipping D. Both A and B
44. First Zn deficiency in India was reported by
    A. Hegdey B. Arnon and stout
    C. Nicholas D. Y. L. Nene
45. Which micronutrient causes lime induced chlorosis?
    A. Mn B. Cu
    C. Fe D. Zn
46. Flow of nitrogen in soil is mainly due to
    A. Mass flow B. Diffusion
    C. Interception D. None of the above
47. Micronutrient flow is mainly a _____ process in soil
    A. Mass flow B. Diffusion
    C. Interception D. None of the above
48. The Fe-protein fraction of nitrogenase is also termed as
    A. Fe-nitrogenase B. Dinitrogenase
    C. Dintrogen oxide D. Dintrogen reductase
49. What is the symptom of molybdenum deficiency in crucifers?
    A. Black rot B. Whip tail
    C. Blossom end rot D. Marsh spot
50. What is the symptom of boron deficiency?
    A. Blossom end rot B. Hollow heart
    C. Darkened plumule D. Blotching
51. Which of the following essential elements acts as catalyst and activates the enzymes, regulates osmotic pressure and flow of plant sap and provides strength to straw
    A. Nitrogen B. Phosphorus
    C. Potassium D. Sulphur

52. The nutrient element which is an integral part of proteins and chlorophyll in plants and whose deficiency first appears on older leaves is

A. Nitrogen B. Phosphorus

C. Magnesium D. Sulphur

53. Which of the following is not a macronutrient?

A. N B. Cu^{++}

C. K D. P^{++}

54. Which element forms part of structure of the chlorophyll molecule?

A. Cu B. Mg

C. Zn D. Co

55. Which of the following is not a trace element

A. Cu B. P

C. Mn D. Zn

56. Which of the following is a micronutrient

A. Mg B. K

C. Ca D. Mn

57. Which of the following element is a component of the middle lamella in plant cells?

A. Chlorine B. Calcium

C. Manganese D. Iron

58. Which one of the following elements in not needed by plant for the normal healthy growth

A. Magnesium B. Mercury

C. Iron D. Calcium

59. Major function of phosphorus is in the formation of

A. Cell membranes B. Cell wall

C. Enzymes D. Carbohydrates

60. Minerals are absorbed by the plants through

A. Pressure flow B. Diffusion

C. Active transport D. Osmosis

61. Magnesium is required for

A. DNA replication B. RNA synthesis

C. Stomatal movements D. Synthesis of chlorophyll

62. Potassium is employed in
   A. Chlorophyll synthesis
   B. Protein synthesis
   C. Cementing synthesis
   D. Opening and closing stomata
63. Calcium is a component of
   A. Middle lamella
   B. Primary walls
   C. Secondary walls
   D. Chlorophyll
64. Both nitrogen and sulphur are required by plants for
   A. Chlorophyll synthesis
   B. Enzymes
   C. Cell wall
   D. Stomata movements
65. Chlorosis results from deficiency of
   A. Chlorine
   B. Sodium
   C. Calcium
   D. Magnesium
66. Micronutrients mainly function as
   A. Osmotic constituents of cell sap
   B. Components of important biochemical reactions
   C. Cofactors of enzymes
   D. Constituents of chlorophyll
67. Critical elements are
   A. Na, K and Ca
   B. N, P and Mg
   C. N, P and K
   D. Mn, B and Mo
68. Macronutrients are elements that
   A. Play major role in plant nutrition
   B. Are required in large quantities in plants
   C. Form large molecules in plants
   D. None of the above
69. Micronutrients/trace elements are those that
   A. Can be removed from the plant without any effect on it
   B. Play a minor role in plant nutrition
   C. Form very small molecules in plants
   D. Are present/required in high quantities in plants
70. In plant mineral nutrition, elements are called macro or micro-elements depending upon their
   A. Relative presence in plant ash
   B. Relative importance in plant growth
   C. Relative amount required in plants
   D. Relative availability in soil

71. Minerals are absorbed in the form of

A. Molecules B. Ions

C. Compounds D. Mixtures

72. Tracer elements are those that are

A. Required in small amount by the plant

B. Radioactive and can be used to investigate a process in the plant

C. First to be traced in the plant

D. Present in traces in the soil solution

73. The absorption of minerals due to difference in the electropotential gradient without use of energy is

A. Active absorption B. Passive absorption

C. Osmotic absorption D. None of the above

74. Passive absorption of mineral salts is not dependent on

A. Diffusion B. Osmosis

C. Donnan equilibrium D. Ionic exchange

75. Active absorption of minerals salts makes use of

A. Ionic exchange B. Carriers

C. Phosphorylation of elements D. None of the above

76. Which of the following does not operate in the carrier concept of active absorption of minerals

A. Electron transport B. Contractile protein

C. Protein lecithin D. Ascending water stream

77. Absorbed minerals are transported to other parts of the plants by

A. Diffusion B. Imbibition

C. Ion exchange D. Water stream

78. A primary deficiency is caused by insufficient by absorption of

A. Magnesium B. Manganese

C. Calcium D. Potassium

79. Downward passage of mineral from upper soil layers to lower soil strata is called

A. Percolation B. Leaching

C. Weathering D. Runaway

80. Soil nitrate is more likely to leach than ammonium due to its
    A. Small size B. Negative charged
    C. Being useless D. Abundance
81. The largest reservoir of nitrogen is
    A. Rocks B. Sea
    C. Air D. Soil
82. The enzymes required for nitrogen fixation is
    A. Nitrogen deaminase B. Nitrodioxidase
    C. Amino acid decarboxylase D. Nitrogenase
83. Hydroponics is growing plants in
    A. Laboratory B. Phytotron
    C. Liquid culture medium D. Solid culture medium
84. Aeroponics is growing plants in
    A. Air B. Satellites
    C. Other planets and space D. Stands with liquid spray of their roots
85. Nodule formation of legume roots is reduced during deficiency of
    A. Sulphur B. Boron
    C. Nitrogen D. Both A and B
86. Little leaf/leaf rosetting is deficiency symptom of
    A. Zn B. Mn
    C. Fe D. B
87. Internal cork of apple/browning of cauliflower is deficiency symptom of
    A. Mo B. B
    C. Cu D. Zn
88. Common free ion in the cell is
    A. Iron B. Potassium
    C. Sulphate D. Phosphate
89. Which of the following are the most abundant elements in the living cells
    A. C, H, S and P B. C, O, N and P
    C. C, H, O and N D. C, H, Mg and Ca
90. A fertilizer has a formula of three figures 15-9-9. They stand for percentage of
    A. N, Ca and Mg B. Mg, P and K
    C. Ca, N and Fe D. N, P and K

91. The raw material most used by the plants is

A. O_2 B. CO_2

C. N_2 D. K

92. Mineral salts which are absorbed by the roots from the soil are in the form of

A. Very dilute solution B. Dilute solution

C. Concentrated solution D. Very concentrated solution

93. Minerals absorbed by roots move to the leaf through

A. Xylem B. Phloem

C. Sieve tubes D. None of the above

94. Plants absorb mineral salts from the soil solution through

A. Semi permeable membrane into the cytoplasm

B. Perforation at the apex of root-hairs only

C. The cell wall which is semipermeable

D. None of the above

95. Which of the following is secondary nutrient?

A. Ca B. Mo

C. Mn D. Zn

96. Which of following is not an essential micronutrient?

A. Boron B. Vandadium

C. Manganese D. Molybdenum

97. Which of the following elements is not required by plant for their healthy normal growth?

A. Calcium B. Magnesium

C. Lead D. Iron

98. Which one of the following essential elements can land plants normally obtained directly from the air?

A. Hydrogen B. Carbon

C. Nitrogen D. Phosphorus

99. Which of the following elements is necessary for translocation of sugars in plants?

A. Iron B. Molybdenum

C. Manganese D. Boron

100. Which of the following is present in the core of chlorophyll molecule?

A. Fe B. Mg

C. K D. Mn

101. Which is not an essential element for plants?

A. Iron B. Potassium

C. Zinc D. Sodium

102. Which one is an inorganic nutrient?

A. Cellulose B. Vitamin

C. Calcium D. Protein

103. Chlorosis in plants occur due to

A. High sunlight intensity

B. Low sunlight intensity

C. Absorption of yellow pigments from the soil

D. Deficiency of Mg and Fe in the soil

104. Most of the plants obtain nitrogen from the soil in the form of

A. Free nitrogen gas B. Nitric acid

C. Nitrites D. Nitrates

105. Nutrients that are required by plants in smaller quantities are considered as

A. Micronutrients B. Macronutrients

C. Mega nutrients D. Chemical nutrients

106. If macronutrients and micronutrients are not available to plants, then the plants

A. Show abnormalities B. Rapid growth of stems

C. Do not grow D. Both A and C

107. Micronutrients include all except

A. Molybdenum B. Chlorine

C. Carbon D. Zinc

108. Nutrients that are required by plants in large quantities are considered as

A. Mega nutrients B. Chemical nutrients

C. Micronutrients D. Macronutrients

109. Micronutrient which is important in transport of sugar, synthesis of enzymes and cell division is

A. Phosphorus B. Boron

C. Potassium D. Sulphur

110. The following micronutrient required for plant growth is

A. Nitrogen
B. Potassium
C. Sulphur
D. Manganese

111. Match the following

a. Nitrogen	1. Energy producer
b. Phosphorus	2. Disease resistance
c. Potassium	3. Plant growth
d. Magnesium	4. Chlorophyll constituent

	a	b	c	d
A.	2	1	4	3
B.	4	3	2	1
C.	3	1	2	4
D.	2	3	1	4

112. Example of mobile nutrient is

A. P
B. K
C. Fe
D. N

113. Which of the following nutrients is required for synthesis of cystine and methionine?

A. Nitrogen
B. Sulphur
C. Phosphorus
D. Manganese (Mn)

114. Magnesium is a constituent of

A. Xanthophyll
B. Anthocyanin
C. Chlorophyll
D. Cytokinin

115. Which nutrient plays a activist and catalytic role in photosynthesis in plants?

A. Magnesium
B. Calcium
C. Molybdenum
D. Manganese

116. Which nutrient helps in the formation of chlorophyll?

A. Calcium
B. Magnesium
C. Molybdenum
D. Manganese

117. Which of the following is a micronutrient?

A. N
B. Ca
C. S
D. Mn

Answer keys

1	A	21	C	41	A	61	D	81	C	101	D
2	B	22	D	42	D	62	A	82	D	102	C
3	A	23	B	43	A	63	A	83	C	103	D
4	B	24	B	44	D	64	B	84	D	104	D
5	D	25	C	45	C	65	D	85	D	105	A
6	B	26	C	46	A	66	C	86	A	106	D
7	D	27	A	47	B	67	C	87	B	107	C
8	C	28	B	48	D	68	B	88	B	108	D
9	B	29	A	49	B	69	B	89	C	109	B
10	C	30	B	50	C	70	C	90	D	110	D
11	B	31	A	51	C	71	B	91	B	111	C
12	C	32	C	52	A	72	B	92	A	112	D
13	C	33	B	53	B	73	B	93	A	113	B
14	B	34	B	54	B	74	B	94	A	114	C
15	D	35	D	55	B	75	B	95	A	115	A
16	A	36	A	56	D	76	D	96	B	116	B
17	B	37	D	57	B	77	D	97	C	117	D
18	D	38	A	58	B	78	D	98	B		
19	C	39	D	59	A	79	B	99	D		
20	A	40	A	60	C	80	B	100	B		

8

Soil Fertility and Evaluation

I. Choose the correct answer

1. NBSS and LUP stands for

   A. National Bureau of Soil Survey and Land Use Planning

   B. National Bureau of Soil Science and Land Use Planning

   C. National Bureau of Soil Survey and Land Use Project

   D. National Bureau of Soil Survey and Land Use Programme

2. NBSS and LUP of ICAR has divided India into _____ agroecological zones using FAO.

   A. 15　　B. 20

   C. 21　　D. 7

3. NDVI equal to

   A. IR-R　　B. IR/R

   C. (IR-R)/ (IR+R)　　D. All of the above

4. All India Soil Survey and land Use Organization was established in the year

   A. 1952　　B. 1956

   C. 1947　　D. 1945

5. The survey which is used for watershed and village development is

   A. Detailed　　B. Reconnaissance

   C. Detailed reconnaissance　　D. Semidetailed

6. Scale used in semi detailed study is

   A. 1:100,000　　B. 1:250,000

   C. 1:50,000　　D. None

7. Frequency of observation for detailed survey is

   A. 1 in 10,000 ha　　B. 1 in 625 ha

   C. 1 in 100 ha　　D. 1 in 25 ha

8. In rapid reconnaissance (for more intensive study) survey distance between field observations is

A. 10 km B. 2.5 km

C. 500m D. 100m

9. The first soil map of India was developed in 1932 by

A. Dokuchaev B. Dhruvanarayana

C. Rambabu D. Scholaskaya

10. The systematic examination, description, classification and mapping of soil of an area is known as

A. Soil survey B. Soil mapping

C. Soil classification D. All of the above

11. Mitscherlich proposed the growth curve in the year

A. 1809 B. 1909

B. 1709 D. 1609

12. Soil fertility is the highest in

A. Thanjavur B. Dharmapuri

C. Namakkal D. Pudukottai

13. Match the following

a. J.B.Boussingault 1. Essentiality of nutrients

b. Justus Von Liebig 2. Father of field experiments

c. J.B.Lawes and J.H.Gilbert 3. Father of agricultural chemistry

d. Arnon and Stout 4. Permanent manurial experiment

	a	b	c	d
A.	3	4	1	2
B.	2	1	4	3
C.	4	3	1	2
D.	2	3	4	1

14. The scales recommended for detailed survey are

A. 1:10000 or 1:25000 B. 1:100000 or 1:250000

C. 1:50000 or 1:75000 D. 1:75000 or 1:100000

15. Who is considered as father of field experiments?

A. Jan Baptist B. Francis Bacon

C. J. B.Boussingault D. Robert Boyle

Answer keys

1	A	11	B
2	B	12	A
3	C	13	D
4	B	14	A
5	A	15	C
6	C		
7	D		
8	A		
9	D		
10	A		

9

Soil Organic Matter and its Decomposition

I. Choose the correct answer

1. Soils containing more than __________ % of organic matter are classified as peats.

   A. 20 B. 30

   C. 40 D. 50

2. In general, soil is composed of ________ % organic matter.

   A. 5% B. 25%

   C. 45% D. 50%

3. Which of the following soil is very rich in organic matter?

   A. Desert soil B. Peaty and organic soil

   C. Laterite soil D. Red soil

4. Organic matter contains about _________ % organic carbon

   A. 32 B. 18

   C. 68 D. 58

5. The C:N ratio in the organic matter of the furrow slice (upper 15cm) of arable soils commonly ranges from

   A. 3:1 to 4:1 B. 6:1 to 7:1

   C. 18:1 to 19:1 D. 8:1 to 15:1

6. There is a net increase in the mineralization of organic nitrogen in soil when

   A. C: N = 20 - 30:1 B. C: N = < 20:1

   C. C: N = 30:1 D. Nitrogen is taken up by the crops

7. The process of converting organic form of nitrogen into inorganic form of nitrogen is known as

   A. Denitrification B. Mineralization

   C. Nitrification D. Ammonification

8. The process of converting organic nitrogenous compounds into ammonia is

A. Nitrification B. Ammonification

C. Mineralization D. Oxidation

9. The conversion of inorganic C by the soil organism into organic forms is called

A. Immobilization B. Reduction

C. Decomposition D. Aminization

10. Sequence of nitrogen cycle is

A. $N_2 \rightarrow NH_4^+ \rightarrow NO_3 \rightarrow N_2 + H_2O$

B. $NH_4^+ \rightarrow N_2 \rightarrow NO_3 \rightarrow N_2 + H_2O$

C. $NO_3 \rightarrow NH_4^+ \rightarrow N_2 + H_2O$

D. $NO_2 \rightarrow NO_3 \rightarrow N_2 \rightarrow NH_4^+ \rightarrow N_2 + H_2O$

11. Example of very slowly decomposing raw organic matter is

A. Sugar B. Cellulose

C. Fat and waxes D. Proteins

12. CEC of humus is about

A. 200-400 C mol (P^+)/kg B. 7-10 C mol (P^+)/kg

B. 5-15 C mol (P^+)/kg D. 25-30 C mol (P^+)/kg

13. Match the following

a. Nitrification 1. *Pseudomonas*

b. Denitrification 2. *Clostridium*

c. Sulphur oxidizing bacteria 3. *Nitrobacter*

d. Ammonifying bacteria 4. *Desulfovibrio*

	a	b	c	d
A.	3	1	4	2
B.	4	3	2	1
C.	2	1	4	3
D.	4	2	1	3

14. Which organic fraction is not soluble in both acid and alkali

A. Fulvic B. Humic

C. Humin D. All of the above

15. Immobilization of sulphur occurs in soil when C: S ratio is

A. <300:1 B. >300:1

C. >400:1 D. >200:1

16. Denitrification is a process of

A. Oxidation B. Reduction

C. Hydration D. Carbonation

17. Microorganism involve in conversion from nitrite to nitrate is

A. *Nitrosomonas* B. *Nitrobacter*

C. *Pseudomonas* D. *Bacillus*

18. Denitrification mostly takes place in

A. Aerobic B. Anaerobic

C. Both D. None of the above

19. For mineralization of P, optimum ratio of C: N: P should be

A. 100:10:1 B. 50:10:1

C. 80:10:1 D. 30:10:1

20. The organic matter of soils is ordinarily obtained by multiplying the organic carbon content by

A. 1.52 B. 1.62

C. 1.72 D. 1.82

21. Conversion of inorganic form to organic forms of nutrient in soil is called as

A. Mineralization B. Immobilization

C. Nutrient fixation D. Nutrient cycle

22. The best example for organic colloid is

A. Humus B. Kaolinite

C. Montmorillonite D. Vermiculite

23. Cellulose content in humus is

A. 5% B. 4%

C. 8% D. 9%

24. The humus fraction soluble in both acid and alkali is

A. Fulvic acid B. Humic acid

C. Humin D. All

25. Under anaerobic or submerged condition nitrogen mineralization stops at
    A. NO_2^- B. NH_4^+
    C. NO_3^- D. N_2
26. Humic acid precipitates at the pH of
    A. 5.0 B. 4.0
    C. 4.8 D. 3.5
27. The humus fraction soluble in alkaline medium and insoluble in acid medium is
    A. Fulvic acid B. Humic acid
    C. Humin D. All
28. Well decomposed organic matter which is mixed deeply into soil is called as
    A. Mor humus B. Moder humus
    C. Mull humus D. All
29. The average composition of humus is
    A. Carbon 30%, oxygen 30%, nitrogen 20%, hydrogen 10%, ash 10%
    B. Carbon 50%, oxygen 35%, nitrogen 5%, hydrogen 5%, ash 5%
    C. Carbon 40%, oxygen 30%, nitrogen 20%, hydrogen 5%, ash 5%
    D. None of the above
30. Average composition of humus includes
    A. Carbon B. Oxygen
    C. Nitrogen D. All the above
31. Humus is a
    A. Fe-Mo complex B. Ligno-protein complex
    C. Iron-protein complex D. Crude fibre – protein complex
32. Humic group of organic matter fraction constitutes
    A. 60-80% of SOM B. 20-30% of SOM
    C. 80-90% of SOM D. 100% of SOM
33. Lignin theory was proposed by
    A. Kononova B. Haigh and Sochtig
    C. Liebig D. Waksman
34. The lignin content in humus is about
    A. 35% B. 45%
    C. 60% D. 25%

35. The final product of breakdown of hemicelluloses is

A. CO_2 + water B. Humus

C. Water D. CO_2

36. The C:N ratio of humus is

A. 40:1 B. 10:1

C. 25:1 D. 100:1

37. To check nitrification, nitrification inhibitors are most useful in

A. Paddy B. Cotton

C. Maize D. None of these

38. To prevent denitrification losses of nitrogen in paddy field, nitrogen should be applied in the

A. Reduced zone B. Oxidized zone

C. Hydronized zone D. Calcified zone

39. Humus enhances the mineral breakdown and increases the availability of some

A. Anions B. Cations

C. Neutral ions D. None of these

40. Humus colloids are composed basically of

A. Carbon B. Nitrogen

C. Helium D. Ozone

41. Which of the following contains highest nutrients?

A. Compost B. Droppings of sheep and goat

C. FYM D. None of these

42. An average well decomposed FYM contains

A. 0.5% K_2O B. 0.2% P_2O_5

C. 0.5% N_2 D. All of these

43. Trench method of FYM preparation is also known as

A. Pit method B. Heap method

C. Dr. B.N. Acharya method D. None of these

44. When organic matter with wide C: N ratio (70:1) is added to the soil, the net effect is the disappearance of mineral nitrogen due to

A. Mineralization B. Immobilization

C. N_2 transformation D. N_2 reduction

45. Match list I with list II and choose the correct options given below

List I	List II
a. *Nitrobacter*	1. Ammonia as substrate
b. *Nitrosomonas*	2. Nitrite as substrate
c. *Thiobacillus*	3. Ferrous as ferric
d. *Ferrobacillus*	4. Sulphur to SO_4

	a	b	c	d
A.	3	4	1	2
B.	3	4	2	1
C.	2	4	1	3
D.	2	1	4	3

46. Conversion of nitrogen to molecular nitrogen is known as

A. Denitrification B. Nitrification

C. Nitrogen fixation D. Ammonification

47. Find out the correct statement

(i) Conversion of organic C into inorganic C is called as mineralization

(ii) Conversion of inorganic C into organic C is called as immobilization

A. (i) alone is correct B. (ii) alone is correct

C. (i) and (ii) are correct D. (i) and (ii) are wrong

48. Sources of enzymes in soil are

A. Microbes

B. Microbes and plant roots

C. Microbes, plant roots and soil animals

D. Microbes, plant roots, shoot and soil animals

49. Phosphotase enzymes play a major role in ________ of organic phosphates in soil

A. Mineralization B. Immobilization

C. Mass transportation D. none of these

50. Humic acid precipitates at the pH

A. 5.0 B. 5.2

C. 4.8 D. 4.5

51. The term humic acid was given by

A. Oden B. Miescher

C. Berzelius D. Mulder

52. What is the percentage of organic carbon in organic matter?
A. 48 B. 58
C. 78 D. 68

53. Transformation of raw organic matter into humus is called
A. Humification B. Brounification
C. Rubrification D. All of the above

54. The process of denitrification involves conversion of nitrite to
A. Nitric oxide B. Nitrous oxide
C. Dinitrogen D. All of the above

55. The conversion of nitrogen into nitrates is known as
A. Nitrogen fixation B. Ammonification
C. Nitrate assimilation D. Nitrogen cycle

56. Soil organic matter a good indicator of
A. Biological health B. Chemical health
C. Physical health D. All of the above

57. The transformation of nitrates to gaseous nitrogen is accomplished by microorganisms in a series of biochemical reactions. The process is known as
A. Nitrification B. Denitrification
C. Nitrogen fixation D. Ammonification

58. In the process of nitrogen fixation, which of the following microorganism is involved
A. Non symbiotic microorganisms only
B. Symbiotic microorganisms only
C. Non symbiotic and symbiotic microorganisms both
D. None of the above

59. ______ play a key role in the transformation of rock to soil
A. Cyanobacteia B. Pectin decomposing bacteria
C. Nitrifying bacteria D. Denitrifying bacteria

60. The groups of bacteria which have the ability to fix nitrogen from air to soil are
A. Symbiotic B. Non symbiotic
C. Both A and B D. None of the above

61. The crops which are involved in nitrogen fixation are

A. Alfalfa and clover B. Soybean

C. Bean and lupine D. All of the above

62. The conversion of molecular nitrogen into ammonia is known as

A. Nitrification B. Denitrification

C. Nitrogen fixation D. Ammonification

63. Among the following which is not an ether soluble compound

A. Fats B. Oil

C. Tannins D. Wax

64. The average C:N ratio of cultivated soil is

A. 8:1 to 15:1 B. 10:1 to 12:1

C. 20:1 to 30:1 B. 4:1 to 9:1

65. What is the C:N ratio for fresh organic materials

A. 400:1 B. 100:1

C. 50:1 D. 20:1

66. What is the optimum pH for composting?

A. 1.5 – 4.5 B. 4.5 – 9.5

C. 2.5 – 4.5 D. 1.5 – 3.5

67. What is the nitrogen content present in neem cake?

A. 5.2% B. 6.5%

C. 4.5% D. 7.8%

68. Match the following and select the correct code

a. Organic manure 1. *Sesbania aculeata*

b. Green manure 2. Compost

c. Green leaf manure 3. *Pongamia glabra*

	a	b	c
A.	2	3	1
B.	1	2	3
C.	2	1	3
D.	3	1	2

69. Which of the following is an edible oil cake used as concentrated organic manure?

A. Groundnut cake B. Neem cake

C. Castor cake D. Calotropis cake

70. Which of the following organic manure contain the highest N content?

A. Sesame cake B. Pungam cake

C. Neem cake D. Press mud

71. Average nutrient content of FYM is

A. 2% N, 1% P_2O_5, 3% K_2O

B. 3% N, 2% P_2O_5, 1.5% K_2O

C. 0.5% N, 0.25% P_2O_5, 0.5% K_2O

D. 2% N, 1.5% P_2O_5, 2.5% K_2O

Answer keys

1	D	16	B	31	B	46	A	61	D
2	A	17	B	32	A	47	C	62	A
3	B	18	B	33	D	48	C	63	C
4	D	19	A	34	A	49	A	64	B
5	D	20	C	35	B	50	C	65	C
6	B	21	B	36	B	51	C	66	B
7	B	22	A	37	A	52	B	67	A
8	B	23	B	38	A	53	A	68	C
9	A	24	A	39	B	54	D	69	A
10	A	25	B	40	A	55	A	70	A
11	C	26	C	41	B	56	D	71	C
12	A	27	A	42	D	57	B		
13	A	28	C	43	C	58	C		
14	C	29	B	44	C	59	A		
15	C	30	D	45	D	60	C		

UNIT V: AGRICULTURAL ENTOMOLOGY

1

Fundamentals of Agricultural Entomology

I. Choose the correct answer

1. In which among the following glands, pheromone is produced in female?

   A. Aphrodisiac glands　　B. Eversible glands

   C. Olfactory glands　　D. Thoracic glands

2. Cursorial type of legs is found in

   A. Aquatic beetles　　B. Mole crickets

   C. Cockroaches　　D. Bugs

3. Fecundity rate of termite is

   A. 60-70 eggs　　B. 600-700 eggs

   C. 6-7 eggs　　D. 6000-7000 eggs

4. Match list I with list II and choose the correct options given below

List I	List II
a. Siphoning	1. Aphids
b. Cheuring type	2. House flies
c. Sponging	3. Beetles
d. Piercing - sucking	4. Butterflies

	a	b	c	d
A.	4	3	2	1
B.	4	2	3	1
C.	3	1	4	2
D.	3	4	1	2

5. Tegmina type of wings is present in which insect?

   A. Dragon fly　　B. Butterflies

   C. Crickets　　D. Bugs

6. Which among the following insects does not improve soil fertility?

   A. Spring tails　　B. Butterflies

   C. Termites　　D. Acada

7. Insects which inject toxins into man and animals that cause irritation, swelling is

   A. Lice B. Houseflies

   C. Mosquito D. Wasps

8. Destructive Insects and Pests Act is formulated in the year

   A. 1912 B. 1915

   C. 1914 D. 1917

9. The International code of Zoological Nomenclature consists of

   A. 57 articles B. 77 articles

   C. 67 articles D. 87 articles

10. Which of the following is not head sclerite

    A. Gena B. Epimeron

    C. Frons D. Vertex

11. Which category of pest occur on the crop throughout the year?

    A. Sporadic pest B. Seasonal pest

    C. Occasional pest D. Persistent pest

12. Tremendous increase in pest population brought about by insecticide is called

    A. Resistance B. Subsistence

    C. Persistence D. Resurgence

13. Which among the following is not a introduced pest?

    A. *Pectinophora gossypiella* B. *Heteropsylla cubana*

    C. *Aleurodicus dispersus* D. *Empoasca kerri*

14. When was insecticidal act enacted

    A. 1912 B. 1919

    C. 1968 D. 1914

15. Chemicals used to control mites are called

    A. Acaricides B. Avicides

    C. Molluscicides D. Rodenticides

16. When was the first pheromone identified?

    A. 1959 B. 1969

    C. 1929 D. 1919

17. Which of the following is associated with articulation of wings
    A. Trochanter B. Phragmata
    C. Tegula D. Scutum
18. The type of eyes found in larvae is
    A. Ocelli B. Stemmata
    C. Compound eyes D. Ommatidia
19. The compound responsible for bioluminescence in insects is
    A. Chitin B. Xanthophylls
    C. Luciferin D. Keratin
20. Filter chamber of homopterans helps in rapid removal of
    A. Salts B. Water
    C. Excretory material D. Nitrogen
21. Systole refers to
    A. Relaxation phase B. Both relaxation and contraction
    C. Contraction phase D. None of these
22. Haemoglobin as blood pigment is found in
    A. Chironomids B. Cochroaches
    C. Calliphora D. Calliflora
23. Detrimental effect of host plant on the biology of insect is known as
    A. Non preference B. Tolerance
    C. Antibiosis D. Resistance
24. Number of segments in the abdomen of collembola is
    A. 10 B. 11
    C. 08 D. 06
25. Anamorphosis is the phenomenon found in
    A. Collembola B. Diplura
    C. Protura D. Thysanura
26. Malphigian tubules are absent in
    A. Protura B. Thysanoptera
    C. Collembola D. Isoptera
27. Base of the compound eye is strengthened by
    A. Ocelli B. Circum ocular suture
    C. Circum ocular sulcus D. Ommatidia

28. National Bureau of Agricultural Insect Resources (NBAIR) is located at

A. New Delhi B. Bangalore

C. Bhubaneswar D. Jabalpur

29. Match list I with list II and choose the correct options given below

List I	**List II**
a. *Aphis craccivora*	1. Coccidae
b. *Thrips tabaci*	2. Pseudococcidae
c. *Coccus viridis*	3. Aphididae
d. *Sacharicoccus sacchari*	4. Thripidae

	a	b	c	d
A.	3	4	1	2
B.	3	1	4	2
C.	4	3	1	2
D.	4	1	2	3

30. In nature, insect pest population is kept under check by factors such as

A. Topographic B. Climate

C. Biotic D. All the above

31. Pest surveillance comprises of

A. One basic component B. Two basic components

C. Three basic components D. More than three components

32. Spread of pest from one field to another is largely determined by

A. Rainfall B. Temperature

C. Humidity D. Wind current

33. National Bureau of Agricultural Insect Resources was established in

A. 1973 B. 1993

C. 1963 D. 1983

34. Match the following

a. Insecticide rule	1. 1946
b. First Quarantine Act	2. 2003
c. Directorate of Plant Protection and Quarantine	3. 1971
d. Plant Quarantine order	4. 1905

	a	b	c	d
A.	2	3	1	4
B.	2	1	4	3
C.	3	4	1	2
D.	4	3	2	1

35. Match the following

a. *Schistocerca gregaria*	1. Bombay locust
b. *Locusta migratoria*	2. Rice grass hopper
c. *Patanga succincta*	3. Desert locust
d. *Hieroglyphus banian*	4. Migratory locust

	a	b	c	d
A.	3	4	1	2
B.	4	3	2	1
C.	2	4	3	1
D.	1	4	3	2

36. Name the category of pest which occurs most frequently with close association with a particular crop.

A. Occasional pest B. Regular pest

C. Seasonal pest D. Sporadic pest

37. Indicate the oviposition site of locusts and grass hopper

A. Leaf B. Soil

C. Stem D. Flower

38. What is the name of the semio chemical which is involved in the intra specific communication?

A. Allomone B. Kairomone

C. Pheromone D. Synomone

39. Give an example for structural pest

A. Epilachna beetle B. Case worm of rice

C. Termite D. Rice grass hopper

40. What is the percentage of annual loss of food in our country due to insect pests, according to conservative estimate?

A. 5 B. 15

C. 30 D. 40

41. What is the worldwide estimated amount of loss (in billion rupees) caused by insect pests to eight crops viz: rice, wheat, barley, maize, potato, soybean, cotton and coffee?

A. 102 B. 182

C. 362 D. 542

42. Name one weed host for fruit sucking moth?

A. *Tinospora cordifolia* B. *Tephrosia purpurea*

C. *Trianthema portulacastrum* D. *Ipomea aquatica*

43. What is the family of *Helopeltis antonii*?

A. Aphididae B. Aleurodidae

C. Cercopidae D. Miridae

44. Match the following (B with A)

A	B
a. *Bactrocera dorsalis*	1. Cicadellidae
b. *Amritodus atkinsoni*	2. Geometridae
c. *Erosomyia indica*	3. Tephritidae
d. *Thalassodes quadraria*	4. Cecidomyiidae

	a	b	c	d
A.	3	1	4	2
B.	4	3	2	1
C.	2	1	3	4
D.	1	3	4	2

45. Name the plant in which alleolopathic substances Allyl isothiocyanate has been reported

A. Garlic B. Sesame

C. Mustard D. Marigold

46. When the population of the pest is found to be always higher than ETL, what is the name of the pest?

A. Sporadic pest B. Potential pest

C. Seasonal pest D. Key pest

47. Examples of durable insect resistance are

A. Hessian fly, stem saw fly, green bugs (wheat)

B. Jassids (cotton)

C. Stem borers and leaf hoppers (Rice)

D. All of these

Answer keys

1	B	11	D	21	C	31	C	41	C
2	C	12	D	22	A	32	D	42	A
3	D	13	D	23	C	33	B	43	D
4	A	14	C	24	D	34	C	44	A
5	C	15	A	25	C	35	A	45	C
6	B	16	A	26	C	36	A	46	D
7	D	17	C	27	C	37	B	47	D
8	C	18	B	28	B	38	C		
9	D	19	C	29	A	39	C		
10	B	20		30	D	40	B		

2

Pests of Field Crops and Their Management

I. Choose the correct answer

2.1. Cereals and millets

1. Hopper burn, a characteristic symptom in rice is caused by

   A. Thrips B. Bugs

   C. Hoppers D. Stem borer

2. The insect causes "silver shoot" in rice

   A. Yellow stem borer B. Gall midge

   C. BPH D. Leaf folder

3. Which one of the following statement is correct?

   Statement 1: Parasitoid recommended for yellow stem borer in rice is *Trichogramma chilonis*

   Statement 2: Dislodging the cases by running a rope over the crop is recommended for rice caseworm

   A. Statement 1 alone is correct B. Statement 2 alone is correct

   C. Both statements are correct D. Both statements are wrong

4. Match the following

   a. Green leaf hopper 1. *Cnaphalocrocis medinalis*

   b. Brown leaf hopper 2. *Nephotettix virescens*

   c. Yellow stem borer 3. *Scirpophaga incertulas*

   d. Leaf folder 4. *Nilaparvata lugens*

	a	b	c	d
A.	4	3	2	1
B.	2	3	4	1
C.	2	1	4	3
D.	4	1	3	2

5. Give classical example for a monophagous borer pest

A. *Cofana spectra* B. *Soggtella furgifera*

C. *Scirpophago incertulas* D. *Chilo partellus*

6. Use of higher seed rate, a cultural method for the control of pest in sorghum

A. Stem borer B. Shootfly

C. Aphids D. Shoot bug

7. Tungro disease of rice is spread by

A. *Nephotettix virescens* B. *Sogatela furcifera*

C. *Nilaparvata lugens* D. *Thrips tabaci*

8. Match list I with list II and choose the correct options given below

List I	**List II**
a. Leaf folder	1. *Soggella fursifera*
b. Mealy bug	2. *Orseolia oryzae*
c. Gall midge	3. *Brevennia rehi*
d. White backed plant hopper	4. *Cnaphalocrocis mainsails*

	a	b	c	d
A.	4	1	2	3
B.	4	3	2	1
C.	3	1	2	4
D.	2	3	4	1

9. Which among the following is the symptom caused by paddy stem borer?

A. Silvery streaks B. Backward rolling

C. Silvery shoot D. Dead heart

10. What is the parasitoid recommended for the management of paddy yellow stem borer?

A. *Trichogramma japonicum* B. *Chrysoperla carnea*

C. *Trichoderma viride* D. *Pseudomonas fluorescens*

11. What is the vector for rice tungro virus?

A. *Hydrellia sasakii* B. *Nephotettix virescens*

C. *Spodoptera mauritia* D. *Nymphula depunctalis*

12. What is the recommended management for maize aphid?

A. Quinalphos @ 1 l/ha B. Carbaryl @ 1 kg/ha

C. Phosalone @ 25 kg/ha D. Dematon @ 20 ml

13. Which among the following pest causes sooty mould on leaves of maize?

A. Web worm B. Earhead bug

C. Shoot bug D. Ash weevil

14. What is the symptom caused by earhead caterpillar in sorghum?

A. Dead heart B. Black mould

C. Shot hole on ear heads D. Chalky appearance of earheads

15. Red mining in sorghum is caused by which pest?

A. Shoot fly B. Pink stem borer

C. Earhead caterpillar D. Shoot bug

16. What is the scientific name of stink bug of pearl millet?

A. *Geromyia penniseti* B. *Chilo partellus*

C. *Nezara viridula* D. *Atherigona approximate*

17. What is the management recommended for the control of root aphid in finger millet?

A. Phosalone @1.25 l/ha B. Carbaryl @ 1kg/ha

C. Quinalphos @ 2l/ha D. Phosphomidon @ 0.5 ml/lit

18. Consider the statements and find out the correct statements

(i) Quantitative survey is useful for enumeration of pest

(ii) Relative sampling is to measure pest in terms of some values compared over time and space

(iii) Emergence trap is used for sucking pest

A. (ii) and (iii) are correct B. (i) and (iii) are correct

C. (iii) alone is correct D. (i) and (ii) are correct

19. Insecticide which cause resurgence of BPH in rice?

A. Endosulfan B. Phorate

C. Carbofuran D. Malathion

20. Economic injury level was defined as " Lowest density will cause economic damage" by

A. C.V. Riley B. Albert *et al*

C. Stern *et al* D. Storey *et al*

21. Increased N fertilizer increases the incidence of ____ in rice

A. Hopper B. Stem borer

C. Leaf folder D. Caseworm

22. Leaf whorl application is used to control

A. Internal borer
B. Leaf feeders
C. Root feeder
D. Flower feeder

23. What is the scientific name of Anguomois grain moth that attack ripening grains of paddy, sorghum and finger millet in the standing crop and the grains in storage?

A. *Plodia interpunctella*
B. *Cadra cautella*
C. *Corcyra cephalonica*
D. *Sitotroga cerealella*

24. Indicate the number of bow traps (Tanjore or Vallanadu) to be kept per acre of rice field for rodent management?

A. 10-15
B. 20-25
C. 40-50
D. 50-60

25. Match the following (B with A).

A	B
a. *Heterodera avenae*	1. Rice root nematode
b. *Anguina tritici*	2. Molya disease of wheat
c. *Hirschmanniella oryzae*	3. Rice white tip nematode
d. *Aphelenchoides besseyi*	4. Wheat gall nematode

	a	b	c	d
A.	3	1	4	2
B.	4	3	2	1
C.	2	1	3	4
D.	1	2	3	4

26. Match the following (B with A)

A	**B**
a. *Bandicota bengalensis*	1. Indian field mouse
b. *Rattus meltada*	2. Indian gerbil rat
c. *Tatera indica*	3. Mole rat
d. *Mus booduga*	4. Grass rat

	a	b	c	d
A.	4	3	1	2
B.	3	4	2	1
C.	1	3	4	2
D.	2	3	4	1

27. Name the vector of corn mosaic and freckled yellows of sorghum

A. Plant lice B. Shoot bug
C. Leaf hopper D. Earhead bug

28. Both macropterous and brachypterous individuals of the sucking pest which causes yellowing of leaves and stunted growth in sorghum crop. Name the pest.

A. *Pyrilla perpusilla* B. *Heterococcus rehi*
C. *Peregrinus maidis* D. *Hysteroneura setariae*

29. What is the pest which has become very serious in maize crop recently?

A. *Spodoptera litura* B. *Spodoptera frugiperda*
C. *Spodoptera mauritia* D. *Helicoverpa armigera*

30. Match the following.

a. *Tetranychus neocaledonicus* 1. Sugarcane blister mite
b. *Oligonychus indicus* 2. Yellow mite (muranai mite)
c. *Aceria sacchari* 3. Red spider mite
d. *Polyphagotarsonemus latus* 4. Sorghum mite

	a	b	c	d
A.	3	4	1	2
B.	4	3	1	2
C.	3	2	4	1
D.	2	4	1	3

31. Match the following

a. Sorghum shoot fly 1. Carbofuran 3G @ 25kg
b. Rice yellow stem borer 2. NPV @ 250 LE/ha
c. Gram pod borer 3. Seed treatment with Imidachloprid 70WS @ 1kg/ha
d. Red hairy caterpillar 4. Quinalphos 1.5D @ 25kg/ha

	a	b	c	d
A.	2	4	1	3
B.	4	3	2	1
C.	3	1	4	2
D.	3	2	1	4

32. Which pest is responsible for 'Corky screw' symptom in pearl millet crop?

A. Leaf beetle B. Stem borer
C. Shoot fly D. Ear midge

33. Grainless glumes with pupal cases attached to the tip of the spikelet of pearl millet earhead. Which insect causes above symptoms?

A. *Chilo partellus* B. *Geromyia pennisetti*

C. *Arthrodes is sp* D. *Nezara viridula*

34. Wilting and drying of plants in patches and black ants around the base of finger millet. Which pest is associated with above symptoms?

A. Root aphid B. White grub

C. Ash weevil D. Flea beetle

35. What is the family of black hairy caterpillar, *Estigmene lactinea* which causes defoliation in finger millet crop?

A. Noctuidae B. Phycitidae

C. Melolonthidae D. Arctiidae

36. Dead heart, red mining in the mid rib, presence of windows in the leaves and bore holes at the base of stem in sorghum crop. Name the pest which causes above symptoms

A. Shoot fly B. Stem borer

C. Gall midge D. Stink bug

37. What is the recommended number of hanging type plastic fish meal traps for sorghum shoot fly management?

A. 5/ac B. 10/ac

C. 15/ac D. 20/ac

38. What is the ETL for sorghum earhead bug? (express as number of bugs / head).

A. 5 B. 10

C. 15 D. 20

39. What is the entomological name of green nettle slug caterpillar (leaf scorpion) on sorghum?

A. *Cryptocephalus schestedii* B. *Thosea aperiens*

C. *Marasmia trapezalis* D. *Monolepta signata*

40. Identify the statement?

Statement 1: Root aphid is a specific pest in finger millet

Statement 2: Scientific name of root aphid is *Tetraneura* sp.

A. Statement 1 alone is correct B. Statement 2 alone is correct

C. Both statements are correct D. Both statements are wrong

41. The nematode which causes ufra symptom in rice crop is
    A. White tip nematode B. Rice root nematode
    C. Rice stem nematode D. Root knot nematode

42. Match the following

Disease	Vector
a. Little leaf of brinjal	1. *Bemisia tabaci*
b. Tomoto leaf curl	2. *Nilaparvata lugens*
c. Rice tungro	3. *Cestius phycitis*
d. Grassy stunt	4. *Nephotettix virescens*

	a	b	c	d
A.	3	4	2	1
B.	2	4	1	3
C.	4	3	2	1
D.	1	4	2	3

43. What is the pest which has become very serious in maize crop recently?
    A. *Spodoptera litura* B. *Spodoptera frugiperda*
    C. *Spodoptera mauritia* D. *Helicoverpa armigera*

44. *Pericallia ricini* is a serious pest of which crop?
    A. Castor B. Sunflower
    C. Groundnut D. safflower

Answer keys

1	C	11	B	21	C	31	C	41	C
2	B	12	D	22	A	32	C	42	A
3	B	13	C	23	D	33	B	43	B
4	D	14	D	24	B	34	A	44	A
5	C	15	A	25	A	35	D		
6	B	16	C	26	A	36	B		
7	A	17	B	27	B	37	A		
8	B	18	D	28	C	37	A		
9	D	19	B	29	B	39	B		
10	A	20	C	30	A	40	C		

2.2. Pulses

1. What is the scientific name of redgram sterility mite
   A. *Exelastis atomosa* B. *Lampides boeticus*
   C. *Helicoverpa armigera* D. *Aceria cajani*

2. Pin head size holes in redgram pod is a symptom of

A. Plume moth
B. Pod fly
C. Blue butterfly
D. Gram pod borer

3. What is the scientific name for blister beetle in blackgram?

A. *Mylabris phalerata*
B. *Bemisia tabaci*
C. *Empoasca kerri*
D. *Riptortus pedestris*

4. What is the ETL adopted for gram pod borer (*Helicoverpa armigera* of bengalgram?

A. 5 early instar larvae/plant
B. 3 early instar larvae/plant
C. 4 early instar larvae/plant
D. 2 early instar larvae/plant

5. What is the ETL adopted for bean aphids in cowpea?

A. 18/2.5cm shoot length
B. 19/2.5cm shoot length
C. 20/2.5cm shoot length
D. 30/2.5cm shoot length

6. What is the ETL adopted for spotted pod borer?

A. 3 larvae/plant
B. 2 larvae/plant
C. 4 larvae/plant
D. 5 larvae/plant

7. In which crop, *Melanagromyza sojae* is present?

A. Cowpea
B. Blackgram
C. Lablab
D. Soybean

8. Example of polyphagous pest is

A. Plume moth
B. Red hairy caterpillar
C. Red cotton bug
D. Gram pod borer

9. The field carry over storage pest in pulses is

A. Pulse pod bug
B. Pulse pod fly
C. Pulse pod wasp
D. Pulse beetle

Answer keys

1	D	6	A
2	B	7	D
3	A	8	D
4	D	9	D
5	A		

2.3. Oil seeds

1. Which among the pest is a capitulum borer of sunflower?
   A. *Helicoverpa armigera* B. *Spodoptera litura*
   C. *Amrasca biguttula* D. *Spilosoma obliqua*

2. Match list I with list II and choose the correct options given below

List I	**List II**
a. *Achaea janata*	1. Sesamum
b. *Asphondylia sesami*	2. Sunflower
c. *Amrasca biguttula*	3. Cotton
d. *Oxycarenus hyalinipennis*	4. Castor

	a	b	c	d
A.	3	1	2	4
B.	4	1	2	3
C.	2	1	3	4
D.	4	3	1	2

3. Consider the statement and choose the correct one
   (i) Groundnut leaf miner : Field looks like burnt appearance
   (ii) Groundnut aphid : Stunting of stem
   (iii) Red hairy caterpillar : Defoliation
   A. (i) and (ii) are correct B. (ii) and (iii) are correct
   C. (i) and (iii) are correct D. All the statements is correct

4. Find out the wrong statement
   (i) Red hairy caterpillar on groundnut is a seasonal pest
   (ii) ETL is always higher than EIL
   (iii) DBM and cotton bollworm are key pests
   A. (i) and (iii) are wrong B. (ii) and (iii) are wrong
   C. (ii) alone is wrong D. (i) and (ii) are correct

5. What is the family of castor slug caterpillar?
   A. Pyraustidae B. Noctuidae
   C. Cochlididae D. Lymantriidae

6. Which pest of castor is mainly used as laboratory host for multiplication of *Trichospilus pupivora*?
   A. *Olene mendosa* B. *Ariadne merione*
   C. *Pericallia ricini* D. *Porthesia scintillans*

7. An important foliage feeding pest of groundnut which undergoes pupal diapause in soil. What is it?

   A. Leaf miner B. Red hairy caterpillar

   C. White grub D. Stem borer

8. What is the family of *Anisolabis stali* (pod borer in groundnut)?

   A. Buprestidae B. Forficulidae

   C. Lygaedae D. Gelechiidae

9. Which is the vector of bud necrosis in groundnut?

   A. *Empoasca kerri* B. *Caliothrips indicus*

   C. *Scirtothrips dorsalis* D. *Frankliniella schultzei*

10. Top leaves rolled and webbed together in vegetative phase-flowers and young capsules are bored at reproductive stage in gingelly. Give the name of pest responsible for above symptoms.

    A. Death head moth B. Leaf hopper

    C. Leaf webber D. Stink bug

11. Name the vector for sesamum phyllody

    A. *Orosius albicinctus* B. *Antigastra catalaunalis*

    C. *Asphondylia sesami* D. *Nezara viridula*

12. Ear wig is an important pest of

    A. Groundnut B. Blackgram

    C. Cotton D. Sunflower

Answer keys

1	A	6	B	11	A
2	B	7	B	12	A
3	D	8	B		
4	C	9	D		
5	C	10	C		

2.4. Cash crops

1. The microbial agent used for the management of sugarcane early shoot borer is

   A. NPV B. GV

   C. CPV D. Bt

2. Which among the following is the internode borer of sugarcane?

   A. *Chilo infuscatellus snellen* B. *Chilo sacchariphagus indicus*

   C. *Scirpophaga excerptalis* D. *Ceratovacuna lanigera*

3. To control whitefly in cotton, the number of yellow sticky traps required per ha is

   A. 20 B. 5

   C. 40 D. 12

4. Whitefly resistant cotton variety is

   A. Supriya B. Kanchan

   C. Amravathi D. All the above

5. Parasite used to control early shoot borer in sugarcane is

   A. *Trichogramma chilonis* B. *Sturmiopsis inferens*

   C. *Gambroides javensis* D. *Ichnemonids*

6. Detrashing is done to control

   A. Early shoot borer B. Internode borer

   C. Top shoot borer D. Woolly aphid

7. Scientific name of cotton boll strainers is

   A. *Dysdercus cingulatus* B. *Bemisia tabaci*

   C. *Amrasca devastans* D. *Spodoptera litura*

8. Name the sex pheromone used for the management of *Pectinophora gossypiella*?

   A. Bombycol B. Gossiplure

   C. Grandlure D. Pherodin SL.

9. The vector for grassy shoot virus in sugarcane is

   A. *Aleurodicus barodensis* B. *Psalis pennatula*

   C. *Melanaphis sacchari* D. *Myzus persicae*

10. The pest which is managed by setting up of yellow sticky trap is

    A. Boll worm B. Cotton stem weevil

    C. Red cotton bug D. Cotton white fly

11. Cotton leaf curl virus is transmitted by

    A. *Phenacoccus solan* *B. Bemisia tabaci*

    C. Aphis gossypii *D. Thrips tabaci*

12. What is the name of the bacterium associated with red cotton bug for staining of the lint?

    A. *Bacillus popilliae* B. *Nematospora gossypii*

    C. *Verticillium lecanii* D. *Pseudomonas flourescens*

13. Which pest is responsible for dead heart, shot holes; mid rib lesions and bunchy top symptoms in cane crop?

A. *Holotrichia consanguinea* B. *Scirpophaga excerptalis*

C. *Chilo partellus* D. *Telicota augias*

Answer keys

1	B	6	B	11	B
2	B	7	A	12	B
3	D	8	B	13	B
4	D	9	C		
5	B	10	D		

3

Pests of Horticultural Crops and Their Management

I. Choose the correct answer

3.1. Fruits

1. Insect which causes semi circular or circular cuttings on the leaves of rose, guava and redgram is

   A. Leaf cutter bee B. Hairy caterpillar

   C. Semi looper D. Chafer beetle

2. The pupation site for fruit flies is

   A. Leaf B. Flower

   C. Stem D. Soil

3. Psyllid – *Diaphorina citri* is a major pest of

   A. Citrus B. Mango

   C. Guava D. Banana

4. Weed host of fruit sucking moth is

   A. *Tinospora cardifolia* B. *Ipomea sp.*

   C. *Abutilon indicum* D. All the above

5. Citrus tristeza virus is transmitted by

   A. Black aphid B. Citrus black fly

   C. Citrus psyllid D. Citrus leaf miner

6. Banding is a special management practice to control

   A. Banana aphid B. Cottony cushion scale of apple

   C. Codling moth of apple D. Fruit sucking moth of citrus

7. Corky scab formation on fruits is a symptom of

   A. *Helopeltis antonii* B. *Indarbella sp.*

   C. *Bactrocera diversus* D. *Conogethes punctiferalis*

8. Mango stem borer incidence can be managed by

(i) Resistant varieties like neelam, himayuddin

(ii) Swabbing with coal tar and kerosene @ 1:2 ratio

(iii) Field release of *Opium compensatus*

A. (ii) and (iii) are correct
B. (i) and (iii) are correct
C. (i) and (ii) are correct
D. All the statements are correct

9. Which of the following statement is incorrect?

A. Mango fruitfly belongs to the family Tephritidae
B. Neelam and Himayuddin are the tolerant varieties of bark borer
C. Potato tuber moth is a introduced pest of potato
D. Methyl eugenol trap is used to control diamond black moth

10. Covering the fruits with polythene bag is a management practice followed for

A. Citrus psyllid
B. Fruit sucking moth
C. Citrus butterfly
D. Leaf miner of citrus

11. Parasitoid to control wooly aphid in apple

A. *Aphelinus mali*
B. *Trichogramma chilonis*
C. *Aspidiotophagus sp*
D. *Opius compensates*

12. Fruit dropping at marble stage in mango is caused by

A. Gaint mealy bug
B. Scales
C. Stem borer
D. Nut weevil

13. Which pest is also a reason for causing sooty mould disease in mango?

A. Shoot borer
B. Hairy caterpillar
C. Red ants
D. Mango hoppers

14. Which among the following is incorrect regarding parasitoid for control of green scale is sapota?

A. *Trichogramma japonicum*
B. *Coccophagus cowperi*
C. *Aneristis sp*
D. *Coccophagus bogoriensis*

15. Which among the following pest transmits greening disease in citrus?

A. Citrus black fly
B. Citrus butterfly
C. Citrus psyllid
D. Citrus aphid

16. For which among the following pest, yellow stick trap is used as control measure in citrus?

A. Black aphid B. Citrus psyllid

C. Citrus leaf miner D. Citrus thrips

17. Match list I with list II and choose the correct options given below

List I	**List II**
a. Rhizome weevil	1. Bunchy top
b. Pseudostem borer	2. Windowing in unfurled leaves
c. Banana aphid	3. Tunneling in rhizome
d. Hairy caterpillar	4. Blackened mass form bore holes

	a	b	c	d
A.	3	4	1	2
B.	3	2	1	4
C.	4	3	2	1
D.	4	1	3	2

18. Rotting of berries and crinkling of leaves in grapes is the symptom caused by which pest?

A. Stem girdler B. Flea beetle

C. Berry plume moth D. Mealy bug

19. Corky scab formation on guava fruit is caused by

A. Fruit borer B. Tea mosquito bug

C. Green scale D. Mealy bug

20. What is the control measure for *Rapala varuna* (fruit borer) of guava?

A. Quinolphos @ 2 l/ha B. Dimethoate 2ml/ha

C. Malathion 0.1% D. Phosalone 0.2%

21. What is the ETL adopted for anar butterfly in pomegranate?

A. 3 eggs/plant B. 8 eggs/plant

C. 7 eggs/plant D. 5 eggs/plant

22. Expand MRL

A. Maximum Residue Level B. Minimum Residue Level

C. Maximum Resistance Level D. Minimum Resistance Level

23. In which stage, mango nut weevil hibernates in between the crevices on the tree trunks?

A. Egg B. Larva

C. Pupa D. Adult

24. What is the ETL for anar butterfly (with bearing capacity of 60 fruits)?

A. 2 eggs/plant B. 5 eggs/plant

C. 10 eggs/plant D. 15 eggs/plant

25. Infested fruit with bore hole plugged with anal segment of the larva; fruit rotting and dropping in pomegranate crop. Which pest causes above symptoms?

A. *Ferrisia virgata* B. *Deudorix isocrates*

C. *Siphoninus phillyreae* D. *Clania crameri*

26. Which aphid is vector of bunchy top of banana and cardamom mosaic?

A. *Pentalonia nigronervosa* B. *Aphis craccivora*

C. *Myzus persicae* D. *Toxoptera aurantii*

27. What is the common name of *Carpomyia vesuviana*?

A. Ber fruit borer B. Ber fruit fly

C. Leaf butterfly D. Hairy caterpillar

28. Rhinoceros beetle damages not only coconut tree, but also one fruit tree in the adult stage what is it?

A. Fig B. Star goose berry

C. Custard apple D. Pine apple

29. What is the specific parasitoid used against *Eriosoma lanigerum* effectively?

A. *Aphelinus mali* B. *Prospaltella perniciosi*

C. *Encarsia formosa* D. *Telenomus rowani*

30. Fruit dropping at marble stage, tunnelled cotyledons, ovipositional injuries and eggs seen on marble sized fruits. What is the name of the monophagous and univoltine pest which causes above symptoms on mango?

A. Fruit borer B. Nut weevil

C. Fruit fly D. Mango hopper

31. Which is the pupation site for fruit flies?

A. Leaf B. Flower

C. Stem D. Soil

32. Which species of aphid is the vector for tristeza virus?

A. *Aphis craccivora* B. *Toxoptera citricidus*

C. *Myzus persicae* D. *Lipaphis erysimi*

Answer keys

1	A	6	C	11	A	16	A	21	D	26	A	31	D
2	D	7	A	12	B	17	A	22	A	27	B	32	B
3	A	8	C	13	D	18	D	23	D	28	D	33	
4	A	9	D	14	A	19	B	24	B	29	A	34	
5	A	10	B	15	C	20	C	25	B	30	B	35	

3.2. Vegetables

1. Yellow leaf mosaic of bhendi crop is spread by
   A. Jassids　　B. Borers
   C. Jassid and borers　　D. None of these
2. What is the recommended management for white fly?
   A. Phosalone 0.7%　　B. Spinosad 45%
   C. Indoxacarb 333 ml/ha　　D. Imidacloprid 100-125 ml/ha
3. Which one of the following is a brinjal variety resistant/tolerant to aphids?
   A. Annamalai　　B. Pusa ruby
   C. Pusa early dwarly　　D. Rashmi
4. Which is the polyphagous dipteran pest recently introduced into India?
   A. Serpentine leaf miner　　B. Sorghum gall midge
   C. Moringa pod fly　　D. Redgram pod fly
5. Bhendi fruit borer can be managed by
   A. Carbaryl 50WP @ 2g/lt　　B. Carbofuran 3G @ 30kg/ha
   C. Phasalone 35EC @ 2ml/lt　　D. Methyl demoton 25EC @ 500 ml/ha
6. Insecticide recommended for sucking pest is
   A. Sevidol 8G @ 2%　　B. Dimethoate @ 0.05%
   C. Quinalphos @ 0.05%　　D. Carbaryl 50WP @750g/ha
7. Chemical used to control snails and slugs in vegetable crops is
   A. Trimedlure　　B. Pherodin SL
   C. Metaldehyde　　D. Bromodiolone
8. Pest which attacks cole crops and belongs to the family of Tenthredinidae is
   A. Mustard aphid　　B. Painted bug
   C. Mustard sawfly　　D. Radish flea beetle

9. Burning the torch to kill larva is a management to control
   A. Bud worm in moringa B. Leaf caterpillar in moringa
   C. Hairy caterpillar of moringa D. Pod fly of moringa
10. Symptoms of pod fly includes
   A. Larva seen in group in tree trunks
   B. Scraping the bark and gnawing foliage
   C. Leaflets reduced to papery structure
   D. Oozing of gummy exudates from fruit
11. Irregular zig-zag tunnels is a characteristic symptom of
   A. Gram pod borer B. Leaf caterpillar
   C. Amaranthus weevil D. Leaf webber
12. Vector of cassava mosaic virus is
   A. Whitefly B. Aphid
   C. Spiralling whitefly D. Thrips
13. Scrapping of epidermal leaf tissues producing whitish patches is a symptom of
   A. Leaf webber B. Cabbage borer
   C. Diamond black moth D. Cabbage green semilooper
14. Field and storage pest in potato is
   A. Black cut worm B. Potato tuber moth
   C. White grubs D. Tobacco caterpillar
15. Use of cut potato tubers as trap at 10 days interval is a management practice for
   A. Tortoise beetle B. Cut worm
   C. Potato tuber moth D. Sweet potato weevil
16. The introduced pest in crucifers is
   A. Mustard saw fly B. Cabbage butterfly
   C. Diamond black moth D. Cabbage borer
17. Trap crop recommended for fruit flies management is
   A. Mustard B. Marigold
   C. Castor D. Ribbed gourd
18. Which pest act as a vector for little leaf of brinjal?
   A. Aphid B. Brown leaf hopper
   C. White fly D. Mite

19. Match list I with list II and choose the correct options given below

List I	List II
a. Brinjal fruit and shoot borer	1. *Scirtothrips dorsalis*
b. Tomato pin worm	2. *Amrasca devastans*
c. Jassids - Bhendi	3. *Leucinodes orbonalis*
d. Thrips	4. *Tuta absoluta*

	a	b	c	d
A.	4	2	3	1
B.	4	3	2	1
C.	3	4	2	1
D.	3	1	2	4

20. Which pest in tomato causes bronzing and webbing symptom?
    A. Striped mealy bug B. White fly
    C. Serpentine leaf miner D. Red spider mite
21. Which is the parasitoid recommended for the management of shoot and fruit borer of bhendi?
    A. *Trichogramma japonicum* B. *Trichogramma chilonis*
    C. *Chelonus blackburni* D. *Trichoderma viride*
22. Which pest is commonly called muranai mite in chilli?
    A. *Polyphagotarsonemus latus* B. *Tetranychus cinnabarinus*
    C. *Aceria cajani* D. *Tetranychus neocaledonicus*
23. Which is the major pest found in onion?
    A. Whitefly B. Aphid
    C. Thrips D. Jassid
24. Crop rotation is effective in controlling which pest of onion?
    A. Thrips B. Onion fly
    C. Earuring D. Mite
25. Which among the following is not used as attractant for pod fly in moringa?
    A. Citronella oil B. Eucalyptus oil
    C. Lactic acid D. Tartaric acid
26. For which pest of moringa, the holes in bark are plugged with chloroform soaked cotton wool.
    A. Hariy caterpillar B. Bark caterpillar
    C. Leaf caterpillar D. Bud worm

27. Methyl eugenol bait is used for which pest?

A. Stem fly B. Leaf miner

C. Fruit fly D. Pumpkin beetle

28. *Plusia peponis* is a serious pest in which crop of cucurbits?

A. Pumpkin B. Summer squash

C. Ashgourd D. Snakegourd

29. What is the insecticide recommended for stem gall fly?

A. Malathion @ 500 ml/ha B. Quinalphos @ 25 kg/ha

C. Chlorpyriphos @ 1 l/ha D. Phosphamidon @ 1 l/ha

30. Bunchy top in cassava is caused by which pest?

A. Spiralling white fly B. White fly

C. Mealy bug D. Scale

31. Which among the following is not a pest of curry leaf?

A. Psyllid bug B. Mite

C. Citrus butterfly D. Bark borer

32. Consider the statement and choose the correct one

(i) Diamond back moth : Scrapping of leaves

(ii) Cabbage borer : Webs the leaves and bore the stem

(iii) Cabbage aphid : Crinkling and cupping of leaves

A. (i) and (ii) are correct B. (ii) and (iii) are correct

C. (i) and (iii) are correct D. All the statements are correct

33. Indicate one pesticide which has been reported to cause resurgence of *Myzus persicae* in brinjal

A. Cypermethrin B. Malathion

C. Phorate D. Lindane

34. What is the name of first instar larva of *Mylabris pustulata* (Blister beetle)?

A. Naiad B. Protonymph

C. Crawler D. Triungulin

35. Which is a typical example for migratory insect pest?

A. Locust B. Rice earhead bug

C. Cumbu root grub D. Diamond black moth

36. Which pest of sweet potato can be managed with mulching with *Clerodendrum infortunatum* at 5 tonnes/ha?

A. Stem borer
B. Sweet potato weevil
C. Tortoise beetle
D. Hairy caterpillar

37. Indicate the number of larval parasitoids *Diadegma semiclausum* to be released per hectare for the management of *Plutella xylostella?*

A. 10,000
B. 25,000
C. 50,000
D. 75,000

38. Indicate the number of yellow sticky traps/ha to attract and kill the adults of sucking pests like whitefly

A. 5
B. 10
C. 15
D. 30

39. What is the name of introduced pest, the larvae of which mine into leaves or bore into tender shoots and developing tubers of potato. Also attack tubers in storage?

A. Cut worm
B. Bihar hairy caterpillar
C. Green leaf beetle
D. Potato tuber moth

40. What is the family of sweet potato weevil?

A. Curculionidae
B. Apionidae
C. Cassididae
D. Hispidae

41. Larvae seen in groups in tree trunks, feed gregariously, scrap the bark and gnaw the foliage of drum stick and defoliation of the tree. Which pest causes above symptoms?

A. Leaf caterpillar
B. Hairy caterpillar
C. Bud worm
D. Bud midge

42. What is the scientific name of amaranthus leaf caterpillar?

A. *Hypolixus trancatulus*
B. *Spoladea recurvalis*
C. *Eretmocera impactella*
D. *Spodoptera litura*

43. Give the name of the introduced pest which scraps the epidermal tissue producing typical whitish patches and advance stage larvae bite holes in the leaves of cole crops

A. Cabbage borer
B. Diamond black moth
C. Leaf webber
D. Cabbage butterfly

44. What is the name of the pest that attacks the cole crops and belongs to the family of Tenthredinidae?

A. Mustard aphid
B. Painted bug
C. Mustard sawfly
D. Radish flea beetle

45. Indicate the family of *Bagrada cruciferarum*

A. Pieridae
B. Agromyzidae
C. Aphididae
D. Pentatomidae

46. Which pest is responsible for cassava mosaic?

A. Whitefly
B. Cassava scale
C. Mealy bug
D. Thrips

47. Withered terminal shoots; bore holes on fruits plugged with excreta; shedding of flower buds; drying of leaves due to boring of petioles by larvae. Which pest causes above symptoms in brinjal crop?

A. Leaf roller
B. Bud worm
C. Stem borer
D. Shoot and fruit borer

48. Skeletonization in brinjal leaves is caused by

A. Ash weevil
B. Hadda beetle
C. Grass hopper
D. Hairy caterpillar

49. Which is the vector of brinjal little leaf disease?

A. *Bemisia tabaci*
B. *Aonidiella aurantii*
C. *Cestius phycitis*
D. *Aspidiotus destructor*

50. Adult moths suck the juice by piercing the fruits. Infested fruits shrink, shrivel, rot and ultimately drop down. Indicate the name of pest responsible for above symptoms in tomato.

A. *Eudocima fullonica*
B. *Spodoptera litura*
C. *Trichoplusia* ni
D. *Euzophera perticella*

51. Indicate the vector of tomato leaf curl disease

A. *Aphis gossypii*
B. *Bemisia tabaci*
C. *Myzus persicae*
D. *Ferrisia virgata*

52. Which pest causes gall like swellings on the stem near the base in bhendi crop?

A. Pod fly
B. Semi looper
C. Stem weevil
D. Grass hopper

53. Oozing of brown resinous fluid from fruits; distorted and malformed fruits. The maggots feed on the pulp of fruits and cause premature dropping of fruits and make them unfit for consumption. Which pest causes above symptoms in cucurbits?

A. *Bactrocera cucurbitae* B. *Baris trichosanthis*

C. *Neolasioptera falcata* D. *Melittia eurytion*

54. What is the name of the pest, adult of which feeds on leaf and flowers and grub feeds on the roots, stem and fruits touching the soil, in pumpkin crop?

A. Hadda beetle B. Grey beetle

C. Pumpkin beetles D. Snake gourd semilooper

Answer keys

1	C	11	C	21	B	31	B	41	B	51	B
2	D	12	A	22	A	32	D	42	B	52	C
3	A	13	C	23	C	33	A	43	B	53	B
4	A	14	B	24	B	34	A	44	C	54	C
5	A	15	D	25	D	35	A	45	D	55	
6	B	16	C	26	B	36	B	46	A	56	
7	C	17	D	27	C	37	C	47	D	57	
8	C	18	B	28	D	38	C	48	B	58	
9	C	19	C	29	A	39	D	49	C	59	
10	D	20	D	30	C	40	B	50	A	60	

3.3. Spices and plantation crops

1. Name the invasive pest on coconut

A. *Oryctes rhinoceros* B. *Rhynchophorus ferrugineus*

C. *Leucopholis coneophora* D. *Aceria guerreronis*

2. Indicate the number of parasitoids to be released per coconut tree for management of black headed caterpillar

A. 2 – 5 B. 10 – 15

C. 20 – 25 D. 30 - 35

3. Central spindle appears cut or toppled fully opened fronds showing characteristic diamond shaped cuttings. Holes with chewed fiber sticking out at the base of central spindle in coconut. These symptoms are caused by the pest in the adult stage. What is it?

A. Red palm weevil B. Rhinoceros beetle

C. Bark weevil D. White grub

4. Name the entomopathogenic fungus used to control the larvae of rhinoeros beetle in manure pit

A. *Beauveria bassiana* B. *Verticillium lecanii*

C. *Metarhizium anisopliae* D. *Farinocystis tribolii*

5. Name the pupal parasitoid recommended against black headed caterpillar of coconut

A. *Aphelinus mali* B. *Goniozus indicus*

C. *Telenomus rowani* D. *Trichospilus pupivora*

6. Chemical used to control rhinoceros beetle in coconut is

A. Sevidol 8G 25g+Fine sand 200g applied thrice in a year

B. Phorate 10G 5g-twice in a year

C. Carbaryl 50WP @ 0.01%

D. All the above

7. Which of the following is correct with respect to management of coconut rhinoceros beetle?

(i) Hooking is done during peak period of population

(ii) Application of naphthalene balls (3-4 balls)

(iii) Application of white muscardine fungus @ 5×10^{11} spores/m^3

A. (i) and (iii) are correct B. (i) and (ii) are correct

C. (ii) and (iii) are correct D. All the statements are correct

8. Match the following

a. Red spider mite 1. Coppery brown discolouration

b. Scarlet mite 2. Upper surface of leaves

c. Purple mite 3. Upward curling

d. Pink mite 4. Under surface of mature leaves

	a	b	c	d
A.	4	3	2	1
B.	2	4	1	3
C.	1	3	4	2
D.	3	1	4	2

9. Identify the statement?

(i) Rhizome scale is a serious pest of ginger

(ii) Rhizome scale can be managed by application of well rotton sheep manure @ 10 t/ha

A. Statement (i) alone is correct B. Statement (ii) alone is correct

C. Both statements are correct D. Both statements are wrong

10. Identify the statement?

Statement (i): Diamond shaped cuttings is a symptom of red palm weevil

Statement (ii): Oozing of reddish brown liquid is a symptom of rhinocerous beetle

A. Statement (i) alone is correct B. Statement (ii) alone is correct

C. Both statements are correct D. Both statements are wrong

11. Specific symptom caused by pollu beetle is

A. Stunted plants B. Withering of plants

C. Curling of leaves D. Hollow berries

12. The pest which causes dead heart symptom in cardamom is

A. *Conogethes punctiferalis* B. *Sciothrips cardamom*

C. *Eupterote cardomomi* D. *Onthophagus sp.*

13. Vector for katte disease of cardmom is

A. *Aphis gossypii* B. *Bemisia tabaci*

C. *Pentalonia nigronervosa* D. *Aceria cajani*

14. Match list I with list II and choose the correct options given below

List I	**List II**
a. Red palm weevil	1. Infest unopened heart leaf
b. Coconut mealy bug	2. Brown patches of nuts
c. Coconut eriophyid mite	3. Webbing of inflorescence
d. Arecanut inflorescence caterpillar	4. Oozing out reddish brown fluid

	a	b	c	d
A.	4	1	2	3
B.	4	3	2	1
C.	3	2	1	4
D.	3	1	2	4

15. Match list I with list II and choose the correct options given below

List I	**List II**
a. Cardamom aphid	1. Quinalphos @ 2ml/lit
b. Cardamom beetle borer	2. Phosalone @ 2 ml/lit
c. Turmeric shoot borer	3. Dimethoate @ 2ml/lit
d. Turmeric rhizome scale	4. Malathion @ 0.1%

	a	b	c	d
A.	2	3	1	4
B.	4	1	4	2
C.	4	3	1	2
D.	2	1	3	4

16. What is the scientific name for coffee brown scale?

A. *Coccus viridis* B. *Xylotrechus quadripes*

C. *Saissetia coffeae* D. *Ariophanta solata*

17. What is the recommended management practice for control of coffee red borer?

A. Green muscardine fungus B. Brown muscardine fungus

C. Pseudomonas fungus D. White muscardine fungus

18. Upward curling of leaves in tea is caused by

A. Red spider mite B. Pink (or) orange mite

C. Purple mite D. Scarlet mite

19. Which pest causes hollow and crumble berries in pepper?

A. Pollu beetle B. Aphids

C. Thrips D. Mussel scale

20. Shedding of berries in pepper is caused by

A. Mussel scale B. Shoot borer

C. Gall thrips D. White talked mealy bug

21. What is the control practice for mites in betel vine?

A. Dimethoate @ 2ml/lit B. Chlorpyriphos @ 2 ml/lit

C. Dicofol @ 0.5 ml/lit D. Quinalphos @ 2 ml/lit

22. Rhinolure and Ferrolure are recommended for coconut rhinoceros beetle and red palm weevil respectively, what type of pheromones they are?

A. Alarm pheromones B. Aggregation pheromones

C. Sex pheromones D. Trail pheromones

23. What is the quantity of trizophols 40% EC recommended for root feeding to control coconut eriophyid mite?

A. 2 ml/10 lit of water B. 5 ml/10 ml of water

C. 15 ml/15 ml of water D. 30 ml/30 ml of water

24. Which pest of coffee occurs both in the field and storage?
    A. White borer   B. Red borer
    C. Shot hole borer   D. Coffee bean beetle
25. What is the name of looper pest on tea?
    A. *Phassus malabaricus*   B. *Biston suppressaria*
    C. *Andraca bipunctata*   D. *Stauropus alternus*
26. What is the family of shoot fly, *Formosina flavipes* affecting cardamom crop (causing dead hearts in seedling)?
    A. Cecidomyiidae   B. Muscidae
    C. Chloropidae   D. Syrphidae
27. Plants become weak, pale and withered in the field. White coloured scales seen scattered on rhizomes and growing buds, shrivelling of rhizomes and buds. Which pest causes above symptoms in turmeric and ginger?
    A. *Aspidiotus hartii*   B. *Chalcidomyia atricornis*
    C. *Stephanitis typicus*   D. *Udaspes folus*
28. What is the family of wild moth, *Cricula trifenestrata* which damages leaves of pepper?
    A. Bombycidae   B. Saturniidae
    C. Eucosmidae   D. Noctuidae
29. Cardamom thrips belongs to the genus of
    A. *Scirtothrips*   B. *Sciothrips*
    C. *Rhipiphorothrips*   D. *Retithrips*
30. Berries with exit holes, affected berries dry up turn dark and hollow and crumble when pressed. Irregular feeding holes on the leaves of pepper crop. Indicate the insect pest which causes above symptoms
    A. Berry gallmidge   B. Top shoot borer
    C. Marginal gall thrips   D. Pollu beetle

Answer keys

1	D	11	D	21	C
2	B	12	A	22	B
3	B	13	C	23	C
4	C	14	A	24	D
5	D	15	B	25	B
6	D	16	C	26	C
7	B	17	D	27	A
8	B	18	B	28	B
9	C	19	A	29	B
10	D	20	D	30	D

3.4. Flower crops

1. Flower shows fading symptom in rose caused by
   A. Thrips B. Aphid
   C. Scale D. Mealy bug
2. What is the control measure for rose scale?
   A. NSKE 5% B. Fish oil resin soap
   C. Neem oil 2% D. Whitex spray 25 g/lit
3. Consider the statement and choose the correct one
   (i) Jasmine budworm - use of light traps
   (ii) Jasmine gallery worm - proper pruning
   (iii) Flower thrips - NSKE 5%
   A. (i) and (ii) are correct B. (ii) and (ii) are correct
   C. (i) and (iii) are correct D. All the statements are correct
4. In chrysanthemum, withering of flower is caused by
   A. Thrips B. Flower feeder
   C. Aphid D. Lacewing bug
5. Netting is done in tuberose to prevent the damage
   A. Red spider mite B. Grasshopper
   C. Aphid D. Bud borer
6. What is the control measure for bud borer in marigold?
   A. Prophenphos @ 2 ml/l B. Fipronil @ 1.5 ml/l
   C. Spinosad @ 0.75 ml/l D. Abamectin @ 0.5 ml/l
7. Which insect causes circular or semi circular cuttings on the leaves of rose, guava, redgram etc.,?
   A. Leaf cutter bee B. Hairy caterpillar
   C. Semi looper D. Chafer beetle
8. Which pest causes felty like hairy out growth (erineum) on the surface of the leaves, tender stem and flower buds in jasmine?
   A. Budworm B. Gallery worm
   C. Jasmine eriophyid mite D. Leaf web worm

Answer keys

1	B	5	B
2	B	6	C
3	D	7	A
4	C	8	C

4

Integrated Pest Management

I. Choose the correct answer

1. National Centre for Integrated Pest Management is located at

   A. Bangalore B. New Delhi

   C. Jabalpur D. Raichur

2. Use of irradiation is a ______ method of pest control.

   A. Chemical control B. Biological control

   C. Legal control D. Physical control

3. Which among the following is not a parasitoid?

   A. Trichogramma B. Bracon

   C. Chelonus D. Chrysopa

4. Match list I with list II and choose the correct options given below

List I	**List II**
a. Egg-larval parasitoid	1. *Bracon hebetor*
b. Larval parasitoid	2. *Tetrastichus israeli*
c. Larval – pupal parasitoid	3. *Chelonus blackburni*
d. Pupal parasitoid	4. *Isotima javensis*

	a	b	c	d
A.	3	4	1	2
B.	3	2	1	4
C.	4	3	2	1
D.	4	1	3	2

5. *Cryptolaemus montrouzieri* was introduced in India against coffee green scale in the year

   A. 1898 B. 1902

   C. 1888 D. 1920

6. In _____ year, three exotic encyrtid parasitoids viz *Acerophagus papayae, Anagyrus loecki and Pseudoplomastix mexicana* against papaya mealy bug *Paracoccus marginatus* was released.

A. 1983 B. 2010

C. 1963 D. 1988

7. What is recommendation of *Cyrtorhinus lividipennis* against hemipterans?

A. 3000-4000/ha B. 50-60 bugs/100m^2

C. 10-12/plant D. 5000-6000/ha

8. *Trichogramma* parasitoids are multiplied on _____ eggs.

A. *Acherontia styx* B. *Agrius cingulata*

C. *Corcyra cephalonica* D. *Sitotroga cerealella*

9. Trichogramma card will consists of _____ eggs.

A. 2 cc B. 0.2 cc

C. 0.6 cc D. 6 cc

10. What is recommended dose of release of *Chrysoperla carnea*?

A. 10000 larva/acre B. 5000 larva/acre

C. 20000 larva/acre D. 50000 larva/acre

11. What is the growth medium for *Trichoderma viride*?

A. Molasses yeast medium B. Potato dextrose agar medium

C. Yeast extract mannitol agar D. King's B medium

12. _____ semi synthetic based medium is used for multiplication of *Helicoverpa armigera*.

A. Cowpea B. Chick pea

C. Blackgram D. Greengram

13. Which stage of larvae is used for mass culture of SLNPV?

A. 1st instar B. 2nd instar

C. 3rd instar D. 5th instar

14. Name the biocontrol agent that is recommended as rice seed treatment and foliar application for the management of rice root and white tip nematodes

A. *Trichoderma viride* B. *Pseudomonas fluorescens*

C. *Paecilomyces lilacinus* D. *Pasteuria penetrans*

15. Give an example for monophagous predator?

A. *Cyrtorhinus lividipennis* B. *Rhynocoris fuscipes*

C. *Coccinella repanda* D. *Rodolia cardinalis*

16. Consider the statement and choose the correct one

(i) 1920 – *Aphelinus mali* introduced from England to control wooly aphid on apple, *Eriosoma lanigerum*

(ii) 1929 – 31 – *Fodolia cardinalis* imported into India to control cottony cushion scale, *Icerya purchasi*

(iii) 1965 – Predator *Platymeris laevicollis* introduced to control Rhinoceros beetle

A. All the statement are correct B. (i) and (ii) alone is correct

C. (ii) and (iii) alone is correct D. (i) and (iii) alone is correct

17. Match list I with list II and choose the correct options given below

List I	**List II**
a. Granulovirus (GV)	1. Green muscardine fungus
b. *Bacillus thuringiensis* (BT)	2. White halo fungus
c. *Verticillium lecanii*	3. Virus
d. *Metarhizium anisopliae*	4. Bacteria

	a	b	c	d
A.	2	4	3	1
B.	4	3	2	1
C.	3	4	2	1
D.	2	3	4	1

18. Which among the following pesticide does not causes pesticide residues?

A. DDT B. BHC

C. Neem cake D. Aldrine

19. BHC was first synthesized by

A. Faraday B. Finkenbrink

C. Zeidler D. Glover

20. Entomological society of India started in

A. 1934 B. 1938

C. 1936 D. 1940

21. Pheromone trap is used to attract

A. Male moths B. Female moths

C. Adults D. Larvae of insects

22. HCN is a

A. Physical poison B. Protoplasmic poison

C. Respiratory poison D. Nerve poison

23. (i) Bhopal gas tragedy was occurred in the year 1994

(ii) In 1953, many people died due to parathion poisoning in Kerala

A. Both are correct B. (i) alone is correct

C. (ii) alone is correct D. Both are wrong

24. Pesticides shall be completely banned from 31st December 2020 are

A. Alachlor B. Dichlorvas

C. Phosphamidan D. All the above

25. Consider the statement and choose the correct one

(i) Netting – for hoppers, grass hopper

(ii) Sticky trap – sucking insects

(iii) Bait trap – shoot fly

A. All the statement are correct B. (i) and (ii) alone is correct

C. (ii) and (iii) alone is correct D. (i) and (iii) alone is correct

26. Chemicals when applied to plant or soil are absorbed by foliage or roots is called _____ type of pesticide.

A. Contact poison B. Systemic poison

C. Stomach poison D. Fumigant poison

27. In Kerala, which pesticide caused health hazard due to aerial spraying of cashew?

A. Methyl isocyanate B. DDT

C. BHC D. Endosulfan

28. A neem product used as insect repellent is

A. Azadirachtin B. Parathion

C. Rotenone D. Endrin

29. Which among the following is entomopathogenic microorganism

A. *Bacillus thuringiensis* B. *Bacillus cereus*

C. Both A and B D. None of the above

30. Important components of insect pest management are

A. Cultural B. Mechanical

C. Biological D. All the above

31. (i) Sex pheromonal system is highly evolved in lepidoptera

(ii) Pheromones are produced by eversible glands at the tip of abdomen of female

(iii) Sex pheromones have low carbon atoms and low molecular weight

A. All are correct B. (i) and (iii) are correct

C. (i) and (ii) are correct D. (iii) alone is correct

32. *Cryptolaemus montrouzieri* was imported from

A. China B. Japan

C. North America D. Australia

33. Scientific name of white muscardine fungus is

A. *Metarhizium anisopliae* B. *Hirsutella thompsonii*

C. *Beauveria bassiana* D. *Verticillium lecanii*

34. Composition of poison bait per hectare is

A. Rice bran 7.5 kg + Jaggery 7.5 kg + Carbaryl 7.5 kg + 7.5 lit of H_2O

B. Rice bran 12.5 kg + Jaggery 1.25 kg + Carbaryl 1.25 kg + water 7.5 lit

C. Rice bran 5.5 kg + Jaggery 2.5 kg + Carbaryl 1.25 kg + water 5 lit

D. Rice bran 10 kg + Jaggery 5 kg + Carbaryl 2.5 kg + 7.5 lit of H_2O

35. The fungus used to control the larvae of rhinoceros beetle in manure pit is

A. *Beauveria bassiana* B. *Verticillium lecanii*

C. *Metarhizium anisopliae* D. *Farinocystis tribolii*

36. What is the organism from which nereistoxin has been isolated?

A. Actinomycetes B. Bacterium

C. Marine annelid D. Fungus

37. Match the following (B with A)

A	B
a. *Hypothenemus* hampei	1. *Verticillium lecanii*
b. *Coccus viridis*	2. *Chelonus blackburni*
c. *Plutella xylostella*	3. *Beauveria bassiana*
d. *Phthorimaea operculella*	4. *Cotesia plutellae*

	a	b	c	d
A.	1	2	3	4
B.	2	3	4	1
C.	2	4	1	3
D.	4	3	2	1

38. Indicate the number of cocoons of *Fulgoraecia melanoleuca* for the management of sugarcane leaf hopper

A. 4000-5000 B. 500-1000

C. 1000-2000 D. 8000-9000

Answer keys

1	A	11	A	21	B	31	C
2	D	12	B	22	C	32	D
3	D	13	D	23	C	33	C
4	A	14	B	24	D	34	B
5	A	15	D	25	A	35	C
6	B	16	A	26	B	36	C
7	B	17	C	27	D	37	C
8	C	18	C	28	A	38	A
9	D	19	A	29	C		
10	C	20	B	30	D		

5

Apiculture

I. Choose the correct answer

1. Which is the most important family which consists of economically important honey bees?

   A. Agaonidae B. Apidae

   C. Anthophoridae D. Megachilidae

2. Which is the domesticated bee species indigenous to India?

   A. *Apis laboriosa* B. *Apis cerana indica*

   C. *Apis florea* D. *Apis dorsata*

3. Match the following (B with A)

A	B
a. *Apis dorsata*	1. Himalayan bee
b. *Apis andreniformis*	2. Little bee
c. Apis *laboriosa*	3. Rock bee
d. *Apis florae*	4. Black dwarf bee

	a	b	c	d
A.	3	4	1	2
B.	4	3	2	1
C.	1	3	2	4
D.	2	3	1	4

4. What is the annual yield from a rock bee colony?

   A. 0-15 kg B. 16-20 kg

   C. 25-37 kg D. 40-47 kg

5. Among the following, which bee species does not build multiple combs?

   A. *Apis cerana indica* B. *Apis andreniformis*

   C. *Apis mellifera* D. *Apis nigrocincta*

6. Which is the world's largest wild species of honey bee?

A. *Apis florea* B. *Apis dorsata*

C. *Apis laboriosa* D. *Trigona iridipennis*

7. What is the normal population expected in an Indian bee colony?

A. 5000 - 6000 B. 7000 - 8000

C. 9000 - 10000 D. 20000 - 30000

8. Corbicula is present in the worker bee

A. Fore legs B. Middle legs

C. Hind legs D. Both fore and middle legs

9. How many pairs of wax glands are present in the abdominal part of worker bee?

A. Two pairs B. Three pairs

C. Four pairs D. Five pairs

10. Indicate the number of ommatidia present in compound eye of drone

A. 4000 B. 5000

C. 6000 D. 8000

11. Match the following (B with A)

A	B
a. Pollen brush	1. Velum
b. Pollen basket	2. Alkaline gland
c. Dufour's gland	3. Corbicula
d. Fibula	4. Scopa

	a	b	c	d
A.	4	3	2	1
B.	3	2	1	4
C.	4	1	2	3
D.	1	2	3	4

12. Who was considered as father of American (or) modern bee keeping and founder of frame hive?

A. Fr. Newton B. L.L.Langstroth

C. Major Hruschka D. Moses Quinley

13. What are the abdominal tersites where the scent glands is situated in the foraging bees?

A. Between 3rd and 4th B. Between 4th and 5th

C. Between 5th and 6th D. Between 2nd and 3rd

14. The ectodermal exudates from the reigning queen is called queen substance which is categorized as

A. Allomone B. Kairomone

C. Allelo chemical D. Pheromone

15. Which glands of worker bee produce bee milk?

A. Mandibular glands B. Lateral pharyngeal glands

C. Acid glands D. Alkaline glands

16. Which type of bee is produced from unfertiliged eggs laid by the queen?

A. Drone B. Queen

C. Worker D. Both queen and worker

17. What is the name given to the resinous substance exuded by buds, leaves and other parts of various trees and shrubs and collected by the foraging bees?

A. Nectar B. Wax

C. Propolis D. Royal jelly

18. Match the following (B with A)

A	B
a. Ren.Fr.Newton	1. Honey extractor
b. Major Hruschka	2. Smoker
c. Langstroth	3. Seven frame hive
d. Moses Quinley	4. Bee space

	a	b	c	d
A.	3	4	2	1
B.	2	4	1	3
C.	2	1	4	3
D.	4	3	2	1

19. How many bee hives are available in India?

A. 2,00,000 B. 3,00,000

C. 4,00,000 D. 6,00,000

20. What is the temperature range in which the bees are most active in foraging?

A. 23-25°C B. 25-27°C

C. 27-29°C D. 30-31°C

21. How many trips the workers make to collect 500-1000 grams of pollen?

A. 2000 B. 4000

C. 6000 D. 8000

22. Who has described two types of dancing by foragers (Round and wag tail dones)?

A. Van Eonden B. Von Frisch

C. Thorpe D. Roleinson

23. Which disease is called Isle of wight disease?

A. Nosema B. Amoebic disease

C. Aocarine D. Sac brood

24. Match the following (B with A)

A	B
a. *Bacillus larvae*	1. Parafoul brood
b. *Bacillus pluton*	2. American foul brood
c. *Bacillus paraalveri*	3. Chalk brood
d. *Ascosphaera apis*	4. European foul brood

	a	b	c	d
A.	2	4	1	3
B.	3	4	1	2
C.	1	2	3	4
D.	2	3	1	4

25. What is the average annual per capita consumption of honey in India?

A. 2.4 g B. 4.4 g

C. 6.4 g D. 8.4 g

26. Among the following, which plant provides a rich supply of nectar?

A. Sweet potato B. Castor

C. Tamarind D. Neem

27. Which enzyme splits the sucrose of nectar into dextrose and levelose?

A. Amylase B. Lipase

C. Invertase D. Protease

28. The whole process of eliminating the moisture by the bees themselves is called as

A. Cooling B. Natural ripening

C. Heating D. Exclusion

29. Which type of bee hive is recommended for bee keeping of introduced species, *Apis mellifera*?

A. A type B. B type
C. C type D. D type

30. How many bee keepers are available in India?

A. 1,00,000 B. 1,50,000
C. 3,00,000 D. 5,00,000

31. Match the following (B with A)

A	B
a. Lesser wax moth	1. *Palarus orientalis*
b. Black ant	2. *Platybolium alvearium*
c. Bee hunter wasp	3. *Achroia grisella*
d. Tenelerionid beetle	4. *Camponotus compressus*

	a	b	c	d
A.	4	1	2	3
B.	3	2	1	4
C.	3	4	1	2
D.	2	1	4	3

32. What is the name of a rectangular box that traps the queen, but allow workers and drones to pass through?

A. Drone trap B. Swarm trap
C. Queen excluder D. Smoker

33. What is the flying speed of foraging bees normally?

A. 5-10 km/hr B. 10-15 km/hr
C. 15-20 km/hr D. 25-30 km/hr

34. Which group of insect pests causes bald brood condition in honey bees?

A. Ants B. Wasps
C. Wax beetles D. Wax moth

35. What is the distance between food source and the hive to perform wag tail dance by foraging bees?

A. Less than 40 metres B. Less than 60 metres
C. Less than 100 metres D. Greater than 100 metres

36. Which crop is found to be a very rich source to supply both nectar and pollen to the bees?

A. Glyricidia B. Maize

C. Cotton D. Sweet potato

37. Give an example for an endoparasitic tracheal mite of an adult bees.

A. *Varroa destructor* B. *Acarapis woodi*

C. *Pyemotes herfsi* D. *Tropilaelaps clareae*

38. Which bee species is considered to be sister species of *Apis florae*?

A. *Apis breviligula* B. *Apis andreniformis*

C. *Apis binghami* D. *Apis nigrocincta*

39. What is the name given for the subsequent swarms?

A. Secondary swarm B. Tertiary swarm

C. Cast swarm D. Fourth swarm

40. What is the protein content (by weight) in the royal jelly?

A. 15-20% B. 20-25%

C. 30-35% D. 40-43%

41. What is the life period of a queen bee?

A. 6 months B. 9 months

C. One year D. Two to three years

42. Which is the major honey producing state in India?

A. Karnataka B. Punjab

C. Tamil Nadu D. Jammu-Kashmir

43. The bees that go out first to find out new sources of pollen, nectar, propolis and water are called as

A. Feeder bees B. House bees

C. Scout bees D. Drifting bees

44. The comb of which honey bee is made up of a dark material called cerumen?

A. Indian bee B. Rock bee

C. Little bee D. Dammer bee

45. What is the bee space recommended for bee hive used for rearing *Apis mellifera*?

A. 7 mm B. 8 mm

C. 9 mm D. 10 mm

46. Match the following (B with A)

A	B
A. Cantharophily	1. Bees
B. Melittophily	2. Small moths
C. Psychophily	3. Butterflies
D. Phalaenophily	4. Beetles

	a	b	c	d
A.	4	3	2	1
B.	3	2	1	4
C.	2	4	3	1
D.	1	2	3	4

47. What is the percentage of dextrose and levulose in the honey?

A. 50-55% B. 55-60%

C. 60-75% D. 80-85%

48. How many weeks the house bees are confined to the hive to attend various duties from the time of emergence?

A. Two weeks B. Three weeks

C. Four weeks D. One week

49. Among the following, which plant is rich in pollen?

A. Banana B. Sorghum

C. Guava D. Soapnut tree

50. How many days, young worker bees feed the larvae in the queen cells with bee milk?

A. Two days B. Three days

C. Four days D. Five days

51. What is an average egg laying capacity per day of the queen bee of *Apis cerena indica*?

A. 100 B. 200

C. 300 D. 500

52. What is the percentage of population of workers in a bee colony?

A. 60% B. 70%

C. 80% D. 90%

53. What is the longevity of an adult worker bee?

A. 45-80 days B. 10-15 days

C. 20-25 days D. 30-35 days

54. What is the name for a mixture of honey and partially digested pollen, fed to the larvae in the worker cells of three days?

A. Propolis B. Bee bread

C. Rastellum D. Scopa

55. What is the honey yield potential (kg/colony/year) of Italian bee under migratory bee keeping conditions?

A. 10-15 B. 20-25

C. 30-35 D. 40-45

56. Indicate the year in which *Apis mellifera* has been introduced into the Punjab?

A. 1962 B. 1970

C. 1990 D. 1992

57. What is the term used to denote the pollination by bees?

A. Spromyophily B. Myophily

C. Melitophily D. Sphingophily

58. Name the disease which has almost wiped out the native colonies (*Apis cerana indica*) in Tamil Nadu?

A. Chalk brood B. Nosema

C. Varroasis D. Thai sac brood virus disease (TSBV)

59. Which group of insects are called as angles in agriculture?

A. Honey bees B. Beetles

C. Moths D. Butterflies

60. Melitophily refers to pollination caused by

A. Wasps B. Bees

C. Beetles D. Hawk moth

61. A single colony of rock bee yields upto

A. 30 kg of honey B. 40 kg of honey

C. 50 kg of honey D. 60 kg of honey

62. Apiculture is a subsidiary occupation and provides additional income to

A. Small farmers B. Marginal farmers

C. Landless labourers D. All the above

63. The ______ of worker bee secretes royal jelly.

A. Mandibular gland | B. Dufour's gland
C. Hypopharyngeal gland | D. Rectal gland

64. How many colonies of bees should be placed per hectare cropped area (Indian honey bee)?

A. 3 /ha | B. 5 /ha
C. 7 /ha | D. 12 /ha

65. Collection of pollen grains from leguminous crops by bees is called

A. Tripping | B. Nipping
C. Stripping | D. Dripping

66. Beekeeping was introduced to South India in the year ______.

A. 1920 | B. 1851
C. 1882 | D. 1911

67. What is the entomological name for Indian honey bee?

A. *Apis florea* | B. *Apis mellifera*
C. *Apis cerana indica* | D. *Apis dorsata*

68. Which among the following is not a good source of pollen and nectar (pasturage)?

A. Maize | B. Mango
C. Sunflower | D. Citrus

69. What is the flight distance travelled by bees to collect pollen / nectar?

A. 1 – 2 km | B. 2 – 3 km
C. 5 – 8 km | D. 8 – 10 km

70. Consider the statement and choose the correct one

(i) Prevent swarming – spring season management
(ii) Provide sugar syrup – summer season management
(iii) Provide new queen to hives – winter season management

A. (i) and (ii) alone are correct | B. (ii) and (iii) alone are correct
C. (i) and (iii) alone are correct | D. All the statements are correct

71. Which one of the following bee yields maximum honey?

A. Rock bee | B. Indian bee
C. Italian / European bee | D. Little bee

Answer keys

1	B	16	A	31	C	46	C	61	C
2	B	17	C	32	B	47	C	62	D
3	A	18	B	33	D	48	B	63	C
4	C	19	D	34	D	49	D	64	B
5	B	20	B	35	D	50	D	65	A
6	C	21	C	36	C	51	D	66	D
7	D	22	B	37	B	52	D	67	C
8	C	23	C	38	B	53	A	68	A
9	C	24	A	39	C	54	B	69	B
10	D	25	D	40	D	55	D	70	D
11	A	26	C	41	D	56	B	71	C
12	B	27	C	42	B	57	C		
13	C	28	B	43	C	58	D		
14	D	29	C	44	D	59	A		
15	B	30	B	45	D	60	B		

6

Sericulture

I. Choose the correct answer

1. What is the position of India in respect of raw silk production in global scenario?

   A. First — B. Second
   C. Third — D. Fourth

2. Which is called Vanya silk ?

   A. Eri — B. Tasar
   C. Muga — D. All the three combined

3. Which silk worm spins cocoons with discontinuous filament?

   A. Mulberry silk worm — B. Tasar silk worm
   C. Eri silk worm — D. Muga silk worm

4. How many persons get remunerative employment throughout the year from one acre of mulberry?

   A. 2 — B. 5
   C. 10 — D. 20

5. Indicate the year in which The Central Silk Board was started?

   A. 1929 — B. 1939
   C. 1949 — D. 1959

6. Which state is called The Silk Bowl of India ?

   A. Tamil Nadu — B. West Bengal
   C. Andhra Pradesh — D. Karnataka

7. Match the following (B with A).

A	B
a. Bombay teal	1. Muga silk worm
b. Soalu	2. Eri silk worm
c. Castor	3. Tasar silk worm
d. Arjun tree	4. Mulberry silk worm

	a	b	c	d
A.	2	3	4	1
B.	4	3	2	1
C.	4	2	1	3
D.	3	2	1	4

8. What is the length of semi hardwood cuttings of mulberry to be used as planting material?
   A. 10-15 cm B. 15-20 cm
   C. 20-25 cm D. 25-30 cm
9. What is the age of mulberry to be used for planting in the main field?
   A. 60-75 days B. 75-90 days
   C. 90-120 days D. 120-140 days
10. Which is the insect pest responsible for tukra symptom in mulberry?
   A. Leaf hopper B. Thrips
   C. Leaf webber D. Pink mealy bug
11. Give an example for subterranean pest attacking mulberry crop
   A. Black scale B. Termite
   C. Spiralling white fly D. Thrips
12. Match the following (B with A)

A	B
a. Pink mealy bug	1. *Bacillus subtilis*
b. Mulberry root rot	2. *Pseudomonas mori*
c. Bacterial leaf spot	3. *Meloidogyne incognita*
d. Root knot nematode	4. *Cryptolaemus montrouzieri*

	a	b	c	d
A.	4	3	2	1
B.	1	2	3	4
C.	2	3	4	1
D.	3	2	1	4

13. Name the rainfed mulberry variety suitable for red loamy soil
   A. MR 2 B. V 1
   C. S 13 D. S 34

14. Which silk is called as Ahimsa silk?

A. Mulberry silk B. Eri silk

C. Tasar silk D. Muga silk

15. Normally how many larvae instars occur in *Bombyx mori*?

A. Two B. Three

C. Four D. Five

16. What is the length of the silk filament in the cocoon of bivoltine race of *Bombyx mori*?

A. 300-400 m B. 400-500 m

C. 500-800 m D. 1000-1600 m

17. Which instar of mulberry silk worm is popularly called as black ant or black worm?

A. I instar B. II instar

C. III instar D. IV instar

18. Match the following (B with A).

A	B
a. Pure mysore	1. Cross breed
b. Kalimponga	2. Bivoltine hybrid
c. Cauvery	3. Multivoltine
d. Chamundi	4. Bivoltine

	a	b	c	d
A.	1	2	3	4
B.	2	3	4	1
C.	3	2	4	1
D.	3	4	1	2

19. How many distinct regions are present in the silk glands of mulberry silk worm?

A. Two B. Three

C. Four D. Five

20. Which region of silk gland secretes major protein of silk, fibroin?

A. Anterior region B. Middle region

C. Posterior region D. Both anterior and middle region

21. What is the proportion of sericin in cocoon shell?

A. 10% B. 20%

C. 30% D. 40%

22. The ideal size of the chopped leaves for II instar mulberry silk worm

A. 0.5 to 2 cm^2 B. 2 to 4 cm^2

C. 4 to 6 cm^2 D. 6 to 8 cm^2

23. What is the size of the cleaning nets used for V instar silk worm larvae?

A. 2 mm^2 B. 5 mm^2

C. 10 mm^2 D. 20 mm^2

24. Indicate the temperature requirement for I instar larvae of mulberry silk worm

A. 26-28°C B. 25-26°C

C. 24-25°C D. 23-24°C

25. What is the optimum density of silk worm larvae for chandriki?

A. 200-300 worms/m^2 B. 400-500 worms/m^2

C. 600-700 worms/m^2 D. 800-900 worms/m^2

26. Match the following (B with A).

A	B
A. Ishiwata glands	1. Cross breed for rainfed areas
B. Herald gland	2. Female larva (sexual mark)
C. BL23 x NB4D2	3. Cross breed for irrigated areas
D. BL24 x NB4D2	4. Male larva (sexual mark)

	a	b	c	d
A.	1	2	3	4
B.	3	1	4	2
C.	4	3	2	1
D.	2	4	1	3

27. Which disease is transmitted to offspring by transvorial transmission from mother moth?

A. Muscardine B. Pebrine

C. Flacherie D. Grasserie

28. Which is used to prevent evaporation of moisture and to maintain high humidity in the rearing bed of young silk worms?

A. Ant well B. Mountages

C. Chop sticks D. Paraffin paper

29. What is the optimum humidity recommended for V instar silk worms?

A. 85% B. 80%

C. 75% D. 70%

30. How many eggs are found in one Disease Free Laying (DFL) of bivoltine hybrid?

A. 300-350 B. 350-450

C. 450-500 D. 500-600

31. How many Disease Free Laying (DFL) can be easily reared per hectare of mulberry under irrigated condition?

A. 1000 B. 1500

C. 2500 D. 4000

32. What is the concentration of chlorine dioxide (general disinfectant) used in silk worm rearing?

A. 1% B. 1.5%

C. 2.5% D. 4%

33. What is the quantity of the bed disinfectant like vijetha recommended for rearing 100 dfls?

A. 1 kg B. 2 kg

C. 3 kg D. 5 kg

34. How many hyper parasitoids (*Nesolynx thymus*) are recommended to kill the uzi fly pupae?

A. One lakh/100 dfls B. Two lakhs/100 dfls

C. Three lakhs/100 dfls D. Four lakhs/100 dfls

35. What is the species of thrips that attack mulberry crop?

A. Thrips tabaci B. *Pseudodendrothrips mori*

C. *Scirtothrips dorsalis* D. *Rhipiphorothrips cruentatus*

36. Name the insecticide that is generally recommended for insect pest management in mulberry crop.

A. Dichlorovos B. Phosphamidon

C. Endosulfan D. Fenthion

37. Match the following (B with A.

B	A
a. Uzi fly	1. *Beauveria bassiana*
b. Pebrine	2. *Borrelina bombycis*

c. Grasserie | 3. *Exorista bombycis*
d. Muscardine (white) | 4. *Nosema bombycis*

	a	b	c	d
A.	4	3	1	2
B.	3	1	2	4
C.	1	2	3	4
D.	2	3	1	4

38. Name the plant, the leaf extract of which is recommended for the management of grosserie disease.
A. *Tridax procumbens* B. *Psoralea corylifolia*
C. *Trianthema portulacastrum* D. *Amaranthus viridis*

39. Indicate the year in which the Central Sericultural Research and Training Institute was established at Mysore.
A. 1943 B. 1948
C. 1962 D. 1972

40. What is the shell ratio of bivoltine races of silk worm?
A. 10% B. 15%
C. 20% D. 30%

41. What is the important symptom of uzi fly attached in the lake instar silk worm larvae?
A. Double cocoons B. Thin and flimsy cocoon
C. Perforated (pierced cocoon) D. Thin end cocoons

42. What is the name given to the cross breed, BL67xCSR3
A. Kabila *B.* Swarnandhra
C. Hemavathy D. Cauvery

43. What is the term used to denote the thickness of silk filament?
A. Epprouvette B. Denier
C. Gridle D. Cellule

44. Where the Central Sericultural Germplasm Research Centre is located?
A. Berhampore B. Hosur
C. Kodathi D. Pampore

45. Which is the bivoltine hybrid that is popular in Tamil Nadu at presently?
A. Nandhi B. Chamundi
C. CSR 2 x CSR 4 D. CSR 18 x CSR 19

46. Give an example for important insect pest that damages the cocoons in the storage (Grainage)

A. Dermestid beetle B. Straw mite

C. Ants D. Nematode

47. The quantity of cocoons required to obtain one kg of raw silk is known as

A. Brins B. Denier

C. Rendilta D. Jette bout

48. The process of killing the pupae without harming the cocoon shell is called

A. Riddling B. Steining

C. Twisting D. Stifling

49. What is the quantity of lime to be applied in the rearing bed during moulting?

A. 10-20 g/m^2 B. 20-30 g/m^2

C. 30-50 g/m^2 D. 70-80 g/m^2

50. Which disease is very common in young age worms?

A. Grasserie B. Flacherie

C. Muscardine D. Aspillosis

51. How much of labour can be saved by adopting shoot method of rearing?

A. 15-25% B. 30-40%

C. 60-70% D. 75-80%

52. What is the recommended quantity of FYM for one hectare of chawki mulberry garden per year?

A. 10 MT B. 20 MT

C. 30 MT D. 40 MT

53. Name the bed disinfectant developed by TNAU, Coimbatore.

A. Suchi B. RKO

C. Uijathe D. TNAU seri dust

54. The variety of mulberry which is unsuitable for rainfed condition is

A. S13 B. S34

C. V1 D. RFS 135

55. Silk fibre is a

A. Carbohydrate B. Fat

C. Protein D. Cellulose

56. Age of mulberry saplings to be used for planting in the main field is
   A. 60-75 days B. 75-90 days
   C. 90-120 days D. 120-140 days

57. Number of larval instars occur in *Bombyx mori* is
   A. Two B. Three
   C. Four D. Five

58. Resistant variety of mulberry to powdery mildew is
   A. Kanva 2 B. S 36
   C. S13 D. MR 2

59. Match the following

a.	*Morus* sp	1. Muga silkworm
b.	Soalu	2. Eri silkworm
c.	Castor	3. Tasar silkworm
d.	Arjun tree	4. Mulberry silkworm

	a	b	c	d
A.	4	1	2	3
B.	3	2	4	1
C.	4	3	2	1
D.	2	1	4	3

60. The rearing house of silkworm should face
   A. North-South B. East – West
   C. Either A or B D. South - North

61. The quantity of cocoons required to obtain one kg of raw silk is known as
   A. Brins B. Denier
   C. Renditta D. Jette hour

62. Chemical used to control uzi fly is
   A. 1% benzoic acid B. 2% propanoic acid
   C. 1% butyric acid D. 5% hypochloric acid

63. The ideal size of chopped leaves for feeding the silkworm during third instar stage is
   A. 0.5 - 1 cm B. 1 - 2 cm
   C. 4 - 6 cm D. 6 - 8 cm

64. Eri silkworms are commercially reared on

A. Mulberry leaves
B. Castor leaves
C. Tobacco leaves
D. None of the above

65. Identify the correct sequence of activities with regard to silkworm rearing

A. Brushing → mounting → chawki rearing → late age rearing
B. Mounting → brushing → chawki rearing → late age rearing
C. Mounting → chawki rearing → late age rearing → brushing
D. Brushing → chawki rearing → late age rearing → brushing

66. Which state produces maximum mulberry silk?

A. Karnataka
B. Andhra Pradesh
C. Tamil Nadu
D. West Bengal

67. Which one of the following is correctly matched with the pebrine disease of silkworm?

A. *Beauveria*
B. *Aspergillus*
C. *Nosema*
D. NPV

68. Consider the statements

(i) Four types of silkworm are reared in India

(ii) 89% of total silk produced in India come from mulberry silk worm

A. Statement (i) and (ii) are wrong
B. Statement (i) is wrong and (ii) is correct
C. Statement (i) is correct and (ii) is wrong
D. Statement (i) and (ii) are correct

69. DFL is related to

A. Silkworm
B. Earth worm
C. Honey bee
D. Soil pests

70. Stifling is the process involved in

A. Apiculture
B. Lac culture
C. Sericulture
D. Vermi culture

71. All silkworms belong to the insect order

A. Hemiptera
B. Lepidoptera
C. Coleoptera
D. Hymenoptera

72. Who isolated and identified the first pheromone, sex attractant from silkworm moths?

A. Karlson and Butenandt B. N.A. Cobb

C. C.V. Riley D. Albert Koebele

73. Ideal temperature for rearing silkworm is

A. 15°C to 20°C B. 25°C to 30°C

C. 10°C to 15°C D. 10°C to 20°C

74. How many cocoons are required to produce 1 kg raw silk?

A. 30,000 B. 20,000

C. 40,000 D. 60,000

75. What is the name of pheromone isolated from females of silkworm?

A. Gossyplure B. Bombykol

C. Helilure D. Spodolure

76. White muscardine disease is caused by

A. *Metarhizium anisopliae* B. *Nosema* sp.

C. *Beauveria bassiana* D. *Granulosis virus*

77. The second largest producer of silk is

A. Nepal B. India

C. China D. Japan

78. In India, mulberry silk is produced mainly in the states of

A. Karnataka. Andhra Pradesh,

B. Tamil Nadu, Jammu & Kashmir and West Bengal

C. Both A and B

D. None of the above

79. The non-mulberry silks are produced in

A. Jharkhand, Chhattisgarh, Odisha and North-Eastern states

B. Tamil Nadu, Jammu & Kashmir and West Bengal

C. Karnataka. Andhra Pradesh

D. None of the above

80. Primary food plant of mulberry silkworm is

A. *Morus indica* B. *M. alba*

C. *M. multicaulis* D. All the above

Answer keys

1	B	16	D	31	C	46	A	61	C	76	C
2	D	17	A	32	C	47	C	62	A	77	B
3	C	18	D	33	C	48	D	63	C	78	C
4	B	19	B	34	A	49	C	64	B	79	A
5	C	20	C	35	B	50	D	65	D	80	D
6	D	21	C	36	A	51	C	66	A		
7	A	22	B	37	A	52	D	67	C		
8	B	23	D	38	B	53	D	68	D		
9	C	24	A	39	C	54	C	69	A		
10	D	25	D	40	C	55	C	70	C		
11	B	26	B	41	C	56	C	71	B		
12	C	27	B	42	D	57	D	72	A		
13	C	28	D	43	B	58	D	73	B		
14	B	29	D	44	B	59	A	74	D		
15	D	30	D	45	C	60	B	75	B		

7

Storage Pests and Their Management

I. Choose the correct answer

1. Damage in rice weevil is caused by

   A. Adult only | B. Grub only
   C. Egg and grub | D. Both adult and grub

2. Example of field and storage pest is

   A. *Callosobruchus chinenis* | B. *Sitotroga cerealella*
   C. *Cylas formicarius* | D. All the above

3. Match the following

   A. Rice moth | 1. Pin head sized bore holes
   B. Cigarette beetle | 2. Rotting of tubers
   C. Khapra beetle | 3. Webbing of food grains
   D. Potato tuber moth | 4. Surface scratching

	a	b	c	d
A.	3	1	4	2
B.	2	1	4	3
C.	4	3	2	1
D.	2	3	4	1

4. Which of the following storage pest release quinines?

   A. Sweet potato weevil | B. Red flour beetle
   C. Fig moth | D. Rice moth

5. Drug store beetle is a storage pest of

   A. Rice | B. Tobacco
   C. Pulses | D. Turmeric

6. Safe storage moisture content is about

   A. > 18% | B. 15-16%
   C. 11-12% | D. 18%

7. Recommended dosage of aluminium phosphide for cover fumigation is

A. 21 tablets/ton of grain
B. 9 tablets/ton of grain
C. 3 tablets/ton of grain
D. 25 tablets/ton of grain

8. Insects can be controlled by

A. Decreasing O_2
B. Increasing CO_2
C. Both A and B
D. Decreasing N_2

9. Optimum temperature for storage is about

A. 13-25°C
B. 25-33°C
C. 35-37°C
D. >40°C

10. Rice weevil larvae feeds on grains

A. Internally
B. Externally
C. Broken grains
D. Scarving grains

11. The bruchid infestation in storage pulses can be treated with neem oil in ratio of

A. 1:50
B. 1:100
C. 1:25
D. 1:5

12. When storage space in godown is not sufficient, food grains are stored in the open air; this method of storage is known as

A. Open storage
B. Closed storage
C. CAP storage
D. Bulk storage

13. Bruchid beetle can cause pod damage in groundnut to the extent of

A. 70-80%
B. 80-90%
C. 90-100%
D. None of the above

14. Hermetic principles are related to

A. Soil pests
B. Foliar pests
C. Spices pests
D. Stored grain pests

15. Which among the following pests attack both field and storage?

A. Rice weevil and sweet potato weevil
B. Rice moth and fig moth
C. Red flour beetle and saw toothed grain beetle
D. Indian meal moth and potato tuber moth

16. Which among the following is not a secondary storage pest?

A. Saw toothed grain beetle
B. Long headed flour beetle
C. Flat grain beetle
D. Indian meal moth

17. Which among the following is not a internal feeder?
    A. Rice weevil B. Tamarind beetle
    C. Rice moth D. Cigarette beetle
18. Which among the following is not a external feeder?
    A. Rice moth B. Khapra beetle
    C. Almond moth D. Pulse beetle
19. Match list I with list II and choose the correct option given below

List I	**List II**
a. Lesser grain borer	1. *Callosobruchus maculatus*
b. Rice moth	2. *Rhyzopertha dominica*
c. Confused flour beetle	3. *Corcyra cephalonica*
d. Pulse beetle	4. *Tribolium surinamensis*

	a	b	c	d
A.	3	1	2	4
B.	2	3	4	1
C.	4	3	2	1
D.	3	4	1	2

20. Which chemical is safest for fumigation to control insects in storage?
    A. Ethylene di bromide B. Nemagon
    C. Alluminium phosphide D. Zinc phosphide
21. Stored grain insect pests can easily be controlled by maintaining temperature at
    A. 135ºF B. 150ºF
    C. 165ºF D. 120ºF
22. Stored grain pests can be killed by _____ hour exposure to 51.5-54.5°C
    A. 2 B. 3
    C. 5 D. 7
23. The best method to control stored grain pests is
    A. Fumigation B. Systemic insecticide
    C. Proper drying and storage D. Biological agents
24. Which of following insect infests the grains in the field and then comes to storage?
    A. *Ephestia cautella* B. *Tribolium castaneum*
    C. *Sitotroga cerealella* D. All of the above

25. Which of the following is not storage pest?
   A. Rodents B. Nematodes
   C. Bacteria D. Fungi

26. The storage pest which has become very serious in maize crop recently is
   A. *Spodoptera litura* B. *Spodoptera mauritia*
   C. *Spodoptera frugiperda* D. *Helicoverpa armigera*

27. Name the family of khapra beetle, a major pest on stored wheat
   A. Cucujidae B. Tenebrionidae
   C. Anobiidae D. Dermestidae

28. What is the ratio of zinc phosphide to be used with baiting for rodent management?
   A. 1:49 B. 1:19
   C. 1:29 D. 1:39

29. What is the dose of malathion 5% dust to be mixed with 100 kg of seed for storage pest management?
   A. 0.5 kg B. 1.0 kg
   B. 2.0 kg D. 3.0 kg

30. Match the following (B with A)

A	B
A. *Sitophilus oryzae*	1. Cigarette beetle
B. *Lasioderma serricorne*	2. Khapra beetle
C. *Pachymeres gonagra*	3. Rice weevil
D. *Trogoderma granarium*	4. Tamarind beetle

	a	b	c	d
A.	2	4	1	3
B.	1	3	2	4
C.	4	3	2	1
D.	2	4	3	1

Answer keys

1	D	6	C	11	B	16	D	21	B	26	C
2	D	7	C	12	C	17	C	22	B	27	D
3	A	8	C	13	C	18	D	23	A	28	A
4	B	9	B	14	D	19	B	24	C	29	B
5	D	10	A	15	A	20	C	25	B	30	A

8

Nematology

I. Choose the correct answer

1. The nematode which feeds on leaf tips of rice is

   A. *Aphelenchoides besseyi* B. *Tylenchulus sp.*

   C. *Rotylenchulus reniformis* D. *Radopholus similis*

2. The major nematode which attacks tuberose is

   A. *Globodera sp.* B. *Meloidogyne incognita*

   C. *Pratylenchus coffeae* D. *Helicotylenchus multicinctus*

3. Which statement is wrong?

   Statement 1: Scientific name of potato cyst nematode – *Globodera rostochiensis*

   Statement 2: Kufri jyoti is a resistant cultivar for potato cyst nematode

   A. Statement 1 alone is wrong B. Statement 2 alone is wrong

   C. Both statements are wrong D. Both statements are correct

4. Match the following

   a. Dagger nematode 1. *Tylenchulus semipenetrans*

   b. Tundu disease 2. *Heterodera avenae*

   c. Molya disease 3. *Xiphinema index*

   d. Slow decline 4. *Anguina tritici*

	a	b	c	d
A.	3	1	2	4
B.	2	1	4	3
C.	4	3	1	2
D.	3	4	2	1

5. Burrowing nematode can be managed by

   A. Malathion @ 0.1% B. Carbofuran 3G @ 40g

   C. Gypsum @ 200kg/ha D. Fenthion @ 0.5%

6. Which of the following statement is true?

   (i) The important components of IPM is exclusion, population reduction and tolerance

   (ii) Target species is the focal point of tolerance

   (iii) Exclusion is a preventive control measure

   A. All the statements are correct B. (i) and (ii) are correct

   C. (ii) and (iii) are correct D. (i) and (iii) are correct

7. Match the following

a. Ectoparasitic nematode	1. *Radopholus similis*
b. Semi-endoparasitic nematode	2. *Longidorus* sp
c. Endoparasitic nematode	3. *Aphelenchoides sp*
d. Leaf and bud nematode	4. *Rotylenchulus reniformis*

	a	b	c	d
A.	2	1	4	3
B.	3	4	2	1
C.	2	4	1	3
D.	2	3	1	4

8. Name the smallest nematode size?

   A. *Heterodera sp* B. *Paratylenchus sp*

   C. *Pratylenchus sp* D. *Meloidogyne spp*

9. Nematodes and wilt disease are major problems in the cultivation of

   A. Chrysanthemum B. Crotons

   C. Crossandra D. Crotalaria

10. Which nematode causes ufra symptom in rice crop?

    A. White tip nematode B. Rice root nematode

    C. Rice stem nematode D. Root knot nematode

11. Give the name of the genus of cyst nematode

    A. *Anguina* B. *Ditylenchus*

    C. *Globodera* D. *Meloidogyne*

12. Give an example for semi endoparasitic nematode

    A. Citrus nematode B. Reniform nematode

    C. Spiral nematode D. White tip nematode

13. What is the name of the chemical that has been imported from West Germany and tested against potato cyst nematode in Nilgiris?

A. DDT B. Fensulfothion

C. Aldicarb D. Carbofuran

14. Which is the chemical pesticide that is presently recommended in majority of situations for the management of phytonematodes?

A. DDT B. DBCP

C. Carbiofuran D. Aldicarb

15. Give the common name for the nematode under the genus *Hoplolaimus*

A. Dagger nematode B. Needle nematode

C. Lance nematode D. Stunt nematode

16. Triploblastic, bilaterally symmetrical, unsegmented, pseudocaelomate, vermiform and colourless organisms are called as

A. Centipedes B. Snails

C. Rodents D. Nematode

17. Give an example for effective acaricide

A. Carbaryl B. Dicofol

C. Phenthoate D. Quinalphos

18. Two varieties of potato viz *Kufri Swarna* and *Kufri Thenmalai* have been released as resistant varieties, which is the pest?

A. Potato tuber moth B. Potato cyst nematode

C. Cut worm D. White grub

19. Give an example for endoparasitic sedentary nematode

A. Lesion nematode B. Rice root nematode

C. Cyst nematode D. Stubby nematode

20. What is the name of chemical which is used against snails and slugs in vegetable crops?

A. Trimedlure B. Pherodin Sl

C. Metaldehyde D. Bromadialone

21. Which nematode is the vector of 'fan leaf' of grapes (NEPO virus)?

A. *Trichodorus pachydermus* B. *Xiphinema index*

C. *Xiphinema americanum* D. *Hoplolaimus indicus*

22. What is the common name for *Achatina fulica*?

A. Field crab B. Giant African snail

C. Tapioca millipede D. Rodent

23. Give the common name for *Ditylenchus dipsaci*

A. Stunt nematode B. Lance nematode

C. Spiral nematode D. Bulb and stem nematode

24. Which among the following is a entomopathogenic nematode?

A. *Meloidogyne incognita* B. *Pratylenchus coffeae*

C. *Radophdus similis* D. *Steinernema carpocapsae*

25. Who is the considered as the Father of Indian Nematology?

A. N.A. Cobb B. A.R.Seshadri

C. Needham D. Kuhn

26. Name the scientist who was responsible for the first report of nematode in India

A. Butler B. Jones

C. Barber D. Dastur

27. Sexual dimorphism is not found in

A. *Tylenchulus* sp B. *Rotylenchulus* sp

C. *Meloidogyne* sp D. *Radopholus* sp

28. *Pratylenchus* sp is commonly called as

A. Lance nematode B. Pin nematode

C. Stunt nematode D. Root lesion nematode

29. Biocontrol agent recommended for seed treatment and foliar application for the management of rice root and white tip nematode is

A. *Trichoderma viride* B. *Paecilomyces lilacinus*

C. *Pseudomonas fluorescens* D. *Pasteuria penetrans*

30. Name the nematode that can be managed by soil solarization of nursery beds by covering with polythene tarps for a fornight.

A. Root knot nematode B. Burrowing nematode

C. Rice root nematode D. Seed gall nametode

31. Match the following (B with A)

A	B
a. *Globodera rostochiensis*	1. Burrowing nematode of banana
b. *Radopholus similis*	2. Root knot nematode (Tomato)
c. *Tylenchulus semipenetrans*	3. Golden nematode of potato
d. *Meloidogyne incognita*	4. Citrus root nematode

	a	b	c	d
A.	1	3	4	2
B.	2	4	1	3
C.	4	3	2	1
D.	1	2	3	4

32. Indicate the polyphagous nematode mainly damaging vegetable crops like tomato, brinjal, bhendi and chilli

A. Cyst nematode
B. Root knot nematode
C. Lance nematode
D. Pin nematode

Answer keys

1	A	6	D	11	C	16	D	21	B	26	C	31	B
2	B	7	C	12	A	17	B	22	B	27	D	32	B
3	B	8	B	13	B	18	B	23	D	28	D		
4	D	9	C	14	C	19	C	24	D	29	C		
5	B	10	C	15	C	20	C	25	A	30	A		

9

Insecticides

I. Choose the correct answer

1. Select the exact expansion for the acronym 'IRM'

   A. Insect Resistance Management

   B. Insecticide Residue Management

   C. Insecticide Resistance Management

   D. Insect Resurgence Management

2. Match list I with list II by using the code given below

List I	List II
a. Physical poison	1. Nitrophenols
b. Protoplasmic poison	2. H_2S
c. Respiratory poison	3. Silica
d. Nerve poison	4. Pyrethrum

	a	b	c	d
A.	3	1	2	4
B.	1	2	3	4
C.	2	1	4	3
D.	3	2	4	1

3. Which one of the following is grouped under fumigants?

   A. HCH B. Aluminium phosphide

   C. Methyl eugenol D. Isopropyl cresols

4. Which one of the following is correctly matched?

   A. Arsenicals - Cycloate B. Carbamates - Hexaflurate

   C. Bipyridylliums - Paraquat D. Phenols - Dalapon

5. Which of the following chemical is most commonly used in India?

   A. Insecticide B. Herbicide

   C. Acaricide D. Fumigant

6. Insecticides Act was passed in the year

A. 1914 B. 1912

C. 1905 D. 1968

7. Organic pesticide isolated from actinomycetes is

A. Avermectins B. Spinosad

C. Imidacloprid D. Vertimec

8. Among the following, which is not an organophosphorus insecticide?

A. Acephate B. Chlorpyriphos

C. Dieldrin D. Fenitrothion

9. Given an example for insectidal formulation banned for manufacture, import and use in India

A. Carbofuran 50% SP B. Carbofuran 3% G

C. Dimethoate 30% EC D. Fenvalerate 20% EC

10. What is the quantity of spray fluid (litres/ha) for high volume sprayers for field crops?

A. 200 B. 400

C. 600 D. 800

11. In which group of insecticides, cholinesterase inhibition is reversible?

A. Organo chlorines B. Organophosphates

C. Carbamates D. Neonicotinoids

12. Give an example for neonicotinoid insecticide

A. Carbosulfan B. Imidacloprid

C. Thiametoxam D. Diflubenzuron

13. Name one insecticide extracted from actinomycetes, *Saccharopolyspora spinosa*

A. Profenofos B. Navaluron

C. Acetamiprid D. Spinosad

14. What is the name of the insecticide extracted from bacterium *Streptomyces avermitilis*?

A. Abamectin B. Cartap

C. Flufenoxuron D. Triazophos

15. Give an example for single dose anticoagulant rodenticide

A. Zinc phosphide B. Alumium phosphide

C. Warferin D. Bromodialone

16. Among the following, which is not a synthetic pyrethroid?

A. Fenvalerate B. Imidaclorprid

C. Cypermethrin D. Permethrin

17. Which group of insecticides acts as agonists of acetyl choline receptor?

A. Organo chlorine B. Synthetic pyrethroids

C. Neonicotinoid D. Insect growth regulator

18. Among the following, which is a non-systemic insecticide?

A. Profenofos B. Phosphamidon

C. Dimethoate D. Methyl demeton

19. Which is the cyclodiene insecticide that has been banned for manufacture, import and use in India?

A. Ethyl parathion B. Fenitrothion

C. Dieldrin D. Phosphamidon

20. When the Central Directorate of Plant Protection and Quarantine was established in India?

A. 1914 B. 1919

C. 1946 D. 1968

21. Give the name of the carbamate insecticide that has been banned for manufacture, import and use in India.

A. Chlordane B. Endrin

C. Aldicarb D. Ethyl parathion

Answer keys

1	C	6	D	11	C	16	B	21	C
2	A	7	B	12	B	17	C		
3	B	8	C	13	D	18	A		
4	C	9	A	14	A	19	C		
5	A	10	C	15	D	20	C		

UNIT VI: PLANT PATHOLOGY

1

Fundamentals of Plant Pathology

I. Choose the correct answer

1. First plant parasitic bacteria was reported by
   A. T.J. Burrill B. Needham
   C. Louis Pasteur D. Leeuwenhoek
2. Fungi, which can grow on living host plant, are called
   A. Obligate saprophyte B. Obligate parasite
   C. Facultative parasite D. Saprophytes
3. *Fusarium* belongs to order
   A. Melaconiales B. Moniliales
   C. Sporobolomycetales D. Cryptococcales
4. Heterocious nature of rust means
   A. A fungus require one host species to complete life cycle
   B. A fungus require two different host species to complete life cycle
   C. Both A and B
   D. None of the above
5. *Pythium* belongs to class
   A. Chytridiomycetes B. Oomycetes
   C. Zygomycetes D. Hypochytridiomycetes
6. *Levillula* is a
   A. Ectoparasitic B. Endoparasitic
   C. Both A and B D. None of the above
7. Modification of floral parts into leafy structures by pathogenic infection is called
   A. Hyperplasia B. Hypertrophy
   C. Phyllody D. Witch's broom

8. Mycoplasma is sensitive to
   A. Pencillin B. Streptomycin
   C. Bavistin D. Tetracycline
9. Plant overgrowth due to increase in size of cells of the tissue
   A. Hypoplasia B. Hypertrophy
   C. Hyperplasia D. All of the above
10. Pectinolytic enzymes of plant pathogens play a major role during pathogenesis in diseases like
    A. Rusts
    B. Downy mildew
    C. Wilts, damping-off and root/foot rots
    D. Powdery mildew
11. *Phyllactinis* causes the disease
    A. Powdery mildew B. Downy mildew
    C. Leaf spot D. Blight
12. Phytophthora belongs to family
    A. Peronophythoraceae B. Pythiaceae
    C. Perenosporaceae D. Albuginaceae
13. *Rhizopus* belongs to class
    A. Oomycetes B. Zygomycetes
    C. Trichomycetes D. Ascomycetes
14. Rust belongs to sub-division
    A. Zygomycotina B. Ascomycotina
    C. Basidiomycotina D. Deuteromycotina
15. Sexual dimorphism means
    A. Males and females are separate
    B. Males and females are morphologically dissimilar
    C. Female possess didelphic ovaries
    D. None of the above
16. The founder of mycology was
    A. Linnaeus B. Anton de Bary
    C. P. A. Micheli D. Saccardo

17. The genera *Claviceps*, *Alternaria* and *Sclerospora* are
    A. Bacteria B. Fungi
    C. MLO D. Virus
18. The organism included in order pernosporales cause the disease known as
    A. Downy mildew B. Smut
    C. Rust D. Powdery mildew
19. The plant disease primarily responsive for the Great Bengal Famine of 1943 was
    A. Blast disease of rice B. Bacterial blight of rice
    C. Udbatta disease of rice D. Brown leaf spot of rice
20. The plant mycoplasmal diseases are transmitted by
    A. Aphids B. Leaf hoppers
    C. Mites D. Above all
21. *Trichodorus* belongs to family
    A. Trichodoridae B. Heteroderidae
    C. Nacobbidae D. Longidoridae
22. *Uncinula* causes the disease
    A. Downy mildew B. Powdery mildew
    C. Blight D. Wilt
23. Virus is transmitted by nematode
    A. *Globodera* B. *Tylenchorhynchus*
    C. *Anguina* D. *Xiphinema*
24. The causal organism *Neovossia indica* produces
    A. Oospores B. Zoospores
    C. Urediospores D. Teliospores
25. Columella is a specialized sterile structure found in sporangium of
    A. *Ulothrix* B. Yeast
    C. *Spirogyra* D. *Rhizopus*
26. Yeast belongs to class
    A. Deuteromycetes B. Basidiomycetes
    C. Zygomycetes D. Ascomycetes

27. Gram positive plant pathogenic bacteria is

A. *Bacillus* B. *Xanthomonas*

C. *Pseudomonas* D. *Corneybacterium*

28. Thread like filaments of fungi is known as

A. Conidia B. Mycorrhiza

C. Sporangium D. Hyphae

29. Which of the following is not a fungal disease?

A. White rust of crucifers B. Black rust of wheat

C. Red rust of tea D. Red rot of sugarcane

30. Gametangial copulation (conjugation) is common in

A. Zygomycetes B. Ascomycetes

C. Phycomycetes D. Deuteromycetes

31. Dikaryon formation is characteristic of

A. Ascomycetes and basidiomycetes

B. Phycomycetes and basidiomycetes

C. Ascomycetes and phycomycetes

D. Phycomycetes and zygomycetes

32. A widely but periodically occurring plant disease is

A. Endemic B. Pandemic

C. Sporadic D. Epiphytotic

33. Fungal hyphae are able to penetrate the host with the help of

A. Mechanical pressure B. Softening by enzymes

C. Both A and B D. Suckers and hooks

34. The disease produced by fungus *Ustilago* is known as smuts because

A. They parasitise cereals

B. The affected host becomes completely black

C. Their mycelium is black

D. They produced sooty mass of spores

35. Spores in sporangia are produced by process

A. Sexual B. Asexual

C. Both of these D. None of these

36. Which one of the following is the largest group of fungi?
    A. Zygomycota B. Ascomycota
    C. Basidiomycota D. Deuteromycota
37. All such fungi in which sexual phase has not been observed are present in
    A. Zygomycota B. Ascomycota
    C. Basidiomycota D. Deuteromycota
38. Solar energy treatment for control of loose smut of wheat was given by
    A. Luthra B. Prevost
    C. Katan D. S. Nagarajan
39. Fungi can be stained by
    A. Saffarine B. Cotton blue
    C. Glycerine D. Lactophenol
40. Fungi usually store the reserve food material in the form of
    A. Starch B. Lipid
    C. Glycogen D. Protein
41. Fungi can be distinguished from algae in fact that
    A. Cell wall is cellulosoic cell wall and chlorophyll is absent
    B. Nucleus is present
    C. Mitochondria are absent
    D. Cell wall is chitinous and chlorophyll is absent
42. Ergot is obtained from
    A. *Rhizopus* B. *Claviceps*
    C. *Albugo* D. *Phytomonas*
43. One of the following is predatory fungus
    A. *Arthrobotrys* B. *Puccinia*
    C. *Fusarium* D. *Alternaria*
44. Fungi usually producing eight spores in a sac like structure belong to
    A. Phycomycetes B. Ascomycetes
    C. Basidiomycetes D. Dueteromycetes
45. One of the following is a heterocious fungus
    A. *Albugo* B. *Phytopthora*
    C. *Puccinia* D. *Ustilago*

46. In some parasitic fungi a globular or hook like structure is formed at the point of contact with the host. This is known as

A. Haustoria B. Appresorium

C. Hold fast D. Hook

47. Fungi which grow on dung is termed as

A. Coprophilus B. Terricolous

C. Saxicolous D. Saxiphilous

48. The fruiting body of *Aspergillus* is called

A. Apothecium B. Perithecium

C. Cleistothecium D. Hypanthodium

49. All fungi are

A. Autotrophs B. Saprophytes

C. Parasites D. Heterotrophs

50. Yeast is unlike bacteria in being

A. Unicellular B. Multicellular

C. Prokaryotic D. Eukaryotic

51. Hyphae are multinucleate and aseptae in

A. Ascomycetes B. Basidiomycetes

C. Zygomycetes D. Dueteromycetes

52. Heterothalism in fungi was discovered by

A. Bessy B. Blackslee

C. Micheli D. De bary

53. Which one of the following enzymes is present in the bacteriophage?

A. Succinic dehydrogenase B. Lysozyme

C. Protease D. Urease

54. Which one of the following viruses contains both DNA and RNA?

A. Cyanophage B. Herpes virus

C. Leuko virus D. Polio virus

55. Viroids have

A. DS-DNA enclosed by protein coat

B. SS-DNA not enclosed by protein coat

C. SS-RNA not enclosed by protein coat

D. DS-RNA enclosed by protein coat

56. Which of the following statements is false?
    A. The bacteriophage has a double stranded DNA molecule
    B. Most plant viruses are RNA viruses
    C. TMV has a double stranded RNA molecule
    D. Most animal viruses are DNA viruses
57. The genetic material in virus is
    A. DNA and RNA B. DNA only
    C. RNA only D. DNA or RNA
58. The simple breaking of mycelium resulting in the formation of a new mycelium from each broken segments is called
    A. Sporing B. Conidiation
    C. Budding D. Fragmentation
59. Akiochi disease is due to
    A. Boron toxicity B. Sulphur toxicity
    C. Zinc toxicity D. Copper toxicity
60. Which of the following is a characteristic of plant virus?
    A. DNA + Protein B. RNA + Protein
    C. DNA or RNA+ Protein D. DNA or RNA+ Protein+ Lipid
61. First Indian Plant Pathologist to study in detail on fungi and plant diseases was
    A. M. J. Thirumalachar B. Prof. Jaichand Luthra
    C. J. F. Dastur D. Dr. Karam Chand Mehta
62. Gene to gene hypothesis was given by
    A. Flor B. Stanley
    C. Julius kuhn D. B. B. Mundkur
63. Destructive Insect Pest Act was passed in
    A. 1912 B. 1914
    C. 1916 D. 1918
64. Potato famine in Ireland (1845) was caused by
    A. *Phytophthora palmivora* B. *Plasmopara viticola*
    C. *Puccinia graminis* D. *Phytophthora infestans*
65. The class ends with
    A. Mycotina B. Mycetes
    C. Oomycetes D. Zygomycetes

66. Leaf curl of tobacco is caused by

A. Nicotina virus Ca-1 B. Nicotina virus-10

C. MLO D. Viroid

67. _____________ proposed a classification of fungi which is now widely accepted

A. Walker (1957) B. Stakman and Harrar (1957)

C. Whittaker (1969) D. Ainsworth (1973)

68. The adjacent cell of the same fungal hypha brought into communication with each other by means of loops is known as

A. Clamp connection B. Appresorium

C. Capsid D. Cleistothecia

69. The imperfect or asexual stage of a fungus is known as

A. Anamorph B. Catamorph

C. Mixomorph D. Biomorph

70. The toxin produced by the fungus of *Drechslera oryzae* , which is highly toxic to rice seedlings is called

A. Cochliobolin B. Biocide

C. Teflatoxin D. Aflatoxin

71. The new name of IPGRI is

A. IBPGR B. NBPGR

C. Biodiversity International D. None of the above

72. Association of fungi with roots of higher plants is known as

A. Lichen B. Mycorrhiza

C. Ascolichen D. Basidiolichen

73. Life cycle of smut fungi was discovered by?

A. Robert Hartig B. Oskar Brefeld

C. J.H. Walker D. Robert koch

74. Which of the following statements is/are correct for eucarpic fungi?

A. Habitat is saprophytic and mycelium coenocytic

B. The reproductive organs arise from a part of thallus while the rest carries out somatic function

C. The entire thallus may be converted into reproductive structure so that somatic and reproductive phases do not occur in some individual

D. All of the above

75. The zygospores are not generally formed in a culture of *Rhizopus* developed from a single spore because of

A. Lack of light

B. Shortage of oxygen

C. Absence of plus (+) and (-) strains of mycelium

D. None of these

76. Perfect stage of a fungus means

A. When the fungus is perfectly health

B. When it reproduces asexually

C. When it forms perfect sexual spores

D. None of these

77. The naked multinucleus mass of protoplasm is called as

A. Mycelium B. Plasmodium

C. Thallus D. Hyphae

78. Which of the following is/are necrotroph (Perthotrophs) fungi?

A. *Sclerotium, Sclerotinia* B. *Botryotinia, Botrytis*

C. *Alternaria, Rhizoctonia* D. All of the above

79. Bulbous base with pointed tip type cleistothecial appendages are found in

A. Oidium B. Erysiphe

C. Phyllactinia D. Both A and B

80. Members of which group of fungi are referred as club fungi?

A. Basidiomycotina B. Ascomycotina

C. Zygomycotina D. None of the above

81. Group/s of basidiomycotina fungi which do not have clamp connection and dolipore septa in its/their mycelium

A. Rust B. Smut

C. Bunt D. Both A and B

82. The rust in which uredial stage is absent is called demicyclic rust. The example of demicyclic rust is

A. Cedar apple rust – *Gymnosporangium juniperi virginianae*

B. Rust of horse parsley (*Smyrnium olusatrum*) – *Puccinia smyrnii*

C. Rust of koa (*Acacia koa)* – *Alelocauda koae*

D. All of the above

83. Which group of fungi is known as fungi imperfection or dustbin fungi?
A. Basidiomycotina B. Deuteromycotina
C. Ascomycotina D. Zygomycotina
84. Amotile sporangiospores (aplanospores) are produced in
A. *Rhizopus* B. *Mucor*
C. Both A and B D. None of the above
85. Trap is found in which fungal genera?
A. *Rhizopus* B. *Claviceps*
C. *Dactylaria* D. All of the above
86. Perithecium is found in which of the fungal genera?
A. *Rhizopus* B. *Claviceps*
C. *Albugo* D. *Dactylaria*
87. Which of the following is characterized by the lack of an observed sexual phase in its members life cycle?
A. Glomeromycota B. Basidiomycota
C. Zygomycota D. Deuteromycota
88. Members of this phylum produce two kinds of haploid spores, one kind being asexually produced conidia
A. Zygomycota B. Ascomycota
C. Basidiomycota D. Glomeromycota
89. The ascomycetes get their name from which aspect of their life cycle?
A. Vegetative growth form B. Asexual spore production
C. Sexual structures D. Shape of the spore
90. Columella is a specialized structure found in the sporangium of
A. *Spirogyra* B. *Ulothrix*
C. *Rhizopus* D. None of these
91. Which pair of the following belongs to basidiomycetes?
A. Puffballs and *Claviceps* B. *Peziza* and stink horns
C. *Morchella* and mushrooms D. Birds nest fungi and puffballs
92. In the fungal classification system ascomycetes come under the division of
A. Gymnomycota B. Mastigomycota
C. Amastigomycota D. Gymnomycota, Mastigomycota

93. In the ascomycete life cycle, meiosis takes place within a
 A. Sporangium B. Ascus
 C. Conidium D. Conidiophore

94. In an ascomycete, the female gametangium is the
 A. Antheridium B. Sperm
 C. Ascogonium D. Ascus

95. Which of the following statements about the deuteromycetes is false?
 A. Most deuteromycetes are clearly basidiomycetes
 B. In some, the sexual phase of the life cycle has not been discovered.
 C. Some have a sexual phase, but it is not the principal basis of classification.
 D. Some have a sexual phase, but the organism is classified because of its resemblance to an organism that lacks a sexual phase.

96. Which of the following statements about the mycelium of the basidiomycota is false?
 A. The primary mycelium is monokaryotic.
 B. The secondary mycelium is dikaryotic.
 C. The tertiary mycelium is dikaryotic.
 D. Clamp connections are characteristic of the monokaryotic mycelium.

97. Members of the phylum basidiomycota that have a peridium belong to the class
 A. Hymenomycetes B. Teliomycetes
 C. Ustomycetes D. Gasteromycetes.

98. In the life cycle of *Puccinia graminis*, dikaryotic hyphae extend downward from the spermogonium and give rise to
 A. Spermogonia B. Spermatia
 C. Aecia D. Uredinia

99. Ergotism is responsible for all of the following except
 A. Hallucinations B. Irish potato famine
 C. Both A and B D. Gangrene

100. Nuclear fusion in basidium is done by process of
 A. Budding B. Meiosis
 C. Mitosis D. Grafting

101. Smut pathogen differs from rust pathogen in having

A. Facultative parasitism B. Obligate parasitism

C. Obligate parasitism D. All of the above

102. Which of the following fungi is commonly known as white mold/stem rotting

A. *Rhizoctonia solani* B. *Sclerotinia sclerotiorum*

C. *Fusarium solani* D. *Albugo candia*

103. Characteristic H-shaped structure of primary sporidia is found in

A. *Neovossia* B. *Ustilago*

C. *Sphaerotheca* D. *Tilletia*

104. Naked asci are produced in the class

A. Discomycetes B. Pyrenomycetes

C. Plectomycetes D. Hemiascomycetes

105. The enlargement of host tissues due to excess cell division is called

A. Hyperplasia B. Hypertrophy

C. Hypoplasia D. Hypotrophy

106. Yeast belongs to class

A. Deuteromycetes B. Basidiomycetes

C. Zygomycetes D. Ascomycetes

107. Dr. B. B. Mundkur is credited for his work on

A. Rust B. Smut

C. Late blight D. Mildew

108. The book Fungi and Plant Diseases was written by

A. Mundkur B. Butler

C. Beijerinck D. Prasad

109. The phenomenon in which a plant tissue infected with one strain of a virus is protected from infection by other strains of the same virus is called as

A. Cross protection B. Cryoscopy

C. Cryotherapy D. Cryobiology

110. A virus that may not destroy the host are called

A. Virulent phage B. Cyanophage

C. Temperate phage D. Lytic cycle

111. _______is inhibition of growth and thereby showing stunting and dwarfing effect on the plants

A. Hyperplasia B. Atrophy
C. Hypertrophy D. Necrosis

112. Phylum plasmodiophoromycetes (Lower fungi) belong to kingdom

A. Chromista B. Protozoa
C. Eumycota D. Mycota

113. Mycosphaerella musicola produces asci within

A. Perithecium B. Apothecium
C. Locules D. Cleistothecium

114. Viruses enter the plant cells through the process of

A. Osmosis B. Pinocytosis
C. Diffusion D. Plasmolysis

115. Dictyospora is a spore with

A. Only horizontal septa
B. Only vertical septa
C. Both horizontal and vertical septa
D. No septa

116. The teliospores of *Sphacelotheca sorghi* causing grain smut of sorghum can remain viable for

A. 2 years B. 4 years
C. 13 years D. < 1 year

117. MLO's (Phytoplasmas) in plant system are translocated through

A. Phloem sieve tubes B. Xylem vessels
C. Cambium tissues D. Plasmodesmata connections

118. LOPAT test is used for the identification of

A. *Xanthomonas* B. *Fluorescent Pseudomonas*
C. *Xylella* D. *Agrobacterium*

119. Bimodal transmission is seen in case of

A. Geminivirus B. Bromovirus
C. Caulimovirus D. Tobamovirus

120. Saccharomycodes ludwigii ascus produces

A. 16 ascospores B. 8 ascospores
C. 4 ascospores D. Large number of ascospore

121. The zygospores formed by the conjugation of gametangia are
   A. Thick walled and black B. Thin walled and blue
   C. Thick walled and blue D. Thin walled and green

122. Who classified fungi under kingdom myceteae of super kingdom eukaryota?
   A. Whittaker B. Copeland
   C. Gregory D. Alexopoulos and Mims

123. Saprophytes and parasites both are found in
   A. Oomycetes B. Chytridiomycetes
   C. Zygomycetes D. All of the above

124. Polyplanetism is found in
   A. *Albugo* B. *Achlya*
   C. *Systopus* D. *Phytophthora*

125. Which of the following are not the members of zygomycetes
   A. *Mucor*
   B. *Choanephora cucurbitarum*
   C. *C. trispora*
   D. *Albugo*

126. Apothecium, fruiting body, is found in
   A. *Claviceps* B. *Peziza*
   C. *Phyllactina* D. *Phytophthora*

127. Receptive region, female reproductive organ in *Aspergillus* is
   A. Stalk B. Trichogyne
   C. Ascogonium D. All of the above

128. Which of the following is an important sex hormone in fungi?
   A. Sirenin B. Antheridiol
   C. Hormone D. All of the above

129. Stanley received Noble prize in 1935 for
   A. Crystallization of TMV B. Discovery of bacteriophage
   C. Discovery of interferon D. All of above

130. Which of the following insect is vector of TMV?
   A. *Myzus persicae* B. *M. pseudosolenoid*
   C. *Microsiphon solanifolii* D. All of the above

131. Bacteriophages were discovered by
A. W.M. Stanley
B. Dmitri Ivanowski
C. Twort and D' herelle
D. Beijerinck

132. Plant viruses can be cultivated by
A. Rubbing virus suspension on leaves
B. Co-culturing virus with protoplast culture
C. Both the above
D. None of these

133. Transmission of bean mosaic virus and necrotic ring spot virus in plants takes place through
A. Suckers
B. Rhizomes
C. Corms
D. Pollen grains

134. The bacteria that causes cancer and gummosis is
A. *Pseudomonas syringae*
B. *Agrobacterium tumefaciens*
C. *Xanthomonas campestris*
D. All of above

135. Father of phytobacteriology is
A. Edward Jenner
B. Robert Koch
C. E.F. Smith
D. Millardet

136. Muller (1961) proposed the role of______in disease resistance in plants?
A. Phytoalexins
B. Phytoalleles
C. Heparins
D. All of the above

137. The pathogen causing a simple interest disease in plant is called?
A. Polycyclic pathogen
B. Phytoalexins
C. Monocyclic pathogen
D. None of the above

138. The pathogen which spread internally throughout the host shows
A. Localized invasion
B. Systemic invasion
C. Resistance
D. No effect

139. The stage when pathogens, after deep dormant phase, again start with the active phase of pathogenesis is called as
A. Perennation
B. Penetration
C. Primary inoculum
D. All of the above

140. Which of the following is not air borne disease in plant?
A. Downy mildew
B. Powdery mildew
C. Late blight
D. Southern blight

141. When will damping off disease of seedlings become very severe?
   A. When the temperature increases
   B. When the temperature decreases
   C. When the moisture content of soil increases
   D. All of above

142. Indicator plant for the diagnosis of Plum Pox Virus (PPV) and Prune Dwarf Virus (PDV) is
   A. *Prunus tomentosa* B. *Papaver somnifera*
   C. Babool D. All of above

143. Techniques used for sampling of air borne pathogen is
   A. Tilak sampler B. Setting plate
   C. Burkard spore trap D. All of the above

144. Chitin and ergosterol, if present in the plants, are indicative of which pathogen
   A. RLOs B. Bacterial
   C. Fungal D. Phytoplasma

145. The first computer simulation programme to simulate early blight, epidemics of tomato and potato was
   A. EPIVEN B. EPIDEMIC
   C. EPIDEM D. MYCOS

146. Which of the following is pathotype specific in plants?
   A. Vertical resistance B. Horizontal resistance
   C. Both the above D. None of the above

147. In India (1914), first quarantine regulation was passed by government under the title?
   A. Destructive Insects and Pests Act (DIP ACT)
   B. Federal Quarantine Act
   C. Seed Act
   D. All of the above

148. The spores which are produced typically by the binucleate mycelium and mainly function as repeating spores for the spread of rust disease in wheat is called
   A. Aeciospores B. Basidiospores
   C. Urediospores D. Teleutospores

149. A sclerotium refers to a modified mycelium which is
A. An underground structure
B. A hard resting body
C. Mainly a food storing organ
D. Easily carried off by wind

150. Target board effect is caused by
A. *Alternaria*
B. *Colletotrichum*
C. *Pyricularia*
D. *Helminthosporium*

151. Only asexual reproduction is found in
A. Ascomycetes
B. Basidiomycetes
C. Oomycetes
D. Deuteromycetes

152. The basidiospores are
A. Exogenous spores
B. Endogenous spores
C. Both A and B
D. None of these

153. *Peziza* is a member of
A. Phycomycetes
B. Ascomycetes
C. Basidiomycetes
D. Deuteromycetes

154. The spermatization takes place in
A. *Neurospora*
B. *Penicillium*
C. *Peziza*
D. *Erysiphe*

155. *Neurospora sitophila* is known as
A. Black mold
B. Red mold
C. Blue mold
D. Green mold

156. The mycelium of *Erysiphe* is
A. Aseptate
B. Septate
C. Both A and B
D. None of these

157. Haplo-diplo-biontic life-cycle is exhibited by
A. Yeast
B. *Mucor*
C. *Penicillium*
D. *Aspergillus*

158. Heterothallism was discovered by
A. Blakeslee
B. Faraday
C. Alexopoulos
D. Gaumann

159. After fusion of sexual gametes in *Mucor*, the resultant structure is known as
A. Oospore
B. Cleistothecium
C. Zygospore
D. Zygote

160. Fungal spores produced asexually at tips or side of hyphae are called

A. Sporangiospores B. Anthrospores

C. Conidia D. Spores

161. What is the mode of nutrition in *Rhizopus*?

A. Autotrophic B. Parasitic

C. Symbiotic D. Saprophytic

162. The brown gills of the mushroom

A. Have no function to perform

B. Are meant for its respiration

C. Help the plant to float in water after heavy rains

D. Bears spores which help in reproduction

163. The rusts are caused by

A. Ustilaginales B. Peronosporales

C. Uredinales D. Erysiphales

164. The name smut diseases is given to those produced by *Ustilago* because

A. Its mycelium is black in colour

B. It parasitizes cereals

C. The host becomes completely black

D. The fungus produces black sooty spore masses

165. In *Phytophthora* the asexual reproductive bodies behave as

A. Conidia

B. Sporangia

C. Conidiosporangia,

D. Both conidia and conidiosporangia

166. A phragmo-basidium means

A. An entire basidium which is fully reproductive

B. A septate basidium which for all purposes is one structure

C. A septate basidium where only one cell is reproductive

D. A septate basidium where both cells are reproductive

167. The classification of the fungi is based mainly on

A. The structure of vegetative mycelium

B. The asexual stage

C. The sexual reproductive stage

D. Both the mycelial structure and sexual stages

168. In the ascomycetes karyogamy occurs within the

A. Ascogonium B. Antheridium

C. Ascus D. Ascogenous hypha

169. The protective covering of sterile hyphae around an ascocarp is termed as

A. Periderm B. Peridium

C. Appendages D. Epiderm

170. Stroma is

A. Compact somatic hyphae with fruit bodies

B. Loosely interwoven hyphae

C. A small hyphal branch

D. A group of spores

171. The fertile portion in the fruiting body of *Lycoperdon* is called

A. Gleba B. Peridium

C. Hymenium D. Gills

172. Diplanetism is exhibited by

A. *Phytophthora* B. *Saprolegnia*

C. *Mucor* D. *Albugo*

173. The process of self-fertilization in fungi is known as

A. Automixis B. Amphimixis

C. Spermatization D. Somatogamy

174. Spore balls are the characteristic feature of

A. *Sapcelotheca* B. *Tolyposporium*

C. *Tellita* D. *Neovassia*

175. Spiroplasma causes

A. Citrus stubborn B. Spike disease

C. Corn stunt D. Both A and C

176. Which one of the following organ of fungus develop into germ tube?

A. Sclerotium B. Rhizoids

C. Haustorium D. Appressorium

177. Naked asci is seen on

A. *Taphrina* B. *Sclerotium*

C. *Erysiphe* D. None of the above

178. Saucer shaped depressed mass of aggregated hyphae

A. Acervuli B. Pycnidia

C. Sporodochia D. Synameta

179. J hook symptom is observed in____________

A. Crown gall B. Banana bunchy top

C. Flat limb D. Anthracnose

180. MLO and spiroplasma are mostly

A. Xylem inhibiting B. Phloem inhibiting

C. Both A and B D. Stomata inhibiting

181. The science which deals with the cause of the plant diseases and nature of the causal agent

A. Etiology B. Aetiology

C. Fertilization D. Both A and B

182. The fungi which transmits the viruses belongs to the class

A. Basidiomycetes B. Oomycetes

C. Zygomycetes D. Plasmodiophoromycetes

183. Renowned scientist Dr. N. E. Borlaug belongs to

A. Entomology B. Agronomy

C. Genetics D. Plant Pathology

184. Fungi imperfecti includes in

A. Basidiomycotina B. Oomycetes

C. Deuteromycotina D. Ascomycotina

185. Which of the following is the type of species of genus begomovirus?

A. Bean mosaic virus B. Bean golden mosaic

C. Cucumber mosaic virus D. Lettuce necrosis virus

186. PLAM is a computerized prediction symptom for

A. Potato late blight B. Pea root rot

C. Peanut leaf spot D. Fire blight of apple / pear

187. Which scientist first crystallized the plant virus?

A. Bawden B. Ivanowski

C. Beijerinck D. Stanley

188. Orobanche is a
   A. Total root parasite B. Semi root parasite
   C. Semi stem parasite D. Total stem parasite
189. Which of the following fungicide is commonly known as Kitteson's killer
   A. Bavistin B. Captan
   C. Carbendazim D. Triadimefon
190. Indian stem rust rules for *Puccinia graminis tritici* was given by
   A. Eriksson B. KC Mehta
   C. Nagarajan and Singh D. E. C. Stackman
191. Who proposed Indian rusts genus mehtamyces?
   A. Mundkur and Thirumalachar B. Mundkur and Kheswala
   C. Capoor *et al.* D. Giri *et al.*
192. The perfect stage of *Rhizoctonia solani* is
   A. *Glomerella tucumanensis* B. *Thanatephorus cucumeris*
   C. *Magnaporthe grisea* D. *Cochliobolus miyabeanus*
193. Normally spherical viruses contain
   A. Higher nucleic acid and lower protein
   B. Higher protein and lower nucleic acid
   C. Lipida
   D. None of the above
194. Suicidal germination takes place in
   A. Dodder B. Striga
   C. Loranthus D. *Dendrophthoe falcata*
195. Specialized feeding hyphae (haustoria) of endomycorrhiza is called
   A. Arbuscules B. Vesicles
   C. Appressona D. Both A and B
196. Claviceps purpurea produces
   A. Allotoxin B. Rubrotoxin
   C. Ergotoxin D. All of these
197. Which one of the following groups consists of systemic fungicides?
   A. Bavistin, Topsin-M, Captan B. Plantvax, Emisan, Calisin
   C. Vitavax, Bavistin, Calisin D. Ziram, Plantvax, Blitox

198. The term fungus was coined by
   A. Gaspard Bauhin B. De Bary
   C. E.J. Butler D. Sadasivan

199. In a long cycled rust "0" stage refers to
   A. Aecium B. Uredium
   C. Pycnium D. Basidium

200. __________ is an example of compound interest disease?
   A. Late blight of potato B. Rust of wheat
   C. Powdery mildew of wheat D. All the above

Answer keys

1	A	26	D	51	C	76	C	101	C	126	B	151	D	176	D
2	B	27	D	52	B	77	B	102	B	127	B	152	B	177	A
3	B	28	D	53	B	78	D	103	D	128	D	153	B	178	A
4	A	29	C	54	C	79	C	104	D	129	A	154	A	179	B
5	B	30	A	55	B	80	A	105	A	130	D	155	B	180	B
6	B	31	A	56	C	81	A	106	D	131	C	156	B	181	D
7	C	32	D	57	D	82	D	107	B	132	C	157	A	182	D
8	D	33	C	58	D	83	B	108	A	133	D	158	A	183	D
9	B	34	D	59	B	84	C	109	A	134	A	159	C	184	C
10	C	35	B	60	B	85	C	110	C	135	C	160	B	185	B
11	A	36	B	61	C	86	B	111	B	136	A	161	D	186	C
12	B	37	D	62	A	87	D	112	B	137	C	162	D	187	D
13	B	38	A	63	B	88	B	113	C	138	B	163	C	188	A
14	C	39	A	64	D	89	C	114	B	139	A	164	D	189	B
15	B	40	C	65	B	90	C	115	C	140	D	165	B	190	C
16	A	41	D	66	B	91	D	116	A	141	C	166	B	191	A
17	B	42	B	67	D	92	C	117	A	142	A	167	D	192	B
18	A	43	A	68	A	93	B	118	B	143	D	168	D	193	A
19	D	44	B	69	A	94	C	119	C	144	C	169	B	194	B
20	B	45	C	70	A	95	A	120	C	145	C	170	A	195	D
21	A	46	B	71	C	96	D	121	A	146	A	171	A	196	C
22	B	47	A	72	B	97	D	122	D	147	A	172	A	197	C
23	D	48	C	73	B	98	C	123	D	148	C	173	D	198	A
24	D	49	D	74	B	99	B	124	B	149	B	174	B	199	C
25	D	50	D	75	C	100	B	125	D	150	A	175	D	200	A

2

Diseases of Field Crops and Their Management

I. Choose the correct answer

2.1. Cereals and millets

1. Rice tungro disease is transmitted by

   A. Aphid B. Whitefly

   C. Green leaf hopper D. Nematode

2. Wheat streak mosaic virus is transmitted by

   A. Aphid B. Whitefly

   C. Leaf hopper D. Mites

3. Charcoal rot disease in sorghum is caused by the pathogen

   A. *Macrophomina sp* B. *Rhizoctonia solani*

   C. *Sclerotium rolfsii* D. *Fusarium moniliform*

4. Sugary disease is common in

   A. Wheat B. Barley

   C. Sorghum D. Rice

5. Southern corn blight epidemic of maize was due to susceptibility of

   A. T- Cytoplasm B. A- Cytoplasm

   C. HD- Cytoplasm D. D- Cytoplasm

6. The downy mildew of pearl millet is caused by

   A. *Sclerospora sorghi* B. *Sclerospora sacchari*

   C. *S. graminicola* D. *Perenospora parasitica*

7. The disease ergot of rye produces sclerotia is caused by

   A. *Claviceps purpurea* B. *C. fusiformis*

   C. *Claviceps sativae* D. All of these

8. Green ear is a disease of

A. Pearl millet B. Red gram

C. Soybean D. Rice

9. Corn stunt disease is caused by?

A. Mycoplasma B. Candida

C. Spiroplasma D. Albugo

10. In blast disease of rice, what will happen if relative humidity falls below 88%

A. Conidia will not be produced B. Dwarf plants will be produced

C. Primary infection increases D. No effect

11. Rice blast pathogen perfect stage is

A. *Pyricularia oryzae* B. *Magnaporthe grisea*

C. *Helminthosporium* D. *Rhizoctonia*

12. Loose smut of barley is/are

A. Internally seed borne B. Externally seed borne

C. Soil borne D. All of these

13. *Barberry vulgaris* is the alternative host for

A. *Hemileia vastatrix* B. *Puccinia recondita*

C. *Puccinia graminis tritici* D. *Melampsora lini*

14. The rice tungro virus contains

A. ss RNA B. ds RNA

C. ds DNA D. Both A and C

15. Alternate host for *Puccinia graminis tritici*

A. *Barberry vulgaris* B. Brinjal plant

C. *Oxalis corniculata* D. Mohania

16. An internally seed borne fungal disease

A. Smut of finger millet B. Red rot of Sugarcane

C. Loose smut of wheat D. Grain smut of sorghum

17. Finger millet variety resistant to neck blast

A. GPU-28 B. Indaf-9

C. Indaf-5 D. MTU-22

18. Tundu disease of wheat is caused by?
    A. Nematode B. Virus
    C. Bacteria D. Nematode and bacteria
19. Molya disease of wheat and barley is caused by
    A. *Heterodera schachtii* B. *Heterodera rostochiensis*
    C. *Heterodera avenae* D. *Heterodera glycines*
20. In plains of India, which wheat rust appears first
    A. Black rust B. Brown rust
    C. Yellow rust D. Orange and yellow
21. Udbatta disease in rice is caused by
    A. *Rhizoctonia oryzae* B. *Pyricularia oryzae*
    C. *Ephelis oryzae* D. *Claviceps oryzae*
22. Alternate host of pearl millet rust is
    A. Brinjal B. Chenopodium
    C. *Glycine max* D. Barberry
23. Covered smut of barley is caused by
    A. *Ustilago hordei* B. *Ustilago avenae*
    C. *Ustilago scitaminea* D. *Ustilago nuda tiritici*
24. Leaf smut of rice is caused by
    A. *Entyloma oryzae* B. *Urocystis tritici*
    C. *Ustilago tritici* D. *Ustilago nuda*
25. The perfect stage of *Helminthosporium* is
    A. *Thanatephorus* B. *Mangnaporthe*
    C. *Cochliobolus* D. *Talaromyces*
26. Smut of pearl millet is
    A. Seed borne B. Soil borne
    C. Air borne D. Seed and soil borne
27. Loose smut of wheat can be effectively controlled by
    A. Crop rotation
    B. Soil treatment with non-systematic fungicides
    C. Seed treatment with systemic fungicides
    D. Spraying the crop with fungicides

28. Yellow ear rot of wheat is caused by

A. *Anguina* B. *Corynebacterium*

C. Both A and B D. *Heterodera*

29. Primary source of infection to green ear disease of pearl millet is

A. Insect B. Soil

C. Air D. Seed and soil

30. Root parasite of pearl millet is

A. Cuscuta B. Striga

C. Orobanche D. Loranthus

31. Smut of wheat is effectively controlled by

A. Bavistin B. Vitavax

C. Benelate D. Thiram

32. *Tolyposorium penicillarie* cause

A. Smut of sugarcane B. Grain smut of sorghum

C. Pearl millet smut D. Head smut of sorghum

33. Tundu disease of wheat is caused by

A. *Anguina* B. *Corynebacterium*

C. Both A and B D. *Heterodera*

34. Ufra disease of rice is caused by

A. *Pratylenchus* B. *Ditylenchus*

C. *Aphelenchoides* D. *Heterodera*

35. Downy mildew in maize cause a typical symptom called

A. Crazy top B. Ergot

C. Green ears D. Brown ears

36. In pearl millet (most favorable conditions for ergot disease

A. RH < 80%, Temperature: 10-15°C

B. RH < 70%, Temperature: 15-20°C

C. RH < 80%, Temperature: 20-30°C

D. RH < 60%, Temperature: 30-35°C

37. What is the scientific name of BPH that cause rice grassy stunt disease?

A. *Nilaparvata oryzae* B. *Nilaparvata lugens*

C. *Aceria cajani* D. *Bemisia tabaci*

38. What is the control measure for downy mildew/grassy top of maize?
    A. Soil application of *Pseudomonas fluorescens* @ 2.5 kg/ha
    B. Soil application of *Pseudomonas fluorescens* @ 2.0 kg/ha
    C. Soil application of *Pseudomonas fluorescens* @ 1.0 kg/ha
    D. Soil application of *Pseudomonas fluorescens* @ 0.5 kg/ha
39. What is the typical symptom of ergot disease in pearl millet?
    A. Snow dew B. Cream to pink honey dew
    C. Yellow to red honey dew D. Brown honey dew
40. How to control the sheath blight (*Rhizoctonia solani*) of rice?
    A. Carbendazim 50 WP @ 200 g/ha
    B. Azoxystrobin @ 100 ml/ha
    C. Carbendazim 50 WP @ 100 g/ha
    D. Carbendazim @ 500 g/ha
41. Which one of the following is the incorrect statement?
    A. Brown spot of rice - *Helminthosporuim oryzae*
    B. Bacterial leaf blight of rice - *Xanthomonas competris* pv. *oryzae*
    C. Leaf blight of maize - *Helminthosporium maydis*
    D. Seedling blight of ragi - *Helminthosporium nodulosum*
42. Which one of the following is a correct statement with respect to grain discolouration in rice?
    A. Avoid heavy phosphatic fertilizer
    B. Avoid heavy potassic fertilizers
    C. Avoid heavy nitrogenous fertilizers
    D. Avoid green manuring
43. What is the optimum date of sowing to control *Puccinia substriata* in pearl millet?
    A. December – May B. June – July
    C. August – September D. October - November
44. Which one of the following rice variety is tolerant to *Pyricularia oryzae*?
    A. CO 43 B. CO 40
    C. CO 47 D. CO 36

45. The term necrosis indicate

A. Curling
B. Blightening
C. Altrophy
D. Death of cells

46. Sexual form of rice blast is

A. *Pyricularia oryzae*
B. *Pyricularia fruitasens*
C. *Magnaporthe oryzae*
D. *Magnaporthe grisea*

47. Match the following

A. Head smut	1. *Sphacelotheca sorghi*
B. Covered kernel smut	2. *Sphacelotheca reiliana*
C. Loose smut	3. *Tolyposporium ehrenbergii*
D. Long smut	4. *Sphacelotheca cruenta*

A. 2 1 3 4
B. 1 2 4 3
C. 4 3 1 2
D. 4 3 2 1

48. Match the following

Target function	**Symptoms induced**
A. Mobilization of stored food	1. Root and foot rot of wheat
B. Absorption of water minerals	2. Damping off and seedling blight
C. Water transport & translocation	3. Leaf curl, whiteness broom
D. Meristematic activity	4. Vascular wilt of cotton

A. 1 2 3 4
B. 2 1 4 3
C. 4 2 1 3
D. 3 1 2 4

49. Black rust of wheat is caused by

A. *Puccinia graminis*
B. *Puccinia recondita*
C. *Puccinia striiformis*
D. *Puccinia glumarum*

50. Which of the following is not correctly matched?

A. Mustard – white rust
B. Paddy – brown spot
C. Wheat – red rust
D. Groundnut – tikka

51. Which type of spores of *Puccinia graminis tritici* infect the barberry plant ?

A. Teliospores
B. Urediospores
C. Aeciospores
D. Basidiospores

52. Frog eye spot of tobacco is a serious disease caused by

A. *Cercospora moricola* B. *C.nigricans*

C. *C.lycopersicum* D. *C.nicotianae*

53. Which is also called as the cancer of wheat

A. Yellow smut B. Loose smut

C. Karnal bunt D. Black rust

54. Sooty and charcoal like powder is shown in case of?

A. Rust B. Downy mildew

C. Smut D. Powdery mildew

55. Prominent foul smell of Karnal bunt is due to

A. Trienthyl amine B. Trimethyl amine

C. Dimethyl amine D. None

56. Famous Indian pathologist, extensively studied about cereal rust

A. K.C. Mehta B. Sadasivan

C. Robert Hartig D. None

57. Based on severity of damage, wheat diseases which have been ranked in the order

A. Brown rust >Loose smut>Stem rust>Karnal bunt

B. Stem rust>Brown rust>Karnal bunt>Loose smut

C. Brown rust>Stem rust>Karnal bunt>Loose smut

D. Karnal bunt>Loose smut>Stem rust>Brown rust

58. *Puccinis graminis* is heterocious fungus because?

A. It completes its life cycle in soil

B. It completes its life cycle on wheat only

C. It completes its life cycle on barbery

D. It completes its life cycle on wheat and barbery

59. Which of the following rust is earlier to appear on wheat in India?

A. Yellow rust B. Brown rust

C. None of these D. Black rust

60. The growth stage at which more attack of sheath blight of rice is seen

A. Grain filling stage B. Booting stage

C. Milking stage D. Active tillering stage

Answer keys

1	C	11	D	21	C	31	B	41	B	51	B
2	D	12	A	22	A	32	C	42	C	52	D
3	A	13	C	23	A	33	C	43	A	53	C
4	C	14	D	24	A	34	B	44	C	54	C
5	A	15	B	25	C	35	A	45	D	55	B
6	C	16	C	26	D	36	C	46	C	56	A
7	A	17	A	27	C	37	B	47	A	57	A
8	A	18	D	28	C	37	A	48	B	58	D
9	C	19	C	29	D	39	B	49	A	59	B
10	A	20	C	30	B	40	D	50	C	60	D

2.2. Pulses

1. High rainfall, humid and cool climate is favourable for _____ disease in soybean.

   A. *Rhizoctonia solani*

   B. *Cercospora sojina*

   C. Charcoal rot (*Macrophomina phaseolina)*

   D. Bacterial blight (*Pseudomonas syringae*)

2. What is the mode of spread of *Cercospora* leaf spot of blackgram?

   A. Water borne B. Air borne

   C. Soil borne D. Seed borne

3. Pathogen which causes pod blight of soybean is

   A. *Colletotrichum truncatum* B. *Colletotrichum lindemuthianum*

   C. *Colletotrichum capsici* D. *Colletotrichum gloeosporioides*

4. In soybean, bacterial blight is controlled by

   A. Seed treatment with bavistin @ 2 g/kg of seed

   B. Seed treatment with carbendazim @ 6 g/kg of seed

   C. Seed treatment with streptocyclin @ 2.5 g/10 kg of seed

   D. Seed treatment with streptocyclin @ 500 ppm

5. Match the following

   A. Fusaruim wilt of redgram 1. Seed treatment with carbendazim at 1 g/kg of seed

   B. Powdery mildew of blackgram 2. Monocrotophos at 500 ml/ha

C. Cowpea mosaic virus — 3. Spray NSKE 5%

D. Collar rot of chickpea — 4. Spot drenching with carbendazim @ 1 g/lit

A. 2 3 4 1 B. 3 2 1 4

C. 4 2 3 1 D. 4 3 2 1

6. The symptoms of circular, black, suncken spots with dark centre and bright red orange margin is due to
   A. *Uromyces phaseoli* of greengram
   B. *Colletotrichum lindemuthianum* of greengram
   C. Cowpea mosaic
   D. *Alternaria alternata* of redgram
7. The vector which causes pigeon pea sterility mosaic virus is
   A. *Aphis gossypii* B. *Bemisia tabaci*
   C. *Aceria cajani* D. *Aphis craccivora*
8. Pigeon pea sterility mosaic virus causes
   A. Disease prevalence B. Reduction in seed germination
   C. Heavy seed abortion D. Reduction in seed quality
9. Wilt of pigeon pea is caused by
   A. *Pythium* B. *Alternaria*
   C. *Colletotrichum* D. *Fusarium*
10. Dry root rot of legumes and beans is caused by
   A. *Erysiphe* B. *Macrophomina*
   C. *Xanthomonas* D. *Phacidiopycnis*

Answer keys

1	A	6	B
2	D	7	C
3	A	8	C
4	C	9	D
5	D	10	B

2.3. Oilseeds

1. Leaf spot or tikka disease of groundnut is/are caused by
   A. *Cercospora arachidicola* B. *Cercosporidium personatum*
   C. Both A and B D. *Drechslera graminea*

2. Systemic fungicide used for the control of Powdery mildew disease
   A. Calixin B. Vitavax
   C. Sulphur dust D. Bavistin
3. Which of the following is a phytoplasma disease?
   A. Sesame phyllody B. Black shank
   C. Vein clearing D. Red rust
4. The vector responsible for peanut bud necrosis in groundnut is
   A. *Aphis craccivora* B. *Thrips palmi*
   C. *Aphis gossypii* D. *Bemisia tabaci*
5. Rust in groundnut can be managed chemically by
   A. Chlorothalonil 100 g/ha B. Hinosan 100 ml/ha
   C. Blue copper 100 g/ha D. Bavistin 100 g/ha
6. Match the following
   A. Early leaf spot 1. *Cercospora personata*
   B. Late leaf spot 2. *Alternaria arachidis*
   C. Stem rot 3. *Cercospora arachidicola*
   D. Alternaria leaf spot 4. *Sclerotium rolfsii*
   A. 1 3 4 2 B. 4 3 1 2
   C. 3 1 4 2 D. 3 1 2 4
7. Phyllody in sesame is caused by
   A. Bacteria B. Insects
   C. Mycoplasma D. Virus
8. *Sclerotium rolfsii* on groundnut can be controlled by fungal antagonists called
   A. *Metarhizium anisopliae* B. *Myrothecium verrucaria*
   C. *Aspergillus niger* D. *Verticillium lecanii*
9. _____ is the mycotoxin which affects the germination of groundnut seed is
   A. Citrinin B. Fumonisin
   C. Ochratoxin D. Aflatoxin
10. White rust is disease of
   A. Bajra B. Wheat
   C. Mustard D. Litchi

Answer keys

1	C	6	C
2	A	7	C
3	A	8	B
4	B	9	D
5	A	10	C

2. 4. Cash crops

1. Top sickness of tobacco is due to the deficiency of
   A. Mg B. Ca
   C. Zn D. Bo
2. Cotton leaf curl virus is transmitted by
   A. Mite B. Whitefly
   C. Aphid D. Plant hopper
3. *Colletotrichum falcatum* causes
   A. Anthracnose of chilli B. Red rot of sugarcane
   C. Sett rot of sugarcane D. Anthracnose of grapes
4. Sugarcane ratoon stunting is caused by
   A. Phytoplasma B. Viroids
   C. *Cavibacter xyli sub sp xyli* D. Virus
5. The perfect stage of *Colletotrichum falcatum* (causes red rot of sugarcane) is
   A. *Glomerella cingulata* B. *Glomerella tucumanensis*
   C. *Glomerella lindemuthianum* D. All of these
6. Treating the setts with aerated steam therapy (AST) at 50°C for 1 hour or in hot water at 50°C for 30 minutes in sugarcane to control.
   A. Sett rot B. Red rot
   C. Rust D. Smut
7. Sap transmissible virus/viruses is/are
   A. Tobacco mosaic virus and sunflower mosaic virus
   B. Leaf curl virus and YMV
   C. Tobacco mosaic virus only
   D. Yellow mosaic virus and sunflower MV

8. Match the following

A. Corn rust	1. *Puccinia arachidis*
B. Coffee rust	2. *Puccinia erianthi*
C. Sugarcane rust	3. *Hemileia vastatrix*
D. Groundnut rust	4. *Puccinia sorghi*

A. 2 4 1 3 B. 4 3 2 1
C. 3 4 1 2 D. 2 3 1 4

9. Which of the following is the incorrect statement?
A. Yellow leaf disease is a viral disease of sugarcane
B. Pustules of rust appear first on the lower surface
C. *Leveillula taurica* causes powdery patches on lower surface
D. Red rot of sugarcane is caused by *Ceratocystis paradoxa*

10. Frog eye leaf spot is an important disease of
A. Tobacco B. Sugarcane
C. *Opium poppy* D. Turmeric

11. Tiger stripe symptom is observed in
A. Fusarium wilt of cotton B. Verticillium wilt of cotton
C. Root rot of cotton D. Boll rot of cotton

12. Major symptom of bacterial blight of cotton is
A. Seedling blight B. Angular leaf spot
C. Black arm D. All the above

13. Orbanche can be managed by using
A. Carbendazim B. Bordeaux mixture
C. Kerosine oil D. Dimethoate

14. Orobanche is a
A. Total root parasite B. Partial root parasite
C. Total stem parasite D. Partial stem parasite

15. Statement 1: Yellow leaf disease is transmitted by *Melanaphis sacchari* in sugarcane
Statement 2: Sugarcane rust is caused by *Puccinia erianthi*
A. Statement 1 alone is correct B. Statement 2 alone is correct
C. Both statements are correct D. Both statements are wrong

16. The whip smut of sugarcane is caused by

    A. *Ustilago maydis* B. *Ustilago hordei*

    C. *Ustilago scitaminea* D. *Ustilago nuda*

17. Sudden and complete wilting in cotton is due to

    A. Root rot by *Rhizoctonia solani*

    B. Root rot by *Rhizoctonia bataticola*

    C. Both A and B

    D. Vascular wilt

Answer keys

1	D	6	D	11	B	16	C
2	B	7	A	12	D	17	C
3	B	8	B	13	C		
4	C	9	D	14	A		
5	B	10	A	15	C		

3

Diseases of Horticultural Crops and Their Management

I. Choose the correct answer

3.1. Fruits

1. The first disease forecasting system in plant pathology was developed for grapevine downy mildew (*Plasmopara viticola*) in the year

   A. 1913 B. 1914

   C. 1915 D. 1916

2. _______ is used to control post harvest diseases in fruits

   A. Ethirimol B. Benomyl

   C. Both A and B D. None of the above

3. The typical symptom of papaya ring spot is

   A. Shoe string B. Topple down

   C. Concentric ring D. Chlorosis

4. Marginal flavescence

   A. *Didymella sp* B. *Phytoplasma*

   C. *Stemphylium* D. *Ascochyta*

5. Bacterial fruit rot of pineapple

   A. *Pantoea ananas* B. Pineapple wilt virus

   C. Heart rot D. Butt rot

6. Flat limb

   A. Guava B. Citrus

   C. Sapota D. Mango

7. *Phytophthora parasitica* causes _________ in pineapple

   A. Heart rot B. Butt rot

   C. Soft rot D. Dry root rot

8. Grape bunch like spores are formed by
   A. *Botrytis sp* B. *Verticillium sp*
   C. *Penicillium sp* D. *Aspergillus sp*
9. Wire stem symptom is observed in
   A. Preemergence damping off B. Postemergence damping off
   C. Foot rot D. Honey comb symptom
10. Pink disease is caused by
   A. *Rosellinia necatrix* B. *Corticium salmonicolor*
   C. *Fusarium sp* D. *Verticillium sp*
11. Papaya leaf curl is transmitted by
   A. *Bemisia tabaci* B. *Aphis gossypii*
   C. *Myzus persicae* D. *Orosius sp*
12. *Phakospora vitis* causes rust of
   A. Pineapple B. Grapes
   C. Apple D. Citrus
13. The disease commonly observed in acidic soil is
   A. Apple mosaic B. Tristeza virus
   C. Banana bunchy top D. Finger and toe disease
14. Peach yellow is caused by
   A. *Fusarium oxysporum* B. Peach yellow virus
   C. Bacteria D. *Candidatus phytoplasma*
15. Pear scab is caused by
   A. *Venturia inaequalis* B. *Venturia pirina*
   C. *Streptomyces scabies* D. *Venturia carpophila*
16. Corm injection is used to manage
   A. Banana bunchy top B. Panama wilt
   C. Burrowing nematode D. Erwinia tip rot
17. The optimum temperature for the attack of foot rot of papaya (*Pythium aphanidermatum*)is
   A. 22°C B. 28°C
   C. 32°C D. 36°C

18. Apple scab is caused by
    A. *Podosphaera leucotricha* B. *Spilocaea pomi*
    C. *Venturia inequalis* D. *Armillaria mellea*

19. *Citrus exocartis* is transmitted through
    A. Infected bud wood B. Budding knife
    C. Seed D. Both knife and bud wood

20. Banana Streak Virus is transmitted by
    A. Mealybug B. Thrips
    C. Whitefly D. Mite

21. *Viscum* spp is a
    A. Partial parasite B. Complete parasite
    C. Root parasite D. Stem parasite

22. Bursting of pseudostem in banana is observed in plants suffering from
    A. Bunchy top B. Panama wilt
    C. Root-knot nematode disease D. Banana streak virus

23. Indicator plant used for citrus tristeza virus
    A. Kagzi lime B. Sweet orange
    C. Trifoliate orange D. Rangapur lime

24. Papaya ring spot is caused by
    A. Poty virus B. Cucumo virus
    C. Como virus D. Tobamo virus

25. NEPO viruses are transmitted by
    A. *Xiphinema index* B. *Trichodorus sp*
    C. *Pythium ultimum* D. *Meloidogyne*

26. Moko disease of banana is caused by
    A. *Fusarium oxysporum f sp. cubense*
    B. *Radopholus similis*
    C. *Ralstonia solanacearum*
    D. *Pentalonia nigronervosa*

27. Diseases which interfers with the conduction of water in plants
    A. Wilts B. Rots
    C. Leaf spots D. Damping off

28. Which is responsible for wood rot?

A. *Erysiphe* B. *Polyporus*

C. *Lycoperdon* D. None of these

29. Anthracnose of grapes is caused by

A. *Elsinoe ampelina* B. *Greenaria viticola*

C. *Plasmopara viticola* D. *Uncinula necator*

30. Exanthema in citrus is the deficiency of

A. Copper B. Manganese

C. Sulphur D. Nitrogen

31. Which fungus cause storage rots of fruits and vegetables

A. *Aspergillus* B. *Penicillium*

C. *Rhizopus* D. *Mucor*

32. Flat limb is a specific disease in

A. Mango B. Sapota

C. Banana D. Guava

33. The percentage of starch solution to control fungal growth of *Capnodium* sp in mango is

A. 1% B. 5%

C. 2.5% D. 3%

34. Composition of bordeaux paste is

A. 1 kg of $CuSO_4$ + 1 kg of lime + 100 lit of water

B. 0.5 kg of $CuSO_4$ + 0.5 kg of lime + 100 lit of H_2O

C. 1 kg of $CuSO_4$ + 1 kg of lime + 10 lit of H_2O

D. 0.5 kg of $CuSO_4$ + 0.5 kg of lime + 10 lit of H_2O

35. Foot rot of papaya is caused by

A. *Phytophthora palmivora* B. *Pythium aphanidermatum*

C. *Peronospora parasitica* D. *Albugo candida*

36. Statement 1: Panama wilt of banana – resistant cultivars like poovan and nendran

Statement 2: Erwinia rot in banana is a fungal disease

A. Statement 1 alone is correct B. Statement 2 alone is correct

C. Both statements are correct D. Both statements are wrong

37. Bacterial disease in plants can be detected mostly by

A. Iodine test B. Tetrazolium test

C. Ooze test D. ELISA

38. Banana bunchy top disease is introduced from

A. Australia B. Fiji

C. Ceylon D. Malaysia

39. CPPTI stands for

A. Commission on Plant Protection Tropical Institute

B. Central Pest Protection Tropical Institute

C. Commission on Pilot Protection Training Institute

D. Central Plant Protection Training Institute

40. Directorate of plant protection, quarantine and storage is located at

A. Ghaziabad B. Ahmedabad

C. Faridabad D. Chennai

41. Plant quarantine order (Regulation of import into India) is promulgated and passed in

A. 2003 B. 2000

C. 2007 D. 1998

42. Match the following

A. Mango malformation 1. Wettable sulphur 0.2%

B. Red rust 2. Maida or starch solution (1%)

C. Powdery mildew 3. NAA @ 100-200 ppm

D. Sooty mould 4. Bordeaux mixture (0.5%)

A. 4 3 1 2 B. 3 4 1 2

C. 2 1 4 3 D. 4 1 2 3

43. Velvetty reddish brown raised pustules is a characteristic symptom of

A. Sooty mould B. Anthracnose

C. Red rust D. Powdery mildew

44. Pathogen of Panama disease of banana is primarily

A. Water borne B. Sucker borne

C. Soil borne D. Seed borne

45. Cedar-apple rust is caused by

    A. *Hemileia vastatrix*

    B. *Melampsora lini*

    C. *Uromyces appendiculatus*

    D. *Gymnosporangium juniperivirginianae*

Answer keys

1	A	11	A	21	A	31	D	41	A
2	C	12	B	22	B	32	B	42	B
3	A	13	D	23	A	33	B	43	C
4	B	14	B	24	A	34	C	44	B
5	A	15	B	25	A	35	B	45	D
6	C	16	D	26	C	36	A		
7	A	17	D	27	A	37	C		
8	A	18	C	28	B	37	B		
9	B	19	B	29	A	39	D		
10	B	20	A	30	A	40	A		

3.2. Vegetables

1. The cauliflower mosaic virus particles contain

    A. RNA B. DNA

    C. Both RNA and DNA D. Either RNA or DNA

2. Avoid copper fungicides which are phytotoxic to

    A. Cucurbits B. Tomato

    C. Brinjal D. None of the above

3. Mild mosaic in potato is caused by

    A. Potato virus X B. Potato virus Y

    C. Both A and B D. None of the above

4. Cauliflower mosaic virus is an

    A. dsDNA B. ssDNA

    C. dsRNA D. ssRNA

5. The genome of tomato leaf curl virus is

    A. ssRNA B. dsRNA

    C. ssDNA D. dsDNA

6. Vertifolia effect was demonstrated in the host and disease of

A. Potato and late blight
B. Wheat and rust
C. Tomato and early blight
D. Pearl millet and downy mildew

7. Silvering disease is a disease of

A. Turnip
B. Carrot
C. Beet root
D. Cabbage

8. Russet scab or black speck of tomato is a symptom of

A. Bangle blight
B. Ring rot
C. Black scurf
D. Grey mold

9. Slippery skin is a symptom of

A. Garlic
B. Apple
C. Banana
D. Onion

10. White mold caused by *Sclerotinia sclerotiorum* is observed in

A. Cabbage
B. Radish
C. Grapes
D. Apple

11. Sett rott of cassava is cauused by

A. *Sclerotium rolfsii*
B. *Fusarium solani*
C. *Phomopsis manihotis*
D. *Diplodia natalensis*

12. *Albugo candida* causes white blisters or white rust of crucifers is a/an

A. Obligate parasite
B. Obligate saprophyte
C. Facultative parasite
D. Facultative saprophyte

13. *Alternaria solani* causes

A. Late blight of potato
B. Wart of potato
C. Early blight of potato
D. Leaf curl of potato

14. *Plasmodiophora brassicae* causes the club root disease of crucifers which can be controlled by

A. Raising pH of soil
B. Decreasing pH of soil
C. Both A and B
D. None of these

15. Little leaf disease of brinjal is caused by

A. *Ustilago*
B. *Chlorobium*
C. Mycoplasma
D. *Albugo*

16. The late blight disease of potato is most serious when the

A. Temperature is high
B. Temperature is low
C. Soil pH is neutral
D. None of the above

17. Abundance of which mineral in plant increases resistance to wilt of tomato?

A. Calcium
B. Phosphorous
C. Boron/ both calcium and phosphorous
D. Both calcium and phosphorous

18. Yellow mosaic of bhendi and mosaic disease of cassava are transmitted by

A. *Aphis craccivora*
B. *Bemisia tabaci*
C. *Myzus persicae*
D. *Toxoptera aurantii*

19. A fungus causing wart of potato is

A. A saprophyte
B. A facultative parasite
C. A facultative saprophyte
D. An obligate

20. Pea rust is caused by

A. *Puccinia*
B. *Uromyces*
C. *Phakospora*
D. *Urocystis*

21. A disease caused by *Colletotrichum circinans* in onion is

A. Black rot
B. Soft rot
C. Black mould
D. Smudge

22. The quarantine act passed by India is

A. Destructive insect and pest act 1914
B. Destructive insect and pest and disease act 1914
C. Pest and disease act 1914
D. Destructive insect and disease act 1914

23. Anthracnose of beans caused by

A. *Colletotrichum lindemuthianum*
B. *Fusarium solani*
C. *Cercospora* sp
D. *Alternaria*

24. Black rot of cabbage is caused by
    A. *Xanthomonas campestris pv. campestris*
    B. *Rhizoctonia solani*
    C. *Xanthomonas campestris pv. vesicatoria*
    D. *Fusarium solani*
25. Leaf shredding and green ear symptoms are noticed in
    A. Downy mildew B. Wilt
    C. Rusts D. Smuts
26. Brown rot of potato is caused by
    A. *Ralstonia solanacearum* B. *Erwinia carotovora*
    C. *Pseudomonas syringae* D. *Streptomyces scabies*
27. Potato spindle tuber disease is caused by
    A. Viroid B. Phytoplasma
    C. Spiroplasma D. Virus
28. Internally seed borne bacterial disease
    A. Black rot of cabbage B. Soft rot of carrot
    C. Pierce disease of grapes D. Citrus canker
29. The spindle tuber disease in potato is caused by
    A. Virus B. MLO
    C. Prion D. Viroid
30. YVMV of okra spreads by
    A. *Bemisia tabaci* B. Aphids
    C. Leaf hopper D. Animals
31. Early blight of potato caused by
    A. *Alternaria solani* B. *Cercospora*
    C. *Rhizoctonia* D. None
32. In which disease of plant, stem rot at soil line with brown to red lesions occurs?
    A. *Rhizoctonia* B. Angular leaf spot
    C. Bacterial blight D. Bacterial spot
33. Which disease of plant is known as ring disease?
    A. Citrus canker B. Black arm of cotton
    C. Wilt of potato D. None of the above

34. White blisters of crucifers is caused by pathogen

A. *Albugo candida* B. *Sclerospora sorghi*

C. *Pythium debaryanum* D. *Plasmopara viticola*

35. Stalk root of onion is caused by

A. Fungi B. Bacteria

C. Nematodes D. Mycoplasma

36. Leaf roll of potato is transmitted by

A. *Myzus persicae* B. *M. pseudosolani*

C. *M. circumflexum* D. All the above

37. Root knot of vegetable is caused by

A. *Meloidogyne* B. *Heterodera*

C. *Pratylenchus* D. *Xanthomonas*

38. Severity of disease club root of cabbage can be reduced by application of

A. Lime B. Gypsum

C. FYM D. Fertilizers

39. Erwinia rot is a

A. Viral disease B. Fungal disease

C. Bacterial disease D. Phytoplasma disease

40. The prominant disease occurs in nursery stage of vegetables is

A. Bacterial wilt B. Mosaic

C. Damping off D. Fusarium wilt

41. Statement 1: Tomato spotted wilt disease is transmitted by *Bemisia tabaci*

Statement 2: Bhendi YMV resistant varieties are Prabhani kranti, Arka anamika and Arka abay

Statement 3: Tobacco virus is transmitted by *Thrips tabaci*

A. All the statements are correct B. (i) and (ii) are correct

C. (ii) and (iii) are correct D. (ii) alone is correct

42. Purple blotch is a important disease of

A. Bhendi B. Turmeric

C. Ginger D. Onion

43. Symptom of white rust in amaranthus is

A. Lesion appear on the stems and seed pods

B. White powdery substance in patches on under surface of leaves

C. Sunken lesions appear on the leaves

D. V shaped spots arising along the margin

44. Club root of crucifers prevalent on soils of

A. Acidic B. Alkaline

C. Neutral D. Both B and C

45. Head quarters of National Plant Quarantine Station is situated at

A. Hyderabad B. New Delhi

C. Bangalore D. Mumbai

46. Black powdery mass of sclerotia is a typical symptom of

A. Charcoal rot B. Collar rot

C. Bacterial blight D. Cercospora spot

47. Downy mildew of crops can be controlled chemically by

A. Imidachlorprid B. Wettable sulphur

C. Mancozeb D. Metalaxyl

48. Which of the following disease is not seed transmissible

A. Potato spindle tuber B. Bean mosaic

C. Tobacco ring spot D. Powdery scab

49. (i) Late blight of potato is a pandemic disease

(ii) Downy mildew is a localized disease

(iii) Wart disease of potato is endemic in Darjeeling

A. (i) and (ii) are correct B. (i) and (iii) are correct

C. All are correct D. (ii) and (iii) are correct

50. Little leaf disease in brinjal is caused by a

A. Virus B. Fungus

C. Phytoplasma D. Bacterium

51. White rust of crucifers is a pseudo-rust because

A. The disease is not caused by basidiomycetous members

B. The colour of the pustule is not red

C. The disease is seen on crucifers

D. The disease is not seen on wheat

52. White rust of crucifer is caused by

A. *Puccinia* B. *Ustilago*

C. *Cystopus* D. *Peziza*

53. Storage fungi that damages the seed in storage is

A. *Aspergillus* spp B. *Colletotrichum* spp

C. *Xanthomonas* spp D. *Pseudomonas* spp

54. Moisture content conducive for storage fungi attack in stored seeds is

A. 10-12% B. 9-10%

C. 13-14% D. 7-8%

55. IPPC stands for

A. Indian Plant Protection Commission

B. International Plant Protection Commission

C. Indian Plant Protection Convention

D. International Plant Protection Convention

56. Example of seed borne disease

A. Damping off B. Root rot

C. Leaf spot D. loose smut

57. Downy mildew of peas is caused by

A. *Albugo candida* B. *Erysiphe polygoni*

C. *Peronospora pisi* D. None of these

Answer keys

1	B	11	D	21	D	31	A	41	D	51	A
2	A	12	A	22	B	32	A	42	D	52	C
3	A	13	C	23	A	33	C	43	B	53	A
4	A	14	A	24	A	34	A	44	A	54	C
5	C	15	C	25	A	35	B	45	B	55	D
6	A	16	B	26	A	36	D	46	A	56	D
7	C	17	D	27	A	37	A	47	D	57	C
8	C	18	B	28	A	37	A	48	D		
9	D	19	D	29	D	39	C	49	B		
10	A	20	B	30	A	40	C	50	C		

3.3. Spices and Plantation Crops

1. Smallest viroid is

A. Coconut cadang B. *Citrus exocortis*

C. SARS D. None

2. Mosaic is the major disease of the spices crop

A. Clove B. Turmeric

C. Cardamom D. Cumin

3. Stem galls of coriander (*Coriandrum sativum*) is caused by

A. *Protomyces macrosporus* B. *Plasmopara viticola*

C. *Peronospora pisi* D. None of these

4. *Exobasidium vexans* which causes

A. Blight of coffee B. Blister blight of tea

C. Blister blight of cocoa D. Red rust of tea

5. Which of the following statement with reference to *Phytophthora* spp. is incorrect?

A. *P. palmivora* causes bud rot in coconut

B. *P. capsici* causes fruit rot in areca

C. *P. arecae* causes nut rot in areca

D. *P. palmivora* causes leaf fall and fruit rot in mandarin

6. The fungus involved with foot rot of pepper is

A. *Phytophthora parasitica* B. *Phytophthora palmivora*

C. *Phytophthora capsici* D. *Phytophthora infestans*

7. Swollen shoot of cocoa is transmitted by

A. *Pentalonia nigronervosa f.sp. caladii*

B. *Pseudococcus njalensis*

C. *Nephotettix cincticeps*

D. *Aphis craccivora*

8. Koleroga of arecanut is controlled by spraying

A. Calixin B. Captan

C. Bordeaux mixture D. Bavistin

9. Effective control for katte disease of cardamom is

A. Eradication and burning of affected clumps

B. Spraying of systemic fungicide

C. Application of *Trichoderma viride* to soil

D. Destruction host

10. Stem galls of coriander is caused by

A. *Fusarium* B. *Alternaria*

C. *Protonaria* D. *Cercospora*

11. Match the following

Crop	**Disease**
A. Cardamom	1. Rhizome rot
B. Turmeric	2. Stem gall
C. Coriander	3. Leaf blotch
D. Ginger	4. Azhukal disease

A. 3 2 4 1 B. 4 3 2 1

C. 3 4 1 2 D. 2 1 4 3

12. Tapering of terminal portion of the trunk is a specific symptom of

A. Tanjore wilt of coconut B. Bud rot of coconut

C. Stem bleeding of coconut D. Kerala wilt of coconut

13. Koleroga is an important disease in

A. Tea B. Coffee

C. Rubber D. Coconut

14. Which of the following statement is incorrect?

A. Abnormal leaf fall is an important disease in arecanut

B. Bracket formation is a symptom of ganoderma wilt in coconut

C. Mahali disease is also known as kolerogo in arecanut

D. Scientific name of blister blight of tea in *Exobasidium vexans*

15. Quick wilt of pepper is caused by

A. *Phytophthora palmivora* B. *Pythium aphanidermatum*

C. *Phytophthora capsici* D. *Fusarium* sp

16. Katte disease of cardamom is transmitted by vector

A. *Bemisia tabaci* B. *Aphis gossypii*

C. *Thrips tabaci* D. *Pentalonia nigronervosa*

Answer keys

1	A	11	B
2	C	12	D
3	A	13	B
4	B	14	A
5	B	15	C
6	C	16	D
7	B		
8	C		
9	A		
10	C		

4

Integrated Disease Management

I. Choose the correct answer

1. Solar treatment is used for

   A. Blast B. Stem rust

   C. Loose smut D. Powdery mildew

2. In Integrated Disease Management (IDM) of tomato, the seeds should be treated with ______ to prevent fungal infection?

   A. Trichoderma (1%) + Imidacloprid (2.5 gm/kg seed)

   B. NPV

   C. Endosulfan (1.5 ml/litre)

   D. All of above

3. Increase in the concentration of CO_2 in soil inhibits the growth of

   A. *Rhizoctonia solani* B. *Ophiobolus graminis*

   C. *Sclerotinia minor* D. All of the above

4. Deficiency of nitrogen makes the plants

   A. Weaker B. Slow growing and aging fast

   C. Susceptible to pathogens D. All of above

5. Application of potash increases

   A. Resistance to water logging B. Frost resistance in plants

   C. Disease resistance in plants D. None of these

6. Exclusion of plant disease by legislation is known as

   A. Disease resistance B. Plant quarantine

   C. Biological control of plant D. Cultural control

7. Components of integrated disease management includes

   A. Surveillance B. Agronomic practices

   C. Host plant resistance D. All the above

8. Trace the logical sequence in effective disease management

   A. Surveillance → quarantine → regulatory → exclusion → use of chemotherapeutants

   B. Surveillance → regulatory → exclusion → quarantine → chemotherapeutants

   C. Quarantine → surveillance → regulatory → exclusion → chemotherapeutants

   D. Quarantine → regulatory → exclusion → surveillance → chemotherapeutants

9. Who developed solar heat treatment for loose smut of wheat caused by *Ustilogo segetum var tritici?*

   A. J.C. Luthra and A.Sattar B. Ramanujan and Co-workers

   C. K.C. Mehta D. G. Rangaswamy

10. Who developed seed plot technique for virus free seed production of potato in Indo-Gangetic Plains?

    A. J.C. Luthra and A.Sattar B. S.N. Dasgupta

    C. Ramanujan and Co-workers D. S. Nagarajan and H. Singh

11. Who formulated Indian stem rust rules for *Puccinia graminis var. tritici*

    A. J.C. Luthra and A.Sattar B. K.C. Mehta Sattar

    C. T.S. Ramakrishan D. S. Nagarajan and H. Singh

12. The first report on use of solar energy for the control of soil-borne disease was published by

    A. J.C. Luthra and A.Sattar B. Katan and Co-workers

    C. M.J. Thirumalachar D. C.D. Mayee

13. Which species of *Aspergillus* produces aflatoxin B1 and B2

    A. *Aspergillus niger* B. *Aspergillus flavus*

    C. *Aspergillus parasiticus* D. Both B and C

14. Which species of *Aspergillus* produces Aflatoxin G1 and G2?

    A. *Aspergillus niger* B. *Aspergillus flavus*

    C. *Aspergillus parasiticus* D. Both B and C

15. Entomopathogenic fungi used to control DBM and codling moth is

    A. *Verticillium lecanii* B. *Nomuraea rileyi*

    C. *Metarhizium anisopliae* D. *Beauveria bassiana*

16. Biocontrol agent used for the control of collar rot of plants caused by *Rhizoctonia solani*

A. *Pasteuria penetrans* B. *Phosphobacteria*

C. *Trichoderma viridi* D. *Bacillus subtilis*

17. Match the following

A. Avoidance 1. Inactivates the inoculums

B. Exclusion 2. Making environment unfavourable for infection

C. Eradication 3. Prevents the introduction of inoculums

D. Protection 4. Prevents infection by means of toxicant

A. 4 3 2 1 B. 2 3 1 4

C. 2 1 4 3 D.1 2 3 4

18. Method of plant disease control was first classified by

A. E.J.Butter B. Mundkur

C. Whetzel D. Baily

19. _____ of plant disease are termed as non-infectious diseases.

(i) Abiotic agents (ii) Biotic agents

(iii) Non-living agents (iv)Primary agents of disease

A. (i) alone is correct B. Both (i) and (ii) are correct

C. (i), (iii) and (iv) is correct D. All are correct

20. Most of plant viral diseases are transmitted by

A. Seed source B. Insects

C. Wind D. Splashing rain

21. Eradication followed to get rid off citrus canker caused by

A. *Xanthomonas campestris* B. *X.arboricola*

C. *X.axonopodis* D. *X.phaseoli*

22. Identify the incorrect pair

A. Hot H_2O treatment – Grassy shoot of sugarcane

B. Hot air treatment – Sugarcane mosaic

C. Soil solarisation – Seed borne pathogen

D. Refrigeration/radiation – Post harvest fungal infections

23. Luthra in 1953 derived a solar treatment method to eliminate the infection of

A. Loose smut B. Flag smut

C. Hill bunt D. Karnal bunt

24. Aerated steam therapy is followed for

A. Grassy shoot of sugarcane B. Sugarcane mosaic

C. Loose smut D. Flag smut

25. Which among the following is used to control nematodes and soil borne pathogens?

A. Inter crop B. Relay crop

C. Catch crop D. Strip crop

26. Resistant variety for sugarcane red rot is

A. COT 104 B. CO 62198

C. C0 85061 D. CO 8201

27. Which among the following means a disease can be eradicated?

(i) Removal of alternate host (ii) Removal of collateral host

(iii) Removal of affected plant (iv) Removal of plant debris

A. (i) and (ii) are correct B. (ii) and (iii) are correct

C. (i) and (iv) are correct D. All are correct

28. Growing resistant variety is a

A. Chemical method of control B. Cultural method of control

C. Trap method of control D. Preventive method of control

29. Which among the following is a best method to control panama wilt of banana?

A. Flood fallowing B. Soil amendment

C. Summer plough D. Adjusting of sowing time

30. What is the best method to control damping off in vegetable like chilli?

A. Depth of sowing B. Spacing adjustment

C. Use of higher seed rate D. Method of sowing

31. Biochemical resistance is observed in which type of onion variety?

A. White onion B. Red onion

C. Yellow onion D. Both B and C

32. Which of the following reduces the longevity of the fungus?

A. Increased N content B. Decreased N content

C. Increased P content D. Decreased P content

33. Which of the following disease can be controlled by raised bed system of nursery?

A. Damping off B. Foot rot of ginger

C. Sheath blight of rice D. Both A and B

34. Which of the following pathogen can be controlled by soil solarisation?

(i) *Pythium* (ii) *Colletotrichum*

(iii) *Fusarium* (iv) *Alternaria*

A. (i) and (ii) are correct B. (i) and (iii) are correct

C. (i) alone is correct D. All are correct

35. HCN in root exudates of sorghum is toxic to

A. *Fusarium udum* B. *Sclerospora sorghi*

C. *Sphacelotheca cruenta* D. *Puccinia purpurea*

36. Mostly viral diseases can be controlled by

(i) Reducing the vector population (ii) Avoid growing in summer season

(iii) Growing resistant variety (iv) Increased seed rate

A. (i) and (ii) are correct B. (ii) and (iii) are correct

C. (iii) and (iv) are correct D. All are correct

37. Application of soil organic amendments suppresses the fungus by

A. Release of O_2 B. Release of CO_2

C. Release of humic acids D. Nutrients release

38. Example of barrier crops

A. Sorghum B. Maize

C. Bajra D. All of these

39. Summer ploughing reduces the spores of

A. *Sclerospora sorghi* B. *Erysiphe polygoni*

C. *Claviceps purpurea* D. *Colletotrichum gloeosporioides*

40. Choose the correct answer

(i) YMV is more prevalent in summer season

(ii) Powdery mildew is more common in winter season

(iii) Bacterial wilt is more prevalent in the presence of RKN

A. (i) alone is correct B. (ii) alone is correct

C. (iii) alone is correct D. All are correct

41. Harvesting season to avoid *Aspergillus flavus* in groundnut is

A. Winter season B. Rainy days

C. Spring D. Autumn season

Answer keys

1	C	11	D
2	A	12	B
3	D	13	D
4	A	14	C
5	C	15	D
6	B	16	C
7	D		
8	A		
9	A		
10	C		

5

Mushroom

I. Choose the correct answer

1. Which among the following is commonly known as oyster mushroom?

   A. *Volvariella* B. *Agaricus*

   C. *Pleurotus* D. *Lentinus*

2. Which of them is a poisonous mushroom?

   A. *Agaricus* B. *Volvariella*

   C. *Pleurotus* D. *Amanita*

3. In Tamil Nadu, major mushroom growing districts include

   A. Kanniyakumari and Ramnad B. Erode and Coimbatore

   C. Kancheepuram and Theni D. Cuddalore and Nagapattinam

4. Mother spawn refers to

   A. Growing mushroom fungus on crop residues

   B. Growing mushroom fungus on straw bed media

   C. Growing mushroom fungus on grain media

   D. Growing mushroom fungus on agar media

5. APK 2 is a

   A. Button mushroom B. Oyster mushroom

   C. Milky mushroom D. Pink mushroom

6. Match the following

   A. Paddy straw mushroom 1. *Calocybe* sp

   B. Oyster straw mushroom 2. *Volvariella* sp

   C. Milky mushroom 3. *Auricularia* sp

   D. Jew's ear mushroom 4. *Pleurotus* sp

   A. 2 4 1 3 B. 4 3 2 1

   C. 3 4 1 2 D. 1 3 2 4

7. Commonly used media for raising pure culture of mushroom

A. MS medium
B. N-free malic acid medium
C. PDA medium
D. AMS medium

8. Medicinal usage of mushroom includes

A. Diabetic
B. Hypertension
C. Anticancerous
D. All the above

9. Mushroom poisoning can be treated by using

A. Benzyl penicillin
B. Secondary metabolites
C. Amanitin
D. Phalloidin

10. Directorate of Mushroom Research is located at

A. Solan
B. New Delhi
C. Coimbatore
D. Ooty

11. Casing in mushroom production refers to

A. Application of sterilized soil + 1000 g/kg of $CaCO_3$
B. Application of sterilized soil + 500 g/kg of $CaCO_3$
C. Application of sterilized soil + 100 g/kg of $CaCO_3$
D. Application of sterilized soil + 10 g/kg of $CaCO_3$

12. Optimum temperature required for growth of milky mushroom is

A. 20-25°C
B. 30-35°C
C. 40-45°C
D. <20°C

13. Volva is present in which mushroom?

A. Button mushroom
B. Oyster mushroom
C. Milky mushroom
D. Paddy straw mushroom

14. What is the toxin present in *Amanita phalloides* poison mushroom?

A. Gyromitrin
B. Phallotoxin
C. Orellanita
D. Coprine

15. Which is the most suitable substrate for mother spawn preparation?

A. Sorghum grains
B. Wheat grains
C. Maize grains
D. Cumbu grains

16. Spawn can be stored up to one month at what temperature?

A. 1-2°C
B. 2-3°C
C. 3-4°C
D. 4-6°C

17. Casing should be done

    A. At the time of spawning
    B. At the time of bed preparation
    C. After completion of spawn
    D. After completion of harvesting

18. Mushrooms are rich in which anti-oxidant?

    A. Selenium
    B. Copper
    C. Magnesium
    D. Boron

19. What should be the percentage of moisture after dehydration of mushroom for storage?

    A. 1-2%
    B. 2-4%
    C. 3-5%
    D. 7-10%

20. Which among the following is a milky mushroom variety?

    A. APK 1
    B. CO 3
    C. Ooty 1
    D. MDU 2

21. What is the light intensity required for production of buttons in mushroom?

    A. 1000-2000 lux
    B. 2000-2500 lux
    C. 2500-3000 lux
    D. 3500-4000 lux

22. Match the following

A. Honey mushroom	1. *Tricholoma matsutake*
B. Sacred mushroom	2. *Armillaria mellea*
C. Pink mushroom	3. *Lentinus edodes*
D. Shiitake mushroom	4. *Psilocybe semilanceata*

    A. 2 1 4 3
    B. 4 2 1 3
    C. 1 3 4 2
    D. 2 4 1 3

23. The incorrect option with respect to the purpose of mixing calcium carbonate in mother spawn preparation is

    A. To remove excess moisture
    B. To neutralize the pH
    C. To avoid caking of grains after sterilization
    D. To avoid contamination

24. Mushroom type which is helpful in fighting against AIDS

    A. Button mushroom
    B. Shiitake mushroom
    C. Oyster mushroom
    D. Paddy straw mushroom

25. The suitable substrate for spawn preparation in mushroom cultivation is

A. Sorghum grains B. Maize grains

C. Wheat grains D. All the above

26. Which of the following is the latest milky mushroom variety released in Tamil Nadu?

A. MDU 2 B. CO 2

C. APK 2 D. PKM 2

27. Diabetic patients are advised to take more of mushrooms as they contain

A. Low protein B. High protein

C. More minerals D. Low carbohydrates

28. Match list I with list II and choose the correct options given below

List I	**List II**
A. Wet bubble	1. Weed moulds
B. Tikki mould	2. Abiotic disorder
C. Phorids	3. Fungal disease
D. Rose comb	4. Pest of mushroom

A. 3 1 4 2 B. 3 4 1 2

C. 4 3 1 2 D. 4 1 3 2

Answer keys

1	C	11	C	21	C
2	D	12	B	22	D
3	B	13	D	23	D
4	C	14	B	24	B
5	D	15	A	25	D
6	A	16	D	26	C
7	C	17	C	27	D
8	D	18	A	28	A
9	A	19	C		
10	A	20	B		

6

Fungicides

I. Choose the correct answer

1. Which of the following fungicide is not a sterol biosynthesis inhibitors ?
   A. Ethirimol B. Triforine
   C. Thiophanate D. Triazoles
2. In general, powdery mildew of crops is managed by
   A. Bavistin B. Copper oxychloride
   C. Vitavax D. Wettable sulphur
3. Foliar application of this fungicide is a waste as it decomposes in light and the fungicide is
   A. Chloranil B. Dichlone
   C. Dinocap D. Dichloran
4. First dithio carbornate fungicide, discovered by Tisdale (1934) was
   A. Maneb B. Thiram
   C. Zeram D. Zineb
5. Inorganic mercury compounds used to eradicate plant pathogens are
   A. $HgCl_2$ B. Hg_2Cl_2
   C. $C_2H_5HgCl_2$ D. Both $HgCl_2$ and Hg_2Cl_2
6. Which of the following are protectant fungicides?
   A. Bordeaux mixture B. Burgundy mixture
   C. Chaubattia paste D. All of the above
7. Damping off and leaf blights are very effectively checked by
   A. Bordeaux mixture B. Burgundy mixture
   C. Thirarn D. Copper oxychloride
8. Von Schmeling and Kulka first time demonstrated the systemic activity of fungicides in
   A. 1956 B. 1966
   C. 1972 D. 1976

9. The Directorate of Plat protection Quarantine and storage was established in

A. 1946 B. 1947

C. 1956 D. 1957

10. Who recommended copper sulphate for seed treatment of wheat against bunt and demonstrated its fungi-toxic value first time

A. Mason B. Benedict Prevost

C. Singh D. P. M. A. Millardet

11. Who introduced burgundy mixture using sodium carbonate in place of lime?

A. Mason B. Narasimhan

C. Singh D. P.M A. Millardet

12. Who discovered bordeaux mixture to control downy mildew of grapevine by using copper sulphate (blue stone) and hydrated lime?

A. Mason B. Narasimhan

C. Singh D. P.M A. Millardet

13. In 1942, which of the Indian scientist developed Chaubattia paste in Almora district (UP) as a wound dressing fungicide and for this he used copper carbonate, lead oxide and linseed oil?

A. Mason B. Narasimhan

C. Singh D. P. M. A. Millardet

14. What is the actual ratio of copper carbonate, lead oxide and linseed oil in chaubattia Paste?

A. 1:1:1.25 B. 1:1:1.5

C. 2:1:2 D. 1:2:2

15. Who discovered first broad spectrum antibiotic streptomycin in 1943?

A. Weindling

B. Von Schmeling and Marshal Kulka

C. S. A. Waksman and A. Schatz

D. S.M. Idris

16. Who discovered first systemic fungicide oxathin?

A. Weindling

B. Von Schmeling and Marshal Kulka

C. S. A. Waksman and A. Schatz

D. S.M. Idris

17. Who developed the concept of vivo toxins and worked out the mechanism of wilting in cotton due to production of fusaric acid by *Fusarium oxysporum* f. sp. *vasinfectum?*

    A. J.F. Dastur B. K.R. Kirtikar

    C. T.S. Sadasivan D. S.N. Dasgusta

Answer keys

1	C	11	A
2	D	12	D
3	B	13	C
4	B	14	A
5	D	15	C
6	D	16	B
7	D	17	C
8	B		
9	A		
10	B		

UNIT VII: AGRICULTURAL MICROBIOLOGY

1

History of Mircobiology

I. Choose the correct answer

1. Father of soil microbiology is
   A. S.N. Winogradsky B. Beijerinck
   C. A. Waksman D. Liebig
2. BGA as nitrogen fixer first demonstrated in India by
   A. P. K. Dey B. Boussingault
   C. Jenny D. R. N. Singh
3. The term mycorrhiza was coined by
   A. Frank B. Hiltner
   C. Ruinen D. Winogradsky
4. Father of bacteriological technique is
   A. Robert Koch B. Gram
   C. Buchner D. Pasteur
5. The first penicillin isolated by Alexander Fleming, penicillin F, is also called
   A. 2-Pentenyl Penicillin B. n-heptyl penicillin
   C. Phenoxy methyl penicillin D. Benzyl penicillin
6. The term vaccine was coined by
   A. Pasteur B. Robert Koch
   C. Jenner D. Jenner and Pasteur
7. Who invented hanging drop method to determine motility of microbes
   A. Pasteur B. Robert Koch
   C. Jenner D. Leeuwenhoek
8. Who developed hybridoma technology for the first time?
   A. Landsteiner B. Fire and Mello
   C. Kohler and Milstein D. D'Herelle

9. Who isolated *Streptococcus pneumonia* for the first time?
   A. Robert Koch B. Edward Jenner
   C. Leeuwenhoek D. Louis Pasteur
10. Who discovered Archaebacteria?
   A. Carl Woese B. Edelmen
   C. Ehrlich D. Pasteur
11. Father of microbiology
   A. A.V. Leeuwenhoek B. Robert Hooke
   C. Robert Koch D. Ivanovsky
12. Father of bacteriology
   A. Anton Van Leeuwenhoek B. Robert Hooke
   C. Robert Koch D. Ivanovsky
13. Nitrification process was discovered by
   A. Schloesing and Muntz (1877) B. Ruinen and Hiltner
   C. Winogradsky and Beijerinck D. Beijernickia and Winogradsky
14. Bacteria responsible for nitrification was isolated by
   A. Winogradsky B. Beijernickia
   C. Ruinen D. Hiltner
15. The first member of the genus Azotobacter was discovered by
   A. M.W. Beijerinck B. Winogradsky
   C. Ruinen D. Hiltner
16. The word rhizosphere and phyllosphere are respectively given by
   A. Hiltner and Ruinen B. Ruinen and Hiltner
   C. Winogradsky and Beijernickia D. None of the above
17. Robert Koch worked on
   A. Diabetes B. Cholera
   C. Malaria D. Tuberculosis
18. First electron microscope was made by
   A. Knoll and Ruska B. Ernest Abbe
   C. Robert Koch D. Anton Van Leeuwenhoek
19. The scientific name of bacterium *Bacillus thuringiensis* owes its origin to Thuringia region in
   A. France B. Germany
   C. USA D. England

20. The lens used in the objective of a compound microscope is
    A. Convex lens
    B. Concave lens
    C. Combination of convex and concave lens
    D. Plano convex lens
21. Unstained live-microbial cells can be studied through
    A. Transmission electron microscope
    B. Phase – contrast microscope
    C. Scanning electron microscope
    D. Light microscope
22. Electron microscope was discovered by
    A. Anton von Leuvenhooke B. Knoll and Ruska
    C. Korenberg D. Robert hooke
23. Who proved that virus could pass through filters with pores small enough to retain bacteria
    A. Stanley B. Ivanowski
    C. Mayer D. Beijerinck

Answer keys

1	A	11	A	21	B
2	D	12	D	22	B
3	A	13	A	23	B
4	A	14	A		
5	A	15	A		
6	A	16	B		
7	D	17	D		
8	C	18	A		
9	D	19	B		
10	A	20	A		

2

Soil Microbes and Their Characteristics

I. Choose the correct answer

1. Microbial population of a soil in general

   A. Decreases with depth B. Increases with depth
   C. Constant throughout the profile D. No specific trend

2. Sulphur reducing bacteria are

   A. *Thiobacillus sp* B. *Bacillus sp.*
   C. *Desulfovibrio sp.* D. None of these

3. The microorganism lies below $< 10°C$ is called

   A. Psychrophiles B. Mesophiles
   C. Thermophiles D. None of the above

4. Thermophiles organism lies in temperature

   A. $> 45°C$ B. $> 25°C$
   C. $< 45°C$ D. $< 25°C$

5. Optimum temperature for mesophile

   A. 10-20°C B. 20-40°C
   C. 40-60°C D. 15-20°C

6. Which organism derive their energy from oxidation of complex organic compound

   A. Heterotrophs B. Autotrophs
   C. Chemotrophs D. Lithotrophs

7. Organism utilize carbon from CO_2 for their cellular synthesis

   A. Hetrotrophs B. Chemotrophs
   C. Autotrophs D. None of the above

8. Most of the soil organism is

   A. Psychrophiles B. Mesophiles
   C. Thermophiles D. All of the above

9. Fungal population is comparatively high in a soil having
   A. Acidic pH B. Neutral pH
   C. Alkaline pH D. Acidic to neutral pH
10. Heterotrophic organisms obtain energy from the biological oxidation of
   A. Organic carbon B. NH_4
   C. SO_4^{-2} D. CO_2
11. Nitrification is mainly carried out by
   A. Heterotrophic organism B. Photoautotrophic organism
   C. Chemoautotrophic organism D. None of the above
12. The microbes, which can survive at the temperature 25 - 30 °C is termed as
   A. Thermophiles B. Mesophiles
   C. Psychrophiles D. Thermophiles
13. The organism, which can survive at the temperature 10 - 15°C, is called
   A. Psychrophiles B. Mesophiles
   C. Thermophiles D. Psychrophiles
14. Urea is mineralized in the presence of enzyme
   A. Co-enzyme B. Peptase
   C. Urease D. All of the above
15. Commonly used method for enumeration of soil microbial population is
   A. Contact slide technique B. Microscopic count
   C. Dilution plate technique D. Microbial respiration
16. Conservation tillage tends to encourage
   A. High microbial population B. Lower number of earthworms
   C. Reduced soil fauna D. None of these
17. The order of microbe population in soil is
   A. Bacteria >Actinomycetes >Fungi >Algae> Protozoa
   B. Actinomycetes> Bacteria >Fungi>Protozoa> Algae
   C. Bacteria> Protozoa> Fungi >Actinomycetes> Algae
   D. Bacteria >Fungi >Actinomycetes> Algae >Protozoa
18. ______ plays a key role in the transformation of rock to soil
   A. Cyanobacteia B. Pectin decomposing bacteria
   C. Nitrifying bacteria D. Denitrifying bacteria

19. The organisms that are able to live in dry conditions are called
    A. Xerophiles B. Osmophiles
    C. Halophiles D. None of the above
20. Organisms most tolerant to moisture stress is
    A. Fungi B. Protozoa
    C. Bacteria D. Actinomycetes
21. Strictly anaerobic bacteria is
    A. *Clostridium* B. *Rhizobium*
    C. *Azotobacter* D. *Azospirillum*
22. Complex compounds produced by roots or through bacterial degradation
    A. Exudates B. Secretions
    C. Mucilages D. Mucigels
23. Murein is present in
    A. *Cyanobacteria* B. *Methanobacterium*
    C. *Halobacterium* D. None
24. Urea degrading bacteria
    A. *Bacillus pasturi* B. *Aspergillus niger*
    C. *Micrococcus sp* D. *Clostridium pasteurianum*
25. Fungi used for bioassay of panthothenic acid
    A. Yeast B. *Neurospora*
    C. *Aspergillus* D. *Mucor*
26. Actinomycetes are
    A. Gram negative, aerobic B. Gram negative, anaerobic
    C. Gram positive, aerobic D. Gram negative, anaerobic
27. Species of mycoplasma are inhabited by
    A. Penicillium B. Tetramycin
    C. Both D. None
28. In endospore staining which one is used
    A. Basic fuschin B. Indian ink
    C. Methylene blue D. Malachite green
29. The species of bacteria, which possesses 250 genes for lipid biosynthesis is
    A. *Mycobacterium genitalium* B. *Mycobacterium tuberculosis*
    C. *Escherichia coli* D. *Haemophilus influenzae*

30. When a virus enters a cell but does not replicate immediately, the situation is called

A. Lysogeny B. Fermentation

C. Symbiosis D. Synergism

31. The viral nucleocapsid is the combination of

A. Genome and capsid B. Capsid and spikes

C. Envelope and capsid D. Capsomere and genome

32. The gram-positive bacteria lack __________ structure/component?

A. Outer membrane B. Murein

C. Teichoic acid D. Plasma membrane

33. Which of the following gram-negative bacteria is not aerobic?

A. *Pseudomonas* B. *Neisseria*

C. *Escherichia* D. None of these

34. Gram-positive bacteria responsible for food poisoning is

A. *Mycoplasma* B. *Pseudomonas*

C. *Clostridia* D. All of these

35. *Thermus thermophilus* is a

A. Gram negative eubacteria B. Gram positive eubacteria

C. Gram negative archaebacteria D. Gram positive archaebacteria

36. Mucopeptide is a component of cell wall in

A. Brown algae B. Red algae

C. Green algae D. Blue green algae

37. ________ is the only bacterial genus where sterols are present in the cell membrane

A. *Escherichia* B. *Mycoplasma*

C. *Chlamydia* D. *Vibrio*

38. Which of the following protein cause the inhibition of transcription of 'nif' gene in nitrogen fixing bacteria

A. Nif B B. Nif A

C. Nif C D. Nif L

39. Among the following which organism is involved in nitrogen fixation with wood trees?

A. *Azotobacter* B. *Frankia*

C. *Azospirillum* D. *Pseudomonas*

40. Bacteria having especially high rate of respiration
    A. *Escherichia coli* B. *Azotobacter*
    C. *Acetobacter* D. *Rhizobium*
41. Number of chromosomes in bacteria is
    A. 1 B. 0
    C. 2 D. Many
42. Microorganism which are associated with non legumes
    A. *Anabaena* B. *Klebsiella*
    C. Both D. None of these
43. Example of chemolithotroph
    A. *Escherichia coli* B. *Bacillus*
    C. *Azotobacter* D. *Nitrosomonas*
44. Iron bacteria which oxidizes ferrous into ferric compound is
    A. *Leptothrix* B. *Beggiatoa*
    C. Both D. None
45. Gram staining was discovered by gram in the year
    A. 1762 B. 1932
    C. 1884 D. 1890
46. Counter stain used in gram staining
    A. Ethyl alcohol B. Iodine solution
    C. Crystal violet D. Safranin
47. Resolving power of electron microscope is ________ times that of light microscope
    A. 10 B. 100
    C. 1000 D. 10000
48. Pseudomorein is present in which organism
    A. *Archaebacteria* B. *Eubacteria*
    C. Eukaryote D. Fungi
49. Mesosomes are well developed in
    A. Gram positive bacteria B. Yeast
    C. Mycoplasma D. Escherichia coli
50. The yeast cell wall is made up of
    A. Glucans B. Mannans
    C. Cellulose and muramic acid D. Glucan, mannan, and chitin

51. The extra chromosomal, circular genetic element capable of self-replication, which is present in bacterial cell__________

A. Genophore B. Chromatophore

C. Plasmid D. Genome

52. The following organism has 'Peritrichous' arrangement of flagella

A. *Pseudomonas aeruginosa* B. *Pseudomonas fluorescens*

C. *Salmonella typhi* D. *Rhodospirillum photometricum*

53. The process of lambda phage mediated gene transfer in *Escherichia coli* is

A. General transduction B. Specialized transduction

C. Abortive transduction D. Transformation

54. Sendai virus enters the host cell by

A. Phagocytosis B. Receptor mediated endocytosis

C. Cell fusion D. Cell fission

55. Exponential growth in bacteria would be expected during

A. Lag phase B. Stationary phase

C. Log phase D. Deceleration phase

56. Among the following which is considered as the best indicator of water pollution

A. *Bacillus* B. *Clostridium*

C. *Escherichia coli* D. *Paramecium*

57. It has been observed that in bacterial colonies, bacteria often secrete toxins at higher population density to check the population size. This phenomenon is termed as

A. Population control B. Allelopathy

C. Intra specific competition D. Quorum sensing

58. A prophage is

A. DNA of lysogenic phase inserted into host chromosome

B. Is a stage of cell cycle

C. Lambda phage DNA

D. Plasmid

59. Transduction has been used extensively for genome mapping for bacteria, which of the following process is useful for gene mapping?

A. Bacterial lysis B. Generalized transduction

C. Specialized transduction D. Site specific recombination

60. In gram staining, the alcohol acts on

A. Teichoic acids
B. Peptidoglycan
C. Periplasm
D. Membrane lipids

61. Bacterial cells can be stained with __________to reveal the presence of lipid inclusions

A. Safranin
B. Methylene blue
C. Tryphan blue
D. Sudan dyes

62. __________ are prokaryotic, but have the ability to carry out oxygenic photosynthesis

A. *Photorhizobium*
B. *Cyanobacteria*
C. *Chlorobium*
D. *Rhodospirillum*

63. Glucose that is taken in by a bacterial cell is made to stay within the cell by

A. Attaching to membranes
B. Immediate utilization
C. Phosphorylation
D. Conversion to fructose

64. The natural resistance in plant is attributed by

A. Polyphenols
B. Thick cell wall
C. Good nutrition
D. High protein content

65. Unicellular prokaryotic microorganism with ray like filaments is

A. Bacteria
B. Fungi
C. Actinomycetes
D. All of the above

66. Cell wall of gram positive bacteria is made up of

A. Amino acid
B. Lipid
C. Pepditogycan
D. Protein

67. Which of following is not found in prokaryotic cell

A. Ribosomes
B. Cell wall
C. Photosynthetic membrane
D. Nucleus

68. Flagellar arrangement when it is cluster of polar flagella

A. Monotrichous
B. Lophotrichous
C. Peritrichous
D. Amphitrichous

69. Efficiency of symbiotic nitrogen fixation depends on

A. Host characteristics
B. Microbial strain characteristics
C. Ecological conditions
D. All of the above

70. Cold loving microbe is known as

A. Mesophile B. Psychrophile

C. Thermophile D. Hyperthermophile

71. Prokaryotic microorganism includes

A. Fungi B. Actinomycetes

C. Bacteria D. Virus

Answer keys

1	A	16	A	31	A	46	D	61	D
2	C	17	A	32	A	47	D	62	B
3	A	18	A	33	C	48	A	63	C
4	A	19	A	34	C	49	A	64	B
5	B	20	D	35	A	50	D	65	C
6	A	21	A	36	D	51	C	66	C
7	C	22	C	37	B	52	C	67	D
8	B	23	A	38	D	53	B	68	B
9	A	24	A	39	B	54	C	69	C
10	A	25	A	40	B	55	B	70	B
11	A	26	C	41	A	56	B	71	C
12	B	27	B	42	C	57	D		
13	A	28	D	43	D	58	A		
14	C	29	B	44	A	59	B		
15	C	30	A	45	C	60	D		

3

Composting

I. Choose the correct answer

1. In natural composting, the quantity of gypsum added for each tonnes is

   A. 25 kg B. 50 kg

   C. 5 kg D. 15 kg

2. In which method, there is anaerobic decomposition to start with, followed by aerobic fermentation?

   A. Indore method B. Bangalore method

   C. Coimbatore method D. Ludhiana method

3. Dominant organisms found in a compost pit are

   A. Thermophilic B. Psychrophilic

   C. Mesophilic D. Psychrophilic and mesophilic

4. Which of the following nutrient is increased by wood ash?

   A. N B. K

   C. P D. S

5. C:N ratio of farm yard manure is

   A. 20:1 B. 40:1

   C. 50:1 D. 80:1

6. The C:N ratio of composted coir pith is

   A. 24:1 B. 112:1

   C. 10:1 D. 30:1

7. Sugarcane trash can be composted easily by using

   A. *Phosphobacteria* B. *Azotobacter*

   C. *Penicillium* D. *Azospirillum*

8. The ideal C:N ratio for composting

   A. 25:1 B. 40:1

   C. 100:1 D. 10:1

9. Recommended rate of TNAU biomineralizer used for composting is
   A. 1 kg/ton of waste   B. 5 kg/ton of waste
   C. 10 kg/ton of waste   D. 2 kg/ton of waste
10. The maturity indices of composting are
   A. Volume reduction   B. Earthy odour
   C. Reduction in particle size   D. All the above
11. Fats, waxes, resins and lignin belong to which category?
   A. Rapidly decomposed   B. Less rapidly decomposed
   C. Very slowly decomposed   D. None of the above
12. The transformation of organic nitrogenous compounds into ammonia is called as
   A. Nitrification   B. Ammonification
   C. Denitrification   D. Fermentation
13. How much molecules of ATP are required to fix a molecule of N_2?
   A. 32 ATP   B. 12 ATP
   C. 16 ATP   D. 8 ATP
14. The organic acids released from decomposing organic matter helps to reduce
   A. Acidity of soil   B. Salinity of soil
   C. Toxic soil   D. Alkalinity of soil
15. The best combination of crop rotation which results in higher organic matter content
   A. Cereals + legumes   B. Malvaceous plants + cereals
   C. Solanaceous crop + cereals   D. Sorghum + bajra
16. The anaerobic decomposition of protein is called as
   A. Putrefaction   B. Proteolysis
   C. Nitrification   D. Mineralization
17. Average nutrient content of well decomposed FYM is
   A. 2:0.5:1.5 (N:P:K)   B. 2.5:1.0:2 (N:P:K)
   C. 0.5:0.2:0.5 (N:P:K)   D. 3:2:1 (N:P:K)
18. Example of green leaf manure
   A. *Crotalaria juncea*   B. *Sesbania aculeata*
   B. *Sesbania grandiflora*   D. *Sesbania rostrata*

19. (i) Coir pith has wider C:N ratio

(ii) The C:N ratio of composted coir pith is 112:1

Choose the incorrect statements?

A. (i) alone is wrong B. (ii) alone is wrong

C. Both are wrong D. Both are correct

20. (i) Humus contains major compounds like carbohydrates, phosphoric acid and some organic acids.

(ii) Humus is soluble in water.

A. Both are correct B. (i) alone is correct

C. (ii) alone is correct D. Both are wrong

21. Green manure crops in 50-60 days can able to accumulate

A. 80 kg N/ha B. 90 kg N/ha

C. 100 kg N/ha D. 60 kg N/ha

22. The composting of coir pith can be speeded up by adding

A. Urea B. Ammonium nitrate

C. Calcium ammonium nitrate D. Ammonium sulphate

23. Within how many days, coir compost will be ready?

A. 30 days B. 40 days

C. 50 days D. 60 days

24. In ______ method of composting, decomposition starting is anaerobic and ends in aerobic.

A. Coimbatore B. Bangalore

C. Indore D. NADP method

25. Which is the ultimate product of decomposition of organic matter?

A. Minerals B. Humus

C. Organic colloid D. Carbon

26. What is added to FYM to make it enriched FYM?

A. Urea B. MOP

C. SSP D. CAN

27. Product of night soil is called

A. Compost B. Dung

C. Mercaptans D. Poudrette

28. Night soil digestion place in India is

A. Nagpur B. Bangalore

C. Hyderabad D. None

29. Starter material for Bangalore method of composting

A. Night soil B. FYM

C. Dung D. Water

30. Composting was first initiated in

A. India B. China

C. England D. None

31. Hippuric acid present in

A. Liquid portion of FYM B. Solid portion of FYM

C. Green manures D. None

32. Persistent binding agents are due to

A. Microbial products B. Humic materials

C. Bacterial products D. Plant material

33. Low quality manure is observed in which type of storage method

A. Heap method B. Pit method

C. Covered pit method D. All

34. Bangalore method of composting is

A. Aerobic method B. Anaerobic method

C. Both D. None of the above

35. Nitrifying bacteria are ______

A. Gram negative B. Minute

C. Rod shaped D. All of the above

36. Soil microorganisms are most active at ______

A. 15-20°C B. 20-25°C

C. 34-36°C D. 40-45°C

37. Which of the following is capable of oxidizing sulfur to sulfates

A. *Thiobacillus thiooxidans* B. *Rhodomicrobium*

C. *Desulfotomaculum* D. *Rhodospirillum*

38. Nitrifying bacteria cannot be isolated directly by the usual techniques employed to isolate heterotrophic bacteri A. The reason may be due to

A. Slow growth
B. Fast growth
C. Medium growth
D. None of the above

39. Bacteria, as a group, are responsible for

A. Nitrogen oxidation
B. Sulfur oxidation
C. Nitrogen fixation
D. All of the above

40. The population of algae in soil is ________ that of either bacteria or fungi

A. Generally smaller than
B. Generally greater than
C. Equal to
D. None of the above

41. The breakdown of cattle manure into biogas is accomplished by which of the following type of bacteria?

A. Hydrolytic
B. Methanogenic
C. Transitional
D. All of the above

42. Which of the following species of different genera of bacteria are not capable of transforming nitrate to nitrogen?

A. *Achromobacter*
B. *Agrobacterium*
C. *Alcaligenes*
D. None of the above

43. For rapid decomposition by microbes, the substrate should have a C/N ratio of

A. 10:20
B. 30:40
C. 60:80
D. 20:30

44. Degree of compost maturity can be assessed by

A. Infrared technique
B. Germination test
C. Both A and B
D. None of the above

45. The microbial ecosystem of soil includes

A. Biotic components of soil
B. Abiotic components of soil
C. Biotic and abiotic components of soil
D. None of the above

46. Amount of dissolved oxygen consumed in five days by biological processes breaking down organic matter

A. BOD
B. AOD
C. COD
D. LOD

47. Greatest producers of organic matter are

A. Crop plants B. Forests

C. Plants of the land area D. Phytoplankton of oceans.

48. The cellulose content in plant tissues is about

A. 20-50% B. 10-30%

C. 1-15% D. 1-10%

Answer keys

1	A	11	C	21	C	31	A	41	D
2	C	12	B	22	A	32	B	42	D
3	C	13	C	23	D	33	A	43	B
4	B	14	D	24	A	34	B	44	C
5	B	15	A	25	B	35	C	45	C
6	A	16	A	26	C	36	C	46	A
7	C	17	C	27	D	37	A	47	D
8	A	18	B	28	A	38	A	48	A
9	B	19	B	29	B	39	D		
10	D	20	B	30	C	40	A		

4

Vermicomposting

I. Choose the correct answer

1. Vermicompost contains

   A. Protease B. Lipase

   C. Amylase D. All

2. Recommended rate of vermicompost for field crops is

   A. 5 tonnes/ha B. 10 tonnes/ha

   C. 5 kgs/ha D. 100 kgs/ha

3. Which one of the following is incorrect?

   A. African worm (*Eudrilus eugeniae*)

   B. Redworm (*Eisenia foetida)*

   C. Indian worm (*Lampito mauritti*)

   D. Asian worm (*Perionyx excavatus*)

4. Common bedding material used for vermicompost?

   A. Fresh tree branches B. Wood ash

   C. Fodder grass D. Horse manure

5. The suitable moisture percentage in vermicomposting

   A. 40% B. 60%

   C. 50% D. None of the above

6. The potassium content in vermicompost is

   A. 0.5-1.5% B. 0.1-0.3%

   C. 0.15-0.56% D. None of these

7. Subsoil deep burrowing species are called

   A. Epigeic species B. Endogeic species

   C. Anecic species D. Ectogeic species

8. The character of earthworm suited for vermicomposting is
   A. High vermin stabilization time
   B. Least stabilization rate
   C. Medium vermin stabilisation time
   D. Very high vermin stabilization time
9. The average percentage of N in vermicompost is
   A. 3 B. 30
   C. 10 D. 15
10. Which is the suitable earthworm for vermicomposting?
   A. *Eudrilus Eugenia* B. *Perionyx excavatus*
   C. *Eisenia foetida* D. *Octochaetona serrata*
11. The chemical used for providing protection to vermibed from ants is
   A. Chloramphenicol B. Griseofulvin
   C. Chlorpyriophosphate D. DDT
12. Vermicompost is biofertilizer which is rich in
   A. Phosphorus B. Calcium
   C. Nitrogen D. All of the above
13. One of the following is not a benefit of vermicompost
   A. Protection of water bodies from pollution
   B. Reduction in microbial activity
   C. Increased availability of minerals
   D. Increased hydration and aeration
14. pH of vermiculture is kept at
   A. Near neutral B. Alkaline
   C. Acidic D. Highly alkaline
15. The vermicompost is ____ in colour.
   A. Red B. Black
   C. White D. Brown
16. How much can worms eat each day?
   A. Half their body weight in food
   B. Equal to the their body weight in food
   C. Double their body weight in food
   D. One fourth of body weight of earthworm

17. What type of worms are the best for vermicomposting?

    A. Blue B. Brown

    C. Red D. Black

18. How long will it take for worm population to double?

    A. 30 days B. 60 days

    C. 90 days D. 120 days

19. What is the ratio of male and female worms required for effective worm reproduction?

    A. 1 male: 1 female B. 1 male: 2 female

    C. 1male: 3 female D. It doesn't matter

Answer keys

1	D	6	C	11	C	16	A
2	A	7	C	12	D	17	C
3	C	8	B	13	B	18	C
4	D	9	A	14	A	19	D
5	B	10	A	15	B		

5

Biofertilizers

1. Choose the correct answer

1. Nitrogen fixing biofertilizers may be used in paddy crop as
   A. Seed treatment B. Seedling root dip
   C. Broadcasting D. All of the above
2. Non-symbiotic N-fixer is
   A. *Rhizobium* B. *Azospirillum*
   C. *Azotobacter* D. *Mycorrhizae*
3. Microbe used to overcome drought condition is
   A. *Azolla* B. Blue green algae
   C. *Aspergillus* D. PPFM
4. Expand PSB
   A. Phosphate solubulising bacteria B. Phosphorus solidifying bacteria
   C. Phosphorus stabilizing bacteria D. Phophorus solubilizing bacteria
5. Type of biofertilizers available in nitrogen form
   A. *Azotobacter* B. AM
   C. Urea D. *Pseudomonas fluorescens*
6. Biofertilizers recommended for field crops (seed treatment)
   A. *Azotobacter* + AM (500g)
   B. *Rhizobium* + Phosphobacteria (200g each)
   C. Visual Azolla medium + *Azotobacter*
   D. AM (1 kg per kg of seeds)
7. What is mycorrhizae?
   A. Sodifying fungus + plants branches
   B. Relationship between soil fungus + plant debris
   C. Mutualistic relationship between soil fungus + plant roots
   D. Relationship between fungus and plant stems + roots

8. Example of associative symbiotic nitrogen fixer?

A. *Beijerinckia* B. *Azospirillum*

C. *Rhizobium* D. *Anabaena azollae*

9. Biofertilizer used for legume crops

A. *Azospirillum* B. *Azotobacter*

C. *Acetobacter* D. *Rhizobium*

10. Who isolated *Azotobacter* as free-living aerobic N_2 fixer?

A. Beijerinck B. Winogradsky

C. M.S.Swaminathan D. Boussingault

11. Swollen deformed *Rhizobium* cells found in root nodule responsible for nitrogen fixation is called

A. Nod-gene B. Sheperd's crook cells

C. Bacteriods D. Nif-genes

12. Stem nodulating *Rhizobium* nodulates in

A. *Sesbania rostrata* B. *Sesbania aculeata*

C. *Sesbania grandiflora* D. *Sesbania speciosa*

13. Nitrogen fixing bacteria in casuarinas

A. *Nostoc* B. *Parasponia*

C. *Frankia* D. *Beijerinckia*

14. CIG (Cross Inoculation Groups) are found in

A. *Azotobacter* B. *Rhizobium*

C. *Azospirillum* D. Both A and B

15. The bacteria which are not present on the rhizoplane, but are abundant in rhizosphere region

A. *Rhizobium* B. *Azospirillum*

C. *Azotobacter* D. All the above

16. Algae is a

A. Photoautotrophs B. Heterotrophs

C. Chemotrophs D. Hemotrophs

17. The species of *Azotobacter* which produce green fluorescent pigmentation in liquid inoculum is

A. *A. chroococcum* B. *A.beijerinckii*

C. *A.macrocytogenes* D. *A.vinelandii*

18. Example of denitrifying bacteria

A. *Nitrobacter* B. *Nitrosomonas*

C. *Pseudomonas* D. *Bacillus*

19. Which of the following nod genes responsible for control of function of all nod genes?

A. Nod B B. Nod C

C. Nod D D. Nod F

20. Example of phyllospheric bacteria

A. *Pseudomonas* sp B. *Nitrosomonus*

C. *Azotobacter* D. *Nitrobacter*

21. Sulphur reducing bacteria is

A. *Desulphovibrio* B. *Thiobacillus*

C. *Beggiatoa* D. *Thiothrix*

22. The optimum temperature for activities of most of the microorganisms is

A. 15-20°C B. 20-25°C

C. 25-35°C D. 35-45°C

23. Sub surface white pellicle formation is a characteristic feature of

A. *Azotobacter* B. *Azospirillum*

C. Phosphobacteria D. *Glucano acetobacter*

24. India – UK nitrogen fixation centre was inaugurated at

A. IISS – Bhopal B. Lucknow

C. Varanasi D. Trivandrum

25. The Government of India implemented central sector scheme called national project on development and use of biofertilizers during which plan?

A. 5th five year plan B. 9th five year plan

C. 10th five year plan D. 1st five year plan

26. Headquarters of National Biofertilizer Development Centre is located at

A. Ghaziabad B. Coimbatore

C. Hyderabad D. Faridabad

27. Expand NPDB
    A. National Programme on Development and use of Biofertilizer
    B. National Progress on Development and use of Biofertilizer
    C. National Project on Development and use of Biofertilizer
    D. National Institute on Development and use of Biofertilizer
28. Shelf life of biofertilizer (carrier based).
    A. 1 month B. 6 months
    C. 1 year D. 9 months
29. Which biofertilizer is also used as a cattle feed
    A. *Mycorrhizae* B. Blue green algae
    C. *Azolla* D. Staghorn fern
30. Recommended rate of blue green algae for rice crop
    A. 50 kg/ha B. 10 kg/ha
    C. 100 kg/ha D. 25 kg/ha
31. Azolla contains _____ per cent protein
    A. 10-15% B. 5 – 10%
    C. 25-35% D. 50-60%
32. The host crop used for the mass production of AM fungi is
    A. Paddy B. Sorghum
    C. Maize D. Finger millet
33. The thickness of polythene bag used for storage of biofertilizer should be of
    A. 25-30 micron B. 50-75 micron
    C. 75-100 micron D. 10-25 micron
34. Quantity of lime added to neutralize the acidity of carrier material is about
    A. 2 g/kg of carrier material B. 10 g/kg of carrier material
    C. 5 g/kg of carrier material D. 25 g/kg of carrier material
35. Biofertilizer recommended for sugarcane crop is
    A. *Azospirillum* B. *Glucano acetobacter*
    C. *Rhizobium* D. *Phosphobacteria*
36. Maximum biofertilizer production capacity is in
    A. Uttar Pradesh B. Madhya Pradesh
    C. Tamil Nadu D. Gujarat

37. The commercial history of biofertilizer began with launch of 'Nitragin' by
    A. Darwin (1876) B. Nobbe and Hilter (1985)
    C. Bonnet (1838) D. Nathan and Smith (1930)
38. In BGA, nitrogen fixation takes place in specialized cells called
    A. Heterocyst B. Bacteriods
    C. Vesicles D. Arbuscles
39. *Rhizobium* is mass cultured by using
    A. Waksmann no 77 media B. King's B broth
    C. N-free malic acid media D. YEMA media
40. Which free living organism fixes atmospheric nitrogen?
    A. BGA B. *Rhizobium*
    C. Nitrobacter D. Nitrosomonas
41. Microorganism responsible for the solubilisation of fixed P is
    A. Blue green algae B. *Azolla*
    C. *Azospirillum* D. Phosphobacteria
42. Symbiotic association of fungal hyphae with plant roots is known as
    A. Mycorrhiza B. Mutual infection
    C. Parasitism D. Lichen
43. Among the following, which organism is a silicate and zinc solubilizer
    A. *Rhizoctonia solani* B. *Pseudomonas striata*
    C. *Gigaspora* sp D. *Bacillus* sp
44. Which organism is in associative symbiotic relationship with graminaceous plant?
    A. *Azospirillum* B. Phosphobacteria
    C. *Rhizobium* D. *Azotobacter*
45. Which organism is called blue green algae?
    A. *Penicillium* B. *Aspergillus*
    C. *Cyanobacteria* D. AM
46. Which is a free floating aquatic fern?
    A. *Glomus* sp B. *Azolla*
    C. *Cyanobacteria* D. *Teridium* sp

47. _______ is a bacteria associated with sugarcane.

A. *Azotobacter* B. *Azospirillum*

C. *Fusarium* D. *Acetobacter*

48. BGA grows best in

A. Upland rice B. Lowland rice

C. Dry seeded rice D. Rainfed rice

49. The most common contaminate of rhizobium isolated from legume root nodule is

A. *Agrobacterium* B. *Azotobacter*

C. *Azospirillum* D. None of these

50. Group of legume plant that develops nodules when exposed to bacteria nodules obtained from the nodules of any member of that plant group is known as

A. Symbiotic promiscuity B. Cross inoculation group

C. Symbiosis D. None of the above

51. If soyabean is being grown for the first time in a field, the seed should be treated with ______ culture

A. *Azospirillium* B. *Azotobacter*

C. *Rhizobium* D. *Phosphobacteria*

52. Which one of the following statements is correct?

A. *Rhizobium* fixes N_2 in soil non-symbiotically

B. *Azotobacter* fixes N_2 symbiotically

C. BGA fixes N_2 in paddy fields under submerged condition

D. *Closterdia* fixes N_2 symbiotically

53. Mycorrhizae infected plants show better ability of absorption of the nutrients, especially

A. Iron B. Manganese

C. Potassium D. Phosphorus

54. Non-symbiotic bacteria fixes _______ amount of N_2 than symbiotic N_2 fixers

A. Less B. More

C. Equal D. Not known

55. Oxidation of sulfur to sulphate is carried out by

A. *Bacillus* spp
B. *Aspergillus* spp
C. *Azotobacter* spp
D. *Thiobacillus* spp

56. Rhizobium infect the host legumes through

A. Epidermal cells
B. Cortex cells
C. Root hairs
D. All of the above

57. Rhizobium after infection converts to a form, which is irregular in shape and is called

A. Spore
B. Cyst
C. Bacteriod
D. None of the above

58. Rhizosphere affects microbial population and nutrient availability by

A. Exerting physical pressure
B. Secreting nutritive metabolites and organic solvents
C. Increasing pore space
D. Changing soil structure

59. The amount of N_2 fixed by *Clostridium* is ______ mg N_2 per gm sugar

A. 15 - 25
B. 7 - 12
C. 2 -7
D. 25 - 50

60. The bacteria considered most important to bring about the conversion of NH_4 to NH_2 is

A. *Nitrosomonas*
B. *Nitrobacteria*
C. Both A and B
D. *Azotobacter*

61. Which of the following is considered as biofertilizer?

A. Farm yard manure
B. Compost
C. Green manure
D. Blue-green algae

62. Denitrification is carried out

A. Usually by facultative anaerobes
B. Predominantly by *Pseudomonas* spp
C. Predominantly by *Bacillus* spp
D. All of these

63. Which of the following soil microorganism is involved in the reduction of sulfates to H_2S?

A. *Thiobacillus thiooxidans*
B. *Desulfotomaculum*
C. *Rhodospirillum*
D. *Rhodomicrobium*

64. Rhizobium first isolated by Beijerinck and named as

A. *Bacillus radicola* B. *Pseudomonas radicicola*

C. *Clostridium* D. None

65. Diatoms are

A. Blue-green algae B. Grass - green algae

C. Yellow - green algae D. Golden - brown algae

66. Leaves of plant used as biofertilizer belong to

A. *Hibiscus* B. Mango

C. *Anabaena* D. *Azolla*

67. Leghaemoglobin is found in

A. Root nodules of legumes B. Mycorrhiza

C. Coralloid roots D. Cyanobacteria

68. Leghaemoglobin takes part in _______

A. Energy release B. Stimulating growth of *Rhizobium*

C. Protecting nitrogenase D. N_2 absorption

69. If wheat field is inoculated with *Rhizobium,*

A. Soil will become nitrogen rich B. Soil will become rich in calcium

C. No effect on soil nitrogen D. Soil will be depleted of nitrogen

70. Heterocyst contains enzyme

A. Pectinase B. Cellulase

C. Nitrogenase D. Phosphorylase

71. A nitrogen fixing blue green algae is

A. *Spirogyra* B. *Rhizobium*

C. *Ulothrix* D. *Anabaena*

72. Aquatic fern which is an excellent biofertilizer

A. *Salvinia* B. *Pteridium*

C. *Azolla* D. *Marsilea*

73. A free living nitrogen fixing bacterium is

A. *Clostridium* B. *Azotobacter*

C. *Rhizobium* D. Both A and B

74. *Azolla* is used as biofertilizer because it

A. Multiplies very fast to produce massive biomass

B. Has association of nitrogen fixing *cyanobacteria*

C. Has association of nitrogen fixing *Rhizobium*

D. Has association of *Mycorrhiza*

75. Biofertilizers include

A. Cow dung manure and farmyard waste

B. A quick growing crop ploughed back

C. BGA/*Anabaena* and *Azolla*

D. All of the above

76. The N content of *Azolla* is

A. 1.0 – 2.0% B. 0.2 – 0.3%

C. 0.01 – 0.02% D. 5.0 – 10.0%

77. The heterotrophic, anaerobic and free-living bacteria is

A. *Pseudomonas* B. *Bacillus*

C. *Rhizobium* D. *Clostridium*

78. A part of nitrogen fixed is excreted as free amino acids in the soil, which was first observed by

A. M.W.Beijerinck B. Virtanen

C. Liebig D. Whitney

79. AM considered as

A. Obligate symbionts B. Facultative symbionts

C. Both A and B D. None

80. Ectotrophic mycorrhizae includes

A. *Amanita* B. *Boletus*

C. Both A and B D. None

81. Maximum nitrogen added to soil by

A. *Rhizobium meliloti* B. *Rhizobium leguminosarum*

C. *Rhizobium japonicum* D. *Rhizobium trifoli*

82. The organism which is leaf inhabitant

A. *Frankia* B. *Klebsiella*

C. *Pseudomonas* D. All

83. Amount of nitrogen fixed by *Azolla*

A. 25-30 kg/ha B. 35-45 kg/ha

C. 50-60 kg/ha D.70-75 kg/ha

Answer keys

1	D	16	A	31	C	46	B	61	D	76	B
2	C	17	D	32	C	47	D	62	D	77	D
3	D	18	A	33	B	48	B	63	B	78	C
4	A	19	C	34	A	49	A	64	A	79	A
5	A	20	A	35	B	50	B	65	D	80	C
6	B	21	A	36	C	51	C	66	D	81	A
7	C	22	C	37	B	52	B	67	A	82	D
8	B	23	B	38	A	53	D	68	C	83	A
9	D	24	A	39	D	54	A	69	C		
10	A	25	B	40	A	55	D	70	B		
11	C	26	A	41	D	56	C	71	D		
12	A	27	A	42	A	57	C	72	C		
13	C	28	B	43	D	58	B	73	D		
14	B	29	C	44	A	59	B	74	B		
15	C	30	B	45	C	60	C	75	C		

6

Applied Microbiology

I. Choose the correct answer

1. The association which involves the exchange of nutrients between two species is referred to as

   A. Mutualism B. Syntrophism

   C. Commensalism D. Antagonism

2. The degradation of complex molecules in soil by fungi for utilization by bacteria is an example of which type of association?

   A. Neutralism B. Mutualism

   C. Commensalism D. Antagonism

3. Which of the following is pollution indicator

   A. Lichens

   B. AM

   C. Plant Growth Promoting Rhizobacteria

   D. All of the above

4. Example for Mn-oxidising bacteria are

   A. *Arthrobacter* B. *Leptothrix*

   C. *Gallionella* D. Both A and B

5. The process of the removal of contaminants and metals using living green plants from soil is known as

   A. Phytoremediation B. Biostimulation

   C. Bioaugmentation D. All of the above

6. Common example of fermented beverage product is

   A. Pickles B. Cheese and yogurt

   C. Bread and buns D. Beer

7. UHT sterilization involves high temperature exposure of objects for

   A. 1-3 seconds B. 1-3 minutes

   C. 1-3 hours D. 10-30 hours

8. Which of the following is used for the commercial production of vitamin B12?

   A. *Propionibacterium* B. *Mycobacterium*

   C. *Brevibacterium* D. None

9. Bacteria which can ferment sugar faster than yeast is

   A. *Clostridium* B. *Zygomonas*

   C. *Thiobacillus* D. *Bacillus*

10. The first antiseptic agent used was

    A. Mercuric chloride B. Carbolic acid

    C. Alcohol D. Hyposolution

11. First antifungal antibiotic is

    A. Aureofungin B. Cyclohexamide

    C. Nystatin D. None of these

12. Milky disease is caused by

    A. *Lactobacillus lactis* B. *Bacillus thuringiensis*

    C. *Bacillus popilliae* D. None of these

13. An antiviral substance produced by animal tissue

    A. Antibody B. Interferon

    C. Antigen D. Virion

14. Fungi used for bioassay of biotin

    A. *Aspergillus* B. Yeast

    C. *Penicillium* D. *Neurospora*

15. Wine turns sour

    A. On exposure to light

    B. Contamination by aerobic *Acetobacter aceti*

    C. Contamination by anaerobic *Lactobacillus lactis*

    D. On prolonged storage

16. The species of *Clostridium* most likely to cause spoilage of canned foods is

    A. *Clostridium sporogenes* B. *Clostridium pasteurianum*

    C. *Clostridium botulinum* D. *Clostridium tetani*

17. Lower BOD of sewage water is an indicator of

    A. Higher amount of toxic elements

    B. Higher acidity

C. Lower organic matter content

D. Higher organic matter content

18. Which property of microorganism is used in bioassay of vitamins?

A. Autotrophy B. Phototrophy

C. Auxotrophy D. Chemoheterotrophy

19. Prions are a type of

A. Viruses B. Proteinaceous particles

C. Yeast like particles D. Viroids

20. The microbial process responsible for the separation of fibres from jute stem

A. Retting B. Fermentation

C. Blanching D. Curing

21. The fungus commonly used for coir pith

A. *Trichoderma* B. *Pleurotus*

C. *Amanita* D. *Agaricus*

22. Vinegar is produced by

A. Acetic acid bacteria B. Lactic acid bacteria

C. Butyric acid bacteria D. Yeast

23. The gelling agent agar-agar is obtained from

A. Fungus B. Red algae

C. Blue green algae D. Brown algae

24. Wood sugar is

A. Glucose B. Mannose

C. Arabinose D. Xylose

25. Name the organism which is predatory on bacteria

A. Virus B. Bdellovibrio

C. Viroid D. Prion

26. Who developed cell free fermentation of modern science?

A. Pasteur B. Koch

C. Buchner D. None of these

27. Principle site for CO_2 fixation in autotrophic prokaryotes

A. Chromosomes B. Carboxyosomes

C. Both D. None of these

28. Antibiotic streptomycin was isolated by

A. Robert Koch B. Flemming

C. Waksman D. Pasteur

29. An aminoglycoside antibiotic is

A. Penicillin B. Streptomycin

C. Tetracycline D. None

30. Microbe involved in fibre retting is

A. *Micrococcus* sp B. *Bacillus subtilis*

C. *Clostridium butrycium* D. *Lactobacillus* sp

31. Magnetosomes are inclusion of ____________ in certain bacteria

A. Iron oxide B. Iron phosphate

C. Iron nitrates D. Iron chlorides

32. The usual mode of gene transfer in bacteria is

A. Transduction B. Conjugation

C. Transformation D. All of the above

33. Which is known as sewage fungus

A. *Cephalosporium* B. *Penicillium*

C. *Leptomitus* D. *Rhizobium*

34. The desire to maintain a safe laboratory environment for all begins with

A. Prevention B. Microbiology

C. Ubiquity D. Accidents

35. Which of the following type(s) of Personal Protective Equipment (PPE) is frequently used

A. Safety glasses B. Gloves

C. Lab coats/Apron D. All of the above

36. Major useful product obtained from microbes is

A. Vitamin B. Single cell protein

C. Antibiotic D. All of the above

37. ___________ is a synthetic antimicrobial drug against *Mycobacterium tuberculosis*

A. Penicillin B. Tetracycline

C. Erythromycin D. Isoniazid

38. Red pigment produced by

    A. *Serratia* B. *Micrococcus*

    C. Both D. None

39. Fermenting organism involved in yogurt is

    A. *Streptococcus* B. *Aspergillus*

    C. *Pediococcus* D. None

Answer keys

1	B	11	C	21	B	31	A
2	C	12	C	22	A	32	C
3	A	13	B	23	B	33	C
4	D	14	D	24	D	34	A
5	A	15	B	25	B	35	D
6	D	16	C	26	C	36	D
7	A	17	C	27	B	37	D
8	A	18	C	28	C	38	A
9	B	19	B	29	B	39	A
10	B	20	A	30	C		

UNIT VIII: CROP PHYSIOLOGY

1

Plant Cell and Anatomy

I. Choose the correct answer

1. Major part of dry weight of a plant is derived from elements obtained from

   A. Soil B. Air

   C. Water D. Decomposing organic matter

2. The largest plant cells are

   A. Xylem vessel cell B. Parenchyma cells

   C. Sieve tube cells D. Sclerenchyma fibers

3. The smallest component of cell is

   A. Microfilament B. Ribosome

   C. Plastid D. Phagosome

4. The smaller cell is metabolically

   A. Less active B. With smaller nucleus

   C. With larger nucleus D. More active

5. Cells metabolically active have

   A. Lower nucleo-cytoplasmic ratio B. Higher nucleo-cytoplasmic ratio

   C. Higher surface: volume ratio D. Both B and C

6. Exception of cell theory is

   A. Protistans B. Algae

   C. Virus D. Mycoplasma

7. The property of cell in which a cell can form many phenotypes is

   A. Totipotency B. Parasexually

   C. Pleuriopotency D. Parthenogenesis

8. Food vacuole in cell is made from

   A. Phagosome + Lysosome B. Phagosome + Feeding canals

   C. Vesicles of a gas vacuole D. None of the above

9. Granules of nucleolus are
   A. Precursors of ribosomes
   B. Precursors of RNA
   C. Precursors of chromosomes
   D. None of the above
10. Nucleolar organizing region (NOR) occurs in the region of
   A. Secondary constriction
   B. Primary constriction
   C. Telomere
   D. Centromere
11. Chromosomes present in eukaryotic cell are composed of
   A. RNA + DNA
   B. DNA + Protein
   C. Only RNA
   D. Only DNA
12. Balbiani rings are called
   A. Coiling of chromonemata
   B. Uncoiling of chromonemata
   C. Both A and B
   D. Enlargements of centromere
13. In case of plant chromosomes, which type of banding techniques used?
   A. C and N
   B. C and G
   C. G and R
   D. Q and G
14. Middle lamella contains
   A. Cellulose
   B. Lignin
   C. Pectate
   D. Cutin
15. A cell's water potential in hypertonic solution
   A. Decreases
   B. First increases and then, decreases
   C. Increases
   D. No change
16. Which of the following phenomenon is responsible for swelling of dry seeds in water?
   A. Capillarity
   B. Adsorption
   C. Endosmosis
   D. All of these
17. The ultra filtration theory to explain the phenomenon of permeability was proposed by
   A. Clowes
   B. Overton
   C. Ruhland
   D. Michaelis
18. Which of the following symbol is used to indicate the osmotic pressure?
   A. ττ
   B. φ
   C. δ
   D. λ

19. Movement of leaves of sensitive plant, *Mimosa pudica* are due to
    A. Thermonasty B. Seismonasty
    C. Hydrotropism D. Chemonasty
20. Phytochrome is involved in
    A. Phototropism B. Photorespiration
    C. Photoperiodism D. Geotropism
21. ATP is
    A. An enzyme which bring about oxidation
    B. An organic compound
    C. A vitamin
    D. A molecule which contains high energy phosphate bond
22. Cellular totipotency is demonstrated by
    A. Only gymnosperm cells B. All plant cells
    C. All eukaryotic cells D. Only bacterial cells
23. The term cell was given by
    A. Robert Hooke B. Tatum
    C. Schwann D. De Bary
24. The membrane around the vacuole is known as
    A. Tonoplast B. Elaioplast
    C. Cytoplast D. Amyloplast
25. A plant cell wall is mainly composed of
    A. Protein B. Cellulose
    C. Lipid D. Starch
26. Lysosomes are known as 'Suicidal bags' because
    A. Parasitic activity B. Presence of food vacuole
    C. Hydrolytic activity D. Catalytic activity
27. Name the organelle which serves as a primary packaging area for molecules that will be distributed throughout the cell?
    A. Mitochondria B. Plastids
    C. Golgi apparatus D. Vacuole
28. Name the outer most boundary of the cell?
    A. Plasma membrane B. Cytoplasm
    C. Nuclear membrane D. None of the above

29. The jelly like substance present inside the cell is known as

A. Cytoplasm B. Ectoplasm

C. Nucleoplasm D. None of the above

30. The main function of centrosome

A. Secretion B. Osmoregulation

C. Protein synthesis D. Formation of spindle fibre

31. Microfilaments are mainly composed of

A. Actin B. Tubulin

C. Myosin D. Chitin

32. Cellulose and hemicellulose which are the constituent of cell wall are synthesized by

A. Lysosomes B. Golgi apparatus

C. Smooth ER D. Rough ER

33. Plasmodesmata connections help in

A. Cytoplasmic streaming or cyclosis

B. Movement of substances between cells

C. Locomotion of unicellular organisms

D. Synchronous mitotic division

34. Cell theory is not applicable to

A. Virus B. Microorganisms

C. Fungi D. Algae

35. According to carrier hypothesis, the specific carriers are present on

A. Plasmalemma B. Tonoplast

C. Endoplasmic reticulum D. Mitochondria

Answer keys

1	B	11	B	21	D	31	D
2	D	12	B	22	B	32	B
3	A	13	A	23	A	33	B
4	D	14	C	24	A	34	A
5	D	15	A	25	B	35	A
6	C	16	D	26	C		
7	C	17	C	27	C		
8	A	18	A	28	A		
9	A	19	B	29	A		
10	A	20	C	30	D		

2

Water Relation and Transport in Plants

I. Choose the correct answer

1. The water readily available to plants for absorption by roots is by

   A. Gravitational water   B. Capillary water
   C. Rain water   D. Hygroscopic water

2. The water potential of pure water at atmospheric pressure is

   A. -2.3 bar   B. +2.3 bar
   C. Zero bar   D. One bar

3. Loss of water from the stomata of leaves are known as

   A. Guttation   B. Exudation
   C. Transpiration   D. Evaporation

4. Plasmolysis occurs due to

   A. Absorption   B. Osmosis
   C. Endosmosis   D. Exosmosis

5. The marine animals that kept in fresh water burst. It shows the process of

   A. Exosmosis   B. Endosmosis
   C. Plasmolysis   D. Deplasmolysis

6. Cooling of plants is caused by

   A. Guttation   B. Photorespiration
   C. Transpiration   D. Assimilation

7. Active uptake of minerals by roots mainly depends on the

   A. Availability of oxygen   B. Temperature
   C. Light   D. Availability of CO_2

8. The hormone which signals the closure of stomata is

   A. Auxins   B. Cytokinin
   C. Gibberellin   D. Abscisic acid

9. Water absorption takes place through

A. Lateral roots
B. Root cap
C. Root hairs
D. Tap root

10. What is the action spectrum of transpiration?

A. Orange and red
B. Green and ultraviolet
C. Blue and red
D. None of these

11. Which one of the following is used for measuring the rate of transpiration?

A. Porometer
B. Osmometer
C. Moll's experiment
D. Potometer

12. Transpiration is least in

A. High atmospheric humidity
B. Good soil moisture
C. High wind velocity
D. Dry environment

13. Stomata open at night and close during day time in

A. Xerophytes
B. Mesophytes
C. Succulents
D. Hydrophytes

14. Which one of the following theories for ascent of sap was proposed by eminent Indian scientist J.C.Bose?

A. Pulsation theory
B. Transpiration pull theory
C. Root pressure theory
D. Atmospheric pressure theory

15. Munch hypothesis is based on

A. Translocation of food due to TP gradient and imbibition force
B. Translocation of food due to turgor pressure (TP) gradient
C. Translocation of food due to imbibition force
D. None of the above

16. The first process by which water enters into the seed coat when a seed is placed in a suitable environment for germination is

A. Osmosis
B. Active transport
C. Absorption
D. Imbibition

17. Which of the following plant material is an efficient water imbibant?

A. Lignin
B. Agar
C. Pectin
D. Cellulose

18. Which of the following experiment is called physiological demonstration of osmosis?
    A. Thistle funnel –whose mouth is tied with egg membrane
    B. Thistle funnel – whose mouth is tied with parchment paper
    C. Bell jar experiment
    D. Potometer
19. Water is lost in a liquid state in some plants through hydathodes. These hydathodes
    A. Remain closed at night
    B. Remain closed during day
    C. Remain always open
    D. Do not show any specificity in opening and closing
20. Passive absorption of water by the root system is the result of
    A. Forces created in the cells of the root
    B. Increased respiratory activity in root cells
    C. Osmotic force in the shoot system
    D. Tension on the cell sap due to transpiration
21. Which of the following helps in ascent of sap?
    A. Root pressure B. Transpiration
    C. Capillarity D. All of above
22. The translocation of organic solutes in sieve tube members is supported by
    A. Cytoplasmic streaming
    B. P proteins
    C. Mass flow involving a carrier and ATP
    D. Root pressure and transpiration pull
23. Potometer works on the principle of
    A. Osmotic pressure
    B. Root pressure
    C. Amount of water absorbed equals the amount transpired
    D. Potential difference between the tip of the tube and that of the plant
24. Minerals absorbed by root move to the leaf through
    A. Xylem B. Phloem
    C. Sieve tubes D. None of the above.

25. Which one increases in the absence of light?

A. Uptake of minerals B. Uptake of water

C. Elongation of internodes D. Ascent of sap.

26. The principal pathway of water translocation in angiosperms is

A. Sieve cells B. Sieve tube elements

C. Xylem vessel system D. Xylem and phloem.

27. In soil, the water available for root absorption is

A. Gravitational water B. Capillary water

C. Hygroscopic water D. Combined water

28. The most widely accepted theory for ascent of sap in trees is

A. Capillarity

B. Role of atmospheric pressure

C. Pulsating action of living cell

D. Transpiration pull and cohesion theory of Dixon and Jolly

29. Water movement between cells is due to

A. Total potential B. Water potential

C. Diffusion pressure deficit D. Incipient plasmolysis.

30. Guttation is mainly due to

A. Root pressure B. Osmosis

C. Transpiration D. Imbibition.

31. The movement of water from one cell of cortex to adjacent one in roots is due to

A. Accumulation of inorganic salts in the cells

B. Accumulation of organic compounds in the cells

C. Water potential gradient

D. Chemical potential gradient.

32. When water enters in roots due to diffusion is termed as

A. Osmosis B. Passive absorption

C. Endocytosis D. Active absorption.

33. Bidirectional translocation of solutes takes place in

A. Parenchyma B. Cambium

C. Xylem D. Phloem

34. With an increase in the turgidity of a cell, the wall pressure will be

A. Fluctuate B. Remain unchanged

C. Increase D. Decrease

35. When a cell is fully turgid, which of the following will be zero?

A. Turgor pressure B. Water potential

C. Wall pressure D. Osmotic pressure

36. The water potential and osmotic potential of pure water

A. 100 and 200 B. Zero and 100

C. 100 and zero D. Zero and zero

37. In soil, water available for plants is

A. Gravitational water B. Chemically bound water

C. Capillary water D. Hygroscopic water

38. The movement of ions against the concentration gradient will be

A. Active transport B. Osmosis

C. Diffusion D. All of the above

39. Passive absorption of minerals depend on

A. Temperature

B. Temperature and metabolic inhibitor

C. Metabolic inhibitor

D. Humidity

40. Stomata of a plant open due to

A. Influx of potassium ions B. Efflux of potassium ions

C. Influx of hydrogen ions D. Influx of calcium ions

41. The translocation of organic solutes in sieve tube members is supported by

A. Cytoplasmic streaming

B. Root pressure and transpiration pull

C. P-proteins

D. Mass flow involving a carrier and ATP

Answer keys

1	B	11	D	21	D	31	C	41	C
2	C	12	A	22	B	32	B		
3	C	13	C	23	C	33	D		
4	D	14	A	24	A	34	C		
5	B	15	B	25	C	35	B		
6	C	16	D	26	C	36	D		
7	A	17	B	27	B	37	C		
8	D	18	B	28	D	38	A		
9	A	19	C	29	C	39	A		
10	C	20	D	30	A	40	A		

3

Mineral Nutrition

I. Choose the correct answer

1. Which of the following is necessary for biological nitrogen fixation?

   A. Copper B. Zinc

   C. Manganese D. Molybdenum

2. The essential element for the synthesis of auxin is

   A. Zinc B. Sulphur

   C. Potassium D. Phosporus

3. The disease "die back of shoots" is caused due to the deficiency of the following microelement

   A. Copper B. Chlorine

   C. Manganese D. Molybdenum

4. Little leaf disease is due to the deficiency of

   A. Nitrogen B. Zinc

   C. Manganese D. Molybdenum

5. Hydroponics is

   A. Growing of aquatic plants

   B. Growing of floating aquatic plants

   C. Soil less cultivation of plants

   D. Growing of plants inside the water

6. Molybdenum is involved in plant metabolism in

   A. Translocation of solutes B. Tryptophan synthesis

   C. ABA synthesis D. Nitrate reduction

7. Plant require Fe and Mg for

   A. Synthesis of chlorophyll B. Opening and closing of stomata

   C. Translocation of carbohydrates D. None of these

8. Plant absorb the element nitrogen in the form

A. Nitrogen gas B. Nitrites

C. Nitrates D. Nitric acid

9. Bacteroid means

A. Dead bacteria B. Living bacteria

C. A bacteria like substance D. Living bacteria, but cannot divide

10. Which of the following bacterium brings about denitrification?

A. *Pseudomonas* B. *Rhizobium*

C. Azotobacter D. Nitrobacter

11. Ion can be accumulated against concentration gradient due to

A. Mass flow B. Active uptake

C. Passive uptake D. Donnan equilibrium

12. Which of the following is essential for nitrogen fixation by leguminous plants?

A. Chlorophyll B. Leghaemoglobin

C. Anthocyanin D. Phycocyanin

13. First experiments related to the method of hydroponics were done by

A. Knop B. Sachs

C. Arnon D. Hill

14. The most widely accepted theory to explain the translocation of carbohydrates in higher plants

A. Root pressure theory B. Osmotic theory

C. Imbibition theory D. Mass flow theory

15. Which element is required for nodulation in legumes?

A. Mn B. Fe

C. Mo D. B

16. Which of the following tissues are involved in water conduction?

A. Xylem and phloem B. Tracheids and tracheae

C. Parenchyma and sclerenchyma D. Xylem fibres and bast fibres

17. Vessels are present in all plants except

A. Pinus B. Rose

C. Gnetum D. Mango tree

18. Xylem consists of
    A. Tracheids, vessels, fibres and parenchyma
    B. Tracheids, vessels and companion cells
    C. Tracheids, fibres and parenchyma
    D. Tracheids, vessels, sieve cells and companion cells
19. Which of the following water conducting element is considered as most advanced
    A. Tracheids B. Multiple vessels
    C. Annular tracheids D. Simple vessels
20. Tracheids and vessels are present in all except
    A. *Marselia* B. *Equisetum*
    C. *Gnetum* D. *Cycas*
21. Wood parenchyma is formed from
    A. Fusiform initials B. Ray initials
    C. Collenchyma cells D. All of these
22. Phloem consists of
    A. Vessels, sieve tube cells, phloem parenchyma, phloem fibres
    B. Sieve tube cells, companion cells, phloem parenchyma, phloem fibres,
    C. Vessels, tracheids, phloem parenchyma, phloem fibres
    D. Vessels, tracheids, sieve tube cells, companion cells
23. Which of the following statement is true about sieve tube cells
    A. Sieve tube cells are nucleated, but devoid of mitochondria and ER
    B. Companion cells are non-nucleated and are regulated by nucleated sieve cell
    C. Sieve tube cells are present in all plants
    D. Companion cells are nucleated and regulate activity of non-nucleated sieve tube cell
24. Which of the following are the examples of phloem fibres
    A. Jute B. Hemp
    C. Flax D. All of above
25. All of the following plant groups posses phloem parenchyma except
    A. Dicots B. Monocots
    C. Gymnosperm D. Pteridophytes

26. Phosphorous and nitrogen ions generally get depeleted in soil because they usually occur as

A. Neutral ions

B. Negatively charged ions

C. Positively charged ions

D. Both positively and negatively charged but disproportionate mixture.

27. Which one is an essential mineral, not constituent of any enzyme but stimulates the activity of many enzymes

A. Zn B. Mn

C. K D. Mg

28. Which of the following element plays an important role in biological nitrogen fixation?

A. Copper B. Molybdenum

C. Zinc D. Manganese

29. Which one of the following elements is almost non-essential for plants?

A. Zn B. Na

C. Ca D. Mo

30. Which of the following is not caused by deficiency of mineral nutrition?

A. Etiolation B. Shortening of internode

C. Necrosis D. Chlorosis

31. When the plants are grown in magnesium deficient but urea rich soil, the symptoms expressed are

A. Yellowish leaves B. Colourless petiole

C. Dark green leaves D. Shoot apex die

32. Plants take zinc in the form of

A. $ZnSO_4$ B. Zn

C. ZnO D. Zn

33. Boron in green plants assists in

A. Activation of enzymes B. Acting as enzyme co-factor

C. Photosynthesis D. Sugar transport

34. Gray spots of oat are caused by deficiency of

A. Cu B. Zn

C. Mn D. Fe

35. If by radiation all nitrogenase enzyme are inactivated, then there will be no

A. Fixation of nitrogen in legumes

B. Fixation of atmospheric nitrogen

C. Conversion from nitrate to nitrite in legumes

D. Conversion from ammonium to nitrate in soil

36. Sulphur is an important nutrient for optimum growth and productivity in

A. Oilseed crops B. Cereals

C. Pulse crops D. Fibre crops

37. A plant requires magnesium for

A. Protein synthesis B. Chlorophyll synthesis

C. Cell wall development D. Holding cells together

38. Choose the correct one regarding Stenberg Effect?

A. Rapid increase in yield with decrease in nutrient concentration

B. Rapid decrease in yield with decrease in nutrient concentration

C. Rapid increase in yield with increase in nutrient concentration

D. Rapid decrease in yield with increase in nutrient concentration

39. The condition in which added nutrients will not increase yield, but can increase nutrient concentration is

A. Critical range B. Toxic

C. Excessive D. Sufficient

40. The plant is absorbing nutrient above the needed concentration i.e., critical range is called as

A. Normal consumption B. Poor consumption

C. Luxury consumption D. Sufficient consumption

41. The movement of nutrients from an area of higher concentration to an area of lower concentration is called

A. Mass flow B. Osmosis

C. Diffusion D. Buffering capacity

Answer keys

1	D	11	B	21	A	31	A	41	C
2	A	12	B	22	B	32	D		
3	A	13	B	23	D	33	D		
4	B	14	D	24	D	34	C		
5	C	15	C	25	B	35	A		
6	D	16	B	26	B	36	A		
7	A	17	A	27	C	37	B		
8	C	18	A	28	B	38	A		
9	D	19	D	29	B	39	D		
10	A	20	D	30	A	40	C		

4

Photosynthesis and Respiration

I. Choose the correct answer

1. Carbon dioxide joins the photosynthetic pathway in

   A. PS I B. PS II

   C. Light reaction D. Dark reaction

2. $NADP^+$ is reduced to NADPH in

   A. PS I B. PS II

   C. Calvin cycle D. Noncyclic photophosphorylation

3. The size of chlorophyll molecule is

   A. Head 15 x 15 A, tail 25 A B. Head 20 x 20 A, tail 25 A

   C. Head 15 x 15 A, tail 20 A D. Head 10 x 12 A, tail 25 A.

4. The substrate for photorespiration is

   A. Phosphoglyceric acid B. Glycolate

   C. Serine D. Glycine

5. In C_4 plants, calvin cycle operates in

   A. Stroma of bundle sheath chloroplasts

   B. Grana of bundle sheath chloroplasts

   C. Grana of mesophyll chloroplasts

   D. Stroma of mesophyll chloroplasts

6. A very efficient converter of solar energy with net productivity of 204 kg/ m_2 or more, the crop is

   A. Wheat B. Sugarcane

   C. Rice D. Bajra

7. Kranz anatomy is typical of

   A. C_4 plants B. C_3 plants

   C. C_2 plants D. CAM plants

8. The first carbon dioxide acceptor in C_4 plants is

A. Phosphoenolpyruvate B. Ribulose 1, 5 diphosphate

C. Oxaloacetic acid D. Phosphoglyceric acid.

9. Photosynthetic pigments found in the chloroplasts occur in

A. Thylakoid membranes B. Plastoglobules

C. Matrix D. Chloroplast envelope

10. Dark reactions of photosynthesis occur in

A. Granal thylakoid membranes

B. Stromal lamella membranes

C. Periplastidial space

D. Stroma outside photosynthetic lamellae

11. During monsoon, the rice crop of eastern states of India shows lesser yield due to limiting factor of

A. CO_2 B. Light

C. Temperature D. Water

12. Ferredoxin is a constituent of

A. PS I B. PS II

C. Hill reaction D. P_{680}

13. Which of the following is used to determine the rate of transpiration in plants?

A. Porometer/hygrometer B. Potometers

C. Auxanometer D. Tensiometer/barometer

14. In terrestrial habitats, temperature and rainfall conditions are influenced by

A. Water transformations B. Transpiration

C. Thermoperiodism D. Translocation

15. Conversion of starch to organic acids is required for

A. Stomatal opening B. Stomatal closing

C. Stomatal formation D. Stomatal activity

16. At constant temperature, the rate of transpiration will be higher at

A. Sea level B. 1 km below sea level

C. 1 km above sea level D. 1.5 km above sea level

17. In guard cells when sugar is converted into starch, the stomatal pore
    A. Closes completely B. Opens partially
    C. Opens fully D. Remains unchanged
18. The enzyme that catalyses carbon dioxide fixation in C_4 plants is
    A. RuBP carboxylase B. PEP carboxylase
    C. Carbonic anhydrase D. Carboxydismutase
19. Photosystem II occurs in
    A. Stroma B. Cytochrome
    C. Grana D. Mitochondrial surface
20. An adaptation for better gaseous exchange in plant leaves is
    A. Hair on lower surface
    B. Multiple epidermis
    C. Waxy cuticle
    D. Stomata on lower surface away from direct sun rays
21. Translocation of carbohydrate usually occurs in the form of
    A. Glucose B. Maltose
    C. Starch D. Sucrose
22. Which one is a C_4 plant?
    A. Papaya B. Pea
    C. Potato D. Maize/corn
23. The carbon dioxide acceptor in Calvin cycle/ C_3 plants is
    A. Phosphoenol pyruvate (PEP) B. Ribulose 1, 5 diphosphate (RuBP)
    C. Phosphoglyceric acid (PGA) D. Ribulose monophosphate (RMP)
24. Maximum solar energy is trapped by
    A. Planting trees B. Cultivating crops
    C. Growing algae in tanks D. Growing grasses
25. Plants, but not animals, can convert fatty acids to sugars by a series of reactions called
    A. Photosynthesis B. Kreb's cycle
    C. Glycolysis D. Glyoxylate cycle

26. During light reaction of photosynthesis, which of the following phenomenon is observed during cyclic phosphorylation as well as non-cyclic phosphorylation?

A. Release of O_2

B. Formation of ATP

C. Formation of NADPH

D. Involvement of PS I and PS II pigment systems.

27. Which of the following pigments acts as a reaction centre during photosynthesis?

A. Carotene

B. Phytochrome

C. P_{700}

D. Cytochrome

28. The 1992 Nobel Prize for medicine was awarded to Edmond H. Fischer and Edwin J.Krebs for their work concerning

A. Reversible protein phosphorylation as a biological regulation mechanism

B. Isolation of the gene for a human disease

C. Human genome project

D. Drug designing involving inhibition of DNA synthesis of the pathogen.

29. The CO_2 fixation during C_4 pathway occurs in the chloroplast of

A. Guard cells

B. Bundle sheath cells

C. Mesophyll cells

D. Spongy parenchyma

30. The primary acceptor, during CO_2 fixation in C_3 paints, is

A. Phosphoenolpyruvate (PEP)

B. Ribulose 1, 5 diphosphate (RuDP)

C. Phosphoglyceric acid (PGA)

D. Ribulose monophosphate (RMP)

31. In C_4 plants, CO_2 fixation is done by

A. Sclerenchyma

B. Chlorenchyma and hypodermis

C. Mesophyll cells

D. Guard cells

32. In C_4 plants, CO_2 combines with

A. Phosphoenol pyruvate

B. Phosphoglyceraldehyde

C. Phosphoglyceric acid

D. Ribulose diphosphate.

33. Photorespiration is favoured by

A. High temperature and low O_2

B. High humidity and temperature

C. High O_2 and low CO_2

D. High CO_2 and low O_2.

34. What will be the number of Calvin cycles to generate one molecule of hexose?

A. 8 B. 9

C. 4 D. 6

35. The correct sequence of electron acceptor in ATP synthesis is

A. Cyt. b, c, a_3, a B. Cyt. c, b, a, a_3

C. Cyt. o, a, b, c D. Cyt. b, c, a, a_3.

36. Gibberellic acid induces flower

A. In short day plants under long day conditions

B. In day neutral plants under dark conditions

C. In some gymnospermic plants only

D. In long day plants under short day conditions.

37. What will be the effect on phytochrome in a plant subjected to continuous red light?

A. Phytochrome synthesis will increase

B. Level of phytochrome will decrease

C. Phytochrome will be destroyed

D. First B then A

38. $NADPH_2$ is generated through

A. Photosystem II B. Anaerobic respiration

C. Glycolysis D. Photosystem I

39. A pigment which absorbs red and far-red light is

A. Cytochrome B. Xanthophyll

C. Phytochrome D. Carotene

40. The core metal of chlorophyll is

A. Ni B. Cu

C. Fe D. Mg

41. Chlorophyll-a molecule at its carbon atom 3 of the pyrrole ring II has one of the following

A. Carboxylic group B. Magnesium

C. Aldehyde group D. Methyl group

42. Phytochrome becomes active in

A. Red light B. Green light

C. Blue light D. None of these

43. Transpiration is least in

A. Good soil moisture
B. High wind velocity
C. Dry environment
D. High atmospheric humidity

44. Which one of the following statements about cytochrome P450 is wrong?

A. It is a coloured cell
B. It is an enzyme involved in oxidation reactions
C. It has an important role in metabolism
D. It contains iron

45. The rate of photosynthesis is higher in

A. Very high light
B. Continuous light
C. Red light
D. Green light

46. The first step for initiation of photosynthesis will be

A. Photolysis of water
B. Excitement of chlorophyll molecules due to absorption of light
C. ATP formation
D. Glucose formation.

47. For the synthesis of one glucose molecule, the calvin cycle operates for

A. 2 times
B. 4 times
C. 6 times
D. 8 times

48. For assimilation of one CO_2 molecule, the energy required in the form of ATP and $NADPH_2$ are

A. 2 ATP and 2 $NADPH_2$
B. 5 ATP and 3 $NADPH_2$
C. 3 ATP and 2$NADPH_2$
D. 18 ATP and 12 $NADPH_2$

49. Which is the first CO_2 acceptor enzyme in C_4 Plants?

A. RuDP carboxylase
B. Phosphoric acid
C. RUBISCO
D. PEP-carboxylase

50. Mg is a component of

A. Chlorophyll
B. Cytochrome
C. Haemoglobin
D. Haemocyanin

51. Which pair is wrong?

A. C_3- maize
B. C_4- kranz anatomy
C. Calvin cycle-PGA
D. Hatch and Slake cycle – O.A.A.

52. Loading of phloem is related to
    A. Increase of sugar in phloem
    B. Elongation of phloem cell
    C. Separation of phloem parenchyma
    D. Strengthening of phloem fiber.
53. Which pigment system is inactivated in red drop?
    A. PS-I and PS-II B. PS-I
    C. PS-II D. None of the above
54. What is true for photolithotrops?
    A. Obtain energy from radiations and hydrogen from organic compounds
    B. Obtain energy from radiations and hydrogen from inorganic compounds
    C. Obtain energy from organic compounds
    D. Obtain energy from inorganic compounds
55. Glycolate induces opening of stomata in
    A. Presence of oxygen B. Low CO_2 concentration
    C. High CO_2 D. CO_2 absent.
56. Cytochrome is
    A. Metallo flavo protein B. Fe containing porphyrin pigment
    C. Glycoprotein D. Lipid
57. Which pigment absorbs the red and far-red light?
    A. Cytochrome B. Phytochrome
    C. Carotenoids D. Chlorophyll
58. In photosynthesis, energy from light reaction to dark reaction is transferred in the form of
    A. ADP B. ATP
    C. RuDP D. AMP
59. Which of the following absorb light energy for photosynthesis?
    A. Chlorophyll B. Water molecule
    C. RuBP D. ADP
60. Main function of lenticel is
    A. Transpiration B. Guttation
    C. Gaseous exchange D. Bleeding

61. Which element is located at the centre of the porphyrin ring in chlorophyll?

A. Calcium
B. Magnesium
C. Potassium
D. Manganese

62. Stomata of CAM plants

A. Are always open
B. Open during the day and close at night
C. Open during the night and close during the day
D. Never open

63. In sugarcane plant $^{14}CO_2$ is fixed in malic acid, in which the enzyme that fixes CO_2 is

A. Ribulose biphosphate carboxylase
B. Phosphoenol pyruvic acid carboxylase
C. Ribulose phosphate kinase
D. Fructose phosphatase

64. Which one of the following is wrong in relation to photorespiration?

A. It occurs in chloroplast
B. It occurs in day time only
C. It is a characteristic of C4 plants
D. It is a characteristic of C_3 plants

65. Which fractions of the visible spectrum of solar radiations are primarily absorbed by carotenoids of the higher plants?

A. Blue and green
B. Green and red
C. Red and violet
D. Violet and blue

66. In C_3 plants, the first stable product of photosynthesis during the dark reaction is

A. Malic acid
B. Oxaloacetic acid
C. 3-phosphoglyceric acid
D. Phosphoglyceraldehyde.

67. Plants adapted to low light intensity have

A. Larger photosynthetic unit size than the sun plants
B. Higher rate of CO_2 fixation than the sun plants
C. More extended root system
D. Leaves modified to spines.

68. Photosynthetic Active Radiation (PAR) has the following range of wavelengths.

A. 340-450 nm B. 400-700 nm

C. 500-600 nm D. 450-950 nm

69. As compared to a C_3 plant, how many additional molecules of ATP are needed for net production of one molecule of hexose sugar by C_4 plants?

A. Two B. Six

C. Twelve D. Zero

70. In photosystem-I, the first electron acceptor is

A. An iron-sulphur protein B. Ferredoxin

C. Cytochrome D. Plastocyanin

71. During photorespiration, the oxygen consuming reaction(s) occur in

A. Stroma of chloroplasts

B. Stroma of chloroplasts and mitochondria

C. Stroma of chloroplasts and peroxisomes

D. Grana of chloroplasts and peroxisomes

72. The first acceptor of electrons from an excited chlorophyll molecule of photosystem II is

A. Iron-sulphur protein B. Ferredoxin

C. Quinone D. Cytochrome.

73. In the leaves of C_4 plants, malic acid formation during CO_2 fixation occurs in the cells of

A. Bundle sheath B. Phloem

C. Epidermis D. Mesophyll

74. The wavelength of light absorbed by Pr form of phytochrome is

A. 680 nm B. 720 nm

C. 620 nm D. 640 nm.

75. Both photosynthesis and respiration in a plant require

A. H_2O B. CO_2

C. CO D. Cytochrome

76. What is the source of energy is respiration?

A. Light B. Water

C. Carbohydrates D. All of the above

77. Green plants manufacture
    A. Sugar, fats, starch and proteins B. Sugar only
    C. Starch only D. Protein and fats
78. Light energy is converted into chemical energy during
    A. Assimilation B. Osmosis
    C. Emulsification D. Photosynthesis
79. The energy stored during photosynthesis is in the form of
    A. ADP B. ATP
    C. AMP D. GTP
80. Intensity of carbon assimilation is great in
    A. Bright light B. Green light
    C. Blue light D. Red light

Answer key

1	D	21	D	41	D	61	C
2	D	22	D	42	D	62	C
3	C	23	B	43	B	63	B
4	B	24	C	44	A	64	C
5	A	25	D	45	C	65	D
6	B	26	B	46	B	66	C
7	A	27	C	47	C	67	A
8	A	28	A	48	C	68	B
9	A	29	C	49	D	69	C
10	D	30	B	50	A	70	C
11	B	31	C	51	A	71	C
12	A	32	A	52	A	72	C
13	B	33	C	53	C	73	D
14	B	34	D	54	B	74	A
15	A	35	D	55	B	75	D
16	D	36	D	56	B	76	C
17	A	37	B	57	B	77	A
18	B	38	D	58	B	78	D
19	C	39	C	59	A	79	B
20	D	40	D	60	C	80	D

5

Physiology of Growth and Development

I. Choose the correct answer

1. What is the maximum period of growth?

   A. Slow growth rate
   B. Steady growth rate
   C. Speedy growth rate
   D. Senescence phase

2. Which apparatus is used for measurement of growth?

   A. Auxanometer
   B. Potometer
   C. Photometer
   D. Hydrometer

3. Which substances are secreted at the apex of plant and they regulate growth of another region?

   A. Enzymes
   B. Hormones
   C. Vitamins
   D. None of the above

4. Which type of growth is seen in plants?

   A. Irreversible
   B. Increase in volume
   C. Local
   D. Reversible

5. Tropic movement is due to

   A. Bidirectional effect of environmental factors on plant parts
   B. Unidirectional effect of environmental factors on plant parts
   C. Multidirectional effect of environmental factors on plant parts
   D. No effect of environmental factors on plant parts

6. Which is the correct sequence for different phases of growth?

   A. Cell formation - cell differentiation- cell elongation
   B. Cell formation – cell elongation- cell differentiation
   C. Cell differentiation- cell elongation- cell formation
   D. Cell differentiation- cell formation- cell elongation

7. What is the period of cell formation to cell differentiation?
   A. Sigmoid graph B. Normal growth period
   C. Maximum growth period D. Grand period of growth
8. What is the required temperature for growth in most of the plants?
   A. 20-30°C B. 35-40°C
   C. 10-15°C D. 15-20°C
9. Spiral developement of tendrils?
   A. Thigmotropism B. Thermotropism
   C. Hydrotropism D. Phototropism
10. With which reaction phytochrome is associated ?
   A. Phototropism B. Photorespiration
   C. Photoperiod D. Geotropism
11. In the absence of light, amount of which of the following is increased?
   A. Absorption of mineral salts B. Absorption of water
   C. Elongation of internodes D. Ascent of sap
12. Vernalization is
   A. Growth graph related to light
   B. Effect of photoperiod on the growth of plant which results flowering
   C. Rapid growth in low temperature
   D. Daily photoperiod
13. What is the colour of phytochrome pigment?
   A. Yellowish green B. Bluish
   C. Red D. Pink
14. How can a biannual plant be converted into an annual plant?
   A. By cold process of seeds B. By giving more light
   C. By giving more oxygen D. By giving more temperature
15. What is responsible for opening and closing of tulip flower?
   A. Photonastic movement B. Geotropism
   C. Thermonasty D. Nictinasty
16. By which reaction growth of cuscuta occurs on host plant?
   A. Thigmotropism B. Chemotropism
   C. Thigmonasty D. Photonasty

17. Which type of meristematic tissue is found in monocot plant for growth?
    A. Intercalary meristematic tissue B. Apical meristem tissue
    C. Lateral meristem tissue D. Meristematic tissue
18. Which of the following is increased in plants as a result of growth?
    A. Dry volume B. Width
    C. Number D. Dry weight
19. Which of the following are criteria for measurement of growth?
    A. Number B. Weight
    C. Volume D. All the above
20. In which phase of growth, size of vacuole increases?
    A. Cell formation B. Cell elongation
    C. Cell difterentiation D. Cell transfer
21. What is the optimum temperature for growth of the plants?
    A. 25 to 30°C B. 28 to 30°C
    C. 0 to 30°C D. 0 to 28°C
22. Which apparatus is used for exact measuring of growth of plants in longitudinal axis?
    A. Measuring scale B. Auxanometer
    C. Manometer D. Sphygmomanometer
23. What is called the effect of daylight on plant ?
    A. Phototropic B. Photoperiodism
    C. Photooxidation D. Photonastism
24. From the given below, which is short day plant?
    A. Paddy B. Wheat
    C. Oat D. Opium
25. Which of the following is long day plant?
    A. Oat B. Soybean
    C. *Vinca* D. Paddy
26. Vernalization means
    A. Growth graph
    B. Flowering at high temperature
    C. Effect of light on growth
    D. Speedy flowering at low temperature

27. Flowering due to low temperature is
    A. Thermonasty
    B. Vernalization
    C. Nutation
    D. Photonasty
28. If temporary light is made available for dark phase of long day plant, what is observed?
    A. Flowering will not occur
    B. Increase in flowering
    C. Decreasing in flowering
    D. No change
29. Which is an essential temperature for more production of wheat by noting effect of low temperature?
    A. 10 to 20°C
    B. 28 to 30°C
    C. 1 to10°C
    D. 25 to 30°C
30. By which condition, flowering take place in short day plant?
    A. Short day and long night
    B. Short day and short night
    C. Short night
    D. Long day and short night
31. Which type of light is required in long day plants for flowering?
    A. Red light
    B. More light than alloted period
    C. Less light than alloted time period
    D. All of the given
32. Where is phytochrome pigment present?
    A. Fungi
    B. Algae
    C. Bryophyta
    D. Phanerogams
33. Which physilogical reaction is essential for development leaf tendril?
    A. Curvature
    B. Nastism
    C. Circumnutation
    D. Tropism
34. Photoperiodism is
    A. Time table of day night based on light
    B. Flowering plant
    C. Effect of length of day on flowering
    D. Irregular growth based on light
35. Motor cells of leaves and grass, shows which type of movement?
    A. Locomotory movement
    B. Growth movement
    C. Nastic movement
    D. Osmotic movement

36. Which activity in plant is observed due to ethylene?

A. Maturation of leaf B. Maturation of fruit

C. Maturation of flower D. Maturation of seed

37. Which of the following type is improper for nastism?

A. Photonasty B. Hydronasty

C. Thermonasty D. Phototropism

38. Which of the following is incorrect for tropism?

A. Phototropism B. Thermotropism

C. Hydrotropism D. Thigmotaxis

39. What is the direction of tropism?

A. Straight B. Oblique

C. Undirectional D. Directional

40. Which of the example is improper for tropic movement?

A. *Volvox* B. Antherozoids of bryophytes

C. Antherozoids of pteridophytes D. *Mimosa*

41. Match the following

Column I	**Column II**
A. *Volvox*	1. Chemotaxis
B. *Mimosa*	2. Phototaxis
C. Antherozoids of bryophytes	3. Movement / tropism
D. Leaf tendril	4. Thigmotropism

A. 1 2 3 4 B. 2 3 4 1

C. 2 4 1 3 D. 4 3 2 1

42. Match the following

Column I	**Column II**
A. Plasmodium of slime mould	1. Ciliary movement
B. Chlamydomonas algae	2. Circular movement
C. Protoplasm of tradenschantia leaf	3. Rotational movement
D. Protoplasm of hydrilla	4. Amoeboid movement leaves

A. 1 2 3 4 B. 4 3 2 1

C. 4 1 2 3 D. 4 2 1 3

43. Match the following

Column I	Column II
A. Zoospore of volvox	1. Thermotaxis
B. Antherozoids of bryophytes and pteridophytes	2. Thigmotaxis
C. Diatoms	3. Phototaxis
D. Zoospores in oedogonium	4. Chemotaxis

A. 1 2 3 4 B. 4 3 2 1
C. 3 4 1 2 D. 3 2 1 4

44. Match the following

Column I	Column II
A. Opening of leaf blade	1. Epinasty
B. Closing of leaves	2. Hyponasty
C. Zigzag movement in apical bud	3. Nutation
D. Spiral and helical growth of tendrilar plants	4. Circumnutation
E. Pulsation in leaflets of indian telegraph plant	5. Variation

A. (P-i), (Q-ii), (R-iii), (S-iv), (T-v) B. (P-v), (Q-iv), (R-iii), (S-ii), (T-i)
C. (P-v), (Q-i), (R-iv), (S-iii), (T-ii) D. (P-v), (Q-i), (R-iv), (S-ii), (T-iii)

45. Match the following

Column I	Column II
A. Phototropism	1. Water
B. Geotropism	2. Gravitation
C. Hydrotropism	3. Light
D. Thigmotropism	4. Touch

A. 1 2 3 4 B. 3 2 1 4
C. 4 3 2 1 D. 3 2 4 1

46. Match the following

Column I	Column II
A. Lotus and sunflower	1. Hydronasty
B. Crocus and tulip	2. Thigmonasty
C. Due to turgidity of leaves	3. Thermonasty
D. Mimosa	4. Photonasty

A. 4 3 1 3 B. 1 2 3 4

C. 2 3 4 1 D. 1 3 2 4

47. Which of the following movement is not related to auxin level?

A. Bending of shoot towards light

B. Movement of root towards soil

C. Nyctinastic leaf movements

D. Movement of sunflower head tracking the sun.

48. Twining of tendrils is due to

A. Thigmotropism B. Seismonasty

C. Heliotropism D. Diageotropism

49. Flowering dependent on cold treatment is

A. Cryotherapy B. Cryogenics

C. Cryoscopy D. Vernalisation

50. Klinostat is employed in the study of

A. Osmosis B. Growth movements

C. Photosynthesis D. Respiration

51. Removal of apical bud results in

A. Formation of new apical bud B. Elongation of main stem

C. Death of plant D. Formation of lateral branching.

52. If the growing plant is decapitated, then

A. Its growth stops

B. Leaves become yellow and fall down

C. Axillary buds are inactivated

D. Axillary buds are activated.

53. Which one among the following chemicals is used for causing defoliation of forest trees?

A. Malic hydrazide B. 2, 4-D

C. Amo-1618 D. Phosphon D

54. Which combination of gases is suitable for fruit ripening?

A. 80% CH_4 and 20% CO_2 B. 80% CO_2 and 20% O_2

C. 80% C_2H_4 and 20% CO_2 D. 80% CO_2 and 20% CH_2

55. The response of different organisms to the environmental rhythms of light and darkness is called

A. Vernalization B. Photoperiodism

C. Phototaxis D. Phototropism

56. The closing and opening of the leaves of *Mimosa pudica* is due to

A. Seismonastic movement B. Chemonastic movement

C. Thermonastic movement D. Hydrotropic movement.

57. If the apical bud has been removed, then the plants develop

A. More lateral branches B. More axillary buds

C. Plant growth stops D. Flowering stops

58. Which plant is LDP?

A. Tobacco B. *Glycine max*

C. *Mirabilis jalapa* D. Spinach

59. What is the best pH of the soil for cultivation of plants?

A. 3.4 – 5.4 B. 6.5 – 7.5

C. 4.5 – 8.5 D. 5.5 – 6.5

60. Which aquatic fern performs nitrogen fixation?

A. *Azolla* B. *Nostoc*

C. Salvia D. *Salvinia*

61. Roots of which plant contains a red pigment which have affinity for oxygen

A. Carrot B. Soyabean

C. Mustard D. Radish

62. Opening of floral buds into flowers is a type of

A. Autonomic movement of variation

B. Paratonic movement of growth

C. Autonomic movement of growth

D. Autonomic movement of locomotion

63. Which one of the following elements is not an essential micronutrient for plant growth?

A. Zn B. Cu

C. Ca D. Mn

64. Match the following

List I	List II
A. Short day plant	1. Barley
B. Long day plant	2. Cotton
C. Day neutral plant	3. Maize

A. 2 1 3 B. 1 3 2
C. 3 2 1 D. 2 3 1

Answer keys

1	C	11	C	21	B	31	B	41	C	51	D	61	B
2	A	12	C	22	A	32	D	42	C	52	D	62	C
3	B	13	A	23	B	33	C	43	C	53	B	63	C
4	A	14	A	24	A	34	C	44	C	54	C	64	A
5	B	15	C	25	A	35	D	45	B	55	B		
6	B	16	A	26	D	36	D	46	A	56	A		
7	D	17	A	27	B	37	D	47	C	57	A		
8	A	18	D	28	A	38	D	48	A	58	B		
9	A	19	B	29	C	39	D	49	D	59	D		
10	C	20	B	30	A	40	C	50	B	60	A		

6

Growth Hormones

I. Choose the correct answer

1. Gibberellin promotes
   A. Seed germination B. Seed dormancy
   C. Leaf fall D. Root elongation
2. Cut or excised leaves remain green for long, if induced to root or dipped in
   A. Gibberellin B. Cytokinin
   C. Auxin D. Ethylene
3. Hormone primarily connected with cell division is
   A. IAA B. NAA
   C. Cytokinin/zeatin D. Gibberellic acid
4. Phototropic and geotropic movements are linked to
   A. Gibberellin B. Enzyme
   C. Auxin D. Cytokinin
5. Abscisic acid controls
   A. Cell division B. Leaf fall and dormancy
   C. Shoot elongation D. Cell elongation and wall formation
6. Phytohormones are
   A. Chemical regulation of flowering
   B. Chemical regulation of secondary growth
   C. Hormones regulating growth from seed to plant
   D. Regulators synthesised by plants and influencing physiological processes
7. Seed dormancy is due to
   A. Ethylene B. Abscisic acid
   C. IAA D. Starch

8. Coconut milk factor is

A. An auxin | B. A gibberellin
C. A abscisic acid | D. A cytokinin

9. Dwarfness can be controlled by treating the plant with

A. Cytokinin | B. Gibberellic acid
C. Auxin | D. Antigibberellin

10. Highest auxin concentration occurs

A. In growing tips | B. In leaves
C. At base of plant organs | D. In xylem and phloem.

11. A chemical believed to be involved in flowering is

A. Gibberellin | B. Kinetin
C. Florigen | D. IBA

12. Which hormone breaks dormancy of potato tuber?

A. Gibberellin | B. IAA
C. ABA | D. Zeatin

13. Hormone responsible for senescence is

A. ABA | B. Auxin
C. GA | D. Cytokinin

14. Cell elongation in internodal regions of the green plants takes place due to

A. Indole acetic acid | B. Cytokinin
C. Gibberellin | D. Ethylene

15. Which of the following prevents the fall of fruits?

A. GA_3 | B. NAA
C. Ethylene | D. Zeatin

16. Which is produced during water stress that brings stomatal closure?

A. Ethylene | B. Abscisic acid
C. Ferulic acid | D. Coumarin

17. The hormone responsible for apical dominance is

A. IAA | B. GA
C. ABA | D. Florigen

18. Abscisic acid causes

A. Stomatal closure | B. Leaf expansion
C. Stem elongation | D. Root elongation

19. Which is employed for artificial ripening of banana fruits?

A. Auxin B. Coumarin

C. Ethylene D. Cytokinin

20. Which hormone is responsible for fruit ripening?

A. Ethylene B. Auxin

C. Ethyl chloride D. Cytokinin

21. Cytokinin

A. Promotes abscission

B. Influences water movement

C. Promotes cell division

D. Induces dormancy

22. Apical dominance is caused by

A. Abscisic acid in lateral bud B. Cytokinin in leaf tip

C. Gibberellin in lateral buds D. Auxin in shoot tip

23. Bananas can be prevented from over ripening by

A. Maintaining them at room temperature

B. Refrigeration

C. Dipping in ascorbic acid solution

D. Storing in a freezer

24. Plants deficient of element zinc, show its effect on the biosynthesis of plant growth hormone

A. Auxin B. Cytokinin

C. Ethylene D. Abscisic acid

25. Which one of the following pairs, is not correctly matched?

A. Gibberellic acid – Leaf fall B. Cytokinin – Cell division

C. IAA – Cell wall elongation D. Abscissic acid Stomatal closure

26. Mowing grass lawn facilitates better maintenance because

A. Wounding stimulates regeneration

B. Removal of apical dominance and stimulation of intercalary meristem

C. Removal of apical dominance

D. Removal of apical dominance and promotion of lateral meristem

27. Leaf fall can be prevented with the help of
    A. Abscisic acid B. Auxin
    C. Florigen D. Cytokinin
28. Which of the following hormones can replace vernalisation?
    A. Auxin B. Cytokinin
    C. Gibberellin D. Ethylene
29. The movement of auxin is largely
    A. Centripetal B. Basipetal
    C. Acropetal D. Both A and C
30. Hormones which control apical dominance are
    A. Auxin B. Cytokinin
    C. Gibberellin D. Polyamine
31. Ethylene is responsible for
    A. Flowering B. Disease in roots
    C. Ripening of fruits D. Formation of fruits
32. Which of the following substance is not related with initiation of growth ?
    A. ABA B. Gibberellin
    C. IAA D. Cytokinin
33. Which group is correct for the growth inducer hormone?
    A. IAA, ABA and cytokinin B. IAA, gibberellin, ABA
    C. IAA, gibberellin, cytokinin D. ABA, ethylene
34. What is the main origin of cytokinin?
    A. Stem apex B. Root apex
    C. Young leaves D. Lateral buds
35. Mention the effect of cytokinin
    A. It induces cell division and retards the process of senescence
    B. It maintains dormancy
    C. It induces senescence
    D. It inhibits cell division
36. Give full form of 2-4-D
    A. 2-4 dichloro phenoxy acetic acid
    B. 2-4 dichloro butyric acid
    C. 2-4 dichloro nepthalic acetic acid
    D. 2-4 dichloro ethylenic acid

37. Which one of the following stimulates growth in the internode region ?

A. Auxin B. Gibberellin

C. Cytokinin D. Abscisic acid

38. Oat coleoptile test is conducted for which hormone ?

A. Abscisic acid B. Gibberellic acid (GA)

C. Indole acetic acid D. Indole naphthalene acetic acid

39. Gibberellin participate in which of the following process?

A. Removal of seed dormancy B. Developing seed less fruit

C. Growth of internodes D. All of the above

40. Zeatin is an example of

A. ABA B. Auxin

C. Gibberrellin D. Cytokinin

41. State the full form of IAA

A. Indole- 3 acetic anhydrase B. Indole-3 acetic acid

C. Indole- 3 aceto acetate D. Indole-3 aceto-acetic

42. Which of the following physiological process performed by gibberellic acid?

A. Dwarfism of tall plant genetically

B. Elongation of short plant genetically

C. Growth in size of stems and root formation

D. Yellowing of young leaves

43. Which of the following is used to enhance colour of fruits and more juice in fruits unnaturally?

A. Sodium chloride B. IAA

C. Ethylene gas D. Kinetin

44. Which hormone is responsible for apical dominance?

A. Auxin B. Cytokinin

C. Gibberellin D. Ethylene

45. When is abscission layer formed?

A. With increased concentration of auxin

B. With decreased concentration of auxin

C. With increased concentration of gibberellin

D. With decreased concentration of gibberellin

46. What is initiative substance of IAA?

A. Tryptophan B. Lucine

C. Tyrosine D. Phenyl alanine

47. What is apical dominance?

A. Growth of apical bud is inhibited due to nearby lateral buds

B. Growth of apical bud is promoted due to removal of nearest lateral buds

C. Removal of apical bud hinders growth of lateral buds

D. Development of lateral buds hinders due to presence of apical bud

48. Which of the following is water stress hormone?

A. Benzyl amino purine B. 2,4- dichlorophenoxy acetic acid

C. Ethylene D. Abscisic acid

49. If apical region of stem is removed from any plant, what is observed?

A. New apical bud formation B. Length of main stem increases

C. Plant dies D. Lateral branches emerges

50. Which of the hormone is synthetic?

A. GA_3 B. GA_2

C. IAA D. 2, 4 - D

51. What is 2-4 D?

A. Weedicide B. Insecticide

C. Rodenticide D. Wormicide

52. How gibberellin accelerates seed germination?

A. By effecting rate of cell division

B. By the synthesis of digestive enzymes

C. Abscisic acid

D. Absorption of water from hard seed coat

53. What is the reason for senescence of leaf?

A. Ethylene B. Abscisic acid

C. Cytokinin D. Auxin

54. Which hormone is responsible for bolting?

A. Auxin B. Cytokinin

C. Gibberellin D. Ethylene

55. Which hormone is synthesized by root and endosperm?

A. Auxin B. Cytokinin

C. Gibberellin D. Ethylene

56. Which hormone is responsible for growth of leaf apex?

A. IAA B. Zeatin

C. Gibberellin D. Ethylene

57. From where auxin was isolated for the first time?

A. Coleoptile of oat B. Sperm cell of herring fish

C. Paddy plant D. Human urine

58. Which of the following should be used for the control of weeds in farms?

A. Cytokinin B. Auxin

C. Gibberellin D. Ethylene

59. Which chemical induces formation of adventitious roots?

A. Gibberellin B. IAA

C. Abscisic acid D. Cytokinin

60. Which is incorrect for the effects of auxin ?

A. Induces +ve phototropism B. Induces growth and length in stem

C. Shows apical dominance D. Induces -ve phototropism in roots

61. Which of the following organic substance is growth inhibitor?

A. IBA B. ABA

C. IAA D. GA

62. From where indole acetic acid, an organic substance was isolated for the first time?

A. Animal fat B. Gibberellin

C. Human urine D. Fish

63. Cytokinin is formed in which of the following region?

A. Region of cell elongation B. Region of senescence

C. Region of cell division D. Region of abscission

64. Which hormone reduces the dominance of apical bud?

A. Auxin B. ABA

C. Ethylene D. Cytokinin

65. Which is incorrect option for cytokinin ?
   A. Retards senescence
   B. Secreted in the region of active cell division
   C. Increases dominance of apical bud
   D. Stimulates cell division
66. Drooping of fruit, after fruit maturation (ripening) shows
   A. Increase in amount of auxin
   B. Decreases in amount of auxin
   C. Reduces in amount of ABA
   D. Increase in gibberrellic acid
67. Which of the following is mismatched statement for effect of auxin ?
   A. It inhibits lateral growth
   B. It induces stem elongation in plant
   C. It induces cell division
   D. It helps in further elongation of some regions
68. Which hormone is essential for initial growth of root?
   A. IBA
   B. GA
   C. ABA
   D. Kinetin
69. Which is the specific use of synthetic auxin in higher concentration?
   A. Weedicide
   B. Inhibits growth of lateral buds
   C. Inhibits initial process of root formation
   D. Regulates cell elongation
70. Which of the following organic chemical is synthetic?
   A. 2-4-D
   B. IAA
   C. GA
   D. IBA
71. Which is required to inhibit germination of food storing part of potato?
   A. ABA
   B. IAA
   C. IBA
   D. GA
72. Auxin induces growth of root, but inhibits growth of
   A. Apical bud
   B. Unfertilized fruit development
   C. Lateral buds
   D. Root
73. What is indicated by any of the developing plant, if it increase / hyperactivity in lateral buds?
   A. It obtains more light
   B. Cytokinin decreases
   C. It stores more food
   D. Auxin decreases

74. From where gibberellin was isolated for the first time?

A. Penicillium B. Asparagus

C. Mucor D. Gibberella

75. Which of the following effect of gibberellin is observed in plant?

A. Long plant shortens

B. Dwarf plant grows in longitudinal axis

C. Induces formation of root system

D. Yellowing of young leaves

76. Which of the following hormone is responsible for cell division?

A. GA B. IAA

C. Cytokinin D. Abscisic acid

77. Garland of green leaves remain green by treatment of which organic chemical?

A. Cytokinin B. Auxin

C. Ethylene D. Gibberellin

78. Which hormone inhibits senescence of vegetative parts and plants?

A. Auxin B. Cytokinin

C. Gibberellin D. Abscisic acid

79. Which is natural growth inhibitor or senescence inducing hormone?

A. IAA B. ABA

C. NAA D. GA

80. Which hormone affects the growth of plant in adverse environmental condition?

A. Abscisic acid B. Ethylene

C. NAA D. 2-4, D

81. Which of the following phenomenon is regulated by abscisic acid?

A. Shoot elongation

B. Origin of cell wall and cell elongation

C. Opening and closing of stomata

D. Abscission of leaf and dormancy

82. Which hormone inhibits formation of new cells?

A. Abscisic acid B. Kinetin

C. Gibberellic acid D. Indole butyric acid

83. Which of the following is responsible for seed dormancy?
A. Abscissic acid B. Ethylene
C. Gibberellin D. Auxin

84. Name the hormone responsible for activity of chlorophyll in leaves.
A. Cytokinin B. Ethylene
C. Gibberellin D. ABA

85. Which of the following is simple, volatile hormone?
A. Ethylene B. ABA
C. IAA D. Cytokinin

86. Which of the following statement about ABA is inappropriate?
A. Induces ripening of fruit B. Inhibits seed germination
C. Induces dormancy of bud D. Closes stomata

87. Which hormone is absent in dormant seed?
A. ABA B. Auxin
C. GA D. Ethylene

88. Which of the following statement is true for abscisic acid?
A. Inhibits transcription of gene B. Opens stomata
C. Reduces senescence D. Acts as weedicide

89. Which of the following is found in high concentration in healthy leaf?
A. Cytokinin B. Gibberellin
C. Auxin D. Ethylene

90. Which hormones are obtained from fungi and fish, respectively?
A. Gibberellin and zeatin B. IAA and IBA
C. Gibberellin and 2-4 D D. Gibberellin and cytokinin

91. Which hormone is essential in pineapple for inducing flowering, without season?
A. Ethylene B. Zeatin
C. Abscisic acid D. NAA

92. Which organic chemicals are included in shoot with photoperiodism?
A. Ethylene B. Cytokinin
C. Auxin D. Gibberellin

93. The hormone produced during adverse environmental conditions is
A. Benzyl aminopurine B. Bichlorophenoxy acetic acid
C. Ethylene D. Abscisic acid

94. The regulator which retards ageing/senescence of plant parts is
A. Cytokinin B. Auxin
C. Gibberellin D. Abscisic acid

95. A plant hormone used for inducing morphogenesis in plant tissue culture is
A. Cytokinins B. Ethylene
C. Abscisic acid D. Gibberellins

96. ABA is involved in
A. Shoot elongation B. Increased cell division
C. Dormancy of seeds D. Root elongation

97. Differentiation of shoot is controlled by
A. High auxin : cytokinin ratio B. High cytokinin : auxin ratio
C. High gibberellin : auxin ration D. High gibberellin : cytokinin ratio

98. Consider the statements
Statement (i): Fraturia has not produced diverse group of phytohormones.
Statement (ii): Ethylene at higher concentration causes inhibitory action for the growth of the plants.
A. Statement (i) and (ii) are wrong
B. Statement (i) is wrong and (ii) is correct
C. Statement (i) is correct and (ii) is wrong
D. All the statements are correct

99. Growth regulators are chemically
A. Organic chemicals B. Inorganic chemicals
C. Minerals D. Vitamins

Answer keys

1	A	16	B	31	C	46	A	61	B	76	C	91	D
2	B	17	A	32	A	47	D	62	C	77	A	92	D
3	C	18	A	33	C	48	D	63	C	78	B	93	D
4	C	19	C	34	B	49	D	64	C	79	B	94	A
5	B	20	A	35	A	50	D	65	C	80	A	95	A
6	D	21	C	36	A	51	A	66	B	81	C	96	C
7	B	22	D	37	B	52	B	67	D	82	A	97	B
8	D	23	C	38	C	53	B	68	A	83	A	98	B
9	B	24	A	39	D	54	C	69	A	84	A	99	A

10	A	25	A	40	D	55	B	70	A	85	A
11	C	26	B	41	B	56	A	71	A	86	A
12	A	27	D	42	C	57	D	72	C	87	C
13	A	28	C	43	C	58	B	73	D	88	A
14	C	29	B	44	A	59	B	74	D	89	C
15	B	30	B	45	B	60	B	75	B	90	D

7

Environmental Stresses

I. Choose the correct answer

1. Under flood condition, the deficiency of ____ occurs.

   A. O_2 B. O_3
   C. CO_2 D. N_2

2. The dosage of brassinolide used to increase photosynthesis activity under stress condition is

   A. 0.5 ppm B. 0.1 ppm
   C. 0.2 ppm D. 0.75 ppm

3. Identify the correct statement

   i) Increase in osmotic pressure permits the plants to utilize better soil moisture.

   ii) Flooding induces stomatal closure.

   iii) Under flood condition, ethylene biosynthesis has increased.

   iv) In saline soil, EC is < 4 dSm^{-1}.

   A. (i) and (ii) are correct B. (iv) alone is correct
   C. (i), (ii) and (iii) are correct D. All the statements are correct

4. Which of the following is correctly matched?

   (i) Salt tolerant crop - Groundnut

   (ii) Semi salt tolerant crop - Rice

   (iii) Sensitive to salt - Cotton

   A. (iii) alone is correct B. (ii) alone is correct
   C. (i) alone is correct D. All the statements are correct

5. Match the following

List I	**List II**
A. Seed hardening	1. PMA (Phenyl mercury acetate)
B. Antitransparent	2. Cycocel

C. Growth retardant 3. KCl
D. Growth promoter 4. GA
A. 2 1 4 3 B. 1 3 4 2
C. 3 2 1 4 D. 3 1 2 4

6. Match the following
A. Stomatal closing type 1. Atrazine or PMA
B. Film forming type 2. Kaolin
C. Reflectant type 3. Cycocel
D. Growth retardant 4. Silicone
A. 3 4 1 2 B. 2 1 3 4
C. 1 4 2 3 D. 4 3 2 1

7. Under drought conditions, plants show increase in
A. Abscisic acid B. Proline
C. Ethylene D. All the above

8. Ephemerals are those plants that can
A. Resist the drought B. Evade the drought
C. Tolerate the drought D. Cannot tolerate the drought

9. Water content in the plant body on fresh weight basis is
A. 10% B. 20%
C. 30% D. 90%

10. Sorghum plant tries to avoid transpiration during day time by
A. Swelling of its leaves B. Drying of leaves
C. Rolling of its leaves D. Shrinking of leaves

11. What do you mean by evaporation?
A. Loss of water from soil surface
B. Loss of water from stem surface
C. Loss of water from plant surface
D. Loss of water from internodal surface

12. How much rainfall is lost through evaporation?
A. 50-60% B. 60-75%
C. 45-60% D. 80-95%

13. In which category, mobileleaf falls?
A. Stomata closing B. Film forming
C. Reflective D. Growth retardant

14. Under dry land conditions, DAP 2% spray is done for which crop?
    A. Groundnut B. Greengram
    C. Sorghum D. Ragi
15. Which of the following is harmful to higher plants?
    A. Phenol carboxylic acid B. Vanillic acid
    C. Dihydroxystearic acid D. All of these
16. ______ is a term used to describe a plant that shows no obvious symptoms, yet the nutrient content is not sufficient to give the top profitable yield
    A. Acute deficiency B. Critical range
    C. Hidden hunger D. Luxury consumption
17. Which of the following nutrient is supplied primarily by mass flow to the plant?
    A. P B. Zn
    C. S D. Cu
18. Diffusion of mineral ions into the root cells of plants is known as
    A. Passive absorption B. Endocytosis
    C. Active absorption D. Exosmosis
19. Which of the following is an anti-transpirant?
    A. PMA B. PAN
    C. IAA D. AUG
20. Phenyl mercuric acetate (PMA) results in
    A. Reduced photosynthesis B. Reduced transpiration
    C. Reduced respiration D. Killing of plants.
21. Stomata open and close is due to
    A. Circadian rhythm
    B. Genetic clock
    C. Pressure of gases inside the leaves
    D. Turgor pressure of guard cells.
22. Opening and closing of stomata is due to
    A. Hormonal change in guard cells
    B. Change in turgor pressure of guard cells
    C. Gaseous exchange
    D. Respiration

23. Example of antitranspirants
A. Kaolin
B. Waxes
C. Phenyl Mercury Acetate
D. All the above

Answer keys

1	A	6	C	11	A	16	C	21	D
2	A	7	D	12	B	17	C	22	B
3	C	8	B	13	B	18	A	23	D
4	C	9	D	14	B	19	C		
5	D	10	C	15	D	20	B		

UNIT IX: SEED SCIENCE AND TECHNOLOGY

1

Seed Biology

I. Choose the correct answer

1. Which one of the following crop is a self pollinated crop?

   A. Tomato B. Bittergourd

   C. Cotton D. Turmeric

2. In which one of the family, the protogyny mechanisms exist?

   A. Malvaceae B. Convolvulaceae

   C. Magnoliaceae D. Leguminosae

3. .... is an example for homogeny

   A. Maize B. Pearl millet

   C. Mirabilis D. Sapota

4. .... avoids cross pollination

   A. Hidden style and ovary B. Hidden filament and pedicel

   C. Hidden stamen and stigma D. Hidden corolla and calyx

5. .... is an example for pollination by beetles

   A. Erythrina B. Bombax

   C. Mango D. Coconut

6. An example for trimonoecious crop is

   A. Brinjal B. Banana

   C. Sunflower D. Ailanthus

7. At the end of pollen tube, there are two nuclei called

   A. Sperm and ovum

   B. Tube nucleus and generative nucleus

   C. Tube nucleus and sperm

   D. Generative nucleus and stigma

8. Flowers like night queen and jasmine emit a sweet scent to attract insects like

   A. Honey bees B. Butterflies

   C. Beetles and moths D. All the above

9. Genetic self-incompatibility tends to increase

   A. Pollen dispersal B. Inbreeding

   C. Pollination D. Cross pollination

10. The female gametophyte of an angiosperm is the

   A. Embryosac B. Ovule

   C. Megaspore mother cell D. Egg cell

11. If a flower is to be pollinated by birds, it should be

   A. Blue B. White

   C. Yellow D. Orange

12. Which of the following is not characteristic of primitive flowers?

   A. Flowering parts are numerous

   B. Flowers are arranged in definite whorls

   C. Petals and sepals are similar

   D. Unfused flower parts

13. When one plants potatoes, the seed pieces are parts of

   A. Stolons B. Adventitious

   C. Tubers D. Suckers

14. Pollen grains on the stigma of a flower reach the egg by forming a

   A. Cotyledon B. Seed

   C. Pollen tube D. Carpel

15. In custard apple

   A. Self pollination is highly likely

   B. Flowers are dioecious

   C. Flowers are monecious

   D. Anthers and stamens may mature at different times

16. According to position of the ovule within the ovary, an ovule may be

   A. Ascending B. Descending

   C. Horizontal D. Vertical

17. An embryosac of angiosperms generally contains

A. Two nuclei B. Three nuclei

C. Four nuclei D. Eight nuclei

18. Epicalyx is the characteristic of the family

A. Gramineae B. Solanaceae

C. Malvaceae D. Compositae

19. Generally embryosac is

A. Monosporic B. Bisporic

C. Tetrasporic D. Octosporic

20. In cruciferae, the stamens are said to be

A. Didynamous B. Tridynamous

C. Tetradidynamous D. Decadynamous

21. In potato, the inflorescence is

A. Helicoid B. Scropioid cyme

C. Umbel D. Raceme

22. The mode of arrangement of ovules in the cavity of ovary is known as

A. Pollination B. Aestivation

C. Placentation D. Fertilization

23. Umbel inflorescence is characteristic of the family

A. Mustard family B. Okra family

C. Pea family D. Coriander family

24. When the ovule bends along the funicle that the micropyle lays close to the hilum, the ovule is said to be

A. Orthotropous B. Anatropous

C. Amphilotropous D. Campylotropous

25. What do you name, if the ovules are arranged at the base of the ovary?

A. Axile placentation B. Marginal placentation

C. Basal placentation D. Parietal placentation

26. A flower is having a reproductive structure that is either functionally male or functionally female. Which one of the following is correct for this statement?

A. Hermaphrodite flower B. Imperfect flower

C. Staminate flower D. Pistillate flower

27. The number of outer layers present in each ovule are

A. 2 B. 3

C. 4 D. 5

28. Sporopollenin is chemically

A. Protein B. Fatty substance

C. Homopolysaccharide D. Heteropolysaccharide

29. Cauliflory is flowers produced

A. On old dormant bud B. On young bud

C. On the axil D. On the branch

30. Each stamen is differentiated into

A. Style B. Stigma

C. Ovule D. Anther

31. The pollen along with pollen tube is known as

A. Microspore B. Pollengrain

C. Megaspore D. Male gametophyte

32. The process of megasporogenesis occurs in

A. Embryosac B. Egg cell

C. Pollensac D. Ovule

33. The first cell division of the plant zygote is typically

A. Longitudinal B. Diagonal

C. Transverse D. Radial

34. Nucellar polyembryony is reported in species of

A. *Brassica* B. *Citrus*

C. *Gossypium* D. *Triticum*

35. Development of embryo either from synergids or antipodal cell is referred to as

A. Apospory B. Adventive embryony

C. Apogamy D. Diplospory

36. Seed is a/an

A. Matured ovule B. Ripened nucellus

C. Immature ovule D. $3/4^{th}$ matured ovule

37. One male gamete fuses with polar nuclei to form

A. Endosperm nucleus B. Embryo

C. Ovary D. Integument

38. Example of crop which reserves food in endosperm is

A. Pulses B. Vegetables

C. Maize D. Oilseeds

39. Give an example for double dormancy

A. *Allium cepa* B. *Acacia nolotica*

C. *Azadirachita indica* D. *Tectona grandis*

40. Incorrect statement about advantages of quality seed

A. Yield increase by 15-20% B. Fetches higher price

C. Genetically and physically pure D. Maximum replanting value

41. Fertilized and matured ovule is

A. Ovary B. Fruit

C. Seedling D. Seed

42. The seed of rice contains 7-8% protein which is located in

A. Aleurone layer B. Husk

C. Inside the endosperm D. Embryo

43. Wind pollination is called as

A. Entanophily B. Zoophily

C. Anemophily D. Hydrophily

44. (AxB)xC is a

A. Single cross hybrid B. Double cross hybrid

C. Three way cross hybrid D. Top cross hybrid

45. Cotton is a

A. Self pollinated crop B. Cross pollinated crop

C. Often cross pollinated crop D. Often self pollinated crop

46. Fertilized matured ovary is

A. Pericarp B. Fruit

C. Seed D. Seedling

47. ____ is a reproductive deficiency of same plants where male organs in hermaphrodite flowers are rendered defunction.

A. Self incompatibity B. Male sterility

C. Cleistogamy D. Chasmogamy

48. Match list I with list II and choose the correct options given below

List I	**List II**
A. Rice	1. Cleistogamy
B. Groundnut	2. Self pollination
C. Water melon	3. Often cross pollination
D. Redgram	4. Cross pollination

A. 4 3 2 1 B. 2 1 4 3

C. 3 4 1 2 D. 2 4 3 1

49. Which of the following crop is pollinated by insects?

A. Sunflower B. Rice

C. Gingelly D. Tomato

50. What is the type of flower in brinjal?

A. Distyly B. Monostyly

C. Tristyly D. Heterostyly

51. Consider the statement and choose the correct answer.

i) Seed is a ripened ovule

ii) Genetic purity of breeder seed is 99.5%

iii) Seed is a carrier of food supply

A. (i) alone is correct B. (ii) alone is correct

C. (iii) alone is correct D. (i) and (ii) are correct

52. Match list I with list II and choose the correct options given below

List I	**List II**
A. Genetic purity	1. Free from pests and diseases
B. Physical purity	2. High germination and vigour
C. Physiological quality	3. Physical contamination
D. Health quality	4. Genetic contamination

	A	B	C	D
A.	4	3	2	1
B.	3	4	2	1
C.	3	2	4	1
D.	1	2	3	4

53. Which of the following fruits undergo parthenocarpy?
    A. Apple B. Mango
    C. Banana D. Jamun
54. What is the term used, if more than one embryo is present in the seed?
    A. Apomixis B. Parthenocarpy
    C. Polyembryony D. Sexual propagation
55. In which crop seed, the aleurone layer is present?
    A. Redgram B. Blackgram
    C. Greengram D. Barley
56. ———————— is formed from outer integument
    A. Tegmen B. Testa
    C. Seed coat D. Pericarp
57. Endosperm is
    A. 1N B. 2N
    C. 3N D. 4N
58. In which crop, the caruncle is present?
    A. Castor B. Wheat
    C. Redgram D. Sesamum
59. In cotton, ———————— is present
    A. Awn B. Caruncle
    C. Hairs D. Aril
60. Which one of the following has folded cotyledon?
    A. Safflower B. Cotton
    C. Sunflower D. Sesamum
61. In which one of the dicot seed, a thin layer of endosperm is present?
    A. Safflower B. Sunflower
    C. Castor D. Sesamum

62. Cucumber, squashes and beans are

A. Monocots
B. Dicots
C. Multicots
D. Ferns

63. The aleurone layer in maize seed is specially rich in

A. Lipid
B. Starch
C. Protein
D. Auxin

64. Cotyledons and testa respectively are edible parts in

A. Cashewnut and litchi
B. Groundnut and pomegranate
C. Walnut and tamarind
D. French bean and coconut

65. Which one of the following is not matched correctly?

A. Plumule-dicot only
B. Two cotyledons-dicot only
C. One cotyledon-monocot only
D. Endosperm-monocot only

66. A seed develops from a (an)

A. Pollen grain
B. Embryo
C. Ovule
D. Ovary

67. What would be the number of chromosomes of the aleurone cells of a plant with 42 chromosomes in its roots tip cells?

A. 21
B. 42
C. 63
D. 84

68. The larger cells near the micropyle develop into

A. Ground meristem
B. Shoot apical meristem
C. A suspensor
D. Protoderm

69. Water makes up about ——————% of a mature seed

A. One to three
B. Five to twenty
C. Twenty -five to forty
D. Forty-five to sixty

70. Double fertilization was first discovered by Nawaschin (1898) in

A. Lilium and Fritillaria
B. Mango and sugarcane
C. Papaya and pea
D. Brassica and candyfruit

71. Far red light is —————— nm

A. 760-860
B. 660-760
C. 560-660
D. 460-560

72. Which one of the following seed germinates on the plant itself after reaching maturity

A. Jack B. Guava
C. Sapota D. Pineapple

73. Adventitious roots grow from

A. Radicle
B. Plumule
C. Hypophysis
D. Any part of the plant body other than the radicle

74. Cork cambium is

A. Pro meristem B. Ground meristem
C. Lateral meristem D. Intercalary meristem

75. —————— is an example for hypogeal germination

A. Bean B. Maize
C. Cowpea D. Soybean

76. Which hormone triggers the *de novo* synthesis of hydrolytic enzyme during imbibition?

A. GA B. ABA
C. IBA D. IAA

77. Germination of seed while it still remains attached with the parent source

A. Ovipary B. Apomixis
C. Vivipary D. Asepsis

78. Development of embryo without fertilization is known as

A. Parthenocarpy B. Parthenogenesis
C. Apomixsis D. None of the above

79. Development of embryo from unfertilized egg is known as

A. Parthenogenesis B. Parthenocarpy
C. Apomixsis D. None of the above

80. Hard seeds are commonly found in families of

A. Amaranthaceae B. Leguminosae
C. Alliaceae D. Solanaceae

81. What is an example for photo dormancy?

A. *Lactuca* B. *Phacetia*
C. *Tectona* D. *Acacia*

82. Which one of the following is a primary dormancy

A. Quiescence B. Endogenous dormancy

C. Thermo dormancy D. Photo dormancy

83. Which one of the following event is a resting stage of seed

A. Quiescence B. Endogenous dormancy

C. Thermo dormancy D. Photo dormancy

84. Which one of the following light condition is most suitable for non-dormant nature of seed?

A. Red / far – red: high B. Red / far – red : Low

C. Red / far – red : very low D. Darkness

85. Which one of the following seeds are bioscarified by sheeps and goats

A. *Acacia purpea* B. *Acacia tomentosa*

C. *Acacia nilotica* D. *Acacia fistula*

86. What is the optimum concentration of KNO_3 recommended by ISTA for breaking seed dormancy

A. 0.1% B. 0.2%

C. 0.3% D. 0.4%

87. Vivipary means

A. Seed germinates inside the fruit while it is still attached to the parent tree

B. Seed germinates as usual

C. Seed dormancy is very long

D. Because of immature seeds

88. Stratification indicates the seed dormancy breaking method with

A. High temperature

B. Low temperature

C. Ultra high temperature

D. Initially low, later high temperature

89. Match the following

A. Scarification 1. Tree crops

B. Hot water treatment 2. Pulses

C. Leaching 3. Coriander

D. Stratification 4. Cole crops

A. 2 1 3 4 B. 3 4 1 2

C. 4 3 1 2 D. 2 4 3 1

90. The crop in which dormancy is advantageous

A. Sesame B. Paddy

C. Blackgram D. Groundnut

91. Covering surrounding embryo contain growth inhibitor hormone for .... dormancy.

A. Physical dormancy B. Mechanical dormancy

C. External dormancy D. Chemical dormancy

92. In which type of dormancy, due to hardness of seed coats or integuments, embryo could not expand during germination?

A. Physical dormancy B. Mechanical dormancy

C. External dormancy D. Chemical dormancy

93. Which type of dormancy is found when seed is impermeable to water or gaseous exchange?

A. Physical dormancy B. Mechanical dormancy

C. External dormancy D. Chemical dormancy

94. Which type of dormancy, inhibits embryo growth and germination in seed?

A. Endogenous dormancy B. Physiological dormancy

C. External dormancy D. Mixed dormancy

95. Which type of dormancy is found in seed causes physiology and external dormancy?

A. Combined dormancy B. External dormancy

C. Physiological dormancy D. Endogenous dormancy

96. What is the type of dormancy in which embryo do not differentiate into various tissue at the time of fruit maturation ?

A. Internal dormancy B. Physical dormancy

C. External dormancy D. Mixed dormancy

97. During physiological and physical condition some changes observed in seed, it is known as

A. Exogenous dormancy B. Endogenous dormancy

C. Combinational dormancy D. Secondary dormancy

98. By which action a seed coat becomes permeable to water

A. Scarification B. Stratification

C. Vernalization D. All of the above

99. By which physiological process water enters into seed coats of seed ?

A. Endosmosis B. Diffusion

C. Plasmolysis D. Imbibition

100. Which of the following is correct option for seed germination?

A. Emergence of radicle from primary root

B. Emergance of primary root from radicle

C. Development of primary root

D. No root formation

101. What is the rate of respiration during seed germination?

A. Slow B. Steady

C. Rapid D. Zero

102. Which of the following group show viviparous germination?

A. *Rhizophora* and *Avicinnia* B. Orchid and *Rhizophora*

C. Maize and bean D. Soybean and *Xanthium*

103. The process of breaking / softening the seed coat is called

A. Caprification B. Clarification

C. Scarification D. Saponification

104. Match list I with list II using the codes given below

List I	**List II**
A. Bulb	1. Gladiolus
B. Corm	2. Onion
C. Rhizome	3. Potato
D. Tuber	4. Turmeric

A. 1 2 4 3 B. 2 1 4 3

C. 1 2 3 4 D. 2 1 3 4

Answer keys

1	A	16	A	31	D	46	B	61	C	76	A	91	D
2	B	17	D	32	D	47	B	62	B	77	C	92	B
3	C	18	C	33	C	48	B	63	C	78	C	93	A
4	C	19	B	34	B	49	A	64	B	79	A	94	B
5	C	20	C	35	C	50	D	65	A	80	B	95	A

6	B	21	A	36	A	51	A	66	C	81	A	96	A
7	B	22	C	37	A	52	A	67	C	82	B	97	C
8	D	23	D	38	C	53	C	68	C	83	A	98	A
9	D	24	B	39	D	54	C	69	B	84	A	99	D
10	C	25	C	40	D	55	D	70	A	85	C	100	B
11	D	26	B	41	D	56	B	71	A	86	B	101	C
12	B	27	A	42	A	57	C	72	A	87	A	102	A
13	C	28	B	43	C	58	A	73	D	88	B	103	C
14	C	29	D	44	C	59	C	74	C	89	A	104	B
15	D	30	D	45	C	60	B	75	B	90	D	105	

2

Seed Production

I. Choose the correct answer

1. Isolation distance for rice hybrid seed production is

   A. 3m B. 100m

   C. 50m D. 1000m

2. What is the seed rate for short duration rice variety?

   A. 60 kg/ha B. 40 kg/ha

   C. 30 kg/ha D. 20 kg/ha

3. Planting ratio for rice hybrid seed production is

   A. 4:2 B. 6:2

   C. 8:2 D. 10:2

4. What is the special technique used to increase the pollination in rice hybrid seed production?

   A. Hand emasculation B. Rubbing

   C. Detasseling D. Rod driving

5. What is the method of hybrid seed production in maize?

   A. Hand emasculation B. Rubbing

   C. Detasseling D. Rod driving

6. The optimum sieve size for grading of maize seed is

   A. 18/64" B. 16/64"

   C. 20/64" D. 4/64"

7. Which one of the following technique is practiced for synchronization of flowering in sorghum?

   A. Late planting B. Staggered sowing

   C. Early sowing D. Supplementary pollination

8. What is the optimum sowing season for sorghum seed production?

   A. October – November B. January – February

   C. August – September D. March - April

9. Which one of the following chemical is used for hardening of pearl millet seeds?

A. 2% KNO_3 B. 2% NaCl

C. 2% KCl D. 2% $CaCO_3$

10. Which technique is followed for hybrid seed production?

A. CMS B. GMS

C. CGMS D. Both A and C

11. What is the spacing for long duration variety of redgram?

A. 90 x 60 cm B. 90 x 45 cm

C. 90 x 30 cm D. 90 x 120 cm

12. Isolation distance for cowpea foundation seed production is

A. 5 m B. 10 m

C. 100 m D. 50 m

13. Which of the following seed treatment is followed for greengram?

A. 1% KH_2PO_4 B. 0.5% $ZnSO_4$

C. $ZnSO_4$ 100 ppm D. 5% $ZnSO_4$

14. What is the percentage of DAP foliar spray applied for redgram?

A. 1% DAP B. 2% DAP

C. 5% DAP D. 0.5% DAP

15. What is the isolation distance followed for FS of pearl millet?

A. 400 m B. 200 m

C. 1000 m D. 600 m

16. Method of hybrid seed production in cotton is

A. Detasseling B. Supplementary pollination

C. Doak's method D. CMS

17. Seed rate of delinted cotton is

A. 15-20 kg/ha B. 7.5-10 kg/ha

C. 20-25 kg/ha D. 3-4 kg/ha

18. Quantity of gypsum applied for groundnut is

A. 400 kg/ha B. 800 kg/ha

C. 100 kg/ha D. 250 kg/ha

19. Maturity index of groundnut is
    A. Inner side of pod turns brown B. Inner side of pod turns black
    C. Rattling sound D. Viviparous germination
20. Fertilizer recommendation for varietal sunflower seed production is
    A. 60:45:45 kg NPK/ha B. 100:50:50 kg NPK/ha
    C. 150:60:60 kg NPK/ha D. 40:20:20 kg NPK/ha
21. Nursery area of paddy is
    A. 400 m^2 B. 1000 m^2
    C. 800 m^2 D. 200 m^2
22. Method of hybrid seed production in castor
    A. Photoperiod based sex expression
    B. Temperature based sex expression
    C. CGMS
    D. GMS
23. Seed yield of gingelly is
    A. 400-450 kg/ha B. 100-200 kg/ha
    C. 200-250 kg/ha D. 300-350 kg/ha
24. Chemical used to reduce flower drop in tomato is
    A. NAA 20-40 ppm B. IAA 20-40 ppm
    C. IBA 20-40 ppm D. ABO 20-40 ppm
25. Quantity of $ZnSO_4$ applied for rice varietal seed production is
    A. 5 kg/ha B. 10 kg/ha
    C. 25 kg/ha D. 40 kg/ha
26. Isolation distance for varietal seed production of brinjal (CS) is
    A. 100 m B. 200 m
    C. 400 m D. 600 m
27. Seed rate for tomato hybrid seed production is
    A. 1000 g B. 500 g
    C. 250 g D. 100 g
28. Optimum age of chilli seedling for transplanting is
    A. 9-10 weeks old seedlings B. 1 week old seedling
    C. 4-6 weeks old seedlings D. 2-3 week old seedlings

29. Method of hybrid seed production in bhendi is
    A. Emasculation and pollination B. GMS
    C. CGMS D. CMS
30. Optimum stage of harvest for seed purpose in bhendi is
    A. Turning of fruits to orange colour
    B. Dry fruits with hairline cracks
    C. Reddening of fruit
    D. Turning of fruit to bright yellow
31. Planting ratio of vegetable hybrid seed production is
    A. 4:1 B. 5:1
    C. 3:1 D. 6:1
32. What is the biocontrol agent used for seed treatment of chilli?
    A. *Azospirillum* B. Phosphobacteria
    C. *Azolla* D. *Trichoderma viride*
33. What is the optimum bulb size for onion seed production?
    A. 10-15 g B. 40-50 g
    C. 10-20 g D. 25-30 g
34. Optimum season for bulb production of onion for seed purpose is
    A. December – January B. January – February
    C. June – September D. October – March
35. Which chemical is used for sex expression in pumpkin?
    A. Ethrel 250 ppm B. GA 250 ppm
    C. IAA 250 ppm D. IBA 250 ppm
36. Method of hybrid seed production in ribbed gourd is
    A. Detasseling B. Use of gynoecious line
    C. Emasculation and pollination D. Remove of fertile plants
37. Maturity index of ash gourd is
    A. Complete ashy coating B. Yellowing of fruit
    C. Cracking of fruit D. Yellowing of fruit stalk
38. Isolation distance for CS production of ribbed gourd is
    A. 1000 m B. 1500 m
    C. 600 m D. 1200 m

39. Spacing for bittergourd seed production is
    A. 2 x 2 m B. 2.5 x 2.5 m
    C. 3 x 3 m D. 1 x 2 m
40. Seed rate for snakegourd is
    A. 0.75 kg/ha B. 1 kg/ha
    C. 0.5 kg/ha D. 0.25 kg/ha
41. Seed replacement rate is 100% for
    A. Varieties of self pollinated crops B. Varieties of cross pollinated crops
    C. Hybrids D. All of these
42. A problem weed, whose seed once mixed with crop seed is extremely difficult to separate is called as
    A. Non parasitic weed B. Objectionable weed
    C. Parasitic weed D. Aquatic weed
43. Example of inseparable crop seed for wheat is
    A. Barley B. Oats
    C. Gram D. All of these
44. *Argemone mexicana* is a inseparable crop seed in
    A. Wheat B. Rape and mustard
    C. Rice D. Cotton
45. Detasseling is done in
    A. Sorghum B. Cotton
    C. Sugarcane D. Maize
46. Male sterility system followed for redgram is
    A. CGMS B. TGMS
    C. PGMS D. GMS
47. Match the following
    A. Shedding tassel 1. Cumbu
    B. Pollen partials 2. Cotton
    C. Selfed bolls 3. Rice
    D. Pollen shedders 4. Maize
    A. 3 1 4 2 B. 2 3 14
    C. 4 1 2 3 D. 4 2 1 3

48. In hybrid seed production, pollination for 100% seed set can be achieved by

A. Supplementary pollination B. Rope pulling

C. Rod driving D. All the above

49. Match the following

A. Detasseling 1. Cauliflower

B. GMS 2. Rice

C. CGMS 3. Redgram

D. Self incomptability 4. Maize

A. 2 4 1 3 B. 2 3 4 1

C. 4 3 2 1 D. 1 3 2 4

50. The quality of gametocide which is not relevant is

A. Its effect should be uniform in whole blooming period

B. Minimum side effect on plant growth

C. Its effectiveness should not be influenced by environment

D. It is contact in nature

51. Maximum percentage of inert matter in maize as per minimum seed standard

A. 0.5% B. 0.2%

C. 2% D. 5%

52. Isolation distance for hybrid maize (FS) is about

A. 800 m B. 400 m

C. 200 m D. 10 m

53. Planting ratio of paddy in hybrid seed production is

A. 10:2 B. 4:2

C. 2:1 D. 12:8

54. Maximum permitted percentage of off type for CS production in sorghum is

A. 0.5% B. 1.0%

C. 0.1% D. None of these

55. Quantity of other crop seeds permitted for CS of bhendi is

A. 5 Nos/kg B. 10 Nos/kg

C. 15 Nos/kg D. 25 Nos/kg

56. Isolation distance for FS of tomato is

A. 400 m B. 600 m

C. 200 m D. 50 m

57. Time isolation is followed for

A. Sorghum B. Rice

C. Cumbu D. Cotton

58. Emasculation in hybrid cotton production is done in

A. Male line B. Female line

C. Sterile line D. Both A and B

59. Pure seed percentage of groundnut CS is

A. 99% B. 98%

C. 97% D. 96%

60. Heliotropism is a special character of

A. Paddy B. Groundnut

C. Sunflower D. Sugarcane

61. Maximum permitted off type in castor for FS is

A. 1.0% B. 0.5 %

C. 2.0 % D. 5.0 %

62. Number of field inspections in chilli is

A. 3 B. 4

C. 1 D. 2

63. Maximum percentage of designated disease in all cole crops (FS) is

A. 0.50 % B. 0.10 %

C. 0.20 % D. 0.05 %

64. Maximum permitted shedding tassel percentage in hybrid maize seed production is

A. 2% B. 1%

C. 0.1% D. 0.5%

65. The isolation distance is higher in

A. Self pollinated crop B. Cross pollinated crop

C. Often cross pollinated crop D. Both A and B

66. Male sterility used in rice hybrid seed production is
    A. Cytoplasmic male sterility
    B. Genetic male sterility
    C. Cytoplasmic genetic male sterility
    D. Both A and B
67. Planting ratio of female to male in cotton hybrid seed production is
    A. 4:2 B. 8:2
    C. 2:1 D. 20:2
68. Identify the incorrect statement
    i) 2, 4-D spraying in brinjal at flowering stage increase fruit set
    ii) Minimum germination percentage of tomato is 70%
    iii) Isolation distance for bhendi FS is 400 m
    iv) Seed rate in TPS production is higher compared to seed tuber production in potato
    A. (iv) alone is incorrect B. (ii) and (iii) are incorrect
    C. All of these D. (i) alone is incorrect
69. The technique used for hybrid seed production in maize is
    A. Emasculation and dusting B. Three line breeding syatem
    C. Detasseling D. Chemical emasculants
70. Unwanted plants growing from seed that remains in the field from a previous crop is termed as
    A. Objectionble weed plants B. Volunteer plants
    C. Pollen shedders D. Rogues
71. What is the minimum genetic purity standard for hybrid seed production?
    A. 90 % B. 95%
    C. 99% D. 100%
72. Which of the following is used as a live barrier in hybrid rice seed production plots?
    A. Sunflower plants B. Cotton plants
    C. Daincha plants D. Castor plants
73. How many number of border rows to be provided on all sides of hybrid pearl millet seed production plot?
    A. 2 B. 4
    C. 6 D. 8

74. Cotton is often cross pollinated crop in which about —— per cent of cross pollination occurs.

A. 25 % B. 40%

C. 50% D. 75%

75. The flower part removed or made non functional during emasculation is

A. Anther B. Calyx

C. Corolla D. Ovary

76. Minimun isolation distance for foundation seed production in rice is

A. Two metres B. Three metres

C. Four metres D. Five metres

77. The isolation distance for certified seed production in cole crops is

A. 1600 m B. 1000 m

C. 500 m D. 100 m

78. In sunflower hybrid seed production, foundation seed requires an isolation distance of

A. 600 metres B. 800 metres

C. 200 metres D. 100 metres

79. 50% fertile plants are removed in hybrid seed production of

A. Sorghum B. Bajra

C. Redgram D. Ragi

80. The minimum isolation distance for foundation seed production of hybrid pearl millet is

A. 200 m B. 400 m

C. 800 m D. 1000 m

81. Presence of 'B' line in 'A' line population in sorghum hyprid seed production plot is called

A. Shedding tassel B. Selfed boll

C. Partials D. Pollen shedders

82. How many number of heads to be counted per count during field inspection of paddy seed crop?

A. 100 B. 500

C. 1000 D. 1500

83. Minimum number of field counts to be taken in an area of 5 ha seed field is

A. 5 B. 6

C. 7 D. 8

84. The major genetic contaminant in maize hybrid seed production plot is

A. Selfed plants B. Partials

C. Pollen shedders D. Shedding tassels

85. What is the planting ratio for sunflower hybrid seed production?

A. 2:1 B. 3:1

C. 4:1 D. 5:1

86. In groundnut, seed multiplication ratio is

A. 1:5 B. 1:6

C. 1:7 D. 1:8

87. Match list I with list II and choose the correct options given below

List I	**List II**
A. Rice	1. Fertile plant
B. Maize	2. Selfed bolls
C. Cotton	3. Pollen shedder
D. Redgram	4. Shedding tassel

A. 4 3 2 1 B. 3 4 2 1

C. 2 1 4 3 D. 4 3 1 2

88. In which field inspection, the area under seed production is verified?

A. Vegetative stage B. Flowering stage

C. Pre harvest stage D. Post harvest stage

89. In hybrid seed production of sorghum, what type of genetic contaminants should be removed and destroyed

A. Diseased plants B. Pest attacked plants

C. Pollen shedders D. Sterile plants

90. Consider the statement and choose the correct answer

(i) 5 field count is taken for 0-5 acres of land

(ii) 1000 plants/head per count are observed in wheat seed field

A. (i) and (ii) are wrong B. (i) and (ii) are correct

C. (i) alone is correct D. (ii) alone is correct

91. Match list I with list II and choose the correct options given below

List I	List II
A. Maize	1. 2 field inspections
B. Paddy	2. 3 field inspections
C. Brinjal	3. 1000 heads per count
D. Sunflower	4. 100 plants/one count

A. 4 3 2 1 B. 2 1 4 3
C. 3 4 1 2 D. 3 4 1 2

92. How many steps are needed to observe 1000 plants, if 25 plants are observed in one step?

A. 30 steps B. 35 steps
C. 40 steps D. 45 steps

93. Consider the statement and choose the correct answer

i) Field standards are general seed certification standards
ii) Seed standards are specific seed certification standards

A. (i) alone is correct B. (ii) alone is correct
C. (i) and (ii) are correct D. (i) and (ii) are wrong

94. Maximum number of ODV permitted in rice certified seed

A. 5 B. 10
C. 15 D. 20

95. Find out the wrong (incorrect) statement.

A. For certified seed of hybrid maize, minimum germination is 80%
B. For foundation seed of redgram, minimum germination is 75%
C. For certified seed of groundnut, minimum germination is 70%
D. For foundation seed of tomato, minimum germination is 60%

96. Match list I with list II and choose the correct options given below

List I	List II
A. Sorghum	1. Tristyly
B. Greengram	2. Capitulum
C. Sunflower	3. Racemose
D. Brinjal	4. Panicle

A. 2 1 4 3 B. 3 4 1 2
C. 3 4 2 1 D. 4 3 2 1

97. Choose the correct answer
    A. Cumbu is protandry
    B. Castor is dioecious
    C. Chilli is monoecious
    D. Cotton is bisexual or hermaphrodite flower

98. In which crop, 6-8 pickings/harvests are carried out
    A. Bhendi B. Brinjal
    C. Cotton D. Bittergourd

99. In which year, first maize hybrid was released?
    A. 1961 B. 1962
    C. 1963 D. 1971

100. Match list I with list II and choose the correct options given below

List I	List II
A. Sorghum FS	1. 100 m
B. Redgram CS	2. 400 m
C. Sunflower FS	3. 30 m
D. Cotton CS	4. 200 m

    A. 4 3 2 1 B. 4 1 2 3
    C. 2 1 4 3 D. 3 4 1 2

101. Ribbed gourd foundation seed production requires ____ isolation distance
    A. 500 m B. 800 m
    C. 1000 m D. 1200 m

102. What is the isolation distance for foundation seed production in bhendi?
    A. 100 m B. 200 m
    C. 300 m D. 400 m

103. Which one of the following is spacing for seed production of short duration variety of rice?
    A. 20 x 30 cm B. 20 x 15 cm
    C. 20 x 20 cm D. 20 x 10 cm

104. What is the foliar spray recommended for blackgram seed production field?
    A. 1% DAP @ 25-35 DAS B. 0.5% DAP @ 25-35 DAS
    C. 1.5% DAP @ 25-35 DAS D. 2.0% DAP @ 25-35 DAS

105. Which spray is recommended to increase female flowers in cucurbit seed production?

A. NAA 250 ppm B. Ethephon 250 ppm
C. GA 250 ppm D. IAA 250 ppm

106. In which year, first seed testing lab was started in Tamil Nadu?

A. 1985 B. 1980
C. 1975 D. 1970

107. What is the isolation distance for hybrid rice seed production?

A. 25 m B. 50 m
C. 100 m D. 75 m

108. In which crop, chemical sex expression is used for hybrid seed production?

A. Tomato B. Brinjal
C. Cauliflower D. Bittergourd

109. Match list I with list II and choose the correct options given below

List I	List II
A. Redgram	1. 3:1 (or) 6:1
B. Castor	2. 4:2
C. Cumbu	3. 6:1
D. Tomato	4. 5:1

A. 2 1 3 4 B. 1 2 3 4
C. 3 4 2 1 D. 4 3 2 1

110. What is the seed yield of hybrid rice?

A. 50 kg/ha B. 100 kg/ha
C. 150 kg/ha D. 200 kg/ha

111. Consider the statement and choose correct answer

i) Method of maize hybrid seed production is detasseling
ii) In redgram hybrid seed production emasculation and dusting is practiced
iii) In cotton hybrid seed production, emasculation and dusting is practiced

A. (i) alone is correct B. (ii) alone is correct
C. (i) and (ii) are correct D. (ii) and (iii) are correct

112. In which hybrid seed production, rod driving is practiced?

A. Rice B. Maize
C. Sunflower D. Cotton

113. What is the seed rate for male and female in maize hybrid seed production?
A. 5:10 kg/ha B. 10:10 kg/ha
C. 15:10 kg/ha D. 10:15 kg/ha

114. What is the suitable season for cumbu hybrid seed production?
A. November-December B. January-February
C. March-April D. May – June

115. Which one of the following is a designated inseparable other crop seed for wheat?
A. Oats B. Pearl millet
C. Finger millet D. Sorghum

116. Which one of the following is the cause for expression of off types?
A. Recessive gene expression B. Dominant gene expression
C. Co-dominant gene expression D. Cytoplasmic expression

117. What is the exact stage of removal of off types in seed field?
A. After pollination B. During fertilization
C. Before pollination D. After fertilization

118. Which one of the following is not a suitable weather for quality seed production?
A. Moderate rainfall B. Moderate wind
C. Optimum temperature D. Humid climate

119. For which crop, the isolation distance is more or higher?
A. Self pollinated crop B. Self fertilized crop
C. Cross pollinated crop D. Often cross pollinated crop

120. Which one of the following weedicide is a post emergence weedicide?
A. Atrazine B. Glyphosate
C. Butachlor D. Pendimethalin

121. Which one of the following is sprayed to pulses for the production of bolder seeds?
A. 2% DAP B. 1% DAP
C. 1.5% DAP D. 2.5% DAP

122. In cotton, spraying of ———— DAP at boll formation increases seed quality
A. 0.5% B. 1%
C. 1.5% D. 2%

123. Which from the following contaminant does not cause physical contamination?

A. Pollen shedders B. Weed seeds

C. Designated diseased plants D. Other crop plants

124. Which one of the following crop can be harvested in single harvest?

A. Cotton B. Tomato

C. Rice D. Chillies

125. Which one of the following is a genetic contaminant in cotton?

A. Selfed bolls B. Crossed bolls

C. Skewed bolls D. Unopened bolls

126. What is the isolation distance for wheat certified seed production?

A. 200m B. 150m

C. 50m D. 3m

127. Which from the following is the rabi season?

A. February – May B. June – September

C. October – January D. November – December

128. For seed production of sunflower, the sowing season is

A. August – September B. April – August

C. October – November D. November

129. Which one of the following is the seed rate for bunchy type groundnut?

A. 50 kg/ha B. 60 kg/ha

C. 100 - 130 kg/ha D. 35-40 kg/ha

130. Which one of the following treatment is adopted for hardening of bajra seeds?

A. 2% KCl B. 0.5% $CaCl_2$

C. 2% KH_2PO_4 D. 100ml H_2SO_4

131. Which one of the following is recommended sieve size for size grading of rice seed?

A. 23/64" B. 8/64"

C. 24/64" D. 27/64"

132. What is permitted weed seed in redgram?

A. 5/kg B. 10/kg

C. 20/kg D. 40/kg

133. For ———————— seed, 75% germination is permitted as minimum standard

A. Wheat
B. Cotton
C. Greengram
D. Castor

134. Production of breeder seed in cotton requires an isolation distance of

A. 20 metres
B. 30 metres
C. 50 metres
D. 75 metres

135. Oat is said to be

A. Cross pollinated crops
B. Self pollinated crop
C. Mixed pollinated crop
D. Often cross pollinated crop

136. Among vegetables, which one of the following crop needs a less isolation distance

A. Brinjal
B. Crucifers
C. Tomato
D. Bhendi

137. ———————— is the isolation distance for F.S of onion

A. 50 m
B. 400 m
C. 1600 m
D. 1000 m

138. Which from the following is the isolation distance for FS of bhendi?

A. 50 m
B. 400 m
C. 1600 m
D. 1000 m

139. Which season is a suitable for certified seed production of bittergourd

A. June – July
B. April – May
C. June – September
D. February – March

140. Which one of the following is a designated disease for muskmelon?

A. Phompsis fruit blight
B. Anthracnose
C. Cucumber mosaic
D. Black leg

141. Which one of the following is the optimum maturity stage of pumpkin?

A. Yellow colouration of fruits
B. Reddish colouration of fruits
C. Ashy coating over the fruits
D. Yellowish browning of fruit rind

142. What is the pure seed percentage of okra?

A. 95%
B. 97%
C. 98%
D. 99%

143. What is seed multiplication ratio in potato and groundnut?

A. 1:4 and 1:8 B. 1:8 and 1:4

C. 1:8 and 1:10 D. 1:10 and 1:8

144. Which one of the following is an example for two line hybrid seed production?

A. Sesamum B. Jute

C. Groundnut D. Cotton

145. An example for chemical hybridizing agent is

A. PEG B. Mannitol

C. MH D. Calcium chloride

146. Which from the following is interspecific hybrid?

A. Varalakshmi B. Sugana

C. Deccan D. Ganga

147. ———— hybrid maize is an example for double cross hybrid

A. Jawahar B. Deccan

C. COH1 D. Ganga

148. Which from the following crop is an example for GMS method of hybrid seed production?

A. Rice B. Redgram

C. Maize D. Cotton

149. Which method is employed for bittergourd hybrid seed production?

A. Pinching of staminate flowers + hand pollination

B. Hand emasculation + manual pollination

C. GMS + bee pollination

D. CMS + natural pollination

150. In ———— hybrid seed production, the barrier isolation is used

A. Sorghum B. Bajra

C. Rice D. Redgram

151. Which from the following is the seed rate for bhendi hybrid seed production?

A. 20 kg A line and 10 kg B line/ha B. 12 kg A line and 5 kg B line/ha

C. 16 kg A line and 9 kg B line/ha D. 4 kg A line and 1 kg B line/ha

152. ———— % urea solution can be sprayed to late parent of sorghum hybrid seed production for enhancing flowering

A. 1 B. 2

C. 3 D. 4

153. Which system is used for hybrid seed production in onion?

A. Dioecious B. Cytoplasmic male sterility

C. Genetic male sterility D. Self incompatibility

154. The hybrids developed by ICAR Institutions and State Agricultural Universities are called

A. Private hybrids B. Institutional hybrids

C. Public hybrids D. Government

155. ———————— deteriorates drastically upon inbreeding

A. Carrot B. Okra

C. Brinjal D. Broccoli

156. What is the isolation distance of certified seed production of lucerne?

A. 400m B. 300m

C. 200m D. 100m

157. Which one of the following substrate is recommended for germination of fodder cowpea?

A. TP/S B. BP/Tp

C. TP/BP D. BP/S

158. The isolation distance for foundation seed production of cumbu-napier hybrid

A. 10m B. 15m

C. 20m D. 25m

159. Headquarters of the Union for the Protection of New Plant varieties is in

A. Thailand B. USA

C. Denmark D. Switzerland

160. At what time, the hand pollination should be carried out to increase seed set in sunflower hybrid seed production?

A. 5-8 am B. 8-11 am

C. 11-1 pm D. 1pm – 4pm

161. Match the following

Crop	**Isolation distance**
A. Rice (Hybrid)	1. 800 m
B. Maize	2. 100 m
C. Bhendi (FS)	3. 200 m
D. Pumpkin (FS)	4. 400 m

A. 4 3 1 2 B. 3 2 1 4
C. 3 4 2 1 D. 2 3 4 1

162. Isolation distance for FS of cole crops like cabbage and cauliflower is
A. 800 m B. 200 m
C. 400 m D. 1600 m

163. Match the following

A. Certified seed	1. 100% Genetic purity
B. Soybean	2. 99% Genetic purity
C. Nucleus seed	3. 97% physical purity
D. Foundation seed	4. 98% Genetic purity

A. 4 3 1 2 B. 3 4 1 2
C. 2 1 4 3 D. 2 4 1 3

164. Seed generation system depends on
A. Rate of genetic deterioration B. Seed multiplication ratio
C. Total seed demand D. All of these

165. Match the following

A. Nucleus seed	1. White tag
B. Breeder seed	2. Azure blue
C. Foundation seed	3. No specific tag
D. Certified seed	4. Golden yellow

A. 2 1 4 3 B. 3 1 4 2
C. 3 4 1 2 D. 4 3 1 2

166. Seed generation system followed for cross pollinated crops/often cross pollinated crops is
(i) 3 GS (ii) 4 GS
(iii) 5 GS (iv) 2 GS
A. (ii) and (iii) B. (i) and (ii)
C. (i), (ii) and (iii) D. Any of these

167. Special class of paddy seed permitted in seed generation system is

A. CS $\rightarrow$ CS I $\rightarrow$ CS II $\rightarrow$ CS III

B. CS $\rightarrow$ CS I $\rightarrow$ CS II

C. CS $\rightarrow$ CS I $\rightarrow$ CS II $\rightarrow$ CS III $\rightarrow$ CS IV

D. CS $\rightarrow$ CS I

168. Progeny of breeder seed is

A. Nucleus seed B. Foundation seed

C. Certified seed D. Registered seed

169. Identify the incorrect statement

(i) Progeny of foundation seed is breeder seed

(ii) Breeder seed is maintained by concerned breeder of sponsoring institute

(iii) CS and FS are certified by certification agency

(iv) Breeder seed is certified by certification agency

A. (ii) and (iii) B. (ii), (iii) and (iv)

C. (i) alone D. (i) and (iv)

170. Identify the incorrect statement about TFL

A. Certification is voluntary for both notified and released varieties

B. Satisfy the minimum field standards

C. Tested for physical purity and germination

D. Seed Inspector alone can take sample

171. The seed which normally used for commercial crop production is called

A. Breeder seed B. Nucleus seed

C. Foundation seed D. Certified seed

172. The tag of certified seed is

A. Azure blue B. White

C. Golden yellow D. Red

173. Tag colour of registered seed is

A. Opal green B. Purple colour

C. White D. Azure blue

174. Seed which is produced by private seed companies is

A. TFL seeds B. Certified seed

C. Foundation seed D. Both A and B

175. Seed which is applicable to notified kinds only
    A. Certified seed B. TFL seeds
    C. Foundation seed D. Both A and C
176. The validity period of certified seed is
    A. 6 months B. 9 months
    C. 10 months D. 12 months
177. Tag size of certified seed is
    A. 12 x 6 cm B. 15 x 7.5 cm
    C. 13 x 6.5 cm D. Any on these
178. Seed certification is for
    A. Breeder seed and certified seed
    B. Certified seed and foundation seed
    C. Certified seed alone
    D. All the above
179. In hybrid seed production, the seed rate of male line is _____ female line.
    A. Higher than B. Lower than
    C. Equal to D. Depends on crop
180. Steps in seed multiplication are as follows
    A. i. Breeder seed, ii. Foundation seed, iii. Registered seed, iv. Certified seed
    B. i. Foundation seed, ii. Certified seed, iii. Breeder seed, iv. Registered seed
    C. i. Certified seed, ii. Breeder seed, iii. Registered seed, iv. Foundation seed
    D. i. Breeder seed, ii. Foundation seed, iii. Registered seed, iv. Certified seed
181. For breeder seed production, colour of tag used while bagging and sealing is
    A. Blue B. Golden yellow
    C. White D. None of the above
182. Tag colour for foundation seeds is
    A. Green B. Blue
    C. White D. Yellow

183. Golden yellow colour tag is used for

A. Nucleus seed
B. Breeder seed
C. Foundation seed
D. Certified seed

184. Which from the following is the progeny of nucleus seed?

A. Certified seed
B. Foundation seed
C. Registered seed
D. Breeder seed

185. Genetic purity for foundation seed is %

A. 100
B. 99.9
C. 99.5
D. 99

186. International Crop Improvement Association (ICIA) in ———— classified seed into different categories.

A. 1964
B. 1946
C. 1963
D. 1972

187. Genetically most pure seed is

A. Nucleus seed
B. Breeder seed
C. Certified seed
D. Foundation seed

188. What is the yield increase, if you use certified seed for sowing?

A. 5-10%
B. 10-15%
C. 15-20%
D. 20-25%

189. Chemical which is not used to create male sterility is

A. Maleic hydrazide
B. Ethrel
C. Sodium methyl arsenate
D. NaOH

190. TIBA is an/a

A. Growth regulator
B. Growth retardant
C. Gametocide
D. Growth promotor

191. Brinjal is a

A. Cross pollinated crop
B. Often cross pollinated crop
C. Self pollinated crop
D. None of these

192. Pearl millet is cross pollinated due to its

A. Protandrous nature
B. Protogynous nature
C. Hermaphrodite nature
D. All the above

193. The level of natural outcrossing in groundnut is

A. 5% B. 10%

C. 15% D. Negligible

194. Tarai Development Corporation was established in the year

A. 1961 B. 1969

C. 1965 D. 1966

195. Blonded seeds are found in

A. Peas B. Cluster bean

C. Pulses D. Cereals

196. Match the following:

A. Calcium	1. Blotching
B. Boron	2. Blossom end rot
C. Molybdenum	3. Hollow heart
D. Potassium	4. Whiptail

A. 4 2 1 3 B. 3 2 4 1

C. 4 3 2 1 D. 2 3 4 1

197. The 17th essential element added for plant growth is

A. Cobalt B. Molybdenum

C. Nickel D. Magnesium

198. Match the following:

A. Nitrogen	1. Integral part of amino acids
B. Phosphorus	2. Building blocks of protien
C. Sulphur	3. Energy storage
D. Magnesium	4. Key element of chlorophyll production

A. 2 3 1 4 B. 4 3 2 1

C. 3 4 2 1 D. 1 3 2 4

199. In which country, CIMMYT is located?

A. America B. Mexico

C. India D. Australia

200. Deficiency symptom of marsh spot is

A. Potassium B. Manganese

C. Boron D. Calcium

201. Which foliar spray is used to control flower shedding?

A. NAA 40 ppm B. NAA 30 ppm

C. NAA 20 ppm D. NAA 10 ppm

Answer keys

1	B	21	C	41	C	61	B	81	D	101	C	121	A	141	D	161	D	181	B
2	A	22	B	42	B	62	A	82	C	102	D	122	D	142	D	162	D	182	C
3	C	23	D	43	D	63	B	83	C	103	A	123	A	143	A	163	A	183	B
4	D	24	A	44	B	64	B	84	D	104	A	124	C	144	D	164	D	184	D
5	C	25	C	45	D	65	B	85	C	105	B	125	A	145	C	165	C	185	C
6	A	26	A	46	D	66	C	86	D	106	D	126	D	146	A	166	B	186	B
7	B	27	D	47	C	67	B	87	B	107	C	127	C	147	B	167	B	187	A
8	A	28	C	48	D	68	A	88	A	108	D	128	B	148	B	168	B	188	C
9	C	29	A	49	C	69	C	89	C	109	A	129	C	149	A	169	D	189	D
10	B	30	B	50	D	70	B	90	B	110	B	130	A	150	C	170	B	190	A
11	C	31	B	51	C	71	B	91	A	111	C	131	A	151	D	171	D	191	C
12	B	32	D	52	B	72	C	92	C	112	A	132	A	152	A	172	A	192	B
13	C	33	B	53	A	73	D	93	B	113	D	133	C	153	B	173	B	193	D
14	B	34	C	54	C	74	A	94	D	114	A	134	C	154	C	174	D	194	B
15	C	35	A	55	A	75	A	95	A	115	A	135	B	155	A	175	D	195	A
16	C	36	B	56	D	76	B	96	D	116	A	136	C	156	D	176	B	196	D
17	B	37	A	57	B	77	A	97	D	117	C	137	D	157	D	177	B	197	C
18	A	38	A	58	B	78	A	98	B	118	D	138	B	158	A	178	B	198	A
19	B	39	B	59	C	79	C	99	A	119	A	139	A	159	D	179	B	199	B
20	A	40	C	60	C	80	D	100	B	120	B	140	C	160	B	180	A	200	B
																		201	A

3

Seed Processing and Quality Enhancement

I. Choose the correct answer

3.1. Seed processing

1. Indented cylinder separator grades the seeds according to the

   A. Weight B. Surface characteristics

   C. Length D. Size

2. Match the following

   A. Specific gravity separator 1. Seed size

   B. Magnetic separator 2. Seed weight

   C. Spiral separator 3. Surface texture

   D. Air screen cleaner 4. Seed shape

   A. 1 4 3 2 B. 4 3 2 1

   C. 2 3 4 1 D. 3 4 1 2

3. Match the following

   Operation **Crop**

   A. Failing and pounding 1. Cereals

   B. Stripping 2. Rice

   C. Animal treading 3. Pulses

   D. Power tiller threshing 4. Groundnut

   A. 1 4 2 3 B. 2 4 1 3

   C. 4 3 1 2 D. 3 4 1 2

4. Find out the incorrect statement.

   (i) Once over harvest Bhendi

   (ii) 6-8 harvest Paddy

   (iii) Once over harvest Paddy

   A. (iii) alone incorrect B. (i) alone is incorrect

   C. (i) and (ii) are incorrect D. All are incorrect

5. Find out the correct statement
   (i) Seed recovery percentage of acid method is 1.0
   (ii) Seed recovery percentage of fermentation method is 1.0
   (iii) Seed recovery percentage of alkali method is 1.5
   (iv) The chemical used in acid method is NaCl

   A. (iii) and (iv) are correct B. (i) alone is correct
   C. (iii) alone is correct D. (i) and (ii) are correct
6. LSU dryer is a
   A. Batch type dryer B. Continuous flow dryer
   C. Column dryer D. Rectangular bin dryer
7. Match the following

A. Spiral separtaor	1. Length of the seed
B. Disc seperator	2. Shape and surface texture
C. Magnetic seperator	3. Shape or rolling ability
D. Cylinder seperator	4. Surface texture and stickiness of seed

   A. 1 2 3 4 B. 3 2 4 1
   C. 2 3 1 4 D. 4 1 3 2
8. Which one of the following is seed upgrading machine?
   A. Debearder B. Destoner
   C. Pre-conditioning/scalper D. Gravity separator
9. Spiral separator works based on the principle of
   A. Shape B. Length
   C. Weight D. Size
10. Which seed processing machine works on the physical characteristics of surface texture?
   A. Spiral separator B. Colour separator
   C. Magnetic separator D. Specific gravity separator
11. Machine which removes husk is name as
   A. Debeader B. Huller
   C. Scalper D. Precleaner
12. Method of pod separation from plants in groundnut is named as
   A. Beating B. Rubbing
   C. Pounding D. Stripping

13. How many pickings are recommended for gourds?
    A. 3-4 pickings B. 4-5 pickings
    C. 6-8 pickings D. 8-9 pickings
14. Which one of the following method is adopted for tomato seed extraction?
    A. Wet seed extraction B. Dry seed extraction
    C. Acid / Alkali method D. Manual extraction
15. The chemical recommended for delinting of cotton seed is
    A. Perchloric acid B. Concentrated sulphuric acid
    C. Diluted sulphuric acid D. Hydrochloric acid
16. For seed extraction in tomato, which acid is used?
    A. Hydrochloric acid B. Acetic acid
    C. Concentrated sulphuric acid D. Diluted sulphuric acid
17. Seed drying is very important to maintain its
    A. Protein content B. Oil content
    C. Viability and vigour D. Chemical composition
18. The maximum temperature for safe drying of orthodox seeds is
    A. 40°C B. 41°C
    C. 42°C D. 43°C

Answer keys

1	C	11	B
2	C	12	D
3	B	13	B
4	C	14	C
5	D	15	B
6	B	16	A
7	B	17	C
8	D	18	D
9	A		
10	C		

3.2. Seed quality enhancement

1. Controlled hydration of seeds is called
    A. Seed hardening B. Seed priming
    C. Seed encapsulation D. Seed pelleting

2. Commonly used priming osmotium is

A. Polyethylene glycol
B. Vermiculite
C. Salt solution
D. *Pseudomonas*

3. Commonly used chemical for encapsulation is

A. Sodium alginate
B. NaCl
C. Sodium pectate
D. NaOH

4. Match the following

A. Inoculant pelleting — 1. Napthalic anhydride
B. Protective pelleting — 2. *Rhizobium*
C. Herbicide pelleting — 3. *Trichoderma*
D. Nutrient pelleting — 4. DAP

A. 3 2 4 1
B. 2 3 1 4
C. 2 1 4 3
D. 4 3 1 2

5. Choose the correct statement

(i) Seed pelleting is done to facilitate precision planting
(ii) Seed colouring is to improve its brand identity and marketing
(iii) Chemical used for seed hardening of pulses is $ZnSO_4$

A. (i) and (ii) are correct
B. (ii) and (iii) are correct
C. (i) and (iii) are correct
D. All are correct

6. Optimum temperature for seed priming is

A. 0-5°C
B. 5-10°C
C. 10-15°C
D. 15-20°C

7. Match the following

A. Seed priming — 1. Taylor
B. Solid matrix priming — 2. Callan
C. Matric conditioning — 3. Khan
D. Biopriming — 4. Malnassy

A. 3 4 2 1
B. 1 3 4 2
C. 4 1 3 2
D. 2 3 4 1

8. Find out the correct statement

(i) Seed fortification involves hydration and dehydration
(ii) Seed hardening involves hydration and dehydration

A. (i) alone is correct
B. (ii) alone is correct
C. Both are correct
D. Both are incorrect

9. Which of the following is an adhesive in seed pelleting?
   A. Lime B. Rock phosphate
   C. *Albizia amara* leaf powder D. Gelatin
10. ______ is a filler used in seed pelleting
   A. Gum arabic B. Gelatin
   C. Gypsum D. Methyl cellulose
11. Find out the incorrect statement
   A. Pelleted seed can't be stored for more than 3 to 4 months
   B. Seed polymer coating is suitable for all type of lands
   C. Active principle in beetroot for seed colouring is betanin
   D. Seed colouring results in breakage
12. Seed pelleting is a
   A. Pre-sowing seed treatment B. Pre-storage seed treatment
   C. Post-storage seed treatment D. Mid-storage seed treatment
13. The priming agent, which does not penetrate the cell wall is
   A. PEG B. Mannitol
   C. NaCl D. Halogens
14. The suitable chemical used for seed hardening of paddy is
   A. HCl (1%) B. KOH (1%)
   C. KH_2PO_4 (2%) D. KCl (1%)
15. Hardening of bajra is done with
   A. 2% KH_2PO_4 B. 2% KCl
   C. Soaking in water D. 100 ppm $ZnSO_4$
16. Chemical used for seed hardening to overcome drought
   A. KH_2PO_4 B. NaOH
   C. $KHPO_4$ D. K_2SO_4

Answer keys

1	B	6	C	11	D	16	A
2	A	7	C	12	A		
3	A	8	B	13	A		
4	B	9	D	14	D		
5	D	10	C	15	B		

4

Seed Certification

I. Choose the correct answer

1. ISTA stands for

   A. International Seed Testing Agency

   B. International Seed Testing Agreement

   C. International Seed Testing Association

   D. International Seed Testing Agenda

2. Sowing report should be submitted within _____ days from the date of transplanting

   A. 30 days　　B. 15 days

   C. 45 days　　D. 7 days

3. Seed certification includes

   (i) Field inspection

   (ii) Seed sampling

   (iii) Seed quality test

   (iv) Verification of seed source

   A. (i), (ii) and (iv) are correct　　B. (iii) and (iv) are correct

   C. (i) alone　　D. All of these

4. Separate application is submitted in case of

   (i) Different varieties

   (ii) Area more than 25 acres

   (iii) Date of sowing differs by 7 days or more

   A. (i) and (ii) alone　　B. (i) alone

   C. (ii) and (iii) alone　　D. All of these

5. Seed certification has

   A. 3 phases　　B. 6 phases

   C. 7 phases　　D. 4 phases

6. Match the following

Area	**Number of counts**
A. 0-5 acres	1. 6 counts
B. 11-15 acres	2. 5 counts
C. 16-20 acres	3. 8 counts
D. 6-10 acres	4. 7 counts

A. 3 4 1 2 B. 2 3 4 1

C. 2 1 4 3 D. 2 4 3 1

7. Identify the correct statement

A. During first inspection, source of the seed is not necessary to be verified

B. Sowing report should be sent in duplicate

C. Presence of B line in A line is pollen partials

D. Example of pollen shedders is rice

8. Maximum number of inspection is

A. 3 B. 2

C. 4 D. None of these

9. Number of plants/count taken for cotton is

A. 500 B. 1000

C. 100 D. None of these

10. Number of plants/earheads counted for tillering crops like rice is

A. 500 B. 1000

C. 100 D. None of these

11. Number of inspections followed for hybrids is

A. 2 B. 3

C. 4 D. Either A or B

12. Match the following

A. Widely spaced crop	1. Germination
B. Field standard	2. 100 plants
C. Seed standard	3. 1000 plants
D. No. of plants/inspection for broadcasted seeds	4. Isolation distance

A. 1 3 2 4 B. 4 32 1

C. 3 1 4 2 D. 2 4 1 3

13. ISTA was formed during the year

A. 1920 B. 1924

C. 1932 D. 1928

14. (i) International seed lot certificate colour is orange

(ii) Headquaters of ISTA is located in Switzerland

(iii) Number of countries registered in ISTA is 70

A. (i) and (iii) are correct B. (ii) and (iii) are correct

C. (i) and (ii) are correct D. All are correct

15. The first seed testing lab was established in 1869 in

A. India B. Europe

C. Germany D. Africa

16. The journal of Seed Science and Technology is published by ISTA since

A. 1925 B. 1956

C. 1973 D. 1960

17. International Seed Testing Congress was held every

A. One year B. Three years

C. Five years D. Ten years

18. Seed village concept is also known as

A. Seed growers approach B. Community area approach

C. Farmer's seed approach D. Compact area approach

19. Seed multiplication ratio is high for

A. Paddy B. Groundnut

C. Ragi D. Pulses

20. The quality seeds which replaces the farm saved seeds is termed as

A. Seed multiplication ratio B. Seed vigour index

C. Seed germination percentage D. Seed replacement rate

21. Match the following

A. Seed rules 1. 1966

B. Seed act 2. 1983

C. Seed control order 3. 1968

D. Essential commodities act 4. 1955

A. 3 1 2 4 B. 4 3 1 2

C. 1 3 2 4 D. 2 3 4 1

22. Seed Act was implemented in the year

A. 1967 B. 1969

C. 1966 D. 1983

23. Notification of varieties comes under _____ of Seed Act.

A. Sec 3 B. Sec 5

C. Sec 8 D. Sec 11

24. Match the following

Sections of Seed Act	**Section**
A. Seed Analyst	1. Sec 4
B. Seed Inspector	2. Sec 12
C. Certification Agency	3. Sec 13
D. State Seed Laboratory	4. Sec 8

A. 2 1 3 4 B. 3 2 4 1

C. 2 3 4 1 D. 4 3 2 1

25. New seed policy was evolved in

A. 1966 B. 1963

C. 1988 D. 1972

26. NSRTC for testing BT cotton only is located at

A. Varanasi B. Nagpur

C. New Delhi D. Bhopal

27. Number of seed testing laboratory in Tamil Nadu is

A. 7 B. 11

C. 8 D. 12

28. National Seed Research and Training Centre is located at

A. Coimbatore B. Varanasi

C. Nagpur D. New Delhi

29. Seed bill was introduced in

A. 2001 B. 2004

C. 2006 D. 1983

30. The period of protection for notified varieties in PPV & FR Act is

A. 9 years B. 15 years

C. 18 years D. 12 years

31. Choose the correct answer

(i) There are 25 sections in Seed Act 1966

(ii) PPV & FR Act was enacted in the year 2001

(iii) National Seed Policy 2002

(iv) New policy on seed development 1988

A. (iii) and (ii) are correct B. (i) and (ii) are correct

C. (i) and (iv) are correct D. (i), (ii), (iii) and (iv) are correct

32. Consider the statements: The state seed certification agencies perform the following functions:

(i) They select seed growers.

(ii) They carry out the requisite field inspections.

(iii) They conduct seed test.

(iv) They guide the seed growers on production, processing and distribution of seeds.

A. (i) alone correct B. (i) and (ii) are correct

C. (i), (ii) and (iii) are correct D. All are correct

33. Number of plants to be counted per count during field inspection in wide-spaced row crops seed field.

A. 100 B. 500

C. 1000 D. 1500

34. For variety release, DUS test is must. Which authority is conducting DUS test?

A. ICAR B. ICRISAT

C. PPV & FRA D. IARI

35. Which one of the following maize variety is a composite variety?

A. African tall B. Deccan

C. Ganga D. COH1

36. Which one of the following is not relevant with respect to seed quality?

A. Embryonic plant B. Non-living organism

C. A dispersal unit D. Beginning and end of plant life

37. In wheat and rice, the genetic purity of a variety can deteriorate due to :

A. Inbreeding

B. Mechanical contamination with seeds of other varieties

C. Delayed segregation

D. Both A and B

38. How SMR is calculated

A. Ratio of seed yield and seed rate

B. Ratio of seed rate and seed yield

C. Ratio of grain yield and seed rate

D. Ratio of seed rate and grain yield

39. How SRR is worked out?

A. (Seed yield / Seed rate) x 100

B. Seed yield / Seed rate

C. (Qty of actual quality seed sown / Qty of quality seed required) x 100

D. (Qty of certified seed required / Qty of certified seed sown) x 100

40. What is seed replacement rate for hybrids?

A. 25% B. 50%

C. 75% D. 100%

41. .... % is replacement rate in India.

A. 10-15 B. 15-20

C. 20-25 D. 25-30

42. Who from the following has suggested the steps for maintaining genetic purity?

A. Baskin and Delouche (1972)

B. Baskin and Baskin (1974)

C. Hartmann and Kester (1968)

D. Harrington and Woodstock (1962)

43. What is the seed renewal period of composite variety?

A. 2-3 years B. 3-4 years

C. 1-2 years D. 1 year

Answer keys

1	C	11	C	21	A	31	D	41	B
2	B	12	D	22	B	32	D	42	C
3	D	13	B	23	B	33	A	43	B

4	D	14	C	24	C	34	C
5	B	15	C	25	C	35	A
6	D	16	C	26	B	36	B
7	D	17	B	27	B	37	A
8	C	18	D	28	B	38	A
9	C	19	C	29	B	39	C
10	B	20	D	30	B	40	D

5

Seed Testing

I. Choose the correct answer

1. Ability of a seed to withstand in field conditions are called

   A. Seed germination B. Seed vigour

   C. Seed viability D. Both A and B

2. Planting value of field is

   A. Pure seed % - Germination % B. Pure seed % x Germination %

   C. Pure seed % / Germination % D. None of these

3. Father of seed testing is

   A. N.A. Cobb B. Frederich Nobbe

   C. Dr. Badrinarayanan D. Hiltner

4. Identify the incorrect statement

   A. A small portion taken from representative sample is called working sample

   B. Submitted sample size is about 1 kg

   C. The working sample size of paddy is 40 kg

   D. Nobbe trier is suitable for sampling a lot in bag

5. The minimum germination percentage of paddy is

   A. 60% B. 75%

   C. 80% D. 90%

6. The minimum number of seeds used for germination test is

   A. 250 B. 400

   C. 1000 D. None of these

7. A specified quantity of seed which is physically identifiable is

   A. Seed certification B. Seed lot

   C. Seed analysis D. Seed testing

8. Which of the following crop has maximum seed lot size?

A. Paddy B. Groundnut

C. Pearl millet D. Maize

9. _____ is to estimate the extent of biotic and abiotic impurities present in seed lot

A. Germination test B. Purity analysis

C. Standard test D. None of these

10. Most practical and basic common method of moisture estimation prescribed by ISTA is

A. Moisture meter B. Hot air oven method

C. Toluene method D. Lyophilization

11. Purity analysis for groundnut is done with

A. Kernels B. Pods

C. Nuts D. Shell

12. RH in STL should be

A. Less than 50% B. Less than 40%

C. Less than 70% D. Less than 90%

13. Which of the following is an indirect method of moisture determination?

A. Hot air oven method B. Moisture meter method

C. Lyophilization D. Toluene method

14. Chemicals used in desiccators are

A. $CaCl_2$ B. Silica gel

C. NaOH D. All of these

15. Temperature range for high constant oven method is

A. $103\pm2^{\circ}C$ B. $130\pm3^{\circ}C$

C. $196\pm2^{\circ}C$ D. $198\pm3^{\circ}C$

16. Most commonly used paper for germination is/are

A. Germination sheet B. Paddy straw paper

C. Filter paper D. Banana – pseudostem paper

17. Germination test method for larger seeds is

A. Top of paper B. Between paper towel medium

C. Sand medium D. All of these

18. Tetrazolium concentration used in viability test is

A. 2% B. 5%

C. 0.5% D. 10%

19. Grow out test is to predict the

A. Physical purity of seed B. Genetic purity of seed

C. Seed viability D. All of these

20. Example of seed viability test

A. Accelerated ageing test B. Brick gravel test

C. Ferric chloride test D. Paper piercing test

21. Seed vigour of cotton can be estimated by

A. Cool germination test B. Cold test

C. Water sensitivity D. Exhaustion test

22. On staining, the colour formed during quick viability test is

A. Blue B. Red

C. Colourless D. Orange

23. National Seed Corporation was set up in

A. April 7, 1963 B. March 7, 1963

C. June 7, 1963 D. January 7, 1963

24. Quick viability test was developed by

A. Hiltner B. Lakon

C. Frederich Nobbe D. None of these

25. (i) The concentration of $FeCl_3$ used for viability testing is 20%

(ii) Indoxyl acetate test is a specific seed viability test for soybean

A. (i) alone is correct B. (ii) alone is correct

C. Both are correct D. Both are wrong

26. Chemical used in accelerated ageing test is

A. KOH B. $FeCl_3$

C. H_2SO_4 D. Tetrazolium

27. Match the following

Seed vigour test	**Examples**
A. Physical test	1. Cold test
B. Biochemical test	2. Seed density
C. Stress test	3. GADA test
D. Performance test	4. Speed of germination

A. 1 3 4 2 B. 2 3 1 4

C. 4 3 2 1 D. 2 1 4 3

28. Pure seed percentage for certified seed in wheat is about

A. 98% B. 95%

C. 99.9% D. 85%

29. As per ISTA standards, final count of seed germination in maize is taken on

A. 7th day B. 14th day

C. 10th day D. 3rd day

30. First Seed Testing Laboratory in India was established in

A. 1969 B. 1961

C. 1983 D. 1971

31. Prechilling treatment required for which crop for breaking dormancy

A. Paddy B. Cauliflower

C. Pulses D. Chillies

32. Standard seed germination percentage for chilli is

A. 45% B. 75%

C. 60% D. 90%

33. Minimum germination percentage is low for

A. Bitter gourd B. Paddy

C. Maize D. Redgram

34. Which of the following test is used to predict the genetic purity of seed ?

A. Potassium nitrate test B. Ferric chloride test

C. Grow out test D. Seed germination test

35. Seed sample taken from laboratory for testing is known as

A. Primary sample B. Composite sample

C. Submitted sample D. Working sample

36. Seed health test may be done through

A. Visual examination B. Washing technique

C. Soaking D. Any one of the above

37. Match the crops with the respective seed tests. Select the correct code

Crop	**Seed test**
A. Sorghum	1. Peroxidase test
B. Wheat	2. NaOH test
C. Soyabean	3. PAGE
D. Cotton	4. KOH Bleach test

A. 4 2 1 3 B. 1 4 2 3
C. 2 3 1 4 D. 4 2 3 1

38. Which is the most useful method of detecting virus infection in seeds?
A. Seed plating B. Phago test
C. ELISA D. None of these

39. The ideal requirements for good seed are
A. Genetic and physical purity
B. Good germination
C. Freedom from diseases and weeds
D. All the above

40. The test used for quick testing of viability of seeds is
A. Phenol test B. Thiourea test
C. Tetrazolium test D. Succinic acid test

41. Seed testing is done for
A. Purity B. Germination
C. Moisture content D. All of the above

42. Which one of the following is a direct vigour test for seeds?
A. Speed of germination B. Tetrazolium test
C. Accelerated ageing test D. Seedling length measurements

43. TZ test is used to estimate
A. Seed moisture B. Seed purity
C. Seed viability D. Genetic purity

44. As per the ISTA rules, the final count for rice seed germination test has to be taken on
A. 4th day B. 7th day
C. 10th day D. 14th day

45. What is the name of the journal published by ISTA?

A. Seed Research | B. Seed Tech News
C. Seed Science and Technology | D. Journal of Seed Technology

46. Number of seeds needed for grow out test is

A. 50 | B. 100
C. 200 | D. 400

47. The colour of ISTA certificate is

A. White | B. Azure blue
C. Orange | D. Opal green

48. Findout the odd one

A. Velvet Roller separator | B. Magnetic separator
C. Inclined draper | D. Gravity separator

49. Under which section of the Indian Seeds Act, 1966 the varieties are notified

A. Se C. 3 | B. Se C. 5
C. Se C. 7 | D. Se C. 9

50. Which year, Indian Seed Act was implemented?

A. 1966 | B. 1967
C. 1968 | D. 1969

Answer keys

1	B	11	B	21	A	31	B	41	D
2	B	12	C	22	B	32	C	42	C
3	B	13	B	23	B	33	A	43	C
4	A	14	D	24	B	34	C	44	D
5	C	15	B	25	C	35	D	45	C
6	B	16	A	26	A	36	D	46	D
7	B	17	C	27	B	37	A	47	C
8	D	18	C	28	A	38	C	48	D
9	B	19	B	29	A	39	D	49	B
10	B	20	C	30	B	40	C	50	D

6

Seed Pathology and Storage

I. Choose the correct answer

6.1. Seed pathology

1. Seed borne fungi can be detected by

   A. Blotter method B. Agar plate method

   C. NaOH seed soak test D. All the above

2. Which of the following is a seed borne viral disease?

   A. Rice tungro disease

   B. Bean common mosaic

   C. Blackgram common mosaic

   D. Bhendi yellow vein clearing mosaic

3. Which one of the following is a bacteria that contaminates seed surface?

   A. *Fusarium oxysporum* B. *Verticillium dahliae*

   C. *Xanthomonas* D. *Aspergillus niger*

4. In which crop, loose smut is a designated disease?

   A. Rice B. Pearl millet

   C. Wheat D. Sorghum

5. Severe infection of tobacco mosaic virus is observed in

   A. Brinjal B. Chilli

   C. Potato D. Tomato

6. For which seed borne disease, 0.2% NaOH test is used to separate infected seed

   A. Head smut of cumbu B. Karnal bunt of wheat

   C. Leaf spot of sunflower D. Brown rot of potato

Answer keys

1	D	6	B
2	B		
3	C		
4	C		
5	D		

I. Choose the correct answer

6.2. Seed storage

1. Safe moisture percentage of a seed is

   A. 8-9% B. 9-10%

   C. < 8% D. > 13%

2. Choose the correct statements

   (i) Orthodox seed can tolerate low temperature

   (ii) Orthodox seed can be dried below 30-35% moisture

   (iii) Example of recalcitrant seeds is rubber and coffee

   (iv) Orthodox seed can be stored for several years

   A. (i) and (ii) are correct B. (i) and (iii) are correct

   C. (i), (iii) and (iv) are correct D. All are correct

3. Optimum seed moisture for storage of paddy is

   A. 7-8% B. 10-12%

   C. > 13% D. < 8%

4. The field carry over storage pest in pulses is

   A. Pulse pod bug B. Pulse pod fly

   C. Pulse pod wasp D. Pulse beetle

5. Which one of the following is a seed treating chemical?

   A. Carbofuran B. Carbendazim

   C. Sevin D. Malathion

6. How much quantity of water is added for slurry treatment of seeds?

   A. 2 ml B. 3 ml

   C. 3 ml D. 5 ml

7. Consider the statement and choose incorrect answer

   (i) Seed disinfection refers to control of surface and external borne pathogens

   (ii) Seed disinfestations refers to control of deep seated and internal pathogens

   A. (i) and (ii) are incorrect B. (i) and (ii) are correct

   C. (i) alone is correct D. (ii) alone is correct

8. What is the optimum temperature and relative humidity for safe storage?

   A. 30°F + 70% RH = 100 B. 40 °F + 70% RH = 100

   C. 50°F + 50% RH = 100 D. 20 °F + 80% RH = 100

9. Match list I with list II and choose the correct options given below

List I	**List II**
A. Recalcitrant seed	1. 30-35% moisture
B. Orthodox seed	2. Cloth bag
C. Moisture vapour proof container	3. 6-12 % moisture
D. Moisture pervious proof container	4. 700 gauge polythene bag

   A. 3 4 1 2 B. 4 3 1 2

   C. 2 4 3 1 D. 1 3 4 2

10. Find out the correct answer

   (i) Moisture vapour pervious containers allows water in the form of vapour and liquid.

   (ii) Moisture vapour proof container will not allow entry of water in the form of vapour and liquid.

   A. (i) alone is correct B. (i) and (ii) are correct

   C. (ii) alone is correct D. (i) and (ii) are wrong

11. Match list I with list II and choose the correct options given below

List I	**List II**
A. Black arm in cotton	1. 36-43% seed loss in storage
B. Rodents	2. *Xanthomonas compestris*
C. Pests	3. 35-72 % loss in storage
D. Black rot in cabbage	4. *Xanthomonas maleacearum*

   A. 4 3 1 2 B. 2 1 4 3

   C. 4 3 2 1 D. 3 4 1 2

12. Match List I with List II and choose the correct options given below

List I	List II
A. Red flour beetle	1. Circular holes
B. Pulse beetle	2. Brown / damaged seed
C. Cigarette beetle	3. Webbing
D. Indian meal moth	4. Irregular holes

A. 4 3 1 2 B. 3 4 1 2
C. 2 1 4 3 D. 3 4 2 1

13. Where Central Rice Research Institute is located?
A. Calcutta B. Cuttack
C. Karnal D. New Delhi

14. IPGRI is located at
A. USA B. UK
C. Japan D. Rome

15. Tea is an example of
A. Recalcitrant B. Orthodox
C. Difficult recalcitrant D. Both A and B

16. Identify the wrongly matched option relevant to moisture content in storage under moisture pervious container
A. Pumpkin - 7.0% B. Capsicum - 8.0%
C. Cotton - 6% D. Maize - 12%

17. At which moisture percentage should the cereal grains be stored?
A. 5-6 % B. 7-9 %
C. 10-15 % D. 8-10 %

Answer keys

1	B	11	A
2	D	12	C
3	B	13	B
4	D	14	D
5	B	15	A
6	D	16	C
7	A	17	D
8	C		
9	D		
10	B		

UNIT X: AGRICULTURAL BIOTECHNOLOGY

1

Agricultural Biotechnology

I. Choose the correct answer

1. The term biotechnology was first coined in

   A. 1919, Karl Ereky B. 1916, Neuberg

   C. 1991, Frederick Sanger's D. 1961, Lipmann

2. Biotechnology is used in areas including

   A. Agriculture B. Bioremediation

   C. Food processing D. All the above

3. Genetic engineering is

   A. Use of cellular enzymes to manipulate DNA

   B. Improve existing/create novel proteins to make useful products

   C. Block or decrease the production of certain proteins

   D. Grow cells/tissues under laboratory conditions to produce an entire organism, or to produce new products

4. Functional genomics is

   A. High-throughput approaches to determine the biological function of all of the genes and their products

   B. Improve existing/create novel proteins to make useful products

   C. Block or decrease the production of certain proteins

   D. Computational analysis of biological data

5. Translational genomics include(s)

   A. Transcriptomics alone

   B. Proteomics alone

   C. Metabolomics and transgenomics

   D. All the above

6. Vaccination was first attempted by

A. Gregor Mendel , 1787 B. Oswald Avery, 1777
C. Colin MacLeod, 1767 D. Edward Jenner, 1797

7. Phages infect

A. Only bacteria B. Only virus
C. Both A and B D. None of the above

8. Genetic engineering is perfected by a technique to cut and paste DNA using restriction enzymes

A. Stanley Cohen B. Herbert Boyer
C. Both D. Francis Crick

9. .... developed the polymerase chain reaction (PCR) technique.

A. Kary Mullis B. Georges Kohler
C. Cesar Milstein D. None of the above

10. First recombinant vaccine approved for human use is

A. Hepatitis B B. Polio
C. Hepatitis C D. Hepatitis A

11. .... is the first genetically modified plant approved for field tests.

A. Virus-resistant tomatoes B. Virus-resistant brinjal
C. Virus-resistant cotton D. None of the above

12. Genetically modified tomatoes were sold in the U.S. for the first time in the year

A. 1994 B. 1971
C. 1991 D. 1930

13. The term totipotency means

A. The capability of a cell to form an individual plant
B. The capability of a cell to form an individual cell
C. Both A and B
D. None of the above

14. Father of plant tissue culture is

A. Duhamel du Monceau B. Morgan, T.H
C. Haberlandt D. Rechinger

15. The embryo culture was first demonstrated by
    A. Robbins
    B. Harrison
    C. Liabach
    D. Kotte
16. Father of micropropagation is
    A. Ball
    B. Harrison
    C. Robbins
    D. Kotte
17. _____ initiated studies on crown gall and tumour formation in plants
    A. White
    B. Braun
    C. Both A and B
    D. None of the above
18. Who demonstrated that virus free plants can be recovered from infected plants through shoot meristem culture?
    A. Morel
    B. Martin
    C. Both A and B
    D. None of the above
19. Anther culture was discovered by
    A. Guha
    B. Maheshwari
    C. Both A and B
    D. None of the above
20. The concept of developmental stages in cultures *in vitro* culture was developed by
    A. Murashige
    B. Skoog
    C. Both A and B
    D. Guha
21. The basic requirements for successful genetic engineering are
    A. Restriction enzymes
    B. Cloning vehicles (vectors)
    C. Detection and selection of cloned genes
    D. All the above
22. Post-zygotic barriers to hybridization are
    A. Failure of pollen to germinate
    B. Poor pollen tube growth
    C. Lack of endosperm development
    D. Failure of stigma to germinate
23. Pre-zygotic barriers to hybridization can be overcome by
    A. *In vitro* fertilization
    B. Embryo culture
    C. Ovule culture
    D. Pod culture

24. Cell differentiation in plants is

A. Irreversible B. Reversible

C. Both A and B D. None of the above

25. The inherent potentiality of a plant cell to give rise to a whole plant is described as

A. Cellular totipotency B. Morphogenesis

C. Organogenesis D. None of the above

26. For a differentiated cell to express its totipotency, it should undergo

A. Dedifferentiation B. Redifferentiation

C. Both A and B D. None of the above

27. The phenomenon of morphogenesis depends on the factors like

A. Polarity B. Differentiation

C. Regeneration of individual cells D. All the above

28. The relatively high level of auxin to cytokinin favoured _________ during organogenesis

A. Root formation B. Shoot formation

C. Both root and shoot formation D. Leaves formation

29. The relatively high level of cytokinin to auxin favoured _________ during organogenesis.

A. Root formation B. Shoot formation

C. Both root and shoot formation D. Leaves formation

30. The genesis of shoot from the explants or calli is termed as

A. Caulogenesis B. Rhizogenesis

C. Organogenesis D. None of the above

31. The somatic embryogenesis was first observed by

A. Steward B. Skoog

C. Reinert D. None of the above

32. The various theories of somatic embryogenesis are

A. Cell isolation theory

B. Differentiation theory

C. Intercellular communication and cytodifferentiation theory

D. All the above

33. _____ is used most successfully to obtain rapid growth of somatic embryos into plants.

A. Auxin B. Cytokinin

C. Gibberellic acid D. None of the above

34. The mineral solution widely used by early investigators was

A. Knop's medium B. MS medium

C. White's medium D. None of the above

35. The medium in tissue culture should provide

A. Nutrients for the survival of the plant cells, tissues and organs under culture

B. Optimal physical condition of pH, osmotic pressure, etc

C. Both A and B

D. None of the above

36. The systematic study of mineral requirements of plant tissue and organs in culture was made by

A. Murashige and Skoog B. Vasil and Hildebrant

C. Nitsch and Nitsch D. All the above

37. The mineral nutrient that plays a vital role in growth and differentiation of cultured tissues is

A. N B. P

C. K D. S

38. Nitrogen is generally supplied in _____ form.

A. NH4 B. NO_3

C. NO_2 D. NH3

39. The optimum concentration of K needed is

A. 2 mM B. 20 mM

C. 200 mM D. 0.2 mM

40. At low nitrogen concentration, presence of _____ element enhances the formation of somatic embryos.

A. K B. P

C. Ca D. Mg

41. Sulphur is provided in the form of

A. Sulphates B. Sulphites

C. Both A and B D. Sulphides

42. The standard carbon source is

A. Sucrose B. Glucose

C. Fructose D. Galactose

43. Universally required vitamin in tissue culture medium is

A. Thiamine HCl B. Pyridoxine HCl

C. Nicotinic acid D. Calcium pantothanate

44. Vitamin (s) used in tissue culture medium is/are

A. Calcium pantothanate B. Pyridoxine HCl

C. Nicotinic acid D. All the above

45. The commonly used auxins in tissue culture are

A. IAA, IBA, NAA, 2,4 D B. BAP, 2-iP, Kinetin, Zeatin

C. GA_3 D. Kinetin, Zeatin

46. The cytokinins are diluted in

A. HCl B. NaOH

C. Both A and B D. H_2SO_4

47. High auxin and low cytokinin ratio favours

A. Initialize root formation, embryogenesis and callus formation

B. Induce formation of adventitive or axillary shoots

C. Chloroplast formation and other processes

D. None of the above

48. The naturally occurring gibberellin is involved in

A. Internode elongation

B. Enhancement of flower, fruit and leaf size

C. Germination and vernalization

D. All the above

49. The gibberellins are soluble in

A. Diluted HCl B. NaOH

C. Cold water D. Hot water

50. Ethylene is involved in

A. Fruit maturation B. Abscission

C. Senescence D. All the above

51. _________ promotes ethylene biosynthesis and epinasty.

A. Brassinosteroids B. Jasmonates

C. Polyamines D. Salicyclic acid

52. Jasmonic acid is a
    A. Methyl ester
    B. Ethyl ester
    C. Ether
    D. Diphenyl ether
53. Abnormal structures developed during organogenesis are called
    A. Organoids
    B. Meristemoids
    C. Both A and B
    D. None of the above
54. Embryo culture is used for
    A. Overcome embryo abortion due to incompatibility barriers
    B. Overcome seed dormancy and selfsterility of seeds
    C. Embryo rescue in distant hybridisation
    D. All the above
55. Total number of stages in micro propagation is
    A. 3
    B. 4
    C. 5
    D. 6
56. The suitable explant for producing virus free plant is
    A. Shoot tip
    B. Leaf bit
    C. Stem bit
    D. None of the above
57. The crucial stage in tissue culture is
    A. Preparative stage
    B. Initiation of culture
    C. Multiplication
    D. Rooting of shoots
58. The oxidation of phenolic compounds leached out from the cut surface of the explant in tissue culture leads to
    A. Browning of the medium
    B. Blackening of the medium
    C. Whitening of the medium
    D. None of the above
59. Ovule culture is first attempted in
    A. Orchidaceae
    B. Fabaceae
    C. Malvaceae
    D. Cruciferae
60. The growth hormone not used in embryo culture medium is
    A. Auxin
    B. Gibberellin
    C. Cytokinin
    D. ethylene
61. The success of embryo culture depends on
    A. Developmental stage of the embryo at isolation
    B. Growth conditions of the mother plant

C. Composition of the nutrient medium

D. All the above

62. *In vitro* fertilization can take place through

A. Stigma fertilization

B. Placental fertilization

C. Fertilization of an isolated ovule without a placenta

D. All the above

63. Endosperm culture is successful in

A. Euphorbiaceae B. Santalaceae

C. Loranthaceae D. All the above

64. Cryopreservation involves the usage of

A. Solid carbon dioxide (-79^{0}C). B. Vapour nitrogen (-150^{0}C).

C. Liquid nitrogen (-196^{0}C). D. All the above

65. The benefits of micropropagation are

A. Rapid multiplication of superior clones

B. Multiplication of disease free plants

C. Cost effective process

D. All the above

66. Dimethyl sulfoxide is used as _____ in tissue culture.

A. Cryoprotectant B. Growth regulator

C. Osmaticum D. None of the above

67. Ono is a somaclonal variety of

A. Sugarcane B. Geranium

C. Alfa alfa D. Citronella

68. Limitation(s) of somaclonal variation is/are

A. Applicable only to those species which regenerate complete plants out of cell cultures

B. Reduced or no regeneration potential

C. Undesirable features like reduced fertility, growth and even overall performance

D. All the above

69. Synthetic seeds are of _____ types

A. Hydrated B. Desiccated

C. Both A and B D. None of the above

70. Gels used for synthetic seed production includes

A. Carrageenan and gelrite B. Gibberellic acid

C. Guargum D. Both A and C

71. Incorporation of activated charcoal in synthetic seed coating improves

A. Conversion and vigour of the encapsulated somatic embryos

B. Increases respiration of somatic embryos

C. Retains nutrients within the hydrogel capsule and slowly releases them to the growing embryo

D. All the above

72. The protoplast isolation by enzymatic method was demonstrated by

A. E.C. Cocking B. Klecker

C. Takebe D. None of the above

73. The most widely used osmotica for protoplast isolation is/are

A. Sorbitol B. Mannitol

C. Both A and B D. None of the above

74. For protoplast fusion, _____ is/are used

A. $NaNO_3$ B. High pH and high Ca^{2+}

C. PEG D. All the above

75. The first report of plant regeneration from isolated protoplasts was from

A. *Nicotiana tabacum* B. *Petunia hybrida*

C. *Zea mays* D. *Sorghum halepense*

76. The somatic hybridisation is used

A. Genetic recombination in asexual or sterile plants

B. Overcoming barriers of sexual incompatibility

C. Both A and B

D. None of the above

77. The first somatic hybrids are produced in

A. *Datura innoxia* B. *Nicotiana repanda*

C. *N. nesophila* D. *N. stockonii*

78. The essential steps in rDNA technology is

A. 4 B. 5

C. 2 D. 7

79. In cDNA synthesis, the eukaryotic _________ is used as a template to generate DNA A.

A. mRNA B. tRNA

C. rRNA D. None of the above

80. The tool for joining DNA molecules is/are

A. Restriction endonucleases B. Ligases

C. Both A and B D. Cleaving enzymes

81. The rDNA technology is used for

A. Gene cloning

B. Creation of transgenic plants and animals

C. DNA sequencing

D. All the above

82. Nucleases act on

A. DNA B. RNA

C. Both A and B D. None of the above

83. The enzymes used in rDNA technology include with star activity is/are

A. Kinase B. Phosphatase

C. Reverse transcriptase D. All the above

84. Plasmids containing phage cos sites are known as

A. Cosmids B. Phasmids

C. Both A and B D. None of the above

85. Yeast artificial chromosomes (YAC) are

A. The largest of the cloning vectors

B. Cloning limit of 100-1000 kb

C. Very low efficiency

D. All the above

86. __________ enzymes unite DNA segments

A. Restriction enzymes B. DNA ligase

C. Nuclease D. None of the above

87. Cloning is mainly used for
   A. Large scale protein production B. Gene therapy
   C. Both A and B D. None of the above
88. Taq polymerase is
   A. Thermostable B. Thermounstable
   C. Thermoliable D. Thermo sensitive
89. The larger the plasmid, __________ is the efficiency with which it is taken up by cells.
   A. Lower B. Higher
   C. Medium D. Constant
90. The natural genetic engineer is
   A. *Agrobacterium tumefaciens* B. *Bacillus subtilis*
   C. *Escherichia coli* D. *Bacillus* sp.
91. T-DNA region of Ti plasmids is
   A. Region A B. Region B
   C. Region C D. Region D
92. The optimum concentration of PEG for DNA transfer is
   A. 15-25% B. 30-40%
   C. 10% D. None of the above
93. Flavr-Savr™ is the GM variety of
   A. Tomato B. Potato
   C. Soyabean D. Aonla
94. Flavr-Savr™, the GM variety of tomato has _____ property
   A. Delayed ripening B. Resistance to fruit borer
   C. Resistant to leaf miner D. Resistance to fungal growth
95. Immunoblot is the other name of
   A. Northern blot B. Southern blot
   C. Western blot D. Eastern blot
96. Eastern blot is a method used to check for the presence of
   A. DNA
   B. RNA
   C. Protein
   D. Protein post translational modification

97. The technique in which nucleic acids or proteins are immobilized onto a solid support is called as

A. Blotting
B. Hybridisation
C. Immobilization
D. Mobilization

98. The phage vectors that contain single site for the insertion of foreign DNA are designated as

A. Insertional vectors
B. Replacement vectors
C. Both A and B
D. Instituional vectors

99. Plasmids capable of promoting their own transfer to a wide range of host are called as

A. Degradative plasmids
B. Cryptic plasmids
C. Stringent plasmids
D. Promiscuous plasmids

100. Relaxed plasmids are also called as

A. High copy number plasmids
B. Stringent plasmids
C. Low copy number plasmids
D. Promiscuous plasmids

101. Plasmids are grouped into __________ major types

A. 2
B. 3
C. 4
D. 5

102. DNA ligase joins the DNA molecule covalently by catalysing the formation of __________ bonds between adjacent nucleotides.

A. Phosphodiester
B. Phosphotriester
C. Both A and B
D. Phosphoester

103. The group of enzymes used in rDNA technology which cleave or cut the genetic material

A. Nucleases
B. DNA ligase
C. Ligase
D. Both B and C

104. The restriction enzymes used abundantly in rDNA technology is

A. Type I
B. Type II
C. Type III
D. Any one of these

105. Varuna is a somaclonal variety of

A. Sugarcane
B. Geranium
C. *Brassica juncea*
D. Citronella

106. Cryopreservation of tissue culture materials in liquid nitrogen is at
A. $-196\,^{0}$ C B. $-190\,^{0}$ C
C. $-96\,^{0}$ C D. $-90\,^{0}$ C

107. The enzyme used in enzymatic method for protoplast isolation is
A. Cellulase B. Pectinase
C. Both A and B D. Nuclease

108. The culturing of single protoplast in liquid media is done by
A. Drop culture method B. Micro chamber culture
C. Multiple drop array technique D. Micro droplet cultures

109. The sonication method was introduced by
A. Crossway and Reich B. Fromm
C. Klein D. Xu

110. Pomato is somatic of
A. Poppy and potato B. Poppy and tamarind
C. Potato and tomato D. Poppy and tomato

111. Preserving germplasm in frozen state is
A. Cryopreservation B. *In-situ* preservation
C. Cold storage D. Vernalisation

112. Disease free plants in micropropagation can be obtained through
A. Meristem culture B. Anther culture
C. Embryo culture D. Cell culture

113. Hairy roots induced *in vitro* by the infection of *Agrobacterium rhizogenes*, are characterized by
A. High degree of lateral branching B. Genetic instability of culture
C. Presence of geotropism D. Poor biomass production

114. In callus culture, roots can be induced by the supply of
A. Auxin and no cytokinin
B. High auxin and low cytokinin
C. High cytokinin and low auxin
D. Auxin and cytokinin equal proportion

115. Plant medium used widely in preparation of culture medium is got from
A. *Cycas revoluta* B. *Cocos nucifera*
C. *Pinus roxburghii* D. *Borassus flabellifer*

116. Flavr savr variety of tomato remains fresh for long because it
   A. Has little polygalacturonase
   B. Abundant polygalacturonase
   C. Has gene for antibiotic resistance
   D. Lacks amylase
117. A major use of embryo culture is in
   A. Clonal propagation
   B. Overcoming hybridization barrier
   C. Production of alkaloids
   D. Introduction of somaclonal variation
118. Tiny fat bubbles used to deliver genes are
   A. Electropores B. Cholesterols
   C. Phospholipids D. Liposomes
119. A true transgenic organisms must carry the transgene in
   A. Every cell B. Somatic cells only
   C. Gametes only D. The cell that originally gets it
120. Transgenic pharming involves using __________ to produce recombinant proteins in
   A. Cows milk B. Bacteria, culture media
   C. Phage, bacteria D. Fungi, culture media
121. Bt toxin producing plants are resistant to
   A. Brown plant hopper B. Round worm
   C. Gall midge D. Pink boll worm
122. Which of the following is not a cloning vector
   A. Helicase B. SV40
   C. PBR322 D. *Escherichia coli* genomic DNA

Answer keys

1	A	26	C	51	A	76	C	101	A
2	D	27	D	52	A	77	A	102	A
3	A	28	A	53	A	78	A	103	A
4	A	29	B	54	D	79	A	104	B

5	D	30	A	55	C	80	B	105	C
6	D	31	A	56	A	81	D	106	A
7	A	32	D	57	C	82	C	107	C
8	C	33	C	58	A	83	D	108	D
9	A	34	A	59	A	84	A	109	D
10	A	35	C	60	A	85	D	110	C
11	A	36	D	61	D	86	B	111	A
12	A	37	A	62	D	87	C	112	A
13	A	38	A	63	D	88	A	113	A
14	C	39	B	64	C	89	A	114	B
15	C	40	A	65	D	90	A	115	B
16	A	41	A	66	A	91	A	116	A
17	C	42	A	67	A	92	A	117	B
18	C	43	A	68	D	93	A	118	D
19	C	44	D	69	C	94	A	119	A
20	A	45	A	70	D	95	C	120	A
21	D	46	C	71	B	96	D	121	D
22	C	47	A	72	A	97	A	122	A
23	A	48	D	73	C	98	A		
24	B	49	C	74	D	99	D		
25	B	50	D	75	A	100	A		

UNIT XI: ENVIRONMENTAL SCIENCE

1

Importance of Environmental Science and Natural Resources

I. Choose the correct answer

1. Salim Ali Centre for Ornithology and Natural history is located at

   A. Pune B. Hyderabad

   C. Kerala D. Coimbatore

2. Who wrote the book Violence of Green Revolution

   A. Vandana Siva B. Sheila Dikshit

   C. Maneka Gandhi D. Arundhathi Roy

3. The biggest award for environmental activities in India is given in the name of an individual. In whose name is it constituted?

   A. Lal Bahadur Shastri B. Morarji Desai

   C. Indira Gandhi D. Kamaraj

4. Expand GIS

   A. Geographical Information System

   B. Geographical Information Source

   C. Geological Information System

   D. Geological Index System

5. MoEF means

   A. Ministry of Energy and Forest

   B. Ministry of Environment and Forests

   C. Ministry of Energy and Fuel

   D. Management of Environment and Forestry

6. Zoological Survey of India is at

   A. Delhi B. Mumbai

   C. Kolkata D. Chennai

7. World Forest day is celebrated on

A. 21st March B. 5th June

C. 1st December D. 7th June

8. The book Silent Spring was written by

A. Madhav Gadgil B. Anil Agarwal

C. Rachel Carson D. E.O.Wilson

9. The Salim Ali Bird Sanctuary is located at

A. Pondicherry B. Thattekad

C. Anakkatti D. Kalakkad

10. Who among the following is commonly called Bird Man of India?

A. Salim Ali B. M.S. Swaminathan

C. M.C. Mehta D. Raphel Emerson

11. What is UNCED?

A. United Nations Conference on Education Development

B. United Nations Conference on Environmental Day

C. United Nations Conference on Environment and Development

D. None of these

12. Earth provides enough to satisfy every man's need, but not for every man's greed words by

A. Tagore B. Gandhiji

C. Nehru D. None

13. All forms of water that comes down on earth, including rain, snow, hail etc., is known as

A. Calcification B. Fixation

C. Precipitation D. Accumulation

14. The ocean covers________ percentage of earth's surface.

A. 51% B. 61%

C. 71% D. 91%

15. Green revolution is associated with

A. Sericulture B. Agriculture

C. Fish culture D. Silviculture

16. The components of LPG are
    A. Methane and Hexane B. Propane and Butane
    C. Ethane and Methane D. Propane and Ethane
17. The portion of the earth and its environment which can support life is known as
    A. Crust B. Biosphere
    C. Exosphere D. Atmosphere
18. What is troposphere?
    A. Portion of air
    B. Portion of water
    C. Lowest layer of atmosphere where we survive
    D. Portion of sky
19. The main energy source for the environment is
    A. Solar energy B. Chemical energy
    C. Bioelectric energy D. Electrical energy
20. Which gas is likely to be reduced in the atmosphere by deforestation?
    A. Carbon dioxide B. Nitrogen
    C. Oxygen D. Sulphur dioxide
21. What are rodenticides?
    A. That kill fishes B. That kill insects
    C. That kill rats D. That kill crocos
22. Which of the following is the most responsible for world water crisis?
    A. Dams B. Floods
    C. Drought D. Population growth
23. The resources that can be replaced by natural ecological cycle is called
    A. Renewable B. Non-renewable
    C. Exhaustible D. Natural
24. The amount of solar radiation reaching the surface of the earth is called
    A. Solar flux B. Reflected light
    C. Minerals D. Solvents
25. The most harmful of ultraviolet radiations are
    A. UV-C B. UV-B
    C. UV-A D. All the above

26. Grassland of USA is referred to as
    A. Prairies B. Steppes
    C. Pampas D. Veldts
27. Extensive planting of trees to increase forest cover is called
    A. Afforestation B. Agroforestry
    C. Deforestation D. Social forestry
28. Soil erosion can be prevented by
    A. Deforestation B. Afforestation
    C. Overgrazing D. Removal of vegetation
29. A renewable source of energy is
    A. Petroleum B. Coal
    C. Nuclear fuel D. Trees
30. Smog is a mixture of
    A. Smoke and fog B. Snow and fog
    C. Snow and dust D. Sulphur dioxide and fog
31. Moisture in the air is known as
    A. Water B. Fog
    C. Snow D. Humidity
32. The capacity to do work is termed as
    A. Power B. Force
    C. Strength D. Energy
33. Ozone layer is present in
    A. Troposphere B. Stratosphere
    C. Mesosphere D. Ionosphere
34. Ozone umbrella is located in which layer of atmosphere
    A. Troposphere B. Stratosphere
    C. Mesosphere D. Ionosphere
35. The unit of total water content of the soil is known as
    A. Holard B. Chraserd
    C. Echard D. All of the above
36. Pedology
    A. Study of water B. Study of air
    C. Study of soil D. None

37. What is deforestation?
    A. Product of forest B. Destruction of forest
    C. Forest Protection D. None
38. Deforestation generally decreases
    A. Global Warming B. Drought
    C. Soil erosion D. Rainfall
39. Which among the following result in the formation of soil?
    A. Radiation B. Weathering
    C. Erosion D. Pollution
40. Mulching helps in
    A. Soil fertility B. Moisture conservation
    C. Improvements soil structure D. Soil sterility
41. Atmospheric humidity is measured by
    A. Auxanometer B. Photometer
    C. Hygrometer D. None
42. Which of the following is a disadvantage of renewable energy?
    A. High pollution B. Available only in few places
    C. High running cost D. Unreliable supply
43. A solar cell is an electrical device that converts the energy of light directly into electricity by the
    A. Photovoltaic effect B. Chemical effect
    C. Atmospheric effect D. Physical effect
44. In hydroelectric power, what is necessary for the production of power throughout the year?
    A. Dams filled with water B. High amount of air
    C. High intense sunlight D. Nuclear power
45. The main composition of biogas is
    A. Methane B. Carbon dioxide
    C. Nitrogen D. Hydrogen
46. Which Ministry is mainly responsible for research and development in renewable energy sources such as wind power, small hydro, biogas and solar power?
    A. Human Resource Development
    B. Agriculture and Farmers Welfare

C. Ministry of New and Renewable Energy

D. Health and Family Welfare

47. Which among the following have a large amount of installed grid interactive renewable power capacity in India?

A. Wind power B. Solar power

C. Biomass power D. Small Hydro power

48. The world's first 100% solar powered airport is located at

A. Cochin, Kerala B. Bengaluru, Karnataka

C. Chennai, Tamil Nadu D. Mumbai, Maharashtra

49. Which of the following is not under the Ministry of New and Renewable Energy?

A. Wind energy B. Solar energy

C. Tidal energy D. Large hydro

50. Where is the largest wind farm located in India?

A. Jaisalmer Wind Park, Rajasthan

B. Muppandal Wind Farm, Tamil Nadu

C. Vaspet Wind Farm, Maharashtra

D. Chakala Wind Farm, Maharashtra

51. Which Indian enterprise has the motto "ENERGY FOREVER"?

A. Indian Renewable Energy Development Agency

B. Indian Non-Renewable Energy Development

C. Indian Agricultural Development

D. Indian Biotechnology Development

52. Which of the below theory is related to non-renewable resources?

A. Game theory B. Phlogiston theory

C. Big Bang theory D. Hotelling's theory

53. The primary composition of coal is

A. Nitrogen B. Carbon

C. Oxygen D. Hydrogen

54. Which Ministry is mainly responsible for refining, distribution, import, export of petroleum products and natural gas in India?

A. Ministry of Petroleum and Natural Gas

B. Ministry of Fossil Fuel

C. Ministry of Non-Renewable Energy

D. Ministry of Oil

55. The most abundantly available fossil fuel in India is

A. Coal B. Natural Gas

C. Petroleum D. Oil

56. Which of the following non-renewable energy is not classified under a fossil fuel?

A. Nuclear B. Petroleum

C. Oil D. Natural gas

57. The major non-renewable energy usage in India is

A. Coal B. Petroleum and other liquids

C. Natural gas D. Nuclear

58. How many Nuclear power stations are there in India?

A. 5 B. 6

C. 7 D. 8

59. Which is the first state in India to make roof top rain water harvesting compulsory to all the houses?

A. Tamil Nadu B. Kerala

C. Assam D. Goa

60. The name given to the diversion channels of the western Himalayas is

A. Phalodi B. Johads

C. Guls or Kuls D. Khadins

61. What is Palar pani?

A. Spring B. Milk

C. River water D. Rain water

62. Which of the following is the major source of fresh water which is available in India?

A. Ocean water B. River water

C. Pond water D. Ground water

63. Narmada Bachao Andolan is related to

A. Tehri B. Bhakra Nangal

C. Sardar Sarovar D. Rihand

64. Which planet is also known as blue planet?

A. Mercury B. Venus

C. Earth D. Mars

65. The rank of India in terms of water availability per person p.a in the world is

A. 130th B. 131st

C. 132nd D. 133rd

66. Ground water is accessed by

A. Drilling wells B. Drip irrigation

C. Check bunds D. Constructing canals

67. Energy in the form of heat and light is obtained by

A. Biomass B. Fossil fuels

C. Sun D. Wind

68. Which among the following is not a conventional source of energy?

A. Solar energy B. Coal

C. Hydro power D. Petroleum

69. India receives _______ amount of solar radiation/sq.m

A. 1-2 kWh B. 3-5 kWh

C. 4-7 kWh D. 8-10 kWh

70. What is the value of solar constant _______ per square cycle?

A. 1.366 kilowatt B. 1.02 killowatt

C. 1.25 killowatt D. 1.425 killowatt

71. What is the mean annual wind speed of the world?

A. 1 - 2 m/s B. 3 – 4 m/s

C. 4 - 5 m/s D. 6 – 7 m/s

72. When did Wildlife (protection) Act enacted?

A. 1952 B. 1976

C. 1972 D. 1987

73. India's first biosphere reserve came into existence in

A. 1988 B. 1989

C. 1986 D. 1987

Answer keys

1	D	16	B	31	D	46	C	61	D
2	A	17	B	32	D	47	A	62	D
3	C	18	C	33	B	48	A	63	C
4	A	19	B	34	B	49	D	64	C
5	B	20	C	35	A	50	B	65	D
6	B	21	C	36	C	51	A	66	A
7	A	22	C	37	B	52	D	67	C
8	C	23	A	38	D	53	B	68	A
9	B	24	A	39	B	54	A	69	C
10	A	25	A	40	B	55	A	70	A
11	C	26	A	41	C	56	A	71	C
12	B	27	A	42	D	57	A	72	C
13	C	28	B	43	A	58	C	73	C
14	C	29	B	44	A	59	A		
15	B	30	A	45	A	60	C		

2

Ecosystem and Biodiversity

I. Choose the correct answer

1. The phenomenon of occurrence of additional species found in the ecotone or transitional zone between adjoining ecosystems is known as

   A. Edge effect B. Root effect

   C. Raman effect D. Coolidge effect

2. The complex network of interconnected food chains is called

   A. Trophic level B. Food web

   C. Ecological pyramid D. Ecology chain

3. The area to which a species is biologically adapted to live is known as

   A. Niche B. Habitat

   C. Succession D. Community

4. The largest brackish water lake situated in Asia is in Orissa. Which is the lake?

   A. Chilka lake B. Vembanad lake

   C. Woolar lake D. Dal lake

5. Ramsar convention refers to the conservation of

   A. Deserts B. Wetlands

   C. Agriculture lands D. Forest land

6. The animal which consumes decaying organic matter is

   A. Carnivore B. Detritivore

   C. Herbivore D. Producers

7. A set of organisms that resemble one another in appearance and behaviour is called as

   A. Exons B. Prions

   C. Species D. Guilds

8. An ecosystem gradually merges with an adjoining one through a transitional zone is called as
   A. Ecological niche B. Ecological footprint
   C. Ecotone D. Shore effect
9. The primary consumers are also called as
   A. Herbivores B. Carnivores
   C. Enzymes D. None of these
10. All the genes of a population is called
   A. Gene pool B. Genome
   C. Gene bunch D. Gene population
11. Favorable morphological and physiological response to a change in environment is called
   A. Preadaptation B. Ecotyping
   C. Formation of ecophenes D. Acclimatization
12. Plants adapted to open, sunny habitats are
   A. Sciophytes B. Heliophytes
   C. Mesophytes D. Epiphytes
13. Study of inter-relationship between organisms and their environment is
   A. Ecology B. Ecosystem
   C. Phytogeography D. Ethology
14. Which one is nature's cleaner?
   A. Consumers B. Producers
   C. Decomposers and Scavengers D. Symbionts
15. The relationship between nitrogen fixing bacteria and leguminous plants is an example for
   A. Parasitism B. Predation
   C. Mutualism D. Commensalism
16. The species that flowers is called as
   A. Gymnosperms B. Bryophytes
   C. Angiosperms D. Algae
17. _____ is an example of bottom feeders .
   A. Cat fish B. Frog
   C. Snake D. Tadpole

18. A hawk that eats a frog is a
    A. Producer
    B. Primary consumer
    C. Secondary consumer
    D. Tertiary consumer
19. An example of lotic system
    A. Pond
    B. River
    C. Lake
    D. Reservoir
20. The word Biophilia was coined by
    A. Dr. Hackel
    B. Dr.Johansson
    C. Dr. Benjamin
    D. E. O. Wilson
21. Lotic ecosystem refers to
    A. Static water system
    B. Ecosystem of flowing water
    C. Ecosystem of estuaries
    D. Deep marine water system
22. Autotrophs are
    A. Consumers
    B. Herbivores
    C. Saprophytes
    D. Producers
23. Organisms which depended on producers for nutrition are called
    A. Autotrophs
    B. Saprophytes
    C. Consumers
    D. Xerophytes
24. The source of atmospheric oxygen is
    A. Nitrogen cycle
    B. Green plants
    C. Water
    D. Carbon cycle
25. Plants which grow in shade are called
    A. Sciophytes
    B. Heliophytes
    C. Oxylophytes
    D. Epiphytes
26. The term ecology was coined by
    A. A.G.Tansley
    B. Ernst Haeckel
    C. Aristotle
    D. Linnaeus
27. Photosynthesis is found in
    A. Producers
    B. Decomposers
    C. Consumers
    D. Scavengers
28. Phytoplankton are
    A. Producers of forest
    B. Producers of lakes
    C. Consumers of ocean
    D. Omnivores

29. Gas released during photosynthesis is
    A. Methane B. Nitrogen
    C. Oxygen D. Carbon dioxide
30. Ecology is
    A. The science that studies the evolution of life
    B. Integrates both social and natural sciences to help us understand how the earth works
    C. The study of the relationships between organisms and their environment
    D. The study of the environment in the absence of humans
31. An example of an abiotic component
    A. Plants B. Soil
    C. Animals D. Bacteria
32. The term 'Eco' implies
    A. Environment B. Ecotone
    C. Ecotourism D. Soil
33. The major reservoir of carbon is
    A. The atmosphere B. Ocean bed
    C. Plant and animals D. Rock
34. Plants which grow in light are called
    A. Sciophytes B. Heliophytes
    C. Oxylophytes D. Epiphytes
35. The simplest aquatic ecosystem can be seen in a
    A. River B. Lake
    C. Pond D. Water Tank
36. What is hibernation and aestivation?
    A. Thermal adaptation shown by animals
    B. Wind adaptation shown by animals
    C. Adaptation of animals to escape from predators
    D. None
37. What is symbiosis?
    A. Study of distribution of related species
    B. Association between members of same species
    C. Association between members of two species
    D. None

38. What is edge species?
    A. The species which occur abundantly in the ecotone
    B. Species on the verge of extinction
    C. Rare species
    D. Endemic species
39. What is lentic habitat ?
    A. Running water habitat B. Standing or still water habitat
    C. Marine habitat D. None
40. What is lotic habitat?
    A. Standing or still water habitat B. Marine habitat
    C. Running water habitat D. Stagnant water
41. What is Plankton?
    A. Microscopic floating organisms – Plants and animals.
    B. Bottom dwelling aquatic organisms
    C. Large plants in water
    D. None
42. The inherent ability of organisms to reproduce and multiply is called as
    A. C value B. Biotic potential
    C. Carrying capacity D. K value
43. North American grassland are called
    A. Pampas B. Prairies
    C. Savannah D. None
44. African grasslands are called
    A. Prairies B. Pampas
    C. Savannah D. None
45. What is desertification?
    A. Conversion of forests into desert
    B. Conversion of croplands into desert
    C. Conversion of grassland into desert
    D. All of the above
46. The first trophic level in a food chain
    A. Green plants B. Herbivores
    C. Carnivores D. Bacteria

47. Sulphur bacteria are examples of

A. Carnivores
B. Heterotrophs
C. Saprophytes
D. Autotrophs

48. Which is an example for sedimentary biogeochemical cycle

A. Oxygen cycle
B. Nitrogen cycle
C. Water cycle
D. Phosphorus cycle

49. Green land biome

A. Tundra
B. Pampas
C. Taiga
D. Thaar

50. Rain during November is more acidic than monsoon rain due to

A. Dissolved CO_2
B. Dissolved SO_2
C. Dissolved NO_2
D. None of the above

51. What is Dendrology?

A. Study of plants
B. Study of butterflies
C. Study of trees
D. None of these

52. An example of one way ecological cycle is

A. Carbon dioxide cycle
B. Water cycle
C. Energy cycle
D. Oxygen cycle

53. What is deep ecology?

A. Protecting nature for its own sake
B. Ecology of deep sea
C. Ecology of forest
D. Ecology of caves

54. The first protected area in India is

A. Silent Valley
B. Corbett National Park
C. Bandipur sanctuary
D. Nagarhole

55. The Indian Parliament passed the Biodiversity bill in the year

A. 2000
B. 2005
C. 2002
D. 2007

56. Which chemical was responsible for Bhopal gas tragedy?

A. Methyl isocyanate
B. Benzene hexachloride
C. Tri nitro toluene
D. Both B and C

57. The destruction of habitat of plants and animals is called
    A. Endemism B. Endangered species
    C. Habitat loss D. Flood
58. Zoos are examples for
    A. *In situ* conservation B. *In vivo* conservation
    C. *Ex situ* conservation D. *Ex vivo* conservation
59. In which Indian state is Corbett National park located
    A. Madhya Pradesh B. Uttarakhand
    C. Kerala D. Tamil Nadu
60. The first national park of Kerala
    A. Aralam B. Kottayam
    C. Idukki D. Iravikulam
61. In which year was Project Tiger launched?
    A. 1973 B. 1964
    C. 1998 D. 1970
62. Earth summit of Rio de Janeiro (1992) resulted in
    A. Compilation of Red list
    B. Establishment of biosphere reserves
    C. Conservation of Biodiversity
    D. IUCN
63. India is primary centre of domestication of
    A. Sheep B. Goat
    C. Water buffalo D. Elephants
64. Lions are found in
    A. Western Ghats B. Corbett National Park
    C. Forests of Madhya Pradesh D. Gir forests
65. National Park associated with rhinoceros is
    A. Kaziranga B. Ranthambore
    C. Corbett D. Valley of flowers
66. Some species of plants and animals are extremely rare and may occur only at a few locations are called
    A. Endemic B. Endangered
    C. Vulnerable D. Threatened

67. The only known breeding colony of the greater and lesser Flamingos in our country is seen in desert.

A. The Great Rann of Kutch B. The Thar

C. Ladakh D. Atacama

68. The drug morphine is extracted from _____ plant.

A. Cocoa B. Belladonna

C. *Opium poppy* D. Tannin

69. Species is known as *Azadirachta indica.*

A. Neem B. Mango

C. Jackfruit D. Banana

70. Which tree is known as flame of the forest?

A. *Zizyphus* B. *Butea monosperma*

C. Jackfruit D. *Pongamia*

71. Which tree is known as Coral tree?

A. *Quercus* B. *Dipterocarps*

C. *Erythrina* D. *Zizypus*

72. Which plants die after flowering?

A. Lotus B. Bamboo

C. Chrysanthemum D. Butea

73. The one-horned Rhinoceros is now restricted to which state?

A. Maharashtra B. Gujarat

C. Assam D. Uttar Pradesh

74. Asiatic lion is found only in ....

A. Gir Forest B. Manas

C. Kasiranga D. Sundarbans

75. ______ is a marine tortoise which shows the unique phenomenon 'arribada'.

A. Olive Ridley B. Star Tortoise

C. Travancore Tortoise D. Both B and C

76. Largest reptile in the world

A. Dragon B. Anaconda

C. Crocodile D. Python

77. Snow leopard is found in which National Park?
    A. Kaziranga B. The Great Himalayan
    C. Bharatpur D. Nagarhole
78. Point Calimere sanctuary is situated in which state?
    A. Tamil Nadu B. Kerala
    C. Karnataka D. Gujarat
79. The movement 'Beej Bachao Andolan' was aimed for the conservation of
    A. Trees B. Shrubs
    C. Crops D. Coconut
80. The Red data book which lists endangered species is maintained by
    A. UNO B. WHO
    C. IUCN D. WWF
81. Which of the following is a biodiversity hot spot in India?
    A. Western Ghats B. Nandadevi
    C. Eastern Ghats D. Aravalli
82. First Biosphere reserve in India
    A. Nilgiri B. Agastyamalai
    C. Eravikulam D. Chinnar
83. Flag ship species of Choolannur sanctuary
    A. Tiger B. Peacock
    C. Elephant D. Rhino
84. Herpetology is a branch of science which deals with
    A. Aves B. Mammals
    C. Reptiles D. Fishes
85. Bears are usually hunted and killed for their
    A. Teeth B. Skin
    C. Gall bladder D. Nails
86. Coral reefs in India can be seen in
    A. Himalayan region B. Andaman and Nicobar Islands
    C. Uttar pradesh D. Maharashtra

87. Which of the following is an extinct species?
A. Tiger B. Lion
C. Dodo D. Ostrich

88. The only ape found in India
A. Gorilla B. Chimpanzee
C. Hoolock gibbon D. Oranguttan

89. Black Buck is a
A. Goat B. Deer
C. Butterfly D. Bird

90. Gharial is a
A. Crocodile B. Cobra
C. Tortoise D. Frog

91. ____ is one of the most endangered species of Indian birds
A. Bee eater B. Paradise fly catcher
C. Owl D. The great Indian bustard

92. Pangolins feed on
A. Ants B. Fruits
C. Leaves D. Roots

93. Many wild plant and animals are on the verge of extinction due to
A. Habitat destruction B. Climatic change
C. Non availability of food D. None of the above

94. The most endangered ecosystem in India
A. Shola forest ecosystem B. Evergreen forest ecosystem
C. Pond ecosystem D. Tundra Ecosystem

95. Eravikulam National Park conserves
A. Lion tailed macaque B. Tiger
C. Elephant D. Nilgiri Tahr

96. First National Park in India
A. Jim Corbertt National Park B. Bandipur National Park
C. Gir National Park D. Sunderbans National Park

97. Agastyamalai Biosphere reserve is in
A. Pathanamthitta B. Thiruvananthapuram
C. Idukki D. Wayanad

98. What is meant by *ex situ* conservation?

A. Conservation of a species by protecting its habitat along with all other species living there

B. Conservation of forest ecosystem

C. Conservation of a species outside its natural habitat

D. Conservation of plants.

99. Killing of animals disturbs

A. Good for ecosystem B. Good for man

C. The balance of nature D. None

100. The state which constituted green bench

A. Kerala B. Tamil Nadu

C. Assam D. Madhya Pradesh

101. The first global environmental protection treaty The Montreal Protocol was signed on Sept. 26.

A. 1985 B. 1990

C. 1981 D. 1987

102. Name the endangered animal which is protected in Rajamalai National Park

A. Chital B. Black buck

C. Nilgiri Tahr D. None

103. Animals and plants are best protected in

A. Zoos B. Botanical gardens

C. National parks D. Sanctuaries

104. The native place of redwood trees?

A. Australia B. Amazon

C. California D. Thailand

105. Biodiversity can be broadly classified into how many types?

A. 2 B. 5

C. 3 D. 4

106. Biodiversity is of importance as it offers

A. Stability of ecosystems B. Stability of atmosphere

C. Stability of species D. Stability of research

107. The loss in biodiversity is not attributed to
   A. Explosion in the human population
   B. Transforming earths surface
   C. Destruction of natural habitats
   D. Use of sustainable products
108. In how many ways, does the conservation of biodiversity work?
   A. 5 B. 2
   C. 3 D. 4
109. Which one of the following is not an *in situ* conservation method?
   A. Zoo B. National Parks
   C. Biosphere Reserves D. Sanctuaries
110. Which is an advantage of *ex situ* conservation?
   A. Cheap method
   B. Conserve large number of species together
   C. Genetic process for breeding/long life
   D. Existence in natural habitat
111. The area of National Parks range between
   A. 0.61 to 7818 kms B. 0.04 to 3162 kms
   C. 0.14 to 3612 kms D. 0.16 to 8718 kms
112. The activities of cultivation of land, timber harvesting is permitted in
   A. Sanctuaries B. National Parks
   C. Biosphere Reserves D. Protected Areas
113. Hot spot areas have
   A. Low density of biodiversity B. Only endangered plants
   C. High density of hot springs D. High density of biodiversity
114. Which one of the following is not a gaseous biogeochemical cycle in an ecosystem?
   A. Carbon cycle B. Phosphorous cycle
   C. Sulfur cycle D. Nitrogen cycle
115. Transfer of energy from source of plants through a series of organism is known as
   A. Food web B. Energy cycle
   C. Food chain D. Biological system

116. The type of ecosystem with the highest mean plant productivity is
A. Tundra
B. Temperate grassland
C. Desert
D. Tropical rain forest

117. An ecosystem which can be easily damaged, but can be recovered after some time, if damaging effect stops will be having
A. High stability and high resilience
B. High stability and low resilience
C. Low stability and low resilience
D. Low stability and high resilience

118. In ecosystem, standing crop refers to
A. All the green plants
B. All the non living materials
C. All living and dead animals
D. All the living materials both animals and plants

119. Which ecosystem produces the highest annual net primary productivity?
A. Tropical evergreen forest
B. Tropical rain forest
C. Tropical deciduous forest
D. Temperate evergreen forest

120. What flows through the ecosystem while matter cycles within them?
A. Energy
B. Force
C. Pressure
D. Wind

121. Total primary production in an ecosystem is known as
A. Gross final production
B. Gross primary production
C. Gross middle production
D. Net primary production

122. Which type of ecosystem accounts for most of the net primary productivity on earth even though it has a low average net primary productivity?
A. Tropical rain forest
B. Desert
C. Tropical evergreen forest
D. Oceans

123. Generally ecosystem consists of how many basic components?
A. One
B. Two
C. Three
D. Four

124. The three functional components interact with each other to form
A. Environmental succession
B. Environmental depression
C. Environmental system
D. Ecology

125. The dominant second tropic level in a lake ecosystem is
A. Phytoplankton
B. Zooplankton
C. Plankton
D. Benthos

126. What is called for the process of breaking down food to yield energy?
   A. Oxidation B. Photosynthesis
   C. Cellular respiration D. Decomposition
127. What are called for organisms which get energy by eating dead organisms?
   A. Decomposers B. Producers
   C. Consumers D. Herbivores
128. Which among the following is a product of photosynthesis?
   A. Glucose B. Carbon
   C. Monoxide D. Nitrogen
129. What is called for an organism that eats both plants and animals?
   A. Omnivore B. Carnivore
   C. Decomposers D. Herbivore
130. Why energy flow is linear in an ecosystem?
   A. Because it flows in air medium
   B. Because it is very particular
   C. Because ecosystem is linear
   D. Because energy flows from one trophic level to the next higher one
131. Flow of nutrients is
   A. Unidirectional B. Rectangular
   C. Cyclic D. Triangular
132. Why plants in forests do not make use of all the light energy available to them?
   A. Because plants do not require energy
   B. Because plants are grown only in the winter season
   C. Because of the absence of chlorophyll
   D. Because sunlight does not fall on the leaves fully
133. Which form of suns energy is trapped by the producers in the energy flow?
   A. Light energy B. Chemical energy
   C. Wind energy D. Pressure energy
134. How many percentage of energy transferred from one trophic level to the next higher level?
   A. 10% B. 20%
   C. 50% D. 100%

135. Into how many areas, the energy that is received by organisms during energy transfer is converted?

A. One B. Two

C. Three D. Four

136. ______ is the science deals with relationship between living organisms and their physical environment.

A. Ecology B. Ecosystem

C. Phyrogeography D. Ethology

137. Salt water comes under ______ type of environment .

A. Terrestrial environment B. Fresh water environment

C. Oceanic marine environment D. Oceanic region

138. ______ explains ecosystem behaviour from individual units.

A. Ecosystem ecology B. Population ecology

C. Marine ecology D. Terrestrial ecology

Answer keys

1	A	21	B	41	A	61	A	81	A	101	D	121	B
2	B	22	D	42	B	62	C	82	A	102	C	122	D
3	B	23	C	43	B	63	D	83	B	103	C	123	B
4	A	24	B	44	C	64	D	84	C	104	C	124	C
5	B	25	A	45	D	65	A	85	B	105	C	125	B
6	B	26	B	46	A	66	B	86	B	106	A	126	C
7	C	27	A	47	D	67	A	87	C	107	D	127	A
8	C	28	B	48	D	68	C	88	C	108	B	128	A
9	A	29	C	49	B	69	A	89	B	109	A	129	A
10	A	30	C	50	B	70	B	90	A	110	C	130	D
11	D	31	B	51	C	71	C	91	D	111	B	131	C
12	B	32	A	52	C	72	B	92	A	112	A	132	D
13	A	33	B	53	A	73	C	93	A	113	D	133	A
14	C	34	B	54	B	74	A	94	B	114	B	134	A
15	C	35	C	55	C	75	A	95	D	115	C	135	C
16	C	36	A	56	A	76	B	96	A	116	D	136	A
17	C	37	C	57	C	77	B	97	B	117	D	137	C
18	D	38	A	58	C	78	A	98	C	118	D	138	B
19	B	39	B	59	B	79	C	99	C	119	B		
20	D	40	C	60	D	80	C	100	B	120	A		

3

Pollution

I. Choose the correct answer

1. Ganga Action Plan in India was launched in the year

   A. 1988 B. 1985

   C. 1980 D. 1978

2. What is the name of the action plan for sustainable development in the twenty first century framed in the Rio Declaration on Environment & Development (1992)?

   A. Action 21 B. Agenda 21

   C. Rio 21 D. Declaration 21

3. The unit of measurement of intensity of sound is in

   A. Decibels B. Lux

   C. Parsec D. Candela

4. Enrichment of water body by nutrients like phosphorus and nitrogen is called

   A. Succession B. Eutrophication

   C. Stratification D. Climax vegetation

5. The worst nuclear accident happened to date is occurred at

   A. Chernobyl in 1986 B. Three Mile Power Plant in 1979

   C. Sellafield in 1957 D. Fukushima in 2011

6. Major cause of ozone depletion is due to which chemical?

   A. Chlorofluorocarbons B. Polyphenols

   C. Dioxins D. Rayon

7. The legally binding international agreement to reduce greenhouse gases by 5% in 2012 is

   A. Vienna convention B. Montreal Protocol

   C. Kyoto Protocol D. None of the above

8. Salinization is

A. Accumulation of salts in water B. Accumulation of salts in soil

C. Accumulation of salts in body D. Accumulation of salts in animals

9. What is oil slick?

A. Boiled oil B. Cooled oil

C. Thin film of oil in sea water D. Oil in deep sea

10. Cigarette smoking exposes one to

A. Sulphur dioxide B. Carbon dioxide

C. Nitrogen peroxide D. Carbon monoxide

11. Ozone hole is a

A. Hole in the atmosphere B. Destruction of ozone layer

C. Hole in the hydrosphere D. Hole in the troposphere

12. Euro II standard refers to

A. Lowering sulfur content in fuel B. Increasing sulfur content in fuel

C. Lowering carbon content in fuel D. Increasing carbon content in fuel

13. Noise is

A. Huge sound

B. Sound of vehicles

C. Undesirable and unwanted sound

D. Sound of crackers

14. What is temporary threshold shift?

A. Inaudible noise

B. Noise that is untolerable

C. Tolerable noise

D. Hearing loss due to excessive noise

15. Acid is an example of

A. Corrosive waste B. Infectious waste

C. Radioactive waste D. Ignitable waste

16. Any unfavorable alteration of the environment is called as

A. Eutrophication B. Environmental pollution

C. Biomagnification D. Bioaccumulation

17. The presence of solid, liquid or gaseous compounds, which may not be normally present, or in excess concentration in the atmosphere is called
    A. Air pollution B. Water pollution
    C. Soil pollution D. Radioactive pollution
18. The historical monument that is affected by acid rain is
    A. Taj Mahal B. Pyramid of Egypt
    C. Pisa Tower D. Golden Temple
19. Acid rain contains
    A. Sulphuric acid B. Hydrochloric acid
    C. Oxalic acid D. Acetic acid
20. Organ affected by pneumonia is
    A. Liver B. Kidney
    C. Heart D. Lungs
21. Name the disease caused by mercury poisoning in Japan
    A. Itai itai B. Xeroderma pigmentosum
    C. Measles D. Minamata disease
22. The place where the worst nuclear disaster took place?
    A. Washington B. Chernobyl
    C. Bhopal D. Japan
23. Torrey Canyon is famous for
    A. Gulf of war B. Industries
    C. Electric potential D. Oil spillage
24. Aquatic life is damaged by
    A. Sound pollution B. Air pollution
    C. Thermal pollution D. All of these
25. Minamata disease is caused by
    A. Air pollution B. Water pollution
    C. Marine pollution D. All of these
26. Acid rain mainly results from
    A. Sulfur dioxide B. Carbon dioxide
    C. Carbon monoxide D. Ammonia
27. Ozone depletion is mostly caused by
    A. CO_2 B. CCL
    C. CFC D. CO

28. BOD of river water is found very high. This means water

A. Is clear B. Is highly polluted

C. Contain algae D. Contain many dissolved minerals

29. Global warming is caused by

A. GHGs B. CFC

C. CH_4 D. NO_2

30. The darkening of the skin due to arsenic poisoning is called as

A. Black syndrome B. Diffuse melanosis

B. Skin scaling D. None of these

31. Boron, zinc and manganese are usually referred to as

A. Micronutrients B. Macronutrients

C. Soil Vitamins D. MBZ nutrients

32. Incineration of municipal waste involves

A. Oxidation B. Deduction

C. Redox action D. Disintegration

33. The famous minamata disease in Japan is due to the accumulation of——in fishes

A. Cadmium B. Mercury

C. Zinc D. Lead

34. Soil pollution is caused by

A. Aerosol B. Ozone

C. Acid rain D. PAN

35. Green house effect is caused by

A. Increase in CO_2 B. Increase in O_2

C. Decrease in O_2 D. Decrease in CO_2

36. ——- is the poisonous gas leaked during Bhopal gas tragedy

A. MIC B. PVC

C. Teflon D. Hydrogen sulphide

37. The term nuclear winter is associated with

A. Nuclear war

B. Nuclear disarmament

C. Nuclear weapon testing

D. After effect of a nuclear explosion

38. The phenomenon of accumulation of non-biodegradable pesticides in human beings

A. Biomagnification B. Bioaccumulation

C. Biodegradation D. Bioremediation

39. Example for a physical pollutant

A. Water B. Air

C. Radiation D. Plant

40. DDT is a ——- pollutant

A. Biodegradable B. Non biodegradable

C. Un-biodegradable D. Naturally degradable

41. Eutrophication results from

A. Agricultural and sewage water B. Vehicle exhaust

C. Pesticides D. Industrial effluents

42. The cause of Bhopal disaster is

A. Methyl alcohol B. Methyl carbonate

C. Methyl isocyanate D. Methyl sulphate

43. What is meant by root zone process?

A. A control measure to prevent water pollution

B. A process by which roots of plants are spread on the ground

C. A control measure to prevent soil pollution

D. None of these

44. Exxon Valdez?

A. Oil Tanker which sank in 1989 along the coast of Alaska and marine life seriously affected

B. A plane which crashed and caused death of human life

C. A ship which wrecked on the coast of India

D. None of these

45. Centre of Modern Nuclear Technology in India is

A. CRAS B. SARC

C. BARC D. None of these

46. What is an incinerator?

A. Furnace used for burning solid waste

B. Furnace used for treating liquid waste

C. Both A and B
D. None of the above

47. Photochemical smog is called
A. Tokyo smog B. London smog
C. Los Angeles smog D. None

48. The combustion of waste in the absence of oxygen is called
A. Haemolysis B. Pyrolysis
C. Hydrolysis D. None

49. The heating of earths atmosphere due to trapped radiation is known as
A. Global warming B. Glass house effect
C. Thermal effect D. Greenhouse Effect

50. Thickness of plastic cover permissible to use
A. 50 microns B. 20 microns
C. 100 microns D. 10 microns

51. A biodegradable plastic developed by Biopak Corporation Australia is
A. Biopol B. Pet
C. Polyester D. PVC

52. Lead in water can cause
A. Eye disease B. Arthritis
C. Kidney damage D. Hair falling

53. Disease aggravated by air pollution is
A. Cholera B. Rheumatism
C. Bronchitis D. Haemophilia

54. Which of the following type of pollution can cause the outbreak of jaundice?
A. Air B. Thermal
C. Water D. Land

55. BOD stands for
A. Biological Oxygen Decrease B. Biotic Oxygen Demand
C. Biological Oxygen Demand D. None of the above

56. Example of secondary air pollutant is
A. O_3 B. CO
C. NO_2 D. CO_2

57. INFOCANE and INFO crop models were developed by
   A. IARI
   B. ICAR
   C. IPCC
   D. Department of Environmental Science
58. Blue baby syndrome is due to the presence of
   A. Excess sulphate in drinking water
   B. Excess chlorine in drinking water
   C. Excess heavy metals in drinking water
   D. Excess nitrates in drinking water
59. Mercury poisoning in water is the reason for
   A. Pellegra B. Minamata disease
   C. Itai-Itai disease D. Scurvy
60. Itai-itai disease is caused by
   A. Pb poisoning B. Cd poisoning
   C. Hg poisoning D. Cu poisoning
61. Which of the following is an indicator of organic water pollution?
   A. BOD B. pH
   C. Salinity D. Eutrophication
62. Eutrophication by sewage pollution refers to the
   A. Nutrient enrichment of freshwater bodies
   B. Nutrient depletion of freshwater bodies
   C. Toxic chemical accumulation in freshwater bodies
   D. Heavy metal accumulation in freshwater bodies
63. Which of the following is the major reason for algal bloom?
   A. Presence of heavy metals B. Contamination by pathogens
   C. Eutrophication D. Soil erosion
64. Which of the following is the major cause of biomagnification?
   A. Eutrophication B. Detergent pollution
   C. Pesticide pollution D. Industrial pollution
65. In filtration, the amount of dissolved solids passing through the filters is
   A. Difference between total solids and suspended solids
   B. Sum of total solids and suspended solids

C. Independent of suspended solids

D. None of the above

66. What is oxygen depleting waste?

A. Organic waste that can be decomposed by aerobic bacteria

B. Organic waste that can be decomposed by anaerobic bacteria

C. Organic waste that can be decomposed by aerobic viruses

D. Organic waste that can be decomposed by anaerobic viruses

67. What is the indicator of pollution in water?

A. Amount of oxygen B. Amount of hydrogen

C. Amount of BOD D. Amount of nitrogen

68. Why certain parts of water bodies contain more number of algae?

A. Due to favorable environment B. Due to run-off of excess fertilizers

C. Due to lack of fertilizers D. Due to water pollution

69. What are water soluble inorganic chemicals?

A. Compounds of pure metals B. Compounds of non-metals

C. Compounds of synthetic metals D. Compounds of toxic metals

70. There is .... class of common water pollutants.

A. Only one B. Two

C. Five D. Several

71. Sediment of suspended matter occurs?

A. When soil is eroded from the air

B. When soil is eroded from the land

C. When soil is eroded from the water

D. When soil is eroded from the rock

72. What is a sediment of suspended matter?

A. Insoluble particles of soil and other solids

B. Soluble particles of soil and other solids

C. Insoluble particles of water

D. Soluble particles of water

73. Where we can find water soluble radioactive isotopes?

A. In radioactive reactor B. In radioactive coolant

C. In radioactive shield D. In radioactive waste

74. What is the main reason for thermal pollution?
   A. Increase in the temperature of the ecosystem
   B. Increase in the chemical content in water
   C. Hot water released by power plants and industries
   D. Pollution causing by vehicles

75. How to minimize water pollution due organic chemicals that release to water bodies?
   A. To remove all the aquatic organisms from the water
   B. To purify water manually and release to the water bodies
   C. Purify the water before enter the water bodies directly from industries
   D. Leave the water bodies without using it

76. The birds lay eggs with shells that are much thinner than normal is an example of
   A. Bioaccumulation B. Mutation
   C. DNA sequence D. Mal nutrition

77. How agricultural management helps in the control of water pollution?
   A. By giving an idea about the use of land management
   B. By increase the water intake
   C. By using poor soil which consumes less water
   D. By encouraging farmers to use more chemicals

78. Why ground water monitoring is important in control of water pollution?
   A. To provide more quantity of water
   B. To increase the chemical contents in the water
   C. To provide good quality of water
   D. To reduce the amount of water supplying from ground water

79. How can we reduce the effluent volume of water to maintain its pollution level?
   A. Increase the upstream flow by low flow augmentation
   B. Decrease the upstream flow by low flow augmentation
   C. Increase the upstream flow by high flow augmentation
   D. Decrease the upstream flow by high flow augmentation

80. What is the pH range of effluent after treatment?
   A. Between 4.4 and 5.5 B. Between 4.8 and 6.1
   C. Between 6.8 and 7.8 D. Between 7.8 and 8.3

81. Why controlled use of water hyacinth is important in controlling of water pollution?
   A. To decrease the BOD level
   B. To increase the BOD level
   C. To maintain the BOD level
   D. To completely vanish the BOD level

82. When did water cess act come into force?
   A. 1973 B. 1975
   C. 1977 D. 1980

83. How many percentage of pollution accounts by sewage and municipal effluents?
   A. 25 B. 50
   C. 75 D. 100

84. What is the full form of NRCP?
   A. National Railway Corporation Pipeline
   B. National Rivers Cleaning Phase
   C. National Roads Cleaning Phase
   D. National River Conservation Plan

85. How many rivers do the National River Conservation Plan covered?
   A. 13 B. 15
   C. 16 D. 18

86. Which plan was launched by the Ministry of Environment and Forests (MoEF) to restoring the water quality and ecology of the lakes?
   A. National Water Conserved Plan
   B. National Lake Conservation Plan
   C. National River Ceremony Plan
   D. National Water Conservation Plan

87. Which is the most polluted river in India?
   A. Ganges B. Yamuna
   C. Sabarmati D. Godavari

88. What is used to convert wastelands into agricultural lands?
   A. Check dams B. Water purifier
   C. Rain harvesters D. Gradonies

89. Which one of the following industries produced sulfur dioxide and flu ash as pollutants?

A. Textile industries B. Cottage industries

C. Thermal industries D. Coal industries

90. Which one of the following is a mechanical means of treating industrial effluents?

A. Oxidation B. Chlorination

C. Recycling of waste D. Sedimentation

91. What is the pH value of normal rain?

A. 1 B. 5.5

C. 8 D. 7

92. For the survival of fish in a river stream, the minimum dissolved oxygen is prescribed.

A. 3 ppm B. 5 ppm

C. 4 ppm D. 10 ppm

93. Which among the following gas from automobiles causes major air pollution in metropolitan cities?

A. CO B. NO_2

C. SO_2 D. N_2

94. In photochemical smog, peroxy benzyl nitrate causes

A. Severe skin irritation B. Severe respiratory problem

C. Severe eye irritation D. Severe headache

95. Consider the statement and choose the correct one regarding causes of global warming

(i) Rapid use of fossil fuel

(ii) Deforestation/clearing of lands

(iii) The use of chloroflurocarbon in electronics

A. All the statements are correct

B. (i) and (ii) are correct

C. (ii) and (iii) are correct

D. (i) and (iii) are correct

Answer keys

1	B	16	B	31	A	46	A	61	A	76	A
2	B	17	A	32	A	47	B	62	A	77	A
3	A	18	A	33	B	48	B	63	C	78	C
4	B	19	A	34	C	49	D	64	C	79	A
5	A	20	D	35	A	50	C	65	A	80	C
6	A	21	D	36	A	51	A	66	A	81	B
7	C	22	B	37	D	52	C	67	C	82	C
8	B	23	D	38	B	53	C	68	B	83	C
9	C	24	C	39	C	54	C	69	D	84	D
10	D	25	C	40	B	55	C	70	A	85	D
11	B	26	A	41	A	56	A	71	B	86	B
12	C	27	C	42	C	57	A	72	A	87	B
13	C	28	B	43	A	58	D	73	D	88	D
14	D	29	A	44	A	59	B	74	C	89	C
15	A	30	B	45	C	60	B	75	C	90	D
										91	B
										92	C
										93	A
										94	C
										95	A

4

Disaster Management and Impact Assessment

I. Choose the correct answer

1. Disasters can be broadly termed as ———types.

   A. 2   B. 4

   C. 5   D. 3

2. The annual flood peaks in India are recorded in months of

   A. June, July   B. July, August

   C. July, September   D. August, September

3. Uttarakhand lies in zone ——— of earthquake prone areas.

   A. 5   B. 3

   C. 4   D. 2

4. To measure flood variability, ———- is used widely.

   A. Flash Flood Magnitude Index   B. Flood Index

   C. Flood Magnitude Index   D. Flash Flood Index

5. How many elements of disaster management are there?

   A. 8   B. 7

   C. 4   D. 6

6. Which of the below is an example of slow-onset disaster?

   A. Earthquake   B. Tsunami

   C. Cyclone   D. Drought

7. The first step in preparedness planning is

   A. Analysis of data collected

   B. Determination of objectives

   C. Determination of strategy

   D. Development of implementing device

8. Tsunami detectors are placed in sea at ——- kms from shore.
   A. 25 B. 100
   C. 50 D. 85
9. How much of India's coastline is vulnerable to disasters?
   A. 5000km B. 5500km
   C. 5700km D. 6000km
10. How much percentage of the landmass is prone to earthquakes in India?
   A. Around 58% B. Around 60%
   C. Around 63% D. Around 65%
11. How many hectares of Indian land are prone to floods and river erosion?
   A. Around 25 million hectares B. Around 30 million hectares
   C. Around 35 million hectares D. Around 40 million hectares
12. When did National Disaster Management Authority formed?
   A. 2000 B. 2005
   C. 2010 D. 2015
13. Under which Ministry National Disaster Management Authority comes?
   A. Ministry of Environment B. Ministry of Foreign Affairs
   C. Ministry of Pollution D. Ministry of Home Affairs
14. Who heads the National Crisis Management Committee?
   A. Prime Minister B. President
   C. Cabinet Secretary D. Ministry of Environment
15. What is called for the manuals that identify the role of each officer in State for managing the natural disasters?
   A. State Relief Manuals
   B. State Environmental Protection Manuals
   C. State Disaster Manuals
   D. State Protection Manuals
16. Who released the first Disaster Management Plan of India?
   A. H.D. Deve Gowda B. Atal Bihari Vajpayee
   C. Manmohan Singh D. Narendra Modi
17. When did the Disaster Management formed?
   A. 2005 B. 2006
   C. 2007 D. 2008

18. When was Asian Disaster Preparedness Center established?

A. 1980 B. 1986

C. 1990 D. 996

19. Where is National Institute of Disaster Management located?

A. Bangalore B. Mumbai

C. New Delhi D. Kanpur

20. Where is International Tsunami Center located?

A. New York B. London

C. Mysore D. Honolulu

21. When do we celebrate as International Day for Natural Disaster Reduction?

A. March 1 B. April 15

C. September 12 D. October 13

22. How many types of impact assessments are there?

A. 5 B. 4

C. 3 D. 6

23. Environmental impacts can of———-types.

A. 3 B. 5

C. 4 D. 2

24. A short term environmental impact assessment (EIA) has a time period of

A. 2-5 years B. 10-15 years

C. 5-10 years D. 5-7 years

25. EIA (Environmental Impact Assessment) commenced in the year

A. 1960s B. 1890s

C. 1880s D. 1950s

26. How many stages are there in EIA?

A. 5 B. 3

C. 2 D. 4

27. Domestic demand for water can be assessed using

A. X.Y.Z B. H.I.J

C. A.B.C D. P.Q.R

28. ——— divided methodologies for EIA into ——— categories.
A. Warner, 4 B. Bisset, 4
C. Warner, 5 D. Bisset, 5

29. Water Act is a main law in action used for EIA formulated in
A. 1981 B.1974
C. 1975 D. 1986

30. The intensity of earthquake is measured in
A. Beaufort scale B. Richter scale
C. Mohs scale D. Joules

31. Natural earthquakes are caused by
A. Earth's crust B. Deep seas
C. Peak mountains D. Forests

32. The word Tsunami is derived from two Japanese words
A. tsu (big) and nami (flow) B. tsu (harbour) and nami (wave)
C. tsu (big wave) and nami (wave) D. None of these

33. The deadliest Tsunami in recorded history took place on
A. 26-Dec-2004 B. 26-Dec-2000
C. 15-Nov-1990 D. 15-Dec-1999

34. Which one of the following cause acid rain?
A. Water pollution B. Soil pollution
C. Air pollution D. Noise Pollution

35. What are two acids formed when gases react with the tiny droplets of water in clouds?
A. Sulphuric acids and nitric acid
B. Hydrochloric acid and nitric acid
C. Sulfurous acid and acetylsalicylic acid
D. Sulphuric acid and hydrochloric acid

36. What is the nature of acid rain?
A. Withstanding B. Protecting
C. Corrosive D. Balancing

37. Which of the following way acid rain affects the plants?
A. By nourishing the nutrients from the soil
B. By increasing the nutrients from the soil

C. By removing nutrients from the soil

D. By balancing the nutrients in the soil

38. What is the result of acid rain when it falls into water bodies?

A. The water becomes acidic

B. The water becomes pure

C. The water increases its nutrients value

D. The water increases its level

39. Which one of the way can prevent acid rain?

A. Increase the emission of sulfur dioxide and nitrogen oxides

B. Decrease the emission of sulfur dioxide and nitrogen oxides

C. Increase in the emission of hydrochloride and phosphate

D. Decrease in the emission of hydrochloride and phosphate

40. The Taj Mahal in India is affected by

A. Fog B. Acid rain

C. Water pollution D. Spoil pollution

41. Which of the following is the best way to reduce acid rain in soil?

A. By adding sulphur to the soil B. By adding nitrogen to the soil

C. By adding oxygen to the soil D. By adding limestone to the soil

42. How can we control acid rain which is causing due to the exhaust fumes on the atmosphere by cars?

A. By burning more fuels B. By using old engine vehicles

C. By using ignition D. By using catalytic converters

43. Which is the most acidic in pH scale?

A. 0 B. 7

C. 10 D. 14

44. Who was the first to use the phrase acid rain?

A. Robert Angus Smith B. Ernest Flower

C. Elmer Joseph Clark D. Christ Ralph

Answer keys

1	A	11	D	21	D	31	A	41	D
2	D	12	B	22	B	32	B	42	D

3	C	13	D	23	D	33	A	43	A
4	A	14	C	24	C	34	C	44	A
5	D	15	A	25	A	35	A		
6	D	16	D	26	D	36	C		
7	B	17	A	27	A	37	C		
8	C	18	B	28	C	38	A		
9	C	19	C	29	B	39	B		
10	A	20	D	30	B	40	B		

5

Waste Water Management

I. Choose the correct answer

1. The term sullage refers to
   - A. Fresh waste water
   - B. Septic waste water
   - C. Toxic waste water
   - D. Waste water from kitchen, laundry
2. Waste water can become septic by the loss of
   - A. Dissolved oxygen content
   - B. Carbon content
   - C. Organic compounds
   - D. Water content
3. Which one of the below is not an attribute of drinking water?
   - A. Aesthetics
   - B. Economic
   - C. Safety
   - D. Source
4. The extent of water treatment depends on how many factors?
   - A. 5
   - B. 2
   - C. 3
   - D. 4
5. What is added to the water treatment tank to settle the colloidal particles?
   - A. Alum
   - B. Alum and lime
   - C. Lime
   - D. Potash
6. Disinfection of water in our country is mainly done by
   - A. Oxygenation
   - B. Hydration
   - C. Chlorination
   - D. Filtration
7. Which minerals and in what form are present in ground water?
   - A. Fe and Mn in ferrous and manganous
   - B. Fe and Cu in ferric and cupric
   - C. Fe and Mn in ferric and manganous
   - D. Cu and Mn in cuprous and manganous

8. How many types of waste water treatment plants are there based on the type of waste water?

A. 5 B. 4

C. 2 D. 3

9. On how many conditions does the intervention of waste water depend on?

A. 5 B. 7

C. 6 D. 4

10. A ground water characteristic has to be monitored at least once in a ____ till design span.

A. Week B. Month

C. Day D. Quarter

11. Ground water samples should be collected at least up to a distance ___ km.

A. 2 B. 3

C. 4 D. 5

12. If no open wells are available, action needs to be taken to provide at least ____ monitoring wells.

A. 1 B. 2

C. 3 D. 4

13. How should the monitoring wells be arranged in the absence of bore wells?

A. One on up gradient and other three on the down gradient

B. One on up gradient and other two on the down gradient

C. One on up gradient and other one on the down gradient

D. One on up gradient and other four on the down gradient

14. The ground water flow direction has to be ascertained periodically and reported at least

A. Once in a year B. Once in two years

C. Once in three years D. Once in four years

15. The directions of the ground water flow have to be established with

A. State Ground Water Board B. Water Control Board

C. PCB D. SPCB

16. The Clean Water Act (CWA) regulates
   A. Discharge of pollutants into the waters of the United States
   B. Discharge of pollutants into the waters of the United Kingdom
   C. Discharge of pollutants into the air of the United States
   D. Discharge of pollutants into the waters of India
17. Section _____ of CWA regulates discharges of hazardous substances.
   A. 311(B)(2)(B) B. 311(B)(2)(A)
   C. 312(B)(2)(A) D. 311(B)(1)(A)
18. The Federal Water Pollution Control Act of 1948 was the first major U.S. law to address water pollution.
   A. 1945 B. 1946
   C. 1947 D. 1948
19. The CWA reduced the amount of pollution from
   A. Point sources B. Non point sources
   C. Chemicals D. Mining
20. The discharge of regulated chemicals into surface waters is controlled by
   A. SARA B. CERCLA
   C. NPDES D. PDAC
21. The maximum amount of pollution that each waterway could absorb is known as
   A. TMDL B. TSML
   C. TDSML D. TDS
22. _____ requires EPA to establish regulations to protect human health from contaminants present in drinking water.
   A. SAWD B. SDWA
   C. ASAW D. SWSA
23. Who is responsible for the clean up of oil spill?
   A. HWS B. APS
   C. Oil Pollution Act D. SARA
24. Which section of CWA regulates land disposal of sludge?
   A. Section 402 B. Section 403
   C. Section 404 D. Section 405

25. Which CWA program controls water pollution by regulating point sources?

A. SPCC B. PCC

C. NPDES D. PDA

26. Which section of CWA is responsible for monitoring of wetlands?

A. Section 402 B. Section 403

C. Section 404 D. Section 405

27. Which CWA program manages non point source pollution?

A. NPSMP B. NSPPP

C. NSGOP D. NPSRA

28. When did CWA come into existence?

A. 1970 B. 1971

C. 1972 D. 1973

29. Sedimentation is a

A. Primary water treatment B. Secondary water treatment

C. Tertiary water treatment D. Final process

Answer keys

1	D	11	D	21	A
2	A	12	D	22	B
3	D	13	A	23	C
4	B	14	C	24	D
5	B	15	A	25	C
6	C	16	A	26	C
7	A	17	B	27	A
8	D	18	D	28	C
9	B	19	A	29	B
10	D	20	C		

6

Soil Waste Management

I. Choose the correct answer

1. Which of the following is used in the production of plastic?
   A. Mercury B. Lead
   C. Vinyl chloride D. None of these
2. What is true about aerobic bacteria?
   A. Flourish in the presence of free oxygen
   B. Consume organic matter as their food
   C. Oxidise organic matter in sewage
   D. All the above
3. The term Municipal Solid Waste (MSW) is generally used to describe
   A. Wastes from industrial processes, construction and demolition debris.
   B. Wastes from private homes, commercial establishments and institutions.
   C. Mining wastes
   D. Agricultural wastes
4. The most serious environmental effect posed by hazardous wastes is.
   A. Air pollution
   B. Contamination of groundwater
   C. Increased use of land for landfills
   D. None of these
5. Problem of solid waste disposal can be reduced through
   A. Recycling B. Lesser pollution
   C. More timber D. Population control
6. Metals are produced as waste in industries like
   A. Skiing B. Mining
   C. Electroplating D. Digging

7. Making new containers from crushed glass helps to

A. Save materials B. Save fuel

C. Both of these D. None of these

8. Social, economical and ecological equity is the necessary condition for achieving

A. Social development B. Economical development

C. Sustainable development D. Ecological development

9. How many major sources of solid waste are there based on their origin?

A. 10 B. 5

C. 9 D. 6

10. Which of the below is not an idea behind solid waste management?

A. Control of waste generation B. Storage and collection

C. Disposal D. Stop waste generation

11. The number of functional components of solid waste management is

A. 5 B. 3

C. 6 D. 4

12. The term ISWM refers to

A. International Solid Waste Management

B. Integrated Solid Waste Management

C. Integrated Solid Waste Machine

D. International Solid Waste Mechanism

13. Under which rule of Government, guidelines for solid waste management are followed today?

A. Municipal Solid Waste Rules, 2000

B. Municipal Solid Waste Rules, 2016

C. Solid Waste Rules, 2000

D. Solid Waste Rules, 2016

14. The average composition of municipal solid waste is

A. 41% organic, 40% inert and 19% recyclable

B. 20% organic, 60% inert and 20% recyclable

C. 30% organic, 20% inert and 50% recyclable

D. 19% organic, 41% inert and 40% recyclable

15. There are __________ ways to treat waste thermally.

A. 5 B. 3

C. 2 D. 6

16. How many types of landfills are there?

A. 3 B. 2

C. 5 D. 4

17. The WHO has classified the biomedical waste into __________ categories.

A. 5 B. 4

C. 3 D. 2

18. Which gas produced in open dumps from the decomposition of biodegradable waste?

A. Ethane B. Methane

C. Propene D. Ethene

19. Which was the first city to have an established system of waste removal?

A. Lahore B. Athens

C. Paris D. London

20. Why burning waste is not an acceptable practice of solid waste management?

A. Because it is very costly

B. Because it requires modern technologies

C. Because it cause several environmental issues

D. Because it requires lot of space

21. What plan should we make to the disposal of solid waste?

A. Integrated waste management plan

B. Recycling of waste management plan

C. Reducing of waste management plan

D. Use of waste management plan

22. The term municipal solid waste is used to describe which kind of solid waste?

A. Hazardous B. Toxic

C. Non hazardous D. Non toxic

23. How many main components are there in integrated waste management?
   A. One B. Two
   C. Three D. Four
24. Which of the integrated waste management is reduced on an individual level?
   A. Source reduction B. Recycling
   C. Disposal D. Burning
25. Which of the following can be recycled many times?
   A. Plastic B. Wood
   C. Organic materials D. Aluminum
26. Why plastics are difficult to recycle?
   A. Because it is very hard material
   B. Because it is very adhesive in its nature
   C. Because of different types of polymer resins
   D. Because of different sizes of plastic
27. How many key characteristics of a municipal sanitary landfill are there?
   A. One B. Two
   C. Three D. Four
28. How does organic material in the buried solid waste will decompose?
   A. By the action of oxidation B. By the action of microorganisms
   C. By the flow of water D. By the soil particles
29. What is called for the process of burning municipal solid waste in a properly designed furnace under suitable temperature and operating conditions?
   A. Landfill B. Recycling
   C. Vermicomposting D. Incineration
30. Why the recycled paper is banned for use in food containers?
   A. Because it creates contamination
   B. Because it creates a lot of spaces
   C. Because paper can be used only one time
   D. Because paper is very thick and can't cover the food containers
31. The 3 R principle in waste management involves
   A. Reduce, Regain, Reuse B. Reduce, Reuse, Recycle
   C. Reduce, Reform, Reset D. Reduce, Retain, Regain

Answer keys

1	B	11	C	21	A	31	B
2	D	12	B	22	A		
3	B	13	D	23	C		
4	B	14	A	24	A		
5	A	15	B	25	D		
6	C	16	A	26	C		
7	C	17	B	27	C		
8	C	18	B	28	B		
9	C	19	B	29	D		
10	D	20	C	30	A		

7

Social Issues and the Environment

I. Choose the correct answer

1. Official date of Earth Day is on
   A. April 22 B. March 21
   C. May 22 D. June 05
2. The World Wetlands Day is celebrated on
   A. February 02 B. February 28
   C. June 05 D. March 21
3. National Maritime Day of India is celebrated on
   A. October 16 B. April 05
   C. March 21 D. May 22
4. World Water Day is celebrated on
   A. May 22 B. June 05
   C. March 22 D. May 11
5. Public awareness of environment creates
   A. Environmental protection B. Environmental degradation
   C. Environmental improvement D. Environmental cultivation
6. Wild life protection act was formulated during the period of
   A. Mrs. Indira Gandhi B. Lal Bahadur Shastri
   C. Rajiv Gandhi D. Morarji Desai
7. Vermicomposting is a natural method of
   A. Producing compost manure B. Producing worms
   C. Managing waste it creates D. Destroying worms
8. Which year was declared as the Water Year by Indian government
   A. 2010 B. 2004
   C. 2007 D. 2000

9. On which date was the Stockholm Conference on Human Environment held?

A. July 6th 1974
B. Aug 8th 1976
C. June 5th 1972
D. Dec 12th 1990

10. Where was the Stockholm conference on Human Environment held?

A. Sweden
B. Austria
C. India
D. Greece

11. The controversial dam across the river Narmada?

A. Sardar Sarovar
B. Hirakud
C. Bhakra-Nangal
D. Sutlej

12. Leader of Narmada Bachao Andolan

A. Vandana Siva
B. Medha Patkar
C. Menaka Gandhi
D. Mayilamma

13. What is meant by GM foods?

A. Growth modified foods
B. Genetically modified food
C. Growth marked foods
D. Good mobility food

14. Who had stated in the Stockholm Conference in 1972 that poverty was the greatest polluter?

A. Indira Gandhi
B. Mahatma Gandhi
C. Rajiv Gandhi
D. Jawaharlal Nehru

15. The movement Pani Panjayath was initiated to conserve waters in the drought prone areas of state.

A. Tamil Nadu
B. Rajasthan
C. Maharashtra
D. Karnataka

16. Which state proposed a ban on all types of polythene packing for the first time in India?

A. Himachal Pradesh
B. Madhya Pradesh
C. Kerala
D. Karnataka

17. The expansion of SPCA

A. Society for the Protection of Common Animals
B. Society for the Prevention of Cruelty to Animals
C. Society for the Prohibition of Cruelty to Animals
D. None

18. Who coined the slogan of Chipko Movement Ecology in permanent economy?

A. Jawaharlal Nehru B. Salim Ali

C. Sunderlal Bahuguna D. Rachel Carson

19. Environmental Protection Act was introduced in the year

A. 1986 B. 1988

C. 1972 D. 1989

20. Rain water harvesting is a major method implemented for

A. Water conservation B. Soil conservation

C. Forest conservation D. Ecological conservation

21. The method of simultaneous integration of trees with agricultural crops is called

A. Agroforestry B. Deforestation

C. Reforestation D. Combined culture

22. Mullaperiyar dam is in the district?

A. Thrissur B. Pathanamthitta

C. Idukki D. Alappuzha

23. What is bagasse? What is it used for?

A. Sugar cane waste – to make paper

B. Biogas – used as fuel

C. Liquid waste – as fertilizer

D. Vermicompost – as fertilizer

24. Example for a biodegradable polymer is

A. Polyethylene B. Polypropylene

C. Poly lactic acid D. Polyester

25. World Ozone day is

A. March 16 B. June 5

C. September 16 D. November 16

26. Utilisation of natural resources in moderate manner to remaining something for the next generation is termed as

A. Resettlement B. Sustainable development

C. Rehabilitation D. Mutual development

27. The expansion on PQLI is
    A. Physical quality of life index
    B. Population quotient of life in India
    C. Poor quality of life in India
    D. Poverty, quality of life in India
28. The anthrax disease is caused by
    A. Virus B. Bacteria
    C. Protozoa D. Helminth
29. Super bugs are
    A. Synthetic bug B. Bacteria
    C. Radio nucleotide D. Industries
30. Salmonellosis is a disease related to consumption of
    A. Chicken B. Eggs
    C. Mutton D. Fish
31. One third of the global cases of tuberculosis is in
    A. Britain B. Sweden
    C. India D. China
32. Causative organisms of malaria
    A. Bacteria B. Fungus
    C. Plasmodium D. Virus
33. What is black lung?
    A. Occupational hazard to the minors
    B. Occupational hazard to navigators
    C. Occupational hazard to pesticide applicators
    D. None of these
34. What is carcinogen?
    A. Drugs for curing infectious disease
    B. Drugs used for curing cancer
    C. Cancer causing agent
    D. Food colourants
35. Birth rate is called
    A. Mortality B. Vital index
    C. Natality D. Viability

36. Infection of HIV is usually detected by which test

A. Elisa test B. Hybridization

C. Gram staining D. None

37. Death rate of the population

A. Mortality B. Viability

C. Natality D. Vitality

38. Based on what the Kyoto Protocol set emission reduction targets for the group of greenhouse gases?

A. Hydrogen equivalents B. Carbon dioxide equivalents

C. Oxygen equivalents D. Nitrogen equivalents

39. With minor exception, which of the following have been phased out completely globally?

A. Carbon dioxide B. Carbon monoxide

C. Chlorofluorocarbons D. Nitrogen dioxide

40. For what production and consumption, phase out schedules the Montreal Protocol has established?

A. Greenhouse emitting gases

B. Global warming emitting gases

C. Ozone layer depleting substances

D. Water level increasing substances

41. How can be determined carbon dioxide equivalents?

A. By multiplying the quantity of the gas by its global warming potential

B. By multiplying the quantity of the gas by its pressure

C. By multiplying the quantity of the water by its global warming potential

D. By multiplying the quantity of the gas by its global cooling potential

42. When did the Kyoto Protocol entered into force?

A. 1997 B. 2000

C. 2005 D. 2009

43. When is the first commitment period for the Kyoto Protocol expired?

A. 2007 B. 2010

C. 2012 D. 2015

44. When did the Montreal Protocol entered into force?

A. 1984 B. 1986

C. 1989 D. 1994

45. What are the substances present in the ozone layer depleting substances controlled by the Montreal Protocol?

A. Either chlorine or bromine B. Either carbon or nitrogen

C. Either chlorine or carbon D. Either carbon or bromine

46. Why hydro fluorocarbons are no harm to the ozone layer?

A. Because they contain chlorine

B. Because they do not contain chlorine

C. Because they contain carbon

D. Because they contain nitrogen

47. Which amendment was agreed to phase down HFCs under the Montreal Protocol?

A. Paris Amendment B. New York Amendment

C. Delhi Amendment D. Kigali Amendment

48. Which one of the following is the objective of Kyoto Protocol?

A. Stabilization and reconstruction of greenhouse gases

B. Protecting the ozone layer from depletion

C. Reducing the CFCs and HFCs usage

D. Increasing the greenhouse gases

49. When the Clean Air Act in United States was came into force?

A. 1950 B. 1960

C. 1970 D. 1980

50. Which of the following action takes place in the formation of ozone?

A. Action of daylight on oxygen B. Action of daylight on nitrogen

C. Action of daylight on hydrogen D. Action of daylight on phosphorous

51. Why ozone within the upper environment is important?

A. Because it provides rain to the earth

B. It protects the earth from the suns harmful ultraviolet radiations

C. It provides good aesthetic view to the atmosphere

D. It protects the earth from floods

52. Which of the following is threat to the ozonosphere?

A. Nitrogen dioxide B. Oxygen

C. CFCs D. Carbon dioxide

53. Which one of the following is a result of ozone layer depletion?
    A. Increase in the oxygen level
    B. Increase in the nitrogen level
    C. Increase in the phosphorous level
    D. Increases in the carbon dioxide level
54. In which layer of atmosphere, ozone is very vital for all vegetation?
    A. Upper atmosphere B. Below atmosphere
    C. Ground level D. Below ground level
55. Which atom released when CFCs molecules are broken from UV radiations?
    A. Oxygen B. Chlorine
    C. Nitrogen D. Arsenic
56. What is the full form of CFCs?
    A. Chlorofluorocarbons B. Chlorine fluorocarbons
    C. Chromate fluorocarbons D. Chlorofluridcarbons
57. Which is the first place where scientist found the thinning of ozone layer?
    A. Atmosphere above Australia B. Atmosphere above Antarctica
    C. Atmosphere above India D. Atmosphere above France
58. Which treaty was signed in 1987 for the protection of ozone layer?
    A. The Montreal Protocol B. The Kyoto Protocol
    C. Ozone Summit D. Wildlife Conservation Act
59. Which one of the following cause ozone layer depletion?
    A. Oxygen B. Mercury
    C. Sodium silicate D. Methyl chloroform
60. Which compound used in fire extinguishers cause ozone layer depletion?
    A. Sodium aluminates B. Phosphates
    C. Halons D. Sulfurous silicate
61. What is called for the phenomenon when the radiation absorbed by the atmosphere is reradiated towards the surface of the earth?
    A. Smog B. Newton effect
    C. Darwin effect D. Greenhouse effect
62. Which of the following result obtain due to cutting down of trees?
    A. Providing more fresh oxygen B. Providing more pure water
    C. Cause greenhouse effect D. Cause increase in the rain

63. Which is the most abundantly found greenhouse gas?
   A. Carbon dioxide B. Water vapor
   C. Methane D. Nitrous oxide
64. Which of the following is not a greenhouse gas?
   A. Water vapor B. Carbon dioxide
   C. Methane D. Ethane
65. When did greenhouse effect discovered?
   A. 1814 B. 1824
   C. 1854 D. 1884
66. Why the temperature inside the car is much warmer than the outside temperature when the car that has been left parked in the sun for a couple of hours?
   A. Due to air pollution B. Due to smog
   C. Due to sudden climate change D. Due to greenhouse effect
67. Which one of the following cause global warming?
   A. Carbon dioxide B. Oxygen
   C. Nitrogen D. Hydrogen
68. How many percent of carbon dioxide increased in the atmosphere since pre-industrial times?
   A. About 10% B. About 20%
   C. About 30% D. About 40%
69. What is the full form of UNFCC with respect to global warming convention?
   A. United Nations Framework Convention on Climate Change
   B. United Nations Federation Convention on Climate Change
   C. United Nations Framework Center on Climate Change
   D. United Nations Federation Center on Climate Change
70. Which one of the following cause global warming?
   A. Radiative forcing B. Earth gravitation force
   C. Oxygen D. Centripetal force
71. Which one of the following is the anthropogenic radiative forcing of climate?
   A. Aerosols B. Cement
   C. Paper D. Glass

72. Which one of the following land use causes global warming?
    A. Increase in the fertility of soil B. Surface reflectance
    C. Forestation D. Adopting organic farming
73. Changes in the composition of the atmosphere is an example of
    A. Internal forcing B. External forcing
    C. Mid forcing D. Gravitational forcing
74. What is the main reason for melting of ice sheets?
    A. Increase in the oxygen content
    B. Global warming
    C. Noise pollution
    D. Decrease in carbon dioxide content
75. Which one of the following is the reason for a sea level rise?
    A. Depression of sea water B. Expansion of sea water
    C. Due to heavy rainfall D. Due to low rainfall
76. What is the full form of IPCC?
    A. Intergovernmental Panel on Climate Change
    B. International Panel on Climate Change
    C. Intergovernmental Protocols on Climate Change
    D. International Panel on Climate Conservation
77. What is the estimation range of the global mean sea level rise by the year 2100?
    A. 0-10 cm B. 4-45 cm
    C. 9-88 cm D. 14-123 cm
78. CO_2 concentration as on January 1, 2019 is about
    A. 409.92 ppm B. 407.05 ppm
    C. 411.72 ppm D. 395.00 ppm
79. Which of the following is not a green house gas?
    A. CH_4 B. CO_2
    C. Ne D. CFC
80. HQ of IPCC (Inter Governmental Panel on Climate change) is situated at
    A. Geneva B. Washington
    C. London D. Newyork

81. Sea level rise because of global warming or greenhouse effect to a height of about

A. 0.3 m B. 0.9 m

C. 0.75 m D. 0.5 m

82. The temperature of earth would be if no greenhouse effect occurs

A. -15°C B. -18°C

C. 18°C D. 40°C

83. The word smog was coined by

A. Issac Newton B. G.J.Mendal

C. H.A.Des Voeux D. Marconi

84. HQ of National Institute of Oceanography is situated at

A. Goa B. Pune

C. New Delhi D. Hyderabad

85. United Nations climate change conference was held in New Delhi on

A. COP 8, Nov 2002 B. COP 10, Dec 2004

C. COP 1, Apr 1995 D. COP 12, Nov 2006

86. The one and only Inter Governmental Panel on Climate Change session was conducted in India is

A. 8th session B. 22nd session

C. 31st session D. 42nd session

87. The IPCC session was conducted recently in Japan

A. May 2019 B. March 2019

C. June 2019 D. April 2019

88. __________ reacts with haemoglobin.

A. Carbon dioxide B. Nitrogen oxide

C. Sulphur dioxide D. Carbon monoxide

89. Holes are caused in the _______ layer of atmosphere

A. Ionosphere B. Stratosphere

C. Exosphere D. Troposphere

90. How many oxygen particles are there in every atom of ozone?

A. One B. Two

C. Three D. Four

91. Which one of the following parameters is considered to determine the reflectance of a vegetation canopy?

A. Solar zenith angle B. Azimuth angle

C. Look angle D. All of these

92. The instruments which provide electromagnetic radiation of specified wave length or a band of wave lengths to illuminate the earth surface are called

A. Sensors B. Passive sensors

C. Active sensors D. None of these

93. Which one of the following frequency regions is a part of suns radiation?

A. Radio frequency region B. Visible frequency region

C. Ultraviolet frequency region D. Infrared frequency region

94. The arrangement of terrain features which provides attributes: the shape, size and texture of objects is called

A. Spectral variation B. Spatial variation

C. Temporal variation region D. None of these

95. The part radiation due to scattered/diffused radiation entering the field of view of a remote sensor other than that from the required target is

A. Reduces the contrast of the image and also its sharpness

B. Increases the contrast of the image, but reduces the sharpness

C. Increases both the contrast and sharpness

D. None of these reduces the contrast, but increases the sharpness

96. Pick up the correct definition from the following with response to GIS.

A. The geometric property which describes the linkage between line features is defined as connectivity

B. The area features which are wholly contained within another area feature is known so containment

C. Common boundary between two areas of a locality is known as adjacency

D. All of these

97. Formation of snow occurs, if the cloud temperature is

A. At the freezing point B. Below the freezing point

C. Just above the freezing point D. None of these

98. The ratio of the total solar radiant energy returned by a planetary body to the total radiant energy incident on the body is called

A. Reflectance B. Albedo

C. Reflectance factor D. None of these

99. Greenhouse gas includes

A. CO_2 B. CH_4

C. N_2O D. All of the above

Answer keys

1	A	16	A	31	C	46	B	61	D	76	A	91	D
2	A	17	B	32	C	47	D	62	C	77	C	92	C
3	B	18	C	33	A	48	A	63	B	78	A	93	A
4	C	19	A	34	C	49	C	64	D	79	C	94	B
5	A	20	A	35	C	50	A	65	C	80	A	95	A
6	A	21	A	36	A	51	B	66	D	81	A	96	D
7	A	22	C	37	A	52	C	67	A	82	B	97	B
8	C	23	A	38	B	53	D	68	C	83	C	98	B
9	C	24	C	39	C	54	A	69	A	84	A	99	D
10	A	25	C	40	C	55	B	70	A	85	A		
11	A	26	B	41	A	56	A	71	A	86	B		
12	B	27	A	42	C	57	B	72	B	87	A		
13	B	28	B	43	C	58	A	73	B	88	D		
14	A	29	B	44	C	59	D	74	B	89	B		
15	C	30	D	45	D	60	C	75	B	90	C		

UNIT XII: AGRICULTURAL ECONOMICS, FINANCE AND AGRI BUSINESS

1

Fundamentals of Agricultural Economics and Theory of Consumer Behaviour

I. Choose the correct answer

1. Economics is the study of mankind in the ordinary business of life. This definition was given by

   A. Adam Smith B. Lord Robbins

   C. Alfred Marshall D. Samuelson

2. The branch of economic theory, that deals with the problem of allocation of resources is

   A. Microeconomics B. Macroeconomics

   C. Econometrics D. None of these

3. A study of how increase in the corporate income tax rate, will affect the natural unemployment rate is an example of

   A. Macroeconomics B. Descriptive economics

   C. Microeconomics D. Normative economics

4. If a point falls inside the production possibility curve, what does it indicate?

   A. Resources are over utilized B. There is employment in the economy

   C. Resources are underutilized D. Both B and C

5. In which type of economy, do consumers and producers make their choices based on the market forces of demand and supply?

   A. Open economy B. Controlled economy

   C. Command economy D. Market economy

6. Under a free economy, prices are

   A. Regulated

   B. Determined through free interplay of demand and supply

   C. Partly regulated

   D. None of these

7. Which of the following falls under microeconomics?

A. National income
B. General price level
C. Factor pricing
D. National saving and investment

8. In a free market economy, when consumers increase their purchase of a goods and the level of ____ exceeds _____, then prices tend to rise.

A. Demand, supply
B. Supply, demand
C. Prices, demand
D. Profits, supply

9. Under inductive method, the logic proceeds from

A. General to particulars
B. Particular to general
C. Both A and B
D. None of these

10. Wealth of Nations was written by

A. Adam Smith
B. John Smith
C. Robbins
D. None

11. _____ shows the various combinations of two product that give the same amount of satisfaction

A. ISO cost curve
B. Indifference curve
C. Marginal utility curve
D. ISO quant

12. Total utility is maximum when

A. Marginal utility is maximum
B. Marginal utility is zero
C. Average utility is maximum
D. Average utility is zero

13. An indifference curve is always

A. Curve to the origin
B. Convex to the origin
C. L-shaped
D. A vertical straight line

14. Marginal utility curve of a consumer is also his

A. Indifference curve
B. Total utility curve
C. Supply curve
D. Demand curve

15. An equilibrium, the slope of indifference curve is

A. Equal to the slope of budget line
B. Greater than the slope of budget line
C. Smaller than the slope of budget line
D. None

16. The law of equal marginal utility considers price of money as

    A. Zero B. Less than one

    C. More than one D. One

17. Marginal utility approach was given by

    A. J.R.Hicks B. Alfred Marshall

    C. Robbins D. A.C. Pigou

18. Indifference curves between income and leisure for an individual are generally

    A. Concave to the origin B. Convex to the origin

    C. Negatively sloped straight lines D. Positively sloped straight lines

19. In case of a right angled indifference curve, the goods are

    A. Perfect complements B. Perfect substitutes

    C. Inferior goods D. Giffen good

20. Indifference curves never intersect each other due to

    A. Different levels of satisfaction B. Same levels of satisfaction

    C. Convex to origin D. Concave to origin

Answer keys

1	C	11	B
2	A	12	B
3	A	13	B
4	C	14	D
5	D	15	A
6	B	16	D
7	C	17	B
8	A	18	D
9	B	19	A
10	A	20	A

2

Theory of Demand and Supply

I. Choose the correct answer

1. Demand for a commodity refers to
   A. Desire for the commodity
   B. Need for the commodity
   C. Quantity demanded for that commodity
   D. Quantity of the commodity demanded at a certain price during any particular period of time
2. In case of an inferior good, the income elasticity of demand is
   A. Positive   B. Zero
   C. Negative   D. Infinite
3. For what type of good does demand fall with a rise in income levels of households?
   A. Inferior goods   B. Substitutes
   C. Luxuries   D. Necessities
4. In case of inferior goods like bajra, a fall in its price tends to
   A. Make the demand remain constant
   B. Reduce the demand
   C. Increase the demand
   D. Change the demand in an abnormal way
5. Movement along the same demand curve shows
   A. Expansion of demand
   B. Expansion of supply
   C. Expansion and contraction of demand
   D. Increase and decrease of demand

6. What is an Engels curve?
   A. Another name of demand curve
   B. Curves showing both demand and supply curves
   C. Curve named after Lord Engels
   D. All
7. Which factor generally keeps the price – elasticity of the demand for a good low
   A. Variety of uses for that good
   B. Its low price
   C. Close substitutes for that good
   D. High proportion of the consumer's income spent on it
8. In case of a straight line demand curve meeting the two axes, the price elasticity of demand at the mid point of the line would be
   A. 0 B. 1
   C. 1.5 D. 2
9. An increase in demand can result from
   A. A decline in the market price
   B. A reduction in the price of substitutes
   C. An increase in income
   D. An increase in the price of complements
10. The supply of a goods refers to
   A. Actual production of goods
   B. Total stock of goods
   C. Stock available for sale
   D. Amount of goods offered for sale at a particular price per unit time
11. Increase or decrease in supply means
   A. Shift in supply curve
   B. Movement along same supply curve
   C. Both A and B
   D. Neither A or B
12. If supply curve is perfectly inelastic, the supply curve is
   A. Vertical B. Horizontal
   C. Upward sloping D. Downward sloping

13. When supply price increase in the short run, the profit of the producer

A. Increases B. Decreases

C. Remains constant D. Decreases marginally

14. Change in the supply of a commodity along with same supply curve may occur due to

A. Change in the price of commodity

B. Change in the price of related goods

C. Change in the future, expectation about the prices of the good

D. Change in the cost of inputs

15. What is the elasticity of supply, when price changes from 15 to 12 supply change from 6 units to 5 units?

A. 0.77 B. 0.87

C. 0.833 D.0.58

16. An perfectly inelastic, supply curve will be

A. Parallel to X-axis B. Parallel to Y-axis

D. Downward slopping D. None of these

17. If the supply of a commodity is perfectly elastic, an increase in demand will result in

A. Decrease in both price and quantity at equilibrium

B. Increase in both price and quantity at equilibrium

C. Increase in equilibrium quantity, equilibrium price remaining constant

D. Increase in equilibrium price, equilibrium quantity remaining constant

18. When change in quantity supplied is proportionate to the change in the price, the producer is

A. Perfectly elastic supply B. Relatively elastic supply

C. Unitary elastic supply D. Perfectly inelastic supply

19. Expansion in supply refers to a situation when the producers are willing to supply a

A. Larger quantity of the commodity at an increased price

B. Larger quantity of the commodity due to increased taxation on that commodity

C. Larger quantity of the commodity at the same price

D. Larger quantity of the commodity at the decreased price

Answer keys

1	D	11	A
2	C	12	A
3	A	13	A
4	B	14	A
5	C	15	C
6	C	16	B
7	B	17	C
8	B	18	C
9	C	19	A
10	D		

3

Determination of Price and Output

I. Choose the correct answer

1. Which of the following is not an essential condition of pure competition?

   A. Homogenous product

   B. Large number of buyers and sellers

   C. Freedom of entry

   D. Absence of transport cost

2. Under which of the following forms of market structure does a firm has no control over the price of its product

   A. Monopoly B. Oligopoly

   C. Monopolistic competition D. Perfect competition

3. Given the relation MR = P(1-1/e) if e>1, then

   A. Marginal revenue > 0 B. Marginal revenue < 0

   C. Marginal revenue = 0 D. None

4. Profits of the firm will be more at

   A. Marginal revenue = Marginal cost

   B. Additional revenue from extra unit equals its additional cost

   C. Both A and B

   D. None

5. What should firm do when marginal revenue is greater than marginal cost?

   A. Firm should expand output

   B. Effect should be made to make them equal

   C. Prices should be curved down

   D. All of these

6. Under monopoly, price discrimination depends upon
   A. Elasticity of supply for commodity
   B. Elasticity of demand for commodity
   C. Size of market
   D. All of above
7. Monopolist can determine
   A. Cost B. Output
   C. Either price or output D. None
8. MR of nth unit is given by
   A. TR_n/TR_{n-1} B. $TR_n + TR_{n-1}$
   C. $TR_n - TR_{n-1}$ D. All of these
9. For maximum profit, the condition is
   A. Average Revenue = Average Cost
   B. Marginal Revenue = Marginal Cost
   C. Marginal Revenue = Average Revenue
   D. Marginal Cost = Average Cost
10. Equilibrium price may be determined through
   A. Only demand B. Only supply
   C. Both demand and supply D. None
11. If price is forced to stay below equilibrium price,
   A. Excess supply exists B. Excess demand exists
   C. Either A or B D. Neither A or B
12. An increase in supply with unchanged demand leads to
   A. Rise in price and fall in quantity B. Fall in both price and quantity
   C. Rise in both price and quantity D. Fall in price and rise in quantity
13. In the long run
   A. Only demand can change
   B. Only supply can change
   C. Both demand and supply can change
   D. None of these
14. A competitive firm in the short run incur losses. The firm continues production, if
   A. Price > Average Variable Cost B. Price = Average Variable Cost
   C. Price < Average Variable Cost D. Price $\geq$ Average Variable Cost

15. Under _____ market condition, firms make normal profits in the long run

A. Perfect competition B. Monopoly

C. Oligopoly D. None

16. A monopolist is able to maximize his profits when

A. His input is maximum

B. He charges a high price

C. His average cost is minimum

D. His marginal cost is equal to marginal revenue

17. Under monopolistic competition, the gross elasticity of demand for the product of a single firm would be

A. Infinite B. Highly elastic

C. Highly inelastic D. Zero

18. When AR = 10 and AC = 8, the firm makes

A. Normal profit B. Net profit

C. Gross profit D. Supernormal profit

19. What are the conditions for the long run equilibrium of the competitive firm?

A. Long-run Marginal Cost = Long-run Average Cost = Price

B. Short-run Marginal Cost = Short-run Average Cost = Long-run Marginal Cost

C. Price = Marginal Revenue

D. All of these

20. Kinked demand curve hypothesis is given by

A. Alfred marshall B. A. C. Pigou

C. Sweezy D. Hicks and Allen

21. Supernormal profits occur, when

A. Total revenue is equal to total cost

B. Total revenue is equal to variable cost

C. Average revenue is more than average cost

D. Average revenue is equal to average cost

22. If under perfect competition, the price line lies below the average cost curve, the firm would

A. Make only normal profits B. Incur losses

C. Make abnormal profit D. Profit cannot be determined

23. The Marginal Revenue curve cuts the horizontal line between Y axis and demand curve into

A. Two unequal parts B. Two equal parts

C. May be equal or unequal parts D. None of these

Answer keys

1	D	11	B	21	C
2	D	12	D	22	B
3	A	13	C	23	B
4	C	14	D		
5	A	15	A		
6	B	16	D		
7	C	17	D		
8	C	18	D		
9	B	19	A		
10	C	20	C		

4

Theory of Production and Cost

I. Choose the correct answer

1. _____ show the overall output generated at a given level of input

   A. Cost function

   B. Production function

   C. ISO cost

   D. Marginal rate of technical substitution

2. If Long-run Average Cost curve falls as output expands, this is due to

   A. Law of diminishing returns B. Economics of scale

   C. Law of variable proportion D. Diseconomics of scale

3. Isoquants are equal to

   A. Product lines B. Total utility lines

   C. Cost lines D. Revenue lines

4. The marginal product curve is above the average product curve when the average product is

   A. Increasing B. Decreasing

   C. Constant D. None

5. Increasing returns to scale can be explained in terms of

   A. External and internal economics

   B. External economics and internal diseconomics

   C. External and internal diseconomics

   D. All of these

6. An isoquant is _____ to an isocost line at equilibrium point

   A. Convex B. Concave

   C. Tangent D. Perpendicular

7. At the point of inflexion, the marginal product is

A. Increasing B. Decreasing

C. Maximum D. Negative

8. Diminishing marginal returns implies

A. Decreasing average variable costs

B. Decreasing marginal costs

C. Increasing marginal costs

D. Decreasing average fixed costs

9. If the marginal product of labour is below the average product of labour. It must be true that

A. Marginal product of labour is negative

B. Marginal product of labour is zero

C. Average product of labour is falling

D. Average product of labour is negative

10. Law of variable proportion is valid when

A. Only one input is fixed and all other inputs are kept variable

B. All factors are kept constant

C. All inputs are varied in the same proportion

D. None of these

11. Opportunity cost is

A. Direct cost B. Total cost

C. Accounting cost D. Cost of foregone opportunity

12. An input increases, average fixed cost

A. Remains constant B. Starts falling

C. Start rising D. None

13. Average fixed cost can be obtained through

A. $AFC = \frac{TFC}{TS}$ B. $AFC = \frac{EC}{TU}$

C. $AFC = \frac{TC}{PC}$ D. $AFC = \frac{TFC}{TU}$

14. AFC curve is

A. Convex and downward sloping B. Concave and downward sloping

C. Convex and upward sloping D. Concave and upward rising

15. A firm's average fixed cost is Rs 20 at 6 units of output what will it be at 4 units of output?

    A. Rs 60 B. Rs 30

    C. Rs 40 D. Rs 20

16. U-shaped average cost curve is based on

    A. Law of increasing cost B. Law of decreasing cost

    C. Law of constant returns to scale D. Law of variable proportions

17. When shape of average cost curve is upwards, marginal cost

    A. Must be decreasing B. Must be constant

    C. Must be rising D. Any of these

18. If total cost at 10 units is Rs 600 for 11th unit. The marginal cost of 11th unit is

    A. Rs 20 B. Rs 30

    C. Rs 40 D. Rs 50

19. Economic cost excludes

    A. Accounting cost + explicit cost

    B. Accounting cost

    C. Explicit cost+ implicit cost

    D. Accounting cost + opportunity cost

20. Which of the following cost curves is never U shaped?

    A. Average cost curve B. Marginal cost curve

    C. Total curve D. Fixed cost curve

Answer keys

1	B	11	D
2	B	12	B
3	A	13	D
4	A	14	A
5	A	15	B
6	C	16	D
7	C	17	C
8	C	18	C
9	C	19	A
10	A	20	D

5

Factors of Production

I. Choose the correct answer

1. In general, capital means
   A. Building B. Machinery
   C. Money D. None
2. The reward paid to capital is
   A. Rent B. Wages
   C. Interest D. None
3. Agriculture is classified under ______ sector
   A. Primary B. Secondary
   C. Tertiary D. None
4. The reward paid to labour as a factor of production is
   A. Rent B. Wages
   C. Profit D. None
5. Investment in education is called ______ capital
   A. Physical B. Human
   C. Money D. None
6. Any work undertaken only for ______ is not regarded as labour
   A. Income B. Reward
   C. Pleasure D. None
7. All the free gifts of nature are termed as
   A. Land B. Labour
   C. Capital D. None
8. The National income of advanced countries are at
   A. High level B. Medium level
   C. Low level D. None

9. Man can change only the ....of land

A. Size B. Uses

C. Nature D. None

10. Labour is

A. Perishable B. Non perishable

C. Ever lasting D. None

11. Efficient labour ______ production

A. Increases B. Decreases

C. Affects D. None

12. Labour is

A. Mobile B. Immobile

C. Stagnant D. None

13. Labour involves ______ elements

A. Human B. Financial

C. Climatic D. None

14. Capital is productive because it yields an

A. Interest B. Income

C. Investment D. None

15. The reward paid to capital is

A. Interest B. Profit

C. Rent D. None

16. Capital is

A. Immobile B. Highly mobile

C. Less mobile D. None

17. Investment in ______ is called human capital

A. Education B. Buildings

C. Monetary instruments D. None

18. All capital is

A. Wealth B. Land

C. Income D. None

19. Most products from the primary sector are

A. Finished products B. Raw materials

C. Natural resources D. None

20. Increasingly becoming important sector is
    A. Primary sector B. Secondary sector
    C. Tertiary sector D. None
21. All labour is
    A. Homogeneous B. Heterogeneous
    C. Lazy D. Intelligent
22. Unemployment due to mechanization of agriculture is
    A. Seasonal B. Structural
    C. Industrial D. Personal
23. A skilled worker is an example of
    A. Entrepreneur B. Capital input
    C. Labour input D. B and C above
24. Labour is hirable but you cannot hire
    A. Capital B. Land
    C. Manager D. Entrepreneur
25. Economic development of a country requires
    A. Skilled labour B. Diplomacy
    C. Abundant natural resources D. A and C of above
26. Which of the following input factor takes risk innovates and coordinates
    A. Capital B. Labour
    C. Productivity D. Entrepreneur
27. The transformation of resources into economic goods and series is called
    A. Technical efficiency B. Input
    C. Production D. Increasing returns
28. The following is not a factor of production
    A. Labour B. Entrepreneurship
    C. Land D. Money
29. Natural environment that can be used for the production of goods and services is
    A. Labour B. Money
    C. Capital D. Natural resources

Answer keys

1	C	11	A	21	B
2	C	12	A	22	B
3	C	13	A	23	C
4	B	14	A	24	D
5	B	15	A	25	D
6	C	16	B	26	D
7	A	17	A	27	C
8	A	18	A	28	D
9	B	19	B	29	D
10	A	20	C		

6

Inflation, Liberalisation, Privatization and Globalization

I. Choose the correct answer

1. When prices are falling continuously, the phenomenon is called

   A. Inflation B. Stagflation

   C. Deflation D. Reflation

2. When too much money classes too few goods, the resulting inflation is called

   A. Deflation B. Demand pull inflation

   C. Cost push inflation D. Stagflation

3. Cause of inflation in India is/are

   A. Deficit financing

   B. Erratic agriculture growth

   C. Inadequate rise in industrial production

   D. All of the above

4. Stagflation means

   A. Inflation with stagnation B. Recession with stagnation

   C. Inflation galloping like stage D. Inflation and increasing output

5. Which is the most effective quantitative method to control inflation in the economy?

   A. Bank rate policy B. Selective credit control

   C. Cash reserve ratio D. Both A and B

6. Which measures are followed by the government for handling inflation?

   A. Monetary measures B. Fiscal measures

   C. Controlling investments D. All of these

7. Inflation is measured on the basis of

A. Wholesale price index
B. Consumer price index
C. Marshall's index
D. All of these

8. When price increases due to increase in factor prices, it is

A. Demand pull inflation
B. Cost pull inflation
C. Stagflation
D. None of these

9. Barter has the defect

A. Goods exchanged are of inferior quality
B. Goods cannot be exchanged for services
C. Lack of common measure of value
D. None of the above

10. Value of money and supply of money are related

A. Inversely
B. Directly
C. Govt. law
D. Are not related

11. Inflation

A. Makes distribution of income equal
B. Makes distribution of income unequal
C. Has no effect on distribution of income
D. Affects only industrial sector

12. _____ refers to relaxation of government restrictions and regulations usually in areas of social and economic policies

A. Privatisation
B. Globalization
C. Disinvestment
D. Liberalization

13. FDI means

A. Forex direct investment
B. Foreign deregulated investment
C. Foreign direct investment
D. Forex deregulated investment

14. EPCG stands for

A. Export Promotion Capital Goods
B. Export Programmer for Credit Generation
C. Exchange Programmer for Consumer Goods
D. Export Promotion Consumer Goods

15. EXIM policy was announced in
    A. 1990 B. 1992
    C. 1995 D. 1998
16. The foreign trade policy has
    A. Started serve from India brand
    B. Identified certain thrust areas for growth
    C. Started duty free export credit
    D. All of the above
17. Disinvestment means selling of a public investment to a
    A. Private enterprises B. Public enterprises
    C. Capital market D. Departmental enterprises
18. 100 per cent privatization in India has taken place of
    A. CMC limited B. Maruti Udyog limited
    C. Centaur hotel D. VSNL
19. Cross holding is a method of
    A. Privatisation B. Globalisation
    C. Disinvestment D. Liberalisation
20. CIF stands for
    A. Cost, insurance, freight B. Cost inclusive of freight
    C. Cost in freight D. Cost, interest, freight
21. Privatization can be achieved by
    A. Leasing B. Franchising
    C. Contracting D. All of these
22. IMF was organized in
    A. 1946 B. 1956
    C. 1966 D. 1976
23. Organization which does not facilitable the process of globalization
    A. IMF B. World bank
    C. Asian bank D. WTO
24. Opening up the economy to the economies of the world so that Indian economy can compute at international level is called as
    A. Liberalization B. Globalization
    C. Privatization D. None of these

25. Exports now finance over ____ of imports

A. 50% B. 60%

C. 70% D. 80%

26. In the 2006-07 budget, the peak rate of custom duty was brought down to

A. 5% B. 10%

C. 12% D. 20%

27. IMF commenced its operation in

A. March 1947 B. April 1947

C. December 1947 D. April 1957

28. Exports now finance over 80% of imports, as compared to 60% in 1985, this situation is achieved due to

A. Liberalization B. Privatization

C. Disinvestment D. Globalization

29. Present membership of WTO is around _____ countries.

A. 135 B. 151

C. 180 D. 184

30. WTO was formed in

A. 1990 B. 1991

C. 1995 D. 2000

31. The other name of World Bank is

A. IDA B. IFC

C. IBRD D. All of these

32. Globalisation of a country's economy would increase its

A. Export B. Import

C. Both A and B D. Foreign exchange reserve

33. Globalisation of Indian economy was initiated in the year

A. 1981 B. 1985

C. 1991 D. 1995

34. Trade liberalisation in India resulted in

A. Increased share of agricultural and allied products in total export earnings.

B. Increase in absolute value of total exports

C. Both A and B

D. None of these

Answer keys

1	C	11	B	21	D	31	C
2	B	12	D	22	A	32	C
3	D	13	C	23	C	33	C
4	A	14	A	24	B	34	B
5	C	15	B	25	D		
6	D	16	D	26	B		
7	B	17	A	27	B		
8	B	18	C	28	D		
9	C	19	C	29	B		
10	A	20	A	30	C		

7

Basic Concepts in Farm Management

I. Choose the correct answer

1. Farm management deals with

   A. Labour allocation alone | B. Farm resource allocation
   C. Insurance allocation | D. All of these

2. Match the following

A. Farm machinery	1. Financial resource
B. Fertilizers, seeds	2. Stock resources
C. Labour	3. Fixed resources
D. Capital	4. Flow resources
A. 4 3 2 1	B. 3 2 4 1
C. 2 3 4 1	D. 3 4 2 1

3. Most useful method of decision making process

   A. Traditional method | B. Technical method
   C. Economic method | D. All the above

4. Characteristics of farm management which is not included

   A. Risk management
   B. Maximizing profit
   C. Use of applied science
   D. Non-integration of enterprises in the farm

5. In long run concept, all the factors used for crop cultivation is

   A. Fixed | B. Variable
   C. Either A or B | D. Both A and B

6. Cost which is also known as sunk cost

   A. Variable cost | B. Fixed cost
   C. Cost of variable inputs | D. Non cash inputs

7. Labour in farm management is an

A. Passive factor
B. Active factor
C. Substitute factor
D. None of these

8. Farm management is a

A. Physical science
B. Biological science
C. Social science
D. None of these

9. The value of seed and plants, manures and fertilizers, insecticides, fungicides and irrigation charges are known as

A. Variable cost
B. Fixed cost
C. Input cost
D. Machinery cost

10. Payment made to labour for its assistance to production is called

A. Rent
B. Wage
C. Interest
D. None of the above

11. Per hectare calculated cost is known as

A. Cost of cultivation
B. Cost of production
C. Cost of farming
D. Total cost

12. Per quintal calculated cost is known as

A. Cost of cultivation
B. Cost of production
C. Cost of farming
D. Total cost

13. Gross Domestic Product (GDP) defined as a value of all

A. Goods and produced in an economy in a year
B. Goods and services in an economy in a year
C. Final goods produced in an economy in a year
D. Final goods and services produced in an economy in a year

14. Which of the following is not component of farm business?

A. Capital
B. Environment
C. Land
D. Management

15. Which of the following is management decision

A. Level of resource use
B. Selection of least cost
C. Enterprise mix
D. All of the above

16. Farming in which multiple farmers run their holdings as a joint enterprise is termed as

A. Cooperative farming | B. Collective farming
C. Communal farming | D. Both B and C

17. Match the following

A. Diversified farming | 1. Investment by business person
B. Specialized farming | 2. More than one enterprise
C. Intensive farming | 3. More labour and capital in small farm
D. Capitalistic farming | 4. Single enterprise

A. 3 2 4 1 | B. 2 3 4 1
C. 2 4 3 1 | D. 4 3 2 1

18. Farming system which involves rearing of animals is called

A. Arable farming | B. Pastoral farming
C. Intensive farming | D. Extensive farming

19. Which of the following is not a system of farming based on ownership and operationship?

A. Dry farming | B. State farming
C. Collective farming | D. Capitalistic farming

20. Diversified farming is

A. Type of farming | B. System of farming
C. Both A and B | D. None of the above

Answer keys

1	B	11	A
2	B	12	B
3	C	13	D
4	D	14	B
5	B	15	C
6	B	16	D
7	B	17	C
8	D	18	B
9	C	19	A
10	B	20	A

8

Cost Concepts

I. Choose the correct answer

1. Maximum net revenue is obtained when

   A. MC > MR　　B. MC < MR

   C. MC = MR　　D. None of these

2. Cost minimization is depended on

   A. Cost of inputs　　B. Output price

   B. Rate of substitution　　D. All the above

3. The resources should be used in crops or enterprises where they bring not the greatest average return, but the greatest marginal returns, is a

   A. Law of return　　B. Cost principle

   C. Laws of equimarginal returns　　D. Principle of variable proportion

4. Fertilizer application in field is an example of

   A. Continuous function　　B. Discrete function

   C. Discontinuous function　　D. Both B and C

5. The incorrect statement about stage III of law of diminishing return is

   A. MPP is negative　　B. Rational stage

   C. EP is negative　　D. Both B and C

6. Elasticity of production is

   A. EP = MPP – APP　　B. EP = MPP + APPP

   C. EP = MPP x APP　　D. EP = MPP/APP

7. Demand for agricultural commodities is

   A. Elastic　　B. Inelastic

   C. Constant　　D. None of these

8. ______ is called as graphical representation of all the various combinations of inputs yielding the same level of output.

   A. Isocost line　　B. Isoquant line

   C. Both A and B　　D. Isorevenue line

9. (i) Fixed cost is dependent of output

   (ii) As output increases, total variable cost and total cost decreases

   (iii) Example of fixed cost is seeds and fertilizers

   A. (i) and (ii) are wrong B. (ii) and (iii) are wrong

   C. (i) alone is wrong D. All the statements are wrong

10. Cost of producing an additional unit of output is called as

    A. Total cost B. Marginal cost

    C. Fixed cost D. Variable cost

11. At break even point,

    A. The total cost and total revenue break is even

    B. The profit is equal to zero

    C. Minimum operation required to meet the total costs

    D. All the above

12. In PMFBY, premium for crops is

    A. Kharif crops 1. 5%

    B. Rabi crops 2. 1.5%

    C. Commercial and Horticulture crops 3. 2%

    A. 3 1 2 B. 2 3 1

    C. 3 2 1 D. 1 3 2

13. If the usage of one product increases, the second product usage is also increases and these products are called

    A. Complementary products B. Supplementary products

    C. Both A and B D. None of these

14. Match the following

    A. Current assets 1. Land and building

    B. Current liability 2. Cash on hand

    C. Fixed assets 3. Rent and taxes

    D. Long term liability 4. Mortgages and land contracts

	A	B	C	D
A.	3	1	2	4
B.	4	2	1	3
C.	2	3	1	4
D.	3	4	1	2

15. When marginal utility is zero, total utility is

A. Maximum B. Minimum

C. Constant D. Either A or B

16. The cost of crop production can be minimized by using economic principle

A. Law of diminishing marginal return

B. Principle of least cost combination

C. Law of variable proportion

D. None of these

17. Principle of equimarginal return is applied when

A. The prices of resources are high

B. The prices of resources are low

C. The prices of resources are equal

D. Either A or B

18. The shape of isoquant for perfect substitutes is

A. Parallel to x-axis B. Linear line

C. Parallel to y axis D. Convex to origin

19. Match the following

A. Tractor loan 1. Marketing loan

B. Motor cycle loan 2. Production loan

C. Key loan 3. Consumption loan

D. Warehouse receipt loan 4. Hypothecation loan

	A	B	C	D
A.	3	4	2	1
B.	2	1	4	3
C.	2	3	4	1
D.	2	4	3	1

20. Which statements are correct with respect to rational stage of classical production function

(i) MPP < APP

(ii) MPP = 0 when stage ends

(iii) E_p = 1 when stage starts

(iv) TPP negative

A. (i), (ii), (iii) and (iv) are correct B. (i), (ii) and (iii) are correct
C. (ii) and (iii) are correct D. (ii), (iii) and (iv) are correct

21. The decision rule drawn from the principle of marginalism is
A. MC > MR B. MC = MR
C. MC < MR D. MC > <MR

22. Which statements are correct with respect to random factor in time series analysis?
(i) Includes all omitted factors
(ii) Tastes and preferences are not included
(iii) Selling costs are included
(iv) Advertisement cost enhances random factor
A. (i) only B. (i) and (ii) are correct
C. (i), (iii), (iv) are correct D. (ii) and (iv) are correct

23. Which cost is said to be unit cost of production?
A. Total cost B. Average fixed cost
C. Average variable cost D. Average cost

24. Elasticity of production is obtained directly from which production function?
A. Linear B. Quadratic
C. Square root D. Cobb Douglas

25. Which statements are correct for continuous production function?
A. Input can be split into small unit
B. Output can be split into small unit
C. Input and output can be split into small units
D. Both input and output cannot be split.

26. The following is not a disadvantage of specialised farming?
A. Failure of crop
B. Increase in the skill of the farmer
C. Non utilisation of productive resources
D. Affects the soil health

27. Line representing various combination of two inputs that can be purchased with given outlay of fund is called as
A. Isoquant B. Isocost line
C. Isorevenue line D. Income curve

28. All small scale units with investments limit in plant and machinery upto _____ irrespective of the location of the unit are called tiny enterprises.

A. 25 lakhs B. 22 lakhs
C. 23 lakhs D. 20 lakhs

29. Agricultural prices commission is now called as

A. Commission on Agricultural Prices
B. Commission on Agricultural Cost and Prices
C. Agricultural Prices and Cost Commission
D. None of the above

30. Taccavi loans are the loans from

A. Private sector B. Government
C. Individual money lender D. All the above

31. Factors influencing elasticity of supply

A. Availability of inputs of production
B. Length of time period
C. Diversification of production activity
D. All the above

32. Loans extended for a period varying from 15 months to 5 years is known as

A. Short term loan B. Medium term loan
C. Long term loan D. Clean loan

33. Minimum size of the farm below which the output of a farm will be too small to maintain the family in a reasonable standard of living is called

A. Reasonable holding B. Minimum holding
C. Economic holding D. High standard holding

34. In NABARD, extent of refinance under various activities includes

A. Pilot rainfed project
B. Waste Land Development Scheme
C. Non farm sector scheme and agro processing promoting units
D. All the above

35. Products are at the maximum for a farm business when output is at a level where

A. MC = AC B. MR=AR
C. MR = AC D. MC = MR

36. The best use of limited resources is studied under the law of

A. Substitution B. Opportunity cost

C. Diminishing returns D. All of the above

37. A farmer can increase his farm income by

A. Increasing production B. Reducing cost of production

C. Both A and B D. None of the above

38. When TPP is maximum, the MPP will be

A. Maximum B. Zero

C. Minimum D. None of the above

39. Maximum profit is obtained at the point, where

A. $MP = AP$ B. $MP < AP$

C. $MP > AP$ D. None of the above

40. Utility of last unit is called

A. Initial utility B. Total utility

C. Marginal utility D. Zero utility

41. MC is given by

A. Slope of TFC B. Slope of TC

C. Slope of AC D. None of these

42. Which statement is true

A. ATC + AVC = AFC B. ATC + MC = AFC

C. ATC + AFC = AVC D. AFC + AVC = ATC

43. As output increases, AC curve

A. Falls B. Rises

C. Remains constant D. All are correct

44. TVC

A. Starts from origin B. Does not start from origin

C. Is parallel to Y-axis D. None of these

45. A farmer decides to stop growing crop A and instead use the land to grow crop B. The amount of potential profit lost by not growing crop A represents the farmer's

A. Opportunity costs B. Variable costs

C. Marginal costs D. Fixed costs

46. The federal government subsidizes the cost of insurance that covers the loss of revenue to a farmer as a result of

A. Damage to a crop due to a severe drought

B. Higher costs for distributing and marketing a product

C. A drop in prices due to oversupply of a commodity

D. Lower prices due to competition with foreign producers

47. Identify the correct statement

A. Net worth statement is known as income statement

B. It is equal to subtracting total liabilities from total assets

C. Anything of value in the possession of the farm business is call liability

D. Net worth ratio is also known as debt equity ratio

48. Detailed physical and financial statement of a farm plan or of a change in farm plan over a period of time is known as

A. Farm planning B. Farm budgeting

C. Financial analysis D. Income statement

49. Good farm plan should be

(i) Flexible

(ii) Maximize the resource use efficiency

(iii) Timely acquisition

(iv) Repayment of farm credit

A. (ii) and (iii) are correct B. (iii) and (iv) are correct

C. (iv) alone is correct D. (i), (ii), (iii) and (iv) are correct

50. Situation in which possible future outcomes are unknown is known as

A. Risk B. Uncertainly

C. Both A and B D. None of these

51. Economist who is awarded with Nobel memorial prize in economic sciences is

A. Hopkins B. Warren F

C. Adam Smith D. Amartya Kumar Sen

52. (i) Short term credit is given for purchase of seeds, fertilizers and pesticides

(ii) Long term credit given for periods more than 5 years to 25 years

(iii) Short term credit is repaid in one installment

(iv) Example of non institutional source of finance is land lords and money lenders

A. (iii) and (iv) are wrong B. (iv) alone is wrong
C. (iii) alone is wrong D. None of these

53. Depreciation depends on
A. Expected life B. Original cost
C. Salvage value D. All the above

54. Match the following

A. Enterprise budgeting — 1. Estimating outcome of part of business
B. Partial budgeting — 2. For specific entity
C. Complete budgeting — 3. Magnitude of cash inflow and outflow
D. Cash flow budgeting — 4. Whole farm business analysis

	A	B	C	D
A.	2	1	4	3
B.	3	4	2	1
C.	2	1	3	4
D.	4	3	2	1

55. Taccavi loans are provided
A. During cropping period B. Before sowing of crops
C. During famine, drought D. At the time of processing

56. Identify the incorrect statement about taccavi loans?
A. Low interest
B. Taccavi loans are granted for long period of time
C. Convenient repayment plan
D. Adequate loan amount

57. Higher level of efficiency denotes
A. System index is more than 100 B. System indeed is less than 100
C. System index is equal to 100 D. None of these

58. Ability of the farm to meet the current liabilities like tax, rent etc., can be measured by
A. Net Capital Ratio B. Current Ratio
C. Loan credit Ratio D. Debt Equity Ratio

59. A good farm record system is

A. Single entry system B. Double entry system

C. Both A and B D. Common record system

60. Allocation of scarce capital resources among competing ends is called as

A. Credit dispention B. Capital rationing

C. Credit distribution D. Capital lending

61. (i) Feasibility of a project can be measured by 3R principle

(ii) If the BCR of particular plan/business is less than 1, then it is worth to invest on project

(iii) If NPW (Net Present Worth) of a project is positive, it is considered as economically feasible project

A. (i) and (iii) are correct B. (iii) alone is correct

C. (i) and (ii) are correct D. All are correct

62. Economic viability of project can be measured by

A. Net present worth (NPW) B. Benefit cost ratio (BCR)

C. Internal rate of return (IRR) D. All the above

63. The advantages of money lenders are

(i) Unrestricted supply of credits

(ii) Timely availability of credit

(iii) Low rate of interest

(iv) Easy access by farmers

A. (i) and (ii) are correct B. (i), (ii) and (iii) are correct

C. (ii) and (iv) are correct D. (i), (ii) and (iii) are correct

64. (i) Scale of finance is the credit limit fixed for each crop

(ii) It is fixed based on the crops cost of cultivation

(iii) It is fixed once a year

A. (i) and (ii) are correct B. (iii) alone is correct

C. (ii) and (iii) are correct D. All are correct

65. Informal sector loans include

A. NABARD B. SBI

C. Money lenders D. Both B and C

66. Repaying capacity of farmer depends on
    (i) Family expenses
    (ii) Amount of income in farm household
    (iii) Pre existing liabilities
    (iv) Margin for the risk factor
    (v) Loan installment
    A. (i), (ii) and (iii) are correct B. (i), (ii) and (iv) are correct
    C. (iii), (iv) and (v) are correct D. All are correct
67. Loan amount gets absorbed in production process and additional income generated is sufficient to repay the entire loan amount is termed as
    A. Non-self liquidating credit B. Self liquidating credit
    C. Both A and B D. None of these
68. Short term loan mainly given for purchase of
    A. Pump set B. Seed
    C. Heavy machinery D. Bullock
69. Which of the following is the equation for determining net worth?
    A. Net Worth = Assets – Liabilities B. Net Worth = Assets + Liabilities
    C. Net Worth = Assets / Liabilities D. Net Worth = Liabilities - Assets
70. Solvency of a business can be determined by evaluating the
    A. Cash flow statement B. Debt to equity ratio
    C. Price to earnings ratio D. Net income
71. Land is considered to be a
    A. Short term asset B. Long term asset
    C. Intermediate term asset D. Short term liability

Answer keys

1	C	16	B	31	D	46	A	61	A
2	D	17	A	32	B	47	B	62	E
3	C	18	B	33	C	48	B	63	D
4	A	19	C	34	D	49	D	64	D
5	B	20	B	35	D	50	B	65	C
6	D	21	B	36	A	51	D	66	D
7	B	22	C	37	D	52	D	67	B
8	B	23	D	38	B	53	D	68	B

9	D	24	D	39	D	54	A	69	D
10	B	25	C	40	C	55	C	70	B
11	D	26	B	41	B	56	D	71	B
12	C	27	B	42	D	57	A		
13	A	28	A	43	D	58	B		
14	C	29	B	44	A	59	B		
15	A	30	B	45	A	60	B		

9

Agricultural Finance and Cooperation

I. Choose the correct answer

1. Agricultural finance mainly concern with
   A. Utilization of funds
   B. Acquisition of funds
   C. Both utilization and acquisition of funds
   D. None of the above
2. National income denotes
   A. Revenue of the government in one year
   B. Sum total of all factor earnings in the country
   C. Revenue of nationalized enterprises
   D. Banks budgetary surplus of the government
3. What is the most important source of money lending to farmers in rural areas
   A. Rural banks B. Local money lender
   C. Nationalized banks D. Cooperative agencies
4. Match the following

Special branches	**Bank**
A. Agricultural development branches	1. Syndicate Bank
B. Rural service centre	2. State Bank of India
C. Farm clinic centre	3. Dena Bank
D. Rural credit and development divisions	4. Indian Overseas branches

   A. 1 3 4 2 B. 4 3 2 1
   C. 2 3 1 4 D. 2 1 4 3

5. Which bank extends financial assistance to small and marginal farmers through DRDA (District Rural Development Agency)?
   A. Commercial Bank B. Private Bank
   C. Corporation Bank D. None of these
6. Bank which are not directly involved in financing to the farmers is
   A. SBI B. NABARD
   C. RBI D. Both B and C
7. Apex institution for agricultural finance is
   A. RBI B. NABARD
   C. RRB D. Commercial Bank
8. Land development banks provide
   A. Short term loan B. Medium term loan
   C. Long term loan D. None of these
9. _____ is to enhance the export of processed agricultural products
   A. MPEDA B. APEDA
   C. NAFED D. NIAM
10. The first type of co-operative societies established in India are
    A. Credit societies B. Farming societies
    C. Marketing societies D. Housing societies
11. The central sector scheme on women in agriculture was launched during
    A. Sixth five year plan B. Seventh five year plan
    C. Eighth five year plan D. Ninth five year plan
12. Which of the following organizations looks after the credit needs of agriculture and rural development in India?
    A. FCI B. IDBI
    C. NABARD D. ICAR
13. Which of the following estimates the National income in India?
    A. Central Statistical Organization B. National Income Committee
    C. Niti Ayog D. Reserve Bank of India
14. Co-operatives for tribes are called as
    A. Multipurpose societies
    B. Savita
    C. Lead bank
    D. Large agriculture multipurpose co-operative societies

Answer keys

1	C	11	B
2	B	12	C
3	B	13	A
4	C	14	D
5	A		
6	D		
7	B		
8	C		
9	B		
10	A		

10

Banking

I. Choose the correct answer

1. Pandiyan bank is sponsored by

   A. Indian Bank B. Indian Overseas Bank

   C. United Bank of India D. Union Bank of India

2. Tamil Nadu Grama Bank is established on

   A. April 2019 C. March 2018

   B. December 2018 D. January 2019

3. Headquarters of Pandiyan Bank is

   A. Salem B. Coimbatore

   C. Virudhunagar D. Chennai

4. Tamil Nadu Grama Bank is sponsored by

   A. Indian Bank B. Indian Overseas Bank

   C. Union Bank of India D. United Bank of India

5. Lead bank in Coimbatore is

   A. Canara Bank B. SBI

   C. Indian Overseas Bank D. Indian Bank

6. Number of subsidiary banks started with State Bank of India in 1959 is

   A. 5 B. 3

   C. 7 D. 9

7. Nationalization of commercial bank is on

   A. June 29, 1969 and July 1975 B. July 19, 1969 and April 1980

   C. April 10, 1969 and June 1980 D. March 15, 1969 and April 1980

8. As on today, the number of nationalized bank in India is

   A. 25 B. 20

   C. 21 D. 14

9. Number of banks commercialized in 1980 is

A. 14 B. 6

C. 20 D. 12

10. Imperial Bank of India was established in

A. 1931 B. 1955

C. 1935 D. 1921

11. Bank which is not nationalized is

A. Union Bank of India B. United Bank of India

C. Nainital Bank D. Vijaya Bank

12. RBI Act was passed in the year

A. 1935 B. 1934

C. 1924 D. 1955

13. Bank rate is about

A. 5.00% B. 5.25%

C. 5.50% D. 5.40%

14. CRAFICARD committee headed by the chairmanship of

A. Narasimham B. Sivaraman

C. Bava D. None of these

15. Lead bank scheme was initiated by

A. RBI B. NABARD

C. Commercial Bank D. Both A and B

16. Match the following

A. Service area approach 1. 1975

B. All India Rural Credit Review Committee 2. 1989

C. Regional Rural Bank 3. 1969

D. RBI nationalization 4. 1949

A. 4 3 2 1 B. 2 4 1 3

C. 2 1 4 3 D. 2 3 1 4

17. Lead bank scheme is for

A. Block B. State

C. District D. Village

18. The first Indian RBI governor is

A. I.G. Patel B. C.D.Deshmukh

C. Osborne Smith D. H.V.R.Iyengar

19. The banks which was merged with Bank of Baroda is

A. Indian Bank and Corporation Bank

B. Punjab National Bank and Canara Bank

C. IDBI and IDFC

D. Dena Bank and Vijaya Bank

20. The bank which prepares district credit plan is

A. Lead bank B. State Bank of India

C. Cooperative bank D. Reserve Bank of India

21. The current Repo rate is about

A. 5.65% B. 5.15%

C. 5.4% D. 6.25%

22. The Bharatiya Reserve Bank Note Mudran Pvt Ltd., headquarters is at

A. Kolkatta B. Bangalore

C. Noida D. Mumbai

23. The bank which is not a customers of NABARD is

A. Schedule commercial bank B. RRB

C. Cooperative banks D. Local area banks

24. Match the following

A. Reverse Repo rate 1. 4%

B. CRR (Cash Reserve Ratio) 2. 5.15%

C. Statuary Liquidity Ratio 3. 18.75%

A. 2 1 3 B. 3 1 2

C. 3 2 1 D. 2 3 1

25. The RRB was formed under the committee of

A. Sivaraman B. Narasimham committee

C. Bava committee D. None of these

26. RRBs are sponsored by schedule commercial bank of about

A. 50% B. 35%

C. 15% D. 25%

27. The service of RRB are not available in the state of

A. Madhya Pradesh and Bihar

B. Andhra Pradesh and Nagaland

C. Goa and Sikkim

D. Uttar Pradesh and Madhya Pradesh

28. Example of non banking financial institutions

(i) Life Insurance Corporation (LIC)

(ii) General Insurance Corporation (GIC)

(iii) Unit Trust of India

(iv) Muthoot Finance Ltd.,

(v) Chit Fund Company

A. (iv) and (v) B. (iii), (ii) and (v)

C. (i), (ii) and (iii) D. All of these

29. Bank which is exempted from maintaining CRR and SLR is

A. NABARD B. Commercial banks

C. RRB D. HDFC

30. The first RRB is named as ______ and is sponsored by ______.

A. Vananchal Gramin Bank, SBI

B. Sutlej Gramin Bank, Punjab and Sind Bank

C. Saptagira Grameena Bank, Indian Bank

D. Prathama Grameen Bank, Syndicate Bank

31. Which of the following is not the function of the RBI?

A. Bankers Bank

B. Custodian of foreign exchange reserve

C. Controller of credit

D. Allotting money directly to farmers for agricultural development

32. At present, how many public sector banks are working in India?

A. 27 B. 25

C. 29 D. 12

33. Who issues metallic coins in India?

A. RBI B. GOI

C. Banks and financial institutions D. All the above

34. Which of the following is issuing currency notes in India?

A. RBI B. GOI

C. Banks and financial institutions D. All the above

35. Village adoption scheme was first conceived by

A. NABARD B. SBI

C. Canara Bank D. RRB

36. NPCI stands for

A. National Payments Consumer of India

B. National Project Consumer of India

C. National Payments Corporation of India

D. National Project Corporation of India

37. Who is sponsor bank for Pallavan grama bank and where is the headquarters?

A. Indian Bank, Salem B. Indian Bank, Cuddalore

C. SBI, Salem D. IOB, Salem

38. The following is not an affiliate body of World Bank

A. IMF B. IFC

C. IDA D. WTO

39. LSMPD was established in India based on the recommendations of

A. Narasimham committee B. Bava committee

C. Nicholson committee D. Mohan Kanda

40. Match the following

NABARD refinances the following projects to the tune of

A. Farm mechanization 1. 100%

B. Biogas 2. 70%

C. Non farm sector schemes 3. 75%

D. Other schemes 4. 50%

	A	B	C	D
A.	3	1	4	2
B.	1	4	3	2
C.	4	2	1	3
D.	4	3	1	2

41. SLR means

A. Statutory Liquidity Ratio
B. Standard Liquidity Ratio
C. Systematic Lending Ratio
D. Subsidized Lending Ratio

42. Regional Rural Banks are financed by

A. Nationalized banks
B. Government of India
C. RBI
D. All the above

43. Which of the following are called Brettonwoods twins?

A. IMF and World Trade Organisation
B. IMF and International Bank for Reconstruction and Development
C. IBRD and World Trade Organisation
D. None of the above

44. The National Bank for Agriculture and Rural Development (NABARD) was established in the year

A. 1970
B. 1975
C. 1977
D. 1982

45. The head office of the NABARD is located in

A. Lucknow
B. Hyderabad
C. New Delhi
D. Mumbai

46. NABARD was established in the

A. Fourth five year plan
B. Fifth five year plan
C. Sixth five year plan
D. Eighth five year plan

47. Which of the following banks were nationalized in 1980?

A. Andhra Bank
B. Vijaya Bank
C. Corporation Bank
D. All the above

48. Consider the following statements and identify the correct answer.

(i) Post nationalization banks were supposed to open more branches in rural and semi-urban areas

(ii) Banks had to provide credit facilities to areas that come under priority sector.

A. (i) alone is correct
B. (ii) alone is correct
C. Both are correct
D. None

49. Consider the following statements and identify the correct answer.

(i) The lead bank scheme owes its origin to Nariman Committee

(ii) Under this scheme, SBI and its subsidiaries only were given the responsibility of development of districts

A. (i) alone is correct B. (ii) alone is correct

C. Both are correct D. None

50. Regional Rural Banks work at

A. Hobli level B. Taluk level

C. District level D. All levels

51. Which of the following is a subsidiary of SBI?

A. State Bank of Hyderabad B. State Bank of Mysore

C. State Bank of Patiala D. All the above

52. In 2001, RBI issued a set of guidelines for private sector. Which of the following is true?

A. Initial paid-up capital should be 200 crore rupees

B. Share of promoters in paid-up capital should not be less than 40%

C. Big corporate houses are not allowed to promote any bank

D. All the above

53. In 2001, RBI issued a set of guidelines for private sector. Which of the following is true?

A. NBFCs with minimum CAR of 12% and with good track record will be allowed to open private banks

B. New banks have to open minimum 25% of branches in rural and semi-urban areas

C. They have to provide minimum 40% of loans to priority sector

D. All the above

54. In 2001, RBI issued a set of guidelines for private sector. Accordingly which bank was issued licence?

A. HDFC Bank Limited B. YES Bank Limited

C. ICICI Bank Limited D. All the above

55. Which of the following banks was not nationalized in 1969?

A. Vijaya Bank B. Canara Bank

C. Bank of India D. Central Bank of India

56. Consider the following statements and identify the correct statements.
    (i) NABARD was set up by an act of Parliament in 1982
    (ii) It facilitates credit for agriculture only
    A. (i) alone is correct   B. (ii) alone is correct
    C. Both are correct   D. None

57. Consider the following statements and identify the correct statements.
    (i) NABARD provides consultancy services.
    (ii) NABARD supervises rural financial institutions
    A. (i) alone correct   B. (ii) alone correct
    C. Both are correct   D. None

58. Which of the following is a function of NABARD?
    A. Monitoring flow of ground level credit to agriculture
    B. Credit planning and monitoring
    C. Formulation of operational guidelines for rural financial institutions
    D. All the above

59. Which of the following institutions is not part of the World Bank community?
    A. IBRD   B. WTO
    C. IDA   D. IFC

60. Which bank is known as banker's bank?
    A. RBI   B. SBI
    C. PNB   D.NABARD

61. A banking system where business is carried on by a bank through a network of branches spread throughout the country is known as
    A. Unit banking   B. Branch banking
    C. Chain banking   D. Group banking

62. .....refers to a system of banking in which two or more independent banks are brought under the control of a holding company
    A. Group banking   B. Chain banking
    C. Deposit banking   D. Investment banking

63. Banking is a system where banks combine both the deposit banking and invest banking functions
    A. Chain banking   B. Deposit banking
    C. Investment banking   D. Mixed banking

64. India's first women's bank The Bharatiya Mahila Bank was inaugurated in which city?

A. Mumabi B. Delhi

C. Kolkata D. Chennai

65. Current deposit is also known as

A. Savings deposit B. Demand deposit

C. Time deposit D. Recurring deposit

66. Which deposits are repayable after the expiry of the fixed period?

A. Demand deposit B. Time deposit

C. Savings deposit D. Recurring deposit

67. ....is a credit facility granted by commercial banks to current account holders

A. Cash credit B. Over draft

C. Discounting of bills of exchange D. Demand loans

68. The process of ....begins with banks lending money out of primary deposit.

A. Credit creation B. Cash credit

C. Debit creation D. Over draft

69. CRR refers to

A. Cash Reserve Ratio B. Credit Reserve Ratio

C. Common Reserve Ratio D. None of these

70. NBFI s refers to

A. Non Banking Financial Industries

B. Non Banking Financial Institution

C. Net Banking Financial Industries

D. Net Banking Financial Institutions

71. DIGC refers to

A. Deposit Industrial Guarantee Corporation

B. Development Insurance Guarantee Corporation

C. Development Industrial Guarantee Corporation

D. Deposit Insurance Guarantee Corporation

72. SLR refers to

A. Statutory Liquidity Ratio B. Stability Liquidity Ratio

C. Safety Liquidity Ratio D. None of these

73. EFT stands for

A. Electronic Fund Transmission
B. Electronic Fund Transfer
C. Electronic Feature Transfer
D. None of these

74. Which bank was introduced first ATM machine in India?

A. RBI
B. HSBC
C. PNB
D. ICICI bank

75. CDM refers to

A. Cash Deposit Machine
B. Credit Development Method
C. Cash Development Method
D. Cash Development Machine

76. ECS refers to

A. Easy Cash Service
B. Electronic Clearing Service
C. Electronic Cash service
D. Easy Clearing Service

77. NEFT refers to

A. National Economic Fund Transfer
B. National Economic Fee Transfer
C. National Electronic Fee Transfer
D. None of these

78. IFSC stands for

A. Indian Financial System Code
B. International Financial System Code
C. Indian Fund Service Code
D. None of these

79. RTGS stands for

A. Real Time Gross Settlement
B. Real Term Gross Settlement
C. Real Time Goal Settlement
D. Real Term Goal Settlement

80. SWIFT stands for

A. Society for Worldwide Internet Financial Telecommunications
B. Solution for Worldwide Interbank Financial Telecommunications
C. Solution for Worldwide Internet Financial Telecommunications
D. Society for Worldwide Interbank Financial Telecommunications

81. CBS stands for

A. Code Banking Solutions
B. Core Banking Solutions
C. Common Banking Solutions
D. Credit Banking Solutions

82. CTS refers to

A. Cheque Truncation System | B. Cheque Transaction System
C. Cheque Truncation Solution | D. Cheque Transaction Solution

83. Credit Information Bureau of India Limited is India's first credit rating agency which was incorporated in the year

A. 1988 | B. 2000
C. 2005 | D. 1995

84. KYC refers to

A. Know Your Customer | B. Know Your Credit
C. Know Your City | D. Know Your Company

85. Delivery of financial services at affordable costs to the disadvantaged low income segments of the society is known as

A. Credit creation | B. Financial exclusion
C. Financial inclusion | D. Consumer credit

86. RBI act came into existence during

A. 1934 | B. 1935
C. 1948 | D. 1945

87. Banking Regulation Act came into existence during

A. 1949 | B. 1934
C. 1956 | D. 1947

88. A cheque bears a date earlier than the date on which it is presented to the bank, it is called as

A. Post-dated cheque | B. Anti- dated cheque
C. Outstation cheque | D. Local cheque

89. A cheque bears a date which is yet to come it is called as

A. Post dated cheque | B. Anti –dated cheque
C. Crossed cheque | D. Self cheque

90. If a cheque presented for payment after three months from the date of the cheque, it is known as

A. Self cheque | B. Mutilated cheque
C. Local cheque | D. Stale cheque

91. If a cheque is torn into two or more pieces and presented for payment, it is called

A. Mutilated cheque | B. Stale cheque
C. Local cheque | D. Self cheque

92. Cancellation of cheque is known as

A. Crossing
B. Opening of crossing
C. Double crossing
D. General crossing

93. MICR refers to

A. Magnetic Ink Character Recognition
B. Magnetic Information Character Recognition
C. Magnetic Ink Code Recognition
D. Magnetic Icon Character recognition

94. Life Insurance Corporation of India was formed in the year

A. 1948
B. 1964
C. 1956
D. 1988

95. The General Insurance Corporation of India was formed in the year

A. 1973
B. 1948
C. 1956
D. 1984

96. General Insurance Corporation of India Act was formed in

A. 1973
B. 1963
C. 1972
D. 1962

97. FDR stands for

A. Fixed Delivery Receipt
B. Fixed Deposit Receipt
C. Final Deposit Receipt
D. Final Delivery Receipt

98. In which year Negotiable Instrument Act was passed?

A. 1981
B. 1956
C. 1881
D. 1984

99. In which types of banking system, several banks joins hands with each other for meeting the credit requirements of the large borrower ?

A. Group banking
B. Consortium banking
C. Net banking
D. None of these

100. The practice of conducting banking transactions from home rather than at bank branches by means of electronic telecommunication is known as

A. Branch banking
B. Group banking
C. Chain banking
D. Home banking

101. NPA means

A. Net Performing Asset
B. Non Performing Asset
C. Net Profit Acceptance
D. None of these

102. Example for Foreign Bank is

A. Centurion Bank
B. City Bank
C. Axis Bank
D. All

103. Bank of Baroda is an example for

A. Private sector Bank
B. Foreign Bank
C. Public sector Bank
D. None of these

104. Federal Bank is a

A. Private sector Bank
B. Foreign Bank
C. Public sector Bank
D. None of these

105. IBRD is also known as

A. Central Bank
B. World Bank
C. Exim Bank
D. All

106. State financial corporation is an example for

A. Industrial Bank
B. Foreign Bank
C. Public sector Bank
D. All

107. …… is a loan for short term temporary financing for business firms.

A. Term loans
B. Bridge loans
C. Cash credit
D. All

108. ……. is a temporary financial arrangement by the bank to draw more than the amount standing to his credit

A. Over draft
B. Bridge loans
C. Cash credit
D. None of these

109. A ….. is a bank line any other bank operating on a small scale without involving credit risk

A. Consortium Bank
B. Payment Bank
C. Small Finance Bank
D. None of these

110. …. bank can accept deposit only, but cannot lend.

A. Consortium Bank
B. Payment Bank
C. Small Finance Bank
D. None of these

111. …… can issue ATM debit cards, but no credit cards.

A. Payment Bank
B. Consortium Bank
C. Small Finance Bank
D. None of these

112. ….. is to perform lending activities among weaker sections of the community.

A. Small Finance Bank
B. Consortium Bank
C. Payment Bank
D. All

113. ….. are norms for banks aimed at mitigating the risk and strengthening the capital structure of the banks of member countries.

A. IRAC rules
B. BASEL norms
C. Capital Adequacy Norms
D. None of these

114. Which of the following is known as plastic money?

A. Credit card
B. Debit card
C. None of these
D. Both of these

115. Debit card means

A. Pay later
B. Pay now
C. Both of these
D. None of these

116. Which type of loans have less prone to the risk of becoming NPA?

A. Retail loans
B. Whole sale loans
C. Gold loans
D. Mortgage loans

117. Which is the fastest possible money transfer system through banking channel?

A. RTGS
B. EFT
C. ATM
D. None of these

118. Which of the banking asset are treated as performing asset?

A. Standard asset
B. Loss asset
C. Doubtful asset
D. Sub standard asset and standard asset

119. When was the banking ombudsman scheme was introduced?

A. 1991
B. 1994
C. 1995
D. 1990

Answer keys

1	B	21	C	41	A	61	B	81	B	101	B
2	A	22	B	42	D	62	A	82	A	102	B
3	C	23	D	43	B	63	D	83	B	103	C
4	A	24	A	44	D	64	A	84	A	104	A
5	A	25	B	45	D	65	B	85	C	105	B
6	C	26	B	46	C	66	B	86	A	106	A
7	B	27	C	47	D	67	B	87	A	107	B
8	B	28	D	48	C	68	A	88	B	108	A
9	B	29	C	49	A	69	A	89	A	109	B
10	D	30	D	50	C	70	B	90	D	110	B
11	C	31	D	51	D	71	D	91	A	111	A
12	B	32	D	52	D	72	A	92	B	112	A
13	D	33	B	53	D	73	B	93	A	113	B
14	B	34	A	54	B	74	B	94	C	114	D
15	A	35	B	55	A	75	A	95	A	115	B
16	D	36	C	56	A	76	B	96	C	116	A
17	C	37	A	57	C	77	D	97	B	117	A
18	B	38	D	58	D	78	A	98	C	118	A
19	D	39	B	59	B	79	A	99	B	119	C
20	A	40	D	60	A	80	D	100	D		

11

Kisan Credit Card

I. Choose the correct answer

1. When did the Government present Kisan Credit Card Scheme?

   A. April 1853 B. August 1998

   C. July 1991 D. November 1995

2. Margin shareholder of Agriculture Insurance Company is

   A. National Insurance Company Ltd

   B. General Insurance Corporation of India

   C. NABARD

   D. The New India Assurance Company Ltd.

3. Pradhan Mantri Fasal Bima Yojana is an example of

   A. Crop insurance scheme B. Rural development scheme

   C. Women empowerment scheme D. Employment scheme

4. Agriculture Insurance Company of India Limited commenced business from

   A. 2005 B. 2003

   C. 2000 D. 1999

5. NAIS stand for

   A. National Agriculture Innovative Scheme

   B. National Agricultural Infrastructure Scheme

   C. National Agricultural Insurance Scheme

   D. National Agricultural and Rural Development Insurance Scheme

6. Kisan Credit Card was introduced by

   A. SBI B. Indian Bank

   C. RRB D. HDFC Bank

7. Institution involved in Kisan Credit Card is

A. Commercial banks B. RRB

C. State cooperative bank D. All the above

8. The committee responsible for KCC scheme is

A. R.V. Gupta B. Sivaraman

C. Narasimham D. Bava committee

9. Kisan Credit Card provides only

A. Long term credit B. Medium term credit

C. Short term credit D. Both A and C

10. Kisan Credit Card introduced in

A. 1995 B. 1998

C. 2000 D. 2003

11. Consider the following statements and identify the correct statements.

(i) The Kisan Credit Scheme was launched in 2015

(ii) The scheme provides adequate and timely credit support to the farmers for their cultivation needs.

A. (i) alone is correct B. (ii) alone is correct

C. Both are correct D. None

Answer keys

1	B	6	B	11	B
2	B	7	D		
3	A	8	A		
4	B	9	C		
5	C	10	B		

12

Agribusiness Management

I. Choose the correct answer

1. Document that describes the type of competition a business will face and the types of customers the business hopes to attract is

   A. Financial plan B. Operating plan
   C. Management plan D. Legal plan

2. Document that projects the income, expenses, and profits of a business over a multi-year period is

   A. Operating plan B. Legal plan
   C. Management plan D. Financial plan

3. The written description of all aspects of an agribusiness is

   A. Management plan B. Business plan
   C. Legal plan D. Financial plan

4. The time between the beginning of a process or project and the appearance of its results is

   A. Lead time B. Benefit
   C. Cost per click D. Spot advertisement

5. A plan of action for a business is known as a

   A. Balance sheet B. Cash flow statement
   C. Budget D. Financial statement

6. A TV advertisement placed on one station in one market is

   A. Spot advertisement B. Lead time
   C. Cost per click D. Benefit

7. A technique for deciding if an advertisement should be placed and for how long is

A. Spot advertisement B. Lead time

C. Cost benefit analysis D. Benefit

8. The total of the product cost plus the markup is

A. Price point B. Loss leader

C. Selling price D. Price skimming

9. Placing a high price on a product because of a lack of competition is

A. Price skimming B. Price point

C. Selling price D. Revenue

10. The total amount received from the product sales is

A. Selling price B. Revenue

C. Price point D. Loss leader

11. What are two goals of product packaging?

A. Preserves Quality B. Marketing and sales

C. Protection and restraint D. Both A and C

12. The demand for pork is determined by

A. The price of pork B. Income of the purchaser.

C. The price of substitute products D. All of the above

13. A dairy cow held for breeding and production purposes is known as a

A. Short term asset B. Intermediate asset

C. Capital asset D. Long-term liability

14. Vertical integration is most common in which of the following agricultural enterprises?

A. Horses B. Beef

C. Grain D. Poultry

15. Which of the following business types allows the most liability protection for the owners?

A. Partnership B. Sole proprietorship

C. Corporation D. Partnership

Answer keys

1	C	11	D
2	D	12	D
3	C	13	C
4	A	14	D
5	C	15	C
6	A		
7	C		
8	C		
9	A		
10	B		

UNIT XIII: AGRICULTURAL MARKETING AND INTELLIGENCE

1

Agricultural Marketing

I. Choose the correct answer

1. Market in which bond, share and securities are bought and sold are called

   A. Consuming market B. Rural market

   C. Forward market D. Capital market

2. Match the following

A. Secular market	1. One seller
B. Monopoly market	2. Permanent one
C. Monopsony market	3. One buyer
D. Monopolistic competition	4. Large number of seller deal in heterogeneous commodity

   A. 2 1 4 3 B. 4 3 2 1

   C. 2 1 3 4 D. 3 4 1 2

3. Marketing is

   A. Economic link between the producers and the consumers

   B. Maintain the balance between demand and supply

   C. Equitable distribution of goods and services

   D. All the above

4. Match the following

A. Terminal market	1. Marketing over the country
B. National market	2. Export purpose
C. Secular market	3. More than one country
D. International market	4. Machineries and manufactured goods

   A. 2 4 1 3 B. 3 4 2 1

   C. 2 1 4 3 D. 4 3 1 2

5. Market is derived from

A. Greek word
B. Latin word
C. French word
D. Both B and C

6. The device used for protection against the price fluctuations which arise in the course of the marketing of commodities is

A. Future trading
B. Contract farming
C. Speculative market
D. Capital market

7. The commodities not suitable for future trading are

A. Commodities having in plentiful supply
B. Commodities having minimum degree of perishability
C. Commodities having heterogenous character
D. Commodities having low demand

8. Number of regulated markets functioning in Tamil Nadu is

A. 268
B. 252
C. 248
D. 272

9. The most common method exists in regulated market is

A. Open auction system
B. Close tender system
C. Moghum sale
D. Dara sale

10. Oligopoly market refers to

A. Differentiated or undifferentiated products or services
B. Few firms are in market
C. Firm may be price maker
D. All the above

11. The agricultural sector contributed to our foreign exchange resources by

A. Earning foreign exchange through export
B. Conserving through import substitutions
C. Both A and B
D. None of the above

12. VAT is

A. Excise tax
B. Income tax
C. Indirect sales tax
D. Direct additional tax

13. Which one of the following is a competitive market?
    A. Perfect market B. Primary market
    C. Capital market D. Wholesale market
14. In pure competitive market, the demand curve is slopping
    A. Downward B. Upward
    C. Straight to X-axis D. Parallel to Y-axis
15. Kinked demand and price rigidity are seen in this market structure
    A. Oligopoly B. Monopoly
    C. Perfect D. Duopoly
16. Match the following:

A. Secular market	1. Demand over entire country
B. Terminal market	2. Cattle market
C. Local market	3. Manufactured goods
D. National market	4. Processing and storage are dominant

	A	B	C	D
A.	3	4	2	1
B.	3	2	1	4
C.	2	3	4	1
D.	3	1	4	2

17. When large number of seller deal in heterogenous and differentiated form of commodity is called
    A. Perfect market B. Oligopoly market
    C. Oligopsony market D. Monopolistic competitive market
18. In convergent form of Cobb-Web cycle, the relationship between E_d and E_s is
    A. $E_d > E_s$ B. $E_d < E_s$
    C. $E_d = E_s$ D. $E_s > E_d$
19. Which of the following is the most competitive market structure?
    A. Perfect competition B. Monopolistic competition
    C. Oligopoly D. Local market
20. Persons who expect that prices will go down in future are
    A. Bulls B. Bears
    C. Retailers D. Whole sellers

21. Persons who expect that price will go up in future are known as
    A. Bulls B. Bears
    C. Whole sellers D. Dalal
22. Prices are settled by pressing the fingers under cover of a piece of cloth is
    A. Private negotiation B. Under cover of a cloth
    C. Sale by sample D. Moghum sale
23. Primary wholesale market, secondary wholesale market and terminal market are the kind of
    A. Wholesale market B. Cooperative market
    C. Both A and B D. None of the above
24. Combination of crop production and milk production activities is an example of
    A. Competitive B. Complementary
    C. Supplementary D. None of the above
25. The regulated market have been established by
    A. Central government B. District Municipal Corporation
    C. State government D. Panchayats
26. A regulated market or controlled market is the provision of goods or services that is regulated by
    A. A government appointed body B. A private person
    C. An NGO D. ICAR
27. Which of the following is correct about regulated markets?
    A. It is common for a regulated market to control natural monopolies such as aspects of telecommunications, water, gas and electricity supply.
    B. Often regulated markets are established during the partial privatization of government controlled utility assets
    C. In a regulated market, the government regulatory agency may legislate regulations that privilege special interests
    D. All the above are correct
28. The storage, pricing and marketing of agricultural commodities is as important for high profits as the process of production so the government since 1951 has laid stress on the development of
    A. Physical markets
    B. On farm and off farm storage structures

C. Facilities for standardization and grading

D. All the above

29. When department of Agricultural marketing started in Tamil Nadu?

A. 1967 B. 1977

C. 1987 D. 1997

30. The word market is derived from which word

A. Greek B. French

C. Latin D. Roman

31. Seaboard markets located at

A. Alappey B. Vishakhapatnam

C. Goa D. Cochin

32. Terminal markets are located at

A. Bangalore B. Hyderabad

C. Nagpur D. Imphal

33. Which crop is traded internationally?

A. Coffee B. Sorghum

C. Bajra D. Groundnut

34. Which of the following is an imperfect market?

A. Monopoly B. Oligopoly

C. Both A and B D. None of these

35. In duopsony market, there will be

A. One buyer B. One seller

C. Two buyers D. Two sellers

36. Converting groundnut into oil creates

A. Place utility B. Form utility

C. Time utility D. Possession utility

37. Transport function of marketing creates

A. Place utility B. Form utility

C. Time utility D. Possession utility

38. Storing milk creates

A. Place utility B. Form utility

C. Time utility D. Possession utility

39. ABC company buying potatoes from XYZ trader results in

A. Place utility B. Form utility

C. Time utility D. Possession utility

40. Quality of agricultural commodities is ensured by

A. AGMARK B. ISI

C. BSI D. ISO

41. International food safety standards are developed by

A. HACCP B. CODEX

C. ECOMARK D. WTO

42. Market where buying and selling is regulated and controlled by state Government is

A. Secular market B. Perfect market

C. Regulated market D. Long term market

43. Match the following:

A. Form utility 1. Storage function

B. Place utility 2. Processing function

C. Time utility 3. Exchange function

D. Possession utility 4. Transportation function

	A	B	C	D
A.	3	4	1	2
B.	2	4	1	3
C.	4	3	2	1
D.	2	1	4	3

44. The characteristics of Agricultural commodities include

(i) Perishable ability

(ii) Seasonality of production

(iii) Bulkiness of product

(iv) Irregular supply

A. (ii) and (iii) are correct B. (iii) and (iv) are correct

C. (i) and (iv) are correct D. (i), (ii), (iii) and (iv) are correct

Answer keys

1	D	11	C	21	A	31	D	41	B
2	C	12	C	22	B	32	A	42	C
3	D	13	A	23	A	33	A	43	B
4	B	14	C	24	B	34	C	44	D
5	B	15	A	25	C	35	C		
6	A	16	A	26	A	36	B		
7	C	17	D	27	D	37	A		
8	A	18	A	28	D	38	C		
9	B	19	A	29	B	39	D		
10	D	20	B	30	C	40	A		

2

Market Structure and Market Channel

I. Choose the correct answer

1. The person in wholesale market who acts as the representative of either a seller or a buyer is known as

   A. Middle man B. Commission agent

   C. Retailer D. Wholesaler

2. Middle man who don't buy and sell directly, but assist in marketing process is

   A. Speculative middle man B. Agent middle man

   C. Facilitative middle man D. Merchant middle man

3. It the time lag between the production and consumption increases, the risk associated with marketing

   A. Decreases B. Increases

   C. Constant D. Either increase or decrease

4. Tariff and tax law changes comes under

   A. Price risk B. Institutional risk

   C. Physical risk D. Storage risk

5. Risk can be minimized by

   A. Improved storage structures

   B. Transferring risk to insurance companies

   C. Fixing maximum and minimum price by the government

   D. All the above

6. Farmers share in consumers rupee is lower for

   A. Paddy B. Pulses

   C. Coarse grains D. Fruits and vegetables

7. Quantity of the produce which the producer (farmer) actually sells in the market is
   A. Marketing margin
   B. Marketed surplus
   C. Marketable surplus
   D. Producer surplus
8. Marketable surplus is called as
   A. Forced sale B. Surplus sale
   C. Voluntary sale D. Both A and B
9. Which of the following is incorrectly matched?
   A. Small and marginal farmers - Marketed surplus > marketable surplus
   B. Large farmers - Marketed surplus < Marketable surplus
   C. Theoretical surplus - Marketable surplus
   D. Theoretical surplus - Marketed surplus
10. Inverse relationship between price and marketable surplus is given by
   A. V.M.Dandekar and Rajkrishna B. P.N. Mathur and M.Ezekiel
   C. Acharya D. Kohls and Uhl
11. Marketable surplus is more in the case of
   A. Rice B. Jowar
   C. Cotton D. Gram
12. Marketable surplus is less in case of
   A. Rice B. Cotton
   C. Sugarcane D. Tomato
13. Commission agents earn their income as
   A. Profit B. Per cent of sales value
   C. Per cent of quantity sold D. Service charge
14. Risk taking is a function of
   A. Agent middlemen B. Merchant middlemen
   C. Speculator D. Facilitative middlemen
15. Price spread is least in marketing of
   A. Rice B. Milk
   C. Green leaves D. Coconut

16. Portion of total produce in stock which the farmer is willing to sale is termed as
    A. Marketable surplus B. Marketed surplus
    C. Marketing margin D. Marketing output
17. Marketed surplus is
    A. Less than the total production B. More than the total production
    C. Equal to total production D. None of the above
18. Knowledge of marketable surplus helps the
    A. Farming population B. Nonfarm population
    C. Both A and B D. Neither A nor B
19. Market conduct includes
    A. Market sharing and price setting policies
    B. Policies aimed at coercing rivals
    C. Policies towards setting the quality of products
    E. Efficiency in the use of resources
20. All the following have positive relationship with marketable surplus except
    A. Size of family B. Size of holding
    C. Quantity of production D. Both A and B
21. Primary function of marketing includes
    A. Procurement B. Transport
    C. Storage D. Banking
22. Secondary function of marketing includes
    A. Assembling B. Grading
    C. Insurance D. Banking
23. Tertiary function of marketing includes
    A. Assembling B. Transport
    C. Storage D. Insurance
24. Physical function of marketing includes
    A. Grading B. Buying
    C. Selling D. Financing
25. Exchange function of marketing includes
    A. Processing B. Transport
    C. Selling D. Standardization

26. Facilitative function of marketing refers to

A. Processing B. Grading

C. Buying D. Financing

27. Physical movement function of marketing refers to

A. Storage B. Creating demand

C. financing D. None of these

28. Ownership movement function of marketing refers to

A. Packaging B. Distribution

C. Negotiation of price D. Supervision

29. Market management function of marketing refers to

A. Distribution B. Rendering advice

C. Determining need D. Financing

30. Wholesalers perform the following functions except

A. Assembling B. Sorting

C. Advancing loans D. None of these

31. Brokers differ from commission agents by

A. Not owning the commodity

B. Providing financial assistance to farmers

C. Services rendered to their clients

D. Earning profit

32. Match the following:

A. Physical function 1. Selling

B. Exchange function 2. Dissemination of market information

C. Tertiary function 3. Processing

D. Facilitative function 4. Banking

	A	B	C	D
A.	3	1	4	2
B.	2	1	4	3
C.	4	3	2	1
D.	4	2	1	3

33. A flour mill opening its retail outlet is an example for

A. Horizontal integration
B. Forward integration
C. Conglomeration
D. Backward integration

34. Pepsico company engaging in tomato procurement directly from farmers is

A. Horizontal integration
B. Vertical integration
C. Conglomeration
D. Forward integration

35. Calculating marketing margin and cost in fresh fruits marketing is meaningful when one follows

A. Lot method
B. Sum of average gross margin method
C. Comparison of prices at successive levels of marketing
D. Both B and C

36. Farmers share in consumer rupee will be the least in marketing of

A. Rice
B. Milk
C. Cotton
D. Gram

37. Price spread will be the least in marketing of

A. Rice
B. Milk
C. Green leaves
D. Coconut

38. Market performance can be estimated by

A. Price spread
B. Marketing efficiency
C. Marketing margin
D. Marketing cost

39. Marketing efficiency can be improved by

(i) Reduction in the marketing cost
(ii) Increase in the satisfaction of consumer at given cost
(iii) Increasing the marketing cost

A. (ii) and (iii) are correct
B. (i) and (ii) are correct
C. (ii) alone is correct
D. All the statements are correct

40. The difference between price paid by consumer and the price received by producer is known as

A. Price spread
B. Marketing efficiency
C. Marketed surplus
D. Marketing surplus

41. Profit earned in marketing functions involved in moving the produce from the production to consumption is

A. Marketing cost
B. Marketing margin
C. Pricing efficiency
D. Farm retail spread

42. Method used to detect marketing margin and cost of perishable commodities is

A. Lot method / consignment method
B. Comparison of prices at successive level of marketing
C. Gross margin method
D. Both B and C

43. Marketing cost and marketing margin includes

(i) Prices of goods i.e., product at different stage of marketing
(ii) Cost of transportation
(iii) Cost of processing
(iv) Cost of operation in marketing

A. (i) and (iii) are correct
B. (iii) and (iv) are correct
C. (i), (ii) and (iii) are correct
D. All the statements are correct

44. The difference between the prices prevailing at successive stages of marketing at a given time is

A. Lagged margin
B. Concurrent margin
C. Recurrent margin
D. Both B and C

45. ______ shows relationship of the firms in a market

A. Marketing margin
B. Market integration
C. Marketed surplus
D. Marketing efficiency

46. Which type of integration reduces the number of middle men in the market?

A. Horizontal integration
B. Vertical integration
C. Diagonal integration
D. Both A and B

47. Choose the correct statements

(i) The wholesaler assuming the function of retailing is an example of backward integration
(ii) When a firm assumes more than one function, it is called as vertical integration
(iii) NAFED is an example of conglomeration integration

A. (i) and (ii) are correct B. (iii) alone is correct

C. (ii) alone is correct D. (ii) and (iii) are correct

48. Marketing cost is lower for

A. Food grains B. Fruits

C. Vegetables D. Flowers

49. The factor which do not cause higher marketing cost is

A. Production area away from markets

B. Necessity of storage from production to consumption

C. Need of processing

D. Increase in consumer income

50. Compared to developed countries, the marketing cost of food grains in India is

A. Lower B. Higher

C. Equal D. None of the above

51. Farmer's share in consumer price is

A. $FS = \frac{\text{Marketing cost}}{\text{Price received by farmer}} \times 100$

B. $FS = \frac{\text{Retail price}}{\text{Price received by farmer}} \times 100$

C. $FS = \frac{\text{Price received by farmer}}{\text{Price given by consumer}} x\ 100$

D. All the above

52. (i) Sum total of all operations involved in the manufacture and distribution of farm supplies, production and distribution called as agribusiness.

(ii) Hindustan Lever Ltd., is an example of conglomerate integration

(iii) Poultry, fruit and vegetable farms come under horizontal integration.

A. (ii) and (iii) are correct B. (iii) alone is correct

C. All the statements are correct D. (i) alone is correct

53. Expansion of firms by consolidating additional marketing functions and activities under a single management is

A. Market integration B. Marketing efficiency

C. Price spread D. Technical efficiency

54. Match the following

A. Production risk	1. Due to fluctuation in price
B. Marketing risk	2. Increase with increase in credit
C. Price risk	3. Based on rainfall distribution
D. Financial risk	4. Based on fluctuation in supply

	A	B	C	D
A.	1	4	3	1
B.	3	4	2	1
C.	3	1	4	2
D.	4	1	3	2

55. The route through which agricultural products move from producers to consumers is known as

A. Marketing information B. Marketing channels
C. Marketing efficiency D. Marketing institutions

56. Individuals, which specialize in performing the various marketing functions and rendering their services, are known as

A. Producers B. Consumers
C. Middle man D. None of the above

57. Individuals who buy goods from whole sellers and sell them to the consumers in small quantities are known as

A. Whole seller B. Retailer
C. Consumer D. Producer

58. Land holding of either 10 or more hectares have been classified as

A. Semi-medium B. Medium
C. Semi-large D. Large

59. In which system of sale, commission agents take the sample of the produce to the shops of buyers?

A. Quotations on samples B. Open auction system
C. Private negotiation D. None of the above

Answer keys

1	B	11	C	21	A	31	C	41	B	51	B
2	C	12	A	22	B	32	A	42	A	52	B
3	B	13	B	23	D	33	B	43	D	53	A
4	B	14	C	24	A	34	B	44	B	54	C
5	D	15	C	25	C	35	A	45	B	55	B
6	D	16	A	26	D	36	C	46	B	56	C
7	B	17	A	27	D	37	C	47	D	57	B
8	A	18	C	28	C	38	B	48	A	58	D
9	D	19	B	29	C	39	B	49	D	59	A
10	B	20	A	30	D	40	A	50	A		

3

Marketing Institutions

I. Choose the correct answer

1. Match the following

A. First Cooperative Society	1. 1963
B. NAFED	2. 1915
C. NCDC	3. 1958
D. Mirdha committee	4. 1965

A. 2 3 4 1 B. 4 3 2 1

C. 2 3 1 4 D. 3 4 1 2

2. GST was implemented in

A. 1th July 2017 B. 6th August 2016

C. 11th May 2018 D. 15th March 2015

3. MPEDA comes under

A. Ministry of Finance

B. Ministry of Fisheries

C. Ministry of Commerce and Industry

D. Ministry of Agriculture and Cooperation

4. Head quarters of Directorate of Marketing and Inspection was established at

A. Ahmedabad B. Faridabad

C. Faziabad D. New Delhi

5. Central Agmark laboratory is located at

A. Jaipur B. Nagpur

C. Bhopal D. Coimbatore

6. AGMARK is effective i.e., amended since

A. 1996 B. 1986

C. 1976 D. 1979

7. The major functions of warehouses include
   (i) Large quantity of agricultural commodities can be stored
   (ii) Financial needs can be rectified
   (iii) Stabilization of agricultural prices
   (iv) Preventing distress sale of commodities
   A. (i), (ii) and (iv) are correct B. (i) and (ii) are correct
   C. (i), (iii) and (iv) are correct D. All the statements are correct
8. Bank responsible for the agricultural produce (Development and Warehousing) corporation is
   A. NABARD B. RBI
   C. SBI D. World bank
9. Match the following

A. General warehouse	1. Airport or seaport
B. Special commodity warehouse	2. Food grains, fertilizers
C. Refrigerated warehouse	3. Cotton, tobacco
D. Boned warehouse	4. Fruits, vegetables

   A. 3 1 4 2 B. 4 3 2 1
   C. 2 3 4 1 D. 3 2 4 1
10. Central Warehousing Corporation was established at
   A. New Delhi B. Mumbai
   C. Calcutta D. Cochin
11. Essential Commodities Act was passed in the year
   A. 1976 B. 1985
   C. 1969 D. 1955
12. AGMARK and BIS standards was
   A. Compulsory
   B. Voluntary
   C. Based on commodities either A or B
   D. None of these
13. Match the following

A. Central Warehousing Corporation	1. 1958
B. State Warehousing Corporation	2. 1963
C. Warehousing Corporation Act	3. 1957
D. Food Corporation of India	4 1965

A. 2 1 4 3 B. 3 1 2 4

C. 4 3 2 1 D. 3 4 1 2

14. World Trade Organisation is located at

A. New York B. Rome

C. Geneva D. London

15. Match the following

A. Coconut Development Board	1. 1942, Bangalore
B. Coffee Board	2. 1987, Kochi
C. Spice Board	3. 1981, Kochi
D. Tobacco Board	4. 1976, Guntur

A. 3 2 4 1 B. 4 3 2 1

C. 3 1 2 4 D. 3 4 1 2

16. The storage capacity of Central Warehousing Corporation as on 2019 is about

A. 10.6 MT B. 10.1 MT

C. 9.7 MT D. 9.67 MT

17. The simplest and easiest form of business organisation in operational point of view in small scale industry is

A. Joint stock company B. Sole proprietorship

C. Partnership D. Cooperative society

18. The upper limit of number of person in partnership organisation of general business is

A. 10 B. 20

C. 35 D. 30

19. Fair and remunerative price for sugarcane is earlier called as

A. Minimum support price B. Statutory minimum price

C. Procurement price D. Both B and C

20. MSP for paddy in 2019-20 is

A. Rs.2550 B. Rs 1750

C. Rs.1815 D. Rs.1700

21. CACP was originally called as

A. Agricultural prices commission

B. Food grain price committee

C. Cooperative agricultural marketing

D. Marketing committee

22. The major objectives of NAFED which is not included

A. To promote the marketing and trading activities

B. To promote inter state and international trade in agricultural and other commodities

C. Agent of the government for the purchase, scale, storage and distribution

D. To market the produce of the members of society

23. Rural godowns in India is constructed and maintained based on the scheme called

A. Gramin Blandaran Yojana B. Gramin Sadak Yojana

C. Rastriya Krishi Vikas Yojana D. None of these

24. Number of kharif crops included in MSP is

A. 14 B. 6

C. 22 D. 7

25. Agreement on agriculture came into effect from

A. January 1, 2015 B. January 1, 1995

C. January 1, 1991 D. January 1, 2003

26. GATT came into force as a result of

A. Bretton woods agreement B. Agreement of agriculture

C. Treaty of misgoverance D. Agreement of tariff and trade

27. GATT stands for

A. Government Agreement on Trade and Tariff

B. General Agreement on Tariff and Trade

C. General Agreement on Trade and Tariff

D. Graduate Agreement on Trade and Tariff

28. GATT was established in

A. 1949 B. 1955

C. 1995 D. 1947

29. Which of the following organisation take over the function of GATT?

A. NCDC

B. World Trade Organisation (WTO)

C. FCI

D. NAFED

30. GST for fresh fruits and vegetables is

A. 0% B. 5%

C. 12% D. 18%

31. Quality of agricultural commodities is ensured by

A. AGMARK B. ISI

C. BSI D. ISO

32. International food safety standards are developed by

A. AACCP B. CODEX

C. ECOMARK D. WTO

33. Which of the following is correct about CACP?

A. CACP recommends MSP in kharif only

B. CACP recommends MSP in rabi only

C. CACP recommends MSP in kharif and rabi

D. CACP doesn't recommended MSP for food grains

34. Building buffer stock is possible by

A. Domestic procurement B. Import

C. Both A and B D. None of these

35. (i) Bonded warehouse are meant for use by exporters and importers only.

(ii) Warhouses help in stabilizing the commodity price by staggering its supply throughout the year.

(iii) All commodities could be stored in the central warehousing corporation godowns.

A. (i) and (iii) are correct B. (ii) and (iii) are correct

C. (iii) alone is correct D. (i) and (ii) are correct

36. (i) Procurement price is higher than MSP

(ii) Procurement price is the price at which the crops are procured

(iii) MSP is a guarantee price for the produce from the government

A. (ii) and (iii) are correct B. (i) and (iii) are correct

C. (ii) alone is correct D. All the statements are correct

37. Contribution of agriculture sector to India's GDP is
    A. 12.0% B. 16.9%
    C. 18.0% D. 16.5%
38. e-NAM ie., Electronic National Agriculture Market was launched in
    A. 2015 B. 2016
    C. 2017 D. 2018
39. NITI Aayog was formed in the year
    A. 2015 B. 2016
    C. 2017 D. 2018
40. The first mega food park was inaugurated in March
    A. 2015 B. 2016
    C. 2017 D. 2018
41. GST on fertilizers is about
    A. 12% B. 0%
    C. 28% D. 18%
42. Chairman of GST council is
    A. Finance minister B. Agriculture minister
    C. External affairs minister D. Rural development minister
43. Products which remain untaxed under GST is
    A. Fresh fruits and vegetables B. Meat products
    C. Dairy products D. All the above
44. (i) GST rate of tea, coffee and sugar is 5%
    (ii) Electricity is not taxed under GST instead by individual state government
    A. (ii) alone is correct B. (i) alone is correct
    C. Both are wrong D. Both are correct
45. The price which announced by GOI on the recommendation of CACP before the harvest of crops is
    A. MSP B. FRP
    C. Procurement price D. None of these
46. Number of commodities covered under AGMARK is
    A. 225 B. 222
    C. 227 D. 221

47. Agmark Act was passed in the year
    A. 1937 B. 1945
    C. 1928 D. 1935
48. Number of cereal crop covered under MSP is
    A. 5 B. 7
    C. 14 D. 12
49. The first state warehouse was setup in
    A. Bihar B. Orissa
    C. Tamil Nadu D. Gujarat
50. The Tamil Nadu State Agricultural Marketing Board was constituted in
    A. 1965 B. 1970
    C. 1985 D. 1975
51. The national level body controlling state agriculture marketing boards is
    A. TNSAMB
    B. National council of state agricultural marketing board
    C. COSAMB
    D. Both B and C
52. The state which has not constituted state agricultural marketing board is
    A. Andhra Pradesh B. Uttarkhand
    C. Karnataka D. Kerala
53. Headquarters of TNSAMB is located at
    A. Coimbatore B. Chennai
    C. Kancheepuram D. Trichy
54. Supporting prices of agricultural commodities are announced by
    A. Agricultural Universities B. ICAR
    C. State Government D. Central Agricultural Costs and Prices
55. Maximum Support Price (MSP) is fixed based on
    A. Average cost of production B. Maximum cost of production
    C. Overall profit D. Total cost of production
56. Levy price applies to
    A. Farmers B. Traders
    C. Farmers and traders D. None

57. Value Added Tax (VAT) was first introduced in

A. Sri Lanka
B. Bangladesh
C. France
D. India

58. The minimum support price system for agricultural commodities was started in the year

A. 1962
B. 1963
C. 1964
D. 1965

59. The new name of Agricultural Prices Commission is

A. Commission for farm costs and prices
B. Commission for agricultural costs and prices
C. Commission for agricultural costs
D. Commission for Kisan costs and prices

60. Match the commodity boards with their headquarters

Board	**Head quarters**
A. Coconut Development Board	1. Bangalore
B. Tobacco Board	2. Kottayam
C. Rubber Board	3. Guntur
D. Coffee Board	4. Kochi

A. 4 3 2 1
B. 4 2 3 1
C. 2 1 3 4
D. 4 1 3 2

61. Who is responsible to announce minimum support price and when it is announced?

A. State Government, after sowing
B. CACP, after sowing
C. Government of India, before sowing
D. Government of India, after sowing

62. The demand for farm inputs is said to be

A. Derived demand
B. Reservation demand
C. Effective demand
D. Ineffective demand

63. The beneficiaries in Small Farmer Development Agency (SFDA) were the farmers who owned land holdings with the size of

A. 7.5 to 10 acres
B. 5.0 to 7.5 acres
C. 2.5 to 5.0 acres
D. Below 2.5 acres

64. First state warehousing corporation was set up in

A. Tamil Nadu B. Bihar

C. Kerala D. Maharashtra

65. The expert group on Agricultural marketing was established under the chairmanship of

A. Acharya B. Dantwala

C. Shankarlal Guru D. Sri RCA Jain

66. APEDA functions under the

A. Ministry of Agriculture

B. Ministry of Food and consumer Affairs

C. Ministry of Commerce and Industry

D. Ministry of Finance

67. In which state of India, the famous cooperative AMUL is situated?

A. Gujarat B. Maharashtra

C. Delhi D. M P.

68. Buffer stock is the stock of food grains procured by the government through

A. IFCI B. FCI

C. IDBI D. FICCI

69. What does food security mean?

A. Availability of food

B. Accessibility of food

C. Availability and accessibility of food to all at all times.

D. Availability, accessibility and affordability of food to all at all the times

70. In which state, ration shops are run by cooperatives in large extent?

A. Assam B. Karnataka

C. Tamil Nadu D. Goa

71. Buffer stock scheme purpose is

A. To save food grains from pest attack

B. To stop price fluctuations

C. To transport the food

D. To deliver the food

72. Agmark act 1937 comes under
A. Dept. of Consumer Affairs, Govt. of India
B. Dept. of Agriculture and Cooperation
C. Dept. of Marketing and Inspection
D. Dept. of Legal Meterology

73. Coffee is adulterated with
A. Saw dust
B. Chicory
C. Ghee
D. All of these

74. Agmark is related with
A. Processing
B. Quality
C. Packaging
D. All above

75. The National Centre for Agricultural Economics and Policy Research is located at
A. New Delhi
B. Kolkata
C. Hyderabad
D. Bhopal

76. Agricultural commodities are graded with
A. ISI
B. Eco-products
C. Agmark
D. Green product

77. Who issues Agmark?
A. Directorate of Marketing and Inspection, Government of India
B. Bureau of Indian Standards (BIS)
C. Ministry of Food Processing
D. Ministry of Statistics

78. At present how many members are in the WTO?
A. 160
B. 164
C. 207
D. 195

79. Where is the headquarter of the WTO?
A. New York
B. Washington DC
C. Geneva
D. Austria

80. Which of the following statement is not true about the WTO?
A. WTO is a permanent organisation
B. Uruguay round gave the birth to the WTO.
C. Ministerial conference is the highest policy making body of the WTO
D. WTO was officially constituted on 1 January 1991

81. Which of the following country is not the member of the WTO?
    A. Iran B. Azerbaijan
    C. Belarus D. None of these
82. Which of the following is not the objective of the WTO?
    A. To improve the standard of living of peoples of the member countries
    B. To enlarge production and trade of goods
    C. To protect environment
    D. To improve the balance of payment situation of the member countries
83. Which of the following body is not related to the WTO?
    A. Dispute settlement body B. Trade policy review body
    C. Council of trade in goods D. Exchange rate management body
84. Which of the following institution is associated with Dunkel proposals?
    A. World Bank B. International Monetary Fund
    C. World Trade Organization D. United Nations Organization
85. Pick the odd man out
    A. MPEDA B. APEDA
    C. NAFED D. DMI
86. Tariffication of all non tariff barriers is related to
    A. Market access commitment B. Aggregate measure of support
    C. Export subsidy D. TRIPS
87. AOA allows unlimited support to activities such as
    A. Pest and disease control
    B. Public stock holding for food security purpose
    C. Domestic food aid
    D. All of these
88. Food Corporation of India was established in the year
    A. 1955 B. 1965
    C. 1972 D. 1975
89. Buffer stock operations does not ensure
    A. Price fall B. Price stabilization
    C. Food security D. None of these

90. Building buffer stock is possible by

A. Domestic procurement B. Import

C. Both A and B D. None of these

91. Which five year plan is responsible for establishment of Agricultural Marketing and Processing Cooperative Societies?

A. First five year plan B. Third five year plan

C. Fifth five year plan D. Seventh five year plan

92. Apex body of cooperative marketing is

A. National Cooperative Development Corporation

B. National Agricultural Cooperative Marketing Federation

C. TANFED

D. FCI

Answer keys

1	B	16	A	31	A	46	A	61	C	76	D	91	A
2	A	17	B	32	B	47	A	62	A	77	A	92	B
3	C	18	B	33	C	48	B	63	C	78	B		
4	B	19	B	34	B	49	A	64	B	79	C		
5	B	20	C	35	D	50	B	65	A	80	D		
6	B	21	A	36	D	51	D	66	C	81	D		
7	D	22	D	37	C	52	D	67	A	82	C		
8	B	23	A	38	B	53	B	68	B	83	D		
9	C	24	A	39	A	54	D	69	D	84	C		
10	A	25	B	40	D	55	A	70	C	85	D		
11	D	26	A	41	A	56	C	71	B	86	A		
12	B	27	B	42	A	57	C	72	A	87	D		
13	B	28	D	43	D	58	D	73	B	88	B		
14	C	29	B	44	D	59	B	74	B	89	D		
15	C	30	A	45	C	60	A	75	A	90	C		

UNIT XIV: AGRICULTURAL EXTENSION AND RURAL SOCIOLOGY

1

Extension Education

I. Choose the correct answer

1. The latin roots for the word 'Extension'

   A. Ex and tension — B. Ex and tensio

   C. Ex and lucco — D. Ex and termo

2. The concept of extension education process was given by

   A. Paul Leagans — B. Van Den Ban

   C. Wilson and Gallup — D. Alexander

3. James Stuart associated with

   A. Extension education — B. University extension

   C. Both A and B — D. None of the above

4. The learning curve in teaching follows a

   A. S-shape — B. U-shape

   C. V-shape — D. L-shape

5. The cone of experience was developed by

   A. Berlo — B. Lewin

   C. Van Den Ban — D. Edgar Dale

6. Who is father of extension in India?

   A. Robert Chambers — B. A.Reddy

   C. C.K.N. Singh — D. D. Berlo

7. Extension is a

   A. One way flow of message — B. Two way flow of message

   C. Non formal education — D. Both B and C

8. Social classes are classified based on

   A. Religion — B. Community

   C. Economic status — D. Political status

9. Extension is a

A. Informal education
B. Out of school system of education
C. Both A and B
D. Formal education

10. The extension activities was started first time in

A. USA
B. Russia
C. Germany
D. India

11. MANAGE stands for

A. National Institute of Agricultural Extension and Management
B. Management of Agricultural Extension
C. National and International Institute of Agricultural Extension and Management
D. Both A and B

12. The important feature of I-kisan portal is

A. E-choupal
B. Portal in regional language
C. Both A and B
D. None of these

13. Which five year plan aimed at attaining self sufficiency in food?

A. Third
B. Fourth
C. Fifth
D. Sixth

14. Sponsoring agency of 'Cyber Extension Project' is

A. NAARM, Hyderabad
B. MANAGE, Hyderabad
C. ICAR, New Delhi
D. GBPUA & T, Pantnagar

15. Consider the statement and choose the correct one regarding extension

(i) Extension utilizes the organizers and leaders to achieve objectives
(ii) It studies social situations of rural society
(iii) It seeks to modify the attitude of people

A. (i) and (ii) are correct
B. (ii) and (iii) are correct
C. (ii) alone is correct
D. (i) and (iii) are correct

16. Where is National Institute of Agricultural Extension and Management located?

A. Pantnagar
B. Rajendranagar
C. Jodhpur
D. Banaras

17. Who is father of extension education?

A. Robert Chamber
B. J.P. Leagans

C. K.N. Singh D. James Stuart

18. Teaching process was given by

A. Wilson and Gallup B. J.P. Leagans

C. K.N. Singh D. James Stuart

19. Important element of learning situation

A. Learner B. Situation

C. Teacher D. Study materials

20. The essential elements of effective learning situation is

(i) An instructor

(ii) Subject matter

(iii) Teaching material

(iv) Learners

(v) Physical facilities

A. (i) and (iii) are correct B. (ii), (iii) and (iv) are correct

C. (i) and (iv) are correct D. All the above

21. Contact farmer is considered as

A. Opinion leader B. Professional leader

C. Official leader D. Lay leader

22. Steps in teaching is shortly called as

A. ALETA B. AIDCAS

C. KPDC D. AIDALS

Answer keys

1	B	11	A	21	A
2	A	12	C	22	B
3	B	13	B		
4	A	14	B		
5	D	15	D		
6	C	16	B		
7	D	17	B		
8	C	18	A		
9	C	19	A		
10	A	20	D		

2

Extension Teaching Methods

I. Choose the correct answer

1. How many elements are there in diffusion of innovations?

   A. 4 B. 6

   C. 3 D. 5

2. Among the following which is not a non projected aids?

   A. Flash cards B. Charts

   C. Pictures D. Slide projector

3. Match the list I with list II and choose the correct one

List I	List II
A. Audio	1. Opaque projector
B. Visual	2. Radio
C. Audio-visual	3. Flash cards
D. Projected aids	4. Drama

   A. 4 3 2 1 B. 2 4 3 1

   C. 2 3 4 1 D. 4 2 3 1

4. Consider the statement and choose the correct one with respect to print media

   (i) It delivers news and information

   (ii) Viewer friendly

   (iii) Periodically updation

   A. (i) and (ii) are correct B. (ii) and (iii) are correct

   C. (i) and (iii) are correct D. All the statements are correct

5. Find out the wrong answer regarding group contact

   A. Lecture meetings B. Office calls

   C. Method demonstration D. Tours

6. Indian state broad casting service was renamed as All India Radio in the year

   A. 1936 B. 1927

   C. 1924 D. 1947

7. The present national coverage of AIR by area is

   A. 90.6% B. 97.3%

   C. 93.6% D. 95.3%

8. When did the television broadcasting started in India?

   A. 1947 B. 1953

   C. 1959 D. 1976

9. In the word 'POSTER' what does the letter 'O' stands for

   A. Objection B. Object

   C. Objective D. Obedience

10. Indian planning commission first established in

   A. 1952 B. 1950

   C. 1947 D. 1953

11. For providing the precise and reliable scientific information in simple language, the extension system used is

   A. Lectures B. Leaflets

   C. Pictures D. Radio talk

12. Find out the incorrect statement

   A. All India Radio comes under Ministry of Agriculture and Farmers welfare

   B. All India Radio also known as Akashvani

   C. Tamil Nadu comes under South zone of Radio Network

   D. Radio Broadcasting in India was started in 1924

13. The best extension method for farmers is

   A. Leaflets B. Folder

   C. Poster D. Demonstration

14. The external service division of All India Radio broadcasts in

   A. 22 languages B. 15 languages

   C. 27 languages D. None of these

15. Example of group contact method of extension teaching method is
    A. Farm and home visits B. Method demonstration
    C. Television D. Personal letters
16. Television is a
    A. Individual contact method B. Group contact method
    C. Mass contact method D. Either B or C
17. The word Television is derived from
    A. Latin B. Greek
    C. French D. Either A or B
18. Television was delinked from All India Radio with full fledged directorate in
    A. 1969 B. 1976
    C. 1986 D. 1981
19. Which of the following method should follow ABC principle?
    A. Exhibition B. Posters
    C. Campaigns D. Hoarding
20. Match the following

A. Interpersonal channel	1. Radio
B. Mass media channel	2. Extension worker
C. Localite channel	3. Between two persons
D. Cosmopolite channel	4. Opinion Leaders

    A. 4 3 2 1 B. 2 1 4 3
    C. 3 1 4 2 D. 3 1 2 4
21. Number of persons in mass contact method is
    A. 1-2 persons B. 2-30 persons
    C. More than 30 persons D. No limit – any of these
22. Skill development through
    A. Result demonstration B. Method demonstration
    C. Field days D. Symposium
23. Which method is more useful for making people aware of the new agricultural technology quickly?
    A. Individual method B. Group contact method
    C. Mass contact method D. None of these

24. The demonstration which shows the value or worth of the new practice is

A. Method demonstration B. Result demonstration

C. Trial demonstration D. Any one of these

25. The best extension method suited to all situation

A. Demonstration B. Campaign

C. Farm publication D. None of these

26. The best extension method to teach a skill involved in the particular practice is

A. Group discussion B. Method demonstration

C. Result demonstration D. Lecture

27. Method demonstration works based on the principle of

A. Learning is believing B. Seeing is believing

C. Learning by teaching D. Learning by doing

28. Mention the stage at which poster is most effective?

A. Awareness B. Interest

C. Trial D. Evaluation

29. Research under participatory technology development is mostly carried out at

A. Experimental farms B. Farmers holdings

C. Research centres D. None of the above

30. Which of the following is not a characteristic of PRA?

A. Quick B. Interactive

C. Team effort D. Rigidity

31. Television is an

A. Audio aid B. Visual aid

C. Audio-visual aid D. None of the above

32. Symposium is a short series of lectures, usually by speaker

A. 1-2 B. 2-5

C. 5-7 D. 7-10

33. Method demonstration focuses on

A. Teaching B. Result

C. Skill D. None of the above

34. _______ is the intense educational activity to create awareness.
    A. Farmer's day B. Campaign
    C. Demonstration D. Study tour

35. A small intense discussion group usually involving 3 persons responding to a specific question or in search of very precise information is called as
    A. Buzz group B. Panel
    C. Colloguium D. Debate

36. A method of motivating the people for adoption of new practice is called as
    A. Method demonstration B. Farmers day
    C. Result demonstration D. ART

37. Which of the following is group contact method?
    A. Seminar B. Panel
    C. Symposium D. All of these

38. The best method for showing the value of new project is
    A. Result demonstration B. Exhibition
    C. Farmers fair D. Meeting

39. Puppet show are included in
    A. Audio aids B. Visual aids
    C. AV aids D. None of these

40. A blog is a fusion of two words
    A. Web and Google B. Web and Log
    C. WAN and LAN D. Glob and Log

Answer keys

1	A	11	B	21	C	31	C
2	B	12	A	22	B	32	B
3	C	13	D	23	C	33	C
4	C	14	C	24	B	34	B
5	B	15	B	25	D	35	A
6	A	16	C	26	B	36	C
7	A	17	B	27	D	37	D
8	C	18	B	28	A	38	A
9	C	19	B	29	B	39	C
10	B	20	C	30	D	40	B

3

Communication Models and Programme Planning

I. Choose the correct answer

1. Match list I with list II and choose the correct one

List I	List II
A. Early adopters	1. 16%
B. Early majority	2. 13.5%
C. Innovators	3. 34%
D. Laggards	4. 2.5%

A. 2 4 3 1 B. 2 3 4 1
C. 4 3 2 1 D. 4 2 3 1

2. Reading newspaper is which level of communication
A. Inter personal B. Intra personal
C. Dyadic D. Intra organization

3. Important function of communication
A. Information B. Influence
C. Integrative D. Persuasive

4. Communication is a _____ word.
A. Greek word B. Latin word
C. French D. None of these

5. The sender and the receiver of message connected with each other by
A. Channels of communication B. Audience
C. Communication obstruction D. Transmitter

6. The process by which an innovation is communicated through certain channels over time among the members is called
A. Adoption B. Diffusion
C. Communication D. Decision

7. Which of the following is not a element in the diffusion of innovations?

A. Innovation B. Communication channel

C. Time D. Noise

8. The term 'Newness' is related with

A. Communication channel B. Social system

C. Innovation D. Decision

9. Degree to which an innovation is perceived as better than other ideas is termed as

A. Complexity B. Compatibility

C. Relative advantage D. None of these

10. Treatment of message is done to message

A. Clear B. Understandable

C. Realistic D. All the above

11. Termination element in channels of communication is

A. Audience B. Speaker

C. Audience response D. Obstructions

12. Match the following

A. Compatibility	1. Difficult to understand and use
B. Complexity	2. Consistent with the existing values
C. Trialability	3. Result of innovation are visible to others
D. Observabity	4. Experimented with on a limited basis

A. 2 3 4 1 B. 3 4 2 1

C. 3 1 4 2 D. 2 1 4 3

13. Who classified the farmers based on their innovativeness ie., Adopter categories?

A. John knight B. Rogers

C. John Williams D. John McMillan

14. _____ are the last to adopt an innovation

A. Innovators B. Early adopters

C. Early majority D. Laggards

15. Find out the correct statement

    i) Individuals first to adopt an innovation is called as innovators

    ii) Aristotle model of communication is the earliest model

    iii) Most applicable model to public speaking is Aristotle's model

    iv) Lasswell model is redescribed / represented by Michael Buhler

    A. (i) and (ii) are correct B. (iii) and (iv) are correct

    C. (iii) alone is correct D. All are correct

16. Match the following

    A. Shannon and weaver model 1. 1960

    B. Osgood – Schrann model 2. 1949

    C. Berlo model 3. 1975

    D. Lasswell model 4. 1948

    A. 2 3 1 4 B. 4 3 1 2

    C. 1 3 4 2 D. 3 1 4 2

17. Find out the incorrect statement

    (i) The percentage of early adopters is 13.5%

    (ii) Early majority adopters are deliberate in nature

    (iii) Innovators are eager to try new ideas

    (iv) Peoples adopt new ideas just before the average number of social system comes under late majority category

    A. (i) alone is incorrect B. (ii) alone is incorrect

    C. (iii) alone is incorrect D. (iv) alone is incorrect

18. The barrier to communication includes

    A. Distortion B. Communication overload

    C. Absence of redundancy D. All the above

19. Sources of obstruction may be due to

    (i) Use of too many channels in a service

    (ii) Failure to use enough channels in parallel

    (iii) Failure to select channels appropriate to the objective of communicator

    (iv) Failure to avoid physical distraction

    A. (ii), (iii) and (iv) B. (iv) alone

    C. (ii) and (iii) D. All of the above

20. The person who acts as a link between higher extension official and farming community is known as

A. Village extension worker B. District Collector

C. KVK Head D. Extension Officers

21. Find out the incorrect statement

A. Communication has multiplier effect

B. Message should be clearly understandable by the audience

C. The message should be attractive in communication

D. Communication is the process by which two or more people exchange ideas, facts and feelings given by John Paul.

22. The main problem with mass communication is

A. Costly B. No local dialect

C. Same information D. Cumbersome

23. Communication barriers include

A. Social B. Semantic

C. Technical D. All of these

24. Source – Transmitter – Signal – Receiver – Destination is the model of communication proposed by

A. Berlo B. Lasswell

C. Shannon and Weaver D. Aristotle

25. The adopter category considered as 'friends and neighbours' by other members in the social system

A. Innovators B. Early adopters

C. Early majority D. Late majority

26. What is the percentage of early adopters in the social system?

A. 2.5% B. 13.5%

C. 34% D. 16%

27. A, B, C's of journalism stands for

A. Accuracy, Brevity and Clarity B. Attractive, Brief and Clear

C. Accuracy, Brief and Clarity D. None of the above

28. In agricultural extension, mass Communication can be done through

A. Bulletin B. Television

C. Newspaper D. All the above

29. Backward flow of communication is

A. Transmission B. Sending

C. Feedback D. Receiving

30. Farmer's behaviour includes

A. Attitude B. Knowledge

C. Skills D. All of these

31. Communication through signals body movement and gestures is

A. Verbal B. Non verbal

C. Group D. Mass

32. The actual physical product of source encounter is

A. Receiver B. Message

C. Channel D. Feedback

33. The process by which individual maintains contact with environment is

A. Perception B. Learning

C. Attitude D. Intelligence

34. Aristotle model of communication contains ____ elements.

A. Five B. Four

C. Three D. Two

35. _____ is an outline of work so arranged for efficient execution of the entire programme

A. Project B. Plan of work

C. Aim D. Objective

36. Which one of the following is not relevant to an extension programme by USDA (1956)?

A. The situation in which the people are located

B. Problems that are a part of local situation

C. Objectives and goals of the local people in relation to country's national problems

D. Recommendations to reach these objectives on a long time basis

37. Who developed extension programme planning model?

A. Leagans (1961) B. Lawrence (1962)

C. Matthews (1962) D. Sandhu (1965)

38. Last stage of programme planning process is

A. Evaluation
B. Auditing
C. Supervision
D. Reconsideration

39. Principles of programme planning is / are

A. It is based on analysis of fact of the situation
B. Based on need and interest of the local people
C. It determines priorities, define objectives and solution which offer satisfaction
D. All of these

40. Farmers first model was put forwarded by

A. Robert Chamber
B. A.A. Reddy
C. Knapp
D. D. Berlo

41. The main mode of extension in the farmers first model is

A. Farmer to farmer
B. Agent to farmer
C. Research to agent
D. Farmer to scientist

42. Which of the following is not true?

A. Programme planning is a spontaneous process
B. Programme planning is an educational process
C. Programme planning is a continuous process
D. Programme planning is a coordinating process

43. Effective extension service is a process of

A. Helping the people which helps themselves
B. Profiting the local leaders
C. Helping the B.D.O
D. All of the above

44. Measuring performance against predetermined goals is called

A. Management
B. Evaluation
C. Measurement
D. Supervision

45. Acceptance and rejection are one of the kinds of

A. Failure of channel
B. Feedback
C. Treatment of message
D. Empathetic feelings

46. PRA was introduced in India by

A. Government department's B. ICAR

C. NGO's D. Ford Foundation

47. For a study of farming system, the best PRA exercise is

A. Transect walk B. Resource mapping

C. Time line D. All of these

48. Who stated 'Extension programme' is a set of clearly defined conceived objectives or ends by analysis and which are to be achieved through extension teaching activity?

A. Lawrence B. Leagans

C. USDA D. Kelsey and Hearne

49. PRA refers to

A. Program for Regional Agriculture

B. Participatory Rural Appraisal

C. Program for Research and Appraisal

D. Project Research Agency

50. A statement of situation, Objectives, Problems and solution is known as

A. Extension program B. Evaluation

C. Plan of work D. Calender of work

Answer keys

1	B	11	C	21	D	31	B	41	A
2	B	12	D	22	B	32	B	42	A
3	A	13	B	23	D	33	A	43	A
4	B	14	D	24	C	34	A	44	B
5	A	15	D	25	C	35	B	45	B
6	B	16	A	26	B	36	C	46	A
7	D	17	D	27	B	37	D	47	B
8	C	18	D	28	D	38	D	48	B
9	C	19	D	29	C	39	D	49	B
10	D	20	A	30	D	40	A	50	A

4

Rural Developmental Programmes

I. Choose the correct answer

1. Who started the National Extension Service (NES)?

   A. Paul Hoffman B. Vinoba Bhave

   C. V.T. Krishnamachari D. S.K. Dey

2. Who recommended Panchayat raj system?

   A. Ashok Mehta B. Balwant Rai Mehta

   C. Kumar Mehta D. Jayaraj Mehta

3. When did Krishi Vigyan Kendra (KVK) established?

   A. 1954 B. 1964

   C. 1942 D. 1974

4. Agri-clinic Yojana was started by

   A. RRB B. RBI

   C. NABARD D. SBI

5. Kisan Credit Card (KCC) was started in the year

   A. 1978-79 B. 1998-99

   C. 1986-87 D. 1972-73

6. When was Kisan Call Centre launched?

   A. 2003 B. 2004

   C. 1999 D. 2000

7. Rural development programmes should be formed to meet

   A. Short term changes B. Emergent situation

   C. Long term changes D. All the above

8. Rural Landless Employment Guarantee Programme (RLEGP) was started in the year

   A. 1978 B. 1983

   C. 1984 D. 1985

9. The basic guide, philosopher and friend in rural development is
   A. BDO B. VDO
   C. Pradhan D. Pramukh
10. The basic unit of development under the IRDP is a
   A. District B. Community development block
   C. Village D. Family
11. Etawah project was started by
   A. S.K.Dey B. Albert Mayer
   C. Mahatma Gandhi D. None of these
12. The project which is merged with National Extension Service is
   A. Nilokheri project
   B. Community Development Programme
   C. Etawah project
   D. IVLP
13. Mazdoor Manzil scheme also known as
   A. Nilokheri project B. Etawah project
   C. Marthandam project D. Sriniketan project
14. The scheme which is implemented in areas where Community Development Programme (CDP) is not covered are
   A. Panchayat raj B. National Extension Service
   C. Mazdoor Manzil D. NATP
15. Community Development Programme was launched in
   A. 1948 B. 1952
   C. 1957 D. 1935
16. The project which was started at Travancore in Kerala is
   A. Sriniketan project B. Etawah project
   C. Sarvodaya movement D. Marthandam project
17. Gurgoan project was established by
   A. B.N.Gupta B. Spencer Hatch
   C. F.L.Brayne D. None of these
18. Which committee were appointed for KVK scheme in 1974?
   A. Narasimham commission B. Mohan Singh Mehta committee
   C. Bava committee D. None of these

19. The objectives of Community Development Programme includes
    (i) Increasing agricultural production
    (ii) Providing recreational facilities and programme
    (iii) Providing programmes for village women and youth
    (iv) Improving housing and family living conditions
    A. (i) and (ii) B. (ii) and (iii)
    C. (iii) D. (i), (ii), (iii) and (iv)
20. Training and visit system was introduced first in the state of
    A. Madhya Pradesh B. Andhra Pradesh
    C. Rajasthan D. Karnataka
21. Package programme is also known as
    A. IADP B. IRDP
    C. TRYSEM D. CADP
22. The short comings of Panchayat Raj is
    A. Rural awakening
    B. Significant progress in the field of primary and secondary education
    C. People get protected water supply
    D. Dilution of their authorities and responsibilities
23. IADP in Tamil Nadu was first implemented in
    A. Kancheepuram B. Kanyakumari
    C. Tanjore D. Trichy
24. Which of the following schemes are merged into Swarnajayanthi Gram Swarzgar Yojana (SGSY) in 1999?
    A. IRDP B. TRYSEM
    C. DWACRA D. All the above
25. Match the following

A. Intensive Agricultural Area Programme (IAAP)	1. 1966
B. High Yielding Variety Programme (HYVP)	2. 1978
C. Integrated Rural Development Programme (IRDP)	3. 1970
D. Drought Prone Area Programme (DPAP)	4. 1964

A. 3 1 4 2 B. 4 3 2 1

C. 4 1 2 3 D. 2 1 4 3

26. Which are the correct statements

(i) IADP was initially implemented in seven districts

(ii) HYVP helped the country in attaining self sufficiency in food

(iii) IAAP helps the scientist to have direct interaction with the farming community

(iv) NATP project is assisted by World Bank.

A. (i) and (ii) are correct B. (ii) and (iii) are correct

C. (i), (ii) and (iv) are correct D. All are correct

27. The agencies ie., project implementing agencies involved in implementation of the ITP component of NATP (National Agricultural Technology Project) are

(i) Directorate of Extension (ii) MANAGE

(iii) SAMETI (iv) ATMA

A. (i) and (ii) B. (ii) and (iii)

C. (ii), (iii) and (iv) D. All of these

28. The main reason for evolution of IRDP is

A. Failure of IADP B. Failure of CDP

C. Failure of NATP D. Failure of IAAP

29. Lab to land programme was implemented in

A. 1969 B. 1989

C. 1979 D. 1999

30. Which of the following is not an Agricultural Development Programme?

A. IADP B. IVLP

C. NATP D. IRDP

31. In which year, Grow More Food Enquiry Committee was formed?

A. 1953 B. 1952

C. 1948 D. 1966

32. In which five year plan, IADP was incorporated?

A. 2nd five year plan B. 3rd five year plan

C. 4th five year plan D. 5th five year plan

33. How much percentage of cultivated area of the country was brought under Intensive Agricultural Development in IAAP?

A. 10 - 15% B. 15 - 20%

C. 20 - 25% D. 25 - 30%

34. In which five year plan, HYVP was implemented?

A. 2nd five year plan B. 3rd five year plan

C. 4th five year plan D. 5th five year plan

35. In which project, ATMA was implemented?

A. NATP B. ITDA

C. IRDP D. IWDP

36. Which one of the following state was not involved in the pilot testing of NATP?

A. Andhra Pradesh B. Tamil Nadu

C. Bihar D. Punjab

37. IWDP means

A. Intensive Wastelands Development Programme

B. Intensive Wastelands Development Project

C. Integrated Wastelands Development Programme

D. Integrated Wastelands Development Project

38. In which period DPAP was launched?

A. 1972 - 73 B. 1973 - 74

C. 1974 - 75 D. 1975 - 76

39. The Etawah Pilot project in Uttar Pradesh was originated by

A. Sir Daniel Hamilton B. Dr.Spencer Hatch

C. Mahatma Gandhiji D. Lt.Col.Albert Mayer

40. IVLP stands for

A. Indian Village Linkage Programme

B. Indian Village Linkage Plan

C. Institutional Village Linkage Programme

D. Integrated Village Lab to land Programme

41. Integrated Child Development Services scheme was started in the year

A. 1976 B. 1975

C. 1977 D. 1980

42. In NABARD, extent of refinance under various activities includes
    A. Pilot Rainfed Projects
    B. Waste Land Development Scheme
    C. Non Farm Sector Scheme and Agro Processing Promoting Units
    D. All the above
43. NARS stands for
    A. National Agricultural Resource System
    B. National Agricultural Revenue System
    C. National Agricultural Research System
    D. National Applied Research System
44. The first KVK was established in
    A. Calcutta B. Ranchi
    C. Coimbatore D. Pondicherry
45. NIRD under Ministry of Rural Development is located at
    A. Calcutta B. Hyderabad
    C. Bangalore D. Chennai
46. The T & V system of extension was introduced into India by
    A. Daniel Benor B. Van den Ban
    C. MS Swaminathan D. C. Subramanian
47. ATMA stands for
    A. Agriculture Technology Management Association
    B. Agricultural Technology Management Agency
    C. Agricultural Technology Mission Agency
    D. None of the above
48. Which of the following statement is incorrect?
    A. TRYSEM is one of the allied scheme of Swarnajayanti Gram Swarozgar Yojana
    B. SAMTI is the apex training institute at state level to give training support to ATMA
    C. Initially FIRKA development scheme was started in 34 FIRKAS
    D. Drought prone area programme was developed in the year 1972.
49. T & V system is a good example of
    A. Extension approach
    B. Training approach

C. Cooperative self help approach

D. Integrated development approach

50. Match the following

A. Sevagram project	1. Haryana
B. Gurgoan project	2. Uttar Pradesh
C. Indian Village service	3. Maharashtra
D. Etawah project	4. Rajasthan

A. 3 1 4 2 B. 1 2 4 3

C. 2 1 3 4 D. 4 3 1 2

51. NAARM is located at

A. New Delhi B. Hyderabad

C. Bangalore D. Cuttack

52. NATP was funded from

A. USA B. World bank

C. GOI D. ICAR

53. State Agricultural Universities in India were setup on the pattern of Land Grant College of

A. UK B. France

C. Italy D. USA

54. The leader of Boodhan movement is

A. Acharya Vinoba Bhave B. Spencer Hatch

C. F.L.Brayne D. T.Prakasam

55. Agriculture was made a state subject through

A. Government of India Act (1919) B. Royal Commission Report (1928)

C. Ford Foundation Report (1959) D. GMF Enquiry Report

56. The first state in India to introduce training and visit system was

A. Punjab B. Rajasthan

C. Tamil Nadu D. Bihar

57. Extension approach in India generally follows the norms of

A. Cooperation B. Participation

C. Prescription D. Mobilization

58. Match the following

A. IADP	1. Poverty programme
B. IRDP	2. Package programme
C. NREP	3. Employment generation
D. SEDA	4. Targeted approach

A. 3 1 4 2 B. 1 2 4 3

C. 2 1 3 4 D. 4 1 2 3

59. IRDP is

(i) 1978

(ii) Family approach

(iii) Emerged due to failure of CDP

(iv) To provide gainful employment and increase the purchasing power of rural people

A. (ii), (iii) and (iv) are correct B. (iv) alone is correct

C. (i), (ii) and (iii) are correct D. (i), (ii), (iii) and (iv) are correct

60. High yielding variety programme has given emphasis on

A. Land reform

B. Package and practices with dwarf varieties

C. Increase production through dry farming

D. None of these

61. The state which has no Panchayat Raj institutions is / are

(i) Mizoram

(ii) Nagaland

(iii) Meghalaya

(iv) Andhra Pradesh

A. (i), (ii) and (iv) B. (ii) and (iii)

C. (iii), (iv) and (i) D. (i), (ii) and (iii)

62. Sponsoring agency of Village Knowledge Centre is

A. M.S.Swaminathan Research Foundation, Chennai

B. MANAGE, Hyderabad

C. NAARM, Hyderabad

D. National Information Centre

63. Who is associated with YMCA?
    A. Spencer Hatch B. F.L.Brayne
    C. S.K. Dey D. Albert Mayor
64. Incharge of the Intensive Agricultural District Programme in district is
    A. Project officer B. Social Welfare officer
    C. District Collector D. District Panchayat Raj officer
65. Krishi Vigyan Kendra's are sponsored by
    A. IARI B. ICAR
    C. State Agricultural Universities D. State Government
66. National demonstrations were started in
    A. 1985 B. 1965
    C. 1948 D. 1970
67. National Extension Service (NES) was started in
    A. 1952 B. 1953
    C. 1995 D. 1976
68. Which of the following is incorrect statement?
    A. KVK is founded by ICAR
    B. It is also known as Farm Science Centre
    C. The number of KVK at present in 716
    D. None of these
69. Need based and skill oriented vocational training to practicing farmers and employed extension personnel is provided through
    A. Training and visit B. KVK
    C. National demonstration D. Lab to land programme

Answer keys

1	D	11	B	21	A	31	B	41	B	51	B	61	D
2	B	12	C	22	D	32	B	42	D	52	B	62	A
3	D	13	A	23	C	33	C	43	C	53	D	63	A
4	C	14	B	24	D	34	C	44	D	54	A	64	A
5	B	15	B	25	C	35	A	45	B	55	A	65	B
6	B	16	D	26	C	36	B	46	A	56	B	66	B
7	D	17	C	27	D	37	C	47	B	57	C	67	B
8	B	18	B	28	B	38	B	48	D	58	C	68	D
9	B	19	D	29	C	39	D	49	A	59	D	69	B
10	C	20	C	30	D	40	C	50	A	60	B		

5

Rural Sociology

I. Choose the correct answer

1. Who has defined sociology as interpretive understanding of social man?

   A. Chitamber　　B. Max Weber

   C. Gillin & Gillin　　D. Bonner

2. Find out the wrong answer

   A. Sociology is the science of rural society

   B. Sociology is study of human beings

   C. Sociology is the science deals with living beings interactions

   D. Sociology deals with principle of cohesion

3. It is the study of sociological life in rural setting – Rural Sociology profounded by

   A. Dahama　　B. Bhatnagar

   C. Desai　　D. Mott

4. Among the following which is not a scope of rural sociology

   A. Rural social institution

   B. Rural planning and reconstruction

   C. Religion and cultural rural society

   D. Rural problems are viewed from isolated angle

5. Who stated the characteristics of Indian Rural Society?

   A. Reddy　　B. Haiman

   C. Henning　　D. Loster

6. Which among the following is not a social institution?

   A. Political　　B. Economic

   C. Religion　　D. Custom

7. Match the list I with list II and choose the correct one

List I	**List II**
A. Partriarchal family	1. Ancestry continues through father
B. Matriarchal family	2. Male is the head
C. Matrilocal family	3. Female is the head
D. Patrilineal family	4. Husband goes to lives with wife's house

A. 3 2 4 1 B. 2 4 3 1

C. 2 3 4 1 D. 4 3 2 1

8. When did Red Cross society started?

A. World war I B. World war II

C. Sepoy Revolt D. Panipat war I

9. Who described the quality of a leader?

A. Dahama and Bhatnagar B. Gillin and Gillin

C. Max Webber and Bonner D. Bohlen and Raudabagh

10. Among the following which is not a characteristic of leader?

A. Autocratic B. Democratic

C. Dictatorship D. Laissez-faire

11. Consider the statement and choose the correct one

i. Urbanization – proportion of people in rural area

ii. Health – number of hospitals per 10000 populations

iii. Clothing – quantity and quality of cloth used per head

A. (i) and (ii) are correct B. (ii) and (iii) are correct

C. (i) and (iii) are correct D. All the statements are correct

12. In motivation, when an incentive (or) goal is artificially introduced, it is called

A. Intrinisic value B. Extrinsic value

C. Economic value D. Historic value

13. Among the following, which is not a technique of motivation

A. Need based approach B. Use of audio visuals

C. Dispersal D. Participation

14. Family is included under

    A. Primary group
    B. Nuclear group
    C. Tertiary group
    D. None of the above

15. _____ is the unit of rural society

    A. Farmers
    B. Village
    C. Women
    D. Extension workers

16. Study of human relationships in rural situations is called

    A. Sociology
    B. Rural Sociology
    C. Rural planning
    D. Both A and B

17. Which one of the following is the rural social organization?

    A. Red cross society
    B. Blue cross society
    C. National social service
    D. Rural social society

18. 4-H club was established in

    A. Russia
    B. Canada
    C. America
    D. Japan

Answer keys

1	B	11	B
2	A	12	B
3	C	13	C
4	D	14	A
5	A	15	B
6	D	16	B
7	C	17	A
8	A	18	C
9	A		
10	C		

UNIT XV: HORTICULTURE

1

Fundamentals of Horticulture

I. Choose the correct answer

1.1. Introduction

1. The cost of cultivation of vegetables is more due to
   A. Labour cost B. Weedicide cost
   C. Fertilizer cost D. Packing cost
2. Second irrigation given to the transplanted crop is called as
   A. Life irrigation B. furrow irrigation
   C. Drip irrigation D. Sprinkler irrigation
3. Farm yard manure generally applied in soil
   A. To increase the porosity
   B. To increase the organic matter content
   C. To increase micro organism
   D. To decrease pathogens
4. Lack of insufficient calcium results in
   A. Blossom end rot B. Flower development
   C. Leaf growth D. Fruit set
5. Development of fruits without seeds is termed as
   A. Vivipary B. Parthenocarpy
   C. Apomixis D. Polyembryony
6. Vegetable crop highly tolerant to water stress is
   A. Tomato B. Potato
   C. Bean D. Amaranthus
7. What is the volume of spray fluid required for spraying 1 ha of the crop
   A. 250 litre B. 350 litre
   C. 400 litre D. 500 litre

8. Which one of the below is a biofertilizer.

A. Urea B. Calcium ammonium nitrate

C. Diammonium phosphate D. Azolla

9. Which one of the following is a slow release fertilizer

A. N- Serve B. Urea

C. DAP D. Potassium sulphate

10. Chemical thinning of fruit is done with spraying

A. Benzyl adenine B. Thiourea

C. Naphthalene acetic acid D. Etheral

11. Which of the following fruit crop is not belongs to temperate region?

A. Apple B. Pea

C. Strawberry D. Lemon

12. Which of the following is growth retardant ?

A. GA3 B. Kinetin

C. ABA D. IBA

13. Which of the following is a tropical fruit crop?

A. Strawberry B. Walnut

C. Sapota D. Citrus

14. In hilly area, the system of fruit planting used is

A. Contour B. Strip cropping

C. Wind strip cropping D. Barrier cropping

15. The Branch of science that deals with study principles of propagation and production of fruits is called as

A. Olericulture B. Floriculture

C. Pomology D. Entomology

16. What is the suitable tool for pruning?

A. Shovel B. Budding knife

C. Bill hook D. Secateur

17. Pomology is derived from

A. Latin B. French

C. English D. Greek

18. First commercial vegetable seed production unit in India was established in 1942 at

    A. Quetta B. Kullu
    C. Nilgiris D. Pusa

19. Father of Horticulture

    A. Thomas Andrew Knight B. Liberty Hyde Bailey
    C. John Lindley D. All of the above

20. Word "Horticulture" is derived from

    A. Latin B. English
    C. Greek D. Italic

21. India is known as home of

    A. Vegetables B. Spices and Medicinal
    C. Fruits D. Flowers

22. Potato is a

    A. Long day plant B. Short day plant
    C. Day neutral plant D. Both B and C

23. Known variety of cauliflower suitable for tolerating high temperature is

    A. Early kumari B. Synthetic
    C. Snowball D. Pusa deepali

24. Which of the following crop requiring higher O_2?

    A. Sugarcane B. Tea
    C. Banana D. Betel vine

25. Soil with low pH is injuries to plants due higher toxicity of

    A. Fe and Mg B. Fe and Ca
    C. Fe and Mn D. Fe and Al

26. Light which promotes seed germination growth is

    A. Green light B. Red light
    C. Blue /Violet light D. Both A and B

27. Match the following

    A. Long day plant 1. Sweet potato
    B. Short day plant 2. Wild kidney bean

C. Day neutral plant 3. Cabbage

D. Intermediate plant 4. Chillies

A. 1 2 3 4 B. 3 1 4 2

C. 4 3 1 2 D. 2 3 4 1

28. The optimum temperature requirement of horticulture crops

A. 45°C – 47°C B. 30°C – 35°C

C. 24°C – 27°C D. 10°C – 15°C

29. The crop suitable for heavy rainfall region is

A. Citrus B. Mango

C. Tea D. Apple

30. Identify the incorrect statement

A. Cold air is heavier than warm air which is known as temperature inversion

B. Dry soil is suitable for Mediterranean herb garden

C. National Research Centre for cashewnut is located at Puttur, Karnataka

D. None of these

31. The number of Agro climatic zones of Tamil Nadu is

A. 15 B. 7

C. 20 D. 21

32. Match the following

A. Vit A 1. West Indian Cherry

B. Vit B1 2. Pomegranate

C. Vit B2 3. Apple

D. Vit C 4. Mango

A. 4 3 2 1 B. 3 2 4 1

C. 2 1 4 3 D. 3 1 4 2

33. Deficiency of calcium causes

A. Beri-Beri B. Pellagra

C. Scurvy D. Rickets

34. Iron content is higher in

A. Karonda B. Dates

C. Spinach D. All of these

35. Single seeded cucurbits vegetables is

A. Chow chow B. Ivy gourd

C. Gherkin D. Pointed gourd

36. Match the following

A. Banana	1. King of flower
B. Apple	2. Sword sucker
C. Tomato	3. Pome
D. Dahlia	4. Early blight

A. 2 1 4 3 B. 4 3 2 1

C. 2 4 3 1 D. 2 3 4 1

37. Which one of the followings is a climacteric type of fruit?

A. Banana B. Citrus

C. Litchi D. Grape

38. Which of the following is non-climacteric type of fruit?

A. Pineapple B. Litchi

C. Grape D. All of these

39. Mango is rich in

A. Vitamin E B. Vitamin B

C. Vitamin C D. Vitamin A

40. A flower having many pistils on the same receptacle develop

A. Multiple fruit B. Aggregate fruit

C. Stone fruit D. All the above

41. Guava, tomato, ber and melons are rich in

A. Vitamin A B. Vitamin B

C. Vitamin C D. Vitamin D

42. Which one of the following prevents soil erosion and reclaim water logged soils?

A. Ber B. Aonla

C. Pomegranate D. All the above

43. Which one of the following fruit crop is well known for its cooling effect?

A. Phalsa B. Sweet lime

C. Jamun D. All the above

44. The word hortus means

A. Fruit B. Culture
C. Garden D. Orchard

45. Who is the father of systematic pomology?

A. Lamarck B. Darwin
C. Mendel D. Decandolle

46. Which of the following fruit is non- climacteric?

A. Persimmon B. Sapota
C. Avocado D. Citrus

47. Rich source of fat (> 21%) is

A. Cashew B. Walnut
C. Almond D. Pecanut

58. Which is the most salt tolerant crop?

A. Mango B. Pomegranate
C. Banana D. Aonla

49. Which fruit has the highest oil content?

A. Peach B. Avocado
C. Olive D. Mango

Answer keys

1	A	15	C	29	C	43	D
2	A	16	D	30	D	44	C
3	B	17	A	31	B	45	D
4	A	18	A	32	A	46	D
5	B	19	D	33	D	47	B
6	C	20	A	34	D	48	D
7	D	21	B	35	A	49	C
8	D	22	B	36	D		
9	A	23	A	37	A		
10	C	24	B	38	D		
11	D	25	D	39	D		
12	C	26	B	40	B		
13	C	27	B	41	C		
14	B	28	C	42	D		

1.2. Area, Production, export and import of horticultural crops

1. More Indian fruits and vegetables are exported to
   A. USA B. UAE
   C. Germany D. Japan
2. The State having the highest productivity of coconut during 2017-18 is
   A. Kerala B. Andhra Pradesh
   C. Tamil Nadu D. Karnataka
3. Arrange the state based on production of flowers is
   A. Tamil Nadu > Karnataka > Andhra Pradesh
   B. Karnataka > Tamil Nadu > Andhra Pradesh
   C. Andhra Pradesh > Karnataka > Tamil Nadu
   D. Kerala > Karnataka > Tamil Nadu
4. The Place were growing apple in plain is
   A. Bangalore B. Pune
   C. Lucknow D. Imphal
5. Major imported vegetables in India is
   i) Onion ii) Okra
   iii) Chillies iv) Ginger
   A. (i) and (ii) B. (ii) and (iii)
   C. (iii) alone D. (ii) and (iii)
6. Major exporter of flower is
   A. Netherlands B. India
   C. Germany D. China
7. Cut flower contribution to total trade in floriculture is
   A. 86% B. 53%
   C. 45% D. 92%
8. Identify the correct statement
   A. India is the largest producer and consumer of cashew nut, tea and spices
   B. Major importer of spices from India is Soviet Union
   C. Average requirement of vegetables per day per head is 80 g
   D. All of these

9. Share of horticulture crops in total export of agricultural commodities is
   A. 30% B. 46%
   C. 37% D. 28%
10. The crop which has maximum production under spices
   A. Garlic B. Chillies
   C. Turmeric D. Nut meg
11. Horticulture contribution to agricultural GDP is about
   A. 30% B. 40%
   C. 15% D. 20%
12. Which country ranks number one position in fruit production in the world?
   A. China B. India
   C. Pakistan D. Brazil
13. Which one of the following state ranks first in spices production?
   A. Tamil Nadu B. Madhya Pradesh
   C. Andhra Pradesh D. Maharashtra
14. In which state, the production of plantation crops is higher?
   A. Tamil Nadu B. Andhra Pradesh
   C. Madhya Pradesh D. Maharashtra
15. Which vegetable is exported in larger quantities during the year 2016-17?
   A. Fresh cabbage B. Fresh cauliflower
   C. Fresh onion D. Fresh potato
16. The export value is higher during the year 2018-19
   A. Processed fruits B. Processed vegetables
   C. Cucumber and gherkins D. None of these
17. State having maximum area under fruit production is
   A. Andhra Pradesh B. Kerala
   C. Tamil Nadu D. Maharashtra
18. Leading vegetable producing state in India (2018-19) is
   A. Madhya Pradesh B. Maharashtra
   C. West Bengal D. Assam
19. Leading flower producing state in India is
   A. Kerala B. Tamil Nadu
   C. Karnataka D. Andhra Pradesh

Answer keys

1	B	11	A
2	B	12	D
3	A	13	B
4	A	14	B
5	D	15	C
6	A	16	A
7	A	17	D
8	A	18	C
9	C	19	B
10	B		

1.3. Organisations involved in horticulture

1. All India Coordinated Vegetable Improvement Project (AICVIP) was started in

   A. 1991-92 B. 1981-82

   C. 1970-71 D. 1960-61

2. Under the All India Coordinated Vegetable Improvement Project (AICVIP), India is divided into agro-climatic zones

   A. 8 B. 12

   C. 18 D. 24

3. New seed policy was launched in

   A. 1982 B. 1992

   C. 1988 D. 1986

4. National Research Centre for Litchi (NRCL) is located at

   A. Pune B. Muzaffarpur

   C. Lucknow D. Kolkata

5. Central Drug Research Institute is situated at

   A. Lucknow B. Mumbai

   C. New Delhi D. Hyderabad

6. International Potato Research Centre at is located at

   A. Shimla B. Peru

   C. Rome D. USA

7. Directorate of Onion and Garlic Research (DOGR) is situated at

   A. Shimla   B. Nasik

   C. New Delhi   D. Lucknow

8. Identify the incorrect statement of APEDA

   A. For export of scheduled products, APEDA registration is mandatory

   B. Financial assistance schemes are avail in APEDA

   C. Registered member can participate in training programme of APEDA

   D. APEDA is exclusive only for agriculture products

9. Commodity boards are comes under

   A. Ministry of Agriculture and Farmer's Welfare

   B. Ministry of Commerce and Industry

   C. Ministry of Food Processing Industries

   D. Either A or C

10. Central Arid Zone Research Institute (CAZRI) is located at

    A. Jodhpur   B. Nagpur

    C. Bikaner   D. Pune

11. HQ of International Society for Horticulture Science (ISHS) is at

    A. USA   B. Belgium

    C. France   D. Brazil

12. Journal "Indian Horticulture" is published by

    A. IIHR   B. IARI

    C. ICAR   D. IGKV

13. National Horticulture Mission was launched during

    A. 2004-2005   B. 2005-2006

    C. 2007-2008   D. 2002-2003

14. Commodity Boards are

    A. Statutory bodies   B. Registered bodies

    C. Controlled by NABARD   D. Controlled by RBI

15. Math the following

    A. Coffee board   1. Cochin

    B. Coconut board   2. Bangalore

    C. Rubber board   3. Kottayam

    D. Tea board   4. Calcutta

A. 3 2 4 1 B. 2 1 3 4

C. 1 2 3 4 D. 4 3 2 1

16. APEDA stands for

A. Agricultural and Processed food products Export Development Authority

B. Agricultural and Processed food products Economy Development Authority

C. Agricultural and Preserved food productions Export Development Authority

D. Agricultural and Preserved food products Environment Development Authority

17. National Research Centre for Banana is located at

A. Kerala B. Tamil Nadu

C. Andhra Pradesh D. Himachal pradesh

18. National Horticulture Board was located at

A. Gurgoan, Haryana B. Bangalore, Karnataka

C. Ajmer, Rajasthan D. Mumbai, Maharashtra

19. National Research Centre for Grapes is situated at

A. Bangalore B. Hyderabad

C. Pune D. Muzaffarpur

20. International Institute of Horticulture is situated at

A. Brazil B. Italy

C. USA D. None of the above

Answer keys

1	C	11	B
2	A	12	C
3	C	13	B
4	B	14	A
5	A	15	B
6	A	16	A
7	B	17	B
8	D	18	A
9	B	19	C
10	A	20	A

1.4. Orchard and its management

1. Which one of the following is a non-insect pest in orchard crops

A. Mites B. Cut worms

C. Weevils D. Aphid

2. The beneficial fungus associated with roots of orchard crops is

A. Phytopthora B. *Rhizobium*

C. Mycorrhiza D. *Pythium*

3. Wind breaks are planted in orchards towards

A. South-West B. North-West

C. North-East D. East-South

4. The main season for planting orchard crop

A. January-February B. June-July

C. March-April D. November-December

5. In hexagonal method of tree planting, more trees can be planted than the triangular method and what is the percentage?

A. 0 B. 5

C. 10 D. 15

6. Planting distance of individual fruit species provides the following advantages

A. Uniform growth

B. Allows easy orchard operation

C. Improper utilization of orchard space

D. Proper supervision

7. The most common method planting orchard crop

A. Ridge and furrow B. Bed

C. Pit D. Ridge

8. Gypsum is used as an amendment for reclaiming

A. Alkali Soils B. Acid Soils

C. Saline D. Saline Alkali Soils

9. Which is the most important factor considered while establishing an orchard?

A. Topography B. Approach road

C. Location D. Availability of water

10. The site for an orchard should be selected
    A. In a new locality
    B. Away from market
    C. In a remote place
    D. In a predominantly fruit growing area
11. In orchard layout, smallest area should be allocated under
    A. Irrigation channels
    B. Roads and path
    C. Manures pit
    D. Farm building
12. Most economic method of irrigation of orchard under water scarcity conditions
    A. Flood system
    B. Ring system
    C. Sprinkler system
    D. Drip system
13. Popular method of orchard planting is
    A. Square system
    B. Digonal system
    C. Hexagonal system
    D. Rectangular system
14. The most common method of budding used for orchard crops
    A. S budding
    B. L budding
    C. Eye budding
    D. T budding
15. The number of plants in an unit becomes almost double of square system in
    A. Rectangular system
    B. Triangular system
    C. Quincunx system
    D. Contour system
16. The term scion and root-stock are used in
    A. Layering
    B. Grafting
    B. Budding
    D. Cutting
17. Ideal water table depth preferred for establishing an orchard is
    A. More than 3
    B. Less than 3
    C. Less than 1
    D. All of these
18. A garden that grows single crop in larger quantities for distant market is called as
    A. Market garden
    B. Nutritional garden
    C. Kitchen garden
    D. Truck garden
19. Which fruit crop is suitable for kitchen garden?
    A. Mango
    B. Papaya
    C. Sapota
    D. Ber

20. In nutritional garden, which perennial vegetable is recommended?
    A. Tapioca B. Elephant foot yam
    C. Ivy gourd D. Bitter gourd
21. Which vegetable is more suitable for commercial garden?
    A. Potato B. Radish
    C. Carrot D. Beet root

Answer keys

1	A	11	A	21	A
2	C	12	D		
3	B	13	A		
4	B	14	D		
5	D	15	C		
6	B	16	B		
7	C	17	A		
8	A	18	D		
9	A	19	B		
10	D	20	C		

1.5. Propagation methods in horticulture

1. Which is the popular and cheapest method of asexual propagation ?
    A. Budding B. Layering
    C. Cutting D. Grafting
2. In a grafted plant, the lower part of plant is known as
    A. Stock B. T-shield
    C. Scion D. Stem
3. What is the latest grafting technology for commercial multiplication of mango?
    A. Stone grafting B. Saddle grafting
    C. Softwood grafting D. Whip and tongue grafting
4. What is the ratio of pot mixture containing red earth, FYM and sand?
    A. 1:2:1 B. 1:1:1
    C. 1:1:2 D. 2:1:1
5. What is the height and diameter of tube pot?
    A. 25 x 32 cm B. 35 x 35 cm
    C. 20 x 27 cm D. 20 x 13 cm

6. Which is the suitable medium for marcottage?
   A. Vermiculite B. Saw dust
   C. Perlite D. Pumice
7. Which of the following crop is propagated by bulbs?
   A. Turmeric B. Banana
   C. Potato D. Onion
8. Asexually propagated crops is
   A. Tomato B. Brinjal
   C. Apple D. Jack fruit
9. Protray are related to
   A. Post harvest B. Nursery
   C. Processing D. Transport
10. Making an incision below a bud to retard its growth
   A. Nicking B. Ringing
   C. Notching D. Thinning
11. Angle formed by attached of a branch to the trunk
   A. Conn B. Crown
   C. Corona D. Crotch
12. Choose the correct statements
   i) NFT was developed initially by India in 1920
   ii) NFT was developed by Dr. Alan Zhang Jr.
   iii) Saline water is not suited for this technique
   A. i) and ii) are correct B. ii) and iii) are correct
   C. All are correct D. iv) All are incorrect
13. Growing media in NFT technique is
   A. Perlite B. Coconut husk
   C. Rock wool D. All of these
14. Base material for hydroponics is
   i) Sand ii) Gravel
   iii) Glass Wool iv) Coir pith
   A. (i) and (ii) only B. (ii) and (iii) only
   C. (iii) and (iv) only D. All of these

15. Suitable fruit crop for kitchen gardening is

A. Lime B. Sapota

C. Mango D. Ber

16. Perennial vegetable suitable for kitchen garden is

A. Passiflora B. Coccinea

C. Pointed gourd D. Chow-chow

17. Area of large nutrition garden is

A. 500 sq.m B. 150 to 200 sq.m

C. < than 100 sq.m D. 1000 sq.m

18. Truck gardening is a _____ type of cultivation.

A. Intensive B. Extensive

C. Moderate D. Both A and B

19. Type of crop grown in market gardening is

A. Colacasia B. Tapioca

C. Elephant foot yam D. Bhendi

20. In vegetable forcing, extreme summer temperature should be reduced by

A. 5 – 10°C B. 20 – 25°C

C. 30 – 35°C D. 15 – 20°C

21. The kitchen garden is designed with following principles as

i) Backyard of the house

ii) Quick growing fruit trees on north side

iii) Never be a shady place

A. (i) alone B. (ii) alone

C. (iii) alone D. All the above

22. Identify the incorrect statement

i) Low technology green houses are less than 3m in total height

ii) No vertical wall for low technology green house

iii) Medium technology green house have roof or side hall ventilation or both

iv) Medium level green house offer superior environment performance

A. (i) only B. (ii) only

C. (iii) only D. (iv) only

23. Most commonly used cladding material in greenhouse is
    A. Poly carbonate cladding B. Fibre glass reinforced polyester
    C. Polythene D. Polyvinyl chloride
24. CO_2 level in sealed green house is about
    A. 200 - 300 ppm B. 350 - 400 ppm
    C. 150 - 200 ppm D. None of these
25. Growing vegetables out of their normal growing season is called
    A. Vegetable forcing B. Truck gardening
    C. Kitchen gardening D. Both A and C
26. Tongue grafting is a modified form
    A. Whip grafting B. Inarching
    C. Saddle grafting D. None

Answer keys

1	D	11	D	21	D
2	A	12	C	22	D
3	C	13	D	23	C
4	D	14	A	24	C
5	D	15	A	25	A
6	A	16	B	26	A
7	D	17	A		
8	C	18	B		
9	B	19	D		
10	A	20	A		

2

Production Technology of Fruit Crops

I. Choose the correct answer

2.1. Tropical fruits

1. Citrus fruits are commonly propagated by
   A. Cutting B. Layering
   C. T-budding D. Tongue grafting
2. Fruit which is cured in smoke for ripening
   A. Apple B. Banana
   C. Orange D. Mango
3. According to CFTRI, papain extraction is the highest during
   A. Rainy season B. Summer
   C. Winter D. All
4. Poor man's apple is
   A. Mango B. Sapota
   C. Guava D. Citrus
5. Match list I with list II and choose the correct options given below

List I	**List II**
a. Mango	1. Rutaceae
b. Citrus	2. Punicaceae
c. Grapes	3. Anacardiaceae
d. Pomegranate	4. Vitaceae

   A. 4 2 1 3 B. 3 1 4 2
   C. 3 1 2 4 D. 4 1 3 2
6. What is the scientific name of jack?
   A. *Carica papaya* B. *Mangifera indica*
   C. *Prunus americana* D. *Artocarpus heterophyllus*
7. Which one of the followings is the variety of sapota?
   A. MDU 1 B. BSR 1
   C. PKM 1 D. KKM 1

8. BSR 1 belongs to which fruit crop?
   A. Aonla B. Custard apple
   C. Pomegranate D. Jack
9. In which season, banana is planted in garden lands?
   A. January – February and June – July
   B. January – February and November – December
   C. July – August and September – October
   D. July – August and May – June
10. Which variety of banana is suitable for culinary purpose?
   A. Monthan B. Robusta
   C. Poovan D. Rasthali
11. Which mango is suitable for export?
   A. Alphonso B. Neelum
   C. Mulgoa D. Banagalora
12. What is the spacing for mango high density planting?
   A. 4 x 4 m B. 6 x 6 m
   C. 3 x 3 m D. 5 x 5 m
13. What is the recent commercial propagation method in mango?
   A. Whip method B. Soft – wood grafting
   C. Stone grafting D. Budding
14. Consider the statements and choose the correct answer
   i) Off season, mulgoa variety
   ii) NAA 20 ppm is recommended for mango fruit retention
   iii) NAA 25 ppm is recommended for mango fruit retention
   A. (i) is correct B. (ii) alone is correct
   C. (iii) is correct D. (i) & (ii) are correct
15. In which month, pruning is done in mango senile orchard?
   A. June B. July
   C. August D. September
16. What type of sucker is used as a planting material in banana?
   A. Water sucker B. Rhizome
   C. Sword sucker D. Peepal
17. How much percent of lindane is mixed with soil while filling the pits for banana?
   A. 1.5% B. 1.0%
   C. 2.5% D. 2.0%
18. How many suckers to be planted in high density planting in banana @ 1.8 x 3.6 m spacing?
   A. 4200 B. 4300
   C. 4500 D. 4600

19. What is the fertilizer dosage for banana grown in garden land?
 A. 150:90:300 g/plant/year B. 210:35:450 g/plant/year
 C. 110:35:330 g/plant/year D. 160:50:390 g/plant/year
20. Bunchy top of banana is caused by
 A. Jassid B. Aphid
 C. Thrips D. Weevil
21. What is the yield of poovan banana?
 A. 30-40 t/ha B. 20-40 t/ha
 C. 50-60 t/ha D. 40-50 t/ha
22. Match the list I and list II and choose the correct answer given below:

List I	**List II**
A. Sweet orange	1. *Citrus aurantitolia*
B. Lemon	2. *Citrus reticulata*
C. Mandrin	3. *Citrus limon*
D. Acid lime	4. *Citrus sinensis*

 A. 4 3 2 1 B. 3 4 1 2
 C. 2 1 4 3 D. 1 2 3 4
23. Which one of the following is a variety of acid lime?
 A. Vikram B. Miruthula
 C. Ranga D. Resmi
24. What is the propagation method followed in sweet orange?
 A. Whip method B. Flute budding
 C. Patch budding D. Soft – wood grafting
25. Which growth regulator is used for banana fruit ripening?
 A. Gibberelic acid B. Ethrel
 C. 2, 4, D D. Zeatin
26. What is the origin of papaya?
 A. Asia B. Japan
 C. Malasia D. Tropical America
27. What is the seed rate for papaya?
 A. 500 g/ha B. 200 g/ha
 C. 400 g/ha D. 700 g/ha
28. Which papaya variety is suitable for papain extraction?
 A. Co 7 B. Co 1
 C. Co 4 D. Co 2
29. Which root stock is used propagation of sapota?
 A. *Mimusops elengi* B. *Manilkhara hexandra*
 C. *Bassia latifolia* D. *Calophyllum inophyllum*
30. Which inter crop is cultivated in sapota plantation?
 A. Redgram B. Gingelly
 C. Lab-Lab D. Groundnut

31. Which one of the followings is the king of fruit?
A. Guava B. Banana
C. Citrus D. Mango

32. Which nutrient deficiency is causing fruit cracking in guava?
A. Iron B. Magnesium
C. Boron D. Manganese

33. Origin of jack is
A. China B. India
C. Malaysia D. Sri lanka

34. Which one of the followings variety belongs to jack
A. PKM 1 B. BSR 1
C. PLR 1 D. KKM 1

35. What is the yield of jack?
A. 10 – 20 t/ha B. 15 – 25 t/ha
C. 50 – 60 t/ha D. 30 – 40 t/ha

36. Match list I with list II and choose the correct answer

List I	**List II**
a. Pomegranate	1. BSR 1
b. Ber	2. Ganesh
c. Custard apple	3. Umran
d. Aonla	4. Balanagar

A. 4 3 2 1 B. 4 2 3 1
C. 3 1 4 2 D. 2 3 4 1

37. What is the spacing for pineapple?
A. 90 x 60 x 30 cm B. 90 x 45 x 30 cm
C. 90 x 30 x 30 cm D. 75 x 60 x 30 cm

38. Which is the major pest in pomegranate?
A. Stem borer B. Fruit borer
C. Aphid D. Mealy bag

39. Consider the statements about pineapple and choose the correct answer.
i) NAA 20 ppm + 2% urea @ 50 ml/plant for flower induction
ii) NAA 20 ppm + 1% urea @ 50 ml/plant for flower induction
iii) NAA 10 ppm + 2% urea @ 50 ml /plant for flower induction
A. (i) & (ii) are correct B. (i) & (iii) are correct
C. (ii) & (iii) are correct D. (iii) alone is correct

40. Harvesting time of custard apple is
A. January – March B. March – May
C. August – October D. May – July

41. Mango belong to the family
A. Anacardiaceae B. Malvaceae
C. Arecaceae D. Caricaceae

42. Regular bearing variety of mango
    A. Banesan B. Neelum
    C. Mulgoa D. Alphonso
43. Fruit drop in mango is regulated by
    A. IBA @ 100 ppm B. GA @ 100 ppm
    C. Alar @ 100 ppm D. NAA @ 100 ppm
44. Mango ranks first in which state in terms of area
    A. Uttar Pradesh B. Andhra Pradesh
    C. Karnataka D. Tamil Nadu
45. Suitable variety for pulp in mango is
    A. Rumani B. Banesan
    C. Bangalora D. Dhas-he-ri
46. Black tip in mango is regulated by
    A. NAA @ 200 ppm B. Borax @ 0.6%
    C. GA @ 100 ppm D. IBA @ 100 ppm
47. Hill banana variety is
    A. Vayal vazhai B. Karpooravalli
    C. Namarai D. Poovan
48. Chemical used to spray to remove seediness in banana is
    A. 2,4-D @ 25 ppm B. CCC 1000 ppm
    C. GA @ 500 ppm D. NAA @ 250 ppm
49. Water requirement for banana is
    A. 900-1200 mm B. 600-700 mm
    C. 800-900 mm D. 1200-1500 mm
50. Mattocking is a special practice in banana followed
    A. Before flowering B. After planting
    C. After harvesting D. Before harvesting
51. Common rootstock used for sweet orange is
    A. Acid lime B. Rough lemon
    C. Karna khatta D. Cleopatra mandasin
52. Origin of acid lime is
    A. Mediterranean B. Mexico
    C. South East Asia D. North America

53. Granulation is commonly observed in citrus spp of

A. Acid lime B. Lemon

C. Sweet orange D. Grape fruit

54. Commonly adopted spacing for mandarin orange is

A. 6 x 6 m B. 7 x 7 m

C. 2 x 2 m D. 3 x 3 m

55. Red flush guava variety is

A. Allakabad safed B. Bapatta

C. Hafsi D. Arka mirdula

56. Guava is commercially propagated by

A. Budding B. Air layering

C. Cutting D. Seeds

57. Cricket ball is a variety of

A. Guava B. Papaya

C. Sapota D. Mango

58. Pomegranate is propagated by commercially by

A. Grafting B. Budding

C. Layering D. Rooted cuttings

59. Type of fruit in pomegranate is

A. Balusta B. Drupe

C. Pepo D. Hesperidium

60. Book entitled Principles of fruit culture was written by

A. B.P.Pal B. B.S.Chundawat and N.L.Sen

C. N.L.Patel D. Prasad and Kumar

61. Removal of male bud in banana is technically called as

A. Tipping B. Disbudding

C. Threshing D. Denavelling

62. Kalipatti is a popular variety of

A. Guava B. Pomegranate

C. Sapota D. Grape

63. Patch budding is generally practiced in

A. Guava B. Sapota

C. Ber D. Aonla

64. The impeded inflorescence or bunch development in banana is referred to as
   A. Chocking   B. Premature bunching
   C. Splitting   D. Abortion
65. Which of the following is not correctly matched?
   A. Mulberry- Apocynaceae   B. Litchi – Sapindaceae
   C. Apple - Rosaceae   D. Phalsa - Tiliaceae
66. Which fruit is also referred as bathroom fruit?
   A. Mango   B. Banana
   C. Persimmon   D. Carambola
67. Seedlessness in lemon (*Citrus limon*) is due to
   A. Self incompatability   B. Parthenocarpy
   C. Parthenogenesis   D. Ovule sterility
68. Basrai dwarf and Amrit sagar are the varieties of
   A. Banana   B. Papaya
   C. Mango   D. Sapota
69. Furete is an important variety of
   A. Avocado   B. Mango
   C. Tomato   D. Banana
70. Pineapple belongs to family
   A. Bromeliaceae   B. Arecaceae
   C. Juglandaceae   D. Anacardiaceae
71. Krishna and kanchan are varieties of
   A. Grape   B. Aonla
   C. Apple   D. Ber
72. Ratna variety of mango is a cross of
   A. Neelum× Alphonso   B. Dashehari × Neelum
   C. Neelum× Dashehari   D. None of these
73. Bullock's Heart is used as a root stock in
   A. Custard apple   B. Fig
   C. Guava   D. Aonla
74. Kinnow is basically a
   A. Tangor   B. Tangerine
   C. Citrange   D. Mandarin

75. Roopa is an improved variety of

A. Guava
B. Litchi
C. Walnut
D. Pomegranate

76. In pomegranate the edible part is

A. Juice epicarp
B. Mesocarp
C. Juice hairs
D. Juice testa

77. Which of the following is the late ripening cultivar of ber?

A. Umran
B. Sindhura Narnaul
C. Kaithli
D. Gola

78. Surinam cherry is used as a rootstock for

A. Sweet cherry
B. Longan
C. Sour cherry
D. Jamun

79. St. George is a rootstock of_________ resistant to

A. Grape, Powdery mildew
B. Grape, Wilt
C. Grape, Phylloxera pest
D. Guava, Anthracnose

80. Oldest propagation method of mango is

A. Inarching
B. Stone grafting
C. Bridge grafting
D. Veneer grafting

81. Which of the following variety of banana is developed by tissue culture technique?

A. Srimanti
B. Basari
C. Harichal
D. Lalvelchi

82. Pineapple contains _________ which are responsible for pineapple flowering

A. Ethyl propionate esters
B. Methyl propionate esters
C. Vitamin C
D. All

83. Papain extracted from immature papaya fruit contain digestive enzyme known as

A. Papainase
B. Acetate
C. Bromelain
D. None

84. *Eriobotrya japonica* is a

A. Tropical fruit
B. Temperate fruit
C. Arid fruit
D. Sub –tropical fruit

85. The February flowering in guava is known as
    A. Hasta bahar B. Mrig bahar
    C. Ambe bahar D. None
86. Spacing followed in custard apple is
    A. 4.5×4.5 mts B. 4×4 mts
    C. 6.5× 6.5 mts D. 5.5× 5.5 mts
87. Activity of ethylene in fruit ripening is maintained by
    A. Mo B. Cu
    C. Fe D. Ca
88. The citrus classification was given by
    A. Bruns B. Tanaka and Swingle
    C. Simmonds D. None
89. The mango hybrid developed by IIHR
    A. Arka Hans B. Arka Jyothi
    C. Arka Aruna D. Arka Vathi
90. Which is used for deblossoming purpose in mango?
    A. NAA B. GA
    C. Paclobutrazol D. ABA
91. Synthetic tetraploid variety of banana is
    A. Bodles Altafort B. Matti
    C. Pisang Lilin D. Dwarf Cavendish
92. Plough crop is common name of the following fruit crop
    A. Walnut B. Cashewnut
    C. Ber D. Date palm
93. Brown turkey is
    A. Root stock of fig B. Root stock of sapota
    C. Root stock of jack fruit D. Variety of avocado
94. Green mould of citrus is caused by
    A. *Penicillium digitatum* B. *Penicillium italicum*
    C. Lemon butterfly D. None
95. A bud mutant cultivar of mango is
    A. Noorjhan B. Rosica
    C. Croton D. Ratna

96. Which one variety of mango is free from spongy tissue?
A. Dasheri B. Ratna
C. Mallika D. Alphonso

97. Banana chips are dried at
A. 70-80°C B. 80-90°C
C. 40-50°C D. 55-60°C

98. Sindhu variety of mango is developed by crossing between which of the parents?
A. Alphonso × Fazali B. Totapari × Alphonso
C. Ratna × Alphonso D. Neelum × Alphonso

99. Papaya variety Surya is produced by crossing between
A. Pusa Nanha× Pusa Dwarf B. Sunrise Solo × Pink Flesh Sweet
C. Solo × Red Flesh D. Pink Flesh Sweet × Sunrise Solo

100. Kinnow is a cross between
A. Willow leaf × King B. King × Willow leaf
C. Both D. None

101. L-49 variety of guava was developed at
A. Maharastra B. Uttar Pradesh
C. Madhya Pradesh D. Rajasthan

102. Self incompatible mango cultivar is
A. Zardalu B. Gulab Khas
C. Krishna Bhog D. Bombay green

103. Pineapple is a variety of which fruit crop?
A. Sweet Orange B. Cherry
C. Litchi D. Pineapple

104. Citrus dieback is caused by
A. Water stress B. Virus + Malnutrition
C. Fungi and other D. None

105. Causal organism of panama wilt of banana is
A. Bacterial B. Fungal
C. Mycoplasma D. None

106. Pineapple is originated in
A. India B. Brazil
C. New zealand D. China

107. Sweet orange is generally trained on
A. Single stem B. Multiple stem
C. Two branches D. None of the above

108. Which is the dwarfing rootstock of guava?
A. French Guava B. Chinese Guava
C. American Guava D. Seedling Guava

109. Jamun has same family as
A. Pomegranate B. Guava
C. Papaya D. Sapota

110. Which fruit crop does not belong to Anacardiaceae family?
A. Mango B. Cashew
C. Pistachionut D. Pecan nut

111. Little leaf in mango is due to
A. Zn deficiency B. Mo deficiency
C. Zn toxicity D. Mo toxicity

112. Bacterial soft rot is caused due to
A. Fermentation of pectin B. Fermentation of sugars
C. Formation of ketones D. Formation of amino acids

113. Which papaya species is resistant to distortion ring-spot virus?
A. *Carica papaya* B. *Carica pentagona*
C. *Carica cauliflora* D. *Carica microcarpa*

114. Gulabi is important cultivar of
A. Strawberry B. Litchi
C. Pomegranate D. Grape fruit

115. Cock's comb is a physiological disorder of
A. Sapota B. Aonla
C. Ber D. None of the above

116. Caprification takes place in
A. Fig B. Ber
C. Avacado D. Date palm

117. The type of fruit in fig is
A. Berry B. Syconus
C. Pome D. Drupe

118. ________ is a mutant, developed through gamma irradiation in papaya
A. Pusa dwarf B. Washington
C. Pusa nanha D. Pusa giant
119. Pusa Majestic is a variety of
A. Papaya B. Gauva
C. Mango D. Citrus
120. The fruit of banana is botanically a/an
A. Pepo B. Berry
C. Pome D. Drupe
121. Chromosome number of mango
A. 2n = 40 B. 4n = 40
C. 3n = 40 D. n = 40
122. Pollination in mango is mainly
A. House fly B. Honey bees
C. Weevil D. Wind
123. Polyembryony variety of mango
A. Vellaicollamban B. Olour
C. Kurukkan D. All of the above
124. Which mango variety is suitable for high density planting?
A. Sindhu B. Amrapali
C. Mallika D. Ambika
125. Seedless variety of mango
A. Mallika B. Safari
C. Ratna D. Sindhu
126. Regulation in mango to some extent can be induced with the application of
A. Paclobutrazol B. ABA
C. Auxin D. Thiourea
127. In papaya, papain contain_____ protein
A. 65.2% B. 82.2%
C. 72.2% D. 55.5%
128. Which crop is called micronutrient loving crop
A. Mango B. Citrus
C. Banana D. Apple

129. Multistorey cropping system is practiced in
   A. Bihar and UP   B. Karnataka and Kerala
   C. J and K   D. Punjab and Gujarat
130. Pink fleshed variety of papaya
   A. Sunrise solo   B. Taiwan
   C. Surya   D. Coorg honey dew
131. Choke throat in banana is due to
   A. High temperature   B. Low temperature
   C. High humidity   D. Low humidity
132. Which fruit is commonly known as Fruit of New World ?
   A. Jackfruit   B. Passion fruit
   C. Avocado   D. Mango
133. Papaya is a native of
   A. Asia   B. India
   C. Brazil   D. Tropical America
134. Kalipatti is the famous variety of
   A. Ber   B. Mango
   C. Sapota   D. Litchi
135. Which of the following is a ripening hormone
   A. GA_3 B. Auxin
   C. Cytokinin   D. Ethylene
136. Seeds are sown immediately after extraction in which fruit
   A. Citrus   B. Ber
   C. Mango   D. Jamun
137. Man-made hybrid is
   A. Pineapple   B. Strawberry
   C. Pomegranate   D. Apple
138. To control mango malformation
   A. NAA   B. IAA
   C. IBA   D. 2, 4-D
139. Papain is used in
   A. Textile industry   B. Meat industry
   C. Both A and B   D. None of the above

140. Citrus canker is a _____ disease

A. Bacterial B. Viral
C. Fungal D. MLO

141. Pollination in walnut is by

A. Wind B. Insect
C. Birds D. None

142. Famous variety of mango for pickle use is

A. Ramkela B. Ratna
C. Totapuri D. Bombay Green

143. Micro-propagation is common in multiplication of

A. Banana B. Orchids
C. Strawberry D. All of the above

144. Bending is practice in guava to encourage

A. Better sprouting B. Better ripening
C. Better fruiting D. Better quality

145. Major cause of mango fruit drop is

A. Lack of pollination B. Low stigmatic receptivity
C. Defective perfect flower D. All of the above

146. Bearing habit of mango is

A. Auxiliary B. Mixed
C. Terminal D. None of the above

147. Most important disease of banana in India is

A. Sigatoka B. Fusarium wilt
C. Bunchy top D. Panama wilt

148. The most common type of jamun grown in North India

A. Paras B. Gulabi
C. Jath Jamun D. Raj Jamun

149. Lalit is an improved cultivar of

A. Guava B. Ber
C. Mango D. Aonla

150. Sweetest variety of mango

A. Dhashe-hari B. Langra
C. Alphonso D. Banganpalli

151. Hen and Chicken a disorder is observed in
A. Grapes B. Mango
C. Litchi D. Banana

152. Modified stem of banana is
A. Sword suckers B. Rhizomes
C. Water suckers D. Corm

153. Which of the following is dwarf variety of mango
A. Amarpali B. Alphanso
C. Dashehari D. Langra

154. Commercially used planting material in pineapple is
A. Seed B. Suckers
C. Slip D. Both A & B

155. Fruit cracking in pomegranate is regulated by
A. Liquid paraffin 1% B. Liquid paraffin 2%
C. Liquid paraffin 3% D. Liquid paraffin 5%

156. One of the common problems associated with citrus cultivation is
A. Virus B. Nematode
C. Sucking pests D. Bacterial diseases

157. Plant protection chemical used to control nematode in citrus
A. Methyl parathion B. Carbofuran
C. Nemagon D. Thiram

158. The optimum spacing adapted for the cultivation of acid lime is
A. 3 – 4 m B. 4 – 5 m
C. 5 – 6 m D. 6 – 7 m

159. The soil type suited for acid lime cultivation
A. Sandy B. Alluvial soil
C. Red D. Loamy soil

160. The soils suited for acid lime cultivation
A. Acid soils B. Alkaline soil
C. Saline soils D. Neutral soil

161. Which one of the following citrus type is monoembryonic
A. Lemon B. Lime
C. Pumelo D. Mandarin

162. The optimum season for budding in citrus

A. September – October B. April – May

C. June – July D. January – February

163. The optimum temperature for the cultivation of acid lime is

A. $20 - 30^0$ C B. $25 - 32^0$ C

C. $30 - 35^0$ C D. $35 - 37^0$ C

164. What is the normal yield of acid lime?

A. 20 t/ha/year B. 25 t/ha/year

C. 30 t/ha/year D. 35 t/ha/year

165. What is the method of propagation for sweet orange?

A. Patch budding B. Ring budding

C. Flute budding D. Forket / patch

166. The optimum spacing adapted for obtaining maximum yield in sweet orange is

A. 6 x 6 m B. 7 x 7 m

C. 8 x 8 m D. 10 x 10 m

167. Mandarin starts bearing from

A. 2 – 3 years after planting B. 3 – 5 years after planting

C. 5 – 7 years after planting D. 7 – 9 years after planting

168. The yield obtained from mandarin orange at the peak season is about

A. 10 – 15 t/ha/year B. 15 – 20 t/ha/year

C. 20 – 25 t/ha/year D. Above 25 t/ha/year

169. The nature of inflorescence found in citrus is mostly of

A. Solitary B. Raceme

C. Cymose D. Panicle

170. The root stock of citrange are sensitive to

A. Heat B. Salt

C. Cold D. Drought

171. The indicator plants employed for the index of tristeza virus is

A. Rough lemon B. Cleopatra mandarin

C. Trifoliate D. Kagzilime

172. Premature drop of leaves and die back of twigs of citrus are associated with the deficiency of

A. S
B. Ca
C. Mg
D. K_2O

173. Scaby lesions on the rinds of the oranges are due to the deficiency of

A. B
B. Fe
C. Cu
D. Zn

174. Rangpur lime when grown in high humid conditions is susceptible to

A. Scab disease
B. Canker
C. Wilt
D. Dieback

175. High acidity in the citrus fruits are due to good supply of soil

A. K_2O
B. Ca_2CO_3
C. $MgCO_3$
D. Na_2CO_3

176. In which form pectin is present in fruits?

A. Protopectin
B. Pectin
C. Calcium pectate
D. None of the above

177. A separate ministry for Food processing was established in

A. 1968
B. 1978
C. 1988
D. 1987

178. The fruit product order FPO license is given by

A. NHB
B. State government
C. Government of India
D. ICAR

179. Processed product in which fruit pieces suspended is called as

A. Jam
B. Marmalade
C. Cordial
D. Jelly

180. Sap burn is a post harvest disorder in

A. Apple
B. Mango
C. Guava
D. Citrus

181. Which method is used for inactivation of microbial growth?

A. Sulphuring
B. Sulphitation
C. Blanching
D. Freezing

182. Fenny is prepared from

A. Grapes
B. Apple
C. Straw berry
D. Cashew apple

183. Germicidal effect of KMS is due to

A. SO_2 B. $K_2S_2O_7$

C. H_2SO_3 D. HSO_2

184. Which of the following system of training of grapes has high cost benefit ratio

A. Bower B. Head

C. Kniffin D. Trellis

185. King of Arid Fruits is called

A. Aonla B. Pomegranate

C. Phalsa D. Ber

186. Fruit of the 21st century is called

A. Jamun B. Ber

C. Aonla D. Bael

187. Queen of Fruits is called

A. Avocado B. Mango

C. Mangosteen D. Ber

188. Arka Krishna is a variety of

A. Pomegranate B. Grapes

C. Guava D. Mango

189. Which variety of grapes is processed for more than 50% rasin production in the world?

A. Gulabi B. Anab-e-shahi

C. Thompson seedless D. Cardinal

190. The spur in Grape is

A. New growth of branch B. Old shoot twig

C. Current season growth D. None

191. Bangalore blue variety of grape is having parents

A. *V.vinefera* × *V.labrusca* B. *V.vinefera* × *V.reticulata*

C. Both D. None

192. Bitterness in grapes fruit juice is due to the presence of

A. Streptocine B. Biteracine

C. Naringin D. None

193. The inception of ripening in grape is termed as
    A. Break even point B. Verasion
    C. Colour break D. Turning stage
194. Ganesh kirti is a variety of
    A. Pomegranate B. Ber
    C. Grapes D. Phalsa
195. Fruit of bael (*Aegle marmelos*) is botanically
    A. Hard shelled berry B. Drupe
    C. Hesperidium D. Stone
196. Example of seeded variety of grapes is
    A. Tas-A-Ganesh B. Muscat
    C. Perlette D. Sonaka
197. Propagation followed in grapes is
    A. Softwood cuttings B. Semi hardwood cuttings
    C. Leaf cutting D. Hardwood cuttings

Answer keys

1	C	41	A	81	A	121	A	161	C
2	B	42	B	82	B	122	A	162	A
3	A	43	C	83	A	123	D	163	A
4	C	44	A	84	D	124	B	164	B
5	B	45	C	85	C	125	D	165	A
6	D	46	B	86	A	126	A	166	B
7	C	47	C	87	B	127	C	167	B
8	A	48	A	88	B	128	C	168	B
9	B	49	A	89	C	129	B	169	A
10	A	50	C	90	A	130	A	170	B
11	A	51	B	91	A	131	B	171	D
12	D	52	C	92	B	132	C	172	B
13	B	53	C	93	A	133	D	173	C
14	B	54	A	94	A	134	C	174	A
15	C	55	C	95	B	135	D	175	B
16	C	56	B	96	B	136	A	176	C
17	A	57	C	97	D	137	B	177	C

18	D	58	D	98	C	138	A	178	C
19	C	59	A	99	B	139	C	179	B
20	B	60	B	100	B	140	A	180	B
21	D	61	D	101	B	141	A	181	D
22	A	62	C	102	B	142	A	182	D
23	A	63	A	103	A	143	D	183	C
24	C	64	A	104	B	144	C	184	A
25	B	65	A	105	B	145	D	185	D
26	D	66	A	106	B	146	C	186	C
27	A	67	A	107	A	147	C	187	C
28	D	68	A	108	B	148	D	188	B
29	B	69	A	109	B	149	A	189	C
30	C	70	A	110	D	150	A	190	C
31	D	71	B	111	A	151	A	191	A
32	C	72	A	112	A	152	B	192	C
33	B	73	A	113	C	153	A	193	B
34	C	74	D	114	B	154	B	194	A
35	D	75	D	115	A	155	A	195	A
36	D	76	D	116	A	156	A	196	B
37	A	77	A	117	B	157	B	197	D
38	B	78	D	118	C	158	C		
39	D	79	C	119	A	159	D		
40	C	80	A	120	B	160	D		

2.2 Temperate fruits

1. The origin of grapes is

   A. South East Asia　　B. Burma

   C. Peru　　D. Black to Caspian sea

2. Give an example for seedless grape

   A. Muscat　　B. Red Globe

   C. Anab – e – shahi　　D. Sonaka

3. What is the common method of growning in muscat grapes?

   A. Telephone system　　B. Arbour system

   C. Single trunk system　　D. Kniffin system

4. What insecticide is sprayed to control mealy bug in grapes?
   A. Methyl dematon @ 2 ml/lit B. Phosphomidan @ 2 ml/lit
   C. Malathion @ 2 ml/lit D. Sevin 50% @ 0.1%
5. What is the botanical name of apple?
   A. *Prunus persica* B. *Prunus salicina*
   C. *Malus pumila* D. *Prunus amnericana*
6. Which is the best root stock for apple?
   A. M 775 B. M 776
   C. M 777 D. M 778
7. What is the ideal season for planting of pear?
   A. January – February B. March – April
   C. January – July D. June – December
8. Wooly aphid infestation occurs in
   A. Cherry B. Plum
   C. Apple D. Peach
9. True fruits like peach, plum, apricot and cherry are known as
   A. Aggregate fruit B. Drupe
   C. Multiple fruit D. All the above
10. Apple, apricot, plum, date, olive and peaches are rich in
    A. Protein B. Minerals
    C. Carbohydrates D. All the above
11. Apple variety indigenous to Kashmir and popular in the region
    A. Rome beauty B. Ambri
    C. Baldwin D. Red delicious
12. The enzyme which is responsible for softening of several types of fruits
    A. Polopolysulphonase B. Catalase
    C. Polyhydrase D. Polygalacturonase
13. Which spectrum of light has direct influence on the colour development of Apple Fruit?
    A. Ultra violet B. Infra red
    C. Far red D. Visible
14. Which of the following is a parthenocarpic grapes variety?
    A. Arka Hans B. Perlette
    C. Black Corianth D. Kali sahibi

15. First successful transgenic fruit plants is produced in which fruit

A. Pear B. Mango

C. Apple D. Walnut

16. T- bar system of training is followed in

A. Kiwi fruit B. Almond

C. Cherry D. Pecanut

17. 'Governer's' wood is the variety of

A. Cherry B. Peach

C. Plum D. Pear

18. National Horticulture Mission (NHM) was started in

A. 2000-01 B. 2003-04

C. 2001-02 D. 2005-06

19. The ultra dwarf rootstock of apple is

A. M-13 B. M-27

C. M-104 D. M-111

20. Winter Banana is the variety of

A. Mango B. Banana

C. Apple D. Pear

21. 'Vared' is a low chilling variety of

A. Apple B. Pear

C. Peach D. Plum

22. Water core is a disorder of

A. Pear B. Peach

C. Quince D. Apple

23. Inflorescence of Pear is

A. Solitary B. Raceme

C. Spadix D. Cyme

24. Rosette of Apple is due to the deficiency of

A. Mo B. Cu

C. Zn D. Fe

25. Frontier is a midseason variety of

A. Peach B. Plum

C. Apricot D. Grapes

26. Best time of pruning of Peach is

A. Mid summer B. Mid winter

C. Autumn D. Spring

27. June drop in Apple is due to

A. Lack of pollination B. Moisture stress

C. Ca deficiency D. Alternate bearing

28. Which of the following is variety of Apricot?

A. Chubattia Anupan B. Chubattia Princess

C. Chubattia Madhu D. Sunheri

29. Black stem is the disease of fruit crop

A. Apple B. Mango

C. Peach D. Litchi

30. Which training system is followed for Pear?

A. Central leader B. Modified central leader

C. Open central D. All

31. Which is the male sterile variety of Peach?

A. Red heaven B. Stark early glow

C. J.H.Hale D. Pratap

32. The flower of the cherry tree is the national symbol of which country?

A. India B. Canada

C. China D. France

33. Apple pips contain

A. Juice B. Vitamin H

C. sodium D. Cyanide

34. Chinese Gooseberry is another name for

A. Cherry B. Plum

C. Kiwi D. Lime

35. There is a museum in Belgium dedicated to

A. Chocolate B. Detective Poirot

C. Strawberries D. Beer

36. The only fruit to have seeds on the outside is

A. Pineapple B. Raspberry

C. Lychee D. Strawberry

37. Because it has a high quercitin content this fruit may help relieve hay fever

A. Raspberry B. Strawberry

C. Melon D. Grape

38. A Loganberry is a cross between a blackberry and a

A. Blueberry B. Raspberry

C. Blackcurrant D. Strawberry

39. According to American research, which fruit is No. 1 when it comes to antioxidants?

A. Blueberry B. Orange

C. Pear D. Cherry

40. Which of the following has the highest sugar content?

A. Watermelon B. Lemon

C. Cherry D. Guava

41. In peaches, cherries, plums, and apricots the edible parts are?

A. Endocarp B. Mesocarp

C. Exocarp D. None of the above

42. Which chemical is used for de-greening of fruit?

A. IBA B. Cytokinin

C. Gibberalic Acid D. Ethylene

43. Colour, Short berries and water berries are disorders of

A. Black berry B. Strawberry

C. Mulberry D. Grapes

44. Bitterness in peach is due to

A. Sugar B. Malic acid

C. Hydrocyanin D. Prunasin acid

45. Which state is known as Apple Bowl?
A. Himachal Pradesh B. Uttrakhand
C. J & K D. Punjab
46. Apple is divided in how much grades
A. 4 B. 8
C. 6 D. 10
47. Bitterpit in Apple is due to the deficiency of
A. Ca B. Zn
C. Mn D. K
48. Cultivated strawberry is
A. Diploid B. Octaploid
C. Hexaploid D. Triploid
49. The constituent responsible for the aroma of Apple is
A. Ethyl-2-methyl B. Eugenol
C. Isopentanol D. Tiaxanol butyrate
50. Optimum spacing followed for apple is
A. 6 x 6 m B. 5 x 5 m
C. 3 x 3 m D. 4 x 4 m
51. Fruit set in apple is increased by
A. Auxin B. Amino ethoxy
C. Ethepon D. Cytokin
52. Commercial propagation method in apple is
A. T-budding B. Air layering
C. Patch budding D. Cuttings
53. Nectarines are groups of peaches in which the fruit has
A. No fuzzy skin B. Waxy skin
C. Fuzzy skin D. None of these
54. The litchi seed lose their viability after removal from within a period of
A. Six months B. Two months
C. One month D. One week
55. Stooling method of propagation is generally used in
A. Walnut B. Apricot
C. Litchi D. Sapota

56. Where was the kiwi fruit first grown?

A. New Zealand B. China

C. Australia D. Chile

57. Which one of these is actually a nut?

A. Peanut B. Walnut

C. Brazil Nut D. Hazelnut

Answer keys

1	D	16	A	31	C	46	A
2	D	17	A	32	C	47	A
3	B	18	D	33	D	48	B
4	A	19	B	34	C	49	A
5	C	20	C	35	C	50	D
6	D	21	A	36	D	51	B
7	D	22	D	37	A	52	A
8	C	23	B	38	B	53	A
9	B	24	C	39	A	54	D
10	B	25	B	40	C	55	C
11	B	26	B	41	B	56	B
12	D	27	B	42	D	57	D
13	A	28	C	43	D		
14	C	29	A	44	D		
15	A	30	B	45	A		

3

Production Technology of Vegetables

I. Choose the correct answer

3.1 Tropical vegetables

1. Formation of abscission layer is maturity index of

   A. Leafy vegetable B. Onion

   C. Tomato D. Musk melons

2. Best quality oleoresin is prepared from

   A. Onion B. Chilli

   C. Castor D. Garlic

3. Tomato fruits for canning are harvested at

   A. Mature green stage B. Red ripe stage

   C. Immature green stage D. Half-ripe/pink stage

4. Which chemical is used for controlling sprouting of onions in storage?

   A. Maleic hydrazide (MH) B. Ethylene (C_2H_4)

   C. GA D. All of these

5. For distant marketing, tomato fruits are harvested at

   A. Immature green stage B. Mature green stage

   C. Turning stage D. Red ripe stage

6. Match list I with list II and choose the correct answer

List I	List II
a. Tomato	1. *Capsicum annuum*
b. Brinjal	2. *Solanum melangena*
c. Chilli	3. *Abelmoschus esculentus*
d. Bhendi	4. *Solanum lycopersicum*

   A. 4 3 2 1 B. 3 4 1 2

   C. 3 4 2 1 D. 4 2 1 3

7. What is the seed rate for hybrid tomato

A. 100 g/ha B. 150 g/ha

C. 125 g/ha D. 1750 g/ha

8. How much quantity of *Pseudomonas fluorescens* used for seed treatment in tomato?

A. 5 g/kg of seed B. 10 g/kg of seed

C. 15 g/kg of seed D. 20 g/kg of seed

9. Which growth regulator is suitable for controlling flower drops in tomato?

A. NAA B. GA

C. IBA D. Cycocel

10. Annamalai variety belongs to

A. Tomato B. Chillies

C. Bhendi D. Brinjal

11. What is the spacing for brinjal?

A. 60 x 30 cm B. 60 x 45 cm

C. 75 x 60 cm D. 75 x 75 cm

12. What is the dosage of *Azospirillum* and Phosphobacteria for basal application in brinjal?

A. 1.0 + 1.0 kg/ha B. 1.5 + 1.5 kg/ha

C. 2.0 + 2.0 kg/ha D. 2.5 + 2.5 kg/ha

13. Fertilizer recommendation for brinjal is

A. 200 : 150 : 100 kg NPK/ha B. 200 : 100 : 100 kg NPK/ha

C. 200 : 75 : 100 kg NPK/ha D. 200 : 75 : 75 kg NPK/ha

14. Which variety belongs to bell pepper released by private sector?

A. Vikram B. Sivaji

C. California wonder D. Indira

15. What is the age of seedlings of chillies suitable for transplanting?

A. 35 – 40 days B. 45 – 50 days

C. 20 – 25 days D. 25 – 30 days

16. How many cells are present in protrays?

A. 100 cells B. 98 cells

C. 96 cells D. 94 cells

17. What is the yield of dry chilli?
    A. 0.5 to 1.0 tons /ha B. 1.0 to 2.0 tons /ha
    C. 2.0 to 3.0 tons /ha D. 3.0 to 4.0 tons /ha
18. Which is the important pest of chilli?
    A. Aphids B. Thrips
    C. Jassids D. Mealy bug
19. Which disease infects the seedlings in the vegetable nursery?
    A. Wilt B. Powdery mildew
    C. Root rot D. Damping off
20. Which season is vulnerable to grow bhendi because of severe infection yellow vein mosaic virus?
    A. Summer season B. Winter season
    C. Rainy season D. Kharif season
21. How many days after pollination, bhendi fruits are to be harvested?
    A. 9 days B. 7 days
    C. 5 days D. 3 days
22. What is the seed rate of bhendi variety?
    A. 6 kg/ha B. 8 kg/ha
    C. 10 kg/ha D. 12 kg/ha
23. How many pheromone traps are kept to control fruit borer in bhendi?
    A. 12 /ha B. 10 /ha
    C. 8 /ha D. 6 / ha
24. Which is the family of onion?
    A. Anacardiaceae B. Malvaceae
    C. Araceae D. Alliceae
25. Which one of the following sprays is done to control leaf spot of onion?
    A. Mancozeb 0.5 g/lit B. Mancozeb 0.75 g/lit
    C. Mancozeb 1.0 g/lit D. Mancozeb 2.0 g/lit
26. Which one of the varieties belongs to bellary onion
    A. Arka kalyan B. CO5
    C. CO4 D. MDU 1

27. Fertilizer dose for bellary onion

A. 110 : 150 : 75 Kg NPK/ha B. 110 : 100 : 75 Kg NPK/ha

C. 100 : 150 : 75 Kg NPK/ha D. 100 : 150 : 50 Kg NPK/ha

28. What is the maturity index for bellary onion?

A. Drying of 50% of top and bending

B. Drying of 60% top and bending

C. Drying of 70% top and bending

D. Drying of 75% top and bending

29. Which is the botanical name of ashgourd?

A. *Cucumis sativus* B. *Cucurbita moschata*

C. *Benincasa hispida* D. *Luffa acutangula*

30. Match list I with list II and choose the correct answer

List I	**List II**
a. Pumpkin	1. India
b. Bottle gourd	2. Indo Burma
c. Bitter gourd	3. South Africa
d. Cucumber	4. Mexico, Peru

A. 3 4 1 2 B. 4 3 2 1

C. 4 3 1 2 D. 3 2 4 1

31. Find out the incorrect answer in the following statements.

A. Seed rate for gherkin is 800 g/ha

B. Seed rate for water melon is 3.5 kg/ha

C. Seed rate for musk melon is 1.5 kg/ha

D. Seed rate for snakegourd is 1.5 kg/ha

32. Which cucurbit is used for salad purpose?

A. Snake gourd B. Bottle gourd

C. Ribbed gourd D. Cucumber

33. Which growth regulator is recommended for increasing femaleness in cucurbits?

A. Ethrel B. Alar

C. TIBA D. NAA

34. What is the concentration of ethrel used to increase the femaleness in cucurbits?

A. 150 ppm B. 200 ppm

C. 250 ppm D. 300 ppm

35. Find out the correct answer in the following statements.

A. Yield of ash gourd is 30 t/ha

B. Yield of water melon is 25-30 t/ha

C. Yield of snake gourd is 25 t/ha

D. Yield of bitter gourd is 24 t/ha

36. What is the alkaloid present in tomato?

A. Solanin B. Curcumin

C. Cucurbitacin D. Trichonellin

37. Match list I with list II and choose the correct answers

List I	**List II**
A. Chilli	1. Allyl propyl disulphide
b. Onion	2. Capsaicin
c. Cucurbits	3. Melangenin
d. Brinjal	4. Cucurbitacin

A. 3 1 2 4 B. 4 3 2 1

C. 3 4 2 1 D. 2 1 4 3

38. Which disease causes severe damage in pumpkin and ashgourd?

A. Powdery mildew B. Damping off

C. Leaf spot D. Wilt

39. Which is the major pest of cucurbits attacking fruits?

A. Fruit borer B. Fruit fly

C. Stem fly D. Stem borer

40. Which one the following vegetables is climacteric

A. Tomato B. Brinjal

C. Bhendi D. Chilli

41. Day-neutral vegetable is

A. Sweet potato B. Chilli

C. Onion D. Potato

42. India is the largest producer in the world

A. Brinjal B. Capsicum

C. Chilli D. Tomato

43. Match list I with list II and choose the correct answer

List I	**List II**
a. Tapioca	1. Gajendra
b. Sweet potato	2. CO1
c. Elephant foot yam	3. Yethapur 1
d. Chinese potato	4. CO5

	a	b	c	d
A.	3	4	1	2
B.	4	3	2	1
C.	2	1	3	4
D.	1	2	4	3

44. Which one of the following is *Amorphophallus paeoniifolius?*

A. Tapoica B. Sweet potato

C. Elephant foot yam D. Chinese potato

45. Which one of the following is a variety of moringa?

A. Jothi B. Ganga

C. PKM 2 D. CO 2

46. How to control fruit fly in moringa?

A. Endosulfan B. Profenophos

C. Metasystox D. Phorate

47. What is the seed rate of amaranthus?

A. 2.5 kg/ha B. 2.0 kg/ha

C. 1.5 kg/ha D. 1.0 kg/ha

48. Study of vegetable is called as

A. Floriculture B. Pomology

C. Olericulture D. Sericulture

49. In which vegetable, vit A is present in higher amount?

A. Brinjal B. Tomato

C. Coriander D. Chillies

50. Which vegetable contains more iron?

A. Tomato B. Chilli

C. Amaranthus D. Snake gourd

51. Chromosome number of bhendi is

A. 2n = 29 B. 2n = 70

C. 2n = 60 D. 2n = 130

52. Resistant variety in bhendi for YMV is

A. Parbhani kranti B. MDU 1

C. CO 1 D. Pusa makhmali

53. Growth regulator used to reduce vegetative growth in bhendi is

A. GA 400 ppm B. CCC 100 ppm

C. Ethepon 100-500 ppm D. NAA 200 ppm

54. Seed rate of brinjal is

A. 50 g B. 100 g

C. 400 g D. 250 g

55. Type of flowers which set fruit in brinjal is

A. Long style B. Short style

C. Pseudostyle D. Both B and C

56. Pusa ruby is the variety of

A. Brinjal B. Bhendi

C. Tomato D. Chilli

57. Suitable season for tomato

A. January – February B. August – September

C. April – May D. February - March

58. The acid that is used for seed extraction in tomato is

A. Phosphoric acid B. Con HNO_3

C. Con H_2SO_4 D. Con HCl

59. Fruit cracking in tomato is due to deficiency of

A. Boron B. Mg

C. Ca D. Manganese

60. Water requirement of tomato is

A. 350-550 mm B. 600-800 mm

C. 300-500 mm D. 400-500 mm

61. The principle component responsible for pungency in chilli is

A. Carotenoid B. Capsaicin

C. Capsaxanthin D. Carica xanthin

62. Chilli variety suitable for rainfed cultivation is

A. CO3 B. Arka Basant

C. Pusa Deepti D. PMK 1

63. Chilli is cultivated as rainfed crop in which district of Tamil Nadu?

A. Erode B. Ramnad

C. Coimbatore D. Theni

64. Pericarp or peel cracking in chilli is due to

A. High temperature and high humidity

B. High CO_2 concentration

C. Mg deficiency

D. Low temperature

65. Fruit drop in chilli is controlled by

A. IBA 50 ppm B. GA 50 ppm

C. NAA 50 ppm D. CCC @ 50 ppm

66. Arka Bindu is the coloured variety of

A. Onion B. Ginger

C. Garlic D. Beet root

67. Environment conducive for bulb formation in onion is

A. Low rainfall B. High rainfall

C. Cool temperature D. Warm temperature

68. Alkaloid present in garlic is

A. Allicin B. Allyl trisulphide

C. Diallyl disulphide D. Allinase

69. Seed rate of moringa is

A. 100 g/ha B. 250 g/ha

C. 650 g/ha D. 500 g/ha

70. Cassava is introduced from

A. Portugal B. French

C. Spanish D. England

71. Central Tuber Crops Research Institute is located at

A. Bangalore B. Yethapure

C. Trivandrum D. Tirupathi

72. Seed forming variety of multiplier or aggregatum onion is

A. Pusa red B. Arka bindu

C. CO 5 D. Agri found white

73. Antinutritional compound is

A. Oxalate B. Chlorophyll

C. Lycopene D. Xanthophylls

74. Isothocynates present in

A. Cole Crops B. Amaranthus

C. Solanaceous Vegetables D. Cucurbits

75. French bean is a native of

A. Mediterranean region B. Asia

C. South and Central America D. None of the above

76. Garden beet belongs to the genus

A. *Beta* B. *Brassica*

C. *Raphanus* D. None of these

77. Puffy fruit in tomato is caused by

A. Viral attack B. Bacterial attack

C. Physiological disorder D. None of these

78. Fruits of wild forms of bottle gourd are bitter in taste due to

A. Solanin B. Tomatine

C. Cucurbitacin D. None of these

79. The type of germination in garden pea is

A. Epigeal B. Hypogeal

C. Hypo-epigeal D. Epi-hypogeal

80. Hisar unnat is a variety of which of the following vegetables?

A. Tomato B. Chilli

C. Okra D. Cowpea

81. The photoperiodic response of spinach is

A. Short day B. Long day

C. Day neutral D. Intermediate type

82. Manjari gota variety of brinjal is popular in

A. Punjab B. Maharashtra

C. Rajasthan D. Uttar Pradesh

83. White heart is a physiological disorder of

A. Carrot B. Beet root

C. Muskmelon D. Watermelon

84. Fluted pumpkin is

A. *Cucumis metuliferus* B. *Cucurbita ficifolia*

C. *Cucurbita argyrosperma* D. *Telfairia occidentalis*

85. The Ty-1 gene conferring resistance to tomato yellow leaf curl virus is derived from

A. *Solanum habrochaites* B. *Solanum pennellii*

C. *Solanum chilense* D. *Solanum lycopersicum*

86. Arka Kirtiman is variety of

A. Tomato B. Onion

C. Chilli D. Brinjal

87. The range of optimum night temperature for tomato fruit set is

A. 5-10^0 C B. 15-20^0 C

C. 25-30^0 C D. 35-40^0 C

88. Phomopsis blight is a major disease of

A. Pea B. Potato

C. Tomato D. Brinjal

89. Following is recommended for maintaining freshness in cut leafy vegetables

A. Auxin B. Cytokinin

C. ABA D. Gibberellin

90. A popular white onion variety

A. Arka pragati B. Arka niketan

C. CO1 D. Arka kalyan

91. Which of the following is the variety of onion?

A. Patna white B. Nasik white

C. Jothi D. Anamika

92. The seed rate of onion is

A. 8-10 kg/ha B. 10-20 kg/ha

C. 20-25 kg/ha D. 25-30 kg/ha

93. Which of the following is not the variety of brinjal?

A. Pant Rituraj B. Pant Samrat

C. Pusa Ankur D. Pant Bahar

94. Diara method of cultivation is common in

A. Cucurbits B. Root crops

C. Cole crops D. Tuber crops

95. Protandrous condition favours cross pollination in

A. Cabbage B. Onion

C. Spinach D. Bottlegourd

96. Soft rot of vegetable is caused by

A. *Verticillium* sp. B. *Erwinia* sp

C. *Fusarium* sp D. None of these

97. Which of the following is the anther mutant variety of tomato?

A. Pusa Ruby B. Pusa Gaurav

C. Pusa Divya D. None of these

98. Diploid apogamy is found in

A. Onion B. Cauliflower

C. Chilli D. Brinjal

99. Sylvia is a edible podded variety of

A. Pea B. Broad bean

C. Lima bean D. French bean

100. Sugar baby watermelon has been introduced in India from

A. USA B. Phillipines

C. Denmark D. Israel

101. Vivek and Tijarti are F1 hybrids of

A. Bottlegourd B. Muskmelon

C. Bittergourd D. Watermelon

102. MLO's causing purple top wilt in potato is transmitted by

A. White flies B. Seed

C. Sap D. Leaf hopper

103. Non-lobing leaf character is used as single recessive marker gene for hybrid seed production in

A. Watermelon B. Muskmelon

C. Cucumber D. None of the above

104. Sex expression in cucurbits is manipulated by

A. $AgNO_3$ B. GA_3

C. Ethrel D. All the above

105. Pleiotropy in okra was found in

A. Calyx colour and petal vein colour

B. Resistance to powdery mildew

C. Pod/plant

D. Resistance to YMV

106. Annapurna is a variety of

A. Amaranth B. Bottle gourd

C. Bitter gourd D. Ridge gourd

107. Pant bahar tomato is resistant to

A. Verticillium wilt B. Fusarium wilt

C. Both A and B D. None of these

108. In onion the type of self-sterility is

A. Genic B. Cytoplasmic-genic

C. Cytoplasmic D. None of the above

109. Which of the following is used as androcide in okra?

A. GA_3 B. MH (0.4-0.5%)

C. NAA D. None of the above

110. CH-1 chilli hybrid is a result of cross between

A. MS-12×Punjab lal B. MS-13×Punjab lal

C. MS-1×Punjab lal D. MS-11×Punjab lal

111. Which of the following is highly tolerant to salt?

A. Ashgourd B. Chilli

C. Tomato D. Okra

112. Momordica dioica is commomly known as

A. Bittergourd B. Kakrol

C. Sweetgourd D. Round melon

113. Which of the following belongs to bulb crop?

A. Carrot B. Shallot

C. Salisfy D. Cucumber

114. Hermaphrodite variety of ridge gourd is

A. Pusa Nasdar B. CO1

C. Satputia D. Jhinga Sorai

115. Which of the following is not the harvesting stage of muskmelon?

A. Half slip B. Non- slip

C. Full slip D. Slip

116. Narendra Amrit is a variety of

A. Muskmelon B. Pumpkin

C. Longmelon D. Watermelon

117. Frog eye rot is physiological disorder of

A. Brinjal B. Chilli

C. Potato D. Tomato

118. Pointed gourd is propagated by

A. Root cutting B. Stem cutting

C. Layering D. None

119. Nidhi is a clonal selection of

A. Cassava B. Sweet potato

C. Coleus D. Potato

120. Which of the following is not a variety of brinjal?

A. Pusa purple long B. Pusa kranti

C. Black beauty D. Pusa red

121. Which of the following is a micronutrient?

A. K_2O B. Zn

C. N D. P_2O_5

122. The average fruit yield of brinjal is

A. 10 – 15t/ha B. 25 – 30t/ha

C. 40 – 50t/ha D. 50 – 60t/ha

123. Brinjal can thrives well PH of

A. 5.5 - 6.0 B. 6.0 – 6.5

C. 6.5 - 7.5 D. 7.5 – 8.0

124. Flowers and fruit yield in brinjal can be improved by foliar spray of

A. Triacontanol B. Superphosphate

C. Urea D. Pendimethalin

125. White fly menace in brinjal is controlled by

A. Neem seed extract B. Neem leaf extract

C. Arappu leaf extract D. Turmeric rhizome extract

126. Important disease that affects the cucurbit leaves

A. Stem rot B. Downey mildew

C. Fruit rot D. Powdery mildew

127. *Rhizobium* treatment is given to seeds for fixing

A. P_2O_5 B. N

C. H_2 D. O_2

128. *Citrullus lanatus* is the botanical name of

A. Pumpkin B. Watermelon

C. Muskmelon D. Bittergourd

129. For increasing the female flowers in cucurbits foliar spray is done with
A. GA_3 B. Cytokinin
C. Ethrel D. NAA
130. The chemical used for improving drought tolerance in vegetables
A. Potassium chloride B. Urea
C. Super phosphate D. Calcium ammonium nitrate
131. Suitable soil type for tomato cultivation
A. Loamy soil B. Clay soil
C. Sandy soil D. Black soil
132. The fruits of tomato are botanically called as
A. Drupe B. Berry
C. Pomes D. Hesperidium
133. The average fruit yield of tomato PKM-1
A. 20 - 25 t/ha B. 30 - 35 t/ha
C. 40 - 45 t/ha D. 60 - 70 t/ha
134. The optimum duration for tomato crop from transplanting
A. 80 - 90 days B. 70 - 80 days
C. 110 - 115 days D. 130 - 140 days
135. The traditional packing method of tomato for long distance
A. Gunny bag B. Paper cartoon box
C. Wooden box D. Bamboo basket
136. The tomato fruit fetches high price in the market because of
A. Sorting B. Size grading
C. Weight grading D. Polishing
137. Exposure of tomato fruits to sunlight results in an injury called as
A. Heat injury B. Sun scald
C. Soaking injury D. Bleaching
138. The common market channel followed for tomato is
A. Farmers→Consumers
B. Farmers→Wholesaler→Consumer
C. Farmers→Wholesaler→Retailer→Consumer
D. Farmers→Retailers→Consumer

139. Quality of tomato fruits can be improved by spray with

A. IAA
B. GA_3
C. Cytokinin
D. Ethrel

140. Canning is a method of

A. Heat processing
B. Non heat processing
C. Sterilization
D. Low temperature treatment

141. Tomato sauce must have not less than

A. 5% T.S.S
B. 10% T.S.S
C. 12% T.S.S
D. 16% T.S.S

142. Which of the following crop is self pollinated?

A. Bottlegourd
B. Cauliflower
C. Radish
D. Tomato

143. The spacing for tomato is

A. 20 x 40 cm
B. 30 x 10 cm
C. 60 x 30 cm
D. 60 x 60 cm

144. Which of the following is not the solanaceous vegetables

A. Tomato
B. Brinjal
C. Chilli
D. Bhendi

145. The family of bhendi/okra is

A. Cruciferae
B. Cucurbitaceae
C. Malvaceae
D. Solanaceae

146. Soil type highly suitable for cultivation of chilli

A. Alluvial soil
B. Sandy soil
C. Red soil
D. Loamy soil

147. The fruit quality of chilli is improved by application of

A. Urea
B. Superphospate
C. Potassium sulphate
D. Calcium chloride

148. Directorate of Onion and Garlic Research (DOGR) is situated at

A. Shimla
B. Nasik
C. New Delhi
D. Lucknow

Answer keys

1	D	41	B	81	A	121	B
2	B	42	C	82	B	122	B
3	B	43	A	83	D	123	C
4	A	44	C	84	D	124	A
5	B	45	C	85	C	125	A
6	D	46	B	86	B	126	B
7	A	47	A	87	B	127	B
8	B	48	C	88	D	128	B
9	A	49	C	89	B	129	C
10	D	50	C	90	A	130	A
11	C	51	D	91	A	131	A
12	C	52	A	92	A	132	B
13	A	53	C	93	D	133	B
14	D	54	C	94	A	134	C
15	A	55	A	95	B	135	D
16	C	56	C	96	B	136	B
17	C	57	A	97	C	137	B
18	B	58	D	98	A	138	C
19	D	59	A	99	A	139	B
20	A	60	B	100	A	140	A
21	C	61	B	101	C	141	D
22	B	62	D	102	D	142	D
23	A	63	B	103	A	143	D
24	D	64	A	104	D	144	D
25	D	65	C	105	A	145	C
26	A	66	A	106	A	146	D
27	A	67	D	107	C	147	C
28	D	68	C	108	B	148	B
29	C	69	D	109	B		
30	B	70	C	110	A		
31	C	71	C	111	A		
32	D	72	C	112	B		
33	A	73	A	113	B		
34	C	74	A	114	C		

35	B	75	C	115	B
36	A	76	A	116	B
37	D	77	C	117	B
38	A	78	C	118	B
39	B	79	B	119	A
40	A	80	C	120	D

3.2. Sub tropical and temperate vegetables

1. Which of the following vegetable contains the highest amount of sodium?

   A. Tomato B. Spinach

   C. Lettuce D. Chow chow

2. Browning in cabbage is due to pressure of enzyme

   A. Polyphenotoxidase B. Catalase

   C. Oxidase D. None of these

3. Carbohydrate content in potato is

   A. 12% B. 22%

   C. 32% D. 42%

4. Consider the statements and choose the correct answer

   (i) Kufri Griraj is variety of potato

   (ii) Ooty 1 is variety of carrot

   (iii) Kufri Jyoti is variety of radish

   A. (i) alone is correct B. (ii) alone is correct

   C. (i) and (ii) are correct D. (iii) alone is correct

5. In carrot, soil moisture in excess quantity causes

   A. Root splitting B. Catface

   C. Whip tail D. Root rot

6. What is the optimum tuber size for planting potato?

   A. 20-30 g B. 15-30 g

   C. 30-50 g D. 50-60 g

7. What is the ideal temperature for potato tuber sprouting?

   A. 5-10°C B. 10-15°C

   C. 15-20°C D. 20-25°C

8. Which nematicide is applied to control golden nematode in potato?
   A. Lindane 1kg/ha B. Phorate 1 kg/ha
   C. Carbendazim 1kg/ha D. Carbofuran 1kg/ha
9. When to stop irrigation during harvesting of potato?
   A. 5 days before harvesting B. 10 days before harvesting
   C. 15 days before harvesting D. 20 days before harvesting
10. At what time thinning is done in radish?
   A. 10 days after sowing B. 15 days after sowing
   C. 20 days after sowing D. 25 days after sowing
11. Seed rate for beet root is
   A. 4 kg/ha B. 6 kg/ha
   C. 8 kg/ha D. 10 kg/ha
12. Match list I with list II and choose the correct answers

List I	**List II**
a. Cabbage	1. 375 g/ha
b. Cauliflower	2. 650 g/ha
c. Knol-khol	3. 4 kg/ha
d. Turnip	4. 1.5 kg/ha

	a	b	c	d
A.	4	3	2	1
B.	3	2	4	1
C.	2	1	3	4
D.	3	1	4	2

13. Match list I with list II and choose the correct answers

List I	**List II**
a. N deficiency	1. Blindnes
b. B deficiency	2. Whip tail
c. Molybdenum deficiency	3. Brown rot
d. Low temperature	4. Buttoning

	a	b	c	d
A.	4	3	2	1
B.	3	2	4	1
C.	2	1	4	3
D.	3	1	4	2

14. Which vegetable is used for salad purpose?
    A. Cauliflower B. Potato
    C. Brinjal D. Lettuce
15. Family of sweet potato is
    A. Marantaceae B. Convolvulaceae
    C. Araceae D. Zingiberaceae
16. _____ type of photoperiodism promotes tuberisation in sweet potato
    A. Long day B. Short day
    C. Carotene D. Lycopene
17. Red colour of beet root is due to
    A. Anthocyanin B. Betacynin
    C. Carotene D. Xanthophyll
18. The word cole crops is derived from
    A. Cole wards B. Cliff cabbage
    C. Cole worts D. Both B and C
19. Scientific name of cauliflower is
    A. Brassica *oleraceae var botrytis*
    B. *Brassica olaraceae var capitata*
    C. Brassica *olaraceae var italica*
    D. *Brassica olaraceae var* gemmifera
20. The economic part of cauliflower
    A. Capitulum B. Curd
    C. Head D. Bundle of leaves
21. Cabbage is originated from the species
    A. *Brassica oleracea var sylvestris*
    B. *Brassica olaracea var capitata*
    C. Brassica chinensis
    D. *Raphanus sativus*
22. Golden acre is the variety of
    A. Cauliflower B. Cabbage
    C. Knol-khol D. Broccoli

23. Knol-khol is originated from

A. Mediterranean region B. Ethiopia

C. China D. Russia

24. Buttoning of cauliflower is due to deficiency of

A. Ca B. Mg

C. Nitrogen D. Mn

25. Carrot belongs to the family

A. Apiaceae B. Brassicaceae

C. Chenopodiaceae D. Solanaceae

26. Variety suitable for processing in potato is

A. Kufri Megha B. Kulfri Chipsona

C. Kufri Red D. Kulfri Moti

27. Purple Vienna is a _____variety of Knol-khol

A. Early B. Late

C. Mid D. All season

28. The heat tolerant variety of potato is

A. Kufri Sindhuri B. Kufri Badshah

C. Kufri Sutlej D. Kufri Surya

29. The probable progenitor of cauliflower is

A. *Brassica rupestris* B. *Brassica cretica*

C. *Brassica montana* D. *Brassica insularis*

30. Napiform roots are found in

A. Onion B. Sweet potato

C. Garden beet D. Carrot

31. The basic chromosome number of amaranthus are

A. x = 14 and 15 B. x = 15 and 16

C. x = 16 and 17 D. x = 17 and 18

32. Approximate number of seeds per gram in cucumber is

A. 10-12 B. 30-35

C. 50-60 D. 90-95

33. Which of the following year was named as "International Year of the Potato" by United Nations?

A. 2008 B. 2009

C. 2010 D. 2011

34. The raised bed in broad bed furrow method is recommended for production of

A. Potato B. Carrot

C. Tomato D. Kharif onion

35. Lettuce drop is caused by

A. *Sclerotina* B. *Bremia lactucae*

C. *Phytoplasma* D. Lettuce mosaic virus

36. Browning is boron deficiency symptoms noticed commonly in

A. Tomato B. Potato

C. Cauliflower D. Brinjal

37. Variety resistant to pithiness in turnip is

A. Pusa swati B. Pusa swarnima

C. Pusa chandrima D. Pusa kanchan

38. Scooping method for flower stalk initiation is followed in

A. Cabbage B. Cauliflower

C. Kale D. Onion

39. Which of the following crops is wind pollinated

A. Spinach B. Tomato

C. Cucumber D. Watermelon

40. Vishesh developed by Hindustan Unilever is a hybrid of

A. Cabbage B. Brussels sprout

C. Cauliflower D. Broccoli

41. Which of the following is male sterile genotype of cauliflower

A. SMSMS B. Nmsms

C. Smsms D. NMsMs

42. Palak is

A. Self pollinated B. Often cross pollinated

C. Cross pollinated D. None of the above

43. Which of the following mechanisms exists in carrot
    A. Heterostyly B. Protandry
    C. Protogyny D. None of these
44. The edible part of Jerusalem artichoke is
    A. Tubers B. Spear
    C. Stem D. Corm
45. Potherbs are generally
    A. Cool season crops B. Rainy season crops
    C. Warm season crops D. None of these
46. Which of the following is not dioecious
    A. Asparagus B. Spinach
    C. Pointed gourd D. Both A and B
47. Herkogamy is observed in
    A. Lima bean B. Capsicum
    C. Tomato D. Lettuce
48. Which of the following crop has the highest respiration rate?
    A. Broccoli B. Cabbage
    C. Onion D. Leek
49. *Sauropus androgynous* (Chekurmanis) belongs to family
    A. Euphorbiaceae B. Solanaceae
    C. Convolvulaceae D. Polgonaceae
50. *Solenostemon rotundifolius* (Chinese potato) belongs to family
    A. Lamiaceae B. Solanaceae
    C. Euphorbiaceae D. Convolvulaceae
51. Which of the following is highly tolerant to soil reaction?
    A. Rhubarb B. Bean
    C. Asparagus D. Carrot
52. Which of the following is not a tuber crop?
    A. Potato B. Cassava
    C. Globe artichoke D. Sweet potato

53. Which of the following toxic substances is present in celery?
    A. Apiin B. Sinigrin
    C. Cucurbitacin D. Choline esterase
54. Blanching is practiced in
    A. Okra (Bhendi) B. Asparagus
    C. Tomato D. Onion
55. Which of the following cucurbits exhibit vivipary
    A. Chow chow B. Cucumber
    C. Pumpkin D. Muskmelon
56. Cultivated single seed cucurbit is
    A. Pointed gourd B. Spine gourd
    C. Spiny gourd D. Chow chow
57. Which vegetable is known as multi-vitamin green?
    A. Amaranth B. Spinach
    C. Asparagus D. Chekurmanis
58. Which of the following types of lettuce has tight head?
    A. Crisp head B. Cos
    C. Butter head D. Latin
59. The eyes of potato are useful for
    A. Nutrition B. Respiration
    C. Vegetative propagation D. Protection from predators
60. Spacing adapted for cultivation of cabbage in plains
    A. 10 x 20 cm B. 20 x 30 cm
    C. 45 x 30 cm D. 45 x 60 cm
61. Blanching in cauliflower is specific to
    A. Covering curds with leaves B. Removing leaves
    C. Picking curds D. Removing buds
62. Carrot is a crop grows well in
    A. Cool season B. Warm season
    C. Dry season D. Dry-humid season

63. The underground part of potato is the modification of

A. Stem B. Root

C. Leaves D. Leafy beds

64. Which of the following is the variety of potato?

A. Pusa Ruby B. Arka Anamika

B. Kufri Jyothi C. Arka Basant

65. The country from where the potato originated

A. Brazil B. Peru

C. Canada D. Ethiopia

66. Potato belongs to the family

A. Euphorbiaceae B. Malvaceae

C. Solanaceae D. Brassicaceae

67. Potato crop can tolerate soil conditions

A. Acidic soils B. Alkali soils

C. Saline soils D. Saline alkali soils

68. Sprouting of potato tuber can be inhibited by

A. Maleic hydrazide B. 2,4,5 – T

C. Ethrel D. Thiourea

69. Vernalization, a low temperature treatment is given to tubers for

A. Inducing dormancy B. Breaking dormancy

C. Reducing flowering D. Inducing tuber development

70. The recommended depth of planting for potato tuber

A. 2 – 3cm B. 10 -15cm

C. 15 - 20cm D. 5 – 10cm

71. Chlorosis in potato can be controlled by application of

A. Fe_2SO_4 B. P_2O_5

C. N_2 D. K_2O

72. Earthing up is a common practice in potato for

A. Better tuber development B. For root development

C. Better aeration D. Nutrient uptake

73. The largest potato growing country with reference to area and production
A. China
B. India
C. UK
D. Poland

74. The country ranking first in potato export
A. USA
B. Russia
C. Netherlands
D. Germany

75. Potato as a vegetable crop was introduced in Nilgiri hills in the year
A. 1800
B. 1822
C. 1850
D. 1900

76. Storage practice adapted for storing potato tubers is
A. Open storage
B. Cold storage
C. High temperature storage
D. Concealed storage

77. The keeping quality of potato tubers is poor when harvested during
A. Monsoon period
B. Spring season
C. Summer season
D. Winter season

78. Potato crop needs irrigation
A. Moderate to heavy
B. Minimum
C. Moderate
D. Heavy

79. Higher tuber yield in potato is recorded in soils of
A. Medium texture
B. Fine texture
C. Coarse texture
D. Heavy texture

80. Potato crop gives good response to liberal application of
A. N_2
B. P_2O_5
C. K_2O
D. Ca

81. Botanically, potato tuber is
A. Underground swollen stem
B. Underground swollen root
C. Modified swollen stem
D. Modified swollen fruit

82. Potato is classified as
A. Cover crop
B. Truck crop
C. Silage crop
D. Support crop

83. Number of eyes /buds/tuber increases with

A. Tuber size B. Tuber weight

C. Tuber volume D. Firmness

84. The carbohydrates produced in the leaves are translocated to tuber and stored as

A. Proteins B. Starch

C. Glucose D. Fructose

85. The cooking quality in potato depends on

A. Sugars B. Protein

C. Phenolic compounds D. Fat

86. The potatoes typically used by the canning industry

A. Big mature tubers B. Small immature tubers

C. Immature tubers D. Mature tubers

87. Sweetening of potato tuber during sprouting is due to

A. Loss of starch

B. Increase in the protein content

C. Increase in the minerals

D. Increase in the sugars

88. The potato tubers that suffers less damage during harvesting are

A. Round tubers B. Oblong tubers

C. Irregular tubers D. Long tubers

89. In potato hollow heart disorder is due to

A. Excessive watering and fertilization

B. Excessive watering and haulm cutting

C. Excessive watering and high temperature

D. Excessive watering and cooling

90. Potato tuber production is the maximum at

A. 15°C B. 20°C

C. 25°C D. 30°C

91. The young potato plant grows best at

A. 16°C B. 20°C

C. 24°C D. 28°C

92. Richest source of mineral in potato tuber

A. Mg B. P_2O5

C. Na D. K_2O

93. Number of tubers per plant is higher at

A. Low night temperature B. Higher night temperature

C. Low day temperature D. High day temperature

94. Tuber initiation in potato is favoured by

A. Short day B. Long day

C. Long short day D. Short long day

95. The average weight of cut seed pieces of potato used for sowing

A. 10 – 15 g B. 20 – 25 g

C. 30 – 40 g D. 40 – 50

96. The optimum plant population for higher yield in potato is

A. 1,11,000 B. 1,20,000

C. 1,50,000 D. 1,00,000

97. The optimum tuber size for higher yield in potato is

A. 15 – 20 mm B. 25 – 35 mm

C. 45 – 55 mm D. 35 – 45 mm

98. Seed rate recommended for round cultivars of potato is

A. 8 - 9 q/ha B. 12 – 15 q/ha

C. 15 – 18 q/ha D. 20 – 23 q/ha

99. The fertilizer schedule for a good seed crop of a potato is

A. 125 : 100 : 100 KgNPK/ha B. 100 : 125 : 100 KgNPK/ha

C. 75 : 100 : 100 KgNPK/ha D. 125 : 75 : 75 KgNPK/ha

100. Seed rate for TPS / ha is

A. 20 g B. 50 g

C. 75 g D. 100g

101. Optimum spacing for transplanting potato seedling

A. 20 x 10 cm B. 10 x 10 cm

C. 15 x 20 cm D. 20 x 30 cm

102. One hectare of seedlings from TPS produces seed tubers to plant in the next season for an area of

A. 5 – 10 hectares
B. 10 – 15 hectares
C. 15 – 20 hectares
D. 20 – 25 hectares

103. Micropropagation in potato aims at producing

A. Virus free plant material
B. Disease free plant material
C. Exploit hybrid vigour
D. Pest resistant cultivars

104. The ideal plant for micropropagation of potato is

A. Seed
B. Leaf
C. Embryo
D. Apical meristems

105. Translocation / conduction of food materials to the developing tubers is improved by application of

A. Urea
B. Super phosphate
C. Potash
D. Calcium

106. The major constraint in cultivation and production of potato is

A. Non availability of fertilizer
B. Unpredictable rainfall
C. Insufficient plant protection measures
D. Non availability of good quality seeds

107. Improper storage conditions of potato leads to

A. Pest infection
B. Fungal infection
C. Weight loss
D. Sprouting

108. The bitter taste and greenness of potato tubers is due to

A. Excessive moisture
B. Exposure to sunlight
C. Low moisture content
D. Treatment with chemicals

109. Seed potato from hilly regions of India is preferred because

A. It is cheaper
B. Good varieties are grown in those regions
C. It has better germination percentage
D. It is disease free

110. Increased stem density in potato results
    A. Reduction in number of tubers
    B. Increase in number of tubers
    C. No variation in number of tubers
    D. Increase in size of the tubers
111. Intensity of blackening after cooking the potato tuber is due to
    A. Gluconic acid B. Chlorogenic acid
    C. Citric acid D. Maleic acid
112. The Stolon formation in potato usually begins at
    A. Upper nodes B. Middle
    C. Root D. Lower nodes
113. The nutrient deficiency in potato is more pronounced in acidic hilly soils and red laterite soils.
    A. Phosphorous B. Potassium
    C. Zinc D. Nitrogen
114. Earthing up in potato cultivation is an important interculture operation done on
    A. 10 – 15 days after planting B. 25-30 days after planting
    C. 40- 50 days after planting D. 50 – 60 days after planting
115. In general, water stress reduces the tuber yield due to
    A. High proportion of big sized tubers
    B. High proportion of medium sized tubers
    C. High proportion of small tubers
    D. High proportion of underdeveloped tubers
116. For potato crop, the phosphotic fertilizers are applied as
    A. Basal B. Top dressing
    C. Both basal and top dressing D. As top dressing in split application.
117. Green manuring of potato is helpful in
    A. Reducing pest damage B. Reducing NPK requirement
    C. Reducing nematode attack D. Reducing disease incidence
118. Seed rate for potato crop depends on
    A. Colour tuber B. Quality
    C. Weight D. Size of the tuber

119. The state with largest area & production of potato

A. Punjab B. Uttar Pradesh

C. Gujarat D. West Bengal

120. The highest percentage of area under potato cultivation is located in

A. Hilly region

B. Plateau regions of peninsular India

C. Indo – gangetic plains

D. Sub tropical plains.

121. The tropics are considered unsuitable for profitable culture of potato mainly due to

A. Sunshine B. Temperature

C. Rainfall D. Relative humidity.

Answer keys

1	C	21	A	41	A	61	A	81	A	101	B	121	B
2	B	22	B	42	C	62	A	82	B	102	C		
3	B	23	A	43	B	63	A	83	A	103	A		
4	C	24	C	44	A	64	B	84	B	104	D		
5	A	25	A	45	A	65	B	85	C	105	C		
6	C	26	B	46	D	66	C	86	B	106	D		
7	B	27	A	47	A	67	A	87	D	107	C		
8	D	28	D	48	A	68	A	88	A	108	B		
9	C	29	B	49	A	69	B	89	A	109	D		
10	A	30	C	50	A	70	D	90	B	110	A		
11	B	31	C	51	A	71	C	91	C	111	B		
12	C	32	B	52	C	72	A	92	D	112	D		
13	A	33	A	53	A	73	A	93	A	113	A		
14	D	34	A	54	B	74	C	94	A	114	B		
15	B	35	A	55	A	75	B	95	C	115	C		
16	B	36	C	56	D	76	B	96	A	116	A		
17	B	37	D	57	D	77	A	97	C	117	B		
18	D	38	B	58	A	78	A	98	C	118	D		
19	A	39	A	59	C	79	C	99	D	119	B		
20	B	40	C	60	C	80	C	100	B	120	D		

4

Production Technology of Spices and Plantation Crops

I. Choose the correct answer

4.1. Spices

1. Location of Indian Institute of spices Research
   A. Trivandrum B. Bangalore
   C. Coimbatore D. Calicut
2. Where is the Research Institute of Cardamom located
   A. Myiladumpara B. Thrissur
   C. Kottayam D. Mannuthi
3. Which of the following is the variety of pepper
   A. Sreekara B. Suhasini
   C. Mridhula D. Ganga
4. Which is the suitable tree species to train as a standard for pepper?
   A. *Gliricidia maculata* B. *Tecoma stans*
   C. *Artocarpus heterophyllus* D. *Punica granatum*
5. Which is the berry borer in pepper?
   A. Thrips B. Pollu beetle
   C. Aphid D. Jassid
6. What is the botanical name for clove?
   A. *Coriandrum sativum* B. *Pimenta officinalis*
   C. *Elettaria cardamomum* D. *Syzygium aromaticum*
7. What is the seed rate for cardamom?
   A. 400 g/ha B. 700 g/ha
   C. 600 g/ha D. 300 g/ha

8. What is the family of cardamom?

A. Zingiberaceae B. Piperaceae

C. Araceae D. Poaceae

9. Which spacing is adopted for cardamom?

A. 3 x 2 m B. 3.5 x 2.5 m

C. 4 x 2 m D. 2 x 1.5 m

10. Which of the following statement is correct in respect of cardamom?

i) Primary nursery alone is sufficient

ii) Secondary nursery is ideal for planting cardamom seedlings

iii) Secondary nursery is not necessary

A. (i) alone is correct B. (ii) alone is correct

C. (i) and (ii) are correct D. (iii) alone is correct

11. What is the ideal planting material for bush pepper?

A. Plagiotropic B. Geotropic

C. Orthotropic D. Seeds

12. What is the dosage of bordeaux mix used to control quick wilt in pepper?

A. 1% B. 1.5%

C. 2.0% D. 2.5%

13. Match list I with list II and choose the correct options given below

List I	**List II**
A. Cardamom	1. BSR 2
B. Turmeric	2. ICRI 1
C. Ginger	3. CO2
D. Coriander	4. Karthika

	A	B	C	D
A.	4	3	2	1
B.	2	1	4	3
C.	4	2	3	1
D.	3	4	2	1

14. Consider the statements and choose correct answer

(i) In cardamom, katte disease is caused by virus

(ii) In cardomon, capsule rot is caused by virus

(iii) In cardomon, Rhizome rot is caused by fungus

A. (i) alone is correct B. (ii) alone is correct
C. (i) and (ii) are correct D. (i) and (iii) are correct

15. While rizhome treatment in turmeric, how much quantity of *Trichoderma viride* is used?
A. 4 g/kg B. 6 g/kg
C. 8 g/kg D. 10 g/kg

16. What is the spacing for turmeric?
A. 45 x 20 cm B. 45 x 25 cm
C. 45 x 10 cm D. 45 x 15 cm

17. What is the weight of seed rhizome of turmeric?
A. 20 - 30 g B. 25 - 30 g
C. 30 - 35 g D. 35 - 40 g

18. What is the fresh rhizome yield of turmeric?
A. 25 - 30 t/ha B. 20 - 25 t/ha
C. 15 - 20 t/ha D. 10 - 15 t/ha

19. What is the season for ginger?
A. November - December B. August – September
C. May - June D. January - February

20. Which one of the followings is a variety of coriander?
A. CO 3 B. PMK 1
C. MDU 1 D. VRI 1

21. Major pest in coriander is
A. Thrips B. Aphids
C. Jassids D. Meally bug

22. Where is the National Research Centre for seed spices located?
A. Varanasi B. Cuttack
C. Anand D. Ajmer

23. Which state is the largest producer of spices?
A. Andhra Pradesh B. Karnataka
C. Kerala D. Tamil Nadu

24. In India, leading cardamom growing state
A. Assam B. Karnataka
C. Maharashtra D. Kerala

25. The chromosome number of *Coriandrum sativum* is

A. 2n=11 B. 2n=33

C. 2n=22 D. None of these

26. Rio-de-generio is an improved variety of

A. Turmeric B. Garlic

C. Ginger D. Large cardamom

27. National Research Centre for Spice came into existence in the year of

A. 1983 B. 1986

C. 1981 D. 1976

28. Clove is a native of

A. India B. Molucas

C. Zanziber D. Africa

29. Black pepper is botanically called as

A. *Piper longum* B. *Piper somniferum*

C. *Piper nigrum* D. None of these

30. Linalool is an important ingredient of

A. Fennel B. Coriander

C. Cumin D. Aniseed

31. Which of the following is an example of root spice?

A. Cinnamon B. Sweet flag

C. Mace D. Nutmeg

32. Rapid multiplication technique in black pepper is developed by

A. CFTRI B. IISR

C. CPCRI D. DCCD

33. Rajendra kranti is a variety of

A. Coriander B. Turmeric

C. Fenugreek D. Cumin

34. Trishna a hybrid released by CIMAP, belong to

A. Citronella B. Palmarosa

C. Lemongrass D. Vetiver

35. Anti-bacterial substance present in injured garlic?

A. Allin B. Allyl-propyl tri-sulfide

C. Allyl-propyl di-sulfide D. Allicin

36. Variety Lam Sel-1 belongs to the group of

A. Fenugreek B. Chilli

C. Cumin D. None

37. Propagation material of clove is called as

A. Seed B. Clove

C. Corm D. Matured unopened flowerbud

38. King of spices is

A. Cardomom B. Pepper

C. Clove D. Nutmeg

39. What is the seed rate of fenugreek?

A. 8 kg/ha B. 10 kg/ha

C. 12 kg/ha D. 14 kg/ha

40. What is the fertilizer dose of fenugreek?

A. 50:25:40 kg NPK/ha B. 50:25:50 kg NPK/ha

C. 50:50:50 kg NPK/ha D. 100:25:40 kg NPK/ha

41. What is the spacing followed for clove?

A. 6 x 6 m B. 5 x 5 m

C. 4 x 4 m D. 8 x 8 m

42. Which one of the following is a dioecious tree spice

A. *Cinnamomum zeylanicum* B. *Syzygium aromaticum*

C. *Pimenta officinalis* D. *Cinnamomum tamala*

43. What is the recent method of propagation followed in nutmeg?

A. Semi hardwood cutting B. Flute budding

C. Chip budding D. Soft wood grafting

44. What is the major oil present in nutmeg?

A. Myristicin B. Ugenol

C. Geraniol D. Cinnamaldehyde

45. Among the following which is the variety of tamrind?

A. Tumkur B. MDU 1

C. KKM 1 D. Paiyur 1

46. Important chemical content of black pepper is

A. Piperine B. Solanine

C. Curcumin D. Limone

47. Match list I with list II and choose the correct options given below

List I	List II
A. Cardamom	1. Rhizome
B. Turmeric	2. Unopened flower bud
C. Nutmug	3. Capsule
D. Clove	4. Mace

	A	B	C	D
A.	4	3	2	1
B.	3	4	1	2
C.	3	1	4	2
D.	1	3	4	2

48. Find out the incorrect answer
A. Black pepper is a king of spice B. Cardamom is a queen of spice
C. Clove is home of spice D. Fenugreek contains diosgenine

49. Nutmeg belongs to the family
A. Myristicaceae B. Myrtaceae
C. Bromelacaeae D. Apiaceae

50. Growth regulator used to increase berry size in pepper is
A. IBA 250 ppm B. NAA @ 400 ppm
C. GA @ 200 ppm D. CCC @ 250 ppm

51. Karimunda is the variety of
A. Cardamom B. Turmeric
C. Ginger D. Pepper

52. Main propagation material in pepper
A. Orthotropic B. Runner shoot
C. Geotropic D. Plagiotropic

53. Spices act
A. 1976 B. 1986
C. 1996 D. 2006

54. Which spice is used in Indonesia for the preparation of special brand of cigarettes?
A. Clove B. Cinnamon
C. Nutmeg D. All spice

55. Navashree and nithyashree are the varieties of

A. Pepper B. Cardamom

C. Cinnamon D. Nutmeg

56. Oil of black pepper contains

A. Phenol B. Alkaloid

C. Terpenes D. Tetracycline

57. Bareja system is associated with

A. Nutmeg B. Allspice

C. Betel vine D. Black pepper

58. Sex form present in betelvine

A. Monoecious B. Dioecious

C. Andromonoecious D. None

59. Commercial part of all spice

A. Whole tree B. Leaves

C. Bark only D. Fruits and leaves

60. Family of clove

A. Myrtaceae B. Apiaceae

C. Alliaceae D. None

61. Self sterile variety of black pepper is

A. Balankotta B. Kalluvalli

C. Both A and B D. None of these

62. Which of the following is the small seeded variety of coriander

A. Karan B. Swathi

C. Sindhu D. Sadhana

63. Which of the following is mutant ginger variety?

A. Surabhi B. Himagiri

C. Rio-de-janerio D. Suruchi

64. Yercaud 1 is the improved variety of

A. Cinnamon B. Clove

C. Nutmeg D. Kokum

65. Rose mary is a
A. Tree spice B. Major spice
C. Herbal spice D. All of the above

66. Karimunda is the variety of
A. Cardamom B. Clove
C. Cumin D. None of the above

67. Drying recovery of white pepper
A. 33% B. 25%
C. 50% D.100%

68. Terbein is the important constituent of
A. Sweet flag B. Cinnamon
C. Nutmeg D. Curry leaf

69. Feathering and scrapped chips are important grades of
A. Clove B. Pepper
C. All spice D. Cinnamon

70. CIMAP is situated at
A. Lucknow B. Jammu
C. Patna D. Agra

71. Which spice has a antioxidant property?
A. Turmeric B. Ginger
C. Black pepper D. Cardamom

72. Rostellum is present in which spice crop
A. Curry leaf B. Kokum
C. Vanilla D. Nutmeg

73. Organization which is related to agricultural marketing is
A. NAFED B. NHB
C. NABARD D. FCI

74. Powdery mildew is a serious diseases of
A. Coriander B. Perennial coriander
C. Cardamom D. None of the above

75. Among the following which is a seed spice
A. Dill B. Caraway
C. Aniseed D. All of the above

Answer keys

1	D	21	A	41	C	61	C
2	A	22	D	42	C	62	A
3	A	23	A	43	D	63	A
4	C	24	D	44	A	64	A
5	B	25	C	45	A	65	C
6	D	26	C	46	A	66	D
7	C	27	B	47	C	67	B
8	A	28	B	48	C	68	C
9	D	29	C	49	A	69	D
10	B	30	B	50	B	70	A
11	A	31	B	51	D	71	A
12	A	32	B	52	B	72	C
13	B	33	C	53	B	73	A
14	D	34	B	54	A	74	A
15	A	35	D	55	C	75	D
16	D	36	A	56	C		
17	B	37	D	57	C		
18	A	38	B	58	B		
19	C	39	C	59	D		
20	A	40	B	60	A		

4.2. Plantation crops

1. What is the commonly grown shade tree in coffee estates?
   A. *Erythirina indica* B. *Melia dubia*
   C. *Grevillea robusta* D. *Tectona grandis*
2. Among the fruits, cashew nut is the richest source of
   A. Carbohydrates B. Protein
   C. Fats D. None
3. The variety of coffee largely grown in India is
   A. Old chicks B. Coorgs
   C. Arabica D. Kents

4. Match list I with list II and choose the correct options given below

List I	List II
A. *Coffea arabica*	1. CTC method
B. *Coffea robusta*	2. God of air
C. *Camellia sinensis*	3. Berry
D. *Theobroma cacao*	4. Parchment

	A	B	C	D
A.	4	1	3	2
B.	3	1	4	2
C.	4	3	1	2
D.	2	3	4	1

5. Where is the Central Coffee Research Station located?
   A. Thadiyankudisai B. Thandikudi
   C. Balaganur D. Wayanad
6. Central Tea Research Station is located at
   A. Valparai B. Coonoor
   C. Munnar D. Tocklay
7. In which month coffee main picking is done?
   A. October B. December
   C. November D. January
8. Which is the main borer in coffee?
   A. Red borer B. Berry borer
   C. Root borer D. White borer
9. Which among the following is the variety of *Coffea arabica*?
   A. Selection 795 B. Selection 20
   C. Selection 274 D. Selection 3
10. Athrey is a variety of which crop?
    A. Cocoa B. Rubber
    C. Tea D. Cinchona
11. Which of the pruning height is incorrect regarding tea?
    i) Rejuvenation pruning (75 cm)
    ii) Hard pruning (30-45 cm)

iii) Light pruning (<65 cm)

iv) Skiffing (5-8 cm)

A. (i), (ii), (iii) & (iv) are incorrect B. (i) alone is incorrect

C. (ii), (iii) & (iv) are incorrect D. (iv) alone is incorrect

12. Where is the National Centre for Cashew located?

A. Vridhachalam B. Anakayam

C. Kottarakara D. Puthur

13. Which of the following is not a variety of cashew?

A. VRI 1 B. Vengurla

C. Anakayam 1 D. KKM 1

14. What is the spacing adopted for high density planting of cashew?

A. 5 x 4 m B. 7 x 7 m

C. 6 x 6 m D. 5 x 5 m

15. What is the major disease in tea?

A. Pink disease B. Brown root rot

C. Blister blight D. Charcoal root rot

16. What is the type of budding followed in cashew?

A. Chip budding B. T- budding

C. Flute budding D. Patch budding

17. What is the family of cocoa?

A. Sterculiaceae B. Malvaceae

C. Rubiaceae D. Fabaceae

18. Which among of the following is a variety of cocoa?

A. West coast tall B. Mangala

C. SVPR 1 D. Criollo

19. In which tree crop, cocoa is commonly grown as an intercrop?

A. Rubber B. Coconut

C. Tamarind D. Nutmeg

20. Match list I with list II and choose the correct options given below

List I	List II
A. Arecanut	1. 7.5 x 7.5 m
B. Coconut	2. 3 x 3 m

C. Rubber 3. 2.7 x 2.7 m

D. Cocoa 4. 5 x 5 m

	A	B	C	D
A.	2	3	1	4
B.	4	3	1	2
C.	3	1	4	2
D.	3	4	1	2

21. Which among the following is the major physiological disorder of cocoa?
    A. Stem canker B. Die back
    C. Charcoal pod rot D. Cherelle wilt
22. Where is the Rubber Research Institute of India is situated?
    A. Kottayam B. Pechiparai
    C. Thrissur D. Kasargod
23. At what angle, tapping is done in budded plants of rubber?
    A. 20° B. 25°
    C. 30° D. 45°
24. What is the modern method of curing in cocoa?
    A. Sun drying B. Sweating boxes
    C. Acetic acid fermentation D. Artificial drying
25. Consider the statements and choose the correct one regarding budding technique in rubber
    i) Green budding implies wind loss
    ii) Crown budding prevent wind loss
    iii) Forkert method is adopted for non-uniformity of budded plants
    A. (i), (ii) and (iii) are correct B. (i) alone is correct
    C. (ii) alone is correct D. (i) and (ii) are correct
26. Which is the Indian rubber variety commonly grown in India?
    A. RRIM 600 B. RRII 105
    C. PCK – 1 D. PB217
27. What is the annual yield obtained from budded plants of rubber?
    A. 500 – 600 kg/ha B. 1100 -1200 kg/ha
    C. 800 -1000 kg/ha D. 400-500 kg/ha

28. VPM 3 is a variety of ________ crop?

A. Coconut B. Arecanut

C. Palmyrah D. Rubber

29. Consider the statements and choose the correct answer regarding coconut variety

i) East coast tall is a tall variety of coconut

ii) CGD is a tender coconut variety

iii) VHC-3 is a coconut hybrid

iv) COD is a oil yielding coconut variety

A. All the statements are correct B. (i) and (ii) alone is correct

C. (iii) alone is correct D. (i) (ii) and (iii) are correct

30. Match list I with list II and choose the correct options given below

List I	List II
A. Coconut sweet sap as neera	1. Oozying of reddish brown fluid and bending of trunk
B. Coconut nutrient tonic @200 ml/palm	2. Bracket formation at the base of trunk
C. Red palm weevil	3. Pathaneer as commercial product
D. Thanjavur wilt	4. Increases coconut yield

	A	B	C	D
A.	4	3	1	2
B.	3	4	1	2
C.	3	4	2	1
D.	4	1	3	2

31. Which is the major disease of Arecanut?

A. Collar rot of seedlings B. Foot rot

C. Koleroga mahali or fruit rot D. Bacterial leaf stripe

32. Which branches of nuts are selected for seed nuts in arecanut?

A. Fourth and fifth branch B. Full bunch

C. First branch and last branch D. Second and third branch

33. Which is the variety of arecanut suitable for Tamil Nadu conditions for obtaining higher yield with quality?

A. Mettupalayam local
B. Mohitnagar
C. Srivardhan
D. Mangala

34. What is the cured type of arecanut used in special occasions in Tamil Nadu?

A. Kalipakku
B. Choor kotta
C. Kottapakku
D. Gotu

35. Central Plantation Crop Research Institute is situated at

A. Calicut
B. Coimbatore
C. Tocklay
D. Karagod

36. Coffee is a —— day plant.

A. Short day
B. Long day
C. Day neutral
D. None

37. Match list I with list II and choose the correct options given below

List I	**List II**
A. National Medicinal and Aromatic Board	1. Kolkata
B. Spices board	2. Bangalore
C. Coffee board	3. Kochi
D. Tea board	4. New Delhi

	A	B	C	D
A.	3	1	4	2
B.	4	1	3	2
C.	4	3	2	1
D.	1	3	4	2

38. Consider the statement and choose the correct answer

(i) Assam ranked first in tea production'

(ii) Karnataka ranked first in coffee production

(iii) Kerala ranked first in rubber production

(iv) Karnataka ranked first in coconut production

A. (i) and (ii) are correct
B. (i) and (iii) are correct
C. (i), (ii) and (iv) are correct
D. (i), (ii) and (iii) are correct

39. NHB is located at (National Horticultural Board)

A. Bangalore B. Gurgaon

C. Kolkata D. Kochi

40. In tea plucking, inclusion of more than two leaves is termed as

A. Coarse B. Rough

C. Tough D. Fine

41. Coconut needs at least ———hours of sunlight per year

A. 2000 B. 1000

C. 1500 D. 500

42. After harvesting oil palm bunches, it has to reach the processing plant within

A. 48hr B. 24hr

C. 40h D. 12hr

43. What is the principle pollinating agent in oil palm?

A. Flies B. Honeybee

C. Weevil D. Birds

44. Which coconut variety is the most suitable for ball copra preparation

A. Lakshadweep micro B. West Coast Tall

C. East Coast Tall D. Gangabondam

45. Brown blast is an important physiological disorder of

A. Rubber B. Tea

C. Coffee D. Cocoa

46. The tall varieties of coconut are sometimes referred to as

A. Nana B. Typica

C. Nana-typical D. Typica –nana

47. What is the branching pattern in cocoa called

A. Sword sucker B. Jorquetting

C. Chupon D. Both B and C

48. Soil stirring practice in coffee is known as

A. Skiffing B. Puddling

C. Scuffling D. None

49. Which part of sandalwood is used for aromatic oil extraction?
A. Stem B. Seed
C. Bark D. Heartwood and roots

50. In cashew nut, ...branching is preferred
A. Extensive B. Intensive
C. Scaffold D. None

51. In coconut husk, the coir: fiber ratio is
A. 80:20 B. 70:30
C. 60:40 D. 55:45

52. Coconut Development Board functions under
A. ICAR B. Central Government
C. Agriculture Ministry D. None of these

53. Oil content is higher in
A. Soybean B. Coconut
C. Oil palm D. None of these

54. Best quality tea in India is grown at
A. Darjeeling B. Nainital
C. Karnataka D. Nilgirs

55. Centre of origin of cocao is
A. Asia B. Africa
C. China D. Brazil

56. Root wilt is a serious disorder of
A. Arecanut B. Coconut
C. Cashew D. Cocoa

Answer keys

1	C	11	B	21	D	31	C	41	A	51	B
2	B	12	D	22	A	32	D	42	B	52	B
3	C	13	D	23	A	33	B	43	C	53	B
4	C	14	A	24	B	34	A	44	A	54	A
5	C	15	C	25	D	35	D	45	A	55	D
6	D	16	D	26	B	36	A	46	B	56	B
7	B	17	B	27	C	37	C	47	B		
8	D	18	D	28	A	38	D	48	C		
9	A	19	B	29	D	39	B	49	D		
10	C	20	C	30	B	40	A	50	B		

5

Production Technology of Flower Crops

I. Choose the correct answer

5.1. Flower crops

1. Gladious is propagated by

   A. Corms B. Bulbs

   C. Suckers D. Buddings

2. King of flower is

   A. Crossandra B. Rose

   C. Jasmine D. Dahlia

3. Most suitable packaging material for cut flowers is

   A. Wooden boxes B. Plastic boxes

   C. Cardboard boxes D. Caretes

4. Emission of ethylene during transportation of cut flowers cause a disorder which is called as

   A. Bud opening B. Sleepiness

   C. Bent neck D. Calyx splitting

5. Which is the precursor of ethylene?

   A. Tryptophane B. Methionine

   C. ABA D. IAA

6. *Tagetus erecta* is a

   A. Rose B. Jasmine

   C. Marigold D. Crossandra

7. Propagation material of tuber rose is

   A. Tuber B. Corm

   C. Bulbs D. Rhizome

8. Spacing for Spanish jasmine is
   A. 1.4x1.4 m B. 1.6x1.6 m
   C. 2.0x2.0 m D. 1.8x1.8 m
9. Growth regulator sprayed to increase flower production in rose is
   A. GA @ 250 ppm B. GA @ 300 ppm
   C. GA @ 350 ppm D. GA @ 400 ppm
10. Age of marigold seedling used for transplanting is
   A. 40-45 days B. 35-40 days
   C. 30-35 days D. 25-30 days
11. Calyx splitting is a major problem observed in
   A. Chrysanthemum B. Carnation
   C. Gerbera D. Gladiolus
12. Propagation material for anthurium is
   A. Bulbs B. Sucker
   C. Root cutting D. Stem cutting
13. Rooting growth regulator in flowers is
   A. NAA B. Cytokinin
   C. GA D. IBA
14. Triploid variety of crossandra is
   A. Lutea yellow B. Sebaculis red
   C. Delhi crossandra D. Lutea orange
15. Red rose variety is
   A. Gold strike B. Movie star
   C. Tajmahal D. Avalanche
16. Temptation is the variety of
   A. Carnation B. Anthurium
   C. Cut chrysanthemum D. Cut rose
17. In Tamil Nadu, Floriculture Research Station is situated at
   A. Coimbatore B. Kodai kanal
   C. Thovalai D. Madurai
18. Pulsing is generally practiced in
   A. Fruits B. Spices
   C. Medicinal plants D. Flowers

19. Match list I with list II and choose the correct answer

List I	List II
A. Crossandra	1. Arka Aradhana
B. Jasmine	2. Lutea yellow
C. Marigold	3. Indira
D. Chrysanthemum	4. MDU 1

	A	B	C	D
A.	2	1	4	3
B.	4	3	2	1
C.	3	4	1	2
D.	4	2	3	1

20. Number 1 cut flower is

A. Jasmine B. Rose

C. Marigold D. Crossandra

21. Which state stands first in flower production in India?

A. Karnataka B. Andhra Pradesh

C. Kerala D. Tamil Nadu

22. Which is the queen of flower?

A. Rose B. Jasmine

C. Tuberrose D. Dahlia

23. Consider the statements and choose the correct answer

(i) Seed rate for marigold is 1.5 kg/ha

(ii) Seed rate for crossandra is 5.0 kg/ha

(iii) For gundu malli, 5400 plants/ha

A. (i) and (iii) are correct B. (ii) and (iii) are correct

C. (i) alone is correct D. (i) and (ii) are correct

24. In which month, pruning is carried out for rose?

A. January – March B. June – August

C. October – December D. April – June

25. In which rose variety, petal shedding occurs?

A. Red rose B. Edward rose

C. Nehru D. Linchan

26. Pruning in mullai is done at a height of

A. 45 cm B. 50 cm

C. 55 cm D. 60 cm

27. Which flower crop is highly infested by aphids?

A. Jasmine B. Marigold

C. Rose D. Orchid

28. Wilt is common in

A. Rose B. Orchid

C. Tuberose D. Crossandra

29. In cut chrysanthemum, at what stage the first pinching is done to induce side branches?

A. 2 weeks after planting B. 3 weeks after planting

C. 4 weeks after planting D. 5 weeks after planting

30. What is the micro nutrient deficiency for calyx splitting in carnation?

A. Boron B. Molybdenum

C. Iron D. Manganese

31. Which one of the followings is a variety of orchid?

A. Sonalika B. Sonora

C. Sonia 17 D. Solamalai

32. Where is the location of IIHR?

A. Coimbatore B. New Delhi

C. Varnasi D. Bangalore

33. Major importer of flowers is

A. Malaysia B. USA

C. Australia D. Srilanka

34. ___________ state is first in area under flower production.

A. Tamil Nadu B. Karnataka

C. Kerala D. Andhra Pradesh

35. Name the propagules for Bryophyllum

A. Bulb B. Rhizome

C. Leaf cutting D. Stem cutting

36. ________________ deficiency causes yellowing and senescence of leaves in gerbera

A. Potassium B. Zinc

C. Nitrogen D. Cadmium

37. Where IARI is located?

A. Coimbatore B. Calcutta

C. New Delhi D. Bangalore

38. In flower arrangement, mass concept of arranging flowers in an even symmetry is named as

A. Eastern style B. Western style

C. Japanese style D. Ikebana style

39. What is the foliage used as filler in flower arrangement?

A. Bottle brush B. Sansievieria

C. Anthurium D. Gladiolus

40. Which method is used mostly for dry flowers preservation to maintain natural colour?

A. Hanging upside down B. Burying in sand or borax

C. Glycerine method D. Pressing

41. Blue colour in roses is due to which of the following pigments

A. Anthocyanin B. Delphinidin

C. Xanthophyll D. None

42. Ancestor of modern roses is

A. Ladakh rose B. Moss rose

C. French rose D. Crimson China rose

43. Directorate of Floricultural Research is located at

A. Hyderabad B. Pune

C. Bengaluru D. New Delhi

44. Odd match with regard to crops and varieties

A. Crossandra–Arka Shreya, Arka Shravya

B. Gladiolus –Arka Amar, Arka Manorama

C. Marigold –Arka Agni, Arka Singara

D. Carnation- Arka Flame, Arka Tejas

45. Cold stratification of rose seeds is done at

A. 6-8°C B. 8-12°C

C. 1-4°C D. 5-10°C

46. First genetically modified blue colour flower in the world is

A. Applause B. Moon Dust

C. Flavr Savr D. Bollgard-I

47. National flower of Guatemala is a/an

A. Rose B. Orchid

C. Lotus D. Chrysanthemum

48. Which of the following is not a short day plant

A. Chrysanthemum B. Poinsettia

C. Carnation D. Marigold

49. Colchicine is used to obtain

A. Haploids B. Doubled haploids

C. Mutants D. Sports

50. Hybrid Polyanthas are derivatives of

A. Hybrid Tea's B. Floribunda's

C. Perpetuals D. Grandifloras

51. Major essential oil component of rose is

A. Citronellol B. Phenyl Ethyl Alcohol

C. Geraniol D. Citral

52. Which is Mutation variety of Jasmine?

A. CO 2 Pitchi B. Bio- 13

C. MTU- 8 D. Co- 9

53. Swarna rekha and Vaibhav are important cultivars of

A. Gladiolus B. Tuberose

C. Lilly D. None of the above

54. Which flowering plant is thornless?

A. *Chaenomeles* sp B. *Pyracantha* sp

C. *Euphorbia milli* D. *Lamprocapnos* sp

55. Largest flower market in the world is

A. Aalsmeer, Netherlands B. Amsterdam, Netherlands

C. Paris, France D. Chicago, USA

56. Largest Flower exporting country is

A. Germany B. Netherlands

C. Australia D. Japan

57. Calyx splitting is a disorder of

A. Rose B. Tulip

C. Carnation D. Chrysanthemum

58. First flower auction was launched at

A. New Delhi B. Bangalore

C. Tamil Nadu D. Kerala

59. Fruit of rose is known as

A. Drupe B. Berry

C. Blastula D. Hip

60. Which practice is followed to increase in flower size?

A. Pinching B. Deblossoming

C. Staking D. All the above

61. Which of the following is used as a cut flower?

A. Carnation B. Gladiolus

C. Marigold D. All of the above

62. Carnation is a

A. Quantitative long day plant B. Quantitative short day plant

C. Short day plant D. Day neutral plant

63. For quality flower production, how much quantity of light is most suitable?

A. 10-30% B. 30-40%

C. 40-50% D. 50-60%

64. Which flower is mostly used for floral crown preparation?

A. Tuberose B. Rose

C. Marigold D. Jasmine

65. Which flower crop is regarded as Queen of East ?

A. China aster B. Carnation

C. Gerbera D. Chrysanthemum

66. Golden shower is propagated through

A. Stem cutting B. Vine cutting

C. Root cutting D. Budding

67. Chrysanthemum is ____________ in growth habit

A. Perennial B. Biennial

C. Annual D. Seasonal

68. Yellow coloured rose species

A. *Rosa foetida* B. *Rosa gallica*

C. *Rosa centifolia* D. *Rosa bourboniana*

69. Per hectare seed rate of marigold is ______ gram

A. 200-300 B. 1250-1500

C. 1000-1200 D. 1500-2000

70. ____________ is the father of rose breeding in India

A. Dr.B.P.Pal B. Mukherjee

C. Bhattachaterji D. None

71. Silver thiosulphate is commonly used for flower longevity in

A. Tulip B. Rose

C. Lily D. Carnation

72. In miniature carnation which operation is mostly followed

A. Staking B. Long day

C. Pinching D. None of these

73. First hybrid in gladiolus was ________________ developed in 1841

A. *Gladiolus gandavensis* B. *Gladiolus psittacinus*

C. *Gladiolus oppositiflorus* D. None of these

74. Cyandin anthocyanin is present in ________________colour

A. Black B. Pink

C. Bluish red D. Yellowish white

75. Which is the most popular variety of rose in protected cultivation in India

A. Grand Gala B. Konfetii

C. First Red D. All of these

76. Chemical defoliation in roses is done by

A. Urea B. Auxin

C. GA D. Copper sulphate

77. Which is not a cultivar of china aster

A. Rakhi B. PG white

C. PG violet D. PG purple

78. Madonna lilly is

A. *Lilium candidum* B. *Lilium pardalinum*

C. *Lilium tigrinum* D. *Lilium auratum*

79. Family Aristolochiaceae, represents

A. Herbaceous annuals B. Perennial shrubs

C. Annual flowering plant D. Climbers

80. The Moribana meaning Piled flowers denoted the arrangement of flowers in

A. Shallow containers B. Deep containers

C. Paper wrappings D. Paper cones

81. In which crop tissue culture is commercially used

A. Rose B. Hibiscus

C. Jasmine D. Orchid

82. Repotting in Orchid is done

A. Every years B. Every 2-3 years

C. 5 years D. 10 years

83. Which annual is of Indian origin

A. Balsam B. Zinnia

C. Phlox D. None

84. Most resistant to nematode among flowers is

A. Rose B. Gladiolus

C. Marigold D. Jasmine

85. Which of following is responsible for spot disease in chrysanthemum?

A. Fungus B. Bacteria

C. Virus D. Mycoplasma

86. Which pigment is responsible for red colour in rose?

A. Globulin B. Anthocyanin

C. Xanthophyll D. All

87. Bougainvillea is propagated by

A. Layering B. Budding

C. Seed D. Grafting

88. Which of the following is sympodial orchid
A. Vanda B. Archis
C. Dendrobium D. None

89. Endosperm is missing in the seed of
A. Carnation B. Orchid
C. Rose D. Chrysanthemum

90. Pinching is generally done in quality production of
A. Gerbera B. Philodendron
C. Gladiolus D. Carnation

91. Gladiolus is sensitive to
A. CO_2 pollution B. Nitrogen deficiency
C. Dust pollution D. Fluoride pollution

92. Pusa Narangi is a variety of
A. Rose B. Carnation
C. Jasmine D. Marigold

93. Poornima and Kamini variety of china aster is released by
A. IIHR-Bangalore B. NBPGR
C. IARI-New Delhi D. TNAU

94. Canna is also known as
A. Indian shot B. African lily
C. Spanish day D. Century plant

95. Which of the following family of flowering plants has the largest species
A. Orchidaceae B. Rosaceae
C. Asteraceae D. Brassicaceae

96. Thornless rose rootstock was developed at
A. IARI B. IIHR
C. NBRI D. BARC

97. Bottom heating in .... cutting enhances rooting percent.
A. Hibiscus B. Rose
C. Bougainvillea D. Dahlia

98. Petal burn in chrysanthemum is due to deficiency of
A. Cu B. Bo
C. Ca D. K

99. Kiss of fire is variety of

A. Rose B. Chrysanthemum

C. Gladiolus D. Carnation

100. Which of the following is a flower preservative?

A. KNO3 B. KMnO4

C. Hg Cl2 D. None

Answer keys

1	A	26	A	51	A	76	D
2	D	27	C	52	A	77	A
3	C	28	D	53	B	78	A
4	B	29	B	54	D	79	D
5	B	30	A	55	A	80	A
6	C	31	C	56	B	81	D
7	C	32	D	57	C	82	A
8	D	33	B	58	B	83	A
9	A	34	B	59	D	84	C
10	D	35	C	60	B	85	A
11	B	36	C	61	D	86	B
12	B	37	C	62	A	87	A
13	D	38	B	63	C	88	C
14	C	39	A	64	A	89	B
15	C	40	B	65	D	90	D
16	B	41	B	66	B	91	D
17	C	42	D	67	A	92	D
18	D	43	B	68	A	93	A
19	A	44	C	69	B	94	A
20	B	45	C	70	C	95	A
21	D	46	A	71	D	96	B
22	A	47	B	72	D	97	B
23	D	48	C	73	A	98	C
24	C	49	B	74	C	99	A
25	B	50	B	75	D	100	A

5.2. Landscaping

1. Art of giving shape to plants resembling to figures is called
   A. Training B. Interculture
   C. Topiary D. Pruning
2. Flower colour of *Antigonon leptopus* is
   A. Blue B. Pink
   C. Yellow D. Dark red
3. Plants used for avenue planting are
   A. Shrubs B. Climbers
   C. Trees D. Annuals
4. *Ficus elastica* is a popular
   A. Flowering tree B. Indoor plant
   C. Cacti D. Climber
5. Popular climber of Indian origin
   A. *Tecoma capensis* B. *Bignonia venusta*
   C. *Gloriosa superba* D. None
6. The term Heaven of man is used for the garden
   A. Japanese garden B. Mughal garden
   C. Italian garden D. None
7. Shade loving plant is
   A. Pansy B. Dieffenbachia
   C. Anthurium D. Both B & C
8. Gardenia is a
   A. Flowering shrub B. Tree
   C. Climber D. None
9. Which is the popular climber of Indian origin
   A. Indian Ivy creeper B. Railway creeper
   C. Glory lilly D. All
10. *Cassia fistula* may take ____ years to flower
    A. 5 B. 10
    C. 15 D. 18

11. In *Cassia nodosa* _______flowers appear in bunches from the nodes all along the branches.

A. Yellow B. Red

C. Pink D. Purple

12. The tree having specific shape is

A. *Millingtonia hortensis* B. *Samanea saman*

C. *Polyalthia longifolia* D. None

13. The garden shows a continuous effect due to

A. Rhythm B. Shape

C. Harmony D. Simplicity

14. The Mandor garden, Jodhpur (Rajasthan) was established by raja

A. Abhai singh B. Ajay singh

C. Hari singh D. Man singh

15. In a formal garden , the imaginary central line is known as

A. Edges B. Axis

C. Focal point D. Hedges

16. Plant suitable for pergolas among the following

A. Tuja B. *Tectona jasminoides*

C. *Jasminum sambac* *D. Ipomoea tuberosa*

17. Xeriscaping is a type of landscaping that uses plants that need very little

A. Clean air B. Sunlight

C. Soil D. Water

18. Plant suitable for topiary is

A. *Tecoma stans* B. *Duranta plumeria*

C. *Thunbergia erecta* D. *Clerodendron inerme*

19. Green facade is the term used in which of the following

A. Vermiculture B. Sericulture

C. Green manuring D. Vertical gardening

20. Plant which is suitable as a central specimen in garden

A. Bougainvillea B. Banyan tree

C. Christmas tree D. Rain tree

21. Plant suitable for bonsai making which is easily available

A. Rain tree B. Banyan tree
C. Acacia D. All of these

22. Main features of English garden

A. Lawn B. Rockery
C. Lanterns D. Borders

23. Thorny fencing plant used as hedge is

A. *Inga dulcis* B. *Duranta plumeria*
C. *Agave americana* D. *Hibiscus rosa-sinensis*

24. Concept of lawn was developed in

A. England B. China
C. Japan D. USA

25. *Cassia fistula* bears ..... flowers

A. Yellow B. Orange
C. Red D. Blue

26. Mobility can be achieved in a garden by planting

A. Perennials B. Annuals
C. Biennials D. All

27. Nahar (flowing canals), the concept of flowing cooling water, is the main feature of

A. Persian garden B. French garden
C. Italian garden D. English garden

28. Which of the following is a landscape garden developed below the ground level?

A. Bag garden B. Moon garden
C. Sunken garden D. Terrace garden

29. Stone lantern is an important feature of

A. Japanese garden B. Mughal garden
C. British garden D. English garden

30. Which principle of gardening is ignored when the large tree is planted near the small building?

A. Proportion B. Balance
C. Rhythm D. All the above

31. The fastest method of lawn making is
    A. Seed sowing B. Dibbling
    C. Turfing D. None of the above
32. Which is not the principle of landscaping?
    A. Rhythm B. Unity
    C. Balance D. Line
33. Lal Bagh Botanical Garden is located at
    A. Delhi B. Agra
    C. Hyderabad D. Bengaluru
34. Lyod Botanical garden is located at
    A. Darjeeling B. Assam
    C. Srinagar D. Pune
35. Which is known as miniature garden?
    A. Mughal garden B. English garden
    C. Japanese garden D. Italian garden
36. Ideal plant for making bonsai
    A. *Ficus benjamina* B. *Tectona grandis*
    C. *Artocarpus altilis* D. *Rosa centifolia*
37. Foliage shrub suitable for building decoration is
    A. *Ipomoea tuberosa* B. *Aralia* sp.
    C. Rhododendron D. *Euphorbia pulcherrima*
38. Indicate the climber with violet colour flower
    A. *Allamanda cathartica* B. *Tecoma rosea*
    C. *Quisqualis indica* D. *Petrea volubilis*
39. Which one of the following is a formal garden?
    A. Mughal B. English garden
    C. Japanese garden D. Chinese garden
40. In which garden, the concept of stone and light arrangement is the main feature?
    A. American garden B. English garden
    C. Japanese garden D. Chinese garden

41. Which flowering annual is suitable for growing in beds of garden?

A. Bryophyllum B. Michaelmus daisy

C. Kochia D. Petunia

42. Flowering annuals used for borders in garden is

A. Plulox B. Cosmos

C. Marigold D. Gaillardia

43. Which ornamental plant is used for edging?

A. *Lantana camara* B. *Meyenia erecta*

C. *Pedilanthus tithymaloids* D. *Iresine* spp

44. Duranda is used for

A. Edges B. Hedges

C. Beds D. Pots

45. Match list I with list II and choose the correct answer

List I	**List II**
A. Tecoma stans	1. White flower
B. Ervatamia coronaria	2. Yellow flower
C. *Caesalpinia pulcherrima*	3. Purple blue
D. *Barleria cristata*	4. Orange scarlet

	A	B	C	D
A.	4	3	2	1
B.	2	1	3	4
C.	2	1	4	3
D.	3	4	2	1

46. For what purpose (or) structure, the climbers are used?

A. Bed B. Border

C. Pot D. Pergola

47. What is the medium for cacti?

A. Gravel B. Soil

C. Cocopith D. Pear moss

48. What do you mean by Astro turf?

A. Natural lawn B. Synthetic lawn

C. Seeding D. Turfing

49. Match list I with list II and choose the correct answer

List I	List II
A. Buffalo grass	1. Hills
B. Chain grass	2. Shade loving
C. Blue grass	3. Salt tolerant
D. Kiku grass	4. Acid tolerant

	A	B	C	D
A.	4	3	2	1
B.	2	3	4	1
C.	3	2	1	4
D.	4	1	2	3

50. Which one the following tree is ideal for home garden?

A. *Delonix regia* B. *Samanea saman*

C. *Cassia fistula* D. *Peltophorum inerme*

51. What shrub is suitable for home garden?

A. *Cassia fistula* B. *Millingtonia hortensis*

C. *Tectona grandis* D. *Ixora coccinea*

52. Match list I with list II and choose the correct answer

List I	List II
A. *Spathodea companulata*	1. Blue flower
B. *Senna spectabilis*	2. White flower
C. *Pterospermum acerifolium*	3. Yellow flower
D. *Jacaranda bilicifolia*	4. Red flower

	A	B	C	D
A.	4	3	2	1
B.	3	4	1	2
C.	2	1	4	3
D.	3	4	2	1

Answer keys

1	C	11	C	21	B	31	C	41	D	51	D
2	B	12	C	22	A	32	D	42	A	52	A
3	C	13	C	23	A	33	D	43	D		
4	B	14	A	24	A	34	D	44	B		
5	C	15	B	25	A	35	C	45	C		
6	C	16	D	26	B	36	A	46	D		
7	D	17	D	27	A	37	B	47	A		
8	A	18	D	28	C	38	D	48	B		
9	D	19	D	29	A	39	A	49	B		
10	B	20	C	30	B	40	C	50	C		

6

Production Technology of Medicinal Plants

I. Choose the correct answer

1. Match list I with list II and choose the correct options given below

List I	List II
A. Senna	1. *Withania somnifera*
B. Aswagandha	2. *Gloriosa superba*
C. Sacred basil	3. *Cassia angustifolia*
D. Glory lilly	4. *Ocimum sanctum*

	A	B	C	D
A.	3	2	1	4
B.	4	3	1	2
C.	3	1	4	2
D.	4	2	1	3

2. What is the major principle found in medicinal coleus?
   A. Saponin B. Vinblastine
   C. Allicin D. Forskholin
3. What is the quantity of seed recovery from glory lilly?
   A. 1500 kg/ha B. 1800 kg/ha
   C. 2000 kg/ha D. 1000 kg/ha
4. What is the main active principle found in *Aloe vera*?
   A. Aloin B. Vincristine
   C. Andragraphidin D. Colchicine
5. Match list I with list II and choose the correct options given below

List I	List II
A. *Acorus calamus*	1. Liliaceae
B. *Aloe vera*	2. Lamiaceae

C. *Withania somnifera* 3. Araceae

D. *Coleus forskholii* 4. Solanaceae

	A	B	C	D
A.	4	3	2	1
B.	4	1	3	2
C.	3	1	4	2
D.	4	3	1	2

6. Match list I with list II and choose the correct options given below

List I	**List II**
A. Senna	1. Vikrasudha
B. Medicinal coleus	2. KKM - 1
C. Aswagandha	3. CO -1
D. Sacred basil	4. Poshita

	A	B	C	D
A.	3	2	4	1
B.	2	3	4	1
C.	4	3	2	1
D.	2	4	1	3

7. Where is the Central Institute for Medicinal & Aromatic plants situated?

A. Srinagar B. Bangalore

C. Anand D. Lucknow

8. Match list I with list II and choose the correct options given below

List I	**List II**
A. Camper basil	1. 60 x 45 cm
B. Aloe	2. 40 x 40 cm
C. Glory lilly	3. 60 x 20 cm
D. Medicinal Coleus	4. 45 x 30 cm

	A	B	C	D
A.	4	3	1	2
B.	3	4	1	2
C.	2	1	4	3
D.	2	3	4	1

9. Consider the statements and choose the correct answer regarding active priniciples

   i) Senna contains the active principle – Sennoside A, B

   ii) Glory lily contains the active principle – Colchicine

   iii) Sacred basil contains the active principles – Menthol

   A. All the statements are correct B. (i) alone is correct

   C. (i) and (iii) are correct D. (i) and (ii) are correct

10. What is the seed rate adopted for Aswagandha?

    A. 3 kg/ha B. 2 kg/ha

    C. 4 kg/ha D. 5 kg/ha

11. Consider the statements and choose the correct answer regarding yield of respective crops

    (i) Aswagandha 150 kg/ha dried root

    (ii) Sacred basil 10-15 tons /ha

    (iii) Coleus 1500 – 2000 kg/ha

    (iv) *Aloe vera* 10000 – 12000 kg/ha

    A. All the statements are correct B. (ii) and (iii) are correct

    C. (i) (ii) and (iii) are correct D. (i) and (iv) are correct

12. What is the botanical name of Keelanelli?

    A. *Phyllanthus amarus* B. *Phyllanthus madraspatana*

    C. *Solanum nigrum* D. *Eclipta alba*

13. What is the active principle of keelanelli?

    A. Curcumin B. Hypophyllanthin

    C. Allicin D. Alloin

14. Family of keelanelli

    A. Malvaceae B. Asteraceae

    C. Euphorbiaceae D. Anacardiaceae

15. Active principle in glory lily is

    A. Sennoside B. Colchicine

    C. Withanine D. Forskholi

16. Mint belongs to the family

    A. Asteraceae B. Lamiaceae

    C. Apiaceae D. Geraniaceae

17. Pragathi is the variety of
    A. Glory lily B. Palmarosa
    C. Lemon grass D. Cintronella
18. Vincristine is an alkaloid present in leaves of
    A. Senna B. Palmarosa
    C. Glory lily D. Periwinkle
19. Medicinal plant used for heart disease is
    A. Pyrethrum B. Geraniol
    C. Fox glove D. Patcholi
20. Citrol (80%) is highly present in
    A. Geraniol B. Lemon grass
    C. Palmarosa D. Senna
21. *Pelargonium graveolens* is a
    A. Citronella B. Geranium
    C. Lemon grass D. Senna
22. Geranium is commercially propagated by
    A. Seed B. Slips
    C. Suckers D. Stem cutting
23. Oldest medicinal plant is
    A. Senna B. Periwinkle
    C. Ashwagandha D. Opium
24. Lancing is done in
    A. Henbane B. Guggal
    C. Ashwagandha D. Opium
25. Which species of ocimum is a source of camphor
    A. *Ocimum kilimandscharicum* B. *Ocimum canum*
    C. *Ocimum sanctum* D. Both A and B
26. Plant products used in Asafoetida
    A. Gum B. Bark
    C. Oleoresin D. Both A and C
27. Arka sanjeevani is the variety of
    A. Medicinal solanum B. Senna
    C. Isabgol D. Digitalis

28. Chetak and kirtiman are variety of
    A. Senna B. Isabgol
    C. Opium D. Henbane
29. National Aromatic and Medicinal Plants Board is situated at
    A. Cochin B. Mumbai
    C. Chennai D. New Delhi
30. Offsets are the propagules to propagate
    A. Aleo B. Agave
    C. Pandanus D. All the above
31. Mucilage is present in which medicinal plant
    A. Yams B. Datura
    C. Isabgol D. Belladona
32. Atropine drug is extracted from
    A. Opium B. Belladona
    C. Datura D. None
33. Which part of *Chrysopogon zizanioides* are used to extract oil
    A. Flowers B. Seeds
    C. Roots D. Leaves
34. God of sleep is a common name of
    A. Isabgol B. Opium
    C. Sarpaganda D. Vetiver
35. Shivalik is the variety of
    A. Isabgol B. Mentha
    C. Periwinkle D. Cymbopogon
36. Harvesting of cinchona is called as
    A. Tapping B. Coppicing
    C. Beheading D. Lancing
37. Nirmal is the variety of
    A. Periwinkle B. Mentha
    C. Isabgol D. Cymbopogon
38. Skin tonic is prepared from
    A. Neem B. Aloe
    C. Senna D. None of the above

39. Eucalyptus is
   A. An aromatic tree B. A medicinal tree
   C. Both D. None
40. Major producer of essential oil in the world
   A. India B. USA
   C. UK D. Brazil
41. *Plantago ovata* is the botanical name of
   A. Senna B. Isabgol
   C. Davana D. Celery
42. *Cymbopogon flexuosus* is botanical name of
   A. Lemon grass B. Vetiver grass
   C. Cintronella grass D. Palmrosa grass
43. Patchouli has —— property
   A. Sedative B. Laxative
   C. Stomachic D. Fixative
44. Mentha contains ___ percent oil.
   A. 0.5-0.6 B.1-2
   C. 5-10 D.10-20
45. Which of the following has a antimalarial property?
   A. Poppy B. Cinchona
   C. Rauvolfia D. Senna
46. Arka upkar is the variety of
   A. Medicinal solanum B. Sarpagandha
   C. Periwinkle D. Medicinal yam
47. *Cymbopogon winterianus* is the botanical name of
   A. Palmarosa grass B. Mentha
   C. Java cintronella grass D. None of the above
48. Which plant is used in treatment of asthma and whooping cough?
   A. Dill B. Davana
   C. Ambrette seed D. Adulsa
49. Diosgenin is used in treatment of
   A. Blood cancer B.HIV
   C. Sexual disorder D. All

50. Indian ginseng is the common name of

A. *Azadirachta indica* B. *Rauwolfia serpentina*

C. *Hemidesmus indicus* D. *Withania somnifera*

51. *Ocimum sanctum* is originated in

A. India B. America

C. Africa D. None

52. *Artemisia pallens* belongs to the family

A. Asteraceae B. Geraniaceae

C. Lamiaceae D. None

53. The active constituent present in davana is

A. Artimisinin B. Davanol

C. Citrol D. Geraniol

54. Mint can be propagated through

A. Stolons B. Suckers

C. Seed D. Both A and B

Answer keys

1	C	11	A	21	B	31	C	41	B	51	A
2	D	12	A	22	D	32	B	42	A	52	A
3	C	13	B	23	B	33	C	43	D	53	A
4	A	14	C	24	D	34	B	44	A	54	D
5	C	15	B	25	D	35	B	45	B		
6	B	16	B	26	D	36	B	46	D		
7	D	17	C	27	A	37	A	47	C		
8	C	18	D	28	C	38	B	48	D		
9	D	19	C	29	D	39	A	49	C		
10	D	20	B	30	D	40	D	50	D		

7

Post Harvest Management of Horticultural Crops

I. Choose the correct answer

1. In squash, what is the percentage of total soluble solids
   A. 20-30% B. 10-20%
   C. 40-50% D. 60-70%
2. Which among the following is incorrect regarding preservatives in squash?
   A. Sodium benzoate B. $KMnO_4$
   C. Potassium metabisulphite D. Citric acid
3. What is the percentage of juice content in cordial?
   A. 25% B. 30%
   C. 15% D. 35%
4. Which among the following value added product is not diluted before serving?
   A. Squash B. Nectar
   C. Cordial D. Jam
5. _____ is the boiling temperature for preparation of jam.
   A. 120°C B. 135°C
   B. 115°C D. 105°C
6. For which among the following value added product pectin content is must for preparation?
   A. Jelly B. Jam
   C. Cordial D. Marmalade
7. In _____ value added product shredded is used as suspended material
   A. Jam B. Squash
   C. Marmalade D. Jelly

8. What is the initial temperature of dehydrator during dehydration of fruit?

A. 66°C B. 43°C

C. 71°C D. 56°C

9. Soaking prepared fresh material in a heavy sugar strong salt solution and then sun drying is called

A. Atmospheric drying B. Shade drying

C. Vacuum drying D. Osmotic dehydration

10. Preservation of food in common salt (or) in vinegar is known as

A. Diffusing B. Pickling

C. Squeezing D. Parboiling

11. What is the pasteurization temperature for sauce?

A. 60-70°C B. 50-60°C

C. 85-90°C D. 100-105°C

12. What is the concentration content of Brix for bar making?

A. 50°Bx B. 30°Bx

C. 40°Bx D. 60°Bx

13. The process of sealing food stuffs in containers by heating them for long storage is

A. Sterilization B. Heating

C. Canning D. Pasteurization

14. Who obtained the first British patent on canning of foods in tin containers?

A. Appert B. Peter Durand

C. Saddington D. William underwood

15. Peeling of fruits and vegetables by dipping them in caustic soda is called

A. Mechanical peeling B. Flame peeling

C. Hand peeling D. Eye peeling

16. Match list I with list II and choose the correct options given below

List I	**List II**
A. Sharp freezing	1. -18°C
B. Quick freezing	2. >-60°C
C. Gyogenic freezing	3. -15 – (-29) °C
D. Freeze drying	4. 0 to 4 °C

	A	B	C	D
A.	3	4	2	1
B.	4	3	1	2
C.	2	3	1	4
D.	4	2	1	3

17. Which chemical is used for de-greening of fruit?
    A. IBA B. Cytokinin
    C. Gibberellic Acid D. Ethylene
18. When the number of intermediaries are ____________, the cost incurred by the consumers will be high
    A. More B. Less
    C. Very high D. High
19. Marketing channel aids in the movement of the produce from the producer to the
    A. Wholesaler B. Retailer
    C. Consumer D. Regulated markets
20. With respect to vegetables marketing, which of the following is correct?
    A. A small portion of the product is kept as seed material.
    B. All of the produce is consumed.
    C. Everything is kept for seed and own consumption.
    D. All of the produce is marketed.
21. The main selling point of vegetable is
    A. Commission markets B. Retail market
    C. Farmers D. Consumers
22. Which one the factors affects the length of the market channel
    A. Price of the product B. Marketability of the product
    C. Quality of the product D. Storability of the product
23. Uzhavar sandi is organized structure and it helps to marking of
    A. Seeds B. Grains
    C. Vegetables D. Stems
24. The vegetables should be marketed immediately because of
    A. Value of the produce B. Perishability of the produce
    C. Price of the produce D. Quality of the produce

25. To prevent vegetable loss during excess yield period, it is necessary to give

A. Suitable packing B. Optimum storage

C. Cold storage D. Value addition

26. Colour changes in vegetables under storage is due to

A. Breakdown of lipids B. Breakdown of carbohydrates

C. Breakdown of proteins D. Breakdown of pigments

27. Ageing and deterioration of vegetables under storage is influenced by

A. Oxygen B. Ethylene

C. Nitrogen D. Carbondioxide

28. The most commonly used gas for vegetable preservation

A. Carbon di oxide B. Sulphur dioxide

C. Oxygen D. Nitrogen

29. Common antioxidant used to enhance the nutritive value of processed vegetables?

A. Gibberellic acid B. Acetic acid

C. NAA D. Ascorbic acid

30. Which market channel is making more benefit to farmers?

A. Farmers → Consumer

B. Farmers → Wholesaler → Consumer

C. Farmers →Wholesaler → Retailer → Consumer

D. Farmers → Retailers → Consumer

31. The maximum market loss expected in vegetables marketing is

A. Loss during transport B. Improper package and handling

C. More time gap to sales D. Perishable

32. The penetrometer instrument is used to indicate

A. Softening of tissues B. Total soluble solids

C. Colour D. Firmness of tissues

33. Storing fruits in low temperature helps in

A. Reducing the respiration B. Increasing the respiration

C. Reducing the water content D. Increasing the firmness

34. Fruit stored in a cold chamber exhibit longer storage life because
    A. Exposure to sunlight is prevented
    B. The concentration of carbon dioxide in the environment is increased
    C. The rate of respiration is decreased
    D. There is an increase in humidity

Answer keys

1	C	11	C	21	B	31	D
2	B	12	A	22	A	32	D
3	A	13	C	23	C	33	A
4	B	14	B	24	B	34	C
5	D	15	D	25	D		
6	A	16	A	26	D		
7	C	17	D	27	B		
8	B	18	A	28	B		
9	D	19	C	29	D		
10	B	20	A	30	A		

UNIT XVI: FORESTRY

1

Importance and Role of Forests

I. Choose the correct answer

1. What is the percentage of forest in India?

   A. 17% B. 33%

   C. 22% D. 24.56%

2. What is the forest cover in India?

   A. 8,02,088 sq.km B. 9,20,555 sq.km

   C. 7,08,273 sq.km D. 6,07,123 sq.km

3. How many types of forest had been recognized by Champion and Seth?

   A. 13 B. 16

   C. 20 D. 17

4. In forest, the standard colour given for the regeneration status excellent (80-100%) is

   A. Red B. Green

   C. Black D. Yellow

5. In forest, the standard colour given for the regeneration status deficient (0-20%) is

   A. Green B. Red

   C. Black D. Yellow

6. Man and biosphere programme was started in the year

   A. 1988 B. 1990

   C. 1975 D. 1971

7. Declaration of reserved forest is possible by IFA, 1927 under sections

   A. 3 to 25 B. 3 to 27

   C. 3 to 30 D. 3 to 33

8. Indian Forest Act contains

   A. 56 sections B. 75 sections

   C. 86 sections D. 90 sections

9. Protected forest declared under Forest Act of

A. 1927 B. 1952

C. 1988 D. 2001

10. Indian Forest Act of 1927 contains

A. 10 chapters B. 13 chapters

C. 15 chapters D. 20 chapters

11. What is the percentage of CO_2 at present in the atmosphere?

A. 0.042 B. 0.050

C. 0.030 D. 0.020

12. Where Forest Research Institute is located in India?

A. Bangalore B. Lucknow

C. Dehradun D. Varanasi

13. National Research Centre for Agroforestry is located at

A. Jhansi B. Jodhpur

C. Bhopal D. Hissar

14. Where is the location of Institute for Forest Genetics and Tree Breeding?

A. Mysore B. Hyderabad

C. Coimbatore D. Kochi

15. Abbreviate JFM

A. Joint Farm Management B. Joint Fisheries Management

C. Joint Finance Management D. Joint Forest Management

16. How much forest cover should be maintained in a country to conserve biodiversity?

A. 24% B. 27%

C. 30% D. 33%

17. Consider the statement and choose the correct answer.

i) 54 lakh seedlings are distributed under massive tree planting program

ii) Vellore, Salem, Erode, Dharmapuri and Trichy districts come under Natural regeneration of sandal in traditional areas.

iii) Forest veterinary units are established in Erode, Krishnagiri and Tirunelveli.

A. (i) alone is correct B. (i) and (ii) are correct

C. (ii) and (iii) are correct D. (i) and (iii) are correct

18. Chipko movement is an example of forest conservation through
    A. Tehri garhwal district B. Uttaranchal
    C. Political issue D. Public awareness & participation
19. Deforestation brings about
    A. Soil erosion B. Weed control
    C. Decreases drought D. Increases drought
20. Deforestation is caused due to
    A. Planting of trees B. Construction of roads
    C. Rainfall D. Silviculture
21. Deforestation is the major causal agent of
    A. Depletion of natural resources B. Environmental pollution
    C. Desertification of habitat D. Genetic erosion
22. Which of the following state has the largest forest cover?
    A. MP B. Kerala
    C. UP D. Tamil Nadu
23. Factor responsible for deforestation is
    A. Over harvest of timber B. Conversion of land into silviculture
    C. Grazing D. Both A and C
24. 500 different plant species can be found in one forest patch in
    A. Eastern ghats B. Amazon
    C. Chhattisgarh D. North American plains
25. Industrialisation resulted in loss of what per cent of forests?
    A. 9.3% B. 3.9%
    C. 19.3% D. 13.9%
26. Deforestation refers to
    A. Planting of trees B. Cultivation of crops
    C. Disappearance of forests D. Regeneration of forests
27. Colonial state regarded forests as
    A. No man's land B. Unproductive and wilderness
    C. Source of revenue D. Sign of balanced ecosystem

28. Which of the following is the reason for forests disappearing near railway tracks?
    A. Wood was used to make railway sleepers
    B. Scorched earth policy of imperial troops
    C. Indiscriminate exploitation by tribals
    D. Indiscriminate cutting of trees by contractors
29. Which of the following is the factor in development of timber plantations?
    A. Natural forests are left untouched
    B. Lands used for cultivation of food crops are converted into timber plantations
    C. Natural forests are cleared to make way
    D. Tribals are encouraged to settle in forest villages
30. Chipko movement is related with
    A. Forest conservation B. Soil conservation
    C. Water conservation D. Wetland conservation
31. Which of the following is not a feature of 'scientific forestry'?
    A. Natural forests are cut down
    B. One type of trees are planted in rows
    C. Area cut is replanted
    D. Forest officials do not survey and estimate the area
32. Forests are categorised by the Forest Act of
    A. 1865 B. 1906
    C. 1927 D. 1878
33. The best forests are
    A. Protected forests B. Village forests
    C. State forests D. Reserved forests
34. Imperial Forest Research Institute was set up in
    A. Dehradun B. Mussourie
    C. Bangalore D. Shimla
35. Which of the following is not a feature of shifting cultivation?
    A. Parts of the forest are cut and burnt in rotation
    B. Seeds are sown in the ashes
    C. Plots cleared are cultivated for a few years and then left fallow
    D. Single crop is grown on these plots

36. Which of the following species of trees are suited for building ships and railways?

A. Sal and semur
B. Teak and mahogany
C. Rosewood and sal
D. Teak and sal

37. What is not a factor in discouragement of shifting agriculture?

A. Land so used can not grow timber
B. It makes it harder for government to calculate taxes
C. Many local communities are displaced
D. There was danger of flames spreading

38. Which of the following was true under colonial rule?

A. Forest people retains customary right of hunt
B. Scale of hunting decreases
C. Scale of hunting increases
D. Killing of large animals is discouraged

39. Which of the following is a new development in forestry?

A. Conservation of forests
B. Collecting timber
C. Scientific forestry
D. Keeping communities away from forests

40. Which among the following is the main reason for survival of some dense forests in India?

A. Conservationists
B. Environmentalists
C. Scientific forestry
D. Villages are protected them as sacred grooves

41. World wild life week is observed during

A. First week of October
B. Last week of October
C. Third week of October
D. First week of September

42. World forestry day is observed on

A. 21st March
B. 5th June
C. 1st December
D. 7th June

43. Chipko movement is started by

A. Engler
B. Sunderlal Bahuguna
C. Medha Patkar
D. None of these

44. Major consumer of wood from forest is

A. Thermal power plant
B. Paper industry
C. Chemical industry
D. None of these

45. What are the three R's that are used to save the environment which includes forest?

A. Reduce, Reuse, Recycle
B. Reserve, Reduce, Recycle
C. Reuse, Reserve, Reduce
D. Reserve, Reuse, Reduce

46. Which community of Rajasthan have religious belief for conservation of forest and wildlife?

A. Haddi
B. Bishnoi
C. Rajput
D. Thakur

47. Which one of the following movement is carried out for the conservation of forests and the environment?

A. Forest movement
B. Ganaga Action Plan
C. Tehri Andolan
D. Chipko Andolan

48. Which of the following is not a principle of Chugach National Forest?

A. The forest service is governed by many existing laws
B. National forest system lands are managed for multiple uses
C. It provides subsistence uses for rural residents of Alaska
D. It doesn't collaborate with interested native Alaskan tribes

49. Which country leads in the producing and consuming of forest products?

A. Nepal
B. Kenya
C. India
D. China

50. Which of the following is not the best way to fight a forest fire?

A. Evacuate from the forest surrounding places
B. Not using water as a fire suppression tool
C. Deploy suppressant foam
D. Create a fire line

51. What is called for the practice of regulating forest resources to meet the needs of society and industry while preserving the forest's health?

A. Environmental protection
B. Sustainable forest management
C. Forest policy framework
D. Unsustainable forest management

52. Which one of the following is a branch of forestry?
    A. Protection forestry B. Deforestation
    C. Forest management D. Restricted forestry
53. Which one of the following is not the best way to stop deforestation?
    A. Planting trees
    B. Not encouraging for recycling the used products
    C. Go paperless
    D. Eat vegetarian meals as often as possible
54. What is considered as lungs of nature?
    A. Rock B. Sun
    C. Water D. Trees
55. How erosion is controlled by forest?
    A. By reducing the sunlight penetration
    B. By reducing the rainfalls force on the soils surface
    C. By reducing the pressure
    D. By increasing the rainfalls force on the soil's surface
56. How forests increase the atmospheres humidity?
    A. By transpiration B. By inspiration
    C. By expiration D. By oxidation
57. Extensive planting of trees to increase the forest cover is called
    A. Afforestation B. Agroforestry
    C. Deforestation D. Social forestry

Answer keys

1	D	11	A	21	C	31	D	41	A	51	B
2	C	12	C	22	A	32	D	42	A	52	C
3	B	13	A	23	D	33	D	43	B	53	B
4	B	14	C	24	B	34	A	44	B	54	D
5	C	15	D	25	A	35	D	45	A	55	B
6	D	16	D	26	C	36	D	46	B	56	A
7	B	17	C	27	B	37	C	47	D	57	A
8	C	18	D	28	D	38	C	48	D		
9	A	19	A	29	C	39	A	49	D		
10	B	20	B	30	A	40	D	50	B		

2

Agroforestry

I. Choose the correct answer

1. Consider the statement and choose the correct answer regarding forms of social forestry

   (i) Community forestry –Forestry on land outside conventional forest

   (ii) Farm forestry –Practice of forestry with development and maintenance of high scenic value

   (iii) Extension forestry –Practice of forestry with development and maintenance of low scenic value

   (iv) Agroforestry – Sustainable land management system

   A. (i) alone is correct B. (ii) and (iii) are correct

   C. (iv) alone is correct D. (i) and (iv) are correct

2. Which among of the following is incorrect regarding projects in social forestry?

   A. Tree cultivation in private lands B. Tank foreshore plantations

   C. Forestry extension D. Pallikaranai marshland

3. Social forestry was first recommended by

   A. Govt. of India

   B. Food and Agriculture Organization

   C. United Nations

   D. National Commission on Agriculture

4. The World Agroforestry Centre is located at

   A. Jhansi B. Nairobi

   C. Dehradun D. Jodhpur

5. Social forestry programme was launched in the

   A. Fifth five year plan B. Sixth five year plan

   C. Seventh five year plan D. Eighth five year plan

6. Agroforestry, the definition implies that
   A. Agroforestry normally involves two or more species of plants at least one of which is a woody perennial
   B. An agroforestry system always has two or more outputs
   C. The cycle of an agroforestry system is always more than one year
   D. All of the above
7. Additionally, there are attributes which theoretically all agroforestry system posses are
   A. Productivity B. Sustainability
   C. Adoptability D. All of the above
8. The major categories of agroforestry are
   A. Agrisilvicultural B. Silvipastoral
   C. Agrosilvipastoral D. All of the above
9. What are MPTs?
   A. The multipurpose tree and shrubs could be defined as trees grown deliberately
   B. Kept and managed for preferably more than one intended use
   C. Usually economically motivated major products
   D. All of the above
10. The multiple benefits of MPTs are
   A. The trees with many uses would be preferred to those with one single use
   B. But in a broad sense every tree has at least the triple functions of protective, productive and socio-economic roles
   C. Both A and B
   D. None of these
11. Protective forestry is
   A. Moderation of micro/macro climatic parameters, checking soil erosion and water run-off
   B. Soil improvement/fertility build up, water conservation and flood moderation
   C. Wildlife habitats
   D. All of the above

12. Productive forestry

    A. Wood: timber, building materials, veneers, chipboards and other panel products, pulp and paper, rayon etc.

    B. Bark: Raw as fuel, dyes, tannins and chemical extraction etc

    C. Both A and B

    C. None of these

13. Energy forestry means

    A. Raw: Firewood

    B. Processed: Charcoal, gases or liquid fuels, chemical stem extractives, resin, oil, paint, varnishes

    C. Leaf: Thatch, fodder, oil, silk, wrapper, medicines, honey, dyes, food

    D. All of the above

14. Social forestry means

    A. It is forestry of people by the people and for the people

    B. The forestry in which the efforts aimed at raising and managing trees for the benefits of rural people

    C. Both A and B

    D. None of these

15. Essential ingredients for the success of community forestry are

    A. Capabilities of the land

    B. The villagers choice of land use

    C. Nature of the support the organizational structure provides

    D. All of the above

16. According to Jeff Romm (1980), essentials for the community forestry programme

    A. The technology must be more suitable and available and must be more productive and ecologicallly sustainable than that already in use

    B. The villagers must feel secured of the benefits

    C. New uses of the land and other resources must be profitable from the villager's point of view

    D. All of the above

17. The main problems faced in implementing community forestry are

A. Villagers feel apprehensive of the programme, which they feel is another version of taking away their land by the government

B. Programme needs community's voluntary cooperation and cannot be imposed on it.

C. Programme should be based on the trust and confidence on both sides

D. All of the above

18. Urban forestry is

A. It is specialized branch of forestry that has the objective of cultivation and management of trees for their present

B. Potential contribution to the physiological, sociological and economic wellbeing of urban society

C. Both A and B

D. None of these

19. Management of urban forest is concerned with management needs of forests in urban areas and with how needs are

A. Whatever is done for the forest to maintain the health and vigour

B. Whatever is done to the forest to prevent undue interference with the society

C. Both A and B

D. None of these

20. Benefits of urban forests are

A. Climate amelioration

B. Environmental engineering uses and architectural uses

C. Aesthetic uses

D. All of the above

21. Benefits of social forestry are

A. Betterment of environment

B. Protection from wind and conservation of moisture

C. Reduction of pollution

D. All of the above

22. The history of agroforestry is

A. Cultivating trees and agricultural crops in intimate combination with one another is an ancient practice that farmers have used throughout the world

B. Until the middle ages, it was the general custom to clear-fell degraded forest, burn the slash, cultivate food crops for varying periods on the cleared areas

C. Plant or sow trees before or along with sowing of crop seeds.

D. All of the above

23. Agroforestry and social forestry both includes

A. Production forestry B. Commercial forestry

C. Afforestation D. Plantation of trees

24. Agroforestry systems can be categorized to sets of criteria

A. Structural basis B. Functional basis

C. Socio-economic basis D. All of the above

25. The framework for classification of agroforestry system and practices are

A. Structure of the system (nature and arrangement of components)

B. Function of the system (role and output of components)

C. Socio-economic seals and management levels of the system

D. All of the above

Answer keys

1	D	11	D	21	D
2	D	12	C	22	D
3	D	13	D	23	D
4	B	14	C	24	D
5	A	15	D	25	D
6	D	16	D		
7	D	17	D		
8	D	18	C		

9	D	19	C
10	C	20	D

3

Classification of Forestry System

I. Choose the correct answer

1. Find out the wrong answer

   A. Tropical moist semi evergreen forest – *Albizia lebeck*

   B. Tropical moist deciduous forest – *Terminalia paniculata*

   C. Tropical dry evergreen - *Avicennia alba*

   D. Tropical thorn forest – *Ziziphus mauritiana*

2. Match list I with list II and choose the correct options given below

List I	List II
A. Tree mangrove forests	1. *Aegialitis rotundifolia*
B. Low mangrove forests	2. *Avicennia officinalis*
C. Salt water forests	3. *Amora cucullata*
D. Brackish water forests	4. *Acanthus ilicifolius*

	A	B	C	D
A.	3	1	4	2
B.	4	1	2	3
C.	2	1	3	4
D.	2	1	4	3

3. Consider the statement and choose the correct answer regarding temperate montane forests

   (i) Montane wet temperate forest –Himalayas, from Nepal to Assam and Nilgris

   (ii) Himalayan moist temperate forest – Develops in higher rainfall areas

   (iii) Himalayan dry temperate forest- Dominated by *Rhododendron,* oaks and conifers

   A. (i) alone is correct B. (ii) alone is correct

   C. All the statements are correct D. (i) and (iii) are correct

4. Among the following which plant species is habitual of alpine forests
   A. Ferns B. Kochia
   C. Artemisia D. *Pyrus communis*
5. The forest which occur in low rainfall area is called as
   A. Evergreen forest B. Deciduous forest
   C. Coniferous forest D. All the above
6. How many parts are there in the forest ecosystem?
   A. One B. Two
   C. Three D. Four
7. On which factor, forest type is mainly dependent?
   A. Abiotic B. Size of the forest
   C. Shape of trees D. Products from the trees
8. Where can we find coniferous forest in India?
   A. Deserts B. River deltas
   C. Grassland D. Himalayan
9. Why most of the sun light does not penetrate to the ground in evergreen forest?
   A. Because of snowfall
   B. Because of trees overlap with each other
   C. Because of less temperature
   D. Because of less rainfall
10. Where can we find thorn forest in India?
    A. Semi-arid regions B. Desert regions
    C. Himalayan regions D. Northeast regions
11. Which of the following type of forest is important for watersheds?
    A. Tropical evergreen forest B. Tropical deciduous forest
    C. Tropical montane forests D. Grassland forest
12. How the tropical rain forest gets the name?
    A. Due to less rain B. Due to heavy rain
    C. Due to moderate rain D. Due to no rain required
13. Where can we find the most feared spider in the world Tarantulas ?
    A. In desert B. In mountains
    C. In tropical rain forests D. In grassland forest

Answer keys

1	C	11	C
2	B	12	B
3	D	13	C
4	D		
5	B		
6	B		
7	A		
8	D		
9	B		
10	A		

4

Silvicultural Practices

I. Choose the correct answer

1. Match list I with list II and choose the correct options given below

List I	List II
A. *Artocarpus heterophyllus*	1. Fire wood
B. *Prosopis juliflora*	2. Food
C. *Dalbergia latifolia*	3. Paper
D. *Eucalyptus*	4. Timber

	A	B	C	D
A.	2	1	4	3
B.	4	3	2	1
C.	3	4	1	2
D.	2	1	3	4

2. Find out the wrong answer

   A. *Dendrocalamus strictus* stem is used as food

   B. *Borassus flabellifer* is used as wind break

   C. *Eucalyptus tereticornis* is used as rayon cloth

   D. *Ailanthus excelsa* is used for match wood

3. How much quantity of fuel wood is consumed in India?

   A. 165 mm^3 B. 170 mm^3

   C. 175 mm^3 D. 180 mm^3

4. Which tree fruit is used as food?

   A. *Acacia nilotica* B. *Melia dubia*

   C. *Termnalia arjuna* D. *Annona squamosa*

5. Which tree is used for plywood making?

   A. *Tectona grandis* B. *Ailanthus excelsa*

   C. *Ceiba pentandra* D. *Cyprus rotundus*

6. What is the per cent of livestock population grazing in forest land?

A. 30% B. 40%

C. 50% D. 60%

7. Match list I with list II and choose the correct options given below

List I	List II
A. *Santalum album*	1. Tans
B. *Madhuca indica*	2. Gums
C. *Acacia mearnsii*	3. Oil seeds
D. *Sterculia urens*	4. Essential oil

	A	B	C	D
A.	1	2	3	4
B.	4	3	1	2
C.	4	1	3	2
D.	1	3	2	4

8. Find out the wrong answer

A. *Leucaena leucocephala*	Fodder
B. *Morus alba*	Lac
C. *Atropa belladonna*	Spices
D. *Diospyros melanoxylon*	Tendu and other leaves

9. Match list I with list II and choose the correct options given below

List I	List II
A. Pesticides	1. *Morus alba*
B. Silk	2. *Populus* sp
C. Latex	3. *Azadirachta indica*
D. Toys	4. *Hevea brasiliensis*

	A	B	C	D
A.	3	1	4	2
B.	3	2	4	1
C.	4	3	2	1
D.	3	4	1	2

10. Which tree is used for making handicrafts

A. Bamboo B. *Acacia nilotica*

C. *Acacia catechu* D. *Casuarina equisetifolia*

11. Which tree charcoal is used for electric batteries?

A. Prosopis charcoal B. Acacia charcoal

C. Albizia charcoal D. Bamboo charcoal

12. Match list I with list II and choose the correct options given below

List I	**List II**
A. Tectona grandis	1. Mimosae
B. Casuarina equisetifolia	2. Graimineae
C. *Dendrocalamus strictus*	3. Casuarinaceae
D. *Acacia nilotica*	4. Verbenaceae

	A	B	C	D
A.	4	3	2	1
B.	3	4	2	1
C.	2	1	3	4
D.	1	2	3	4

13. What is the family of *Azadirachta indica*?

A. Mimoseae B. Gramineae

C. Meliaceae D. Verbenaceae

14. Well drained stony soil is suitable for which crop?

A. *Tectona grandis* B. *Casuarina equisetifolia*

C. *Acacia nilotica* D. *Dendrocalamus strictus*

15. Up to what altitude, *Tectona grandis* is grown

A. 600 m B. 800 m

C. 1000 m D. 1200 m

16. What is the optimum soil for *Acacia nilotica*?

A. Alluvial soil B. Black soil

C. Red soil D. Gravel soil

17. Teak seed is known as

A. Samara B. Drupe

C. Berry D. Pome

18. Which one of the following seed treatment is suitable for *Acacia nilotica*?

A. Alternate wetting and drying B. Cold water soaking

C. Hot water soaking D. Alkali treatment

19. Recommended seed treatment for germination improvement of teak is

A. Alternate wetting and drying B. Cold water soaking

C. Acid method D. Alkali treatment

20. What is the seed rate for *Tectona grandis*?

A. 0.25 kg/m^2 B. 0.50 kg/m^2

C. 0.75 kg/m^2 D. 1. 0 kg/m^2

21. Which tree seed is very short lived?

A. *Tectona grandis* B. *Acacia auriculiformis*

C. *Azadirachta indica* D. *Acacia nilotica*

22. Consider the statement and find out wrong answer

A. Optimum seedling age for planting of *Ailanthus* is 2 years old

B. 4 months old seedlings are planted in *Acacia auriculiformis*

C. 10 months old seedlings are planted in *Dendrocalamus strictus*

D. 1 year old seedlings are planted in *Casuarina equisetifolia*

23. What is the stump size of teak for planting?

A. 2.0 cm shoot and 22.5 cm root B. 2.5 cm shoot and 22.5 cm root

C. 2.5 cm shoot and 22.0 cm root D. 2.5 cm shoot and 23.0cm root

24. Which tree is susceptible to water logging conditions and wind break?

A. *Alianthus excelsa* B. *Acacia nilotica*

C. *Tectona grandis* D. *Casuarina equisetifolia*

25. Match list I with list II and choose the correct options given below

List I	**List II**
A. Australian wattle	1. 3.7 x 3.7 m
B. Casuarina	2. 2 x 2 m
C. Solid bamboo	3. 5 x 5 m
D. *Azadirachta*	4. 5 x 5 m

	A	B	C	D
A.	4	3	2	1
B.	3	4	2	1
C.	2	1	3	4
D.	1	2	3	4

26. For tannin, *Acacia nilotica* is felled at the age of
    A. 5-10 years B. 10-15 years
    C. 15-20 years D. 20-25 years
27. Rotation period of *Ailanthus* is
    A. 5 years B. 10 years
    C. 15 years D. 20 years
28. What is the timber yield of teak?
    A. 6000 m^2/ha B. 6200 m^2/ha
    C. 6500 m^2/ha D. 6700 m^2/ha
29. *Leucaena leucocephala* fixes nitrogen in the range of kg/ha/year
    A. 100-200 B. 100-300
    C. 100-400 D. 100-500
30. In which part of India, the first taungya plantation started
    A. North Bengal B. South Bengal
    C. East Bengal D. All of these
31. In which direction, hedge row intercropping is raised?
    A. South-East B. North-South
    C. East-West D. West-East
32. Freshly cut wood contains ______ per cent moisture
    A. 50% B. 75%
    C. 25% D. 100%
33. Taungya system is followed in area having rainfall of
    A. 1200-1500 mm B. 1500-2000 mm
    C. 2000-2500 mm D. 2500-3000 mm
34. In India, average size of home garden is
    A. 1-2 ha B. 2-3 ha
    C. 2-4 ha D. 2-5 ha
35. Root of trees contains (%) total living biomass of
    A. 10-15 B. 15-20
    C. 20-25 D. 20-30
36. Van-Mahotasav was started in the year
    A. 1947 B. 1950
    C. 1955 D. 1960

37. In India, plantation forestry was started in
A. 1840 B. 1842
C. 1848 D. 1849

38. Nitrogen fixing ability of Casurina is due to
A. *Rhizobium* B. *Azatobactor*
C. *Frankia* D. All of these

39. *Dendrocalamus strictus* is referred as
A. Male bamboo B. Female bamboo
C. Culm bamboo D. All of these

40. The valerian oil is obtained from
A. Leaves B. Bark
C. Stem D. Root

41. The Indian copal tree is
A. *Acacia nilotica* B. *Vateria indica*
C. *Tectona grandis* D. *Madhuca indica*

42. How many bamboo species are found in India?
A. 125 B. 136
C. 145 D. 140

43. Salai gum is obtained from
A. *Acacia nilotica* B. *Pterocarpus marsupium*
C. *Shorea robusta* D. *Boswellia serrata*

44. The regular tapping resin tree is
A. *Pinus wallichiana* B. *Pinus roxburghii*
C. *Diospyros melanoxylon* D. *Boswellia serrata*

45. Felling cycle of bamboo is
A. 3-4 years B. 4-5 years
C. 5-6 years D. 5-10 years

46. Golden or yellow bamboo is
A. *Dendrocalamus strictus* B. *Bambusa vulgaris*
C. *Bambusa tulda* D. All of these

47. Most suitable species for cricket bat is
A. *Bombax ceiba* B. *Salix alba*
C. *Populus deltoides* D. *Dalbergia sissoo*

48. The leading country in growing softwood timber in the world is
A. India B. Srilanka
C. Russia D. Kenya

49. The standard length of the axe handle is
A. 60 cm B. 80 cm
C. 90 cm D. 100 cm

50. A snag is a
A. Standing dead tree B. Standing live tree
C. Felled tree D. Felled log tree

51. Selling standing timber is called a
A. Salvage sale B. Stumpage sale
C. Timber sale D. All of these

52. National newsprint and paper mills is established at
A. Nepanagar B. Nagpur
C. Bhopal D. Dehradun

53. Black dammer is
A. *Vetaria indica* B. *Hopea odorata*
C. *Canarium strictum* D. *Agathis loranthifolius*

54. The NTFPs are abundant in
A. Wet evergreen forest B. Dry deciduous forest
C. Tropical rain forest D. Tropical moist forest

55. Sapwood is rich in
A. Starch B. Cellulose
C. Resins D. Gums

56. Institute of Wood Science and Technology is located at
A. Dehradun B. Jhansi
C. Bhopal D. Bangalore

57. Tylose are present only in
A. Hard wood B. Soft wood
C. Semi-hard wood D. All of these

58. Fibre saturation point for most tropical timber ranged between
A. 6-8 B. 10-15
C. 12-20 D. 20-25

59. Growth of the terminal end of the stem is called
   A. Auxiliary growth B. Terminal growth
   C. Shoot growth D. All of these

60. Red rust in *Eucalyptus* is caused by
   A. Bacteria B. Algae
   C. Viruses D. MLO

61. In India, lac is mainly produced in
   A. Kerala B. Karnataka
   C. Bihar D. Tamil Nadu

62. Spike is a common disease of
   A. Rosewood B. Sandalwood
   C. Hardwood D. Softwood

63. The cause of heart rot and Dutch elm disease is
   A. Bacteria B. Algae
   C. Viruses D. Fungus

64. A fire which runs through the top of living tree bushes is called
   A. Surface fire B. Ground fire
   C. Crown fire D. Creeping fire

65. Wilting of sissoo is caused by
   A. *Fusarium solani* B. *Fusarium oxysporum*
   C. *Phytophthora infestans* D. *Fusarium rolfsii*

66. A fire away from the main fire which started by flying spark is called as
   A. Top fire B. Spot fire
   C. Control fire D. Uncontrol fire

67. A nongrass like herbaceous plant is called a
   A. Herb B. Shrub
   C. Fern D. Hedge

68. Pink disease is related to
   A. Teak B. Sandalwood
   C. Sal D. Pine

69. Find out the incorrect statement

A. Silvicultural system - Forest tree crops are tended, harvested and replaced by new trees.

B. Forest mensuration is the rule of action

C. Forest management – application of techniques and economics of forest estate

D. Forest utilization – it is harvesting, conversion and disposal

Answer keys

1	A	11	D	21	C	31	C	41	B	51	B	61	C
2	B	12	A	22	B	32	D	42	B	52	A	62	B
3	C	13	C	23	B	33	A	43	D	53	C	63	D
4	D	14	B	24	A	34	D	44	B	54	B	64	C
5	A	15	D	25	C	35	C	45	A	55	A	65	A
6	C	16	A	26	C	36	B	46	B	56	D	66	B
7	B	17	B	27	B	37	B	47	B	57	A	67	C
8	C	18	C	28	C	38	C	48	C	58	C	68	B
9	A	19	A	29	D	39	A	49	C	59	D	69	B
10	A	20	D	30	A	40	D	50	A	60	B		

5

Wasteland Management

I. Choose the correct answer

1. Which among the following tree species is not suitable for shelter belt?

   A. *Casuarina equisetifolia* B. *Eucalyptus tereticornis*

   C. *Tectona grandis* D. *Acacia nilotica*

2. Match list I with list II and choose the correct options given below

List I	List II
A. Improved fallow species	1. Production of wood, fodder and food products in shifting cultivation
B. Taungya system	2. *Jhum* (or) *Podu* cultivation
C. Multispecies tree garden	3. Intercrops grown in hedge row
D. Alley cropping	4. West Bengal

	A	B	C	D
A.	2	4	1	3
B.	2	3	1	4
C.	4	3	1	2
D.	4	1	2	3

3. Consider the statement and choose the correct answer

   (i) Multipurpose trees and shrubs on farm lands – *Leucaena leucocephala, Cocos nucifera, Ricinus communis.*

   (ii) Crop combination with plantation crops – Cocoa + Coconut

   (iii) Agroforestry fuel wood production – *Ricinus communis, Citrus aurantifolia, Citrus limonium*

   A. (i) alone is correct B. (ii) alone is correct

   C. (i) and (ii) are correct D. (iii) alone is correct

4. What are the trees used for protein bank?

A. *Acacia nilotica* and *Leucaena leucocephala*

B. *Tectona grandis* and *Eucalyptus tereticornis*

C. *Samanea saman* and *Peltophorum inerme*

D. *Pongamia pinnata* and *Callistephus lanceolatus*

5. Which is the correct combination of home garden?

A. *Sesbania grandiflora* – woody species

B. Banana – woody species

C. *Anacardium occidentale* – woody species

D. *Psidium guajava* – herbaceous species

6. What is the ideal width for shelter belt?

A. 70 m B. 50 m

C. 80 m D. 30 m

7. Which one of the following class deals with soil that does not have erosion hazard or little erosion?

A. Class 2 B. Class 3

C. Class 4 D. Class 5

8. Land use class deals with very severe limitations, not suitable for cultivation and useful for grazing forestland and wild life is

A. Class 7 B. Class 6

C. class 5 D. Class 4

9. Which sub class deals with soil which has major climate hazard?

A. Sub class e B. Sub class w

C. Sub class c D. Sub class s

10. Sub class w deals with

A. Soils have susceptibility to erosion B. Soils have excess water hazard

C. Soils have root zone limitations D. Soils have climate hazard

11. Classes which are not suitable for cultivation

A. Class 1, 2, 3 B. Class 4, 5

C. Class 6, 7, 8 D. Both B and C

12. Class of land that are highly suitable for use under irrigation is

A. Class 1 B. Class 2

C. Class 5 D. Classes 6

13. Which of the following capability classes are not assigned with sub classes?
    A. 1 and 7 classes
    B. 1 and 6 classes
    C. 1 and 8 classes
    D. 1 and 5 classes
14. The land capacity classes suited for cultivation is
    A. 5 to 8
    B. 2 to 4
    C. 1 to 4
    D. 6 to 8
15. According to land capability classification, the soils which are not suitable for crop cultivation belong to
    A. Class 1
    B. Class 3
    C. Class 4
    D. Class 8
16. What is the ideal tree height on the upwind side and the downwind side protection for wind break?
    A. 50m tall, 150m upwind and 600m downwind side
    B. 20m tall, 100m upwind side and 500m downwind side
    C. 30m tall, 300m upwind side and 700m downwind side
    D. 40m tall, 300m upwind side and 800m downwind side
17. Match list I with list II and choose the correct options given below

List I	**List II**
A. Saline soil	1. *Dalbergia sisoo* + Sugarcane
B. Alkaline soil	2. *Acacia planifrons* + *Sorghum bicolor*
C. Waterlogged soil	3. *Butea monosperma* + *Eleusine coracana*
D. Gravel soil	4. *Bambusa bamboo* + *Vetiveria zizanioides*

	A	B	C	D
A.	3	1	2	4
B.	2	1	4	3
C.	3	1	4	2
D.	2	4	1	3

18. What is the average grain diameter of sand in sand dune formation?
    A. 0.05 to 0.07 cm
    B. 0.04 to 0.06 cm
    C. 0.03 to 0.05 cm
    D. 0.02 to 0.04 cm
19. Inland sand dunes are present in
    A. Chennai
    B. Madurai
    C. Bikaner
    D. Bangalore

20. Which species is used as protection against sand dunes?

A. *Tectona grandis* B. *Prosopis spicigera*

C. *Acacia catechu* D. *Dalbergia sissoo*

21. The most common tree species used for sand stabilization is

A. *Acacia catechu* B. *Dalbergia sissoo*

C. *Azadirachta indica* D. *Prosopis juliflora*

22. Match list I with list II and choose the correct options given below

List I	List II
A. Rainfall zone 15-30 cm	1. *Parkinsonia aculeata*
B. Rainfall zone 40 cm and above	2. *Cordia gharaf*
C. Rainfall zone 30-40 cm	3. *Cenchrus setigerus*
D. Rainfall zone 40cm and above	4. *Lasiurus sindicus*

	A	B	C	D
A.	4	3	2	1
B.	3	4	2	1
C.	2	1	3	4
D.	1	2	3	4

23. Find out the wrong answer

A. *Cassia siamea* is suitable for mine burden reclamation

B. *Simarouba glauca* is suitable for mine burden reclamation

C. *Pinus roxburghii* is suitable for temperate hill regions

D. *Acacia melanoxylan* is suitable for sub-tropical hills.

Answer keys

1	C	11	C	21	D
2	A	12	A	22	A
3	C	13	C	23	B
4	A	14	C		
5	C	15	D		
6	B	16	B		
7	D	17	C		
8	A	18	D		
9	C	19	C		
10	B	20	B		

UNIT XVII: FARM MACHINERY AND RENEWABLE ENERGY

1

Tractors, Power Tillers and Energy Source Equipments

I. Choose the correct answer

1. The first tractor plant in India was set up by
   A. Hindustan B. HMT
   C. Ford D. Eicher
2. Expand PTO
   A. Power train output B. Power turn off
   C. Power take off D. Power train off
3. Mechanization possibility is strongly influenced by
   A. Farm size B. Cost of farm power
   C. Availability of suitable machines D. All of the above
4. Increasing or decreasing the speed of the engine is controlled by
   A. Brake B. Throttle lever
   C. Clutch D. Gear
5. The single cylinder engine is generally used in
   A. Tractor B. Stationary engine
   C. Motor cars D. Power tiller
6. Which of the following types of internal combustion engine is generally used as portable engine for pumping and electricity generation?
   A. Spark ignition B. Stationary
   C. Vertical single cylinder D. All of these
7. The two stroke engine is
   A. Diesel engine B. Gas engine
   C. Petrol engine D. Steam engine

8. Diesel engine works on principle of
   A. Diesel cycle B. Otto cycle
   C. Carnot cycle D. Adiabatic cycle
9. Flywheel is made of
   A. Cast iron B. Aluminium alloy
   C. High carbon steel D. Low carbon steel
10. Charge of battery is measured in terms of
   A. Density of electrolyte B. Weight of electrolyte
   C. Specific gravity of electrolyte D. Mass of electrolyte
11. Brakes works on principle of
   A. Friction B. Vibration
   C. Sliding D. Suction
12. Thermal efficiency of the diesel engine varies from
   A. 25% to 32% B. 32% to 38%
   C. 40% to 50% D. 50% to 60%
13. The compression ratio of petrol engine is
   A. 4 to 8:1 B. 14 to 20:1
   C. 8 to 15:1 D. 14 to 22:1
14. Which type of wheel is used in tractor?
   A. Disc wheel B. Wire wheel
   C. Split wheel D. Alloy wheel
15. The purpose of tyre rotation on automobiles is to
   A. Avoid ply separation B. Equalize wear
   C. Get better ride D. Reduce wear
16. At what temperature, the hot water comes from engine to radiator?
   A. 50-60° B. 65-75°
   C. 80-90° D. 100-110°
17. Where the clutch is located?
   A. Between gearbox and differential
   B. Between engine and gearbox
   C. Between engine and differential
   D. Between differential and wheels

18. Which country has invented power tiller?

A. India B. China

C. Philippines D. Japan

19. Which type of tractor the power tiller is?

A. Walking type tractor B. Running type tractor

C. Speed type tractor D. Slow speed type tractor

20. What is the operational capacity of harvesting by tiller harvester?

A. 0.5 acre B. 1.0 acre

C. 1.5 acres D. 2 acres

21. Which one of the tillage machinery operates using kerosene?

A. Bull dozer B. Tractor

C. Power tiller D. Digger

22. When to lubricate the power tiller?

A. Every 25 hrs B. Every 50 hrs

B. Every 75 hrs D. Every 100 hrs

23. The draft control is based on

A. Depth of plough B. Furrow bar pull

C. Depth and draft D. Width of plough

24. The application of engineering and technology in agricultural operations to do a better way to improve productivity is

A. Custom hiring B. Farm mechanization

C. Farm machinery D. All of the above

25. When ploughing one hectare of land once by bullocks having 15 cm. furrow width, has to walk about (km)

A. 55 B. 65

C. 66 D. 67

26. The field capacity (ha/day) of traditional implements is about

A. 0.3-0.4 B. 0.4-0.5

C. 0.5-0.6 D. 0.6-0.7

27. A man can develop

A. 0.1 hp B. 0.5 hp

C. 0.75 hp D. 1.0 hp

28. The average force that a bullock can exert
    A. 1/5th of their body weight B. 1/10th of their body weight
    C. 1/20th of their body weight D. 1/25th of their body weight
29. Medium size bullock can develop
    A. 0.50 to 0.75 hp B. 0.75 to 1.0 hp
    C. 0.75 hp to 1.1 hp D. 1.0 to 1.5 hp
30. The thermal efficiency of diesel engine varies between
    A. 25 and 32 per cent B. 32 and 38 per cent
    C. 32 and 40 per cent D. 40 and 45 per cent
31. The thermal efficiency of petrol engine varies between
    A. 25 and 32 per cent B. 30 and 35 per cent
    C. 32 and 38 per cent D. 30 to 40 percent
32. The size of the tractor is dependent on
    A. Furrow number B. Furrow size
    C. Furrow spacing D. Both furrow number and spacing

Answer keys

1	D	11	A	21	D	31	A
2	C	12	B	22	D	32	D
3	D	13	B	23	B		
4	B	14	A	24	B		
5	B	15	B	25	C		
6	B	16	C	26	A		
7	C	17	B	27	A		
8	A	18	D	28	B		
9	A	19	A	29	A		
10	C	20	D	30	B		

2

Tillage and Irrigation Equipments

I. Choose the correct answer

1. Disc plough is forced into the ground by

   A. Suction — B. Its own weight

   C. Its shape — D. Its size

2. Which of the following is not a primary tillage implement?

   A. Mould board plough — B. Disc plough

   C. Chisel plough — D. Cultivator

3. Which of the following is not a function of mould board plough?

   A. Cutting the furrow slice — B. Lifting the soil

   B. Turning the furrow slice — D. Deep ploughing

4. Sub soiler plough is best suited for

   A. Deep ploughing — B. Breaking hard pan

   C. Making ditches — D. Inter cultivation

5. Sub soilers are operated at maximum depth of

   A. 30 - 40 cm — B. 45 - 75 cm

   C. 75 - 90 cm — D. 10 - 20 cm

6. Which of the following is a primary tillage implement?

   A. Cultivator — B. Sweep

   C. Mould board plough — D. Harrow

7. Which of the following tillage implements is preferred where the soil is rough and stony

   A. Mould board plough — B. Disc plough

   C. Puddler — D. Cultivator

8. The width covered by the cultivator depends on the

   A. Type of soil — B. Row spacing of crop

   C. Speed of the tractor — D. Skill of the operator

9. The angle at which the plane of the cutting edge of the disc is inclined to a vertical line is called

A. Disc angle B. Tilt angle

C. Cutting angle D. Plough angle

10. What is the advantage of disc plough?

A. Shallow ploughing B. Non deep ploughing

C. Surface ploughing D. Deep ploughing

11. The churning of soil in the presence of excess water by means of an implement is known as

A. Puddling B. Tilling

C. Harvesting D. Trampling

12. Up to what depth a chisel plough operates?

A. 10 to 15 cm B. 15 to 30 cm

C. 25 to 35 cm D. 60 to 70 cm

13. Cage wheels are equipped with tractor while puddling operation to

A. Increase the coverage B. Reduce the sinkage of wheels

C. Reduce the initial cost D. Reduce the weeds

14. The perpendicular distance between point of share and lower position of the head of the plough is called as

A. Vertical clearance B. Horizontal clearance

C. Throat clearance D. Plough size

15. How many discs are available in the disc plough?

A. 1-4 B. 1-5

C. 1-6 D. 1-7

16. What is the maximum working depth of subsoiler?

A. 0.5 m B. 1 m

C. 1.5 m D. 2 m

17. In a submersible pump,

A. The motor is fixed in ground and pump in water

B. Both motor and pump is placed in the ground

C. Both motor and pump is submerged in water

D. The motor is fixed in water and pump in ground

18. The size of Parshall flumes is determined by its
    A. Throat length B. Throat width
    B. Floor width D. Floor length
19. Sprinklers when not in use, should be stored in a
    A. Hot place B. Wet place
    C. Cool and dry place D. Hot and dry place
20. Emitters are important component of which type of irrigation?
    A. Drip irrigation B. Sprinkler irrigation
    C. Furrow irrigation D. Border irrigation
21. The sprinkler irrigation is not suitable for
    A. Cotton B. Rice
    C. Ground nut D. Tomato
22. Land levelling is not essential for
    A. Furrow irrigation B. Canal irrigation
    C. Sprinkler irrigation D. Drip irrigation
23. Which one of the following is the surface water source of irrigation?
    A. Open well B. Submersible well
    C. Springs D. Lakes
24. Which of the following pumps is not suitable for irrigation?
    A. Centrifugal pump B. Submersible pump
    C. Vertical turbine pump D. Reciprocating pump
25. Impeller is an important component of
    A. Centrifugal pump B. Reciprocating pump
    C. Jet pump D. Propeller pump
26. The main advantage of drip irrigation is
    A. Less cost B. Water saving
    C. More labour D. It can be adopted for all crops
27. Improved type of land leveler is
    A. Scraper B. Ridge
    C. Planks D. Wooden logs
28. Power operated bed former is useful for the crops like
    A. Rice B. Grass
    C. Cotton D. Maize

29. Name the place where the bund former was originally developed?

A. New Delhi B. Coimbatore

C. Bangalore D. Lucknow

30. Land leveling is necessary for

A. Drip irrigation B. Sprinkler irrigation

C. Rasing irrigation D. Furrow irrigation

31. Land leveling otherwise called as

A. Harrowing B. Cultivating

C. Smoothing D. Winnowing

32. In which wood, the bund former is manufactured?

A. Bamboo B. Teak

C. Neem D. Karvel

33. What is the maximum angle of transporting soil in uphill?

A. 5° B. 10°

C. 15° D. 20°

34. Which one of the following is soil auger?

A. Reaper B. Digger

C. Manure spreader D. Baler

35. Where the laser transmitter is mounted?

A. Mounted in the field B. Mounted on tractor

C. Mounted on leveler bucket D. Mounted on draw bar

36. Which is the no till method of ploughing?

A. Planting B. Cultivating

B. Ploughing D. Discing

Answer keys

1	B	11	A	21	B	31	C
2	D	12	C	22	C	32	D
3	D	13	B	23	D	33	C
4	B	14	C	24	D	34	B
5	B	15	D	25	C	35	A
6	C	16	D	26	B	36	A
7	B	17	C	27	A		
8	B	18	B	28	D		
9	B	19	C	29	B		
10	D	20	A	30	D		

3

Sowing and Transplanting Equipments

I. Choose the correct answer

1. The dropping of seeds in a furrow lines in continuous flow is

   A. Drilling B. Planting

   C. Drippling D. Hill dropping

2. The equipment used for dropping the seeds in continuous flow is

   A. Seed drill B. Planter

   C. Transplanter D. Random seeder

3. A seed metering mechanism, the smaller operating for smaller seed is?

   A. Cup feed mechanism B. Cell feed type mechanism

   C. Brush feed mechanism D. Vertical cell wheel mechanism

4. Seed drill is used for sowing

   A. Small seeds B. Bolder seeds

   C. Seedlings D. Plants

5. Placing two or more seeds in a hole by some implement is called as

   A. Broadcasting B. Dropping

   C. Drilling D. Dibbling

6. Which box is used to drop the fertilizers in the seed drill?

   A. Small box B. Medium box

   C. Large box D. Big box

7. The procedure for testing seed drill for correct seed rate is

   A. Metering B. Calibration

   C. Seed drill D. Adjustment

8. Planters are useful for planting of

   A. Small seeds B. Medium seeds

   C. Large seeds D. Very small seeds

9. Dibbler is a

A. Seed drill B. Planter

C. Transplanter D. Automatic transplanter

10. How many raised beds can be made at a time by a sugarcane planter?

A. One B. Two

C. Three D. Four

11. At what horse power, the rice transplanter operates

A. 2 hp B. 4 hp

C. 6 hp D. 8 hp

12. What is the optimum height of rice seedlings used for transplanting by paddy transplanter?

A. 5 to 10 cm B. 10 to 15 cm

C. 10 to 20 cm D. 15 to 20 cm

13. Deep furrow is made to plant

A. Groundnut B. Potato

C. Maize D. Sugarcane

14. Cotton planter is useful only for planting the following seed

A. Kapas seed B. Fuzzy seed

C. Acid delinted seed D. Waxy seed

15. A single row seed cum fertilizer drill is suitable for planting

A. Maize B. Cumbu

C. Sorghum D. Ragi

16. Ridge planting is most suitable for

A. Low rainfall areas B. Average rainfall areas

C. High rainfall D. Dryland areas

17. What is the percentage of sett saving due to sugarcane transplanter ?

A. 35% B. 40%

C. 50% D. 60%

18. What crop is planted using National multi crop ridge planter?

A. Rice B. Sorghum

C. Ragi D. Maize

19. Planter is different from seed drill in respect to

A. Power transmission	B. Metering mechanism
C. Furrow opener	D. Dibbler

20. What is the optimum depth of water for paddy transplanter?

A. 2 cm	B. 3 cm
C. 4 cm	D. 5 cm

21. What is the major difference between seed drill and planter?

A. Row to row spacing

B. Seed to seed spacing

C. Both row to row spacing and seed to seed spacing

D. Row to seed spacing

Answer keys

1	A	11	B	21	C
2	A	12	C		
3	C	13	B		
4	A	14	C		
5	D	15	A		
6	A	16	C		
7	B	17	B		
8	C	18	D		
9	B	19	B		
10	B	20	D		

4

Spraying Equipments

I. Choose the correct answer

1. The chemical tank is made up of

   A. Aluminium B. Stainless steel

   C. Plastic D. Cardboard

2. Nozzle body is made up of

   A. Brass B. Aluminium

   C. Copper D. Steel

3. The application rate of ULV sprayer is

   A. Up to 5 litres/ha B. 5-10 litres/ha

   C. 10-15 litres/ha D. Above 15 litres/ha

4. The nozzle used for chemical spraying of weedicides is

   A. Hollow cone B. Solid cone

   C. Flat fan D. Flooding

5. Hand operated sprayer are operated at pressure (kg/cm^2) of

   A. 1-7 B. 7-10

   C. 10-15 D. 15-20

6. Power sprayers are operated by

   A. Internal combustion B. External combustion

   C. Diesel D. Gas

7. Knapsack sprayer is recommended for spraying of

   A. Large area B. Medium area

   C. Medium to large area D. Small area

8. The simple and most commonly used agitation method for agitating the chemical solution in the tank is

   A. Hydraulic agitator B. Mechanical agitator

   C. Gas agitator D. Air agitator

9. Fan nozzles are also called as

A. Centrifugal B. Flooding

C. Rotary D. Two fluid atomizer

10. While cleaning of the sprayer, which part is to be cleaned frequently?

A. Valve B. Nozzle housing

C. Nozzle cap D. Filter

11. The recommended spray volume for low volume spraying is

A. <100 litres/ha B. 100 - 500 litres/ha

C. >500 litres/ha D. 500 – 1000 litres/ha

12. The extra high speed engines used in knapsack sprayers are powered by

A. Kerosene B. Diesel

C. Petrol D. Dual fuel

13. Power sprayers are operated at a pressure of

A. 5 - 10 kg/m_2 B. 10 - 20 kg/m_2

C. 20 - 55 kg/m_2 A. > 55 kg/m_2

14. In electrostatic spraying, the total volume of liquid to be sprayed over one hectare is

A. < 1 litres B. 50 litres

C. 100 litres D. > 100 litres

15. The height of spray for rotary type hand sprayer for effective spraying is

A. 5 meters B. 10 meters

C. 3 meters D. 8 meters

16. Which one of the following nozzle is used in foam spraying?

A. Vertical fan nozzle B. Solid cone nozzle

C. Window type nozzle D. Air aspirating nozzle

17. Capacity of ultra low volume sprayer is

A. 150 lit/ha B. 100-150 lit/ha

C. 5-10 lit/ha D. 1-5 lit/ha

18. Type of nozzle used for higher application rate and speed is

A. 40-80 psi (Hollow cone) B. 15-30 psi (Flat fan)

C. 5-25 psi (Flood jet) D. Disc type

19. For spraying at higher heights, the sprayer used is

    A. Boom sprayer B. Knapsack sprayer

    C. Rocker sprayer D. Power sprayer

20. The droplet size of mist sprayer is about

    A. 100-250 μm B. 50-100 μm

    C. 0.5 – 50 μm D. > 250 μm

Answer keys

1	C	6	A	11	B	16	D
2	A	7	D	12	C	17	D
3	A	8	A	13	C	18	C
4	C	9	B	14	B	19	C
5	A	10	D	15	C	20	B

5

Harvesting and Threshing Equipments

I. Choose the correct answer

1. Optimum moisture content of crop for better threshing is

   A. 5 – 10% B. 12 – 15%

   C. 15 – 20% D. 20 – 30%

2. A reaper is used for

   A. Cutting crop B. Cutting and windrowing

   C. Cutting and threshing D. None

3. An olpad thresher is operated by

   A. Pair of bullock's B. Tractor

   C. Manually D. Electric motor

4. The mower are designed to cut

   A. Wheat B. Paddy

   C. Mustard D. Grasses

5. Optimum operating cylinder speed for the power operated maize sheller is

   A. 200 – 400 rpm B. 400 – 600 rpm

   C. 600 – 800 rpm D. 1000 – 1200 rpm

6. Length of cut for silage ranges from

   A. 2 – 4 cm B. 5 – 10 cm

   C. 15 – 20 cm D. 20 – 25 cm

7. Most commonly used threshing mechanism on the grain combine is

   A. Rasp bar cylinder B. Spring tooth cylinder

   C. Spike tooth cylinder D. Peg tooth cylinder

8. Paddy can be harvested with the recommended moisture content of

   A. 5 – 10% B. 16 – 30%

   C. 20 – 30% D. Greater than 30%

9. A device used for manual harvesting crop is
   A. Sickle B. Reaper
   C. Mower D. Combine
10. A machine used to cut herbage crops and leave them in swath is
   A. Reaper B. Mower
   C. Combine D. Baler
11. The average threshing out turn of a paddy thresher in kg/hr is
   A. 500 B. 800
   C. 650 D. 1000
12. A thresher causes more seed damage if
   A. Speed is increased B. Clearance is increased
   C. Feed rate is reduced D. Speed is reduced
13. Axial flow thresher utilizes
   A. Spike tooth cylinder B. Hammer mill type
   C. Peg tooth cylinder. D. Rasp bar cylinder
14. A machine used for cutting of cereal crops is
   A. Reaper B. Combine
   C. Mower D. Windrower
15. The material that is left by the harvesting machine in row is known as
   A. Swath B. Stubble
   C. Straw D. Combine
16. A machine used to cut crops and deliver them in a uniform manner in a row is
   A. Combine B. Reaper
   C. Reaper binder D. Windrower
17. Animal operated potato digger is suitable for digging out tubers
   A. Without removal of vines B. After removal of vines
   C. Without removal of leaves D. After removal of leaves
18. What is the digging efficiency of groundnut digger?
   A. 98.6% B. 88.6%
   C. 78.6% D. 68.6%
19. How much labour and time is saved by using animal drawn potato digger?
   A. 20% B. 30%
   C. 40% D. 50%

20. Self propelled combine harvester is provided with

A. Powering engine B. Petrol engine

C. Diesel engine D. Kerosene engine

21. Maintenance work in combine harvester is to be carried out

A. Every 2 hours B. Every 3 hours

C. Every 4 hours D. Every 5 hours

22. The operating speed of combine harvester in field varies from

A. 2 – 6.4 kmph B. 2 – 8 kmph

C. 4 – 10 kmph D. 4 – 12 kmph

23. The grain that is carried over the rear of the sieve with chaff and blown out of the combine harvester is

A. Cylinder loss B. Rack loss

C. Sieve loss D. Drum loss

24. The cutting platform of combine harvester operates at height above ground is

A. 6.5 – 8 cm B. 7.5 – 9 cm

C. 8.5 – 11 cm D. 9.5 – 12 cm

25. An assembly which diverts the straw coming from cylinder towards straw walker is

A. Front beater B. Rear beater

C. Straw walker D. None of these

Answer keys

1	B	11	C	21	D
2	A	12	A	22	A
3	C	13	D	23	C
4	D	14	A	24	B
5	C	15	B	25	B
6	A	16	D		
7	B	17	B		
8	C	18	A		
9	A	19	C		
10	B	20	C		

6

Post Harvest Equipments

I. Choose the correct answer

1. From the most of the wheat mills, the yield of flour can be obtained about
   A. 60% B. 65%
   C. 75% D. 80%
2. Head rice recovery in parboiled rice is due to
   A. Hardening of starch B. Swelling of starch
   C. Gelatinization of starch D. None of these
3. The percentage of husk received from paddy is
   A. 10 B. 15
   C. 22 D. 26
4. The differential speed of rolls of wheat mill is
   A. 2:1 B. 2.5:1
   C. 3:1 D. 3.5:1
5. To separate mustard seed from wheat, the best type of separator is
   A. Indented cylinder separator B. Specific gravity separator
   C. Centrifugal separator D. Spiral separator
6. A scalper is used for
   A. Grading the material B. Rough separation of material
   C. Removing of stones D. Fine separation of material
7. Types of pulse milling are
   A. Dry and wet B. Hot and dry
   C. Wet and humid D. Rough and smooth
8. Natural air drying is recommended, if the RH is below
   A. 100% B. 70%
   C. 60% D. 80%

9. Pulses are the major source of

A. Vitamins B. Protein

C. Carbohydrate D. Fat

10. Polishing of rice is also known as

A. Whitening B. Pearling

C. Scouring D. All the above

11. Polishing of rice in vertical cone polisher is based on

A. Abrasion B. Friction

C. Impact D. None of these

12. Method of conveying granular materials with high speed of air current is called as

A. Belt conveyor B. Screw conveyor

C. Pneumatic conveyor D. Bucket elevator

13. First cleaning operation after threshing is called as

A. Screening B. Scalping

C. Washing D. Grading

14. Break rolls and reduction rolls are used in

A. Rice milling B. Wheat milling

C. Burr milling D. Spice grinding

15. Engle berg huller removes _________ from paddy

A. Husk B. Bran

C. Husk and bran D. Brokens

16. Oil content in parboiled rice bran is ________ raw rice bran

A. Very less than B. Less than

C. Same as D. More than

17. For optimum centrifugal discharge in bucket elevator, the centrifugal force should be__________ the force of gravity

A. Equal to B. Less than

C. Greater than D. Less than (or) equal to

18. In screw conveyor, the pitch of standard screw is _________ its diameter

A. Less than (or) equal to B. Less than

C. Equal to D. Greater than

19. LSU type dryer was developed in

A. India | B. England
C. USA | D. Canada

20. Specific gravity separator is used for grading the grain on the basis of

A. Same size but different specific gravity
B. Same size and same specific gravity
C. Different size but different specific gravity
D. Different size and same specific gravity

21. The moisture content of paddy at the time of milling should be in the range of

A. 9-10% | B. 11-12%
C. 13-14% | D. 66-78%

22. LSU drier is an example of

A. Continuous non mixing type dryer
B. Continuous flow dryer
C. Columnar type dryer
D. Continuous mixing type dryer

23. Inclined belt separator separates grains based on

A. Size | B. Shape
C. Color | D. Specific gravity

24. Cracked seed from whole seed is removed by

A. Blower | B. Aspirator
C. Magnetic separator | D. Colour separator

25. Parboiling of paddy is a ___________ treatment.

A. Hydrothermal | B. Thermal
C. Light | D. None

26. In rice polishing

A. A coating is applied on the outer surface of brown rice
B. A layer of bran is removed from brown rice
C. A layer of starch is removed
D. Only husk is removed

27. Shelling out turn of paddy in rubber roll sheller is about

A. 85% B. 87%

C. 96% D. 95%

28. Break rolls have

A. Smooth surface B. Corrugated surface

C. Rough surface D. Hole in surface

29. Milling refers to the

A. Cleaning and grading

B. Separating, size reduction and polishing

C. Dehusking, splitting

D. Removing of husk and bran layers

30. Stone separator is a form of

A. Specific gravity separator B. Velvet roll separator

C. Magnetic separator D. Disc separator

31. R-Pockets are present to separate desirable grains in

A. Velvet roll separator B. Disc separator

C. Intended cylinder separator D. Spiral separator

32. In spiral separator, the adjustable component for separation is

A. Slope of deck B. Rate of feeding

C. Air flow rate D. None of these

33. Lack of flexibility is the main limitation of

A. Spiral separator B. Belt separator

C. Disc separator D. Magnetic separator

34. The vibratory screens are agitated by

A. Eccentric unit B. Belt and pulley

C. Chain and sprocket D. None

35. The capacity of the hand operated decorticator is

A. 2-3 bags B. 4-5 bags

C. 5-6 bags D. 7-8 bags

36. What is the capacity of mechanical decorticator developed by Maharashtra state?

A. 50-55 bags B. 60-65 bags

C. 70-75 bags D. 75-80 bags

37. Which one of the following is the rice polisher?
A. Disc sheller B. Cone type polisher
C. Puller type sheller D. Decorticator

38. What is the purpose of cleaning of grains?
A. To remove good grains B. To upgrade grain quality
C. To remove impurities D. To remove good seeds

39. What is the optimum temperature used for forced air drying of different crops?
A. 20° C B. 30° C
C. 45° C D. 55° C

40. What is the function of second screen in the cleaner cum grader?
A. Grading B. Scalping
C. Aspiration D. Upgrading

41. What is the milling capacity of hammer mill?
A. 200 – 400 kg/hr B. 400-750 kg/h
C. 400 – 1000 kg/hr D. 400 – 1500 kg/hr

42. Removal of silver skin and the bran layers of brown rice is called as
A. Hulling B. Pearling
C. Polishing D. Whitening

43. What substance is used for glazing of rice
A. Fructose B. Glucose
C. Galactose D. Sucrose

44. What is the function of first screen in the cleaner cum grader?
A. Aspiration B. Scalping
C. Grading D. Upgrading

45. The combination of roasting and stewing is called
A. Braising B. Blanching
C. Sauteing D. Simmering

46. What is the temperature required for poaching?
A. 120 and 140°F B. 130 and 160°F
C. 120 and 150°F D. 160 and 180°F

47. Where is National Institute for Food Technology Entrepreneurship and Management located?

A. Lucknow B. Sonepat

C. Jodhpur D. Panipat

Answer keys

1	C	11	A	21	C	31	B	41	C
2	C	12	C	22	D	32	B	42	D
3	C	13	B	23	B	33	A	43	B
4	B	14	B	24	B	34	A	44	B
5	D	15	C	25	A	35	D	45	A
6	C	16	D	26	B	36	B	46	D
7	A	17	A	27	D	37	B	47	B
8	C	18	C	28	B	38	C		
9	B	19	C	29	D	39	C		
10	A	20	A	30	A	40	A		

7

Renewable Energy

I. Choose the correct answer

1. Improved form of dome type of biogas plant
   A. Deenabandhu — B. Community biogas plant
   C. Village model — D. Floating type
2. Solar energy is used for
   A. Solar water heater — B. Solar distillation
   C. Solar water pumping — D. All the above
3. Renewable source of energy is
   A. Exhaustible — B. Inexhaustible
   C. Nuclear based — D. Biogas
4. Gas formed in biogas plant is
   A. Dithane — B. Ethane
   C. Indane — D. Methane
5. In agriculture, wind energy is mainly used for
   A. Water pumping — B. Harvesting
   C. Fertilizer application — D. Sowing / planting
6. One hp is equal to
   A. 246 watts — B. 250 watts
   C. 746 watts — D. 1000 watts
7. Energy is released from fossil fuels when they are
   A. Pumped — B. Cooled
   C. Burned — D. Pressurized
8. In the production of wave energy which form of energy is used?
   A. Potential energy — B. Kinetic energy
   C. Solar energy — D. Wind energy

9. In hydroelectricity power
   A. Kinetic energy is transferred to potential
   B. Potential energy is transferred to kinetic
   C. Solar energy is transferred to wind energy
   D. Wind energy is transferred to solar energy
10. Energy in the form of heat and light is obtained by
   A. Biomass B. Fossil fuels
   C. Sun D. Wind
11. SI unit for energy is
   A. Watt B. Kilogram
   C. Newton D. Joule
12. Trapped heat inside the earth is known as
   A. Heat energy B. Kinetic energy
   C. Geothermal energy D. Thermal energy
13. The energy sources whose net energy yield is zero
   A. Primary energy sources B. Secondary energy sources
   C. Supplementary energy sources D. All of these
14. The energy sources which produce no net energy are
   A. Secondary energy sources B. Primary sources
   C. Commercial energy D. Non- commercial energy
15. Which of the following is a renewable source of energy?
   A. Coal B. Hydropower
   C. Natural gas D. Petroleum
16. If you are using biomass as a source of energy, you might be
   A. Heating with coal. B. Heating with natural gas.
   C. Heating with petroleum. D. Heating with a wood stove.
17. Which of the following is not a form of kinetic energy (energy of motion)?
   A. Chemical energy B. Electrical energy
   C. Heat energy D. Sound energy
18. Which of the following has nothing to do with hydropower?
   A. Burning B. Gravity
   C. Sun D. Water cycle

19. Which of the following is not a fossil fuel?
    A. Biomass B. Coal
    C. Natural gas D. Petroleum
20. Which of the following is not related to energy efficiency?
    A. Useful energy B. Heat
    C. Energy transformations D. Kilowatts
21. Which among the following source of energy pollutes air?
    A. Water source B. Fossil fuels
    C. Solar energy D. Wind energy
22. Methane gas released from rotting garbage is known as
    A. Biogas B. Synthetic gas
    C. Organic gas D. Gobar gas
23. Biomass fuel is_______ largest source of energy
    A. 1st B. 2nd
    C. 3rd D. 4th
24. Biogas consists of _______ % of carbondioxide
    A. 10-20% B. 20-30%
    C. 30-40% D. 40-50%
25. What is the calorific value of biogas?
    A. 2000 to 2500 kcal/kg B. 3000 to 3500 kcal/kg
    C. 4000 to 4500 kcal/kg D. 5000 to 5500 kcal/kg
26. From 1 kg of cow dung + equal quantity of water gives _______ litre biogas
    A. 0.01 m^3 B. 0.02m^3
    C. 0.03 m^3 D. 0.04m^3
27. Consider the statement and choose the correct one
    (i) Floating drum model – KVIC type
    (ii) Fixed dome type – Deenabandu model
    (iii) Floating drum model – Janata model
    A. (i) and (iii) are correct B. All are correct
    C. (i) and (ii) are correct D. (ii) and (iii) are correct

28. What is the gas holding capacity of deenabandhu biogas model?

A. 20% B. 33%

C. 25% D. 30%

29. Biogas mantle lamps consumes energy ______ per hour

A. 1 – 2 cft B. 2 – 4 cft

C. 3 – 4 cft D. 4 – 5 cft

30. 100 kg of feed stock yields ______ litres of ethanol

A. 15 B. 20

C. 42 D. 32

31. The calorific value of producer gas is

A. 500 – 600 kcal/m^3 B. 650 – 750 kcal/m^3

C. 750 – 850 kcal/m^3 D. 950 – 1200 kcal/m^3

32. What is the gasification rate of gasifier?

A. 125 – 250 kg/h/m^2 B. 100 – 120 kg/h/m^2

C. 175 – 225 kg/h/m^2 D. 150 – 215 kg/h/m^2

33. A country is said to be in water stress, when annual water supplies drop below ______ per person.

A. 1200 cubic meters B. 1000 cubic meters

C. 1500 cubic meters D. 1700 cubic meters

34. Which among the following is not a horizontal axis wind turbine?

A. Dutch wind mill

B. Multi blade water pumping wind

C. Giromill

D. High speed propeller type wind mill

35. Which among the following state does not have thermal power stations?

A. Uttar Pradesh B. Madhya Pradesh

C. West Bengal D. Kerala

36. Methanogens requires pH of about

A. 6.5 to 8 B. 4.5 to 6

C. 8.5 to 11 D. None of these

37. Common energy source in Indian villages is

A. Electricity B. Coal

C. Sun D. Wood and animal dung

38. Both power and manure is provided by

A. Nuclear plants
B. Thermal plants
C. Biogas plants
D. Hydroelectric plants

39. Which of the following statement is not true about composition of biogas

A. It is composed almost exclusively of methane and carbon dioxide
B. It also contains with traces of H_2S, N_2, H_2 and CO
C. It also contains with traces of O_2 and Cl_2
D. Both A and B

40. Which of the following is used to derive energy from wind

A. Wind anemometer
B. Wind screen
C. Wind mills
D. Milling machine

41. Electricity is generated in the windmills in

A. Rotors
B. Gear system
C. Generators
D. Transformers

42. What is the average service life of solar panel?

A. 0 – 5 years
B. 5 - 10 years
C. 10 – 15 years
D. 15 – 20 years

43. In solar air heater, the solar energy is converted to

A. Electric energy
B. Tidal energy
C. Wind energy
D. Thermal energy

44. What is the percentage of fire wood saving due to smoke less chulhas?

A. 5 – 15%
B. 10 – 25%
C. 20 – 35%
D. 30 – 45%

45. The velocity required to operate wind mill is more than

A. 5 km per hour
B. 10 km per hour
C. 5 miles per hour
D. 10 miles per hour

46. The power produced from a wind speed 6.4 to 37 km per hour by windmill varies from

A. 0.1 to 0.5 hp
B. 0.1 to 0.9 hp
C. 0.5 to 1 hp
D. 1 to 9 hp

47. The rate of doing work at the rate of 4500 kg.m per minute is

A. hp
B. Kw
C. Kwh
D. Watt

48. The energy source which provide a net supply of energy is

A. Primary energy sources
B. Secondary energy sources
C. Renewable energy sources
D. All of these

49. Which of the following forms of energy is a renewable resource?

A. Synthetic oil
B. Breeder fission
C. Biomass
D. Oil shale

50. Which of the following forms of energy was a low long term (next 50 years) estimated availability?

A. Low temperature heating from solar energy
B. Synthetic oil and alcohols from coal
C. Photovoltaic production of electricity
D. Coal

51. Which of the following energy sources produces the most electricity in the United States?

A. Coal
B. Hydropower
C. Natural gas
D. Uranium (nuclear power)

52. What is the per cent of the average home's electric bill for lighting?

A. About 10%
B. About 20%
C. About 30%
D. About 40%

53. Methane percentage of biogas varies from

A. 5 to 10%
B. 10 to 25%
C. 30 to 40%
D. 45 to 70%

54. The ratio of cow dung and water for making slurry to feed the biogas plant is

A. 1:2
B. 4:5
C. 3:2
D. 1:5

55. In biogas plant, how much temperature is maintained for biogas production

A. 20°C
B. 35°C
C. 15°C
D. 10°C

Answer keys

1	A	11	D	21	B	31	D	41	C	51	A
2	D	12	C	22	A	32	C	42	D	52	A
3	B	13	C	23	B	33	D	43	D	53	D

4	D	14	A	24	C	34	C	44	C	54	A
5	A	15	B	25	D	35	D	45	B	55	B
6	C	16	D	26	D	36	A	46	B	56	
7	C	17	A	27	C	37	D	47	A	57	
8	B	18	A	28	B	38	C	48	A	58	
9	B	19	A	29	B	39	C	49	C	59	
10	C	20	D	30	C	40	C	50	C	60	

UNIT XVIII: LIVE STOCK AND POULTRY REARING

1

Livestock Rearing

I. Choose the correct answer

1. Match the following

A. Milch breed		1. Jersey
B. Dual breeds		2. Sindhi
C. Draught breed		3. Ongole
D. Exotic breed		4. Kangayam

	A	B	C	D
A.	2	3	4	1
B.	4	3	2	1
C.	2	1	4	3
D.	1	3	4	2

2. Half moon appearance of horns are seen in

A. Ongole B. Gir

C. Kangayam D. Hallikar

3. The unsuitable method of milking is

A. Stripping B. Full hand method

C. Knuckling D. Modern milking

4. Colour of jersy breed is

A. Spotted black and white B. Reddish fawn

C. Silver grey and iron gray D. Steel black

5. The vaccum pressure used in machine milking is

A. 350 – 400 mm Hg B. 450 – 500 mm Hg

C. 250 – 275 mmHg D. 500 – 600 mm Hg

6. Match the following

A. Viral disease 1. Pebrine

B. Bacterial disease 2. Muscardine

C. Fungal disease — 3. Flacherie

D. Protozoan disease — 4. Emit foul smell

	A	B	C	D
A.	4	3	2	1
B.	2	1	4	3
C.	2	3	4	1
D.	3	4	2	1

7. Metabolic disease in cows after calving is
   A. Bloat
   B. Black quarter
   C. Milk fever
   D. Anthrax

8. Symptoms of bloat in cattle is
   A. Die without showing any symptom
   B. High rise of temperature
   C. Drooling of saliva and loss of appetite
   D. Excess intake of fresh legumes lead to gas formation in stomach/ rumen

9. Cattle disease which is susceptible to man is
   A. FMD
   B. Anthrax
   C. Milk fever
   D. Rinder pest

10. National Dairy Research Institute is located at
   A. Karnal
   B. Bhopal
   C. Hyderabad
   D. Lucknow

11. Cattle breed suitable for milking is
   A. Kangayam
   B. Amritmahal
   C. Sindhi
   D. Ongole

12. System of housing suitable for temperate and heavy rainfall region is
   A. Loose housing
   B. Stanchion barn
   C. Either A or B
   D. Milking barn

13. For milking cows, the green grass requirement is
   A. 1.25 kg
   B. 2.5 kg
   C. 5 kg
   D. 10 kg

14. Average production of Holstein Friesian is
A. 4500 kg/lactation B. 6500 kg/lactation
C. 2500 kg/lactation D. 5000 kg/lactation

15. Per capita availability of milk in India during 2017-18
A. 376 g/day B. 337 g/day
C. 355 g/day D. 322 g/day

16. Which position India stands in milk production (2018)?
A. 1st B. 2nd
C. 3rd D. 4th

17. Which animal is best for milching purpose?
A. Sahiwal B. Kangayam
C. Bargur D. Umblachery

18. Which state in India is the highest milk producer?
A. Tamil Nadu B. Gujarat
C. Uttar Pradesh D. Rajasthan

19. What is the per capita availability of milk in Tamil Nadu?
A. 320 g/day B. 310 g/day
C. 300 g/day D. 355 g/day

20. National Dairy Development Board is located at
A. Anand B. Karnal
C. Hyderabad D. Banagalore

21. Which is the oldest method of livestock rearing?
A. Mixed farming B. Semi intensive
C. Integrated farming D. Extensive

22. What is the temperature and time required for low temperature long time method of pasteurization of milk?
A. 72°C and 15-20 min B. 63°C and 30 min
C. 80°C and 15 min D. 57°C and 15 min

23. Which among the following method of milking should be avoided?
A. Stripping B. Fisting
C. Full hand milking D. Machine milking

24. Right time for insemination in buffaloes is ___ hours after the beginning of heat symptoms?

A. 4 B. 12

C. 20 D. 28

25. In cattle shed, inner width of manger should be

A. 30 cm B. 60 cm

C. 90 cm D. 120 cm

26. What space should be provided for per cow in manger?

A. 2 to 2 ½ ft B. 0.5 to 1 ft

C. 1 to 2 ft D. 5 to 6 ft

27. If the cows are housed in a covered (or) partially covered yard, but milking in batches in a special milking house called milking parlour. What is called?

A. Loose housing barn B. Stanchion barn

C. Open air barn D. Pen barn (or) isolation barn

28. How many animals can be maintained in single row system of housing in cattle?

A. >15 animals B. <15 animals

C. 15 – 20 animals D. 25 animals

29. Buffalo calves should be fed with colostrums percentage of its body weight

A. $1/10^{th}$ B. $1/20^{th}$

C. $1/15^{th}$ D. $1/5^{th}$

30. At what age of the calf, the dehorning (disbudding) should be done?

A. 2 weeks of age B. 9 weeks of age

C. 10 weeks of age D. 8 weeks of age

31. What is the minimum age of heifer for breeding?

A. 10 months B. 12 months

C. 14 months D. 15 months

32. What is quantity of dry fodder to be fed to heifers?

A. 5 kg B. 3 kg

C. 7 kg D. 9 kg

33. What is the thumb rule for feeding lactating animals with concentrate?

A. 200-300g/kg milk production B. 100-200g/kg milk production

C. 450-500g/kg milk production D. 300-350g/kg milk production

34. What is the contribution of work bullocks to the total energy requirement for agricultural sector?

A. 28 million hp B. 80 million hp

C. 70 million hp D. 8 million hp

35. Which among the following is a non contagious disease?

A. Anthrax B. Hypocalcemia

C. Rinderpest D. Aflatoxicosis

36. Which among the following is not zoonotic disease?

A. Brucellosis B. Rabies

C. Black quarter D. Tuberculosis

37. What is the quantity of concentrate in total drymatter of cattle feed?

A. 1/3 B. 2/3

C. 3/4 D. 1/4

38. What is the sperm count in one ml of semen?

A. 1 lakh B. 2 lakh

C. 1 million D. 1000 million

39. Splenic fever is another name for

A. FMD B. Anthrax

C. Cowpox D. Mastitis

40. Which element is deficient in milk?

A. Mg B. Ca

C. Fe D. P

41. Expulsion of placenta should be within

A. 2 - 3 hr B. 4 - 8 hr

C. 6 - 8 hr D. 10 - 12 hr

42. Roughage contain moisture up to

A. 15 - 20% B. 5 - 10%

C. 10 - 15% D. 20 - 25%

43. Gestation period of cow is days

A. 283 - 285 B. 290 – 292

C. 142 - 145 D. 152 - 154

44. Mating of the related individual with 4-6 generation is known as
A. Inbreeding B. Line breeding
C. Close breeding D. Outcrossing

45. The largest part of ruminant stomach is
A. Omasum B. Abomasum
C. Rumen D. Reticulum

46. Casein form of total milk proteins is
A. 60 - 65 % B. 70 - 71 %
C. 42 - 45 % D. 80 - 83 %

47. Galactopoiesis is
A. Milk secretion B. Maintenance of lactation
C. Milk let down D. Ceasing of lactation

48. Immunity is caused by
A. Lymphocytes B. Basophils
C. Eosinophils D. All

49. Best pH for semen preservation is
A. 6.4 B. 7.4
C. 7.2 D. 6.8

50. Shortest period of estrous cycle is
A. Estrus B. Proesturs
C. Metestrus D. Diestrus

51. The fat content of double toned milk is
A. 0.5% B. 1.5%
C. 3.0% D. 4.5%

52. Milk share consumed for whole milk purpose is
A. 1/2 B. 3/4
C. 2/3 D. 1/3

53. The major advantage of weaning in cows is
A. To get clean milk B. To get strong calves
C. To get continuous milk D. Increase milking efficiency

54. Thick horns, broad dished forehead and short face are present in
A. Haryana B. Kankrej
C. Tharparkar D. Nagori

55. Oogenesis and spermatogenesis are a major physiological action of (hormone released from pituitary gland).

A. Thyrotropin B. Prolactin

C. Follicle stimulating hormone D. Oxytocin

56. Which type of the ligament is primarily responsible for the udder breaking down?

A. Lateral suspensory B. Median suspensory

C. Both A and B D. None of these

57. Failure of the retractor penis muscles to relax and to allow the penis to extend from the sheath is known as

A. Cryptorchidism B. Scrotal hernia

C. Impotentia coeundi D. Free martin (neuter)

58. The number of pre molar teeth in cattle

A. 6 B. 8

C. 10 D. 12

59. Life span of cattle is

A. 10 - 15 yrs B. 15 - 20 yrs

C. 20 - 25 yrs D. 25 - 30 yrs

60. Ongole is a breed of

A. Cow B. Buffalo

C. Goat D. Sheep

61. Cow milk's protein is called as

A. Zein B. Lactalbumin

C. Casein D. Albumin

62. Average period of lactation in buffalo is

A. 145 days B. 175 days

C. 281 days D. 332 days

63. Toda is a breed of

A. Sheep B. Goat

C. Cattle D. Buffalo

64. Paneer is a

A. Concentrated milk product B. Fermented milk product

C. Coagulated milk product D. Dried milk product

65. Methylene Blue Reduction Test (MBRT) is conducted to know the efficiency of

A. Toned milk B. Double toned milk

C. Sterilized milk D. Pasteurized milk

66. Buffer value of milk is due to

A. Protein B. Fat

C. Lipid D. Carbohydrate

67. Which of the following vitamins is most resistant on heat treatment of milk?

A. Vitamin A B. Vitamin C

C. Vitamin B1 D. Vitamin B12

68. White revolution is related to

A. Cotton B. Milk

C. Rice D. Sheep

69. Enzyme coagulated milk product is

A. Paneer B. Dahi

C. Cheese D. Chhana

70. Colostrum feeding is necessary for

A. Increasing protein B. Easy to digest

C. Disease resistance D. All

71. Mainly draught breed of cattle is

A. Gir B. Sahiwal

C. Amrit Mahal D. Kankrej

72. Temperature required for artificial vagina

A. 41°C B. 39 °C

C. 45°C D. 32 °C

73. Toggenberg is native of

A. Europe B. Switzerland

C. Africa D. USA

74. Tharparkar is native of

A. Haryana B. Rajasthan

C. Pakistan D. Gujarat

75. 'Operation flood' is related to
    A. Opium B. Cotton
    C. Rice D. Milk
76. Body temperature of cow is
    A. 98.2°C B. 45.6°C
    C. 38.5°C D. 34°C
77. Temperature for LTLT pasteurization is
    A. 61 - 63°C B. 42 - 49°C
    C. 62 - 65°C D. 51 - 65 °C
78. Cattle plague is another name for
    A. Anthrax B. Rinderpest
    C. FMD D. Cowpox
79. Longest phase of oestrus cycle is
    A. Proestrus B. Estrus
    C. Metestrus D. Diestrus
80. Gestation period in buffalo is
    A. 280 days B. 310 days
    C. 270 days D. 420 days
81. Jersy is native of
    A. Denmark B. England
    C. Holland D. USA
82. Initiation of milk secretion is called
    A. Lactogenesis B. Galactogenesis
    C. Galactopoiesis D. None
83. Chemical used for dehorning is
    A. NaCl B. Caustic potash
    C. Oxalic acid D. NaOH
84. Milk vein in cows contains
    A. Water B. Blood
    C. Milk D. Milk and blood
85. To remove milk stone is used
    A. Alkali B. Alcohol
    C. Acids D. Acetone

86. The best age of dehorning is

A. 1 week B. 4 weeks

C. 8 weeks D. 16 weeks

87. Better quality khoa is prepared from

A. Buffalo milk B. Cow milk

C. Sheep milk D. Camel milk

88. Total Digestible Nutrients in legume fodder is

A. 10 - 15% B. 15 - 30%

C. 30 - 40% D. 40 - 50%

89. Hormone for milk secretion is

A. Oxytocin B. ACH

C. Prolactin D. TSH

90. Undescended condition of the testes into the scrotal sac is known as

A. Cryptorchidism B. Free martin

C. Scrotal hernia D. Impotentia coeundi

91. Buffalo share in total milk production in India is

A. 55 % B. 42 %

C. 60 % D. 65 %

92. Corn silage, pasture, and hay are examples of what type of feed?

A. Leguminous B. Roughages

C. Concentrate D. None

93. What is the normal respiration rate for cattle?

A. 40-45/minute B. 50-55/minute

C. 10-30/minute D. 58-63/minute

94. Cattle keepers are in centre position in dairy industry because

A. They carry good varieties of cattles

B. They prepare different types of milk products

C. Their products are sold at national in dairy industry

D. They have brought white revolution in dairy industry

95. Who was pioneer of dairy industry in Gujarat?

A. Fahian B. Haber

C. Verghese kurien D. Venus

96. Where Imperial Veterinary Research Institute is located?

A. New Delhi
B. Izatnagar
C. Chennai
D. Kolkata

97. Central Cattle Breeding Farms were established during the

A. 3rd Five year plan
B. 4th Five year plan
C. 5th Five year plan
D. 7th Five year plan

Answer keys

1	A	16	B	31	C	46	D	61	C	76	C	91	A
2	B	17	A	32	B	47	B	62	C	77	A	92	B
3	C	18	C	33	C	48	A	63	D	78	B	93	C
4	B	19	C	34	C	49	D	64	C	79	D	94	A
5	A	20	A	35	B	50	A	65	D	80	B	95	C
6	D	21	D	36	C	51	B	66	A	81	B	96	B
7	C	22	B	37	A	52	D	67	A	82	A	97	B
8	D	23	B	38	D	53	A	68	B	83	B		
9	B	24	B	39	B	54	B	69	C	84	B		
10	A	25	B	40	C	55	C	70	D	85	C		
11	C	26	A	41	D	56	B	71	C	86	B		
12	B	27	A	42	C	57	B	72	C	87	A		
13	C	28	B	43	A	58	D	73	B	88	C		
14	B	29	C	44	A	59	C	74	C	89	C		
15	A	30	A	45	C	60	A	75	D	90	A		

2

Poultry Rearing

I. Choose the correct answer

1. Suitable layer breed is

A. Plymouth B. Vencobb

C. Rhode island red D. Leghorn

2. Important viral disease of poultry is

A. Ranikhet disease B. *Colibacillosis*

C. Salmonellosis D. Coccidiosis

3. Calcium content given to poultry in the range of

A. 50-100 g/bird/month B. 10-25 g/bird/month

C. 150-200 g/bird/month D. 250-500 g/bird/month

4. Brooder house temperature is approximately

A. 10°C B. 20°C

C. 35°C D. 50°C

5. Poor litter management in poultry causes

A. Colibacillosis B. Coccidiosis

C. Ranikhet disease D. Haemophilus

6. Central Poultry Development Organisation and Training Institute was established at

A. Hisar B. Bangalore

C. Bikaner D. Hyderabad

7. First Veterinary and Animal Science University was established at Chennai in

A. 1993 B. 1989

C. 1974 D. 2008

8. Vaccine used to control ranikhet disease in poultry is

A. Marek's vaccine B. La Sota

C. R_2B D. Thiamine

9. Major expenditure in poultry rising is

A. Shed cost B. Feed cost

C. Medicine cost D. Labour cost

10. Temperature requirement of chicks is higher during

A. 1st week B. 2-3rd week

C. 3-4th week D. 5th week

11. In colder parts of country, the poultry house should face

A. South B. North

C. North D. West

12. Poultry feed should be composed of _____ of protein source.

A. 10-15% B. 20-25%

C. 30-35% D. 40-45%

13. At what age of chick, ranikhet disease strain 'F' lasota is vaccinated?

A. 1 day B. 5-7 days

C. 10-14 days D. 8th week

14. Chalk like diarrhoea is a symptom of which poultry disease

A. Salmonellosis B. Infectious coryza

C. Coccidiosis D. Colibacillosis

15. Goose stepping is a deficiency caused by

A. Ca and Mg B. Zn and Mg

C. Ca and P D. Mg and P

16. Match list I with list II and choose the correct options given below

List I	**List II**
A. Semi-intensive	1. 0.5 sq ft
B. Deep litter	2. 1 sq ft
C. Cage system (Single)	3. 3 to 4 sq ft/bird
D. Cage system (Colony)	4. 7 hens/ m^2

	A	B	C	D
A.	3	4	1	2
B.	3	4	2	1
C.	4	3	1	2
D.	4	3	2	1

17. Which among the following is not suitable for backyard poultry?

A. Giriraja B. Krishna – J

C. Gramalakshmi D. Vencobb

18. What is the quantity of calcium given to layers in feed for 100 birds?

A. 2-5 kgs B. 15-20 kgs

C. 5-10 kgs D. 10-15 kgs

19. What is total quantity of feed consumed by broilers up to its 6 week of age?

A. 2 kg B. 3 kg

C. 4 kg D. 5 kg

20. What is the body temperature of day old chick?

A. 95°F B. 28°F

C. 98°F D. 103°F

21. Which of the following is advantage of chicken farming?

A. Initial investment is a little lower than layer farming

B. Rearing period is 6 – 7 weeks only

C. Broilers have high feed conversion efficiency i.e. least amount of feed is required for unit body weight gain in comparison to other livestock

D. All the above

22. Poultry includes

A. Chicken B. Ducks

C. Geese and turkey D. All the above

23. The first phase in the life of poultry is called

A. Growing period B. Birth period

C. Development period D. Maturity period

24. Which of the following is indigenous poultry breed of India?

A. Phulbani B. Kalahandi

C. Dumasil D. All the above

25. World's number 1 egg producer is

A. New Hampshire B. Leghorn

C. English class D. Rhode Island Red

26. Rinderpest is caused by
A. Bacteria B. Virus
C. Parasite D. Mould

27. Estrogen, progestron and relaxin hormones are secreted from
A. Ovary B. Adrenal
C. Pituitary D. Thyroid

28. Average fertile life of an egg is
A. 12 - 24 h B. 1 - 2 days
C. 3 - 4 days D. 5 – 6 days

29. Curled toe paralysis is caused due to
A. Vitamin A B. Vitamin C
C. Vitamin B2 D. Vitamin B12

30. Egg shell is made up of
A. $Ca(OH)_2$ B. $Ca_3(PO_4)_2$
C. $CaCO_3$ D. CaO

31. Most popular poultry in USA is
A. Plymouth Rock B. New Hampshire
C. Rhode Island Red D. Brahma

32. Egg production starts in poultry at the age of
A. 5 1/2 months B. 3 1/2 months
C. 4 months D. 6 months

33. Marek's disease is found in
A. Cattle B. Poultry
C. Sheep D. Goat

34. Yellow colour of egg is due to
A. Carotene B. Anthocyanin
C. Vitamin B D. Xanthophyll

35. The moisture content of paneer should not be more than
A. 70 % B. 65 %
C. 60 % D. 55 %

36. During incubation, testing of egg should be done at
A. 10th day B. 15th day
C. 18th day D. 21th day

37. The feed cost as the percentage of total cost of commercial poultry production is

A. 30-40 B.40-50

C. 60-70 D. Above 90

38. Egg is low in

A. Calcium B. Vitamin C

C. Both A and B D. Phosphorus

39. The hatchery should be situated at least ....ft away from other poultry houses.

A. 100ft B. 500ft

C. 1000ft D. None of the above

40. Which of the following methods is not used for sexing of chicks?

A. Rapid and allow feathering

B. Identification of rudimentary testes in cloaca

C. Barring and non- barring

D. Comb shape

41. Rotating eggs from side to side over a ....degree angle improve hatchability.

A. 90 degree B. 120 degree

C. 180 degree D. Both A and C

42. Denaturation of proteins in chicken occurs in

A. Oesophagus B. Proventriculus and gizzard

C. Crop and pancreas D. Small and large intestine

43. Maintenance of normal cerebrospinal fluid pressure is physiological function of

A. Riboflavin B. Pyridoxine

C. Retinol D. Folic acid

44. Length of ovulatory cycle in birds is

A. 10-12h B. 20-22h

C. 25-26h D. 30-32h

45. The sperm host glands of avian oviduct are located at ....of oviduct

A. Vagina B. Uterus

C. Uterovaginal junction D. Magnum

46. Chicken sperms are able to utilize..........for energy purpose

A. Glucose B. Fructose

C. Both A and B D. None

47. For maximum egg production, the photoperiod is ....

A. 8 h B. 14 h

C. 18h D. 22h

48. FSH and LH hormones are released from the following organ

A. Adrenal cortex B. Ovary

C. Anterior pituitary D. Posterior pituitary

49. The weight of an functionally mature ovary of hen is

A. 5-10g B. 10-20g

C. 20-30g D. 30-40g

50. Body weight of female bird at 72 week of age is _____ g.

A. 1600 g B. 2300 g

C. 1700 g D. 12000 g

51. What is the height of roof over hanging in poultry shed (in summer)?

A. 2 – 3 ft B. 1 – 2 ft

C. 6.5 – 7 ft D. 3 – 5 ft

52. _____ improves the shell quality of eggs

A. Sodium bicarbonate B. Potassium bicarbonate

C. Magnesium bicarbonate D. Calcium bicarbonate

53. For a good layer, the moulting pattern is

A. Late and rapid B. Early and slow

C. Late and slow D. Early and rapid

54. What is the per capita availability of egg in India?

A. 30 eggs/year B. 50 eggs/year

C. 60 eggs/yeat D. 70 eggs/year

55. Match the following

Vitamin deficiency in poultry	**Symptoms**
A. Vitamin A	1. Crazy chick disease
B. Vitamin D3	2. Rickettsia
C. Vitamin E	3. Xerophthalmia
D. Choline	4. Poor feed utilization

	A	B	C	D
A.	3	2	1	4
B.	3	4	2	1
C.	4	3	2	1
D.	2	1	4	3

Answer keys

1	D	11	A	21	D	31	A	41	A	51	D
2	A	12	B	22	D	32	A	42	B	52	A
3	A	13	B	23	A	33	B	43	C	53	A
4	C	14	A	24	D	34	D	44	C	54	D
5	B	15	B	25	B	35	A	45	C	55	A
6	B	16	B	26	B	36	C	46	A		
7	B	17	D	27	A	37	C	47	B		
8	B	18	C	28	A	38	C	48	C		
9	B	19	C	29	C	39	C	49	C		
10	A	20	D	30	C	40	B	50	C		

3

Sheep and Goat Rearing

I. Choose the correct answer

1. Which among the following sheep breed is suitable for southern regions?

   A. Merino — B. Keezhakaraisal

   C. Balangir — D. Gurez

2. What is the common space requirement for adult sheep/head?

   A. $0.5m^2$ — B. $0.9\ m^2$

   C. $1\ m^2$ — D. $12\ m^2$

3. Which exotic sheep breed is suitable for wool purpose?

   A. Karakul — B. Merino

   C. Ramnad white — C. Trichy black

4. Which among the following is not a suitable tree fodder for goat?

   A. Subabul — B. Glyricidia

   C. Pungam — D. Sesbania

5. Which among the following is not a viral disease of sheep and goat?

   A. Blue tongue — B. Sheep pox

   C. Food and Mouth Disease — D. Enterotoxemia

6. Skin allergy in sheep and goat is caused by

   A. Tape worm — B. Round worm

   C. Fluke — D. Tick

7. Chegu is a

   A. Indian sheep breed — B. Indian swine breed

   C. Indian goat breed — D. Exotic buffalo breed

8. Genus of goat is

   A. Ovis — B. Capra

   C. Bos — D. Bubalus

9. Most popular fine wool breed of world is
   A. Rambouillet B. Lincoln
   C. Corriedale D. Merino
10. Morocco leather produced from skin of
   A. Camel B. Horse
   C. Sheep D. Goat
11. Maximum producer of wool is
   A. Rajasthan B. Haryana
   C. U.P. D. Punjab
12. Browsing is common feature of
   A. Horse B. Sheep
   C. Cow D. Goat
13. Angora is a native of
   A. Europe B. Turkey
   C. Holland D. India
14. Tallest breed of sheep is
   A. Deccani B. Bikaneri
   C. Nellore D. Nilgiri
15. Finest wool in Rajasthan is produced by
   A. Magra B. Sonadi
   C. Nali D. Chokla
16. Sheep breeding depends mainly on
   A. Season B. Age
   C. Environment D. None
17. When two breeds are crossed alternatively, it is known as
   A. Criss crossing B. Triple crossing
   C. Back crossing D. None
18. Goat's share in milk production in India is
   A. 3.5 % B. 5 %
   C. 10 % D. 15 %
19. Goat tissue vaccine (GTV) is used against
   A. Food and mouth diseases B. Rinderpest
   C. Haemorrhagic septicaemia D. Black quarter

20. Pashmina is produced from

A. Chegu B. Changthangi

C. Both A and B D. Gaddi

21. Synchronization of heat (controlling heat) is desired in

A. Goat B. Sheep

C. Cow D. Buffalo

22. Ergosterol is a precursor of vitamin

A. A B. B

C. D2 D. E

23. Which of the following glands secrete oxytocin?

A. Thyroid B. Ovary

C. Pituitary D. Adrenal

24. How much space should be provided for each ewe?

A. About 20 sq. ft B. <20 sq. ft

C. 10 sq. ft D. None

25. What sheep breed has all black head and legs?

A. Marino B. Pashmina

C. Surti D. Suffolk

26. How old before lambs begin to eat dry feed?

A. 2-3 weeks of age B. 4-5 weeks of age

C. 7 weeks of age D. None

27. What are sheep keds?

A. Flies B. Lice

C. Ticks D. A or B Both

28. How many years does the average ewe remain productive?

A. 5-6 years B. 2-3 years

C. 9-10 years D. Above 10 years

Answer keys

1	B	11	A	21	B
2	C	12	D	22	C
3	B	13	B	23	C
4	C	14	C	24	A
5	D	15	D	25	D
6	D	16	A	26	A
7	C	17	A	27	C
8	B	18	A	28	A
9	D	19	B		
10	D	20	C		

4

Swine Farming

I. Choose the correct answer

1. Which of the following type of pigs are found in India?
   A. Wild pigs B. Domesticated indigenous pigs
   C. Exotic pigs D. All the above
2. Ghungroo is a / an
   A. Indian sheep breed B. Indian swine breed
   C. Indigenous pig D. Indian goat breed
3. Which of the following is correct about duroc breed of pig?
   A. Pigs of this breed have considerable variations in colour
   B. Durocs have a medium body length and slightly dished face
   C. This breed is known for lean meat
   D. All the above
4. Salted meat of pig is known as
   A. Bacon B. Beef
   C. Pork D. Chicken
5. Large white yorkshire is breed of
   A. Sheep B. Goat
   C. Pig D. Horse
6. Gestation period for swine is
   A. 120 days B. 105 days
   C. 114 days D. 100 days
7. Swine fever is a
   A. Bacterial disease B. Viral disease
   C. Fungal disease D. Protozoan disease

8. National Research Centre on Pig is located at
   A. Guwahati B. Nagpur
   C. Lucknow D. Gurgoan
9. Large white yorkshire is a exotic breed of
   A. UK B. USA
   C. Japan D. None of these
10. Most extensively used exotic breed of pig in India is
   A. Landrace B. Large white yorkshire
   C. Hampshire D. Duroc
11. Method of feeding sows and gilts before breeding is known as
   A. Farrowing B. Castration
   C. Weaning D. Flushing
12. The average length of oestrous cycle in pig is
   A. 7 days B. 14 days
   C. 21 days D. 27 days
13. Generally in breeding boars, the ratio of boar and sow may be
   A. 1:10 B. 1:25
   C. 1:50 D. 1:5
14. Pigs thrive well in temperature range of
   A. 10-14°C B. 15-17°C
   C. 20-25°C D. 30-35°C
15. Average floor space requirement of boar is about
   A. 6.0-7.0 m^2/animal B. 0.9-1.2 m^2/animal
   C. 1.3-1.8 m^2/animal D. 1.8-2.7 m^2/animal
16. Creep feeding is done to
   A. Boar B. Sow
   C. Piglets D. All the above
17. Swine fever belongs to genus of
   A. Pestivirus B. Potovirus
   C. Geminivirus D. Potyvirus
18. Castrated male pig is known as
   A. Barrow B. Sow
   C. Boar D. Gilt

19. Baby pig anaemia is due to _____ deficiency.
    A. Ca B. Fe
    C. Mg D. Both A and B
20. Landrace breed of pig is a native of
    A. UK B. USA
    C. Denmark D. Japan
21. Reddish diamond shaped discolouration on body is a symptom of
    A. Swine fever B. Swine erysipelas
    C. Brucellosis D. Tuberculosis
22. In 20th livestock census, contribution of pigs is about
    A. 1.69% B. 13.87%
    C. 0.237% D. 8.23%
23. Example of indigenous pig breed in India
    A. Duroc B. Nicobari
    C. Hampshire D. Both a and b
24. Leading pork producer in the world is
    A. USA B. China
    C. UK D. Japan
25. Rank of India in pig population in the world is
    A. Second B. Third
    C. Fourth D. Fifth
26. Carcass yield of pig is high about
    A. 50-55% B. 60-80%
    C. 85-90% D. 40-50%
27. Average meat yield of indigenous breed of pig is
    A. 78 kg B. 38 kg
    C. 15 kg D. 56 kg
28. Pig population is the highest in the state of
    A. Jharkhand B. Tamil Nadu
    C. Assam D. Kerala
29. Ghungroo breed of pig is a native of
    A. Meghalaya B. West Bengal
    C. Assam D. Tripura

Answer keys

1	D	11	D	21	B
2	C	12	C	22	A
3	D	13	B	23	B
4	A	14	C	24	B
5	C	15	A	25	D
6	C	16	C	26	B
7	B	17	A	27	B
8	A	18	A	28	C
9	A	19	B	29	B
10	B	20	C		